The Religious Context of Early Christianity

A Guide to Graeco-Roman Religions

HANS-JOSEF KLAUCK

Translated by
Brian McNeil

FORTRESS PRESS
MINNEAPOLIS

THE RELIGIOUS CONTEXT OF EARLY CHRISTIANITY
A GUIDE TO GRAECO-ROMAN RELIGIONS

Fortress Press edition 2003

The publishers gratefully acknowledge the support of Inter Nationes (Bonn, Germany) in the preparation of the English translation.

Cover image: Greek domestic altar from Italy; located in the J. Paul Getty Museum
(Los Angeles, California), inv. #86.AD.598; terracotta, c. 400–375 BCE;
photo © K. C. Hanson 2002. Used by permission.
Cover design: Jessica Thoreson

ISBN: 0-8006-3593-0

09 08 07 06 05 04 03 1 2 3 4 5 6 7 8 9 10

Manufactured in Great Britain

The Religious Context of Early Christianity

A Guide to Graeco-Roman Religions

HANS-JOSEF KLAUCK

Translated by
Brian McNeil

FORTRESS PRESS
MINNEAPOLIS

THE RELIGIOUS CONTEXT OF EARLY CHRISTIANITY
A GUIDE TO GRAECO-ROMAN RELIGIONS

Fortress Press edition 2003

The publishers gratefully acknowledge the support of Inter Nationes (Bonn, Germany) in the preparation of the English translation.

Cover image: Greek domestic altar from Italy; located in the J. Paul Getty Museum
    (Los Angeles, California), inv. #86.AD.598; terracotta, c. 400–375 BCE;
    photo © K. C. Hanson 2002. Used by permission.
Cover design: Jessica Thoreson

ISBN: 0-8006-3593-0

09 08 07 06 05 04 03 1 2 3 4 5 6 7 8 9 10

Manufactured in Great Britain

Contents

Contents

Preface

> Let us for a moment suppose that modern Europe were to witness the believers abandoning the Christian churches in order to venerate Allah or Brahma, to observe the commandments of Confucius or Buddha, to accept the fundamental principles of Shintoism; let us imagine a great congeries of all the races of the world, with Arabic mullahs, Chinese literary scholars, Japanese bonzes, Tibetan lamas, Hindu pandits preaching at one and the same time fatalism and predestination, the cult of ancestors and the adoration of the divinised ruler, pessimism and redemption through self-annihilation, while all these priests built temples in foreign styles in our cities and celebrated their various rites in them – this dream (which the future may perhaps one day see realised) would give us a rather accurate picture of the religious confusion which characterised the ancient world of Constantine.
>
> (F. Cumont, *Die orientalischen Religionen im römischen Heidentum,* reprint Darmstadt 1975, 178f.)

It almost seems as if Franz Cumont, the great Belgian historian of Hellenistic-Roman religion, had developed prophetic gifts alongside all his other talents, when he wrote these lines at the beginning of our century. Now that we have reached the end of the century, we find ourselves confronted by the slogan of the 'multicultural' society, which will always be a multireligious society too. Against this background, it is even easier to draw the analogy which Cumont drew: early Christianity too sought its path in a multireligious world, and if we are to achieve a correct understanding of the literary bequest of early Christianity, it is absolutely necessary to know the outlines of that world.

The following presentation has a modest goal, namely to give students of theology the necessary information in this field. It concentrates on the Graeco-Roman sphere; it does not deal with Judaism, with which Christianity has a quite different (because much closer) relationship. The Introduction gives more detailed orientation about the goal, the criteria of selection and methodological questions. Here I should like only to observe that I have taken a conscious decision in favour of an illustrative style of work that is problem- and text-oriented. This means that in dubious cases, I have preferred not to discuss a possible theme, but rather to present and discuss in detail individual instructive texts. For this reason, I consistently refer to bilingual editions that are readily accessible, and to collections of texts and anthologies which provide the stimulus to the student's own further work along these paths.

One of my main problems has been how to deal with the voluminous secondary literature. My guiding principle has been to cite the older and important works, including many 'classics', and modern works which indicate the present state of scholarship. I myself am more painfully aware than anyone else of how fragmentary all this remains in the face of an immeasurable field of possibilities.

This book was written in German, when I was professor of New Testament exegesis at the University of Würzburg. It appeared in two volumes in 1995 and 1996 as part of a series of theological textbooks, and students and colleagues alike soon (to my surprise) acclaimed it as very helpful. In his kind review, Hans Dieter Betz wrote: 'Translated, revised and adapted for the English-speaking readership, this work would make an enormously valuable tool for all those who are fascinated by the study of early Christianity in the context of the Graeco-Roman culture but who presently lack a comprehensive and detailed summary of the current state of research' (*JBL* 116 [1997] 359). At that time, the planning of the English edition was already under way, but considerable time and effort were required before this could appear. The present book is in effect not only a translation, but a revised and updated edition of the original work.

The main bulk of the task was of course the translation itself (see below), but besides that, copious new references were added to editions of classical texts indicating translations into English, which it is hoped will considerably enhance the usefulness of the book to English-speaking readers. The secondary literature has been brought up to date, including new titles from 1995–8 and some from 1999. Mistakes noted by readers and reviewers of the German edition had to be corrected, and the original two volumes have been combined into a single volume, necessitating a reorganisation of the bibliographies and the index. Another factor was my own move from Würzburg to Munich, where I succeeded my teacher Joachim Gnilka as professor. Living for some time surrounded by boxes of books does not facilitate work like this!

I am grateful to all those who helped launch this work in the English language, above all to the editors of 'Studies of the New Testament and Its World' for accepting my book for their distinguished series. Especial thanks are due to John Barclay, who gave the decisive impetus and helped with the adaptation of the bibliography, and to the staff of the renowned Scottish publisher T&T Clark for taking the risk involved in the publication of a long academic book. But above all, my biggest thanks are due to my translator, Brian McNeil (who incidentally lives in the same German town as I do). He has done a marvellous job in putting into perfectly readable English a German text which is very compressed, and therefore sometimes complicated. Once again he has fulfilled the task of bridge-builder between the German-speaking and the English-speaking theological worlds.

Munich, May 1999   H.-J.K.

Abbreviations

1. Primary Sources

Aeschylus,	*Ag.*	*Agamemnon*
	Prom.	*Prometheus Bound*
Ambrosiaster,	*Quaest. VNT*	*Quaestiones Veteris et Novi Testamenti*
Apollodorus,	*Bibl.*	*Bibliotheca*
Appian,	*Bell. Civ.*	*Bellum Civile*
Apuleius,	*Apol.*	*Apologia*
	Flor.	*Florida*
	Met.	*Metamorphoses*
Aelius Aristides,	*Or.*	*Orationes*
Aristophanes,	*Ach.*	*Acharnians*
	Pl.	*Plutus*
	Ra.	*Ranae (Frogs)*
Aristotle,	*Eth. Nic.*	*Nicomachean Ethics*
	Pol.	*Politics*
Arnobius,	*Adv. Nat.*	*Adversus Nationes*
Artemidorus,	*Oneirocr.*	*Oneirocriticon (Interpretation of Dreams)*
Athenaeus,	*Deipnosoph.*	*Deipnosophistae*
Catullus,	*Carm.*	*Carmina*
Cicero,	*Att.*	*Ad Atticum*
	Divin.	*De Divinatione*
	Dom.	*De Domo Sua*
	Fam.	*Ad Familiares*
	Nat. Deor.	*De Natura Deorum*
	Phil.	*Philippics*
	Quint. Fratr.	*Ad Quintum Fratrem*
	Rep.	*De Re Publica*
	Tusc.	*Tusculan Disputations*
Clement,	*Exc. Theod.*	*Excerpta ex Theodoto*

	Protr.	*Protrepticus*
Demosthenes,	*Or.*	*Orationes*
Dio Chrysostom,	*Or.*	*Orationes*
Diogenes Laertius,	*Vit. Phil.*	*Lives of the Philosophers*
Dionysius,	*Ant. Rom.*	*Antiquitates Romanae*
Epictetus,	*Diss.*	*Dissertationes*
	Ench.	*Encheiridion*
Euripides,	*Alc.*	*Alcestis*
	Ba.	*Bacchae*
	Hel.	*Helen*
	Hipp.	*Hippolytus*
	Iph. Taur.	*Iphigeneia in Tauris*
Eusebius,	*Hist. Eccl.*	*Historia Ecclesiastica*
Firmicus Maternus,	*Err. Prof. Rel.*	*Errores Profanarum Religionum*
Gen		Genesis
Herodotus,	*Hist.*	*Histories*
Hesiod,	*Op.*	*Opera et Dies*
	Theog.	*Theogonia*
Hippolytus,	*Ref.*	*Refutation of All Heresies*
Homer,	*Il.*	*Iliad*
	Od.	*Odyssey*
Hom. Hymn Dem.		Homeric Hymn to Demeter
Horace,	*Ars Poet.*	*Ars Poetica*
	Ep.	*Epistulae*
	Sat.	*Satires*
Ignatius,	*Eph.*	*To the Ephesians*
Irenaeus,	*Adv. Haer.*	*Adversus Haereses*
Jerome,	*Ep.*	*Epistulae*
Josephus,	*Ant.*	*Antiquitates Judaicae*
	Ap.	*Contra Apionem*
	Bell.	*Bellum Judaicum*
	Vit.	*Vita*
Juvenal,	*Sat.*	*Satires*
Livy,	*Urb. Cond.*	*Ab Urbe Condita*
Lucian,	*Alex.*	*Alexander*
	Philops.	*Philopseudes (Lover of Lies)*
Lucretius,	*Rer. Nat.*	*De Rerum Natura*
Macc (1, 2, 3, 4)		Maccabees (1, 2, 3, 4)

Origen,	*C. Cels.*	*Contra Celsum*
Ovid,	*Met.*	*Metamorphoses*
Pausanias,	*Graec. Descr.*	*Graeciae Descriptio*
Petronius,	*Sat.*	*Satyricon*
Philo,	*Abr.*	*De Abrahamo*
	Decal.	*De Decalogo*
	Flacc.	*In Flaccum*
	Leg. Gai.	*Legatio ad Gaium*
	Spec. Leg.	*De Specialibus Legibus*
Philostratus,	*Vit. Ap.*	*Vita Apollonii*
Pindar,	*Pyth.*	*Pythia*
Plato,	*Alcib.*	*Alcibiades*
	Apol.	*Apologia*
	Charmid.	*Charmides*
	Euthyphr.	*Euthyphro*
	Leg.	*Leges*
	Phaed.	*Phaedo*
	Phaedr.	*Phaedrus*
	Polit.	*Politicus*
	Resp.	*Respublica (The Republic)*
	Symp.	*Symposion*
Pliny (elder),	*Hist. Nat.*	*Naturalis Historia*
Pliny (younger),	*Ep.*	*Epistulae*
Plotinus,	*Enn.*	*Enneads*
Plutarch,	*Alc.*	*Alcibiades*
	Alex.	*Alexander*
	Amat.	*Amatorius Liber*
	Aristid.	*Aristides*
	Cons. Uxor.	*Consolatio ad Uxorem*
	Def. Orac.	*De Defectu Oraculorum*
	E ap. Delph.	*De E apud Delphos*
	Fac. Orb. Lun.	*De Facie in Orbe Lunae*
	Gen. Socr.	*De Genio Socratis*
	Is. et Os.	*De Iside et Osiride*
	Lys.	*Lysias*
	Pomp.	*Pompeius*
	Pyth. Or.	*De Pythiae Oraculis*
	Quaest. Conv.	*Quaestiones Conviviales*
	Sept. Sap. Conv.	*Septem Sapientium Convivium*

	Ser. Num. Vind.	*De Sera Numinis Vindicta*
	Suav. Viv. Epic.	*Non Posse Suaviter Vivi secundum Epicurum*
	Thes.	*Theseus*
	Tit.	*Titus*
Porphyry,	*Abst.*	*De Abstinentia*
	Ant. Nymph.	*De Antro Nympharum*
Ps		Psalm(s)
Ps.-Lucian	*Astrol.*	*De Astrologia*
Ps Sol		Psalms of Solomon
Seneca,	*Ben.*	*De Beneficiis*
	Brev. Vit.	*De Brevitate Vitae*
	Cons. Marc.	*Consolatio ad Marciam*
	Ep.	*Epistulae*
	Oed.	*Oedipus*
	Tranq. An.	*De Tranquillitate Animi*
	Vit. Beat.	*De Vita Beata*
Sib		Sibylline Oracles
Sir		(Jesus ben) Sirach
Stobaeus,	*Ecl.*	*Eclogae*
Suetonius,	*Aug.*	*Augustus*
	Calig.	*Caligula*
	Claud.	*Claudius*
	Div. Jul.	*Divus Julius*
	Dom.	*Domitian*
	Tib.	*Tiberius*
	Vesp.	*Vespasian*
	Vitell.	*Vitellius*
Tacitus,	*Ann.*	*Annales*
	Hist.	*Historiae*
Tertullian,	*Apol.*	*Apologeticus*
	Bapt.	*De Baptismo*
	Praesc. Haer.	*De Praescriptione Haereticorum*
Ps.-Tertullian,	*Adv. Omn. Haer.*	*Adversus Omnes Haereses*
Theophrastus,	*Char.*	*Characteres*
Tob		Tobit
Vergil,	*Aen.*	*Aeneid*
	Ecl.	*Eclogues*

Georg.	*Georgics*
Wis	Wisdom of Solomon

For Abbreviations of Nag Hammadi texts see p. 446f.

2. Collections of Sources

BGU	Aegyptische Urkunden aus den Staatlichen Museen zu Berlin: Griechische Urkunden
CIL	Corpus Inscriptionum Latinarum
CIMRM	M. J. Vermaseren, *Corpus inscriptionum et monumentorum religionis Mithriacae*
FGH	F. Jacoby, *Die Fragmente der griechischen Historiker*
FVS	H. A. Diels, *Die Fragmente der Vorsokratiker*
IG	Inscriptiones Graecae
IGRR	R. Cagnat et al., *Inscriptiones Graecae ad Res Romanas*
ILS	H. Dessau, *Inscriptiones Latinae Selectae*
LSAM	F. Sokolowski, *Lois sacrées de l'Asie Mineure*
LSCG	F. Sokolowski, *Lois sacrées des cités grecques*
LSCS	F. Sokolowski, *Lois sacrées des cités grecques. Supplément*
NHC	Nag Hammadi Codex
OGIS	W. Dittenberger, *Orientis Graeci Inscriptiones Selectae*
PGrM	K. Preisendanz, *Papyri Graecae Magicae*
POxy	Oxyrhynchus Papyri
PTebt	Tebtunis Papyri
RecUB	Reclams Universal-Bibliothek, Stuttgart
SEG	Supplementum Epigraphicum Graecum
SIG	W. Dittenberger, *Sylloge Inscriptionum Graecarum*
SVF	J. von Arnim, *Stoicorum Veterum Fragmenta*

3. Periodicals, Series, Collective Works

These follow S. Schwertner, *Internationales Abkürzungsverzeichnis für Theologie und Grenzgebiete*, Berlin 2nd edn. 1992.

General Bibliography

Secondary literature is cited in the text only with the name of the author (in unclear cases, also with a shortened form of the title). The reader should first consult the bibliographical list at the beginning of the section in question, where one will find either full details or else a reference back to a previous list (cited as L1 etc); the same method is used in the footnotes.

List 1. The study of religion

P. Antes, 'Religion in den Theorien der Religionswissenschaft', *HFTh* 1 (1985) 34–56.

E. Durkheim, *The Elementary Forms of Religious Life: A Study in Religious Sociology*, London and New York 1995; French original 1912.

R. B. Gladigow and H. Kippenberg (eds.), *Neue Ansätze in der Religionswissenschaft* (FRW 4), Munich 1983.

B. Grom, *Religionspsychologie*, Munich and Göttingen 1992.

F. B. Jevons, *An Introduction to the History of Religion*, London 9th edn. 1927.

G. Lanczowski (ed.), *Selbstverständnis und Wesen der Religionswissenschaft* (WdF 263), Darmstadt 1974.

——*Einführung in die Religionswissenschaft*, Darmstadt 2nd edn. 1991.

G. van der Leeuw, *Religion in Essence and Manifestation*, 2 vols., Gloucester, Mass. 1967.

U. Mann (ed.), *Theologie und Religionswissenschaft: Der gegenwärtige Stand ihrer Forschungsergebnisse und Aufgaben im Hinblick auf ihr gegenseitiges Verhältnis*, Darmstadt 1973.

J. Z. Smith, *Map is not Territory: Studies in the History of Religions* (SJLA 23), Leiden 1978.

F. Stolz, *Grundzüge der Religionswissenschaft* (KVR 1527), Göttingen 1988.

G. Sundén, *Die Religion und die Rollen: Eine psychologische Untersuchung der Frömmigkeit*, Berlin 1966.

A. Vergote, *Psychologie religieuse*, Brussels 1966.

J. Waardenburg, *Religionen und Religion: Systematische Einführung in die Religionswissenschaft* (SG 2228), Berlin 1986.

M. Weber, *Gesammelte Aufsätze zur Religionssoziologie*, vols. 1–3 (UTB 1488–90), Tübingen 7th–9th edns. 1988; the most relevant essays in vol. 1 have been translated as *The Protestant Ethic and the Spirit of Capitalism*, London 1930, and *From Max Weber: Essays in Sociology*, ed. H. H. Gerth and C. Wright Mills, 2nd edn. London 1991.

——*The Sociology of Religion*, London 1965.

F. Whaling (ed.), *Contemporary Approaches to the Study of Religion*, vols. 1–2 (RaR 27–8), Berlin etc. 1984, 1985.

G. Widengren, *Religionsphänomenologie* (GLB), Berlin 1969.

List 2. History of Greek and Roman religion

F. Altheim, *A History of Roman Religion*, London 1938.

M. Beard, J. North and S. Price, *Religions of Rome*, vol. 1: A History, Cambridge 1998.

U. Bianchi and M. J. Vermaseren (eds.), *La soteriologia dei culti orientali nell'Impero Romano* (EPRO 92), Leiden 1982.

F. Bömer, *Untersuchungen über die Religion der Sklaven in Griechenland und Rom*, vols. 1–4 (AAWLM.G), Mainz 1957–63; vol. 1 also Wiesbaden 2nd edn. 1981; vol. 3 also Stuttgart 2nd edn. 1990 (as FASk 14).

J. N. Bremmer, *Götter, Mythen und Heiligtümer im antiken Griechenland*, Darmstadt 1996.

R. van den Broeck and M. J. Vermaseren, *Studies in Gnosticism and Hellenistic Religions* (EPRO 91), Leiden 1981.

L. Bruit Zeidman and P. Schmitt Pantel, *La Religion grecque*, Paris 2nd edn. 1991.

W. Burkert, *Structure and History in Greek Mythology and Ritual*, Berkeley 1979.

——*Homo Necans: The Anthropology of Ancient Greek Sacrificial Ritual and Myth*, Berkeley 1983.

——*Greek Religion*, Oxford and Cambridge, Mass. 1985.

——'Griechische Religion', *TRE* 14 (1985) 235–53.

F. Cumont, *The Oriental Religions in Roman Paganism*, London 1911, reprint New York 1956.

J. Dalfen, G. Petersmann and F. F. Schwarz (eds.), *Religio Graeco-Romana* (Festschrift W. Pötscher) (GrB.Suppl. 5), Graz and Horn 1993.

L. Deubner, *Attische Feste* [1932], Vienna 2nd edn. 1966; reprint Hildesheim 1969.

M. P. J. Dillon (ed.) *Religion in the Ancient World: New Themes and Approaches*, Amsterdam 1996.

E. R. Dodds, *The Greeks and the Irrational*, Berkeley 1966.

L. R. Farnell, *The Cults of the Greek States*, vols. 1–5, Oxford 1896–1909.

J. Ferguson, *The Religions of the Roman Empire* (AGRL), London and Ithaca 1970.

A. J. Festugière, *Études de religion grecque et hellénistique* (BHPh), Paris 1972.

M. L. Freyburger-Galland et al., *Sectes religieuses en Grèce et à Rome dans l'Antiquité païenne* (Realia), Paris 1986.

J. Geffcken, *The Last Days of Greco-Roman Paganism*, Amsterdam and Oxford 1978.

F. Graf, *Greek Mythology: An Introduction*, Baltimore 1993.

O. Gruppe, *Griechische Mythologie und Religionsgeschichte*, vols. 1–2 (HAW V/2.2–2), Munich 1906.

J. E. Harrison, *Prolegomena to the Study of Greek Religion*, Cambridge 3rd edn. 1922, reprint Princeton 1991.

O. Kern, *Die Religion der Griechen*, vols. 1–3, Berlin 1926–38, reprint 1963.

K. Latte, *Römische Religionsgeschichte* (HAW 5.4), Munich 2nd edn. 1992.

J. H. W. G. Liebeschuetz, *Continuity and Change in Roman Religion*, Oxford 1979.

R. MacMullen, *Paganism in the Roman Empire*, New Haven 1981.

L. H. Martin, *Hellenistic Religions: An Introduction*, Oxford 1987.

R. Muth, *Einführung in die griechische und römische Religion*, Darmstadt 1988, 2nd edn. 1998.

M. P. Nilsson, *Griechische Feste von religiöser Bedeutung mit Ausschluss der attischen*, Leipzig 1906, reprint Darmstadt 1957.

——*Geschichte der griechischen Religion*, vols. 1–2 (HAW V/2.1–2), Munich 3rd edns. 1977, 1974.

A. D. Nock, *Essays on Religion and the Ancient World*, vols. 1–2, Oxford 1972.

R. M. Ogilvie, *The Romans and their Gods in the Age of Augustus*, London 1969.

R. Parker, *Miasma: Pollution and Purification in Early Greek Religion*, Oxford 1983.

F. Pfister, *Die Religion der Griechen und Römer mit einer Einführung in die vergleichende Religionswissenschaft: Darstellung und Literaturbericht (1918–1929/30)* (JKAW.Suppl. 229), Leipzig 1930.

E. des Places, *La Religion grecque: Dieux, cultes, rites et sentiments religieux dans la Grèce antique*, Paris 1967.

S. Price, *Religions of the Ancient Greeks*, Cambridge 1999.

H. E. Schmitt and E. Vogt (eds.), *Kleines Wörterbuch des Hellenismus*, Wiesbaden 1988.

W. Speyer, *Religionsgeschichtliche Studien* (Collectanea 15), Hildesheim 1995.

P. Stengel, *Die griechischen Kultusaltertümer* (HAW 5.3), Munich 3rd edn. 1920.

Z. Stewart, 'La religione', in R. B. Bandinelli (ed.), *La società ellenistica* (Storia e Civiltà dei Greci 8), Milan 1977, 501–616.

J. Toutain, *Les Cultes païennes dans l'empire romain*, vols. I/1–3 (BEHE.R 20, 25, 31), Paris 1905–20, reprint Rome 1967.

R. Turcan, *Les Cultes orientaux dans le monde romain* (Histoire), Paris 2nd edn. 1992.

M. J. Vermaseren (ed.), *Die orientalischen Religionen im Römerreich* (EPRO 93), Leiden 1981.

H. S. Versnel (ed.), *Faith, Hope and Worship: Aspects of Religious Mentality in the Ancient World* (SGGR 2), Leiden 1981.

U. von Wilamowitz-Möllendorf, *Der Glaube der Hellenen*, vols. 1–2, Darmstadt 5th edn. 1976.

G. Wissowa, *Religion und Kultus der Römer* (HAW 4.5), Munich 2nd edn. 1912, reprint 1971.

List 3. The milieu of earliest Christianity

H. D. Betz, *Lukian von Samosata und das Neue Testament: Religionsgeschichtliche und paränetische Parallelen* (TU 76), Berlin 1961.

——*Hellenismus und Urchristentum: Gesammelte Aufsätze*, vol. 1, Tübingen 1990.

——*Antike und Christentum: Gesammelte Aufsätze*, vol. 4, Tübingen 1998.

R. Bultmann, *Primitive Christianity in its Contemporary Setting*, London 1956.

C. Clemen, *Religionsgeschichtliche Erklärung des Neuen Testaments: Die Abhängigkeit des ältesten Christentums von nichtjüdischen Religionen und philosophischen Systemen*, Giessen 2nd edn. 1924, reprint Berlin 1973.

A. Deissmann, *Light from the Ancient East*, 2nd edn. London 1927.

M. Fédou, *Christianisme et religions païennes dans le Contre Celse d'Origène* (ThH 81), Paris 1988.

E. Ferguson, *Backgrounds of Early Christianity*, Grand Rapids 1987, 2nd edn. 1993.

A. J. Festugière, *L'Idéal religieux des Grecs et l'Évangile* (EtB), Paris 2nd edn. 1932, reprint 1981.

——and P. Fabre, *Le Monde gréco-romain au temps de Notre-Seigneur*, vols. 1–2 (BSCR 73/74), Paris 1935.

J. Finegan, *Myth and Mystery: An Introduction to the Pagan Religions of the Biblical World*, Grand Rapids 1989.

R. L. Fox, *Pagans and Christians in the Mediterranean World from the Second Century AD to the Conversion of Constantine*, Harmondsworth 1988.

W. L. Knox, *Some Hellenistic Elements in Primitive Christianity* (SchLBA 1942), London 1944.

H. Koester, *Introduction to the New Testament*, vol. 1: *History, Culture and Religion of the Hellenistic Age*; vol. 2: *History and Literature of Early Christianity*, Philadelphia and New York 1982, 2nd edn. (of vol. 1) 1995.

B. Lang, *Sacred Games: A History of Christian Worship*, New Haven 1997.

J. Leipoldt and W. Grundmann (eds.), *Umwelt des Urchristentums*, vol. 1: *Darstellung des neutestamentlichen Zeitalters*, Berlin 8th edn. 1990.

E. Lohse, *The New Testament Environment*, London 1976.

B. J. Malina, *The New Testament World: Insights from Cultural Anthropology* [1981], Louisville 2nd edn. 1993.

J. Martin and B. Quint (eds.), *Christentum und antike Gesellschaft* (WdF 649), Darmstadt 1990.

B. F. Meyer and E. P. Sanders (eds.), *Jewish and Christian Self-Definition*, vol. 3: *Self-Definition in the Greco-Roman World*, Philadelphia 1982.

A. D. Nock, *Conversion: The Old and the New in Religion from Alexander the Great to Augustine of Hippo*, Oxford 1933, reprint 1952.

H. Preisker, *Neutestamentliche Zeitgeschichte* (STö.H 2), Berlin 1937.

K. Prümm, *Religionsgeschichtliches Handbuch für den Raum der altchristlichen Umwelt: Hellenistisch-römische Geistesströmungen und Kulte mit Beachtung des Eigenlebens der Provinzen*, Freiburg i.Br. 1943, reprint Rome 1954.

C. Schneider, *Geistesgeschichte des antiken Christentums*, vols. 1–2, Munich 1954.

W. Speyer, *Frühes Christentum im antiken Strahlungsfeld: Ausgewählte Aufsätze* (WUNT 50), Tübingen 1989.

J. E. Stambaugh and D. L. Balch, *The Social World of the First Christians* (LEC 2), London and Philadelphia 1986.

P. Wendland, *Die hellenistisch-römische Kultur in ihren Beziehungen zum Judentum und Christentum* (HNT 2), Tübingen 4th edn. 1972.

R. L. Wilken, *The Christians as the Romans Saw them*, New Haven 1984.

D. Zeller, *Christus unter den Göttern: Zum antiken Umfeld des Christusglaubens* (Sachbücher zur Bibel), Stuttgart 1993.

List 4. Collections of texts and pictures

C. K. Barrett, *The New Testament Background: Selected Documents*, London 1957.

M. Beard, J. North and S. Price, *Religions of Rome*, vol. 2: *A Sourcebook*, Cambridge 1998.

K. Berger and C. Colpe, *Religionsgeschichtliches Textbuch zum Neuen Testament* (TNT 1), Göttingen 1987; rev. Engl. edn.: M. E. Boring et al., *Hellenistic Commentary to the New Testament*, Nashville 1995.

L. Boffo, *Iscrizioni greche e latine per lo studio della Bibbia* (BSSTB 9), Brescia 1994.

D. R. Cartlidge and D. L. Dungan, *Documents for the Study of the Gospels*, Cleveland etc. 1980.

V. Ehrenburg and A. H. M. Jones, *Documents Illustrating the Reigns of Augustus and Tiberius*, Oxford 2nd edn. 1955.

H. Freis, *Historische Inschriften zur römischen Kaiserzeit von Augustus bis Konstantin* (TdF 49), Darmstadt 2nd edn. 1994.

H. Geist and G. Pfohl, *Römische Grabinschriften* (TuscBü), Munich 2nd edn. 1976.

J. Hengstl, *Griechische Papyri aus Ägypten als Zeugnisse des öffentlichen und privaten Lebens* (TuscBü), Munich 1978.

G. H. R. Horsley (ed.), *New Documents Illustrating Early Chritianity*, vols. 1–6, Macquarie University 1981–92; vols. 7–8 (ed. S. R. Llewelyn), Macquarie University 1994, 1998.

R. Kieffer and L. Rydbeck, *Existence païenne au début du christianisme: Présentation de textes grecs et romains*, Paris 1983.

K. Latte, *Die Religion der Römer und der Synkretismus der Kaiserzeit* (RGL 5), Tübingen 2nd edn. 1927.

J. Leipoldt, *Die Religionen in der Umwelt des Urchristentums* (BARG 9–11), Leipzig 1926.

———and W. Grundmann (eds.), *Umwelt des Urchristentums*, vol. 2: *Texte zum neutestamentlichen Zeitalter*, Berlin 7th edn. 1986; vol. 3: *Bilder zum neutestamentlichen Zeitalter*, Berlin 6th edn. 1988.

R. MacMullen and E. N. Lane, *Paganism and Christianity, 100–425 CE: A Sourcebook*, Minneapolis 1992.

M. P. Nilsson, *Die Religion der Griechen* (RGL 4), Tübingen 2nd edn. 1927; Eng. trans. *A History of Greek Religion*, Oxford 1949.

R. Penna, *L'Ambiente storico-culturale delle origini cristiane: Una documentazione ragionata* (La Bibbia nella storia 7), Bologna 2nd edn. 1986.

G. Pfohl, *Griechische Inschriften als Zeugnisse des privaten und öffentlichen Lebens* (TuscBü), Munich 2nd edn. 1980.

A. Rumpf, *Die Religion der Griechen* (BARG 13–14), Leipzig 1928.

L. Schumacher, *Römische Inschriften* (Latin/German) (RecUB 8512), Stuttgart 1988.

Introduction

1. The broader task

What contribution does a knowledge of the milieu of the New Testament from an intellectual, religious, cultural, social and political perspective make to our understanding of the New Testament writings, and what light does this knowledge shed on the birth of earliest Christianity? This question, as such, is certainly not new. The modern scholar is constantly surprised, when studying the patristic and mediaeval interpretation of the Bible, to see how often these exegetes quote classical authors and make fruitful use of them to explain the biblical texts. This tendency became stronger at the beginning of the modern period in the context of the Reformation, since many of the Reformers had had an excellent human-istic education (for example, Calvin's earliest published study was a commentary on Seneca's *De Clementia*). With the Enlightenment, the consideration of the historical context was elevated to a methodological principle – what one might call an initial step towards the formation of the historical-critical method, something that has remained until the present day one of the presuppositions of this method that is taken for granted (even if it is not often stated explicitly). One of the early representatives of this method, Johann Jakob Wettstein, gave this a classical formulation in the eighteenth century.

Wettstein was a Protestant minister in Basle who lost his parish office because he began text-critical work on the New Testament. He then went to Amsterdam, at that period the Mecca of all liberal spirits, and published there in 1751/2 his two-volume edition of the New Testament, which has been continually reprinted ever since, and has remained indispensable because of the never-superseded collection of parallels from the classical authors in his footnotes. An appendix to the second volume contains a short treatise *De Interpretatione Novi Testamenti*, the seventh rule of which runs as follows:[1]

---

[1] J. J. Wettstein, *Novum Testamentum Graecum*, vol. 2, Amsterdam 1752, reprint Graz 1962, 878. Translation follows W. G. Kümmel, *The New Testament: The History of the Investigation of its Problems*, London 1973, 50. For a new version of Wettstein's work, see now G. Strecker and U. Schnelle (eds.), *Neuer*

1

'Another rule is much more useful and more easily comprehended: If you wish to get a thorough and complete understanding of the books of the New Testament, put yourself in the place of those to whom they were first delivered by the apostles as a legacy. Transfer yourself in thought to that time and that area where they first were read. Endeavour, so far as possible, to acquaint yourself with the customs, practices, habits, opinions, accepted ways of thought, proverbs, symbolic language, and everyday expressions of these men, and with the ways and means by which they attempt to persuade others or to furnish a foundation for faith. Above all, keep in mind, when you turn to a passage, that you can make no progress by means of any modern system, whether of theology or of logic, or by means of opinions current today.'

Even after more than two hundred years, this remains a very respectable and impressive programme; indeed, it only gains methodological support from the help of the modern theory of literature, which is orientated towards communication: texts display not only internal reference (in relation to structures within the text itself), but also external reference (in relation to circumstances outside the text); they tacitly presuppose the entire cultural knowledge of the period at which they were composed, so that a knowledge of the implied cultural codes is also necessary, if they are to be fully understood.[2] There is simply no possibility of a full *tour d'horizon* of the vast perspectives that open up here. In the nature of things, thanks to the fragmentary character of our sources, all that one will be able to do will be to work with examples in the hope that this takes us some of the way. We will have to be content with approximate evaluations.

2. An earlier programme

List 5.

W. Bousset, 'Die Religionsgeschichte und das Neue Testament', *ThR* 7 (1904) 265–77, 311–18, 353–65; 15 (1912) 251–78.

Wettstein: Texte zum Neuen Testament aus Griechentum und Hellenismus vol. 1: Texte zur Briefliteratur und zur Johannesapokalypse, Berlin 1996; cf. H. J. Klauck, 'Wettstein, alt und neu: Zur Neuausgabe eines Standardwerks', *BZ* NF 41 (1997) 89–95.

[2] See e.g. the section on 'Kulturelles Wissen als zusätzliche interpretatorische Prämisse' in M. Titzmann, *Strukturale Textanalyse: Theorie und Praxis der Interpretation* (UTB 582), Munich 1977, 263–330.

H. Gunkel, *Zum religionsgeschichtlichen Verständnis des Neuen Testaments* (FRLANT 1), Göttingen 1903.

K. Holl, *Urchristentum und Religionsgeschichte* (SASW 10), Gütersloh 1925.

H.-J. Klauck, *Herrenmahl und hellenistischer Kult: Eine religionsgeschichtliche Untersuchung zum ersten Korintherbrief* (NTA NF 15), Münster 2nd edn. 1986.

G. Lüdemann and M. Schröder, *Die religionsgeschichtliche Schule in Göttingen: Eine Dokumentation*, Göttingen 1987.

G. Lüdemann (ed.), *'Religionsgeschichtliche Schule': Facetten eines theologischen Umbruchs*, Frankfurt a.M. 1996.

K. Müller, 'Die religionsgeschichtliche Methode: Erwägungen zu ihrem Verständnis und zur Praxis ihrer Vollzüge an neutestamentlichen Texten', *BZ* NF 29 (1985) 151–92.

H. Paulsen, 'Synkretismus im Urchristentum und im Neuen Testament', in W. Greive and R. Neumann (eds.), *Neu glauben? Religionsvielfalt und neue religiöse Strömungen als Herausforderung an das Christentum*, Gütersloh 1990, 34–44 (the whole volume is very relevant to the problematic of syncretism).

J. Z. Smith, *Drudgery Divine: On the Comparison of Early Christianities and the Religions of Late Antiquity* (JLCR 14), London 1990.

A. J. M. Wedderburn, *Baptism and Resurrection: Studies in Pauline Theology against its Graeco-Roman Background* (WUNT 44), Tübingen 1987.

If one wishes to study the origin of a form of religion and its fundamental texts, an obvious first step is to examine the general religious climate in its milieu. The history of religions school did this at the beginning of our century in its study of the non-Jewish religions of the classical period.

In the 1880s several young Protestant theologians and exegetes came together in Tübingen with the shared conviction that the New Testament must be interpreted with a much stronger emphasis on its Hellenistic, pagan presuppositions. One must investigate the extent to which Christianity in its initial phase was exposed to the influences of the Hellenistic syncretism of the imperial period (this technical term refers to the blending of various forms of religion in the classical period: cf. Paulsen). Among this founding generation – to mention only a few prominent names – we find such exegetes as Hermann Gunkel, regarded as the founder of form-historical criticism, Wilhelm Bousset, and

History of religions

Johannes Weiss (to whom we are indebted for an epoch-making commentary on 1 Corinthians). This group succeeded relatively quickly in elaborating and spreading their ideas through publications, public lectures and academic teaching. Thus, for example, they founded their own series of commentaries in which the texts of the Old and New Testaments were explained in a brief and universally accessible form on the basis of the presuppositions of the history of religions. (This is why this series of commentaries very soon received the name of the 'heretical Bible' in conservative circles.) They also inaugurated the series of 'Religionsgeschichtliche Volksbücher' (popular books on the history of religions, cf. Brückner and Heitmüller in List 59), which enabled them to communicate their insights to a wider public. This school reached its zenith around the turn of the century, and remained identifiable as an independent theological movement until *c.* 1920–30.

The representatives of the history of religions school had no hesitation in deriving much of what was generally seen as specifically Christian, and as an original creation on the part of Christians, from the religions of the surrounding milieu (further information in II/G). There is no doubt that they judged many questions too straightforwardly here, unduly simplifying complicated situations, so that they became guilty of a number of exaggerations. But this does not affect the fruitfulness of the questions they asked. Understandably, violent reactions to such views followed: against this school, every kind of dependence on non-Christian religions was denied, and indeed every similarity and comparability was rejected, since Christianity must prove its originality and its superiority in every respect. The increased tendency from the 1930s onwards to explain as much as possible in earliest Christianity on the basis of the Old Testament and contemporary Judaism must also be seen as a response to the challenge from the history of religions school. This viewpoint found its definitive expression in the monumental *Commentary on the New Testament from the Talmud and Midrash* in several volumes by Paul Billerbeck and in many of the articles in the ten-volume *Theological Dictionary of the New Testament*; here, however, a dubious methodology often takes as a criterion for the Judaism of the first century CE rabbinic writings which must be dated to a considerably later period. Besides this, the fascination exercised by new methods such as form criticism and redaction criticism, as well as dialectical theology's pendulum swing against the liberal theology which had been inspired by the earliest work of the history of religions school, meant that for a while, the question posed by this school moved completely into the background. Such paradigm shifts are repeatedly experienced in scholarship.

We need not examine the question whether one may already go so far as to speak of a new paradigm shift, but it is surely unmistakable that there is a new awareness that the question of the history of religions is both fruitful and necessary. Ultimately, we are not helped here by antitheses such as Judaism *or* Hellenism, autonomy *or* independence. Let me develop this point a little.

It is of course perfectly true that the Jesus movement has its roots in Palestinian Judaism, which was deeply marked by the Old Testament. On the other hand, it is not a matter of chance that all the New Testament writings were composed in Greek – not translated into Greek. It was the Greek and Roman cities of the Mediterranean area that quickly allowed Christianity to gain a foothold, and it was in them that Christianity could display its greatest successes in numerical terms. Besides this, Judaism was numerically strong in the Hellenistic Diaspora, involved in varying degrees of dialogue with the Gentile milieu, and this process of confrontation had led to the adaptation of a certain amount of non-Jewish thought. Thus one cannot set up an antithesis between the Jewish milieu and the non-Jewish milieu; in order to achieve a convincing overview, one must work in all these fields, and the sheer volume of the material makes a division of labour imperative here.

One would impose an unnecessary restriction on one's ability to get a proper perspective on this material, if one were a priori to subordinate everything to the question of a possible dependence – whether particular reasons led one to seek to demonstrate that certain phenomena were originally non-Christian, or an apologetic prejudice led one to dispute the existence of any foreign influence whatsoever. A convincing approach to the texts will avoid both these impasses. The first requirement is to grasp the phenomena in themselves, to present them and to evaluate them. In establishing comparisons, one must distinguish with care between similarities and dependencies. One must establish both the historical plausibility and the de facto existence of dependencies; but one must also evaluate and explain structural similarities. It is only in a comparison that the differences and the specific characteristics of each text genuinely emerge. The critical eye will see clearly that the specific characteristic of Christianity in many cases is to be found less in the details and the individual aspects than in the total pattern and in the unifying centre-point, which gives structure to the Christian universe of meaning. Besides this, the acceptance and assimilation of foreign influences can also be assessed positively, as a sign of the integrative power of the Christian faith, which is capable of fusing the different elements together.

Here we touch upon a question that the modern theology of mission treats under the heading of the inculturation of Christianity.[3] The older praxis of mission too was familiar with the requirement of an adaptation or accommodation: the missionaries were to adapt to the way of life, language, clothing, etc., of the local culture, so that the gospel would not appear to be a foreign import. Obviously, the demand that the gospel be inculturated goes further: the local bearers of each culture ought (and themselves do in fact wish) to develop their own theology which formulates anew, indeed incarnates anew, the gospel on all levels in the forms of expression proper to their own milieu. This is also intended as a contribution to the transformation of the cultures from within, thereby giving due weight to the corresponding perspective of an evangelisation of cultures. For the two belong inseparably together: the inculturation of the gospel and the evangelisation of cultures. In an ideal situation, one may hope that this will enrich the treasury of faith of the entire Church.

One can also apply this perspective of an inculturation of the gospel to the earliest phase of the theological history of the first Christians, carried out in the tension between the patrimony of the Old Testament and Judaism on the one hand, and the horizon of the thought of the Graeco-Roman world on the other. The minimal and at the same time most general consequence of this fact is the requirement that one present at least this non-Jewish horizon for the reception of the Christian proclamation of the gospel.

To take this path will also allow us to overcome some of the impasses of the history of religions school, since this was not interested in the entire horizon for the reception of the gospel, but restricted its investigations primarily to those points where it suspected 'dependencies' and 'influence'. This path does however involve us in two new difficulties, for our broad starting point means that the field of discussion takes on immeasurable dimensions. Thus criteria of selection are demanded in the picture that we draw; and, even

---

[3] See H. Waldenfels, HRGF 169–73; A. Quack, HRWG II, 283–9; P. Stockmeier, 'Die Inkulturation des Christentums', *LS* 39 (1988) 99–103; K. Hilpert and H. Ohlig (eds.), *Der eine Gott in vielen Kulturen: Inkulturation und christliche Gottesvorstellung (Festschrift für G. Hassenhüttl)*, Zurich 1993.

more fundamentally, we need an approximate description of what the term 'religious phenomena' means, and how these can be identified.

3. Elements from social theory

List 6.

F. X. Kaufmann, *Religion und Modernität: Sozialwissenschaftliche Perspektiven*, Tübingen 1989.

T. Luckmann, *The Invisible Religion*, New York 1967.

H. Lübbe, *Religion nach der Aufklärung*, Graz 1986.

N. Luhmann, *Funktion der Religion* (Theorie), Frankfurt a.M. 1977.

H. G. Soeffner, *Die Auslegung des Alltags*, 2: *Die Ordnung der Rituale* (stw 993), Frankfurt a.M. 1992.

We begin with the latter of these, but we do not wish to make the mistake of adding yet another attempt to the list of the many attempts at a definition of religion.[4] It suffices for us to use an operable, general description which adopts elements from the theory of systems (with Niklas Luhmann as one of its chief representatives). In this context, religion is understood as a social system of signs with very precise functions within society, which it alone can supply.

Thus it contributes (*a*) to furnishing the necessary reduction of the possibilities of action with meaningful justifications. To put this more fully: the individual faces a theoretically endless wealth of possibilities of action (e.g. the choice of profession or of a life-partner), and the reaction is a feeling of dizziness; one could always have the suspicion that one has preferred the poorer option and rejected the better possibility. In order that the individual may not completely despair, the number of alternatives must be reduced to a comprehensible cluster that can be mastered; and once the decision has been taken, it needs continually to be stabilised. Here it is helpful to know that it is the will of a higher power that I take this path and remain faithful to it.

Religion also makes (*b*) an indispensable contribution to coping with experiences of contingency, which occur when a path comes to its end, when nothing more can be done and no alternatives are at hand. Death – one's own and that of others – occupies the foremost place here, but one may also mention illness, accidents, or failure in one's professional work or

---

[4] Cf. the bibliography in L1; on what follows, cf. especially Stolz; Whaling; and the introductory articles in HRWG I.

in relationships between human persons. Within a theory that is guided by the image of the frictionless functioning of the system as a whole, there opens up at this point a gap where religion finds its place. It takes away from death a part of its terror, by making the promise of a dwelling of the dead in Elysium, in fellowship with the immortal divinity. It directs the sick to healing gods like Asclepius or to workers of miracles who come into action with their therapies. Processes of specialisation begin.[5] In order to carry out its tasks, religion constructs symbolic worlds composed of mythical narratives, of ritualised gestures, of pictures and buildings, of roles, of objects of piety, texts of prayer, and other elements. These have a character specific to the individual culture, and thus can be very different in practice from one culture to another, but they share the function of facilitating communication about the so-called 'ultimate questions' of life.

Franz-Xaver Kaufmann makes an even more differentiated analysis when he identifies six functions of religion, which he describes as follows (cf. Kaufmann 84–8): 1. the establishing of identity (*inter alia* through affective ties and coping with fear); 2. the guidance of action (i.e. directing the believer's behaviour in exceptional situations, where custom does not suffice); 3. coping with contingency (see above); 4. social integration (religion as the 'glue' of society); 5. cosmicisation (i.e. the establishing of a unified framework within which to interpret and understand the world, as a counterweight to meaninglessness and chaos); 6. a distancing from the world (here we find e.g. the protest of the prophets or the withdrawal of the monks into the wilderness). This more complicated framework could also be applied without difficulty to the classical world, in order to identify the bearers of the various offers and contributions made there. But ultimately, priority must be given to the individual phenomena, which must be described and decoded in case studies (cf. the critique of the tendencies to generalisation of the theory of systems and the portrait of the 'sociological leveller' on the other side, by Soeffner 17–19).

A system-theoretical description of religious phenomena, if it remains conscious of its own limitations, makes no affirmations about claims to truth and absoluteness, whether positive – which could not in any case be expected of such a description – or negative. It cannot, of course, be denied that this model has a tendency to reduce religion to something else, and ultimately to dissolve it into culture and society. Despite the danger of circular arguments,

---

[5] Thus, for example, the divine pair of brothers, the Dioscuri, were responsible in the classical period for rescuing those in peril on the sea: cf. Acts 28:11.

the way to avoid this tendency is to take seriously what those personally involved say about themselves. Thus we will also have to pay heed to what the persons of a particular cultural sphere at a given point in time themselves understood under the headings of religion, faith, piety and the experience of the divine, where they recognised the working of numinous powers and where they saw a transcendence that went beyond purely innerworldly horizons. An exclusive concentration on this interior view (as was customary in the earlier academic study of religion) cannot be recommended, because we should then lack objective criteria for our description;[6] but taken together, the approaches from the outside and from the inside provide sufficiently secure parameters for work in the history of religions.

4. Biblical paradigms

The long excursus on the Gentile veneration of gods in Wis 13–15 seems to repay attention as an historical paradigm for the way in which the Jewish faith in God provided a perspective to confront the phenomenon of religion.[7] It bears witness to an ability to make acute observations, to an intense intellectual confrontation, to a high level of reflection, and to a knowledge of the contemporary discussion among philosophers. Despite all his stringency, the author does not engage in a blindly ferocious polemic, but strives for a differentiated view of the fundamental problematic. In his diagnosis, religion, in the widest sense of this word, has its origin in the managing of experiences of contingency in nature and in human life. This means:

1. The human person feels powerless in the face of the omnipotence of nature, and thus is inclined to deify the powers of nature (Wis 13:1–9).

2. The human person experiences painful losses in the course of life: the death of a beloved child, of one's wife, of parents and friends. The elevation of the dead to the status of heroes and gods is an attempt to come to terms with this (14:15).

3. People need someone or something to turn to when they seek help – we may take a storm at sea as an example of this kind of immediate predicament.

---

[6] I note only in passing that these indications bring us into the dispute between a functionalist and a substantialist way of looking at religion; on this, cf. Luckmann, above all the foreword by H. Knoblauch (in the German translation *Die unsichtbare Religion*, Frankfurt a.M. 1977), which brings the discussion up to date (7–41), and the afterword (164–83).

[7] Cf. M. Gilbert, *La Critique des dieux* (L80).

For want of better possibilities, they make their own god for themselves, and then invoke its aid (13:10–14:11).

4. Human beings are fascinated by the military and political power that imposes its will against every obstacle and imposes its own boundaries. They cannot avoid interpreting such a power in religious categories. This results in the cult of rulers and emperors (14:16–20).

5. In the case of the Egyptians' cult of animals, however, the author's hermeneutical endeavours break down (15:14–19). Others go a step further here, such as Philo, who holds that initially those animals were venerated which were especially useful to human beings for particular reasons, animals that were necessary to human survival or which provided particular benefits to human beings (*Decal.* 77).

6. A move is taken towards reflecting on religion as a social system of signs, in its significance for the shared life of society, although mostly in the negative sense that a false veneration of gods goes hand in hand with a false societal praxis (14:21-31).

The author of the Book of Wisdom leaves no doubt in the reader's mind that he is undertaking an evaluation on the firm foundation of the biblical faith in God. But he does not proceed in a purely deductive manner, as would have been possible here on the basis of the Bible's prohibition of images; instead, he attempts by an inductive method to shed light on the reality of the world and of experience. This is the genuinely sapiential element in his starting point, even when he is dealing with the Gentile belief in gods.

Our choice of the areas of study in this book is not only dictated by considerations of space, but is guided to a certain extent by external considerations: in the light of the New Testament, with a view to a better understanding of its texts, we discuss matters that appear especially informative and which therefore are continually mentioned (more or less explicitly) in exegetical research. It would be easy to use the secondary literature as the basis for a list of relevant terms, but here we follow a biblical text, viz. Luke's Acts of the Apostles, as our example:[8]

In Samaria, the first missionaries meet a man called Simon, whom Luke portrays as a magician (Acts 8:9) but whom the early Church fathers see as

---

[8] Cf. B. Wildhaber, *Paganisme populaire* (L80); H.-J. Klauck, 'With Paul in Paphos and Lystra: Magic and Paganism in the Acts of the Apostles', *Neotest.* 28 (1994) 93–108; Idem, *Magie und Heidentum in der Apostelgeschichte des Lukas* (SBS 167), Stuttgart 1996.

an ancestor of gnosis. The Ethiopian whom Philip baptises (8:26–40) and the centurion Cornelius in Caesarea (10:1–48) were already open vis-à-vis Judaism. Herod Agrippa puts on mannerisms that fit the cult of rulers (12:21f.). The proconsul Sergius Paulus on Cyprus has a Jewish magician and (perhaps) astrologer at his court (13:4–12). In Lystra, Paul and Barnabas barely escape from the plan of the priest of 'Zeus outside the city', viz. a ceremonial sacrifice of a bull to them (14:11–18). In Philippi, Paul encounters a girl with a spirit of augury (16:16–18). In Athens he is enraged at a city that is full of the images of idols, he holds discussions with Stoic and Epicurean philosophers, he discovers an altar to the 'unknown God', and comes suspiciously close to the Stoa in the words he uses in his sermon (17:16–34). In Ephesus, where Jewish exorcists try their luck with the name of Jesus, the believers are filled with repentance and burn their books of sorcery, while the silversmiths present a united front in the name of the great goddess Artemis in their attack on Paul (19:11–40). The inhabitants of Malta begin by looking on Paul as one cursed by the goddess of vengeance, and then acclaim him as a god (28:1–6). We meet the language of the mystery cults – to cast our net a little wider – in 2 Cor 12:4 (ἄρρητα ῥήματα), in Phil 4:12 (μεμύημαι) in 2 Pet 1:16 (ἐπόπται), and possibly in Col 2:18, since 2:8 also speaks in a polemical context of a philosophy (φιλοσοφία). Finally, the Pastoral Letters attack a 'gnosis that is falsely given that name' (1 Tim 6:20).

If we extrapolate only the concepts that are mentioned here, we have already essential components of the material that will be discussed with the appropriate brevity in the following chapters. First comes a general chapter on expressions of religion in public life (temple, sacrifice, feasts, priesthood), in groups, in the private house, and in individual life. Then we turn to the mystery cults, which have been the object of so much discussion. There follow astrology, augury, the belief in miracles and sorcery, as well as the cult of rulers and emperors, and the philosophy of the early imperial period in its religious dimensions. Last of all comes a chapter on gnosis. There may be disagreement about whether this belongs together with these other topics; but gnosis turns up with regularity in exegesis as a somewhat nebulous matter, and it has at some periods been an essential determinant of the debate about the history of religions. Thus the intended readers of this book ought certainly to be interested in knowing whether or not a gnosis existed before and outside Christianity.

Chapter I
Daily Life and Liminal Experiences: Civic and Domestic Religion

A. The sacrificial cult

Let us once again choose Acts 14:8–18 as our starting point. In the city of Lystra in Asia Minor, the populace deduce from a miracle of healing that the two Christian missionaries Paul and Barnabas are Zeus and Hermes, who have appeared in human form. The priest of the temple of 'Zeus outside the city' brings bulls decked with garlands and wants, along with the crowd, to offer a sacrifice to them. A number of vacant points in this narrative demand to be filled out with supplementary information. What kind of temples were this one and others? What was the task of the priest, and how were priests recruited? What was the normal procedure in a sacrifice? To what extent were the people involved in it? To which divinities were sacrifices offered? What kind of expectations lay behind the praxis of sacrifice?

We shall take certain texts in the next sections to exemplify the way in which these questions were dealt with. Sometimes this will involve very long journeys into little-known areas. But we should bear in mind that the sacrificial praxis was a social and religious reality of the first order in the whole of classical antiquity. It was something taken for granted in life. Sacrifices were offered in Judaism too, although concentrated here on the temple in Jerusalem, which was in full function until its destruction in 70 CE. It is probable that the Jewish Christians from Palestine initially continued to take part in the temple sacrifices in the city of Jerusalem after Easter, and that the detachment of Christians from the temple, linked to a corresponding new interpretation of Jesus' death on the cross, began only in the group of Hellenistic Jewish Christians in Jerusalem. At any rate, one of the contingent historical parameters for the birth of Christianity was the fact that it took on its first form in a sacrificial culture. Not only does sacrifice remain alive in Christianity as a theological and spiritual category; it even achieves a stable position in the heart of Christian thought and Christian piety. All these reasons make it appear worthwhile to pay closer attention to the fundamental issues involved.

1. The sacrificial rite

(*a*) The normal form

List 7.

G. J. Baudy, 'Hierarchie oder: Die Verteilung des Fleisches', in B. Gladigow and H. G. Kippenberg, *Ansätze* (L1) 131–74.

G. Berthiaume, *Les Rôles du mágeiròs: Étude sur la boucherie, la cuisine et le sacrifice dans la Grèce ancienne* (Mn.S 70), Leiden 1982.

J. Casabona, *Recherches sur le vocabulaire des sacrifices en Grec, des origines à la fin de l'époque classique* (Publications des Annales de la Faculté des Lettres NS 56), Aix-en-Provence 1966.

M. Detienne and J. P. Vernant (eds.), *The Cuisine of Sacrifice among the Greeks*, Chicago 1989.

S. Eitrem, *Opferritus und Voropfer der Griechen und Römer* (Videnskapsselskapets Skrifter, II, Hist.-Filos. Klasse 1914, 1), Kristiana (Oslo) 1915, reprint Hildesheim 1977.

R. Hägg (ed.), *Ancient Greek Cult Practice from the Epigraphical Evidence*, Stockholm 1994.

V. J. Rosivach, *The System of Public Sacrifice in Fourth-Century Athens* (ACSt 34), Atlanta, GA 1994.

I. Rudhard and O. Reverdin (eds.), *Le Sacrifice dans l'antiquité* (EnAC 27), Geneva 1981.

F. Rüsche, *Blut, Leben und Seele: Ihr Verhältnis nach Auffassung der griechischen und hellenistischen Antike, der Bibel und der alten Alexandrinischen Theologen. Eine Vorarbeit zur Religionsgeschichte des Opfers* (SGKA.E 5), Paderborn 1930.

P. Stengel, *Opferbräuche der Griechen,* Leipzig and Berlin 1910.

A. Thomsen, 'Der Trug des Prometheus', *ARW* 12 (1909) 460–90.

The normal form of sacrifice for Greeks and Romans was the so-called slaughter-sacrifice which was followed by a sacrificial meal. The Homeric epics (which have justifiably been called the 'Bible of the Greeks') furnish us with some fine early examples. Although of course the epics are not ritual texts, the sequence described in them does agree in its fundamental traits with the later ritual, while a few details change. Three key texts will serve as the basis for our further discussions.[1]

---

[1] Translations from Homer: Martin Hammond, *The Iliad*, London 1987; E. V. Rieu, revised by D. C. H. Rieu, *The Odyssey*, London 1991.

Examples of texts

1. In the course of their journey to Troy, the Greeks carried off the daughter of Chryses, the old priest of Apollo, as a captive, but Apollo compels them by means of a plague in the camp to return her to her home. This is done by a delegation led by Odysseus, who also bring an expiatory hecatomb with them.[2] The priest receives his daughter back at the altar and then asks his god Apollo to take away the curse from the Greek army and to cease punishing them. The sacrificial ritual is described as follows (*Iliad* 1.458–68):

> When they had offered prayers and sprinkled the barley grains, first they pulled back the victims' heads and slaughtered them and flayed them: and they cut out the thigh-bones and covered them with fat, folding it twice over, and placed pieces of raw meat on top. The old man burnt them on cut firewood, and poured libations of gleaming wine, while the young men stood by him with five-pronged forks in their hands. Then when the thighs were burnt up and they had tasted the innards, they chopped the rest into pieces and threaded them on spits, roasted them carefully, and then drew all the meat off. When they had finished their work and prepared the meal, they set to eating, and no man's desire went without an equal share in the feast.

2. The first sacrifice in the *Odyssey* to be mentioned is the sacrifice of a cow which Nestor offers to the goddess Athene when he is visited by Telemachus, who is looking for his father Odysseus; here we find some additional details, such as the gilding of the cow's horns (*Od.* 3.436f.). Once again we have the sprinkling of the sacred barley. New elements here are e.g. the cutting off and burning of some hair from the animal's brow and the ritual exulting or shouting on the part of the women who are present (*Od.* 3.445–63):

> The old charioteer Nestor now started the ritual with the lustral water[3] and the scattered grain, and offered up his earnest prayers to Athene as he began the sacrifice by throwing a tuft of hair from its head on the fire. When they had prayed and sprinkled the barley meal, Nestor's son, the high-spirited Thrasymedes, stepped up and struck. The axe cut through the tendons of the heifer's neck and it collapsed. At this, the women raised their celebratory cry – Nestor's daughters and his daughter-in-law, and his honoured wife Eurydice, Clymenus'

---

[2]   The term 'hecatomb' properly denotes a sacrifice of one hundred (ἑκατόν) bulls (βοῦς), but it is employed in a more general sense simply to designate an especially large and solemn sacrifice.

[3]   This is used to wash the hands: cf. *Iliad* 1.449.

eldest daughter. The men lifted the heifer's head from the trodden earth and held it up while that leader of men, Peisistratus, cut its throat. When the dark blood had gushed out and life had left the heifer's body, they swiftly dismembered the carcass, cut out the thigh bones in the usual way, wrapped them in folds of fat and laid raw meat above them. The venerable king burnt these on the firewood, sprinkling red wine over the flames, while the young men gathered round with five-pronged forks in their hands. When the thighs were burnt up and they had tasted the inner parts, they carved the rest into small pieces, pierced them with skewers and held the sharp ends to the fire till all was roasted.

3. The third example takes us into the domestic sphere, where an evening dinner with the external forms of a sacrificial meal is held. Odysseus arrives back incognito, disguised as an old beggar, on Ithaca, his island home, and is hospitably received by the swineherd Eumaeus. They spend the day in a lively conversation, but without Odysseus letting himself be recognised. Our scene begins when evening comes (*Od.* 14.413–38):

> The worthy swineherd called out to his men. 'Bring your best hog. I want to slaughter it for a guest I have here from abroad. And we'll enjoy ourselves, after all we've put up with looking after the white-tusked boars all this time, while other people live for nothing off our work.' He then chopped some firewood with his sharp axe, and his men dragged in a fatted five-year-old hog and held it by the hearth. The swineherd, who was a good and virtuous man, did not forget the immortals, but began the ritual by throwing a tuft of hair from the white-tusked victim into the fire and praying to all the gods that the wise Odysseus might come back to his home. Then he drew himself up and struck the animal with a piece of oak which he had left unsplit. The hog fell stunned. They slit its throat, singed its bristles, and deftly cut the carcass up. The swineherd cut pieces from all the limbs as a first offering to the gods, placed them with raw fat on the thigh bones, sprinkled them with barley meal and threw them all on to the flames. Then they chopped up the rest of the meat, pierced it with spits, roasted it thoroughly, and after drawing it off the spits heaped it up on platters. The swineherd, with his characteristic fairness, stood up to divide it into helpings. He carved and sorted it all out into seven portions, one of which he set aside, with a prayer, for the Nymphs and for Hermes, Maia's son, and distributed the rest to the company. But he gave Odysseus the portion of honour, the hog's long chine.

Systematisation

If we make a formal system out of the data in these texts, we find the skeleton of the normal form of slaughter sacrifice with sacrificial meal among the Greeks (and in all essential points among the Romans too), which must be partly filled out with information from other sources. When a sacrifice is to be made for any reason, the first thing to be done is to select the animal; the choice depends on the occasion, on the particular deity to whom homage is to be paid, and on the possibilities available to the persons involved. No doubt, the sacrifices of bulls and cows in our initial examples represent the most costly procedure, one that was correspondingly rare de facto. It will have been more common to sacrifice pigs (as in the case of Eumaeus) or goats, and even more common to take a sheep (cf. our proverbial 'sacrificial lamb'). The Romans had a complete solemn sacrifice of purification which they called *suovetaurilia*, because it involved swine (*sus*), sheep (*ovis*) and cattle (*taurus*). Poultry were used too; thus, the dying Socrates recalls with his very last words that 'we still owe Asclepius a cock' (*Phaed.* 66 [118a]). It is always a case of edible animals (so that for example no horses or dogs are mentioned in this context), and of domestic animals, not booty that is hunted. The animal selected must be unblemished (cf. Seneca, *Oed.* 299f.: 'Lead to the altar a bull with a pure white back and a heifer whose neck has never been bowed under a crooked yoke'), and the animal should go freely, not under coercion, when it is led in procession to the place of sacrifice. The animal is decked with ribbons and garlands, even in some cases by the gilding of its horns; the participants too set garlands on their heads. A flute-player provides the musical accompaniment.

When they arrive at the place of sacrifice, where a fire is already burning, the group of participants goes in a ring around the altar. All purify their hands with water from a spring or a river. The animal too may be sprinkled with water (less commonly, with wine). This provokes it to jerk its head, and this is interpreted as a nod of consent. But most importantly, those making the sacrifice scatter barleycorn (as in Homer) or (among the Romans) salted coarse meal (*mola salsa*, from which the verb *immolare*, 'to sacrifice', is derived) on the animal and on the altar. The sacrificial priest cuts some of the hair from the brow of the animal and throws it on to the fire. Then he prays to the deity to whom the sacrifice is being offered. In the case of large animals, one of the participants stuns it with a powerful blow to its forehead from the sacrificial axe, from a hammer or a heavy piece of wood. The throat of all the beasts, large and small, is slit, so that the blood can spurt freely from the carotid artery. The ritual sacrificial cry of the women (ὀλολυγή) accompanies this, which is the kernel of the slaughter. Some of the blood lands on the altar, while the rest simply flows on to the earth and must be cleared up later on.

The dead animal is now flayed with specialist skill and divided into portions. In Homer, the edible inner parts were at once roasted on the fire and eaten; among the Romans, this became the place for haruspicy, viz. the consulting of the innards (see III/B, 1(b) below). The bones, covered in fat and sprinkled with wine, were burnt on the altar for the gods (the small pieces of meat, mentioned in Homer, fell out of use later on). The properly sacrificial act now gives way to the meal held by those celebrating the feast. The meat for this meal is roasted on spits, or else cooked in pots (cf. the triad of sacrificial knife, roasting-spit and cooking vessel in Herodotus, *Hist.* 2.42.3). A part of the meat belongs to the temple or to the priest. If too much is left over, it can be taken home, or it is sold on the meat market.

Taken as a whole, the fundamental structure can appropriately be described as follows: 'Animal sacrifice is a ritualised slaughter followed by a meat meal.'[4] A number of details must be investigated in greater detail, and this will be done to some extent in the following paragraphs. Where, for example, does this ritual take place? The first two examples from Homer speak only of altars, and we tend usually to associate temples too with the mention of altars. Who conducts the ritual? In general terms, persons who enjoy respect in society: in our initial examples, the priest of Apollo, the king with his sons and followers, the chief herdsman at the court. In the further course of history, this passes more and more into the hands of specialists and functionaries. Here we must ask about the role of the priests. On what occasions is a sacrifice offered? Our examples are basically of spontaneous actions that arise from the specific situation: the return of the daughter who had been lost, the visit of the son of a companion in arms, the hospitable welcoming of a stranger. But there also existed fixed occasions for sacrifice on the public festivals, as well as regular sacrifices in the daily temple round. To which deities are sacrifices offered? We have seen sacrifices offered in official rituals to Apollo and Athene, who are members of the Olympic pantheon, but we have also heard of all the gods, of Hermes and of the Nymphs. We must investigate this further. What is the provenance of this rite, and who is responsible for its exact observation? The general answer has to be: everything is based on the νόμος, i.e. inherited customs and usages, an unwritten law. The correct sequence of

[4] W. Burkert, *Religion* (L2) 103.

the ritual is mediated societally and derives from the tradition that has been handed down through the generations. The essential thing here is not a handbook that one might consult, nor a schooling in the correct way to carry out rituals of sacrifice, but imitation, taking one's own place in the inheritance that was handed down and was seldom called into question.

Problems

The only remarkable point we will discuss here is the portioning of the sacrificial matter: the edible meat and the skin, i.e. everything that can be used, belongs to the human beings, while the main thing the gods receive is merely bones and fat, and perhaps blood, if the human beings so wish. More precisely, all that the gods enjoy is the steam of the fat as it rises upwards in the smoke of the sacrificial fire, as the satirist Lucian mockingly observes in an essay that is critical of sacrifices (*De Sacrificiis* 9):

> They look down to the earth and look carefully in all directions to see if they can find a fire that has been lit, or clouds of smoke that bring them the smell of sacrifices that their noses so much like. If someone offers a sacrifice to them, they look on this as a delightful treat that is given to them, all opening their gullets as wide as possible in order to gulp down the stinking smoke as if it were something delicious, and they lick like greedy flies the blood poured out on the altars. But if they eat at home, their meal consists of nectar and ambrosia.

Lucian does indeed indirectly note here that the gods do not genuinely need the food of sacrifices, because the only thing they consume is the heavenly food of nectar and ambrosia; but this fundamental relativisation of the sacrificial praxis did not account satisfactorily for the unequal distribution of the parts. The narrative of Prometheus' deceit, as related by Hesiod in his *Theogony* (535–57; cf. Thomsen), attempts to explain how this came about. Prometheus succeeds in getting the better of Zeus by wrapping the valuable meat in the skin of the animal and covering it with the stomach, so that it looks unappealing, whereas he lays out the white bones and the gleaming fat attractively. When Zeus is offered the choice, he opts for the fat and the bones. According to Hesiod, he does this intentionally, although he knows perfectly well what Prometheus has in mind. But there doubtless lies an earlier version of the myth behind Hesiod, in which Zeus was quite simply duped. But even this early stage of the narrative is secondary in comparison to the sacrificial praxis which is in question here: the aim is to supply at a later period a reason for this strange custom. We can see in this a kind of guilt-feeling vis-à-vis the gods, or a surprise at the way the ritual was carried out; but certainly also relief that things had turned out this way and not otherwise, for human beings have a much more imperative need than do the gods of the meat and the skin of animals, in order to be able to live. The guilt is deftly cast upon Prometheus as the author of this custom, and he had already received his vicarious punishment for this transgression (as is well known, since he had also stolen fire from heaven and given it to human beings, he was chained to a rock in the Caucasus; an eagle came regularly and ate his liver, which always grew afresh, until finally Hercules freed him from his torments). We may already at this point venture to suppose that behind all the mythical patterns of explanation the origin of the ritual of slaughter-sacrifice may have been human beings' need to get meat.

The closest parallels to this Graeco-Roman sacrificial praxis, in terms of the sequence of actions, are found in the slaughter-sacrifice in the Old Testament, called *zebach(im)* in Hebrew. It is only here that we find the same sequence of slaughter, blood rite, burning of the part that belongs to the divinity, and a feast. Many differences in individual points also exist: thus, the divinity receives a more generous portion in the Old Testament than among the Greeks, so that there is no room for the idea of a Promethean deceit. Only the Jewish tradition knows the principle that excludes absolutely every human drinking of blood. Nevertheless, we may observe a striking similarity, which has already given rise to a variety of hypotheses. We must assume complicated links at an early cultural stage in the Mediterranean area.

(*b*) Special forms

List 8.

H. Dohrmann, *Anerkennung und Bekämpfung von Menschenopfern im römischen Strafrecht der Kaiserzeit* (EHS.R 1850), Frankfurt a.M. etc. 1995.

D. Gill, 'Trapezomata: A Neglected Aspect of Greek Sacrifice', *HThR* 67 (1974) 117–37.

D. D. Hughes, *Human Sacrifice in Ancient Greece*, London and New York 1991.

M. H. Jameson, '*Theoxenia*', in R. Hägg (ed.), *Cult Practice* (L7) 35–57.

F. Schwenn, *Die Menschenopfer bei den Griechen und Römern* (RVV 15.3), Giessen 1915.

W. Speyer, 'Das letzte Mahl Jesu im Lichte des sogenannten Eidopfers', in Idem, *Christentum* (L3) 477–92.

We begin with the discussion of some special forms, so that we can get at least an approximate view of the whole panorama of ideas about sacrifice in the classical period.

The sacrifice of gifts

As well as meat, other natural products belong to the sacrificial cult, e.g. wine, oil, honey and milk, as well as bread, cakes and many kinds of baked articles. They can also function as independent gifts made in sacrifice; in the case of liquids, they can for example be libations, i.e. the gift of a drink, when either some wine is poured out on to the earth for the divinity and the rest is drunk by the offerer (σπονδή), or the vessel is completely emptied out on to the earth (χοή). In other cases these natural products may be presented in sacrifices of the first-fruits, when examples of each fruit are offered in special vessels.

Annihilatory sacrifices

We are familiar from the Old Testament with the burnt offering, or more precisely an annihilatory sacrifice in which the flames consume the entire matter of the sacrifice and thus it is naturally impossible to hold a sacrificial meal. Similar annihilatory sacrifices, occupying a less prominent position, are found also among the Greeks and the Romans, primarily in expiatory rites and in the cult of the gods of the underworld. A further distinguishing mark is that in annihilatory sacrifices sometimes even domestic animals that are not edible and wild animals caught by hunters are burnt – in extreme cases, even burnt alive.[5]

The ritual of oath and covenant

Once again it is the *Iliad* that shows us an ancient ritual of oath when a binding agreement is concluded. An individual combat between the protagonists Menelaus (on the Greek side) and Paris (on the Trojan side) is to bring the final decision in the war. Agamemnon makes a binding agreement with Priam about this: he slits the throat of two lambs and their

---

[5]   Cf. the strange ritual of burning in honour of Artemis Laphria (an Olympian goddess) in Patrae, related by Pausanias in the imperial period: *Graec. Descr.* 7.18.11–13; on this, cf. W. Burkert, *Religion* (L2) 62f.

blood flows on to the ground. Wine is poured over this, and the words of the oath are spoken (*Il.* 3.299f.; 4.159f.):

> Whichever side first offends against these oaths, may their brains spill on the ground as this wine is spilled ...
>
> There can be no failure of an oath, of the blood of lambs and the unmixed libations and the giving of right hands, in which we trusted.

The effectiveness of the ritual is based first on the supposition that a partner who breaks the covenant will (magically) draw down the curse upon himself, i.e. that the same will happen to him as to the slaughtered animal and the wine that was poured out (cf. Speyer). A covenant meal is not required here, and in fact does not suit the original mood of the scene. But gradually such a meal was introduced, through a blending of the pure ritual of oath-taking with the normal form of sacrifice and with the praxis of blood brotherhood that we find in a number of peoples. This blending leads ultimately to horror stories such as those that were told about Catiline, who was said to have made a covenant with his fellow plotters by killing a boy and eating his entrails (Dio Cassius 37.30.3) or else by drinking his blood mixed with wine (Sallust, *Catiline* 22.1–3).

At the same time, we find here traces of human sacrifice (cf. Schwenn; Hughes; Dohrmann), which was certainly very much the exception in the historical period but is firmly anchored both in the mythical tradition and in those sensational narratives beloved of rumours and of novelists (the classical novels too have some horrifying descriptions of genuine or fictional human sacrifices).

Theoxeny (giving hospitality to gods)

The classical period included among the sacrificial cult in the broad sense also theoxeny, the ritual hospitality shown to gods, or giving them food. This occurred in temples and in the open air, as a private and as a public action, on fixed days and on particular occasions. The requisites are a table to receive the food and a couch on which the decorated images of the gods are given a place.[6] This special form is called *lectisternium* in Latin (from *lectus*, 'resting-place', and *sternere*, 'to spread out', take one's place). Livy tells of *lectisternia* that were held when the auguries were unfavourable, in

---

[6] A Greek example is the inscription SIG 3/583 = LSAM 32 from Magnesia (196 BCE), according to which twelve statues of the gods were placed on three couches; on this cf. O. Kern, *Religion* (L2) III.177.

21

times of drought, plague, and military defeats. They were accompanied by meals held among the citizenry (*Urb. Cond.* 5.13.6–8):[7]

> By means of a solemn meal for the gods [*lectisternium*] which was then [401 BCE] held throughout a period of eight days for the first time in the city, the college of two members which was responsible for the rites pacified Apollo and Platona, Hercules and Diana, Mercury and Neptune on couches made ready [*stratis lectis*] with coverings and cushions, with all the splendour that could be achieved at that time. This ceremony was also carried out in private. It is said that the doors were open in the whole city, that absolutely everything stood in the antechambers for general use, that persons known and unknown, as they happened to come by, were invited as guests everywhere, that people spoke in a friendly and polite manner even with their enemies, and contention and strife abated. In the space of these days, even the prisoners had their fetters removed ...

This action included the hope that the invited deity would (so to speak) appear in person and eat the meal, which was presumably eaten in reality by the priests or the participants. According to Kurt Latte the *lectisternia* were new forms of piety 'which gave the broad masses a more direct possibility than the traditional cult of the gods, of coming close to the gods and assuring themselves that the favour of the gods was certain'.[8]

We can distinguish from these *lectisternia*, which were held on particular occasions, the continuous serving of food to the gods in the temples (see Gill, or his source text Dionysius of Halicarnassus, *Ant. Rom.* 2.23.5: 'I have seen how they set out meals for the gods in sacred houses, barley bread, cakes, wheat and first-fruits on old wooden tables, in baskets and earthenware vessels'). The idea of a meal taken in fellowship by gods and human beings may be indicated in such rites, but it is never clearly stated; where it does find clear expression, it is transposed into mythical spheres and times, as in Homer where the gods enjoy the hospitality of the far-off Ethiopians and Phaeacians (*Il.* 1.423f. and frequently), or in Hesiod, who says about the earliest age: 'At that time the meals were in common, immortal gods and mortal human beings had the same customs' (frag. 1 Merkelbach-West).

---

[7] On this text cf. also L. Fladerer, *Livius: Ab urbe condita / Römische Geschichte. Liber V/5. Buch* (RecUB 2035), Stuttgart 1993. B. O. Foster, *Livy: History of Rome*, vol. 3 (LCL 172), Cambridge, Mass. and London 1924.

[8] *Religionsgeschichte* (L2) 242.

However, the old view continues to live on in the theoxenies that the gods depend on receiving nourishment from human beings, that one must feed them so that they can keep up their strength and remain alive. This was a point that the scorn of the satirists could attack, as we already find in Aristophanes' comedy *The Birds*, where Prometheus tells how 'the gods of the barbarians cry aloud for sheer hunger' and threaten 'to make war on Zeus on high, unless he puts an end to the trade barrier and allows the free import of sacrificial meat' (1520–4).

2. Temples and altars

List 9.
S. E. Alcock and R. Osborne (eds.), *Placing the Gods: Sanctuaries and Sacred Space in Ancient Greece*, Oxford 1994, pb. 1996.
N. Marinatos and R. Hägg (eds.), *Greek Sanctuaries: New Approaches*, London 1993 (with detailed bibliography [192–227]).
E. M. Orlin, *Temples, Religion and Politics in the Roman Republic* (Mn. S 164), Leiden 1996.
G. Roux, *Temples et sanctuaires*, Lyons 1984.
J. E. Stambaugh, 'The Functions of Roman Temples', *ANRW* II/16.1 (1978) 554–608.

The tables for the regular meals of the gods were in the interiors of the temples: the altars for the slaughter sacrifices stood outside, before the entrance. The Greek language has two different terms, τράπεζα for the table and βωμός for the altar. We see here characteristics of the temple complexes of the classical period, which have little in common with what we today think of as rooms for divine worship or church buildings. The typical ideal basic form of a classical temple is as follows: in the middle of an oblong quadrilateral, with steps leading up to it, lies a closed room, the *cella*, into which light falls through an opening in the ceiling or through a high door giving on to the east. Against the back wall, usually somewhat higher up, stands the statue of the god or goddess to whom the temple is dedicated (sometimes two gods were involved, less frequently a larger number). There are scarcely any other articles of inventory in this central part of the temple, apart from the τράπεζα for the gods' meal, a small incense altar and some votive gifts. At any rate, the *cella* is definitely not a room for the believers to gather, nor a place of sacrifice. There may be other smaller rooms behind the *cella* for the use of those employed in the temple, or for storing utensils. The temple treasury was often located here too; this consisted of votive gifts, financial contributions and dues that were levied, and amounted to a considerable value (one of the functions of temples was as banks in which money could be deposited for safe keeping, or loans could be made against a payment of interest). Before the *cella* was an antechamber giving on to the open air; a pillared portico, similarly open, ran around it.

The interior of the temple stood in solemn silence, since it was only from time to time that a visitor entered it; the worship was carried on outside, before the main entrance. It was here that the slaughter-sacrifices, described above, were made; here stood the sacrificial altar on which the sacrificial fire burned. In the earliest period, sods of grass or stones were built up in layers to serve as altars; we also find altars composed of the ashes that piled up from the remains of earlier sacrifices. It was only rarely that altars reached the imposing size of the altar of Zeus in Pergamum (which can be admired today in the Museum Island in Berlin) or of Augustus' altar of peace, the *ara pacis*. Mostly we find rather small, virtually square or else round altar blocks of marble and stone. Larger animals were not slaughtered on such altars, but near them. It sufficed to sprinkle the altar with blood, to cast sacred barley into the fire and to burn the god's portion in the fire. The preparation and the eating of the sacrificial meat also took place in the open air, rather like a picnic. But many temples also had their own kitchen and dining rooms (examples are the temple of Asclepius and the temple of Demeter in Corinth).[9]

The entire temple complex lay within a distinct space called *temenos* (from τέμνω, to 'cut' or 'cut out', indicating here the specially demarcated sacred area). Areas with a spring or a small group of trees tended to be chosen. Springs and groves could also be considered as sacred places in their own right, where the divinity let its presence be felt (cf. Ovid, *Fasti* 3.295–8: 'There lay a grove at the foot of the Aventine, dark from the shadows of the oak trees. Whoever saw it would have said: "A divinity lives

---

[9] See M. Lang, *Cure and Cult in Ancient Corinth: A Guide to the Asklepieion* (American Excavations in Old Corinth: Corinth Notes 1), Princeton 1977; N. Bookidis, 'Ritual Dining in the Sanctuary of Demeter and Kore at Corinth: Some Questions', in O. Murray (ed.), *Sympotica: A Symposium on the Symposion*, Oxford 1990, 86–94, or Idem, 'Ritual Dining at Corinth', in Marinatos and Hägg 45–61.

here." Grass grew in its midst, and the channel of an ever-flowing spring came out of the rock, covered over with green moss.')[10]

The above description can also be applied, in its essential points, to the Jerusalem temple, with the difference that no image of the god stood in its interior, but only the ark of the covenant, possibly as the relic of an ancient throne on which the divinity sat. Apart from this, the rules about access were laid down with particular severity: there was an outer court for Gentiles, a court for the women, a court for the men, and no one was allowed to enter the innermost area except the high priest, and he only once a year. Similar regulations, i.e. the exclusion of specific groups and an inaccessible inner sphere, a so-called *adyton*, existed in non-Jewish temples too, but there they were not the normal case. Participation in the sacrificial celebration was not linked to any very high preconditions, so that long preparatory phases with difficult rituals are the exception, apart from in the mystery cults (see Chapter II below). But some notions of taboo did become established, leading to a minimum of prescriptions regarding purity; sexual continence for brief periods could be made a presupposition, as in the following instructive example from the temple of Athene in Pergamum (133 BCE):[11]

> Whoever wishes to visit the temple of the goddess, both the dweller in the city and everyone else, must have abstained from intercourse with his own wife or with her own husband on the same day, and with another woman or another man on the previous day, and must carry out the necessary ablutions; likewise, such a person must not have come into contact with the burying of a corpse or the delivery of a woman in labour on the previous day; if he comes from a funeral feast and burial, he is to sprinkle himself on all sides and go through the door where the basins of water are set up, and he will be pure on the same day.

3. Gods and images of gods

List 10.

P. Desideri, 'Religione e politica nell' "Olimpico" di Dione', *QSt* 15 (1980) 141–61.

P. F. Dorcey, *The Cult of Silvanus: A Study in Roman Folk Religion* (CSCT 20), Leiden 1992.

[10] See also the fine description of a sacred grove in Pliny the Younger, *Ep.* 8.8.1–7.

[11] SIG 3/982.9 = LSAM 12.

G. Lieberg, 'Die theologia tripertita in Forschung und Bezeugung', *ANRW* I/4 (1973) 63–115.

L. R. Lind, 'Roman Religion and Ethical Thought: Abstraction and Personification', *CJ* 69 (1973/4) 108–10.

C. R. Long, *The Twelve Gods of Greece and Rome* (EPRO 107), Leiden 1987.

R. Muth, 'Vom Wesen römischer "religio"', *ANRW* II/16.1 (1978) 290–354.

G. Radke, *Zur Entwicklung der Gottesvorstellung und der Gottesverehrung in Rom* (Impulse der Forschung 50), Darmstadt 1987.

A. Sprague-Becker, 'The theologia tripertita in Dio Chrysostom's Olympian Oration', *CIW* 87 (1993) 50–4.

The entire interior of the temple was thought of as a dwelling for the divinity, which was represented by its cultic image; other statues of gods could also be present as votive gifts. Some of these cultic images were not especially attractive wooden figures of a venerable age (ξόανα), but more modern votive gifts and statues (ἀγάλματα) were frequently splendid works in bronze or marble, or gold and ivory with a core of hardwood. The gods were portrayed in human form, and there were very many of them. This anthropomorphic polytheism among the Greeks drew on two sources for its basic orientation: early epic poetry and then the plastic arts. Herodotus expresses the former when he writes: 'Hesiod and Homer created the genealogy of the gods in Greece and gave them their sobriquets, distributing offices and honours among them and shaping their figures' (*Hist.* 2.53.2).

This was developed by the Roman authors Mucius Scaevola and Varro in the first century BCE to the so-called *theologia tripertita* (cf. Lieberg). They made a distinction between the mythical theology of the poets, the political theology of the statesmen, which is found in the laws concerning religion and in the religious basis which is given to law as a whole, and the physical or metaphysical theology of the philosophers whose task it is to reflect on the essence of the divine. This categorisation, with which Plutarch too is familiar about 100 CE (*Amat.* 18 [763c–f]), is in another form the basis of the Olympian speech which Dio Chrysostom (cf. Desideri; Sprague-Becker) gave in 97 (or 101 or 105) CE at the games at Olympus, where Pheidias' mighty statue of Zeus, one of the seven wonders of the world, stood in the interior of the temple.

According to Dio, the idea of a divine being is something with which all human persons are born, posited along with the very gift of reason, from the earliest times (*Or.* 12.27). This innate idea develops in the encounter with the wonders of nature and leads to the process of conceptualisation (28–32). Dio himself summarises it thus:

> We have mentioned, as the primal source of the idea of God and the supposition of the existence of a divine being, an idea innate in all human beings, a consequence of the realities that genuinely exist. It has not come into existence through error or chance, but has always been exceedingly powerful and constant; it has arisen among all peoples and continues to exist. It is indeed something held in common and shared by the entire rational world.

The elaboration of this idea has been the work of (*a*) the poets, (*b*) the legislators, (*c*) the representatives of the plastic arts, who are mentioned in all their variety (44), and finally (*d*) the philosophers. A rhetorical device permits Dio to let the sculptor Pheidias speak here. He appeals to Homer as the source of what he has created: all he has done is to transpose the descriptions of the gods in the epics out of the medium of language into the plastic work of art. As Dio's mouthpiece, Pheidias also explains why human beings long for images of the gods (60f.):

> The rational human being does indeed venerate all these [heavenly apparitions]; he takes them to be blessed gods whom he sees from afar. But because of the inclination they feel towards the divine, all human beings have a powerful longing to venerate and celebrate the deity from near at hand, to draw close to it and touch it with gestures of imploration, to sacrifice to it and crown it with wreaths. For just as immature children, when they are separated from their father or mother, are filled with yearning and desire and often stretch out their hands in dreams to the parents who are not present, so do human beings behave in relation to the gods. For they are entirely right to love the gods because of the good things they have received and because they are related to them, and they wish in every way to be with them and to have close relationships with them.

The comparison makes it clear that a distance remains, as in the world of dreams; thus the god is not wholly absorbed into his image, and is not simply identical to it. The Presocratic philosophy had already warned against such confusions. In an important excursus on the philosophy of religion in his *Natural History,* Pliny the Elder, roughly a contemporary of Dio, criticised the search for the image and form of the divinity as a sign of human weakness (*Hist. Nat.* 2.14).

In Homer the gods not only look like human beings; they also behave like them, loving, suffering, hating, and engaging in conflicts among themselves. They have family relationships; they intervene in human life to help or to punish. Often the heaven of the gods seems like a version of segments of human society, projected into the supraterrestrial sphere. But the gods remain distinguished from human beings by (*a*) superior knowledge, (*b*) superior, though not totally boundless, power, and (*c*) immortality. Taken together, they represent the fundamental forms of a pluriform ordered reality which confronts the human person with a great variety of demands.[12]

The number of such gods can potentially be multiplied without any limits, especially when one considers that abstract terms too could be personified and become divine figures – cf. for example Dikē, 'Justice', a daughter of Zeus, or Peithō, the divinised art of persuasion. But the number of well-known deities who enjoyed general veneration remained rather small. Most of them live as a family clan on the cloud-capped peak of the divine mountain Olympus in the north of Thessaly (this is why they are called the 'Olympian gods'). Classical attempts at systematisation prefer to work with the number twelve (cf. Long). Although this system does not quite cope with the complex reality, we can use it as a criterion to provide orientation when we list the most important Greek deities (the rough equivalent in Rome is in brackets):

1. *Zeus* (*Jupiter*), father of gods and of human beings;

2. *Hera* (*Juno*), his consort;

3. *Poseidon* (*Neptune*), brother of Zeus and lord of the seas;

4. *Athene* (*Minerva*), goddess who protected the city of Athens; according to the myth sprung from the head of Zeus, an armed virgin and fighter, but also one who cared for women and helped them;

5. *Apollo*, son of Zeus, dwelling *inter alia* at Delphi as god of the oracle, mostly portrayed as a man in the flower of his youth;

6. *Artemis* (*Diana*), his twin sister, mistress of animals and goddess of the hunt;

7. *Aphrodite* (*Venus*), goddess of love;

---

[12] Thus H. Kleinknecht, *TDNT* 3.68; no less a scholar than K. Rahner (*Schriften zur Theologie*, vol. 1, Einsiedeln 3rd edn. 1958, 104) accepts this formulation and makes it his own.

8. *Hermes* (*Mercury*), messenger of the gods, patron of merchants and of thieves, who also leads the souls of the dead to the underworld;

9. *Hephaistos* (*Vulcan*), the smith, a god of fire and of craftsmen's work;

10. *Ares* (*Mars*), the fearsome god of war – and somewhat apart from the others, because seldom mentioned by Homer, but exceptionally important for the mystery cults, for example:

11. *Demeter* (*Ceres*), the goddess of corn;

12. *Dionysus* (*Bacchus*), the god of wine.

Some gods are missing from this list, such as Hades/Pluto, the god of the underworld, since he lived elsewhere than on the mountain of the gods. The handbooks of the religious history of Greece and Rome present the individual divine figures in monographic form in individual chapters, relating their myths, describing their cult and outlining their functions, but we cannot develop these themes here. We add only one observation about Roman religion (cf. Muth; Lind). In general, especially for the earlier stages, it would be necessary to make sharper distinctions; among the Romans, for example, the mythical stories about the gods and the images of the gods do not play the same central role as among the Greeks. They recognised and identified a divinity by what it did. A fine example of this is the two-headed god Janus, god of the opened and of the closed door, for whom no equivalent exists in the Greek Pantheon. It was his responsibility whether crossing a threshold had good or bad consequences. Virtually every action could be conceptualised and divinised in this way among the Romans, and this led to a superabundant plethora of names. The assimilation to the Greek pantheon, which in very many cases did not succeed with perfect smoothness (with a corresponding evaluation of the importance of the divinities who were required for this process of assimilation), began at the end of the third century BCE. The result was that, in the early imperial period, there were no longer two systems that simply stood alongside one another: many interconnections were made, and they seemed interchangeable.

P. F. Dorcey's study of the Roman god Silvanus is an example of how individualities were maintained. This god of agriculture, of forestry, of hunting and of borders is the Roman divinity most frequently attested by inscriptions, but he had no public cult of his own, i.e. no state temple, no feast, and no holy day. He was especially popular in the second and third centuries CE among the simple populace in the cities, something that assuredly betrays a nostalgic longing for the world of the countryside and a hope of escaping from the wretchedness of the cities (cf. Dorcey 32).

An insistence on the correct carrying out of the ritual was also characteristic of Roman religion, and remained so. The ceremonies must be correct down to the very last detail, and nothing might be altered in them. The cultic personnel had the responsibility for this, and it could carry out its ritual tasks validly even without the participation of the public, i.e. of the people.

4. Priests

List 11.

M. Beard and J. North (eds.), *Pagan Priests: Religion and Power in the Ancient World*, London 1990.

A. Bendlin et al., 'Priesthoods in Mediterranean Religions', *Numen* 40 (1993) 82–94 (review of Beard and North).

R. S. J. Garland, 'Religious Authority in Archaic and Classical Athens', *ABSA* 79 (1984) 75–123.

A. and I. König, *Der römische Festkalender der Republik: Feste, Organisationen und Priesterschaften* (RecUB 8693), Stuttgart 1991, 105–34.

J. Scheid, 'Les Prêtres officiels sous les empereurs julio-claudiens', *ANRW* II/16.1 (1978) 610–54.

L. Schumacher, 'Die vier hohen römischen Priesterkollegien unter den Flaviern, den Antoninen und den Severern (69–253 n.Chr.)', *ANRW* II/16.1 (1978) 655–819.

G. J. Szemler, 'Priesthoods and Priestly Careers in Ancient Rome', *ANRW* II/16.3 (1986) 2314–31.

In the examples from Homer, persons enjoying social respect were responsible for performing sacrifice: the king, the army leader, the master of the house. This possibility continued to exist, but as time went on a specialisation became unavoidable and the office of priest emerged – something significantly different among the Greek and Romans from what we, under the influence of a long Christian tradition, tend to associate with this concept.

We begin with Plato, in the work of his old age on the constitution of the city state, where priests and priestesses are envisaged as having charge of the temples (*Leg.* 6.7 [759a–760a]). They receive this office by the casting of lots, so that the decision appears to be left to the divine guidance of events. Those chosen by lot must however submit to yet another examination, which determines whether they are free of physical blemish and are of legitimate birth, coming from a respectable family, and also free of blood guilt and of similar crimes; this last requirement applies to their parents too. Plato has this office last for only one year, and he sets the threshold of a relatively high age, sixty years, for those who attain it; this may be because sexual continence was demanded for the period of direct priestly activity, and it was thought that this was easier at a more advanced age. The state was to charge two or three treasurers with the chief responsibility for inspecting the temple treasury and the temple area. Plato defines the task of the priestly caste as follows: 'according to the sacred utterance of tradition, it knows how to bring to the gods, by means of sacrifices, gifts in which they take pleasure, and likewise to help us through prayers so that the gods fulfil our wishes' (*Polit.* 29 [290c]).

It follows that every irreproachable, free and healthy male citizen of the state (and correspondingly also every female citizen) was capable of assuming such an office, if the lot fell on him. This also means that such a task was carried out only alongside one's main professional occupation, and that it was not the defining substance of the priest's life.

What did priests have to do? Their activity was locally tied to one particular temple and one particular divinity, and this alone sufficed to prevent the development of a general concept and a priestly order with clearly defined contours. Within their temple area, the priests bore the responsibility for the organisation and for the frictionless performance of the sacrificial celebrations which they led, and in which they spoke the prayer. Other cultic officials and slaves assisted them in this in the larger temple complexes. The age limit which Plato envisaged was certainly not observed everywhere. As well as the decision by the casting of lots, we find other possibilities, such as an election by the people. Many priestly offices were also inherited within a family, or else – especially in Asia Minor and on the islands – acquired by purchase. Inherited and purchased offices were often not subject to a limit of one year or the period of one feast, but were held for an entire lifetime. The purchase can be illustrated by a law about the priesthood in the temple of Asclepius in Chalcedon from the period between 100 BCE and 100 CE:[13]

> [The priest of Asclepius] is to wear a garland during the feasts, and is to go to the public meals ... The priesthood is to be purchased by one who is bodily intact and has the right to take on a public office. But it should also be permissible to buy the priesthood for one's son; otherwise, it is not allowed to

---

[13] Cf. SIG 3/1009 = LSAM 5.

purchase it for another person than one's own self ... When he has paid the entire price of the purchase, he is to be installed in his office; he himself must pay the cost of the ceremony of installation. The priest is to open the temple daily. But he is also to see that the portico at the temple of Asclepius is kept clean. He is to receive the revenues from the month of Machaneios onwards. The price of purchase ... amounts to 5,038 drachmas, 4 oboli. The purchaser is Matris, the son of Menios.

One who purchased such an office hoped that it would bring him public honours and an increase in his social prestige. Special seats were reserved for priests in the city theatre. The inscription just quoted indicates that the priests drew revenues from their activity. In terms of natural produce, a part of the sacrificial gifts fell to them: a thigh of the sacrificial animal and the gifts that were laid on the sacred table. The skins of the sacrificial animals also represented a monetary value, and precise accounts were kept of this. We have some inscriptions that consist only of accounts of the sale of the skins of sacrificed animals.[14] The income from the sale belonged to the state, but the priests too received a share in it, depending on particular circumstances. The temple area too could bring in revenues; donations were made. Sometimes an official residence was made available within the temple area. On the other hand, a priest could also become liable to very heavy expenditure: in this inscription, he is required to pay from his own pocket for the celebrations on the occasion of his installation.

Many similarities existed between Greeks and Romans in the sphere of the individual temple for individual deities, but here a considerably higher social prestige attached to the official priestly offices, to which the state entrusted the care for the oversight and the carrying out of the official exercise of religion.[15] Such a lifelong priesthood was an indispensable part of every political career, and one must remember that it was correspondingly coveted by many people. The new members were chosen by the priestly colleges themselves, by the senate or by the emperor. Very few indeed managed to acquire more than one priestly office; Julius Caesar united in his own hands the task of *pontifex maximus* and that of an augur,

[14] Cf. e.g. SIG 3/1029 (in M. P. Nilsson, *Religion* (L4) 71).

[15] Cf. Pliny the Younger, *Ep.* 4.8.1f., where he rejoices that he has become an augur, 'first of all because it is fine to satisfy the requests of the Princeps even in less significant matters; but also because this priesthood in itself is ancient and sacred, and the fact that it is bestowed for a whole lifetime also confers on it something venerable and special'.

but the emperor Augustus constituted a great exception when he succeeded in acquiring all the important priesthoods for himself – something that in its turn also helped him to widen his power base, which was sometimes threatened. Augustus himself notes in his account of his deeds: 'I was *pontifex maximus* and augur, belonged to the colleges of the *quindecemviri sacris faciundis* and the *septemviri epulonum*, I was a member of the Arval Brothers, *sodalis Titius* and *fetialis*.'[16]

The name *pontifex* means a 'builder of bridges'; the origin of this office was the inspection and maintenance of bridges. There were sixteen pontiffs, with the *pontifex maximus* at their head as the highest Roman authority in questions of religion. They regulated problems of the calendar and laid down the festal days, and were available to give counsel on questions of doubt relating to religious matters. The *augurs* had the task of interpreting premonitory signs. On the basis of the flight of birds and the way in which hens picked at their seeds they ascertained favourable or dangerous omens (see III/B.1(*b*) below). The *quindecemviri sacris faciundis* ('fifteen men with responsibility for the sacred actions to be performed') studied the books of the Sibylline Oracles and had the inspection of the foreign cults that penetrated Rome from the entire Mediterranean area. The *septemviri epulonum* were seven men who were masters of ceremonies and organised official meals on great holidays, also providing the ritual food for the gods on these occasions. These are the four great Roman priestly colleges. Some other specialists follow: the Arval Brothers (from *arva,* 'seed ground') carried out a very ancient agrarian ritual, with processions through the meadow in a sacred grove, and were also active in the imperial cult from the first century CE onwards. The *sodales Titii,* i.e. the companions of the legendary king Titius Tatius from Roman pre-history, are otherwise unknown to us. It seems that Augustus himself revived them, but it is uncertain what their function was. The *fetiales* too had disappeared for several centuries before Augustus called them back to life. They were responsible for declaring war on a foreign tribe, a

---

[16] *Res Gestae* 7; cf. (also for what follows) the text with explanations and bibliography in E. Weber, *Augustus: Meine Taten/Res Gestae Divi Augusti* (TuscBü), Munich and Zurich 5th edn. 1989; M. Giebel, *Augustus: Res gestae/ Tatenbericht* (RecUB 9773), Stuttgart 1975, reprint 1991; see M. Beard et al., *Religions*, vol. 1 (L2) 186–92. F. W. Shipley, 'Res Gestae Divi Augusti', in Idem, *Velleius Parterculus: Compendium of Roman History* (LCL 152), Cambridge, Mass. and London 1924, reprint 1979, 332–405.

declaration accompanied by the symbolic action of throwing a wooden lance into the territory of the enemy; they also made peace in the form of a sacrifice to confirm an oath.

5. Feasts

(a) Overview

List 12.

M. Beard et al., Religions, vol. 2 (L4) 60–77.

F. Bömer, *P. Ovidius Naso: Die Fasten*, vols. 1–2 (WKLGS), Heidelberg 1957.

L. Deubner, *Feste* (L2).

W. Fauth, 'Römische Religion im Spiegel der "Fasti" des Ovid', *ANRW* II/16.1 (1978) 104–86.

J. G. Frazer, *Ovid: Fasti* (LCL 253), rev. by G. P. Goold, Cambridge, Mass. and London 1989.

A. and I. König, *Festkalender* (L11).

M. P. Nilsson, *Feste* (L2).

R. M. Ogilvie, *Romans* (L2) 78–107.

V. J. Rosivach, *System* (L7) 9–67.

J. Rüpke, *Kalender und Öffentlichkeit: Die Geschichte der Repräsentation und religiösen Qualifikation von Zeit in Rom* (RVV 40), Berlin 1995.

H. H. Scullard, *Festivals and Ceremonies of the Roman Republic*, London 1981.

J. E. Stambaugh, *The Ancient Roman City* (Ancient Society and History), Baltimore 1988, 221–4.

H. S. Versnel, *Inconsistencies in Greek and Roman Religion*, II: *Transition and Reversal in Myth and Ritual* (SGRR 6.2), Leiden 1993, 136–227.

The Graeco-Roman world had no weekly feast day like the Jewish sabbath or the Christian Sunday, but there were a large number of feast days with varying degrees of significance, spread at irregular intervals over the entire year. Fragments of a long sacral inscription with the official calendar (LSCS 10; LSCG 16–17) give us especially good information about the festal cycle of the city of Athens (cf. Deubner). The main feast each year was the 'Panathenaia' in honour of the city goddess Athene, at the beginning of the year in August. A new garment for the goddess, woven by the women in the preceding months, was bound like a sail to the carriage of a ship and accompanied in a festal procession through the city to the temple of Athene on the Acropolis, where an old wooden statue of the goddess was clothed with it. On the occasion of the great Panathenaia, held every four years, the allied cities and the colonies which had been founded from Athens also sent delegations to Athens with sacrificial animals and gifts. Another popular feast was the *anthestēria*, a three-day festival in honour of the wine god Dionysus, held early in the year with a ritual drinking competition on the second day. The victor was the one who first emptied a pitcher containing more than two litres of wine.

Ovid described and explained in his *Fasti* (cf. Bömer; Frazer) the Roman festal year with its more than one hundred and fifty feast days, many of which however were not celebrated with any special solemnity, but required only certain ceremonies in a state temple. Unfortunately, only the first six books survive, covering the period from January to July (a full description is given by Ogilvie). Thus, *inter alia*, we do not have Ovid's description of the well-known feast of Saturnalia in December, a kind of Roman carnival with public sacrificial feasts and a temporary loosening of the ordering of society (cf. Versnel). Pliny writes in one of his letters that he has built for himself a soundproofed room on his country estate where he can study undisturbed even at the time of Saturnalia, while the domestic personnel make a din in the other parts of the building (*Ep.* 2.17.24).

We shall study in closer detail only two Attic feasts of medium significance, the *Thargelia* and the *Buphonia*, because they will help to illustrate the controversies in modern scholarship with regard to the meaning and the origin of the practice of sacrifice.

(*b*) Individual examples

List 13.
W. Burkert, *Homo Necans* (L2) 135–43.
L. Deubner, *Feste* (L2) 158–98.
F. Schwenn, *Menschenopfer* (L8) 26–59.
J. P. Vernant, 'A General Theory of Sacrifice and the Slaying of the Victims in the Greek *Thusia*', in Idem, *Mortals and Immortals: Collected Essays*, ed. F. I. Zeitlin, Princeton 1991, 290–302.

Thargelia
Thargelion is the name of one of the Athenian summer months. A somewhat obscure text attributed to Hipponax, a poet of the sixth century

BCE, describes the rite said to have been performed on the 6th/7th of this month each year:[17]

> This is what happened to the 'scapegoat', how purification was carried out in ancient times: when disaster struck a city, inflicted by the wrath of the gods – whether hunger or plague or other damage – they offered as sacrifice the one who was uglier than all the others, as purification and 'scapegoat' for the city afflicted by suffering. At a place not far distant [from the city] they made him take his position, then gave him cheese and bread as well as dried figs. Then they hit him on his penis seven times with onions and wild figs and everything else that grows on uncultivated trees. Finally they burned him on these woods that grew wild, and scattered all the ashes into the sea and into the winds, in expiation (as I have said) for the city afflicted by suffering. It is Hipponax who gives a masterly description of this whole custom.

Parallel traditions speak of two 'scapegoats', or else tell of a poor man who is given the best treatment with feasts for a time and then suffers the same fate. As an alternative to burning, he is thrown down from a rock, unless people were satisfied with chasing the 'scapegoat' from the territory of the city with stones and blows. The latter is probably to be judged as more in keeping with what actually happened; the relics of a genuine human sacrifice, which can still be glimpsed, presumably belong only to the mythical substratum.

The word translated here as 'scapegoat' is φάρμακος (a masculine form) in Greek. A φάρμακον (neuter) is a medicine or a poison. This name on its own suffices to interpret the human vicarious representative as a means of salvation and expiation; this is strengthened by the use of the word 'purification' (καθαρμός) in the text. Nilsson's translation 'scapegoat' ('Sündenbock') is suggested by the comparable rite in the Old Testament, and there are indeed parallels in Lev 16, although there it is an animal that is laden with the guilt of the whole people and is chased into the wilderness – not a human being. This ritual of elimination is significantly different from the basic form of sacrifice that we have seen hitherto; we shall return to this point below.

Buphonia

Towards the end of the year, i.e. roughly in July, the city of Athens celebrated the *dipolieia*, a feast for Zeus as the god of the city, at which a

[17] Frags. 5–11 West.

rite called *buphonia* (killing of the bull) was practised. We know the sequence of events from the long account in Porphyry[18] and some other sources. Bulls were led in a circle round the altar, and the first beast to eat of the sacrificial barley was slaughtered with an axe. The slayer ran away, while those remaining flayed and parted the beast, roasted its flesh and ate it. Then the skin of the bull was stuffed and set in front of a plough in such a way that it seemed as if the animal wanted to go out to work in the fields. Finally a court trial was held at which all blamed each other for its death, until the knife was found guilty and thrown into the sea.

The forms are those of a normal slaughter-sacrifice. The special point is that a genuine 'comedy of innocence' (Burkert) is performed. The bull itself is guilty of all that happens to it, because it was too hasty in eating the barleycorn. The responsibility is distributed among the entire community of the city and then, within this group, among the lifeless tools. There is even a pretence that the sacrificial animal comes back to life. It almost seems as if sacrifice, this common fact of daily life, is nevertheless the repository of deep-seated feelings of guilt, and that it is permissible to express these feelings in this particular instance.

6. Theories of sacrifice

List 14.

G. Bader, *Symbolik des Todes Jesu* (HUTh 25), Tübingen 1988 (*inter alia* on Burkert and Girard).

W. Burkert, *Wilder Ursprung: Opferritual und Mythos bei den Griechen* (Kleine Kulturwissenschaftliche Bibliothek 22), Berlin 1990.

——*Homo Necans* (L2).

E. Ferguson, 'Spiritual Sacrifice in Early Christianity and its Environment', *ANRW* II/23.2 (1980) 1151–89.

R. Girard, *Violence and the Sacred*, London and Baltimore 1977.

——*Le Bouc émissaire*, Paris 1981.

H. Hubert and M. Mauss, *Sacrifice: Its Nature and Function*, London 1964; French original in *Mélanges d'histoire des religions* (Travaux de ASoc), Paris 2nd edn. 1929, 1–130, also in M. Mauss, *Oeuvres*, vol. 1, ed. V. Karady (Collection 'Le Sens commun'), Paris 1968, 193–307.

B. Lang, *Sacred Games* (L3).

---

[18] *De Abstinentia* 2.29f. (according to Theophrastus).

K. Meuli, 'Griechische Opferbräuche', in *Phyllobolia* (*Festschrift P. von der Mühll*), Basel 1946, 185–288; also in Idem, *Gesammelte Schriften*, ed. T. Gelzer, vol. 2, Basle and Stuttgart 1975, 907–1021.
R. Parker, *Miasma* (L2) 257–80.
W. R. Smith, *Lectures on the Religion of the Semites: The Fundamental Institutions*, London 3rd edn. 1927.
F. T. van Straten, 'Gifts for the Gods', in H. S. Versnel, *Worship* (L2) 65–151, esp. 83–8.

(a) Sacrifice as gift

A term for sacrifice that is also found in the New Testament is δῶρον, 'gift' (Mt 5:23f.). Plato gives precisely this definition *(Euthyphr.* 14c): 'Sacrificing means giving something to the gods [δωρεῖσθαι].' A widespread view, also serving Hubert and Mauss as the starting point for their classic studies, understands sacrifice as a gift to the divinity: something valuable, something that can be consumed, is withdrawn from one's own use and presented as a gift to the gods. This might sometimes happen without any ulterior motive, but it might also have the intention of supplying nourishment to keep the god alive, or of stimulating the god to give effective help. This second possibility comes somewhat closer to a rather different intention, which can be summed up in the proverb *do ut des*, 'I give in order that you give in return': the human person proposes an exchange, giving something but expecting to receive something from the gods in return, e.g. help in a situation of distress, or material prosperity. Finally, the gift can also serve to appease the wrath of the gods and to reconcile them with human beings anew.

This last idea, the reconciliation of an angry deity, can most easily be linked to the burnt sacrifices or annihilatory sacrifices in which the entire matter of the sacrifice is a victim to the flames, so that a genuinely painful renunciation is entailed. But in view of the destructiveness involved in this kind of sacrifice, it is difficult to speak of a gift. It is also problematical when the attempt is made to link the character of exchange with the normal form of slaughter-sacrifice, since, as has been shown above, the gods are given such a poor share that the human persons must employ the story of Prometheus' treachery to appease their resulting guilty conscience. Perhaps one could interpret the simple form of a sacrificial gift, or the giving of food to the gods, in this way; but here too the appropriateness of this line of understanding is disturbed by the fact that it is often human beings – the priests, the temple personnel, or those celebrating the feast – who eat the gifts made ready for the gods. Thus the shrewd slave in Plautus' comedy *The Pot of Gold* says: 'I will offer you, goddess Fides, a whole vessel full of honeyed wine as a sacrifice. That is what I will do; but then I will drink it myself' (621–3).

(*b*) Sacrifice as *communio*

Earlier scholarship (cf. Smith) tended for a while to favour the theory of a communion sacrifice, which is no longer so popular. According to this, the fundamental idea in a sacrifice is table fellowship between gods and human beings. The ideal picture of a sacrificial action which Plutarch sketches at one point seems to point in this direction, but it says something rather different if one reads it more closely: 'For that which is delightful in the feasts is not the quantity of wine or the roasted flesh, but the good hope and the belief that the god is present with his help and accepts what is taking place' (*Suav. Viv. Epic.* 21 [1102a]).

Plutarch speaks of the presence of a god at the sacrifice, but not directly of his participation in the meal. In normal circumstances, this presence was surely conceived of rather differently: the god would have been seen as the host who receives the sacrificial gifts and generously hands them back to the human persons. In the theoxeny, on the other hand, the deity takes on the role of the guest, but there the immediate participation by human persons was not so prominent. The two pictures do indeed converge, and explicit meals shared by gods and human beings were occasionally staged (see B, 2(*c*) below). Nevertheless, the idea of the god sharing directly in the human person's table fellowship comes more from a mythical ideal than from experienced reality. Too many data in the contrary sense prevent us from accepting this as the fundamental idea underlying all sacrificial praxis.[19]

(*c*) Scapegoat mechanisms

René Girard's interpretation of sacrifice has recently given rise to much debate. His starting point is the readiness for violence that is latent in every society: in order that society be not totally lacerated by this and drawn into

---

[19] See also A. D. Nock, *Essays* (L2) 582: 'although a god was now guest, now host, man kept his distance'.

internecine struggle, the potential for aggression must be allowed a release from time to time. At periodic intervals this aggression is directed against outsiders to whom the responsibility for all ills is attributed. They are then chased and killed. This procedure involves a high expenditure, since it costs human lives; in the long term, it cannot be maintained. This is why it is detached from the societal outsiders and transposed by means of the mechanism of *mimēsis* (imitation) on to animals, which are offered in sacrifice. There is no problem in institutionalising the bloody sacrifice of animals and repeating this at regular intervals. It has acquired all the values once attached to the original drama. It ties down the aggressive violence and serves as a societal 'glue'.

It is obvious that the classic 'scapegoat' is the inspiration for this interpretation; or, putting it differently, that it is in fact a correct interpretation of scapegoat rituals, whether the Greek *thargelia* with human beings as *pharmakoi*, or the genuine scapegoat in the Old Testament. And it is immediately obvious why this hypothesis is attractive to those who wish to engage in a theological adaptation and Christological development (cf. Bader). But I fail to see what all this has to do with the normal form of slaughter sacrifice among the Greeks and Romans. One has the impression that essentially different realities have simply been equated with one another.

(*d*) An explanation in terms of tribal history

At present it is the genetic model of Meuli and Burkert that most convincingly explains the origin of the slaughter-sacrifice. The 'comedy of innocence' in the *buphonia* shows what is involved here. Initially, the sacrifice is nothing more than a ritualised slaughter, something that has survived as a relic from the prehistorical and early-historical hunting period with some modifications deriving from the agrarian cultures. The ritual of sacrifice has an exculpatory function and diminishes the guilt feelings that the human being experiences when an animal is killed – one must kill in order to eat and to survive, but one knows that killing always implies guilt and that one has the possibility of exterminating the other forms of life thereby. Farmers have in addition the constant contact with their domestic animals which fall victim to the knife that slays them. Many individual details, such as the piling up of the skulls on the altar and the temple wall, or the special way of treating the bones, which to begin with are preserved, just as the preservation of the skin and of course a fortiori the stuffing of the bull in the *buphonia*, indicate the ideal that the animal should remain uninjured – it is to survive, at least in the sense that its species never dies out. Connected with all these feelings is the idea that the sacrificial animal agrees to its own offering in sacrifice, since it willingly goes in the sacrificial procession to the place of sacrifice and makes its assent known through an artificially induced nodding of its head (cf. Plutarch, *Quaest. Conv.* 8.7.3 [729f]: 'Even today great care is taken that an animal should not be slaughtered before a drink offering is poured over it and it nods in assent').

Probably we must suppose that originally every act of slaughter was a sacrifice. The role of the gods in this process gradually intensified, and came into the foreground at a relatively late point – though as far as our knowledge is concerned, this is in fact the earliest historical time of which we have knowledge. The praxis itself still betrays the older preliminary stages, since one essential aspect of sacrifice for Greeks and Romans is that it permits them to get hold of meat.

The force of this hypothesis is that it gives a satisfactory explanation of many striking particularities of the sacrificial praxis, such as the apparent disadvantage of the gods. Naturally – this is the limitation of the hypothesis – not even in the historical period that we can study were those who offered sacrifice conscious of such interconnections, and this means that it is an explanation offered from the outside, more like a theory of systems dealing with the history of tradition, rather than an explanation offered from the inside by the self-understanding of those personally involved. To ascertain what those involved actually felt, we can retain as the lowest common denominator what Plutarch says (see above under (*b*)): namely, the experience of some kind of presence of the divine, combined with the very tangible joyful feast.

Thus the general term 'sacrificial praxis' covers a number of phenomena, some of which display no significant mutual contacts, while some are in fact mutually contradictory. This makes the search for a universally valid theory impossible; we must be content with partial answers which shed light on partial aspects. In this sense, one can link Girard's hypothesis with the mechanism of the scapegoat, but only with it; Burkert's model reveals one essential aspect of the slaughter sacrifice and makes its provenance clearer. Traces of the expectation of *communio* and of a *do ut des* attitude will be discovered elsewhere, as well as the character of gift.

The consequence is that if one adopts sacrificial categories in Christian theology, one must bear in mind precisely which contents and presuppositions one associates with these; it would surely be disadvantageous to speak

41

in general, undifferentiated terms of 'sacrifice'. No matter how one wishes to interpret Jesus' death on the cross as a sacrifice, one must affirm that the familiar forms of sacrifice do not completely fit this, so that the death on the cross explodes the already-existing concepts of sacrifice from within, and did in fact entail something that amounts to the end of all sacrifices. This should lead us to reflect further on what the spiritualisation of sacrificial terms, already known in the non-Christian classical period (cf. Ferguson), really means. What does it mean to 'sacrifice' money, or what does 'the sacrifice of one's life' mean? How far is this metaphor, how far reality?

B. The associations

We have chosen 'religion in the city and in the home' as our guiding theme in this chapter, and within this programme we have hitherto concentrated above all on the public exercise of religion in city and state, in the centre of which stood sacrifice with all its associated feasts, buildings and cult personnel. En route from the public character of the *polis* to the interior sphere of the house, we encounter on the threshold something that exists in its own right, smaller than the city, often at home in one house, but yet larger than the family: the private association. Most associations of the Hellenistic-Roman period are, at least in terms of their external form, cultic associations, and this makes them not only interesting, but essential matter of study for the history of religions. We shall first look at the phenomenon as a whole and the relevant terminology, and then turn to instructive individual examples. With regard to the religious life of the associations we need not speak at great length, because it will quickly be seen that here the traits familiar to us from the public exercise of religion are reproduced in all their essentials.

1. Outward manifestations and terminology

List 15.
F. M. Ausbüttel, *Untersuchungen zu den Vereinen im Westen des Römischen Reiches* (Frankfurter Althistorische Studien 11), Kallmünz 1982.
W. M. Brashear, *Vereine im griechisch-römischen Ägypten* (Xenia 34), Constanz 1993.

W. S. Ferguson, 'The Attic Orgeones', *HThR* 37 (1944) 61–140.

P. Hermann, J. H. Waszink, C. Colpe and B. Kötting, art. 'Genossenschaft', *RAC* 10 (1978) 83–155.

J. Kloppenborg and S. Wilson (eds.), *Voluntary Associations in the Graeco-Roman World*, London 1996.

G. La Piana, 'Foreign Groups in Rome during the First Centuries of the Empire', *HThR* 20 (1927) 183–403, esp. 225–81.

W. Liebenam, *Zur Geschichte und Organisation des römischen Vereinswesens: 3 Untersuchungen*, Leipzig 1890, reprint Aalen 1964.

R. MacMullen, *Roman Social Relations 50 BC to AD 284*, New Haven 1974, 72–87.

O. M. van Nijf, *The Civic World of Professional Associations in the Roman East* (Dutch Monographs on Ancient History and Archaeology 17), Amsterdam 1997.

F. Poland, *Geschichte des griechischen Vereinswesens* (Preisschriften ... der Fürstlich Jablonowskischen Gesellschaft 38), Leipzig 1909, reprint 1967.

M. San Nicolò, *Ägyptisches Vereinswesen zur Zeit der Ptolemäer und Römer*. Erster Teil: *Die Vereinsarten*. Zweiter Teil: *Vereinswesen und Vereinsrecht* (MBPF 2), Munich 2nd edn. 1972.

M. L. Strack, 'Die Müllerinnung in Alexandrien', *ZNW* 4 (1903) 213–34.

E. Ziebarth, *Das griechische Vereinswesen* (Preisschriften ... der Fürstlich Jablonowskischen Gesellschaft 34), Leipzig 1896, reprint Wiesbaden 1969.

(*a*) Description of the phenomenon

'In the period of his political powerlessness, ruled officially or unofficially by the will of the Romans, the Greek displays an unparalleled enthusiasm for membership of associations ... the city no longer has any dominant role to play, since the empire has taken its place ... on the ruins of the πόλις in the larger unity of the empire there grows up the association' (Strack 223–5). Thus the classical voluntary association comes to full flower in the Hellenistic and the Roman periods, thanks also to the destruction of the structure of the *polis* and to the political superiority first of Alexander the Great and his successors, and then of the Romans. Social life withdraws into the association, with structures on a more personal scale. The lower limits on membership are about ten to twenty persons, the upper limits from around one to two hundred. Most associations have a relationship to a god and his cult, even if this remains a rather external trait (Strack 224: 'Almost every Greek association had a fairly close link to one or other god or hero, quite irrespective of whether it pursued religious, scientific, artistic, societal or sociable aims'). The names of many associations are formed on the basis of the name of a god. The god of wine, Dionysus, was especially popular, for obvious reasons: the veneration of Dionysus permitted drinking parties to be held. We find traces of this in association names like Διονυσιασταί (the 'Dionysiasts') and the coining of similar names – the 'Sarapiasts' were an association in honour of the Graeco-Egyptian god Sarapis, the 'Soteriasts' an association in honour of a redeemer god. It was possible for gods to whom little attention was paid in the public cult to find their place in the associations, and the private cultic association was the ideal organisational form for foreign cults from the Orient which sought to establish themselves in Greece or Rome.

A major element in the life of the association was the sacrificial feast and common meal held at regular intervals, each year on the feast of the god or of the foundation, once a month or even more frequently, depending on the aim and the statutes of the association. We find the basic structure of religious praxis in the associations too: a sacrifice as the preparation for a meal. External conditions had to be met, in order to fulfil this: appropriate rooms were required for the assembly and the celebration. In other words, a house was needed as premises for the association. Persons responsible for the preparation and performance of the ritual had to be appointed, and thus structures, functions and offices arose. In the course of time a rich flora of titles came into existence, with regard both to the names of the associations themselves and to the description of the internal organisation of an association. We shall look in the next section at the most important terms, and thus grasp more about the historical development and the internal differentiation of this phenomenon.

(b) The terminology

The oldest Athenian associations about which inscriptions inform us (e.g. SIG 3/1095–7; 1100–2; LSCS 20.125) come from the fifth century BCE. Their members were called ὀργεῶνες (cf. Ferguson), a word connected with ὄργια, a word that in Greek denotes 'the sacred work' and does not yet have the negative overtones that we associate with the word 'orgy'. Freely translated, the ὀργεῶνες are 'sacrificial companions', i.e. people who come together in order to celebrate a sacrificial meal in common.

Aristotle uses other, more direct terms for associations when he speaks of forms of fellowship (*Eth. Nic.* 8.9.5 [1160a19–25]):[20]

> Some fellowships [κοινωνίαι] seem to exist for the sake of enjoyment, such as the cultic associations [θιασωτῶν] and the dining clubs [ἐρανιστῶν]. For these exist to celebrate the sacrifices and to spend time together ... They organise sacrifices and meetings [συνόδους] in connection with these; this allows them at one and the same time to venerate the gods and to find pleasant relaxation for themselves.

This text provides us with examples of typical concepts, first of all κοινωνία 'fellowship' (*communio*), a general term for all forms of community, sometimes best translated as 'corporation'. Connected with this is the neuter τὸ κοινόν, 'that which is held in common, the association', used in the associations relatively frequently to denote the common concerns of the association, its funds, and simply the association itself. Thus one could say: τὸ κοινὸν τῶν Διονυσιαστῶν, 'the association of the adherents of Dionysus'. Then we find in Aristotle the term θίασος, translated into English as 'religious guild'; the dictionary defines this as the name of a group concerned with the holding of feasts, a society which came together to organise sacrifices, processions and other ceremonies in honour of a god, and had a good time in doing so. This is the most important single term for associations. Alongside this we have ἔρανος, linked (possibly at a secondary stage) by classical authors with the verb ἐράω, 'to love'. Ἔρανος designates primarily a meal shared by friends, with each contributing something; in a derived sense it then applies to associations with common funds. It is often translated as a 'dining club'. Aristotle also employs the word σύνοδος for the meetings; this was often used, above all in Egypt, to designate the association itself.

We also find the terms συσσίτιον and ἑταιρία. The former are especially well attested in Sparta, where they were dining associations, sacrificial fellowships, and military units. This word, also used elsewhere as the name for an association (e.g. Polybius 20.6.6), is derived from σῖτος ('grain' and hence more generally 'nourishment') and hence itself gives prominence to the aspect of eating in common. Ἑταιρίαι are groups of friends (from ἑταιρός, 'companion'). The name τεχνῖται is derived

---

[20] Cf. F. Dirlmeier and E. A. Schmidt, *Aristoteles: Nikomachische Ethik* (RecUB 8586), Stuttgart 2nd edn. 1983; H. Rackham, *Aristotle: Nicomachean Ethics* (LCL 73), Cambridge, Mass. and London 1926.

from τέχνη ('art', 'craft') and this was used above all by associations of artists, e.g. actors in the theatre who joined together and virtually always chose Dionysus, the god of the theatre, as their patron. Nor should one forget the association of millers in Alexandria (cf. Strack). One is distantly reminded of the guilds and professional associations of the middle ages, although the realities were not the same.

The most commonly used term in the Latin sources for all the variety of Roman associations is *collegium*. The Romans were suspicious of associations that were free of control, so they defined more clearly than the Greeks the link to official tasks, the legal control and (if one wishes to use this word) the censorship of the associations. When the misuse of the freedom of association represented a threat, it was rigorously limited. Thus Pliny the Younger, when governor in Asia Minor, was not allowed to form any guilds of craftsmen. These were intended only to serve as public firemen (*Ep.* 10.33.3), but Trajan was afraid that they would develop into politically subversive ἑταιρίαι (34.1). This prohibition affected the Christians of Asia Minor too, as we see from Pliny's famous letter about them (96.7).

With regard to the internal differentiation which will be documented in greater detail in the following examples, we wish at this point to note only a few concepts that are of interest when we take a look at Judaism and Christianity. The assembly of the members of an association can be called συναγωγή, 'synagogue', in non-Jewish sources too (LSCG 177.93f.; 135.20). This is not particularly surprising, since the basic meaning of this word is merely 'to lead together', 'a coming together'. One of the officials of the association is a γραμματεύς, who does the work of a secretary. Indeed, his office can 'be considered to some extent as typical of the whole world of the associations' and 'is even more widespread than that of the treasurer' (Poland 383). We also find πρεσβύτεροι, 'elders', as office-bearers in Egyptian associations. One must also note in this context the fact that ἐκκλησία is employed exceedingly seldom in the associations. In the copious material he has collected, Poland has only three texts (332) where ἐκκλησία denotes the official assembly of the association members, in an obvious analogy to the assembly of the citizens of the *polis*. Beneath this unmistakable reserve in terminology there no doubt lies an awareness of the distinction between the private association and the public assembly of citizens.

The associations as a whole certainly embraced members from wide sections of the populace, but we should see the tendency in the individual associations rather in terms of social homogeneity. People who came together in an association already were in contact with one another for other reasons because of family links, or similar professions, the same geographical origin, or membership of the same social class. Women and slaves were certainly admitted to some associations of free men, but we also know of some associations that were only for slaves or for freedmen. Such homogeneous associations had a stabilising effect; they did not tend to promote social integration. Thus they could give slaves the sense of belonging together, and heighten their self-consciousness, but they could do nothing to bridge the gulf between free men and slaves.

It is difficult to make a selection from the plethora of individual examples, especially since it is not always possible to draw clear boundaries marking them off from the family cult, the domestic cult, or the cult of the dead. In what follows, I present only texts that have already been studied on a number of occasions in specialist exegetical literature.

2. Individual examples

(a) Epicteta's foundation

List 16.
B. Laum, *Stiftungen in der griechischen und römischen Antike: Ein Beitrag zur antiken Kulturgeschichte*, vols. 1–2, Leipzig 1914, reprint Aalen 1964; in II.43–52 as no. 43, the text following IG XII/3 no. 330 with German trans.; a portion of this is also found in LSCG 135.
A. Wittenburg, *Il testamento di Epikteta* (Università degli studi di Trieste. Pubblicazioni del Departimento di scienze dell'antichità 4), Trieste 1990 (with an Eng. trans. too).

We begin with the foundation of an association devoted to the memory of the dead. The inscription which informs us about this was found on the Greek island of Thera and comes from the period around 200 BCE. Its contents are as follows:

A woman named Epicteta from the island of Thera had lost her husband and her two sons. Near the sanctuary of the Muses which her husband had built for the first of the sons who had died (cf. lines 8–13: 'my husband Phoenix, who also built the sanctuary of the Muses for our deceased son Cratesilochus and had the reliefs and the pictures of himself and of Cratesilochus made for the pillars'), she establishes a heroes' grove for the three deceased and founds a cultic association consisting of the male relatives – called τὸ κοινόν (e.g. line 203 and many other places) – with a large capital sum. Out of the interest the men are to organise a memorial celebration each year. New members must pay their admission charge by financing a part of the celebration out of their own pockets. The men come to this celebration with their wives and children for a space of three days. On the first day they offer sacrifice to the Muses, on the second day to Epicteta and Phoenix, the couple who have been given the status of heroes, and on the third day to the two sons, who have been given the same status. The oldest son at any given period from among the descendants of Epicteta's daughters is to exercise the 'priesthood of the Muses and the heroes' (lines 57f.).

Epicteta laid all of this down in a testament which was given fixed form in an inscription. A solemn resolution of the association thus called into existence ratifies the testament and adds some further regulations, e.g. that in the period between the meal and the συμπόσιον a drink offering is to be made to the Muses, to the couple and to their sons, and that each guest is to receive three cups of wine. Precise sacrificial regulations determine what is to be burnt for the founder heroes: only the customary portion for the gods (line 190: 'the part of the sacrifice that is considered to be consecrated'), as well as cakes, loaves and fish. A clause prevents the association, once it has come into being, from dissolving itself (lines 255–67: 'The only exception [to this] is a resolution about dissolving the association. It is not to be permitted for anyone to propose this either by word of mouth or in writing ... But if such a proposal is made by word of mouth or in writing, it is invalid, and whoever has spoken thus or made this proposal is to be expelled from the association and also pay a penalty of five hundred drachmas'). There are two offices, properly so-called: an overseer[21] and a treasurer. It seems that the members took turns in presiding at the sacrifices. A commission is specially charged with resolving problematic cases, and finally an archivist is mentioned (lines 279f.: γραμματοφύλαξ), who has a casket in which he keeps the wooden tablets with the testament and the statutes; these were also 'chiselled on the base of the votive gifts in the sanctuary of the Muses' (lines 275f.).

---

[21] ʼΕπίσσοφος in Greek (line 203 and frequently); on his tasks, see *inter alia* lines 203f.: 'The one chosen shall summon an assembly (σύλλογον) each year on the second day of the feast.'

(*b*) The worshippers of Zeus most High

List 17.

C. Roberts, T. Skeat and A. D. Nock, 'The Guild of Zeus Hypsistos', *HThR* 29 (1936) 39–88.

M. San Nicolò, *Vereinswesen* (L15) II.206f.

J. Ustinova, 'The Thiasoi of Theos Hypsistos in Tanais', *HR* 31 (1991) 150–81.

A papyrus leaf (PLondon 2710 = SGUÄ 7835), dated by those who have studied it to the end of the Ptolemaic period (69–57 BCE) contains the statutes of a cultic fellowship in Egypt, or possibly the sketch for such statutes or an abbreviated copy for the use of the members. After giving the date at the head of the document, the statutes begin with a formulaic wish:

> We wish good fortune. The statutes which the members of the association [σύνοδος] of Zeus most High gave themselves, so that these should enjoy validity. Acting according to their regulations, the first thing they did was to choose as their president Petesuchos, the son of Teephbennis, an educated man worthy of the place and of the men [i.e. of the other members] for one year from the above-mentioned month and day, so that he may organise once a month for all who pay their contribution a drinking feast in the sanctuary of Zeus, at which they are to make a drink offering and pray in the assembly room and [are to carry out] the other customary rites for the king as god and lord. All are to obey the president and his assistant in matters concerning the fellowship, and they are to be present at those occasions and meetings and assemblies [συναγωγάς] and excursions which are enjoined upon them. And none of them is to be permitted ... to form factions [σχίσματα] or to leave the fraternity of the president for another fraternity. No one is to ask questions at the drinking feast about the origins of another member, or to show contempt for him or gossip about him or make accusations against him or reproach him, or to refuse his participation for the [current] year or place any obstacle in the way of the common drinking feasts ...

Some further lines have become illegible through the increasing deterioration of the papyrus towards its end; these seem to contain a further regulation of the way contributions were to be paid. The duty of attendance and good behaviour at the events held in common appear to have been prized highly, precisely in face of the risk that the drinking feast could take a bad turn and result in excesses and quarrels. The membership must be maintained for at least one year. The text warns against the formation of internal groups or parties (employing a word that Paul uses at 1 Cor 1:10 in a similar context). A minimum of loyalty is required of each one. The religious goal of the association – to venerate Zeus in his temple as the highest god, and alongside him to venerate the Egyptian king as *Kyrios* – seems somewhat artificial. The degree of internal organisation can only be called rudimentary: it suffices to have a president, elected for one year, and an assistant who helps him.

(c) The *Iobacchae* in Athens

List 18.
R. L. Fox, *Pagans* (L3) 85–8.
E. Maass, *Orpheus: Untersuchungen zur griechischen, römischen, alt-christlichen Jenseitsdichtung und Religion*, Munich 1895, reprint Aalen 1974, 14–71.
L. Morretti, 'Il regolamento degli Iobacchi ateniesi', in *L'association dionysiaque dans les sociétés anciennes: Table ronde . . .* (CEFR 89), Rome 1986, 247–59.
G. Scheuermann, *Gemeinde im Umbruch. Eine sozialgeschichtliche Studie zum Matthäusevangelium* (FzB 77), Würzburg 1996, 17–20, 29–43 (on this inscription).
M. N. Tod, *Ancient Inscriptions: Sidelights on Greek History. Three Lectures*, Oxford 1932, reprint Chicago 1974.

Βάκχος (with *Bacchus* its equivalent in Latin) is one of the names of the god Dionysus. 'Io' was used as an exclamation in the worship of the god. The *Iobacchae* are worshippers of Dionysus who formed a cultic association in honour of their god in Athens; more precisely, they carried out a mystery cult to which only initiates – which in this case means little more than members of the association – were given access. The text of the statutes was given definitive form in an inscription shortly before 178 BCE, but has a rather long prehistory. In social terms, this group belonged to a higher class, since their patron was none other than the millionaire Herodes Atticus.

The inscription[22] begins, referring to itself (so to speak), with the minutes of the assembly of the association at which the present statutes

---

[22] Text: SIG 3/1109 = LSCG 51; English trans. in Tod and in M. W. Meyer, *Mysteries* (L30) 96–9; R. MacMullen and E. N. Lane, *Paganism* (L4) 69–72.

came into force. The members' cries of assent are noted down: 'Long live the most exalted priest Herodes Atticus!', 'Now we are the first of all the Bacchic fellowships!' (lines 24–7). The statute begins with regulations for admission of members and for admission charges (lines 32–41). It is laid down that meetings should be held on the ninth of each month, on the foundation day and on both the regular and the extra feasts of Dionysus (lines 42–7). Expulsion from the assembly of the group is threatened if the monthly contributions are not paid (lines 48–53). In somewhat unsystematic fashion, new details about the method of admission are added here (lines 53–62). In the assembly 'no one is permitted to sing or make uproar or applaud, but each one is to speak and play the role assigned to him in calm and in good order, under the leadership of the priest or the Archibacchus' (lines 63–7). The text mentions several times the importance of paying one's dues on time and of punishments (lines 68–72, 96–107), as well as respectable behaviour (lines 73–95: no fights, no making of accusations against one another, etc.; cf. lines 108–10). A priest has the charge of leadership (lines 111–17), assisted in the sacrifice by an *Archibacchus* (a 'chief worshipper of Dionysus', lines 118–21). The following scenario represents a particularity of this group (lines 121–7):

> And when the portions are divided up, then the priest, the deputy priest, the Archibacchus, the treasurer, the Bucolicus, Dionysus, Korē, Palaemon, Aphrodite and Proteurhythmus are to consume them; and these names [i.e., roles] are to be assigned by lot among all the members.

Alongside the five office-bearers of the association – the priest, his deputy, the *Archibacchus*, the treasurer, and perhaps one who leads in the dance – five gods or heroes are mentioned, both well known (Dionysus; Korē, the girl; Aphrodite) and less familiar (the hero Palaemon; Proteurhythmus, perhaps as an ad hoc creation, a personification of a melody and of its composer). Those association members on whom the lot falls apparently put on the masks of the relevant deities and perform a theoxeny, as representatives of the association's gods, with the five office-bearers as representatives of the association. Thus there is a visual portrayal of the idea that the gods themselves are guests at the meal of the association.

We need only mention in addition that there are persons who see that order is maintained (the *Eukosmos* in lines 94f. and 136–46; the 'horses' as supervisors of the room in line 144); that the meetings take place in a building that belongs to the association, with its own dining room; that the members are asked to make a special contribution in the case of family events and when they receive public honours (lines 127–36); that the above-mentioned treasurer can decide on his own responsibility whether he requires a secretary (γραμματεύς, lines 155–9); and that it is an obligation of honour to be present at the funeral of a fellow member (lines 159–63).

(d) The *cultores Dianae* in Lanuvium

List 19.
F. M. Ausbüttel, *Untersuchungen* (L15).
F. Bömer, *Untersuchungen* (L2) I.87–98: 'Begräbnisvereine'.
R. MacMullen, *Roman Social Relations* (L15) 78f.
——and E. N. Lane, *Paganism* (L4) 66–9.
A. Müller, 'Sterbekassen und Vereine mit Begräbnisfürsorge in der römischen Kaiserzeit', *NJKA* 15 (1905) 183–201.

The classical town of Lanuvium lies in Italy, not far from Rome. An inscription in two parts found there (cf. ILS 7212), dated 9 June 136 CE, presents the statutes of an association that calls itself a *collegium* and whose members understand themselves as *cultores Dianae et Antinoi*. Diana is well known as the goddess of the hunt. Antinous was the lover of the emperor Hadrian. After he drowned in the Nile in 130 CE, the emperor imme-diately gave him the status of a hero. A dominant though not exclusive concern of the association was to see that its members were given a proper burial. For this reason, older research spoke of a 'funerary association' (cf. Bömer), but more recent scholarship suggests greater caution on this point (cf. Ausbüttel), because this would be to undervalue the other aims of the association.

The introductory section informs us about how the association came into existence. A respected citizen, Lucius Caesennius Rufus, put up fifteen thousand sesterces, and the association can cover a large part of its expenses from the interest on this sum. The monthly contribution of five asses, amounting to about fifteen sesterces per year, strikes one as small, but the admission charge (payable only once) amounted to the considerable sum of one hundred sesterces. The introduction also quotes from an edict of the Roman senate. It is a matter of dispute whether this edict gives a general permission for the foundation of associations of this kind, or refers precisely to this individual case.

Among the individual regulations, we should note the following: if a member dies within twenty miles from the city, three men are to be selected to go there and see to the burial on the spot. All their costs are to be reimbursed, including the travel expenses (I, lines 26–33). If one of the members dies as a slave and his master or mistress refuses out of malice to hand over the corpse, the funeral ritual is nevertheless to be held with a picture of the dead person (II, lines 3f.). If someone commits suicide, no expenses are to be paid out for him (II, lines 5f.). When a slave is set free, he must pay one amphora of good wine to the association (lines 7f.). Festival meals are held on the birthday of the patron Caesennius, of his father, his mother, and his brother, on the birthday of Antinous who has been declared a hero, and on the birthday of Diana, which is likewise the foundation day of the association (lines 11–13). Four *magistri cenarum* are nominated every year, following the order of the dates of their admission to the list of members, and these are responsible for preparing the simple meals (line 15: 'some amphoras of good wine, for each member a loaf costing 2 asses, four sardines, sausages, warm water and the service'). There is also an office lasting for five years, to which one is elected; the one chosen is dispensed from all contributions during his time of office and receives a double portion in all the distributions (lines 16–20). Controversies are to be dealt with in the *conventus*, a business meeting (lines 23f.), so that they may not disturb the agreeable atmosphere at the meals on feast days. Financial penalties are exacted for disturbances of good order (lines 25–8).

One could add many further testimonies, but we have already clearly seen a number of constant elements. These include both the offices and the meals, and the striking concern for good order (cf. 1 Cor 14:40).

3. A view from the outside

List 20.
M. Klinghardt, *Gemeinschaftsmahl und Mahlgemeinschaft: Soziologie und Liturgie frühchristlicher Mahlfeiern* (TANZ 13), Tübingen 1996.
T. Schmeller, *Hierarchie und Egalität: Eine sozialgeschichtliche Untersuchung paulinischer Gemeinden und griechisch-römischer Vereine* (SBS 162), Stuttgart 1995.
M. Weinfeld, *The Organizational Pattern and the Penal Code of the Qumran Sect: A Comparison with Guilds and Religious Associations of the*

Hellenistic-Roman Period (NTOA 2), Fribourg (Switzerland) and Göttingen 1986.

But how were the associations of the classical period seen from the outside – i.e., in our case, from the standpoints of Judaism and Christianity? What links exist? From a Jewish perspective, Philo severely criticises the life of the associations in the great city of Alexandria in his indictment of the city prefect Flaccus. Philo sees the ringleaders at work in the milieu of the associations (*Flacc.* 136f.):

> There exist in the city associations [θίασοι] with numerous members, and there is nothing healthy in their fellowship [κοινωνία], which is based on unmixed wine, drunkenness, feasts and the unbridled conduct which results from these. The inhabitants call them assemblies [σύνοδοι] or simply couches [κλῖναι]. Isidore has the first place in almost all these associations, as leader of the feast and of the couches.

After such a devastating judgement, need we look around for further testimony? There can be no doubt that the self-assessment of Judaism and Christianity prevented them from simply setting themselves on the same level as private cultic associations; but there is sometimes a considerable gap between one's self-assessment and the assessment made by other people. We must reflect on the fact that common terms from the life of the associations are also employed in Greek-speaking Judaism. Moshe Weinfeld has compared the forms of organisation and the penal code of the Qumran community with the professional and cultic associations of the Hellenistic-Roman world, and comes to the conclusion that exact parallels exist in the Hellenistic-Roman associations to almost everything in these two fields that is found in Qumran. An outsider could have the impression that Jewish groups were like cultic associations that came from the East and venerated a highest god, and the same is true of the Christian communities in the Graeco-Roman cities. They too seemed to the neutral observer to be mystery associations of a newly-imported oriental deity, with members who met in private houses where they celebrated common meals (cf. Klinghardt). This challenged Christians to do their utmost to clear up this confusion. One possibility here was to call themselves an ἐκκλησία, another the intensification of social integration and Christian charitable activity.

C. Religio domestica

1. Preliminary questions of vocabulary and social history

List 21.

S. Dixon, *The Roman Family* (Ancient Society and History), Baltimore and London 1992.

J. F. Gardner and T. Wiedemann, *The Roman Household: A Sourcebook*, London 1991.

W. K. Lacey, *The Family in Classical Greece*, London 1968.

D. Lührmann, 'Neutestamentliche Haustafeln und antike Ökonomie', *NTS* 27 (1981) 83–97.

D. M. MacDowell, 'The οἶκος in Athenian Law', *CQ* 83 (1989) 10–21.

H. Moxnes (ed.), *Constructing Early Christian Families. Family as Social Reality and Metaphor*, London and New York 1997.

B. Rawson (ed.), *The Family in Ancient Rome: New Perspectives*, London 1986.

I. Richarz, *Oikos, Haus und Haushalt: Ursprung und Geschichte der Haushaltsökonomik*, Göttingen 1991, 15–42.

P. Spahn, 'Oikos und Polis: Beobachtungen zum Prozess der Polisbildung bei Hesiod, Solon und Aischylos', *HZ* 231 (1980) 529–64.

——'Die Anfänge der antiken Ökonomik', *Chiron* 14 (1984) 301–23.

J. E. Stambaugh, *City* (L12) 157–82.

A. Strobel, 'Der Begriff des "Hauses" im griechischen und römischen Privatrecht', *ZNW* 56 (1965) 91–100.

U. Victor, *[Aristoteles] ΟΙΚΟΝΟΜΙΚΟΣ: Das erste Buch der Ökonomik – Handschriften, Text, Übersetzung und Kommentar – und seine Beziehungen zur Ökonomikliteratur* (BKP 147), Königstein 1993.

D. Wachsmuth, 'Aspekte des antiken mediterranen Hauskults', *Numen* 27 (1980) 34–75.

Latin sources (Cicero, *Dom.* 51.132; Suetonius, *Claud.* 12.1) employ the concept of *religio domestica*, 'household religion', for cult forms that were exercised in private. Despite its importance (Wachsmuth 34: 'The domestic cult is both one of the oldest cults of the world religions and one of the most enduring'), this subject 'has been strikingly neglected in scholarship up to the present. We have no general monograph for Greek or for Roman religion' (ibid.). We begin with some preliminary linguistic and social-historical information.

In Greek the house is called οἶκος or οἰκία (with no essential difference between the two nouns); in Latin there are two more widely divergent terms available: *domus* and *familia*. These terms cover two distinct areas. The 'house' indicates first of all the building, the dwelling house, but also the family, from the nuclear family consisting of parents and children (which modern scholarship shows to have been the normal case in the classical period, just as it is today) to the larger family which included slaves, relatives, friends and clients. It is not difficult to see the element that links these: a family, especially an influential large family, will normally also dwell in an appropriate building.

There is complete agreement that the house in this wider sense, integrating both perspectives, was the most important social and economic structure of the classical world. It served as a building-block and as a model for the elaboration of larger political units. Already Aristotle noted a close structural similarity between *oikos* and *polis*, house and city-state. The *polis* functioned like a large house, and it is also directly linked to the houses by the fact that the heads of these houses had a seat and a voice in the full assembly of the citizens of the city (*Pol.* 1.2.1 [1253b1–10]):[23]

> And since it is now clear of what elements the *polis* is composed, we must first speak about the domestic economy [περὶ οἰκονομίας], for every *polis* consists of households [ἐξ οἰκιῶν]. The domestic economy in turn is articulated in terms of the parts of which the household itself is constituted. In its full form, a household consists of slaves and free persons. Each unit should first be investigated by looking at its smallest components. In the case of the household, these first and smallest components are: master and slave, husband and wife, father and children. Thus we shall first consider these three relationships to see how they are, and how they ought to be.

One can also gauge the significance attached to the house from the fact that a specific literary genre developed in the classical period consisting of

---

[23] Cf. F. F. Schwartz, *Aristoteles: Politik. Schriften zur Staatstheorie* (RecUB 8552), Stuttgart 1989; H. Rackham, *Aristotle: Politics* (LCL 264), Cambridge, Mass. and London 1934.

texts with the title οἰκονομικός, the right 'administration of the household', or περὶ οἰκονομίας, about the right 'domestic economy'.[24] It is noticeable that these economic texts are interested above all in the role of the master of the house, who appears in various social relationships: as husband of the wife, as father of the children, and as master of the slaves. This is enough to let us sense the undisputed authoritarian position which was attributed above all by Roman law to the *pater familias*, the head of the family.

2. The domestic practice of the cult

List 22.
C. Bergemann, *Politik und Religion im spätrepublikanischen Rom* (Palingenesia 38), Stuttgart 1992, 3–85.

J. R. Clarke, *The Houses of Roman Italy 100 BC–AD 250: Ritual, Space, and Decoration*, Berkeley 1991, esp. 1–29.

D. P. Harmon, 'The Family Festivals of Rome', *ANRW* II/16.2 (1978) 1592–1603.

M. P. Nilsson, 'Griechische Hausaltäre', in Idem, *Opuscula Selecta* III (Skrifter utgivna av Svenska Institutet i Athen 8° 2.3), Lund 1960, 265–70.

——'Roman and Greek Domestic Cults', ibid. 271–85.

D. G. Orr, 'Roman Domestic Religion: The Evidence of the Household Shrines', *ANRW* II/16.2 (1978) 1557–91.

H. J. Rose, 'The Religion of a Greek Household', *Euphrosyne* 1 (1957) 95–116.

M. Vandoni, *Feste pubbliche e private nei documenti greci* (TDSA. Serie papirologica 8), Milan and Varese 1964.

D. Wachsmuth, 'Aspekte' (L21).

---

[24] Cf. Richarz; Victor. One of the earliest treatises of this kind is Xenophon's *Oikonomikos* (cf. G. Audring, *Xenophon: Ökonomische Schriften* (SQAW 38), Berlin 1992; E. C. Marchant, *Xenophon: Memorabilia and Oeconomicus* (LCL 168), Cambridge, Mass. and London 1923). New Testament exegesis has paid special attention to this genre in the context of the discussion about the 'Haustafeln' (household codes) and in the debate about the position of slaves in the earliest Christian communities.

C. K. Williams II, 'The City of Corinth and its Domestic Religion', *Hesp.* 50 (1981) 408–21.

(*a*) Towards a fundamental evaluation

The great significance of the domestic cult within the total structure of Greek and Roman religion corresponds to the societal value of the domestic fellowship as an elementary form of life and economy.[25] Here we may begin with a passage from Cicero's speech for his own house,[26] about which Dietrich Wachsmuth says: 'In the whole of classical literature there is no more penetrating or precise paraphrase of the religiosity of the classical house' (43; cf. also Bergemann). Nevertheless we must be acquainted with the *Sitz-im-Leben* of this speech before the court, if we are to evaluate correctly its statements about the religious value of the house.

Publius Clodius Pulcher, one of Cicero's political enemies, had acquired Cicero's beautiful house on the Palatine for himself when Cicero was exiled in 58 BCE. He erected a statue of a god on this site and had the place consecrated for it. One year later, Cicero returned from his exile and wanted to repossess his house. He finally succeeded in doing so, thanks to two speeches and a series of negotiations, but there were problems, because his enemy asserted that the house was now a *locus sacer* and could no longer be handed over to profane use. Cicero had to demonstrate the existence of a principle that dwelling houses of private citizens were not consecrated; unlike temples, they are and remain profane dwellings. He also attempted to show what high emotional and also religious values attach to a house, and that precisely for this reason it should not simply be expropriated from its owner.

According to Cicero, the religious value and the consequent right to protection do not come into being through any consecration of the building, but through the forms of religious praxis that are carried out with pious intention by those who dwell in it. A 'holy' house is a 'pious' house that excels in the careful praxis of the domestic cults. This (in Wachsmuth's view) is how the word *sanctus* in the famous quotation from

---

[25] On a city that is also interesting from the perspective of the New Testament, viz. Corinth, cf. Williams.

[26] Cf. M. Fuhrmann, *Marcus Tullius Cicero: Sämtliche Reden*, vol. 5 (BAW), Munich and Zurich 1978, 202–79; N. H. Watts, *Cicero: Orations*, vol. 11 (LCL 158), Cambridge, Mass. and London 1923, 132–311.

Cicero is to be understood: it is, so to speak, in quotation marks (*Dom.* 41.109):

> Quid est sanctius, quid omni religione munitius quam domus unius cuiusque civium? Hic arae sunt, hic foci, hic di penates, hic sacra, religiones, caerimoniae continentur: hoc perfugium est ita sanctum omnibus, ut inde abripi neminem fas sit.

> What is a 'sanctum' to any higher degree, what more protected by every religious practice, than the house of each one of the citizens? Here we find in one and the same place the altars, here the hearths, here the household gods, here the cults, religious practices, and the ceremonies. This place of refuge is so much a 'sanctum' for everyone that it is not permissible to tear anyone away from his house.

This text presents us with a number of questions for study: what kind of altars were found in houses? What is the meaning of the hearth? What are we to understand under 'household gods'? What ceremonies and religious customs have their specific location in the house? The next section presents only a few indications about these matters.

(*b*) Individual forms

Household gods

We begin with the household gods, which existed in great numbers among the Greeks and the Romans. Here we must mention first of all Zeus, 'father of gods and of men' (this is his fixed attribute in Homer), who had a special significance for the earthly house, as a kind of supraterrestrial 'father of the house' with two particular roles: as (*a*) Zeus Herkaios and (*b*) Zeus Ktēsios. (*a*) *Herkaios* is derived from ἕρκος, the boundary enclosing a farm. Zeus Herkaios functioned as the god of a family's dwelling, which was surrounded by a fence. (*b*) *Ktēsios* is derived from κτᾶσθαι, 'to acquire', or from κτῆμα, 'possession'. As Ktēsios, Zeus watches over the possessions and contributes to their increase.

At his side in the house we find above all Hestia, goddess of the hearth and of the fire that burnt upon it, goddess of domesticity and of family concord. The corresponding Latin goddess is *Vesta*, who has a central place in the Roman domestic cult, as well as in the state cult (the well-known 'Vestal virgins' are charged with watching over the sacred fire of Vesta, as patron goddess of concord in the city, in her ancient temple on the Capitol).

Besides this, the Romans venerated as household gods the Penates, whom we have encountered in Cicero's text, and the Lares. Scholars disagree about the precise provenance of these gods. Probably the Penates (the singular form is never used) are connected, if not linguistically then at least materially, with *penus*, the store of goods kept in the house, and with the storage room; while the Lares (the singular is also found: *Lar familiaris*) embody the spirits of the dead members of the family or else, according to another view, are originally protective spirits of particular places. In one of his prologues, Plautus puts the household god himself on the stage (*Aulularia* 1–25):

THE HOUSEHOLD GOD [emerging from Euclius' house]: So that no one may wonder who I am, I will put it briefly: I am the *Lar familiaris* of the house out of which you have just seen me come. I have possessed and watched over this house for many years now, already for the father and the grandfather of the man who lives in it now ... He [i.e. the present owner] has only one daughter. She sacrifices incense or wine to me every day, or prays in some way to me again and again, decorating me with garlands.

House altars

House altars (cf. Nilsson) with small images of the god are attested for the early stages of Greek religious history, i.e. for the Minoan and the Mycenaean periods. So-called household shrines (cf. Orr) were found in many houses in the excavations in Pompeii and Herculaneum, two cities which were covered by lava when Vesuvius erupted in 79 CE and which therefore reflect conditions in the first century CE. These shrines are niches in the wall on which small statues of the gods were placed, or else wooden cupboards which were hung on the wall for the same purpose. Copies of temples, set on plinths, and wall paintings depicting divine beings belong to the same sphere, as do portable house altars, hundreds of which were found in Pompeii. Most of these household shrines were consecrated to the Lares, hence their name *lararium*. In Petronius' *Satyricon*, the hero enters the house of his rich host Trimalchio and sees immediately behind the entrance 'an imposing chest [*grande armarium*] in the corner, with silver Lares [*Lares argentei*] standing in its little chapel [*aedicula*]' (29.8).

Domestic religious rituals

The domestic ritual takes on a particular intensity at the daily meal. A small portion of everything placed on the table belongs to the gods. Among the Greeks, the transition from the meal to the drinking feast involved a sequence of three ritual drink offerings, one of which was made to the *Agathos Daimōn*, who stands for the good spirit of the house and is often represented by the tame house snake. Plutarch calls the table where guests are welcomed to a meal 'an altar of the gods of friendship and of hospitality'; to remove it would amount to 'breaking up the household' (*Sept. Sap. Conv.* 15 [158c]). A sacrificial gift to the Roman Penates was placed on a *patella* at the household meal. Anything that fell from the table belonged to the dead and was thrown into the fire. Ovid writes (*Fasti* 6.305–10):

> In older days it was the custom to sit on long benches before the hearth, and it was believed that the gods were present at the meal ... Even into our own days, a trace of this old custom has survived: a clean vessel bears the food that is sacrificed to Vesta.

Other occasions for domestic rites arose in the course of the year and in the important events of human life. Birth, growing up, marriage and death leave their mark on family life and are accompanied by religious rites in the house (cf. Harmon). According to Athenaeus, the ancient cooks were also specialists for the family sacrifices, and this was important at weddings, for example (*Deipnosoph.* 14 [659d]: 'Thus it is not in the least paradoxical that the cooks [μάγειροι] of old were also experienced in the ritual of sacrifice, since they presided at the sacrifice on the occasion of marriages and other feasts'). Suetonius praises the emperor Claudius' modesty in his private conduct, giving as an example Claudius' refusal to have the betrothal of his daughter and the birth of a grandson celebrated in public (something he could have done at state expense). These were marked merely *religione domestica*, i.e. with domestic rites in the imperial palace (*Claud.* 12.1).

(*c*) Criticism and determination of the relationship between public and private

Despite all this, the domestic cult did not enjoy unreserved popularity among the philosophers and politicians. We also hear the voice of criticism, especially from Plato, who would have preferred to forbid domestic sacrifices:[27]

---

[27] *Leg.* 10.16 (909e).

> The following law is to apply to all, without any exception. No one is allowed *to have a private sanctuary in his own house.* But if someone feels moved to offer a sacrifice, he should carry out this intention in one of the public sanctuaries and hand over the sacrificial gift to the priests and priestesses, whose duty it is to see that all pollution is avoided. United with them, he and all those who wish to take part should make his prayers to heaven.

Plato bases his negative standpoint on the superstition of women and of sufferers who otherwise would establish sanctuaries wherever they found themselves, and on the abuse that such domestic sanctuaries allow trespassers against the gods to commit. The punishments threatened in Plato's text for transgressions go as far as the death penalty where godlessness is proven. This principle did not succeed in establishing itself in such a sharp form, although it certainly lay in the interest of the state to keep control over private cults. Little danger seems to have been feared, as long as the family kept strictly to its own limits, i.e. to the area of the house and to the traditional domestic rituals; the problems began when the boundary separating the family from the association was crossed, and when exotic forms of religion from the East were introduced. Livy describes this danger for Rome as early as the year 429 BCE (*Urb. Cond.* 4.30.9–11):

> Not only were the bodies attacked by the plague; varied superstition made its way into human spirits too, mostly from the outside, when people exploited those afflicted by religious madness, by claiming to be seers and introducing new sacrificial customs into *the houses*, until finally the leading men among the citizens were moved to shame at the generality of the populace. For they saw in *every block of houses* and *in every little sanctuary* alien and unknown expiatory sacrifices intended to beseech the gods to show favour. Therefore the aediles were charged to see that only the Roman gods were worshipped, and this in no way other than that inherited from the fathers.

This leads us to the question of the fundamental relationship between domestic and public cult. Wachsmuth is correct to formulate it thus: there exist both parallelism and antagonism. Parallelism, because the domestic cult (like the associations) reproduces to a greater or lesser extent certain fundamental forms of religious praxis known from the state cult, above all sacrifice in its various forms. But these forms could not be controlled and standardised in the houses, and this situation could lead to antagonism. The domestic cult also has emphases which act as a counterweight to the official cult, because the exercise of religion in the house has a direct link to one's personal life. Rites accompany the great and small crises, the difficult points of transition, and the accustomed rhythm of the sequence of the seasons and the alternation of day and night. The domestic cult had also an antagonistic effect above all by providing a detour along which foreign cultic forms could become established. This happened first of all in houses, from which they were diffused in an underground manner until they emerged into the public world as stable, independent realities.

One could follow many connecting lines from the house, for example to the associations with their meeting rooms, to the mystery cults which in part were practised in houses, or to the philosophical schools which met in a house around the head of the school. Here we shall follow up only one line: the opening of the house on to the public sphere in the form of a private sanctuary and of private cults which went beyond a purely domestic worship.

3. Private sanctuaries

(a) The cult of Sarapis on Delos

List 23.
H. Engelmann, *The Delian Aretalogy of Sarapis* (EPRO 44), Leiden 1975.
M. Totti, *Ausgewählte Texte der Isis- und Sarapisreligion* (SubEpi 21), Hildesheim 1985, 25–8.
O. Weinreich, *Neue Urkunden zur Sarapis-Religion* (SGV 86), Tübingen 1919.
L. M. White, *The Social Origins of Christian Architecture*, vol. 1: *Building God's House in the Roman World. Architectural Adaptation among Pagans, Jews and Chistians* (HThS 42), Valley Forge 1996, 32–40.

The history of the cult of Sarapis on the Mediterranean island of Delos provides us with a perfect example of how, despite much resistance, a foreign cult could get a foothold in the Greek world through the commitment of a family that made use of a variety of buildings. The story covers three generations from c.280 to 200 BCE. An Egyptian priest called Apollonius emigrated from the city of Memphis and settled on the island of Delos, which was an important trade centre but also the sacred territory of the Greek god Apollo. It therefore seemed unlikely that it would be easy to import foreign gods.

Nevertheless, Apollonius the Elder had a small statue of the god Sarapis in his luggage. He rented rooms on Delos, and set up the statue in one of the rooms of this lodging so that he could venerate it. As was common in

Egypt, his priesthood was inherited by his son Demetrius. Clearly, they succeeded in winning over other immigrants from Egypt to the worship of Sarapis, and gradually the rented lodging became too small. A modest wealth had been amassed, and this allowed the realisation of bold plans. The decisive break came under the grandson, Apollonius the Younger. The god revealed to him in a dream that he no longer wished to live in the rented lodging, but wanted a proper temple. The grandson acquired a suitable piece of ground and built a 'temple' on it, though this was a very modest building; the archaeologists who excavated it say that it was of poor quality. The temple properly so-called has only the size of a room: 4.10 × 3.20 metres. Beneath this was a crypt with a well, certainly for purposes of the cult. The complex is completed by a courtyard (12 × 6 metres), a small portico as entry area, and two larger rooms, one of which ($c.40 \text{ m}^2$) seems suitable as a dining room.

This development, culminating in a cultic building (even if only a modest one), met with resistance, and Apollonius the Younger was suddenly involved in legal proceedings; it is probable that conservative forces who saw themselves as under obligation to the god Apollo and did not want to tolerate the foreign cult had laid charges against him, and that Apollonius had neglected to obtain the authorities' official permission for this complex (something that was not necessary for the worship of Sarapis in a private dwelling). Besides this, he seems to have infringed on a neighbouring plot of land with his buildings. Severe penalties threatened the priest, but his accusers were surprisingly peaceful in the courtroom – perhaps the presence of a large number of Egyptians in the courtroom had cowed them. Apollonius the Younger got off scot-free, and he attributed this to the miraculous intervention of the god Sarapis, who had previously made this revelation to him in a second dream: 'Our cause will win.'

We know about this because Apollonius the Younger set up a column in the courtyard of the temple complex when all was over. On this was an inscription giving information about the family history and the revelations in his dreams and ending with a long aretalogy, i.e. a listing of the miraculous deeds of the god Sarapis.

(*b*) A private cult in Philadelphia

List 24.
S. C. Barton and G. H. R. Horsley, 'A Hellenistic Cult Group and the New Testament Churches', *JAC* 24 (1981) 7–41.

K. Berger and C. Colpe, *Textbuch* (L4) 274–6; M. E. Boring et al., *Hellenistic Commentary* 468f.

S. K. Stowers, 'A Cult from Philadelphia: Oikos Religion or Cultic Association?', in A. J. Malherbe, F. W. Norris and J. W. Thompson (eds.), *The Early Church in Its Context: Essays in Honor of E. Ferguson* (NT.S 90), Leiden 1998, 287–301.

O. Weinreich, *Stiftung und Kultsatzungen eines Privatheiligtums in Philadelphia in Lydien* (SHAW.Ph 1919,16), Heidelberg 1919.

From the first century BCE we have the statute of a private cult in Philadelphia in Asia Minor. This text was first published in 1914, but a long time passed before exegetes noticed it. The block containing the inscription (the text SIG 3/985 = LSAM 20) is 98 cm high and at a guess 35–40 cm broad; the whole of the right margin has broken away, and we shall see that this fact is important when we attempt to interpret the text as a whole. In terms of its contents, we can divide the text into four parts of varying length.

1. In the first part (lines 1–11), the founder Dionysius presents himself: he 'gives men and women, free and slave access to *his own house*' (lines 4f.). The goals of his foundation are good health, prosperity, and a good name. Zeus has communicated to him while he was asleep the ordinances which are to realise these goals; as so often, here too the form of revelation in a dream is meant to legitimate the contents of what is stated. From line 6 onwards, deities are listed.

First come Zeus Eumenēs (the adjective means benevolent or kind), his female companion Hestia (typical of a domestic cult, cf. *supra*), and 'the other saving gods' (which could for example refer to the Dioscuri, the pair of divine brothers). Some of the names mentioned next are abstract concepts personified as gods: Eudaimonia (good health), Ploutos (wealth), Aretē (virtuousness), Hygieia (health; cf. the first line), Agathē Tychē (good fate, the goddess of luck), Agathos Daimōn (the good spirit of the house, cf. *supra*), Mnēmē (remembrance), the Charites or Graces (three goddesses who bring blessings) and Nikē (the goddess of victory, who will help the whole undertaking to become established and make its way victoriously).

Here, if we count the group designations 'saving gods' and 'Graces' as each one name, we have altogether twelve gods, whose altars have been set up by Dionysius in his house (line 11). He does not mention the images or statues which presumably went along with the altars. When one hears this, one automatically pictures a large, free-standing building with twelve or more life-size statues and the corresponding altars, but this need not be the case – here we need only recall the domestic shrines in Pompeii. Such shrines would allow the entire pantheon to be accommodated in one spacious room, and there would be sufficient space at the entrance to such a room for the inscription, which is *c*.1 metre high.

2. The long second part lists the individual ordinances. Ritual customs both old and new are mentioned (lines 12–14: 'To carry out the consecrations and the purifications and the mysteries in accordance with the customs of the fathers, and as is written here'; cf. also the sacrifices, line 55). An oath is required on entering this house (presumably, that is, on entering for the first time), which signifies entering the cultic fellowship. This oath speaks of the avoidance of certain moral offences which are listed in a negative catalogue of vices (lines 12–15):

> On entering this house, men and women, free and (domestic) slaves, are to swear by all the gods that they will not knowingly become acquainted with or use any deceit against man or woman, nor any poison that is harmful to human beings, nor magical words with evil intent. With regard to love potions, abortifacients or means of contraception, they will not themselves use them, nor advise another to use them, nor be an accomplice in their use. They will not cease in any way to be well disposed towards this house. And if anyone does or plans any of these things, they will neither permit this nor pass it over in silence, but will reveal it and oppose it.

The continuation of this text shows that the morality involved here is relatively strict. Sexual intercourse with boys is rejected, just as are adultery and the violation of a virgin. If one takes the text completely literally, the only loophole remaining for men is in the sphere of prostitution and vis-à-vis unmarried female slaves. There is a clear intent to strengthen family ties and to ward off magic that could inflict danger. There are points of contact here, in substance and also in terminology, with the medical ethics of that period. If a member of the cultic fellowship transgresses these prescriptions, he is threatened with temporary exclusion from the celebrations and above all with 'evil curses from the gods' (lines 43f.) or with severe divine punishments (line 50). To those who are obedient, the gods 'will show favour and will always give them those good things that gods are accustomed to give the human beings who love them' (lines 46–8). Both of these, reward and punishment, are conceived in innerworldly terms here.

3. In the third part (lines 50–60) something new comes on the scene, when we are told: 'These ordinances were laid at the feet of Agdistis, the most holy guardian and lady of this house [οἰκοδέσποιναν τοῦδε τοῦ οἴκου]', for this Agdistis is a manifestation of the mother deity from Asia Minor, who appears under various names. According to lines 54f. she has the task here of 'inspiring a good attitude in men and women, free and slave, so that they may obey what is written here'. This means that Agdistis must be seen in connection with the customs inherited from the fathers (line 14). As the original goddess of the house, she stands for an earlier phase of the religious life in Dionysius' family; in the new pantheon, her place is taken by the domestic goddess Hestia. Nevertheless, Agdistis was not simply forgotten, any more than the customs of the fathers were forgotten. She herself is to see to it that the new rules laid down in our inscription, which have the basic aim of giving the right structure to family life, are accepted and followed by the members of the extended cultic fellowship. This theological reasoning results in the following directive, which shows how it can be checked whether the commandments are being kept (lines 55–60):

> At the sacrifices, both the monthly and the yearly sacrifices, those who have confidence in themselves, both men and women, are to touch this inscription on which the god's ordinances are written, so that it may be clearly seen who obeys the ordinances and who does not obey them.

This confirms our supposition that the inscription was placed at the entrance to the cultic room. Anyone who is guilty and yet touches it, must know that the divine retribution will swiftly descend upon him. He must understand every misfortune and every piece of bad luck that he encounters from now on as the divine penalty for this wickedness.

4. The conclusion in lines 60–5 is a prayer addressed to Zeus as judge, which envisages the founder Dionysius himself touching the inscription in this way, and puts the expectation of an innerworldly salvation into words again:

> Zeus Sōtēr, graciously and benevolently receive Dionysius' act of touching, and in your favour grant him and his family a good reward, health, rescue, peace, safety on land and on sea . . .

Let us sum up: Dionysius with his family had worshipped the goddess Agdistis in his house as domestic goddess and protectress. Acceptance of this goddess entailed also the acceptance of a system of traditional moral attitudes. But then a modernising shift occurs, with threefold consequences: Agdistis as an inspiring power moves into the background and yields her position to a new, larger Graeco-Hellenistic pantheon with visible altars and images; the older tradition is developed into an articulated statute with new elements drawn from medical ethics and strongly related to the family; at the same time, Dionysius opens his house to like-minded visitors, presumably drawn primarily from neighbouring and related households. The house of Dionysius develops in the city of Philadelphia into a centre and place of support for people who share his moral ideas about the family and the household; they wish to obey these and therefore join together in a cultic fellowship under the protection of suitable deities.[28]

D. The cult of the dead

List 25.

A. H. Armstrong, *Expectations of Immortality in Late Antiquity* (AqL), Milwaukee 1987.

G. Binder and B. Effe (eds.), *Tod und Jenseits im Altertum* (Bochumer Altertumswissenschaftliches Colloquium 6), Trier 1991.

E. F. Bruck, *Totenteil und Seelgerät im griechischen Recht: Eine entwicklungsgeschichtliche Untersuchung zum Verhältnis von Recht und Religion mit Beiträgen zur Geschichte des Eigentums und des Erbrechts* (MBPF 9), Munich 2nd edn. 1970.

F. Cumont, *Recherches sur le symbolisme funéraire des Romains* (BAH 35), Paris 1942.

——*Lux perpetua*, Paris 1949.

A. Dieterich, *Nekyia: Beiträge zur Erklärung der neuentdeckten Petrusapokalypse*, Leipzig and Berlin 2nd edn. 1913, reprint Darmstadt 1969.

G. Gnoli and J. P. Vernant, *La Mort, les morts dans les sociétés anciennes*, Cambridge and Paris 1982.

---

[28] For a comparison with the New Testament (house fellowship, catalogue of vices, Gal 3:28, the question of offices, rites, etc.), see Berger and Colpe (L24).

M. Herfort-Koch, *Tod, Totenfürsorge und Jenseitsvorstellungen in der griechischen Antike: Eine Bibliographie* (Quellen und Forschungen zur antiken Welt 9), Munich 1992.

R. Herzog, 'Fest, Terror und Tod in Petrons Satyrica', in W. Haug and R. Warning (eds.), *Das Fest* (Poetik und Hermeneutik 14), Munich 1989, 120–50.

H. von Hesberg, *Römische Grabbauten*, Darmstadt 1992.

K. Hopkins, *Death and Renewal* (Sociological Studies in Roman History 2), Cambridge 1983.

S. C. Humphreys and H. King (eds.), *Mortality and Immortality: The Anthropology and Archaeology of Death*, London 1981.

D. C. Kurtz and J. Boardman, *Greek Burial Customs*, London 1971.

J. Leipoldt, *Der Tod bei Griechen und Juden*, Leipzig 1942.

F. Pfister, *Der Reliquienkult im Altertum*, vols. 1–2 (RVV 5.1–2), Giessen 1909, 1912.

W. Pötscher, 'Die "Auferstehung" in der klassischen Antike', *Kairos* 7 (1965) 208–15.

E. Rohde, *Psyche: The Cult of Souls and Belief in Immortality among the Greeks*, London 1925.

E. Samter, 'Antike und moderne Totengebräuche', *NJKA* 15 (1905) 34–45.

H. Sonnemanns, *Seele – Unsterblichkeit – Auferstehung: Zur griechischen und christlichen Anthropologie* (FThSt 128), Freiburg i.Br. 1984.

Since death, one's own and that of other people, is a horizon that accompanies human life and inescapably limits it, dealing with death is a decisive test of the efficiency of the religious factor within a societal system. The strategies developed to cope with death cover all the three levels with which we have worked up to this point: first of all, they affect the house to which the dead person belonged, but we have already seen that the concern for the burial and the memory of the dead could be the dominant interest at the foundation of an association (see B, 2 above), and it suffices to recall the funerary celebration of the first of those who fell in the Peloponnesian War (Thucydides 2.34.1–18), followed by the great funeral address by Pericles, to see that this also had a public character. Death even creates its own literary genres, in the funerary address (*epitaphios logos*) and in the literature of consolation. We shall discuss the question of particular hopes for a life after death in connection with the mystery cults (see Chapter II below). We will also have occasion to discuss in greater detail the eschatology of the various philosophical schools (see Chapter V), and there we shall see the form that Plutarch gave to the Platonic myths of a dimension on the far side of death. One can say in a certain sense that death is omnipresent in the picture that we are drawing – also in sacrifice, or in the declaration of posthumous heroic status, to which we must return in connection with the cult of rulers – since death intervenes in almost all the dimensions of life.

A further point of entry is offered here by the cult of the dead. How did people deal with the dead? What rites were developed for their burial, for the care of their graves, for the maintenance of their remembrance? What do these rites accomplish within the structure of society, and what statements do they make about the mode of existence proper to the dead? Here once again we must distinguish between the consciousness of those who carry out such rites, and the statement of the ritual itself. Certainly, it is very difficult to grasp the consciousness of those who celebrate the rite, whereas the rites permit some objectifying statements, if one knows how to decipher them; a modern analogy could be the Christian burial rite, with texts and ceremonies profoundly marked by the Jewish and Christian hope of a resurrection of the dead, even if it has long been the case that not all the participants in the ritual share this conviction.

1. The funeral ritual

List 26.

F. Bömer, *Ahnenkult und Ahnenglaube im alten Rom* (ARW.B 1), Leipzig and Berlin 1943.

J. Bremmer, *The Early Greek Concept of the Soul*, Princeton 1983.

L. Morris, *Death-Ritual and Social Structure in Classical Antiquity* (Key Themes in Ancient History), Cambridge 1992.

A. D. Nock, 'Cremation and Burial in the Roman Empire', in Idem, *Essays* (L2) 277–307.

R. Parker, *Miasma* (L2) 32–73.

E. Rohde, *Psyche* (L25) 3–54, 156–216.

A. Schnapp-Gourbeillon, 'Les funérailles de Patrocle', in G. Gnoli and L. P. Vernant, *La Mort* (L25) 77–88.

(a) A burial ceremony

As our starting point we choose the great burial ceremony that is prepared for Patroclus, the fallen comrade of Achilles, in the penultimate Book of the *Iliad* (23). It begins with a lamentation over the dead man, with the transition to a mourning meal; in the course of the preparation of this meal, the blood of the slaughtered animals is poured over the corpse (23.34). During the following night the soul of Patroclus appears in a dream to Achilles as he sleeps, and complains (23.69–74):

You are asleep, and you have forgotten me, Achilles. You were never neglectful of me while I lived, but you are in my death. Bury me as quickly as can be, so I can pass through the gates of Hades. The ghosts, the phantoms of the dead, are keeping me away, they will not let me cross the river to join their number, but I am left wandering in vain along the broad-gated house of Hades.

Achilles would like to embrace his comrade once again and stretches out his hands to him in longing, but 'the ghost vanished away under the earth like smoke, squeaking' (23.100f.). Astonished, Achilles remarks (23.103–7):

Ah, so there does remain something of a man even in the house of Hades, a ghost [ψυχή] and a semblance [εἴδωλον] of him, but without real being at all. All night long the ghost of poor Patroclus has stood over me weeping and lamenting, and has told me all that I must do – it looked wonderfully like the true man.

We note that the soul appears here only as a poor 'copy' of the dead, resembling him indeed, but without any vital force (on funerary vases, the dead are sometimes depicted as small beings with wings, in a form like that of human beings, but much smaller and almost transparent). An existence in Hades, though not in the least attractive, seems nevertheless preferable to their unstable wanderings. The soul of Patroclus finds rest only when Achilles gives his corpse to the flames on the following day. Together with him – in the form of an annihilatory sacrifice that is typical of the cult of the dead – sheep, bulls, horses and dogs are burnt in the flames, and the cruel high-point is the burning of twelve Trojan prisoners of war, whom Achilles himself murders with this in view (23.175f.). The smouldering ashes are put out with wine, then the blanched bones of Patroclus are gathered and placed in a golden urn, above which a mound of earth will be heaped up. Immediately after this, contests and games take place, and at the end of the day festive meals are held on each of the ships.

(b) Funeral rituals

This classic example allows us to see fundamental patterns of the later ritual of the dead which was held in a simplified form whenever a member of the family died. The striking concern for the rest of the dead soul has also its hidden side, and this hidden motif has probably as much importance as the motif that is mentioned openly – in other words, the ritual serves to give the living peace from the intrusions of the wandering souls, who can become intrusive and dangerous. It is in the interest of the living to aim at a clear demarcation between the realm of life and the realm of death, so that the border transit between the one side and the other is limited as much as possible. This is the source of the fundamental fact that all those who come into contact with death are thereby polluted, so that complex processes of purification are necessary (cf. Parker). Even the goddess Artemis shows that she is subject to this law, when she tells her beloved Hippolytus, as he is dying: 'And now farewell! I may not look on dead persons, my face is polluted by the breath of the dead' (Euripides, *Hipp.* 1437f.).

Laws were enacted to lay down the standard elements of the celebration of the dead; one of their intentions was to hinder a disproportionate splendour in the funeral arrangements (e.g. SIG 3/1218 = LSCG 97). The corpse is washed, anointed, clothed in white garments, strewn with flowers – i.e. is thus declared to be clean – and the bier is set up in the entrance hall of the house. Mourning women sing songs of lamentation, strike their breasts and tear their hair. At the entrance to the house stands a vase with water for the purifying ablutions; the old fire in the hearth is quenched, and a new fire kindled later. After a period lasting from one to two days, the funeral procession accompanies the bier on which the dead person lies, out to the necropolis outside the city. Priests do not accompany this funeral procession, since that was not a part of their duties – this strikes us as strange, but it was taken for granted in the classical period. Sophocles showed impressively in his *Antigone* that the burial of the dead was the first commandment of *pietas*. But burial customs and practices change. As we have seen, the corpse of Patroclus was burnt. This is criticised by Lucretius, the Roman adherent of Epicureanism, in his didactic poem *De Rerum Natura*:[29]

---

[29] See H. Diels and E. G. Schmidt, *Lukrez: Von der Natur* (TuscBü), Munich and Zurich 1993; W. H. D. Rouse and M. F. Smith, *Lucretius* (LCL 181), Cambridge, Mass. and London rev. edn. 1982.

For if it is something bad to be torn in death by the jaws and bites of wild animals, I cannot see how it should not be bitter to be roasted on a pyre in hot flames, or to suffocate in honey, or to become rigid by reason of the cold when one lies on the level of the icy stones, or to be crushed from above, injured by the weight of the earth [that lies on one] (3.888–93).

Although more exotic forms did exist, the two normal forms were cremation and burial in the earth. In the first century CE burial was dominant in the entire eastern half of the empire, including Greece and Asia Minor, while the opposite development had taken place in the western half of the empire, including the capital, Rome. Here corpses were cremated, and then the urns were placed in places such as catacombs (which were not a Christian invention). We need not investigate in detail how this geographical distribution occurred, and what factors led to this development in two different directions; but we must note that this equilibrium was not maintained. A movement towards greater unification started from the East, so that burial became increasingly common in the West too, until this was the dominant form c.200 CE, so that the third century of the Common Era knows virtually only burial of the dead in the earth. Judaism and Christianity had accepted only burial, linking this to their hope for a resurrection of the dead. Scholars agree that neither Judaism nor Christianity played a decisive role in these global tendencies. Nevertheless it was a fortunate circumstance that the exclusive attitude of Jews and Christians on this point did not have to establish itself against opposition, but encountered a universally accepted practice (cf. Morris 68: 'it can hardly be denied that this ritual unity and its fortuitous overlap with the Jewish customs which the Christians favoured must have aided the spread of the new faith').

2. The underworld

List 27.

H. D. Betz, *Lukian* (L3) 81–99.

G. Dietz, 'Der Mythos von Odysseus in der Unterwelt: Zu den Jenseits-vorstellungen in den Epen Homers', *BSIM* 22 (1989) 5–42.

C. Sourvinou-Inwood, *'Reading' Greek Death: To the End of the Classical Period*, Oxford 1996, 10–107.

Bibliography in Lists 25 and 26.

Book 11 of the *Odyssey* contains the *Nekyia*, Odysseus' journey to the underworld, which had a greater influence than any other text on ideas about Hades (Aeneas' journey to the underworld in Book 6 of Vergil's *Aeneid* could be compared with this, as far as the Roman world is concerned). At the entrance to the underworld, which is in a mythical country and is continuously covered by a dark mist, Odysseus summons the souls of the dead in the following manner (*Od.* 11.24–37):

> I drew my sharp sword from my side and dug a trench as long and as wide as a man's forearm. There I poured libations to all the dead, first with a mixture of honey and milk, then with sweet wine, and last of all with water. Over all this I sprinkled some white barley . . . When I had finished my prayers and invocations to the communities of the dead, I took the sheep and cut their throats over the trench so that the dark blood poured in. And now the souls of the dead came swarming up from Erebus.

The steaming, warm blood of the sacrificial animals entices the souls out of the underworld. For a short period, fresh blood infuses them with a new vital force, and this is why they thirst for it. In this manner, Odysseus wants to find out something about his own future from the Theban seer Teiresias (11.90–6): in other words, he is practising necromancy, summoning the dead and putting questions to them. Although she tastes the blood, Odysseus is unable to take hold of the soul of his dead mother. She escapes from his clutches three times (11.207f.), and gives the following explanation:

> It is the law of our mortal nature, when we come to die. We no longer have sinews keeping the bones and flesh together; once life has departed from our white bones, all is consumed by the fierce heat of the blazing fire, and the soul slips away like a dream and goes fluttering on its ways.

The continuation of this scene presents many of the characters of the mythical tradition, who pass by Odysseus and exchange some words with him. Thus, for example, the soul of Achilles complains about the mode of existence in the underworld: 'the dead live on as mindless disembodied ghosts [εἴδωλα]' (11.475f.). He himself 'would rather work the soil as a serf on hire to some landless impoverished peasant than be king of all these lifeless dead' (11.489–91). Towards the end of the book Odysseus also sees those who are being punished in the underworld, including Tantalus – the water reaches to his chin, but he can never drink of it, because it withdraws as soon as he bends down – and Sisyphus: again and again he must roll the mighty rock up to the summit, from which it always rolls down again (11.582–600). He also sees Heracles, but only his εἴδωλον, since Heracles himself has been given a place among the immortal gods and shares the meals at their table (11.601–4).

Thus the common idea of the impotent shadows who lead an empty existence in a dark realm under the earth into which their corpses were lowered[30] (cf. Sheol in the Old Testament) is filled out in two ways. First, terrifying images of the cruel punishment of particularly wicked persons are offered, and these can be explained as a projection into the life after death of penalties that would be genuinely meaningful only if they were inflicted on the body while the sinner was alive on earth; the purpose of this projection is to make possible a *just* outcome for earthly existence. Secondly, a reward for exceptional good deeds and increased piety ought to correspond to the penalties for the wicked, but the *Odyssey* is very reserved here: only in the case of Heracles do we see such a possibility. Here we must also mention Elysium, a paradisal dwelling place to which only a few are admitted. It remains unclear where this lies, and how one should conceive of the state of existence of those who are there. Mostly, it is called the island of the blessed, localised in mythical regions beyond the sea. In older myths, those who attain to Elysium are taken there bodily, transported from the earth before their death, but we also find some who enter Elysium after death. The development after Homer tends more and more to transpose the dwelling place of the souls into the starry heaven (see below). Precisely in the sphere of eschatology, where human beings do as a matter of fact hold incompatible convictions at one and the same time, we must not make any demands for strict logic and total consistency.

3. Giving the dead food and the meal celebrating the dead

List 28.

H. D. Betz, *Lukian* (L3) 71–4.
P. A. Février, 'Kult und Geselligkeit: Überlegungen zum Totenmahl', in J. Martin and B. Quint, *Christentum* (L3) 358–90.

---

[30] Cf. Cicero, *Tusc.* 1.36: 'For since the bodies fall into the earth and are covered with earth (which is why one speaks of them as "buried"), it was believed that the dead would continue their life under the earth. This view led to great errors, and the poets have only made these errors greater.'

75

E. Freistedt, *Altchristliche Totengedächtnistage und ihre Beziehung zum Jenseitsglauben und Totenkultus der Antike* (LQF 24), Münster 1928.

H.-J. Klauck, *Herrenmahl* (L5) 76–88.

T. Klauser, *Die Cathedra im Totenkult der heidnischen und christlichen Antike* (LF 9), Münster 2nd edn. 1971.

G. Koch, *Sarkophage der römischen Kaiserzeit*, Darmstadt 1993.

E. Maass, *Orpheus* (L18) 205–46.

A. D. Nock, 'Sarcophagi and Symbolism', in Idem, *Essays* (L2) 606–41.

R. N. Thönges-Stringaris, 'Das griechische Totenmahl', *MDALA* 80 (1965) 1–99.

R. Turcan, 'Les Sarcophages romains et le problème du symbolisme funéraire', *ANRW* II/16.2 (1978) 1700–35.

(*a*) Sacrifices for the dead

If we detach what Odysseus does at the entrance to the underworld from the special intention of necromancy, what we have is a feeding of the dead, or a sacrifice for the dead. One goes to the grave of the dead, places food and drink there and summons the dead to the meal with invariable formulae of invitation ('Arise, N.N., eat and drink and enjoy yourself'). We find prescriptions governing sacrifices in connection with the dead, e.g. that one should dig a ditch on the western side of the grave and pour in water and oil. In some graves, vertical pipes, designed to receive drink offerings, led directly into the earth; the same purpose was served by cylindrical vases with no bottom, which were placed on the grave. Liquids were preferred because their seeping into the soil provided a striking image of the process of penetrating down to the dead. Lucian confirms that such customs continued to enjoy unbroken popularity in the second century CE, when he gives them an ironic twist in a number of writings that are important evidence about the cult of the dead and belief about an afterlife.[31]

> But what are people looking for there, that leads them to anoint the gravestones and hang garlands of flowers on them? Some people set fire to funeral pyres beside the grave mound and dig ditches in the earth. But why do they throw this quantity of food into the fire, and why – if I see aright – do they pour wine and honey into the ditches? (*Charon* 22).

[31] Apart from *Charon* and *De luctu*, from which I quote, cf. also *Menippus sive Necyomantia, Cataplus sive Tyrannus, Dialogi mortuorum, Verae historiae* 2.5–32.

And they are nourished by the libations and sacrifices for the dead that we offer on their graves, so that a dead person who has not left behind on earth any friend or relative must abide in a state where his hunger is not satisfied, thus cutting a very sorry figure among the other dead (*De Luctu* 9).

The sacrifices for the dead take place on fixed dates: among the Greeks, on the third, the seventh or ninth, and the thirtieth day (presumably reckoned from the day of burial rather than from the day of death); among the Romans, on the day of burial, on the ninth day, and each year on the birthday of the deceased. As well as these, general yearly days of remembrance of the dead were introduced. In Athens these were linked with the *Anthestēria* at the end of February; in Rome the *Parentalia* for one's deceased parents were observed in February, and the *Lemuria* in May for the deceased of the entire household fellowship. Ovid gives the impression that the *Lemuria* gave prominence to the appeasing of dangerous spirits of the dead (*Fasti* 5.429–44), while he emphasises that the dead have only modest needs when he speaks of the *Parentalia* (*Fasti* 2.533–9):

Celebrations take place at the graves too. Appease the souls of your ancestors! Bring little gifts to the cemeteries! The dead wish only a little – pious gratitude is more pleasing than a costly gift. The Styx down below is not the dwelling place of any greedy gods. A tile covered by sacrificial garlands suffices, with fruits scattered about, a few grains of salt and bread moistened in wine, and some loose violets.

Two potential meanings for the feeding of the dead have been indicated above: the appeasing of the spirits of the dead and the conviction that the dead depend on the living for nourishment to sustain their existence in the afterlife. Another driving force could have been the wish to deny the reality of death by continuing table fellowship: by giving the dead a share of one's own food, one maintains a link with them. At the very least, this can help the process of mourning, separating the living step by step from the dead (cf. the way in which the feeding of the dead takes place at staggered intervals!).

(*b*) The funeral meal

It may be easier to grasp this last-mentioned motif for holding table fellowship with the dead if we consider the funeral meal which takes place in the framework of the funeral ceremonies, but in the house of mourning rather than in the cemetery itself. In Greece it is called περίδειπνον, because the meal is held 'around the dead'; in Rome it is called *silicernium*. Another function of the funeral meal was to end the mourning fast of the relatives and to restore them to life; once again, it is Lucian who tells us this (*De Luctu* 24):

> At length comes the funeral feast. All the relatives come and console the parents of the dead person and compel them to eat something again – though one must say (by Jove!) that they are only too willing to be compelled, after a three days' fast, since they can hardly bear their hunger any longer ... Thus at length they begin to eat, although initially completely ashamed to do so ...

At Trimalchio's dinner in Petronius' *Satyricon* a guest who arrives late excuses his delay by saying that he had to take part in this kind of funeral meal, and that the table was very well decked (*Sat.* 65.11: 'But it was very pleasant, although we were obliged to pour the half of what we drank over his bones'). We should also mention briefly the memorial meal, which served to keep the memory of the dead person alive even across longer stretches of time. One of the fundamental tasks of the association which Epicteta founded on the island of Thera (see B, 2(*a*) above) was to hold this memorial meal, and we shall see it again among the Epicureans, who recognised no other form of life after death than a continued existence in human memory.

(c) The meal for the dead

Distinct from the above, since a different terminology is employed, is the meal for the dead (cf. Thönges-Stringaris). Pictorial representations, reliefs of meals for the dead, present a fundamental type that can be described as follows (cf. UUC III no. 18): a man is portrayed lying on a couch before a dining table, with a woman on a throne and a naked boy as cupbearer. A large vessel of wine can be recognised, and the man who rests on the couch stretches out a cup to the boy. On the table are loaves and fruit. Prostrate figures, smaller than the reclining man, may also be portrayed: their lesser size is an indication that they have been taken from the realm of the living. It is not easy to interpret this picture: it has been identified as a scene from daily life, as a meal in the afterlife, as an image of a dead person who enjoys his memorial sacrifice, as a funeral meal. The reclining man has been considered to be one of the normal dead, or a hero, or even a god. Probably the correct view is that the surviving members of the family, in the picture and in reality, surround the bed of the dead person and (as indicated above) share their own food and nourishment with him, in order to reduce the brutality of death's separation.

We also find the meal in the afterlife, with the dead person reclining at table in the other world, though this is less common, so that one should not interpret the relief of the meal for the dead in this sense. We find this projection into the future above all in the world of the mystery cults (see Chapter II below). The interpretation of the relevant symbols in sarcophagus art is disputed (cf. Turcan). The main iconographic evidence for the meal in the afterlife is a cycle of pictures from a Roman cemetery[32] reproducing ideas from the cult of Sabazios – not, as has sometimes been supposed, art influenced by Christianity, although we find there an *angelus bonus* who leads the deceased Vibia into the Elysian fields, where she participates in the meal of the *bonorum iudicio iudicati*, i.e. those who have passed safely through judgement. (Borrowings from Judaism should not be excluded, as is clear from the very fact of the name of the god.)

4. Epigrams on graves

List 29.
A. J. Festugière, *L'Idéal* (L3) 142–60.
H. Geist and G. Pfohl, *Grabinschriften* (L4).
P. Hoffmann, *Die Toten in Christus: Eine religionsgeschichtliche und exegetische Untersuchung zur paulinischen Eschatologie* (NTA NF 2), Münster 3rd edn. 1978, 44–57.
R. Lattimore, *Themes in Greek and Latin Epitaphs* (Illinois Studies in Language and Literature 28.1–2), Urbana 1942, reprint 1962.
R. Merkelbach and J. Stauber, *Steinepigramme aus dem griechischen Osten*, vol. 1, Stuttgart 1998.
W. Peek, *Griechische Vers-Inschriften*, vol. 1: *Grab-Epigramme*, Berlin 1955.
——*Griechische Grabgedichte* (SQAW 7), Berlin 1960.
G. Pfohl, *Inschriften* (L4).

In order that the total picture we are painting here should not be excessively cautious, and thereby also misleading, it should be emphasised

---

[32] Cf. UUC III nos. 68–70; F. Cumont (plate 4.1 in French edition: *Les Religions Orientales dans le Paganisme Romain*, Paris 1929); cf. also Maass.

that not only can a broad sceptical tendency be discerned, but that this was most probably the dominant attitude of most people vis-à-vis death. We see this not least from the many thousands of funeral epigrams which have survived. A small number do indeed display the conviction that became popular following Homer, namely that the souls of the righteous are light and therefore ascend to heaven; this can be linked with forms of a hope for astral immortality that has the souls living in the heavens, or identifies them with stars (cf. Aristophanes, *Peace* 832f.: 'And did you not see anything like what people say – that we become stars in the air after we die?', cf. Hoffmann). But it has been estimated that only at most 10 per cent of the funerary epigrams contain even a hint of a hope for an afterlife. That is not a high total, even when one reflects on the limitations imposed by the genre, and bears in mind that the de facto silence of funeral epigrams about future hopes need not necessarily exclude such hopes. But food for thought is provided by those epigrams that bear clear traces of resignation. We quote here three variations of one formal type that is often found:[33]

οὐκ ἤμην, γενόμην, οὐκ ἔσομ'
οὐ μέλει μοι. ὁ βίος ταῦτα.

I did not exist, I came into being, I will not exist any more.
I do not care – that's life.

Non fui, non sum, non curo
(abbreviated as: n.f.n.s.n.c.)

I did not exist, I do not exist, I do not care.

Nil fui, nil sum;
et tu, qui vivis,
es bibe lude veni.

I was nothing, I am nothing;
and you who [now] live,
eat, drink, play, come!

This brings us finally to Paul, who writes (1 Cor 15:32), 'If the dead are not raised, then let us eat and drink, for tomorrow we are dead.' Here he himself picks up an older slogan which puts in a nutshell how a great many people in his own day perceived their life.

---

[33] Cf. nos. 434f. in Geist; no. 31 in Pfohl; Festugière 158 n. 2; Peek, *Grabgedichte* no. 453.

Chapter II
The Fascination of the Mysterious: The Mystery Cults

A. Approaching the phenomenon

List 30.

W. D. Berner, *Initiationsriten in Mysterienreligionen, im Gnostizismus und im antiken Judentum*, theological doctoral dissertation, Göttingen 1972.

U. Bianchi, *The Greek Mysteries* (IoR XVII/3), Leiden 1976.

——and M. J. Vermaseren (eds.), *Soteriologia* (L2; with numerous relevant essays).

Bibel und Kirche 45 (1990), Heft 3: *Mysterienkulte* (= 117–58).

W. Burkert, *Ancient Mystery Cults*, Cambridge, Mass. 1987.

F. Cumont, *Religions* (L2).

F. Dunand et al., *Mystères et syncrétismes* (EtHR 2), Paris 1975.

L. F. Farnell, *Cults*, vols. 3–5 (L2).

M. Giebel, *Das Geheimnis der Mysterien: Antike Kulte in Griechenland, Rom und Ägypten*, Zurich and Munich 1990.

J. Godwin, *Mystery Religions in the Ancient World*, London 1981.

K. H. E. de Jong, *Das antike Mysterienwesen in religionsgeschichtlicher, ethnologischer und pyschologischer Beleuchtung*, Leiden 2nd edn. 1919.

O. Kern and T. Hopfner, art. 'Mysterien', *PRE* 16 (1935) 1209–1350.

H.-J. Klauck, *Herrenmahl* (L5).

B. M. Metzger, 'A Classified Bibliography of the Graeco-Roman Mystery Religions 1924–1973 with a Supplement 1976–1977', *ANRW* II/17.3 (1984) 1259–1423.

M. W. Meyer, *The Ancient Mysteries: A Sourcebook. Sacred Texts of the Mystery Religions of the Ancient Mediterranean World*, San Francisco 1987; new ppb. edn. 1999.

K. Prümm, art. 'Mystères', *DBS* 6 (1960) 10–225.

R. Reitzenstein, *Hellenistic Mystery Religions: Their basic ideas and significance*, Pittsburgh 1978.

C. Riedweg, *Mysterienterminologie bei Platon, Philon und Klemens von Alexandrien* (UaLG 26), Berlin 1987.

N. Turchi, *Fontes Historiae Mysteriorum Aevi Hellenistici* (Ricerche e testi di storia e letteratura religiose 3), Rome 1923.

H. R. Willoughby, *Pagan Regeneration: Study of Mystery Initiations in the Graeco-Roman World*, Chicago 1929, reprint 1960.

D. Zeller, art. 'Mysterien/Mysterienreligionen', *TRE* 23 (1994) 503–26.

In the argumentation of the history-of-religions school, which we have discussed in the Introduction, the Hellenistic-Roman mystery cults played a decisive role; in our evaluation, we shall return to this point. We shall first attempt to come closer to the phenomenon by investigating the terminology and then asking what mystery cults are and looking at the appearance they present, their development and their history. After this, we turn to five individual cults, which count among those most widespread in antiquity and those best known in the modern period: the mysteries of Eleusis, of Dionysus, of Attis, of Isis, and of Mithras.

If our presentation aimed at completeness, we should certainly have to speak of other cults, large and small, often tied to one locality. Here we mention only a few: the mysteries of the 'great gods', the *Cabiri*, with their centre on the island of Samothrace off the Thracian coast,[1] the mysteries of Zeus Panamaros in Asia Minor,[2] or the mysteries of Andania in Messenia, whose gods Pausanias gives an honourable second place after those of Eleusis (*Graec. Descr.* 4.33.5); an inscription from the year 92 BCE records the external sequence of events at these mysteries.[3] But the texts chosen should allow the most important and fundamental characteristics to be illustrated sufficiently.

1. The terminology

List 31.

G. Bornkamm, 'μυστήριον, μυέω', *TDNT* 4.802–28.

---

[1] Cf. e.g. Giebel 89–114; S. G. Cole, 'The Mysteries of Samothrace during the Roman Period', *ANRW* II/18.2 (1989) 1564–98.

[2] Cf. H. Oppermann, *Zeus Panamaros* (RVV 19.3), Giessen 1924; P. Roussel, 'Les mystères de Panamara', *BCH* 51 (1927) 123–37; a more recent presentation in L. Wehr, *Arznei der Unsterblichkeit* (L157) 356–66.

[3] SIG 3/736 = LSCG 65; trans. UUC II.89f.; Meyer 51–9; cf. M. P. Nilsson's remark about this, *Geschichte* (L2) II.97: 'The mysteries appear much more as a

H. Dörrie, 'Mysterien (in Kult und Religion) und Philosophie', in M. J. Vermaseren, *Religionen* (L2) 341–62.

E. R. Goodenough, 'Literal Mystery in Hellenistic Judaism', in *Quantula-cumque* (*Festschrift for K. Lake*), London 1937, 227–41.

J. D. B. Hamilton, 'The Church and the Language of Mystery: The First Four Centuries', *EThL* 53 (1977) 479–94.

A. E. Harvey, 'The Use of Mystery Language in the Bible', *JThS* NS 31 (1980) 320–36.

H. Krämer, 'Zur Wortbedeutung "Mysteria"', *WuD* 6 (1959) 121–5.

C. Riedweg, *Mysterienterminologie* (L30).

J. Z. Smith, *Drudgery* (L5) 54–84.

H. von Soden, 'ΜΥΣΤΗΡΙΟΝ und *sacramentum* in den ersten zwei Jahrhunderten der Kirche', *ZNW* 12 (1911) 188–227.

When we speak of mystery cults, we adopt a vocabulary that was already common in the classical period. Classical authors too call particular forms of religion 'mysteries' (μυστήρια), mostly employed in the plural, and this has come via the Latin loanword *mysterium* into a number of European languages as 'mystery' (cf. *mystère* in French, *mistero* in Italian, *misterio* in Spanish, etc.).

It is not yet completely clear what the provenance and the fundamental meaning of the word μυστήριον are. The verb μυεῖν, 'to initiate', is a secondary formation created to provide a corresponding verb. Another verb tends to be proposed as the origin of the noun, viz. μύειν, 'to close', 'to keep closed', more specifically to keep the mouth or the lips closed, i.e. to be silent. It is suggested that the root μυ– is onomatopoeic, i.e. that it copies the inarticulate sound (a kind of *mu*) one would make if one attempted to speak with lips closed. According to the usual rules for the formation of Greek words, μυστήριον could be derived from this verb, and thus the etymology would shed light on an essential characteristic of the mysteries: they are something about which one may not speak, but must hold one's tongue and be silent. But this derivation is not certain.[4]

---

popular festival that must be regulated in terms of what went on, and controlled by the police, than as a religious celebration'; extended to the mysteries as a whole by R. MacMullen, *Paganism* (L2) 23f.; on Andania cf. also L. Ziehen, 'Der Mysterienkult von Andania', *ARW* 24 (1926) 29–60.

[4] W. Burkert, *Mystery Cults* (L30) 137 n. 36: 'may be just popular etymology'.

Among the Greeks μυστήριον remained a religious term until late antiquity. We find only seldom and in late contexts a profane employment of this noun in the sense of the secrets of daily life. But from Plato onwards, we find a second line of development where μυστήριον is used as a metaphor for philosophical matters.

In Plato's *Symposium* Socrates relates that the seeress Diotima has told him that he can indeed be initiated (μυηθείης) into the *eros* of philosophical thinking, but she does not know whether he will attain the higher stages of initiation, namely perfection (τέλεα) and the mysterious vision (ἐποπτικά, *Symp*. 28 [209e–210a]). The path of philosophical knowledge resembles the gradual penetration into the μυστήριον, and this surrounds philosophy with the aura of a religious consecration, no doubt a primary aim here. Detached from cultic practices, the concept of mystery takes on more the sense of a secret teaching.

Along complex paths, the concept of μυστήριον entered the theological vocabulary of Judaism and Christianity too. The bridge was built in the Hellenistic-Jewish wisdom literature. In the Book of Wisdom we find both polemic against the pagan cults and the adaptation of μυστήριον to the author's own theological language.

Wis 14:15 is polemic: 'A father, consumed with grief at an untimely bereavement, made an image of his child, who had been suddenly taken from him; he now honoured as a god what was once a dead human being, and handed on to his dependants secret rites (μυστήρια) and initiations (τελετάς)', as is 14:23: 'For whether they kill children in their initiations (τελετάς), or celebrate secret mysteries (μυστήρια), or hold frenzied revels with strange customs'. Wis 12:3ff. anachronistically makes use of the vocabulary of the mysteries, when it castigates the worship of idols by the Canaanites whom the people of Israel found when they took possession of the land: 'Those who lived long ago in your holy land you hated for their detestable practices, their works of sorcery and unholy rites, their merciless slaughter of children, and their sacrificial feasting on human flesh and blood.' We find the positive reception of the terminology at Wis 2:22, where it is stated that the fools 'did not know the secret purposes of God', and at 6:22: 'I will tell you what wisdom is and how she came to be, and I will hide no secrets from you, but I will ... make knowledge of her clear', and 8:4, where Wisdom is called 'an initiate (μύστις)' in the knowledge of God.

Both these lines of development are determinative for Philo of Alexandria too: in his writings we find both polemic against pagan mystery cults and a reception of the vocabulary of mystery in order to describe the value of revelation and the dignity of the process whereby theological knowledge is attained; for the latter, Philo can pick up the metaphorical use of μυστήριον in Greek philosophy from Plato onwards.

The concept of mystery is first filled out with a particular substance through Jewish apocalyptic (cf. Dan 2:28: 'There is a God in heaven who reveals mysteries, and he has disclosed to King Nebuchadnezzar what will happen at the end of days'). Thus its mysteries are eschatological, concerning God's plans about the events of the end time, its precise date, and the premonitory signs. As mysteries, these lie hidden with God and are shown and explained only to chosen seers like Daniel, who transmits them to a circle of the elect. The cultic element is not present here, where the didactic element is predominant; the esoteric quality is preserved, and the specific character here is the eschatological substance.

Μυστήριον is employed twenty-eight times in the New Testament. Here the concept is indebted for its contents to apocalyptic, with one important addition: viz., that the eschatological mystery has been disclosed, and consists in the salvation that God has wrought in Jesus Christ. It is in this sense that Mk 4:11 speaks of the μυστήριον τῆς βασιλείας τοῦ θεοῦ, 'mystery of the kingdom of God'. One senses the presence of the eschatological contents at Rom 11:25, for example: 'I do not want you to be ignorant of this mystery', referring to the following instruction about the fate of Israel in the end time. The so-called literary pattern of revelation is important here: God has now revealed to his holy ones the mystery that was hidden from all eternity (e.g. Col 1:26). It is only from the fourth century CE on that μυστήριον is used in the Greek-speaking Church for the sacraments and the liturgy. Thus the cultic element, which is an aspect of this concept because of its provenance, once again takes on at least some importance.

2. Phenomenology

List 32.

W. Burkert, *Mystery Cults* (L30).

J. Croissant, *Aristote et les mystères* (BFPUL 51), Liege and Paris 1932.

H. P. Müller, 'Sterbende und auferstehende Vegetationsgötter? – Eine Skizze', in *ThZ* 53 (1997) 74–82.

R. Reck, *Kommunikation und Gemeindeaufbau: Eine Studie zur Entstehung, Leben und Wachstum paulinischer Gemeinden in den Kommunikationsstrukturen der Antike* (SBB 22), Stuttgart 1991, 136–42.

C. Riedweg, *Mysterienterminologie* (L30).
A. Tresp, *Die Fragmente der griechischen Kultschriftsteller* (RVV 15.1), Giessen 1914.
R. Turcan, 'Initiation', *RAC* Lfg. 137 (1996) 87–159.
H. S. Versnel, *Transition* (L12) 15–88.
See also the other secondary literature in L30.

(*a*) Secret cults

It may sound a rather simple point, but the first thing to be said about mysteries is that they are *secret cults*. This sets them in a relationship to something else, viz. to the public cult in the city state, but also to the daily domestic ritual which was not secret. Mystery cults are averse to openness; they take place in secret, often at night. They are not universally accessible, but are reserved to a particular group of initiates. This contrast suggests the conclusion that there existed in the religious sphere a need for intimacy which the large-scale celebrations could not satisfy, as well as a need for something extraordinary that could not be found in the routine of daily life. But mysteries, even as secret cults, remain precisely forms of the cult, and thus related to this (Burkert 10: 'Mystery initiations were an optional activity within polytheistic religion'). Many of the cultic possibilities which we have already seen are replicated in the mysteries: sacrifices, ritual meals, rites of purification, processions, the veneration of statues of the gods. This means that the boundaries are imprecise, with a variety of transitional forms.

(*b*) Initiation

The selection which is necessary for the constitution of a limited circle of participants in the mysteries takes place through *initiation* (in Latin, the technical term for the mystery cults is *initia*). This initiation, an essential mark of every mystery cult, could take place on one occasion, or in a succession of different stages from the lowest to the highest level of consecration. The rites employed here varied considerably in their individual details, as did the conditions of admission and the way in which the preparation was structured.

(*c*) Sequence of events

A threefold distinction among the elements involved in the *sequence* of events in the celebration of the mysteries was made already in the classical period: δρώμενα, δεικνύμενα, λεγόμενα (thus e.g. Plutarch, *Is. et Os.* 3.68 [325c; 378a]), whereby the first (cf. the word 'drama') denotes that which is carried out, the external performance of the liturgy. The 'things shown' are objects: cultic objects that are displayed, for example by the hierophant, whose name comes from this function of making visible (φαίνεσθαι) the holy things (τὰ ἱερά). The third category of 'things said' refers to all that is said in the course of the action, in the sense of acclamations and short interpretative utterances, not in the sense of a didactic discourse or a lengthy instruction. The individual cults are indeed based on longer mythical narratives about the gods, but these were either handed on in the course of the preparation (cf. Reck 137: '*digital elements* [explanation, instruction], however, do not belong to the performance of the mysteries, properly so called, but to the preparation of those to be initiated'), or else could be presupposed as something known from the general store of knowledge of myths. The celebrations of the mysteries themselves, as 'collective, symbolic-esoteric communicative actions with a primarily analogous character, on the basis of old (to some extent eastern) myths' (Reck, ibid.) were governed by Aristotle's definition of their essential character: 'Those initiated are not to learn something, but to experience something' (frag. 15 Rose, 3rd edn.: οὐ μαθεῖν τι δεῖν ἀλλὰ παθεῖν). Something is meant to happen to them and with them.

(*d*) Commands to keep silence (*disciplina arcani*)

The initiation was not the only constitutive element of the mystery cult: equally central was the corresponding command to keep silence about what happened in the celebration of the mysteries. What one had experienced there must not under any circumstances be told to other people. Infringements of this obligation to maintain silence were punished, even on some occasions (by the state) with exile or death. Nevertheless we are told that the atheistic poet-philosopher Diagoras of Melos intentionally revealed what happened in the mysteries, thus making them ridiculous and keeping many from letting themselves be initiated. Authors and orators enjoyed alluding more or less openly to the mysteries, testing and straining the boundaries of what was permitted. The myths on which the mysteries were based were not secret. Inscriptions give us information about dates, places, the number of participants, and the organisation. So many individual details could be related without infringing the obligation to secrecy, that it was possible in the classical period to write monographs about the mystery cults (cf. Tresp 9, 28). The Church fathers did not feel themselves bound by the *disciplina arcani*, and we owe to them an important part of the surviving testimonies, even if they are not impartial, and must therefore be read with due critical caution. It has been shown in the case of Clement of Alexandria that at one central point he does nothing other than transcribe a pagan handbook περὶ μυστηρίων (Riedweg 118–20).

One can also ask whether there was in fact so much that could be betrayed. It is probable that the experience of the initiate could not withstand the light of day, because it would inevitably seem mere banality to the eye of critical analysis. Thus the obligation to secrecy would have a formal and social function, rather than being dictated by considerations of substance. This obligation confers on the whole process the aura of the mysterious, thereby making it more attractive (Reck 140: 'The secret of the success lies presumably in the balanced relationship between the publicly known and the hidden').

(e) Myth and rite

The best way to tackle the question of what the aim of the performance of the mysteries was, or in other words what kind of salvation the mystery cults promised, is to attempt to determine the relationship between myth and rite. Every cult is based on its own divine myth, which narrates what happens to a god; in most cases, he has to take a path of suffering and wandering, but this often leads to victory at the end. The rite depicts this path in abbreviated form and thus makes it possible for the initiand to be taken up into the story of the god, to share in his labours and above all in his victory. Thus there comes into being a ritual participation which contains the perspective of winning salvation (σωτηρία). The hope for salvation can be innerworldly, looking for protection from life's many tribulations, e.g. sickness, poverty, dangers on journey, and death; but it can also look for something better in the life after death. It always involves an intensification of vitality and of life expectation, to be achieved through participation in the indestructible life of a god (cf. in general terms Burkert 11: mysteries 'aimed at a change of mind through experience of the sacred').

A theological text from late antiquity (fourth century CE), Sallustius, *De diis et mundo* (ed. G. Rochefort, CUFr) 4.9, gives valuable insight into the understanding of time which lies behind the myth and its actualisation in the rite: 'These events [he has just spoken of Attis] never occurred in reality, but they exist always [ταῦτα δὲ ἐγένετο μὲν οὐδέποτε, ἔστι δὲ ἀεί]. The understanding sees them all simultaneously, but the tongue mentions first the one, then the other.' Despite its superficial narrative structure, the myth is not relating historical events, but is making known eternal and immutable Being. It is only language that develops in a chronological sequence what the understanding recognises as a timeless unity. The fact that the myth is in principle not bound to any unique historical event makes it easier to conceive of a continual recapitulation of the sequence of events, thereby giving the initiand the possibility of entering into this cyclical sequence.

3. History

List 33.
O. E. Briem, *Les Sociétés secrètes de mystères* (BH 315), Paris 1951, 24–96.
W. Koppers, 'Zum Ursprung des Mysterienwesens im Licht von Völkerkunde und Indologie', *ErJb* 11 (1944) 215–75.
See also secondary literature in L30.

Scholarly attempts to shed light on the prehistory of the mystery cults have taken two directions. They have been (*a*) derived ethnologically from old initiation ceremonies such as those that can still be observed in the modern period among African tribes, or from the secret societies of primitive cultures, where hunters and warriors united in bands that inspired terror; or else (*b*) scholars have taken their starting point in those myths that display an 'agrarian substratum', i.e. have sowing and harvest as their themes, and they have explained the mysteries as magic connected with vegetation, with the aim of influencing the fertility of the earth. This at any rate is a stage that has long been superseded, if we look at the cults that are historically accessible: in one case, that of Eleusis, we can follow the cult from the seventh century BCE to the fourth/fifth century CE, i.e. for more than a millennium. Most of the cults came into being within this period, especially in the last two centuries BCE and the two first centuries CE. The influence from the east can be seen more and more strongly from the third century BCE onwards, as the very names of the new mystery gods indicate: Cybele and Attis from Asia Minor, Isis from Egypt, Mithras from Persia (although certain critical reservations are necessary here). Despite this syncretistic trait, one cannot simply call the mysteries an oriental import –

the existence of the Eleusinian cult in the classical period is important evidence pointing in the opposite direction, and Eleusis seems in many respects to have been the normative model for what was elaborated in the later cults.

Confronted with such a lengthy period, it does not seem very meaningful to invoke only one factor to explain the attractiveness of mystery cults, which knew violent ups and downs. Dissatisfaction with the public cult could find other expressions too, e.g. in placing the emphasis on domestic cult forms, in the foundation of a private cultic association which certainly need not always have been a group connected with the mysteries, in criticism of the entire notion of faith in the gods, or in letting philosophy give form to one's life. Social upheavals too will certainly have played a role: while these made possible a greater personal freedom and possibility of choice, they also entailed increasing isolation and made life riskier.[5] The golden age of the mystery cults runs from the second to the fourth century CE, the period in which one can most plausibly speak of a diffused yearning for redemption and for immortality as something typical of the age – a widespread attitude that was propitious to Christianity also. The later in time we look, and certainly in the third and fourth centuries CE, the more must we assume that new attention is being paid to the mystery cults in conscious rivalry to Christianity, as this religion grew stronger.

B. The mysteries of Eleusis

List 34.

P. Boyancé, 'Sur les mystères d'Éleusis', *REG* 75 (1962) 460–82.

B. Dietrich, 'The Religious Prehistory of Demeter's Eleusinian Mysteries', in U. Bianchi and M. J. Vermaseren, *Soteriologia* (L2) 445–71.

H. P. Foley (ed.), *The Homeric* Hymn to Demeter: *Translation, Commentary and Interpretive Essays*, Princeton 1994.

P. Foucart, *Les Mystères d'Éleusis*, Paris 1914.

F. Graf, *Eleusis und die orphische Dichtung Athens in vorhellenistischer Zeit* (RVV 33), Berlin 1974.

---

[5] Burkert, *Mystery Cults* (L30) 11: 'But for those who took part in the chances and risks of individual freedom that had come into existence in the Hellenic world, the mysteries may have been a decisive "invention": cults which were not prescribed or restricted by family, clan, or class, but which could be chosen at will, still promising some personal security through integration into a festival and through the corresponding personal closeness to some great divinity.'

K. Kerényi, *Eleusis: Archetypal Image of Mother and Daughter*, London and New York 1967.

W. F. Otto, 'Der Sinn der eleusinischen Mysterien', *ErJb* 7 (1939) 83–112.

A. W. Persson, 'Der Ursprung der eleusinischen Mysterien', *ARW* 21 (1922) 287–309.

G. Sfameni Gasparro, *Misteri e culti mistici di Demetra* (StRel 3), Rome 1986.

F. Wehrli, 'Die Mysterien von Eleusis', *ARW* 31 (1934) 77–104.

Other secondary literature, some important, in following bibliographical lists.

Eleusis, home of the most celebrated mystery cult of antiquity, lies about twenty to thirty kilometres west of Athens on a bay of the Mediterranean. Between Athens and Eleusis runs the holy road, beginning near the potters' cemetery in the city and leading to the sanctuary of the mysteries. It is not possible to state anything with certainty about the prehistory of the cult; at most, one can still see traces of ancient indigenous agrarian rites tied to this place.

1. The Homeric Hymn to Demeter

List 35.

K. Clinton, 'The Sanctuary of Demeter and Kore at Eleusis', in N. Marinatos and R. Hägg, *Sanctuaries* (L9) 110–24.

H. P. Foley (ed.), *Hymn* (L34).

N. J. Richardson, *The Homeric Hymn to Demeter*, Oxford 1974.

A. Weiher, *Homerische Hymnen* (TuscBü), Munich 3rd edn. 1970, 6–33.

The so-called Homeric Hymn to Demeter, which contains the aetiological foundational myth of Eleusis, dates from the seventh/sixth century BCE. 'Aetiological' means that the myth explains in a narrative form how what is performed in the rite came into being, and anchors this in the pre-historical story of the gods. Thus when we read the text of the hymn, which is part of a collection subsequently attributed to the great poet Homer, we must note where it allows us to see the ritual of the mysteries.[6]

---

[6] This is how Richardson too argues in his commentary. Clinton takes a somewhat different position: the older version of the hymn refers only to the

91

The starting point of the mythical events is as follows: Hades/Pluto, the god of the underworld, snatches off Korē/Persephone, the daughter of Demeter (Latin *Ceres*, also called Deo in the text). The goddess searches for her in desperation, wanders over the earth unrecognised, and after many vain journeys finally arrives at Eleusis in the outward form of an old woman. Here she meets at the well the four daughters of the royal couple, who help her to find a position in the palace as nurse and servant. This is how her reception in the palace is described (Hom. Hymn Dem. 192–211):

> But the mother of the year, Demeter garlanded about with fruit, did not want to sit on the splendid armchair, but remained in silence and lowered her eyes, until finally Iambe with her appropriate wisdom pushed a hard seat in her direction and threw upon it a fleece that shone as if it were of silver. Demeter sat down on this, held her shawl over her eyes with her hands and so sat for a long space upon the seat, without saying anything. She greeted no one, whether with words or with gestures; she did not laugh, she did not eat, she did not drink, since she was filled with yearning and grief for her daughter with the low-slung girdle, as she sat there. Finally Iambe with her appropriate wisdom used jokes and sometimes also mild mockery to bring the mighty and holy one to smile at last, to laugh, to open her kindly heart. Even later on she loved Iambe because of her busy liveliness. But Metaneira [the queen] filled the goblet and offered her honey-sweet wine; but the goddess declined and said that she was not allowed to drink red wine: one should mingle barley and water with tender mint, so that she might sip that. The queen mixed the drink [κυκεῶν, *kukeōn*] as she was bidden, and gave it to the goddess. Deo took it for the sake of the sacred custom and drank it.

This passage alludes to four elements from the introduction to the celebration of the mysteries properly so-called. (1) We have pictorial representations which attest that participants in the Eleusinian mysteries sat with veiled heads on a stool covered with a fleece (something that originally was a ritual of bereavement). (2) Fasting was an element of the preparatory phase for this. (3) Songs with jokes and mockery, an attempt to lighten the spirits that likewise comes from a bereavement ritual, have a place in the processions in the mystery rites. (4) We shall look more closely

---

better-known *Thesmophoria* in Athens, a women's feast at which piglets were thrown into a crevice in the earth. Their decayed remains were later taken up to be used as dung for the fields. The later mysteries are given a place only in the final redaction of the poem, without being genuinely integrated into the text.

later at the special drink (*kukeōn*); but already here we find the significant closing line: Demeter drinks this 'for the sake of the sacred custom' (Richardson 225 translates: 'for the sake of the rite'). Demeter thereby founds a particular rite, while at the same time acting as the prototype of all future initiates, herself performing what she has instituted. 'For the sake of the sacred custom' therefore means: in order to institute a rite, to maintain it and observe it, to practise it beforehand and to give training in it.

From now on, Demeter takes care of Demophon, the son of the Eleusinian king. The child prospers greatly under her care, but the goddess uses a special method here, which does not meet with universal approval (239–46):

> But each night she put him in the midst of a raging fire, as if he were a piece of wood; the parents did not know about this, although they were most astonished at the way he grew to early maturity day by day, upright like a god. Now the immortal and eternal Demeter had made him young; but Metaneira, already fully dressed, went incautiously one night out of the fragrant bedroom in order to see him. She saw, and cried out and smote herself on both her thighs, in anxiety for her son, with her feelings in a wild delusion.

This 'trial by fire' could have made the child immortal. Thus immortality appears to be a theme of the mysteries too, and it is clear that fire has a function in this. But in the myth, the goddess is unable to carry out her plan, after she has been observed carrying out her secret, almost magical action. In an epiphany scene, she makes herself known and asks, before she leaves Eleusis, that a temple be built in her honour. She promises the foundation of the mystery cult (273: 'But I myself will establish sacred initiations [ὄργια]').

The initial thread of the narrative, which has temporarily been lost to sight, is now resumed. Demeter, the goddess of cereals, still looking for her daughter, goes on strike, preventing the grain from growing and causing a famine which also affects the gods, since human beings are no longer willing to sacrifice to them. Through the intervention of Zeus, a compromise is reached that satisfies Demeter: from now on, Persephone spends a third of the year with her husband in the underworld, and two thirds with her mother and the other immortal gods. The closing passage links the various themes together, and contains another reference to the future mysteries (473–89): the goddess

> then went to the kings who have the responsibility for justice, and showed the sacrificial worship first to Triptolemus and then to Diocles the master of the

horse, also to Celeus the leader of the warriors, the force of Eumolpus, and all the gods, describing the exalted initiations [ὄργια] ... No one is permitted ever to do harm to these, to investigate them or divulge them; for great awe of the gods puts an end to all human speech. Blessed is that dweller on earth who has seen such things! But one who does not offer the sacrifices, or who avoids them, will never share in such a joy – he decays in mouldy darkness. Now that the heavenly goddess had instituted all this, they left for Olympus, to the seat of the other gods. Now they both dwell there with Zeus, master of the lightning, venerable and sublime. Most blessed are the dwellers on earth to whom these two show kindness and love; they soon send Ploutos into their great house as hearth-companion, and he gives mortals rich possessions.

Later ages looked on Triptolemus, 'the one who ploughs three times', as *the* cult hero of Eleusis. He was the first to learn from the gods how to cultivate arable land, so that he became the founder of civilisation. Eumolpus, 'the one who sounds well', gave the name to one of the two families of priests at Eleusis who provided the cultic functionaries over many centuries. The hierophant was chosen from the ranks of the Eumolpides: his task was to utter the secret formula at the high-point of the celebration in a melodious voice, in a singing tone. As well as the commandment in line 478 to keep silence, we should also note the two macarisms. The first, probably the later in terms of the historical development, makes a negative statement about what happens after death: the one who refuses to be initiated will decay in mouldy darkness in the underworld. The second and earlier macarism promises those who are allowed to enjoy the favour of the two goddesses that Ploutos will visit them. Things go well with the one who has Ploutos, the personified god of wealth, as a member of the household: such a person has material prosperity and enjoys happiness here and now. Expressed in the world of ideas of the primary level of action of the mythical narrative, such innerworldly hopes could be satisfied e.g. by a rich corn harvest stored in well-filled barns.

2. The Eleusinian Synthēma

List 36.
A. Delatte, *Le Cycéon, breuvage rituel des mystères d'Éleusis* (CEA), Paris 1955 = BCLAB 5.40 (1954) 690–752.
S. Eitrem, 'Die eleusinischen Mysterien und das Synthema der Weihe', *SO* 37 (1961) 72–81.

A. Körte, 'Zu den eleusinischen Mysterien', *ARW* 18 (1915) 116–26.
R. G. Wasson, A. Hofmann and C. A. P. Ruck, *The Road to Eleusis: Unveiling the Secret of the Mysteries*, New York 1978.

About eight or nine hundred years later, Clement of Alexandria quotes a 'password' of the Eleusinian mystery cult, in which some elements have survived with an astonishing continuity (*Protr.* 21.2 [16.18–20 GCS 56]):

κἄστι τὸ σύνθημα 'Ελευσινίων μυστηρίων –
ἐνήστευσα,
ἔπιον τὸν κυκεῶνα,
ἔλαβον ἐκ κίστης,
ἐργασάμενος
ἀπεθήμην εἰς κάλαθον
καὶ ἐκ καλάθου εἰς κίστην.

And this is the *synthēma* of the Eleusinian mysteries:
I fasted,
I drank the drink that was mixed (*kukeōn*),
I took something from the coffer,
I fiddled with it,
I put it away in the basket
and then took it out of the basket and put it in the coffer.

(*a*) *Synthēma*

A *synthēma* or *symbolon* (the term Clement employs elsewhere) looks back on the mysteries and summarises a section of what has been performed. Its function is like that of a code word or a military password: the initiate could authenticate his identity by using it, either when he was admitted to the next stage of consecration or in daily life. This could become a matter of life and death, as we see from Apuleius' defence when he was accused of magic and brought before the court. When it was demanded that he divulge his 'souvenirs' of various mystery cults (the word *signa* here means 'objects'), he replied: 'If by any chance there is someone here present who has been initiated into the same mysteries then let him give me the password (*signum*), and then you may hear the secrets I guard' (*Apol.* 56.7). Apuleius is our chief witness for the mysteries of Isis, which will be described below.

(b) Kykeōn

It is clear that fasting and the drinking of the *kykeōn* belong closely together in the *synthēma*, as in ancient medicine: this drink prevents the stomach ache that would otherwise result from eating too much after a feast. But above all, as in the Hymn to Demeter, the first nourishment that the goddess takes after her fast is this mixed drink. Ovid expresses very well the link to the ritual of the mysteries when he says: 'Since the goddess breaks her fast at nightfall, the initiates today likewise hold their meal by starlight' (*Fasti* 4.535f.).

What is a *kykeōn*? In very general terms, as in the hymn, it is a mixture of barley gruel, water, and an aromatic herb. The name comes from the fact that this mixture must be stirred (Greek κυκᾶν) before being drunk, because otherwise the solid components fall to the bottom of the cup. We also know of richer recipes: in the *Iliad*, a maid mixes for old Nestor a drink of wine, honey, onions, barley meal and goats' cheese (*Il.* 11.624–41), and the sorceress Circe does the same in the *Odyssey*, only with the addition of some poison (*Od.* 10.234–6).

The last point is not without interest, since some modern scholars have attributed a toxic or narcotic effect to the *kykeōn*, also in the case of Eleusis. Thus a drug in the *kykeōn* would explain the participants' feeling of drunkenness, and this would also explain why the celebration of the mysteries made such a great impact. In concrete terms, it is suggested that a powder of dried hallucinogenic fungi was used, or else opium (since poppy capsules are found in the iconography of the goddess Demeter). Another hypothesis is that the grain employed had been affected by ergot, which has a toxic effect and releases LSD (Wasson et al.). Perhaps one should also bear in mind that when barley gruel is mixed with water, it begins sooner or later to ferment, and thus can have a mildly intoxicating effect. But the great majority of specialist literature is probably correct in arguing against the suspicion that narcotics were involved.[7]

The use of barley gruel as a fundamental component points back to a period at which the art of fine milling and baking was not yet known, but people demanded more than simple grains of cereal. In the classical period the *kykeōn* was looked on as a typically uncultivated meal of country people. This fits well with the basic agrarian mood of the earliest stratum of the myth. We will often find that 'survivals' from earlier cultural stages

---

[7] See e.g. Richardson (L35) 345; W. Burkert, *Mystery Cults* (L30) 108–9, with bibliography; M. Giebel, *Geheimnis* (L30) 34.

have been preserved in the mysteries as sacred actions, and now are employed functionally as an alternative that is set up in antithesis to the world that actually exists. The drinking of the *kykeōn* is not at the centre of the action of the mysteries, and one should accordingly be very cautious about invoking quasi-sacramental interpretations.[8]

(c) Coffer and basket

Although the Hymn to Demeter does not mention the *cista mystica* known from a number of mystery cults, the coffer containing secret cult objects, its existence in Eleusis is attested epigraphically and iconographically,[9] and this disposes of scholarly attempts to eliminate it from Eleusis and locate it in the Alexandrine cult of Demeter. The basket no doubt comes from agriculture. Instead of 'I fiddled' (ἐργασάμενος), the conjecture 'I tasted' (ἐγευσάμενος) has been proposed:[10] the drinking of the *kykeōn* would be followed by a second act consisting of the tasting of a mystical food. But even this would not explain why something from the coffer is taken up and laid down. Older scholarship (cf. e.g. Körte) favoured the idea that the contents of the coffer and the basket had a sexual symbolism, e.g. as images of the phallus and the womb: the 'fiddling' with them would mean bringing them into contact with one another and thus carrying out an act of generation that affected the initiate himself, who thus became a child of the god. In principle, one would not wish to exclude the possibility of such an action in the mystery cults of the classical period, but a more recent interpretation happens to fit Eleusis better (cf. Delatte). This picks up a remark by Theophrastus (in a text quoted by Porphyry, *Abst.* 2.6) that when those of old learned how to grind grain, they hid in secret places fine utensils used for this, and regarded them as something holy. Mortars and pestles are used to grind cereals. The grains fly off into a vessel, and thus one has for example the barley meal that is necessary for the preparation of

---

[8] Cf. L. Deubner, *Feste* (L2) 80: 'without doubt possessing sacramental significance'; F. B. Jevons, *Introduction* (L1) 364–66, goes even further. His interpretation follows Sigmund Freud's pattern (in *Totem and Tabu*): in the yearly act of eating a meal prepared from the totem of the clan, i.e. cereal, those who ate 'partook of the body of their deity'.

[9] Cf. U. Bianchi, *Mysteries* (L30), ill. 25, where Demeter herself sits on the coffer.

[10] First in the classic work by C. A. Lobeck, *Aglaophamus sive de theologiae mysticae Graecorum causis libri tres*, Copenhagen 1829, reprint Darmstadt 1961, 25.

the *kykeōn*. By fiddling around with these two objects from coffer and basket, that is with mortar and pestle, the initiate takes part symbolically in the process of obtaining the food that he requires for his life, but which can be obtained only by a destructive intervention in nature (making the grains fly off into the vessel) – an example of the dialectic of death and life, and of the increase in vitality which it was hoped the mystery ritual would bestow.

3. The three stages of the initiation

List 37.

K. Clinton, *The Sacred Officials of the Eleusinian Mysteries* (TAPhS NS 64.3), Philadelphia 1974.

S. Eitrem, 'Die vier Elemente in der Mysterienweihe', *SQ* 4 (1926) 39–59; 5 (1927) 39–59.

R. M. Simms, 'Myesis, Telete, and Mysteria', *GRBS* 31 (1990) 183–95.

The *synthēma* summarises intermediary stages on a longer path that has three main stations: the μύησις (initiation), the τελετή (perfecting), and the ἐποπτεία (vision); recently, Simms has proposed a different structure with only two stages, and μύησις as the overarching concept embracing τελετή and ἐποπτεία.

(a) Myēsis

The initiation took place individually and thus was not bound to the main annual feast. It could be held in the following locations: the forecourt of the sanctuary at Eleusis; the Eleusinion, a subsidiary temple above the Agora in Athens; or the small mysteries celebrated in springtime in Agrae near Athens, once independent but later subordinated to Eleusis and given a preparatory function vis-à-vis the Eleusinian cult. The initiation was carried out by the Eleusinian cult personnel, with the intention of purifying and instructing the initiand. He sits for this on a stool covered with a fleece (cf. the Hymn) and veils his head with a cloth.[11] A winnowing fan, such as is used at threshing to separate chaff from corn, is held over his head (purification by air); a torch is brought near him (purification by fire). Then comes an instruction about certain matters (the cultic myth, liturgical formulae, the behaviour appropriate at the main celebration?).

---

[11] Cf. U. Bianchi, *Mysteries* (L30), ill. 49.

Access to the initiation was made generously available even to women, slaves and foreigners, but only in particular exceptional instances to children, viz. to the so-called παῖδες ἀφ' ἑστίας, 'children from the hearth' (cf. Clinton 98–114), who perhaps represented Demophon in the trial by fire. An inscription (SIG 2/587.207) indicates that the total cost, including that of the accompanying sacrifice, was 15 drachmas. The preferred sacrificial animal was the piglet; in view of the well-known fertility of this domestic animal and of other sacrifices of piglets among the Greeks, one may suspect the presence of fertility rites in the background here.

Aristophanes employed the 'mystical little piglets' (*Ach.* 747) in a number of his plays for purposes of parody. For example, when one of his characters faces the threat of death, he says: 'Lend me quickly three drachmas for a little piglet. I must get myself initiated before I die' (*Peace* 374f.). When the slave Xanthias hears the choir of the initiated in the underworld, he thinks like a practical man and presumes that roast pork will be there too: 'Persephone, holy and highly honoured! How mystical the pork smells here!' (*Ra.* 337f.).

(b) Perfecting and vision

The great mysteries in turn are divided into two phases, τελετή and ἐποπτεία, with at least one year's interval between them. We do not know how this sequence of different stages of consecration was organised in practical terms. It is possible that they were held at different stages in the centre of the main celebration, which we shall study in greater detail below, or that the initiates of the first grade were required to leave the room at a particular point (perhaps veiling their heads).

Precisely this element of initiation by stages became exceedingly popular. Ultimately, via Pseudo-Dionysius the Areopagite, it influenced Christian mysticism too: cf. the division of the mystical path into three stages of purification, illumination, and mystical unification.

4. The main feast

List 38.
W. Burkert, *Homo Necans* (L2).
K. Clinton, *Officials* (L37).
——*Sanctuary* (L35) 116–19.

M. Giebel, *Geheimnis* (L30).

G. E. Mylonas, *Eleusis and the Eleusinian Mysteries*, Princeton 1961.

(a) Chronology

The main feast was held in the month of Boedromion (September/October). On the 13th/14th the ephebes fetched the sacred objects in Eleusis and brought them in closed coffers to the Eleusinion in Athens. On the 15th the herald made the 'proclamation' (πρόρρησις) in the 'colourful hall' in the market place, excluding murderers and barbarians from the celebration of the mysteries (cf. the imitation of this in Aristophanes, *Ra.* 352–70: 'Let whoever is a layman in such a mystery, one whose mind is unenlightened, keep reverent silence and stay far away from our consecrated choirs'). On the 16th the cry went forth: 'Come to the sea, initiates!' There all the adepts bathed (purification by water). On the 19th the great procession with the sacred objects in their containers made its way from Athens to Eleusis, arriving there towards evening. When the participants arrived, the goddess herself gave them on the *Niinnionpinax*[12] a cup that may have held the *kykeōn*; this makes sense, if the previous day had been spent in fasting. It is a matter of scholarly controversy whether all that now followed took place in one night (from the 19th to the 20th), or whether two or three nights were available. The conclusion is a great sacrifice of bulls, with a festal meal for all the participants on the day of their return home.

(b) The night of initiation

When we attempt to describe more precisely the centre of the night of initiation, it helps to begin by looking at the architecture of the sacred precincts in Eleusis – not so much the two sanctuaries of Hades/Pluto or the temple of Demeter, but the *telestērion* itself, the sanctuary of the mysteries, a quadratic roofed building which went through several stages of development. It is unlike all other known Greek temples, with its large roofed assembly room which at the time of Pericles (fifth century BCE) could seat almost three thousand persons. Inside stood the *anaktorōn*

---

[12] U. Bianchi, *Mysteries* (L30), ill. 35; UUC III no. 44.

(meaning roughly: 'the house of the ruler'), a small stone shrine built on an outcrop of stone with a construction leading up to an opening in the roof. The *anaktoron* is one of the relatively rare altar forms, with cavities, which one can envisage as an exceptionally large free-standing hearth. A great fire burnt in the *anaktoron* in Eleusis, making necessary the construction and the opening in the roof, so that the smoke could escape. This allows us to infer with some certainty that effects of fire and light played an essential role in the night of the mysteries. The great hall of the *telestērion* was shrouded in darkness when the crowd arrived and took their places. At a given moment, the *anaktoron* opened and flames shot upwards. The hierophant showed some sacred object in the light of these flames and proclaimed the secret of the mysteries in a loud voice.

Reconstructions of the subsequent sequence of events must be considered as rather less probable. For example, the episode in the Hymn about the boy Demophon in the fire has led to the supposition that the sacrifice of a child was the original, unutterable secret of the mysteries, from which a spiritualised message was later derived: viz., that the path to life always leads via death (Burkert, *Greek Religion* [L2] 286–88). The Church father Hippolytus relates what a gnostic says about Eleusis (*Ref.* 5.8.39f.):

> But the Phrygians also call him [the perfect human being] the ear of corn that is cut when it is green, and according to the Phrygians, the Athenians do the same when they celebrate the Eleusinian mysteries and show the initiates in silence the great, wonderful and most perfect secret of the initiation, namely a reaped ear of corn ... The hierophant himself celebrates the sacred, unutterable mysteries by night in the great celebration at Eleusis and cries with a loud voice: 'The Lady has borne a holy boy, *Brimo* bore *Brimos*', that is to say, the strong one has borne the strong one.

Thus the sacred object would be the reaped ear of corn (at a time when the fields had long been harvested). The lady Brimo would be Demeter or Persephone, and the boy Brimos could be Ploutos, personified wealth, or the initiate himself who becomes a child of the deity when he is summoned and permitted to see. If we suppose that magic connected with rain was performed on the following day, in which two great vessels of water were poured out towards the north and the east with the onomato-poeic incantation ὕε κύε ('Rain, be fruitful!'), then we should have a unified interpretation that also made sense of the barley gruel and the utensils for grinding the grain. The modern observer may ask whether all this elaboration was necessary when the contents of the mystery were so simple, but we must surely assume that the experience as such – which we cannot genuinely recapture today – had a very high value for the participants.[13]

Another suggestion is that statues of the gods were displayed in the light of the fire as it blazed up: ancient small images of the gods from the Mycenaean period or large, majestic statues of the deities of the Eleusinian mysteries, which evoked reactions of wonder when they were seen in the glow of the fire (cf. the concluding epiphany of Demeter in the Hymn). Since we need dates for at least two events, the τελετή and the ἐποπτεία, we need not play off one possibility against another: to look on a cultic image is in fact the realisation of what one would most naturally expect of an ἐποπτεία.

Besides this, the Church fathers assume that genuine cultic dramas were performed in Eleusis. With the intention of discrediting the mysteries as a place where sexual excesses went on, they bring in the *hieros gamos*, the 'sacred marriage' between the goddess and a male human partner (according to Hesiod, *Theog.* 969–71, Ploutos, the god of wealth, is born of the union between Demeter and the farmer Iasion, consummated on a freshly ploughed field; the child Brimos would have his place here too).[14] But it is also possible that the abduction of Persephone, her mother's search for her and her return from the underworld may have been portrayed. One witness, regarded as very reliable, indicates that the hierophant smote a huge gong when he summoned Korē (Apollodorus FGH 244F110b). However, the *telestērion* did not have even a rudimentary stage, nor was there any pit or crypt that could have been used to portray a descent into Hades (for this reason, Mylonas 261–3 transposes the cult drama into the open air; Giebel 40f. suggests that the grotto of Hades was used). The only actors available to put on the liturgical-ritual pantomime were the three

---

[13] Cf. the noteworthy observation by N. J. Richardson, *Hymn* (L35) 25f.: 'the analogy of Christian church ceremonies shows quite clearly that the spoken words of the priest, together with a few actions, the display of sacred objects, and something as simple as the sounding of a bell, are all that is needed to suggest to the worshipper the sense and significance of the sacred narrative.'

[14] Cf. in general G. Freymuth, 'Zum Hieros Gamos in den antiken Mysterien', *MH* 21 (1964) 86–95; A. Avagianou, *Sacred Marriage in the Rituals of Greek Religion* (EHS 15. Classics 54), Frankfurt a. M. 1991.

official *personae*: the hierophant from the family of the Eumolpides, the *daduchos* ('torchbearer') and the *hierokēryx* ('herald of the sacred') from the family of the Kerykes.

We find surprising confirmation of this from another quarter. A technical expression for betraying the mysteries is ἐξορχεῖσθαι, 'to dance out' the mysteries. Alcibiades, an Athenian nobleman and adherent of Socrates, notorious for his unbridled way of life, was accused of sacrilege against the mysteries, because he portrayed them at a drinking party with two friends: the accusers 'said that someone called Theodoros had played the part of the herald and Poulytion the part of the torchbearer, while Alcibiades took the role of the hierophant and the others present at the drinking party played the initiates' (Plutarch, *Alc.* 19.1). Thus Alcibiades 'imitated the mysteries and represented them in his house for those who were present at his drinking party' (ibid. 22.3). This means that this was possible with three persons, i.e. without any great expenditure.

5. The contents and meaning of the mysteries

List 39.
L. J. Alderink, 'The Eleusinian Mysteries in Roman Imperial Times', *ANRW* II/18.2 (1989) 1457–98.
K. Clinton, 'The Eleusinian Mysteries: Roman Initiates and Benefactors, Second Century BC to AD 267', *ANRW* II/18.2 (1989) 1499–1539.
C. Gallant, 'A Jungian Interpretation of the Eleusinian Myths and Mysteries', *ANRW* II/18.2 (1989) 1540–63.
M. Giebel, *Geheimnis* (L30).
M. P. Nilsson, 'Die eleusinischen Gottheiten', in Idem, *Opuscula Selecta* II (Skrifter utgivna av Svenska Institutet i Athen 8° 2.2), Lund 1952, 542–623.

Let us begin once again with the myth. Persephone spends a third of the year under the earth and two thirds above it, emerging in the spring when the earth begins to blossom. Her mother Demeter is the goddess who protects the growth of corn. The philosophers of antiquity who interpreted the myths already saw clearly that this is a coded version of the cycle of vegetation: Persephone in the underworld corresponds to the period in which that which is sown rests under ground, and her return symbolises the beginning growth. (Nilsson has proposed a different interpretation: the third of the year in the underworld is the period in which the corn rests in the storage vessels below the earth, and Persephone's return portrays the date when the corn is fetched out to be sown anew. Most scholars do not follow him here.) It is vital to human existence that nothing disturbs the functioning of this rhythm, but since it often appears at risk, the cult intends to ensure its continual success. The older macarism at the end of the Hymn, promising a rich store of corn, refers to this. A second anthropological perspective is superimposed upon this: the human person, threatened by transience and death, is to receive a share in the vital force of nature, which is ever renewing itself. The agrarian world of ideas could generate images that made it possible to cope with the death that is the human lot (cf. Jn 12:24).

As well as these two special levels of understanding, scholars have proposed other, more general interpretations. The mysteries are understood to speak of fundamental human problems, of social tensions surrounding birth, marriage, and bereavement, etc., and the transformation of these (Alderink); or their ritual makes it possible to encounter one's own unconsciousness (Gallant); what is involved is 'the rediscovery of a lost context of existence as a whole, which the initiate misses' (Giebel 27). To some extent, this is a question of nuances. Let us at any rate hold fast to the point that Eleusis made an important contribution to the development of individual eschatology among the Greeks. The hope which finds expression in the mysteries is orientated to a better destiny in the afterlife. Apart from the later macarism in the Hymn (see above), we have other texts of the same genre, viz. Pindar, frag. 121 Bowra: 'Blessed is the one who has seen this before descending below. He knows the end of life, and also knows the beginning given by the gods'; and Sophocles, frag. 837 Radt (from a lost drama about the Eleusinian herald Triptolemus): 'Thrice blessed are those mortals who have seen this consecration and then go to Hades. For them alone is there life there, but for the others everything is ill.' To these early testimonies we can add a later voice from the first/ second century CE, Plutarch (frag. 178 Sandbach):

> First come false paths and a laborious wandering around on this side and that, fearsome paths in the darkness with no goal, then before the end itself come utter terror, shuddering, trembling and sweat and horror. After this, a wonderful light appears to him, realms full of light and meadows welcome him, where awe-inspiring sounds and dances, sacred songs and heavenly spectacles are performed. The one who is now made perfect walks freely among these, relieved of cares, and joins enthusiastically the company of holy and pure men,

looking down on the uninitiated mass below who trample and press upon one another in mud and mist, because they are afraid of death and do not believe in the good that comes in the afterlife, since they are fettered to wretchedness on earth below.

For our knowledge of the mystery ritual, which this polyvalent text presupposes, it is important to note the initial movement of seeking, wandering about in terror, until this ends when the wonderful light shines forth. The mythical substratum – the goddess's act of seeking and finding – and its ritual recapitulation are mirrored in the subjective feelings of the initiate. At yet a further stage of derivation from the original, all this serves as an image for what happens to the soul in death. The faith connected with the mysteries envisions only for the initiate the paradisal existence which is described in the next section of the text, which can be compared favourably with the image of a colourless existence in a Homeric realm of shadows. One should interpret it as a sign of this particular form of expectation of an afterlife, when golden ears of corn are placed in the grave alongside the dead, or *pithoi* are used for the burial, viz. large storage vessels for corn which are sunk into the earth.

But this also brings us to the ethical question: is one's destiny in the afterlife decided only by the fact of having been initiated, without taking into account one's character and conduct? Critics pointed this out; the Cynic Diogenes put it very trenchantly when he said, 'It would be ridiculous if Agesilaus and Epaminondas thrashed about in the mud while useless people dwelt on the island of the blessed merely because they had undergone an initiation' (Diogenes Laertius, *Vit. Phil.* 6.39). Other philosophers, such as the Stoic Epictetus (*Diss.* 3.21.14f.), emphasise the necessity of the right attitude and the pedagogical effect of the mysteries:

One should come with sacrifices and prayers after having purified oneself and prepared oneself inwardly to approach sacred rites of a venerable age. Only so have mysteries any effect. Only so do we attain the insight that all of this was established by those of old to train us and to improve our life.

In the modern discussion about the ethics of the Eleusinian mysteries, some scholars deny that they had any moral effect whatsoever, while others exaggerate their deep spiritual character in such a way that they appear superior to Christianity. Nilsson proposes a compromise when he observes: 'the mysteries permitted the growth of a morality of peaceful and just social life and the piety of a cultured people which should not be underestimated'.[15]

In 395 CE Eleusis was destroyed by Christianised Goths under Alaric, who thereby put an end to a millennial history that had seen a large number of initiates. Increasingly, these included also non-Athenians and non-Greeks, especially Romans, who even included Roman emperors (cf. Clinton). Nevertheless, despite all its importance, the Eleusinian cult knew boundaries. The essential link to one particular place implies a limit on the possibilities of development; Eleusis neither engaged in missionary activity nor founded subordinate sanctuaries of equal significance.[16] Politically speaking, Eleusis was very closely linked to the Athenian city state. The initiates returned to their daily lives without having assumed new ties, and also without having become members of cultic associations, as was the case with some of the newer mystery cults. No 'community' or 'church' was formed in Eleusis.

C. The cult and mysteries of Dionysus

List 40.

T. H. Carpenter and C. A. Faraone (eds.), *Masks of Dionysus* (Myth and Poetics), Ithaca 1993.

A. J. Festugière, 'Les Mystères de Dionyse', in Idem, *Études* (L2) 13–63.

H. Jeanmaire, *Dionysos: Histoire du culte de Bacchus* (BH 269), Paris 1951.

F. Matz, *ΔΙΟΝΥΣΙΑΚΗ ΤΕΛΕΤΗ: Archäologische Untersuchungen zum Dionysoskult in hellenistischer und römischer Zeit* (AAWLM.G 1963,15), Mainz 1964.

P. McGinty, *Interpretation and Dionysos: Method in the Study of a God* (RaR 16), The Hague 1978.

W. F. Otto, *Dionysus: Myth and Cult*, Bloomington 1965.

---

[15] *Geschichte* (L2) I.667.

[16] Naturally, this does not mean that the cult of the Eleusinian goddesses Demeter and Persephone was not carried out elsewhere, or that this could not have taken on forms like that of the mysteries even outside Eleusis. Examples from cities which were significant for the history of the earliest Christians are Ephesus (SIG 3/820; NDIEC IV.94f.), and Corinth (N. Bookidis and R. S. Stroud, *Demeter and Persephone in Ancient Corinth* [American Excavations in Old Corinth: Corinth Notes 2], Princeton 1987).

R. Turcan, *Cultes* (L2) 289–324.

Dionysus, the son of Zeus and Semele, is the most polymorphous of the Greek gods (cf. Cicero, *Nat. Deor.* 3.58: 'Dionysos multos habemus'; Plutarch, *E ap. Delph.* 9 [389b]: πολύμορφος). His figure and his cult are closely linked with *ecstasy*, i.e. the human person's transcendence of the narrow boundaries of the self, and *enthusiasm*, i.e. the state of being filled by God, and finally with *mania*, the intoxicating madness which bursts the bounds of what is normal through conspicuous behaviour. More clearly than in the case of the mysteries of Eleusis, we must differentiate between the public forms of the cult and the mysteries which are a special variant of this.

1. The Bacchae of Euripides

List 41.

E. Buschor and G. A. Seeck, *Euripides: Sämtliche Tragödien und Fragmente*, vol. 5 (TuscBü), Munich 1977, 255–353.

E. R. Dodds, *Euripides*, Bacchae, Oxford 2nd edn. 1960.

D. Ebener, *Euripides: Tragödien*, vol. 6 (SQAW 30.6), Berlin 2nd edn. 1990, 107–96.

J. E. Harrison, *Prolegomena* (L2) 479–572.

A. Henrichs, 'Changing Dionysiac Identities', in B. F. Meyer and E. P. Sanders, *Self-Definition* (L3) III.137–60, 213–36.

——'Die Maenaden von Milet', *ZPE* 4 (1969) 223–41.

J. Kott, *The Eating of the Gods: An Interpretation of Greek Tragedy*, London 1974.

R. S. Kraemer, 'Ecstasy and Possession: The Attraction of Women to the Cult of Dionysos', *HThR* 72 (1979) 55–80.

H. Oranje, *Euripides' Bacchae: The Play and Its Audience* (Mn.S 78), Leiden 1984.

R. Seaford, 'Dionysiac Drama and the Dionysiac Mysteries', *CQ* 31 (1981) 252–75.

H. S. Versnel, ΕΙΣ ΔΙΟΝΥΣΟΣ: The Tragic Paradox of the *Bacchae*', in Idem, *Inconsistencies in Greek and Roman Religion*, I: *Ter Unus. Isis, Dionysos, Hermes. Three Studies in Henotheism* (SGGR 6), Leiden 1990, 96–205.

Here we can take Euripides' drama *Bacchae*, first performed *c.*405 BCE, as our guiding text. It tells of how the cult of Dionysus penetrated Thebes, despite the vain efforts of Pentheus, the king of the city, to prevent it. Dionysus himself appears in human form, and Pentheus falls victim to the unrestrained violence of the female worshippers of the god (in the middle ages, this drama was interpreted as a Christian mystery play, with a hidden reference to Christian ideas). It should be stated that our interpretation of the text – in which materials from the myth and ritual of the cult of Dionysus[17] are pressed into the service of what the poet wishes to say (cf. Oranje) – goes somewhat beyond Euripides' own intention, in view of the questions that interest us in this book.

(a) The god of wine

Euripides never tires of emphasising that Dionysus is the god of wine. He associates him, as the inventor of wine, with Demeter, goddess of corn (*Ba.* 274–84):

> Mortals venerate two gifts as the highest good:
> the gift of Demeter, or mother earth (call her what you like),
> who nourishes them with dry fruit;
> then came the son of Semele, equal in rank,
> and invented the drink made of grapes
> and brought this to wretched mortals,
> soothing the pain for everyone who empties the cup of the vine;
> bringing sleep that lets one forget all the labour of the day.
> No one else brings such help in suffering.
> This god is poured as a libation to the gods [οὗτος θεοῖσι σπένδεται θεός].

The bold image in the last line refers to the libation in which some wine is poured on to the earth in honour of Zeus and the other gods. Was Dionysus himself present in the wine? Vines, grapes and wine are traditionally signs of his epiphany (e.g., *Ba.* 142f., 707). This is the basis for the Dionysiac wine miracles in the Hellenistic period. Wine is said to flow from a spring in the month of January in the temple of Dionysus on the island of Andros (Pliny, *Hist. Nat.* 2.213). In Elis priests place three empty vats in the temple and lock the door – the next morning, the vessels are full of wine (Pausanias, *Graec. Descr.* 6.26.1f.). We need not go into the

---

[17]   F. Graf, *Mythology* (L2) 175: '*Bacchae* is an enactment of Dionysiac rites in the guise of mythical narrative'; more detail in Seaford.

details of how this was accomplished; presumably some kind of mechanical tricks were involved.

It should be noted that the myths accompanying wine and its god do not only have positive contents. Icarus, who was taught viniculture by Dionysus himself, is murdered by the country people who taste wine for the first time and think that they have been poisoned (Apollodorus, *Bibl.* 3.192). According to a scholion on Clement of Alexandria, *Protr.* 4.4, those treading the grapes sang a song about how Dionysus was torn to pieces. Burkert observes here: 'The most obvious myth would be that Dionysos, the god of wine, was himself killed and dismembered to serve as wine for sacramental drinking.'[18] A text in Cicero does seem to demolish this hypothesis completely: 'When we call corn *Ceres* [Latin for Demeter] and wine *Liber* [Latin for Dionysus], we employ a common metaphor. Or do you think that anyone is so devoid of reason as to believe that the thing which nourishes him is a god?' (*Nat. Deor.* 3.41); but the question remains how far one may see Cicero's sceptical view as truly representative.

(b) Sparagmos and Omophagia

In their first song, the chorus in Euripides praise Dionysus with the following words (*Ba.* 135–40):

> It is a pleasant sight in the mountains when he is tired by his furious running and sinks down to earth in the sacred clothing of the deerskin, thirsting for the raw food (ὠμοφάγον), the blood of the kid.

The god himself performs the *ōmophagion*, i.e. the eating of raw meat, yet another survival of an older cultural stage, and at the same time something that breaks through the civilised world of everyday life; this is why he is also called 'eater of raw food' and 'the one who rips human beings apart', for this is how one gets hold of raw meat – living animals, in the extreme case even a living human being, are torn apart. In the *Bacchae*, this is done by the women, who like to fall into a Dionysiac rapture (cf. Kraemer) and go out into the mountains (*Ba.* 735–47):

> And they tore apart whatever did not have wings to fly away. With no iron tool in their bare hands, they tore the cattle apart, so that many milch cows cried out as they came to a pitiable end in the women's merciless arms. Calves were cut in pieces there in the same way, and many a rib and hoof was cut off and flew through the air, getting caught in the branches of the fir-trees and dripping their

[18] *Religion* (L2) 238.

bloody dew. The bulls began by lowering their sharp horns for a wild thrust, but they were soon overthrown by the hands of a thousand women, and their flesh was divided up in less time than it takes for your royal brow to twitch in horror.

Here we may mention an inscription from 276 BCE which contains the cultic statutes of an association (*thiasos*) of believers in Dionysus. This speaks of an *ōmophagion* which only the priestess of Dionysus is permitted to set forth (LSAM 48.2f.: μὴ ἐξεῖναι ὠμοφάγιον ἐμβαλεῖν μηθενὶ πρότερον [ἢ ἡ ἱέ]ρεια . . .). Probably this refers to small pieces of raw meat which were distributed to those taking part in the sacrifice, either to be eaten or to be deposited in sacrificial cavities or baskets, a rite that has been substituted for the bloody act of tearing a living animal to pieces. It seems that the wildness of the episode in the myth has been repressed, while the act itself is retained in a form that is ritualised and therefore can be transmitted to coming generations (cf. Henrichs, 'Maenaden').

The high-point in Euripides is the following hair-raising sequence of events. Pentheus creeps up on the Maenads in order to observe secretly what they do. He is discovered, and the women, who know no restraint, tear him to pieces under the leadership of his own mother, Agaue. While his grandfather Cadmus gathers together the pieces, Agaue brings his head in triumph into the city and issues invitations to a horrific festival meal, presumably with the remains of Pentheus as the main course (to adopt Dodds' dry tone, 211). We must note here that Dionysus can also appear in the form of a bull. We also register that Dionysus and Pentheus are assimilated in the *Bacchae*; they are in any case cousins, thanks to the mythical genealogy which makes Semele the human mother of Dionysus. If one assesses all the evidence, one can support the hypothesis that Pentheus functions in the *Bacchae* as Dionysus' *doppelgänger* or representative. He takes upon himself the lot that was meant for the god.

(c) Theophagy?

We have now seen a god who can assume the form of a beast and enjoys eating raw meat; his devotees tear living animals to pieces; his representative is dismembered and served as food. If we combine these three elements, we have the rite which the *Bacchae* has turned into a drama. The devotees of Dionysus dismember a sacrificial animal and consume the raw mouthfuls, believing that by eating the bloody flesh they receive the god into themselves. The boundaries between god, human being, and animal become fluid. This appears illogical, but it fits the ecstatic trait which is fundamental to the Dionysiac religion with its bursting of personal limits. What the academic study of religion calls theophagy, 'eating a god', appears to be at least approximately realised in the cult of Dionysus (this is the influential interpretation by Harrison 487f. et al.; in his very instructive contribution with its wealth of material, Henrichs is sceptical on this point: 'Identities' 159f.).

(d) The language of the mysteries

A number of passages in the *Bacchae* make it clear that the cult of Dionysus could also organise itself and present itself as a mystery cult. One of the characteristic macarisms is found early on, in the first song of the chorus (*Ba.* 72f.: 'Thrice blessed is the one who knows the consecrations'). We also hear the pure language of the mysteries in a dialogue between Pentheus (*Ba.* 471: 'What is the secret meaning of the orgies?') and Dionysus (472: 'It is imparted only to those initiated'). This secrecy gives rise to suspicions: Pentheus understands 'orgies' in the pejorative sense with which we are familiar today and makes disparaging statements about their celebration (*Ba.* 221–4):

> There the women drink wine from full tankards, and then one after the other they all slink off into quiet corners in the arms of their sexual partners. They call it the sacrificial worship of Bacchus, but their real god is Aphrodite.

In a fragmentary chorus song from the drama *The Cretans*, Euripides brings together ideas from several cults, but the substratum from the cult of Dionysus and the mysteries can still be seen clearly (frag. 472.9–15 Nauck):

> I lead a holy life, since I became an initiate of Zeus of Mount Ida and shepherd of Zagreus [= Dionysus] who revels by night. I have carried out the festal meal of raw meat [ὠμοφάγους]. I swung the torch of the Great Mother in the mountains. Now that I have become holy, I call myself a devotee of Bacchus.

2. The mystery cult

List 42.
L'Association dionysiaque dans les sociétés anciennes: Actes de la table ronde … (CEFR 89), Rome 1986.
R. A. Bauman, 'The Suppression of the Bacchanals: Five Questions', *Hist* 39 (1990) 334–48.

A. Bruhl, *Liber Pater: Origine et expansion du culte dionysiaque à Rome et dans le monde romain* (BEFAR 175), Paris 1953.

W. Burkert, 'Bacchic *Teletai* in the Hellenistic Age', in T. H. Carpenter and C. A. Faraone, *Masks* (L40) 259–75.

S. G. Cole, 'Dionysus and the Dead', ibid. 276–95.

L. Foucher, 'Le Culte de Bacchus sous l'empire romain', *ANRW* II/17.2 (1981) 684–702.

A. Geyer, *Das Problem des Realitätsbezuges in der dionysischen Bildkunst der Kaiserzeit* (Beiträge zur Archäologie 10), Würzburg 1977.

W. Heilmann, 'Coniuratio impia: Die Unterdrückung der Bacchanalia als ein Beispiel für römische Religionspolitik und Religiosität', in *Der altsprachliche Unterricht* 28.2 (1985) 22–41.

J. Kloos and P. Duff, 'The Phallus-Bearing Winnow and Initiation into the Dionysiac Mysteries', *JRelSt* 16 (1989) 65–75.

R. Merkelbach, *Die Hirten des Dionysos: Die Dionysos-Mysterien der römischen Kaiserzeit und der bukolische Roman des Longus*, Stuttgart 1988.

M. P. Nilsson, *The Dionysiac Mysteries of the Hellenistic and Roman Age* (Skrifter utgivna av Svenska Institutet i Athen 8°, 5), Lund 1957.

J. M. Pailler, *Bacchanalia: La répression de 186 av. J.-C. à Rome et en Italie: Vestiges, images, tradition* (BEFAR 270), Rome 1988.

R. J. Rousselle, *The Roman Persecution of the Bacchic Cult, 186–180 BC*, New York 1982.

E. Simon, 'Zum Fries der Mysterienvilla bei Pompeji', *JDAI* 76 (1961) 111–72.

A. Vogliano and F. Cumont, 'La Grande Iscrizione Bacchica del Metropolitan Museum', *AJA* 37 (1933) 215–63.

G. Zuntz, 'Once more the So-called "Edict of Philopator on the Dionysiac Mysteries" (BGU 1211)', *Hermes* 91 (1963) 228–39, also in Idem, *Opuscula Selecta*, Manchester 1972, 88–101.

(*a*) How widespread was the cult?

Three 'snapshots' will allow us to see something of the history of the mysteries of Dionysus in the classical world.

Ptolemy IV Philopator

The cult and the mysteries were the object of special promotion by the rulers of the successor kings to Alexander the Great in Syria and Egypt. According to 3 Maccabees, Ptolemy IV Philopator even attempted to compel the Jews of Alexandria to take part in the Dionysiac mysteries, or to threaten them with branding with a symbol of Dionysus (3 Macc 2:27–30):

> 'All Jews shall be subjected to a registration involving poll tax and to the status of slaves. Those who object to this are to be taken by force and put to death; those who are registered are also to be branded on their bodies by fire with the ivy-leaf symbol of Dionysus, and they shall also be reduced to their former limited status.' In order that he might not appear to be an enemy of all, he inscribed below: 'But if any of them prefer to join those who have been initiated into the mysteries, they shall have equal citizenship with the Alexandrians.'

The same king ordered that all the Dionysiac mystagogues in Egypt were to come to Alexandria within ten days to be inscribed in lists, declaring their 'genealogy' (i.e. 'to state who had transmitted the mysteries to them, back to the third generation'), and to deposit a written scroll with an account of the sacred doctrine they used.[19] Clearly, the king intends his decree to create order amidst the proliferation of the many Dionysiac cult communities in his country.

PGourob, Sabazios
No less a scholar than Wilamowitz has linked this decree of Ptolemy Philopator with the Gourob papyrus (now in Dublin).[20] This fragment of a mystery book from the third century BCE speaks in line 3 of a τελετή, contains invocations of Eleusinian and Orphite gods, mentions the eating of sacrificial flesh (line 14), and drinking (line 25). In the same breath it speaks of the 'shepherd of cattle' (βούκολος), who is elsewhere known to us as one of the functionaries in the Dionysiac associations, and of a *synthēma* (lines 25f.). Finally, towards the end it speaks of dice, mirrors, and other toys of the child Dionysus in the mystical basket (lines 28–30). The cultic formula 'god through the bosom' (line 24: θεὸς διὰ κόλπου) can be explained on the basis of the Sabazios mysteries, where the initiates drew a snake through their clothes, hinting at sexual union with the god. The celebrated 'garland' oration of Demosthenes contains a passage that is significant for the history of religion, in which the great orator mercilessly

---

[19] BGU 1211 or SGUÄ 7266; cf. only Zuntz and F. Dunand in *L'association* 99–101.
[20] Text etc. FVS 1в23; O. Kern, *Fragmenta* (L43) no. 31; cf. U. von Wilamowitz, *Glaube* (L2) II.373; M. L. West, *Poems* (L43) 170f.

mocks his opponent in the courtroom, because of his participation in secret mysteries. This text refers to the cult of Sabazios, often equated with Dionysus, and also mentions snakes (*Or.* 18.259f.):[21]

> Grown to man's estate, you read aloud to your mother from the written texts at the initiations into the mysteries ... At night you clothed the initiands in the calf skin and mixed the drink for them, you purified them and scoured them with pottery and clay. After the purification, you told them to stand up and say: 'I have fled that which is worse and found that which is better.'[22] ... Then in the day time you led the noble throng [θίασος], garlanded with fennel and poplar leaves, through the streets. You took hold of tame snakes and swung them over your head, crying out: εὐοῖ σαβοῖ and ὑῆς ἄττης ἄττης ὑῆς ...

The scandal of the Bacchanalia

Like Ptolemy IV Philopator, the Roman senate too found it necessary to create public order. The great Bacchanalian scandal took place in 186 BCE in Rome, which the Dionysiac mysteries had penetrated from the south of Italy. We have a detailed account by Livy, though rather in the style of a diverting novel.[23] The beginning of his description is colourful enough (8.3–8): a Greek from the lower classes, who specialised in secret nocturnal cultic practices as 'secret priest and soothsayer', first brought the mysteries to Etruria. More and more people were enticed to take part, because 'the joys of wine and of food' accompanied the ceremonies. As the hour grew later, men and women, young and old, began to indulge in 'excesses of every sort'. This culminated in deeds of murder, but all the 'violence remained undiscovered, since the howling and the tambourines and cymbals made so much noise that nothing could be heard of the victims of rape and murder as they cried for help'.

Livy fills many pages in this tone, and some of his formulations sound rather strange: sometimes after the murders, not even a corpse remained to be buried (8.8); initiands were handed over to the priests like sacrificial

---

[21] For further details see the instructive commentary by H. Wankel, Heidelberg 1976; on Sabazios cf. S. E. Johnson, 'The Present State of Sabazios Research', *ANRW* II/17.3 (1984) 1583–1613. On the mysteries in his cult cf. e.g. NDIEC I.21 (no. 3, lines 9f.).

[22] Cf. W. Burkert, *Mystery Cults* (L30) 19: 'This, then, must have been the immediate experience of successful mysteries: "feeling better now" ... All those everyday needs and hopes were met by practitioners with rituals evidently well attuned to psychic receptivity.'

[23] *Urb. Cond.* 39.8.3–19.7.

victims (10.7) or were in fact slaughtered (13.11). The principal witness expresses her fear that the initiates will tear her to pieces with their bare hands as a punishment for her betrayal (13.5). This is probably to be judged a half-understood echo of *sparagmos* and *ōmophagia*, especially since Livy furnishes further indications that this movement had an ecstatic element.

The senate reacted severely, with pursuit and punishment of those involved – Livy speaks of seventy thousand persons affected, of suicides and many death sentences – and with an official resolution which is preserved in an inscription. This edict does not intend to make the worship of Dionysus per se impossible, but it hedges it about with so many clauses and restrictions that it cannot grow to an underground movement that would threaten the state. Some excerpts from the *Senatus Consultum de Bacchanalibus*:[24]

> None of them is permitted to possess a sanctuary of Bacchus. Should any declare that they absolutely must possess a sanctuary of Bacchus, they are to come to the city praetor in Rome, and after our senate has heard them, it will take a decision upon this matter, provided that at least one hundred senators are present at this debate ... No man is permitted to be a priest. Neither man nor woman is permitted to be president. They are not allowed to have funds held in common ... From now on, they are not permitted to bind themselves by oath or vow or contract or promise, nor to make mutual obligations. No one is to hold celebrations in secret ... A maximum of five persons, men and women, is allowed to hold the celebrations; there may not be more than two men and three women among them, unless the city praetor and the senate permit this, under the conditions set out above ... If any persons have acted contrary to the prescriptions written above, they are to be charged with a crime deserving capital punishment.

[24] The text has often been published and translated: CIL I 2/581; ILS 18; UUC II.83f.; L. Schumacher, *Inschriften* (L4) 79–83; H. J. Hillen, *T. Livius: Römische Geschichte. Buch XXXIX–XLI* (TuscBü), Munich and Zurich 2nd edn. 1993, 340–3; E. T. Sage, *Livy: History of Rome*, vol. II (LCL 313), Cambridge, Mass. and London 1936, 258–67; Heilmann 38–41; K. Latte, *Religion* (L4) 21f.; among the secondary literature, cf. Bauman; Bruhl 82–126; Cumont (L02); M. L. Freyburger-Galland et al., *Sectes* (L2) 171–206; detailed discussion in Pailler; cf. now G. Scheuermann, 'Der Bacchanalienskandal in Rom (186 v.C.): Die Inschrift von Tiriolo und der Bericht des Livius', MF 94 (1994) 174–201.

Villas in which the mysteries were held; the inscription from Torre Nova

It was only under Caesar that the restrictive policy of the senate was relaxed. A broadly new type of Dionysiac mysteries came into existence in the imperial period, more in keeping with the civic life of those who had the status of citizens, more moral and less strange and threatening. The Roman upper classes accepted the mysteries, and it is this group who owned the so-called mystery villas, the best known of which is without doubt the Villa Item in Pompeii.[25] One room is decorated with frescoes which display motifs from the ideas associated with Dionysus, e.g. the uncovering of a phallus which rises up from a corn winnow filled with fruit. It is supposed that the mysteries were celebrated in this room and that the wall paintings record particular excerpts from the myth and the rite. An inscription from Torre Nova in Italy (*c.*150 CE) allows us to learn something of the organisation of such a mystery community. The inscription presents a list of over five hundred members, arranged according to rank and grade within the cult. This community consisted of a senatorial family, their slaves, and their clients. The high priestess is Agrippinilla, mistress of the house.[26] We should also recall here the association of the Athenian *Iobacchae* (see I/B,2(*c*) above), whose relationship to the Dionysiac mysteries is revealed inter alia by its members' predilection for drinking wine in pleasant company, but under social control.

(*b*) Ritual and contents

The elaboration of the ritual of the Dionysiac mysteries was free, and varied according to time and place, but an outline can be discerned. As a preparation for the initiation, the initiand was given instruction: the most important practices were explained from a written scroll. A further precondition was a ten days' period of fasting and sexual abstinence. The consecration took place at night, preferably in the grotto of Bacchus or in a suitably furnished room in a private house. The initiands undergo a bath of

[25] Illustrated e.g. in UUC III nos. 52–4; U. Bianchi, *Mysteries* (L30) nos. 90–2; cf. Simon.

[26] Cf. Vogliano and Cumont; text also in L. Moretti, *Inscriptiones Graecae Urbis Romae I*, Rome 1968, no. 160; described by J. Scheid in *L'Association* 275–90; cf. B. H. McLean, 'The Agrippinilla Inscription: Religious Associations and Early Christian Formation', in Idem (ed.), *Origins and Method: Essays in honour of J. C. Hurd* (JSNT.S 86), Sheffield 1993, 239–70.

purification and swear an oath that they will observe the strictest silence. Other details are mentioned: they are crowned with garlands of the white poplar (a tree that grows in the underworld), they are struck with rods, and soil or powered plaster is scattered over them as part of a purification by the four elements. The torches, the corn winnow, and the indispensable coffer seem to have been adopted from Eleusis. After the consecration, nocturnal celebrations of the members of the cult are held at regular intervals, involving disguises, the representation of portions of the myth, and processions, accompanied by dancing and music, festal meals and drinking parties.

What did the participants expect to get out of this? In general, once again we can say: an encounter with the divine, partaking of a superior vitality, transcendence of the unsatisfactory boundaries of daily life. The Dionysiac mysteries also increasingly tend to hope for a better life after death. According to an inscription from a cemetery in Cumae in Campania (fifth century BCE), the special role of the initiates is expressed already in their burial: 'No one may be buried here except the one who belongs to the initiates of Bacchus.'[27] Centuries later Plutarch expresses his confidence, when he writes to console his wife after the death of their child, that she will overcome the temptation to fall into an Epicurean nihilism in face of the fate of the dead child, because of the mystical symbols of the cult of Dionysus – both are initiates, and therefore they share the knowledge of these matters (*Cons. Uxor.* 10 [611d]). It is well known that Dionysus himself could take on traits of an underworld god; it is related that he fetched his mother Semele up from the underground, something apparently recalled in the celebration of the mysteries. The contents of every hope were a paradise beyond death, a celebration of the mysteries without end.

3. Orphism

List 43.

R. Baumgarten, *Heiliges Wort und Heilige Schrift bei den Griechen. Hieroi Logoi und verwandte Erscheinungen* (ScriptOralia 110), Tübingen 1998, 70–121.

[27] SEG IV.92; LSCS 120; also in G. Pfohl, *Inschriften* (L4) 18, as no. 12; O. Kern, *Fragmenta* (L43) 43, as no. 180; cf. R. Turcan in *L'Association* 227–46.

H. D. Betz, ' "Der Erde Kind bin ich und des gestirnten Himmels". Zur Lehre vom Menschen in den orphischen Goldblättchen' in Idem, *Antike und Christentum* (L3), 222–43.

P. Borgeaud (ed.), *Orphisme et Orphée: en honneur de Jean Rudhardt* (Recherches et Rencontres. Publications de la Faculté des lettres de Genève 3), Geneva 1991.

W. Burkert, 'Orpheus und die Vorsokratiker: Bemerkungen zum Derveni-Papyrus', *AuA* 14 (1968) 93–114.

S. G. Cole, 'New Evidence for the Mysteries of Dionysus', *GRBS* 21 (1980) 223–38.

F. Graf, *Eleusis* (L34).

——'Dionysian and Orphic Eschatology: New Texts and Old Questions', in T. H. Carpenter and C. A. Faraone, *Masks* (L40) 239–58.

W. K. C. Guthrie, *Orpheus and Greek Religion: A Study of the Orphic Movement* (Methuen's Handbooks of Archeology 6), London 2nd edn. 1952.

J. E. Harrison, *Prolegomena* (L2) 455–674.

O. Kern, *Orphicorum Fragmenta*, Berlin 3rd edn. 1972.

M. J. Lagrange, *Les Mystères: L'Orphisme* (= Introduction à l'étude du Nouveau Testament IV: Critique historique 1) (EtB), Paris 2nd edn. 1937.

I. M. Linforth, *The Arts of Orpheus*, Berkeley 1941.

E. Maass, *Orpheus* (L18).

A. Olivieri, *Lamellae aureae Orphicae* (KIT 133), Bonn 1955.

K. Tsantsanoglou and G. M. Parássoglou, 'Two Gold Lamellae from Thessaly', *Hell.* 38 (1987) 3–16 (with bibliography in n. 1).

M. L. West, *The Orphic Poems*, Oxford 1983.

G. Zuntz, *Persephone: Three Essays on Religion and Thought in Magna Graecia*, Oxford 1971, 275–393.

The Dionysiac mysteries are connected by eschatology to Orphism (we often find the combined term 'Orphic-Dionysiac mysteries' in the secondary literature). Orphism takes its name from Orpheus, the mythical poet and singer who sought to rescue his wife Eurydice from the underworld, and who is sometimes counted as the founder of all the mystery cults. In the heart of the myth of these cults stands the tearing of Dionysus to pieces by the Titans, who eat the divine child. Zeus sends a flash of lightning and destroys the Titans who have devoured Dionysus. The soot in the smoke that then flies upwards is the material out of which human beings are made: thus they contain in themselves, from their very origin, both the titanic/evil and the divine/good, since the smoke contained both these – directly, the remains of the Titans, but also indirectly trace-elements of Dionysus (although the latter is found only in the Neoplatonic interpretation). The human being must expiate the guilt of the Titans here on earth through rites of purification and right conduct (e.g. a strict vegetarianism), for otherwise heavy punishments must be expected in the underworld.

Since the Derveni papyrus with its allegorical commentary from the Presocratic period on a theogeny of Orpheus was discovered in 1962, scholarly opinion once again tends to posit an earlier origin for parts of the myth which become visible only in late antiquity in the celebration of the myth in the ritual.[28] The text speaks of μύσται (11.5.8) and deals directly (though polemically) with the mysteries. Plato draws an unattractive picture of the devotees of the Orphic cultic practices, writing that 'charlatans and soothsayers' wander around, 'with books of Musaeus and Orpheus in their hands – so they say – in accordance with which they perform their rites' in order to preserve the living and the dead from the terrible penalties of the afterlife (Resp. 2.7 [364b–365a]). He seems to judge them somewhat more positively in the Phaedo, where his account ends with the utterance from the mysteries: 'Many indeed bear the wand, but few experience the Bacchic enthusiasm' (Phaed. 13 [69D]). In Theophrastus, the superstitious man goes every month with his wife and children to the 'priests of Orpheus' in order to be initiated (Char. 16.11).

The Orphic-Dionysiac hope in an afterlife is given a special expression in texts scratched on gold plates from the fourth/third centuries BCE onwards which have been found as funerary gifts in southern Italy, Greece and Crete.[29] These serve as passports for the dead, since they include among other things instructions for the route the dead person must take in the underworld; how he should reach a spring among the white cypresses (according to B 1–2 in Zuntz' enumeration), from which however he may

---

[28] Preliminary publication in ZPE 47 (1982) Anhang 1–12; cf. West 75–115 (with bibliography); Burkert.

[29] Texts: FVS 1B17–21; Kern 104–8 no. 32; better in Zuntz; on new discoveries in Hipponion (with an unambiguously Dionysiac colouring) and Thessaly (two examples in the form of ivy leaves on the breast of a dead woman), cf. inter alia Tsantsanoglou and Parássoglou; translation of two examples in M. P. Nilsson, Religion (L4) 52.

not drink, and what he is to reply to the guardians who watch over the cool water from the lake of recollection, viz. 'I am a son of the earth and of the starry sky.' We also find macarisms, which in this case go so far as to deify the initiate, as well as references to his union with the goddess of the underworld, whether as adoption, as sacred marriage, or merely as fellowship in a meal and allusions to a ritual of initiation in which milk was used (A 1):

> As pure I come here from among those who are pure, O goddess who rule over Hades ... I am happy to have fled from the care that encompasses me and weighs me down ... I have gone down into the womb of Despoina, the mistress in Hades ... 'You are happy and blessed, you shall be a god instead of a mortal.' I hastened like a young kid to the milk.[30]

The so-called Orphic hymns, 87 poems addressed to various gods, belong to the second century CE. Dionysiac elements are found for example in no. 45: 'Come, blessed Dionysus, emitting fire, with the forehead of a bull ... you of the many names who rule all things, you who delight in swords and blood and sacred maenads.'[31] These hymns may have been used as a prayer book in a cultic community in Asia Minor (West 28f.).

Unlike Eleusis, the Dionysiac mysteries were not tied down to specific places and times; this must be emphasised. They did not require any special sanctuary or any exclusive priestly family. Their external appearance changed, so that they often could take on the form of a cultic association in which women played an important part. All this facilitated the geographic diffusion of the mysteries in the Mediterranean world in classical times.

D. The cult of Attis

List 44.
F. Cumont, *Religions* (L2) 46–72.
E. N. Lane (ed.), *Cybele, Attis and Related Cults: Essays in Memory of M. J. Vermaseren* (Religions in the Graeco-Roman World 131), Leiden 1996.
M. W. Meyer, *Mysteries* (L30) 111–54.

[30] Not, as in many of the older translations: 'I have fallen into the milk as a kid', cf. Tsantsanoglou and Parássoglou 13.
[31] Ed. W. Quant, Berlin 2nd edn 1962; here following UUC II.86; cf. also West; a selection in M. W. Meyer, *Mysteries* (L30) 101–9.

G. Sanders, 'Kybele und Attis', in M. J. Vermaseren, *Religionen* (L2) 264–97.

G. Sfameni Gasparro, *Soteriology and Mystic Aspects in the Cult of Cybele and Attis* (EPRO 103), Leiden 1985.

G. Thomas, 'Magna Mater and Attis', *ANRW* II/17.3 (1984) 1500–35.

R. Turcan, *Cultes* (L2) 35–75.

M. J. Vermaseren, *Corpus Cultus Cybelae Attidisque*, vols. 1–7 (EPRO 50), Leiden 1977–89.

'The cult of Attis' is a convenient title, but we must at once specify that de facto another entity is dominant in this form of religion across wide areas, namely the *magna mater*, a mother divinity originally from Asia Minor, usually called Cybele (her Syrian equivalent is called *inter alia* Atargatis).[32] We can follow with some precision her penetration of Greece and Rome. Inscriptions from 284–70 BCE document the existence of the private sanctuary of an association of worshippers of the Phrygian mother in Piraeus near Athens (LSCG 48 and frequently). During the Second Punic War, in 204 BCE, the Sibylline Oracle promised the Romans the help of the goddess in the struggle against Hannibal. 'They lacked such a motherly protectress in their own divine heaven',[33] and so they brought the goddess to the city in the form of a black meteoric stone from Asia Minor, and erected a temple to her on the Palatine (in addition to Livy, cf. Ovid, *Fasti* 4.247–348). But this remained an isolated enclave until the cult of Attis achieved a public resonance under Claudius (see below).

1. The myth

List 45.

H. Hepding, *Attis, seine Mythen und sein Kult* (RVV 1), Giessen 1903.

P. Lambrechts, *Attis: van herdersknaap tot God* (VVAW.L 24.46), Brussels 1962.

See literature in L44.

The numerous variants of the myth can be reduced to two basic forms. According to the first version, the young Attis is so highly honoured by the mother of the gods that Zeus becomes jealous and sends a wild boar which

---

[32] On this Syrian goddess apart from the fundamental source text (Ps.-Lucian's *De Dea Syria*) cf. above all F. Bömer, *Untersuchungen* (L2) III.84–109.

[33] M. Giebel, *Geheimnis* (L30) 124.

attacks Attis while he is hunting, and kills him. The second version attained wider popularity: Cybele burns with love for Attis, but when he desires to marry the king's daughter, or becomes romantically involved with a nymph, the jealous mother of the gods makes him lose his reason, so that he castrates himself and dies (cf. Ovid, *Fasti* 4.223–46, with an aetiological glimpse of the rites). In other conclusions, Attis survives the castration; or else the goddess asks Zeus to restore him to life, but is granted only that the corpse of Attis should remain incorrupt: his hair continues to grow and his little finger can move (Arnobius, *Adv. Nat.* 5.7). One can scarcely call this a 'resurrection' of Attis, although it is possible that this is how it was seen in late antiquity in the confrontation with Christianity. A number of possible meanings have been suggested for the strange action of self-castration: making the earth fertile, a cultic act of procreation, assimilation to the female goddess, an expression of yearning for the lost androgynous unity, or an action that makes possible the uninterrupted cultic purity that was required for service in the sanctuary. Psychologists will discern here fear of the power of the female to swallow up the male, and fear of the castrating aspect of the excessively powerful maternal imago.

2. The cult

List 46.

J. Carcopino, *Aspects mystiques de la Rome païenne*, Paris 4th edn. 1941.

F. W. Cornish, *Catullus* (LCL 6), Cambridge, Mass. and London, rev. edn. (by G. P. Goold) 1988.

W. Eisenhut, *Catull* (TuscBü), Munich and Zurich 10th edn. 1993, 98–105.

H. Graillot, *Le Culte de Cybèle, mère des dieux, à Rome et dans l'empire romain* (BEFAR 107), Paris 1912.

B. Kollmann, 'Eine Mysterienweihe bei Aretaios von Kappadokien', *Ph.* 137 (1993) 252–57.

A. Rousselle, *Porneia: On Desire and the Body in Antiquity*, Oxford 1988, 121–8.

(a) The self-mutilation

The most striking particularity of the cult of Attis – and often mocked – was the ritual self-infliction of wounds through incisions in the skin (also known from other cults, such as that of the 'dancing dervishes'), going as far as self-castration, which the future adepts of the cult carried out on their own bodies at the height of an orgiastic celebration with a sharp stone or a potsherd, after loud music and wild dance had put them into a trance (cf. especially Rousselle, with attempts at an explanation). A poem of Catullus (c.87–54 BCE) gives a particularly clear illustration of this (*Carm.* 63):

> Attis sped through the high sea with the keel of the hasty ship;
> when his swift foot gladly touched the Phrygian grove
> and entered the dark woods where the goddess dwells,
> wild ecstasy deprived him of his senses
> so that he took a sharp stone and severed his member from his groin.
> When he then perceived that his limbs now lacked virility,
> and his fresh-flowing blood still dampened the earth,
> at once with her[34] white arms she seizes the hollow drum;
> with it, Cybele, she has consecrated herself to your service [*initia*].
> With tender fingers she struck the tightened skin of the bull
> and she began to lead her companions in song, while her body swayed: 'Hasten
>   on high to the mountain wood, you Gallae of Cybele ...
> Chase weariness from your spirits, my companions, and follow me now
> to the Phrygian seat of Cybele, to the Phrygian grove of the goddess;
> where the sound of the cymbals resounds, where the hollow drum sounds its
>   hollow note,
> where the Phrygian flautist blows a muffled tone on the bent reed,
> where the maenads toss their heads on their necks as they swing the ivy,
> where she holds sacred festal orgies with a wailing cry,
> where the unsteady throng of the goddess meanders through the open field –
> there let us hasten at once to the rhythm of the dance!'
> Great goddess, goddess Cybele, lady of the mountain range,
> keep your sacred madness far from my house:
> make other people ecstatic, make other people rage.

The concluding wish of the poet, to be spared from such forms of religious excess, is understandable. We may infer from the death of Attis in the myth that some adepts paid for their self-mutilation with their lives. Survivors became a 'Galla' (the designation of the priests in the service of Cybele, perhaps taken from the name of a river in Asia Minor). Some continued to carry out the service in a sanctuary, while others went about the land with

---

[34] From this point on the Latin text employs adjectives with feminine endings to speak of Attis.

a like-minded throng. Apuleius gives us a very negative description of such mendicant priests of the Syrian mother goddess (*Met.* 8.26.1–30.5).

(*b*) The main feast at Rome

From the reign of the emperor Claudius (in the middle of the first century CE) onwards the annual celebration of Attis in the spring became one of the most popular Roman feasts. We mention only three of its elements: (1) a pine tree was cut down in the sacred grove, and bows of wool with cultic objects, including cymbals and hollow drums, were wound about it. On 22 March (*arbor intrat*), *dendrophoroi*, 'tree-bearers', carried the tree-trunk through the streets of the city to the temple. (2) 24 March was the *dies sanguis*, blood day, on which the excesses already described took place. (3) 25 March was called the day of joy (*hilaria*, cf. Catullus, *Carm.* 63.18: 'Give joy [*Hilarate*] to our mistress by running in the speed enthusiasm bestows'); psychologically speaking, this was assuredly a reaction, after the expressions of sadness had spent themselves. Thus the structure is that of a polarity between sadness and joy, death and life, even without any formal concept of resurrection.

3. Formulae and rites of the mysteries

List 47.

C. A. Forbes, *Firmicus Maternus: the Error of the Pagan Religions* (ACW 37), New York 1970.

K. Hoheisel, *Das Urteil über die nichtchristlichen Religionen im Traktat 'De errore profanarum religionum' des Julius Firmicus Maternus*, philosophical dissertation, Bonn 1972.

R. Joly, 'L'exhortation au courage (θαρρεῖν) dans les mystères', *REG* 68 (1955) 164–70.

R. Turcan, *Firmicus Maternus: L'erreur des religions païennes* (CUFr), Paris 1982.

K. Ziegler, *Julius Firmicus Maternus Senator: Vom Irrtum der heidnischen Religionen* (Das Wort der Antike 3), Munich 1953.

The existence of mysteries of Attis is attested from about the first century BCE onwards. Clement of Alexandria (*Protr.* 15.3 [13.12f., GCS 56]) gives us the *synthēma*, which is patterned on the Eleusinian cultic formula:

ἐκ τυμπάνου ἔφαγον.

ἐκ κυμβάλου ἔπιον.
ἐκερνοφόρησα.
ὑπὸ τὸν παστὸν ὑπέδυν.

I ate from the hollow drum,
I drank from the cymbal,
I bore the *kernos*,
I went into the inner chamber.

A τύμπανον is a drum over which animal skin is stretched, to be held in the hand. A cymbal is a small basin of bronze; these were carried in pairs, so that one could be struck against the other. Both instruments belong to the indispensable paraphernalia of the cult of Attis, where they were used to create the exciting rhythms and the shrill music. They appear with a different function, as plate for food and cup for drink, in the ritual of admission. The *kernos*, a pottery vessel shaped like a ring, with numerous small bowls, was used for sacrifices of the first fruits. When the initiate has passed through these stages, he comes to the goal in the innermost room of the sanctuary. 'Inner chamber' recalls the bridal chamber, and this is why some scholars hold that a sacred marriage between the initiate and the goddess took place; this may be connected with another element in the mysteries of Attis, viz. with the two thrones, on one of which the initiand sat with veiled head, while the other was presumably meant for the goddess.

We have also a second witness to the *synthēma* of the mysteries of Attis: Julius Firmicus Maternus, a Sicilian of senatorial rank, who first wrote a book about astrology and later, after his conversion to Christianity about 350 CE, composed the *De Errore Profanarum Religionum*, in which he appeals to the emperor to extirpate paganism. He gives the following evidence about the mysteries of Attis (18.1):

> In one particular temple, the person condemned to death says, in order to gain admittance to the inner chambers: 'I have eaten from the hollow drum, I have drunk from the cymbal and I have thoroughly learned the secrets of religion.' In the Greek language this is: ἐκ τυμπάνου βέβρωκα, ἐκ κυμβάλου πέπωκα, γέγονα μύστης Ἄττεως [I have become an initiate of Attis].

The phrase 'the person condemned to death' should be understood as referring to the pagan who (as such) is condemned to spiritual death – not to the initiate who is about to have a fictitious experience of death. If we compare Firmicus Maternus to Clement, we see that he omits ἐκερνοφόρησα and brings the entry into the inner chambers to an earlier point in the ritual. Whereas the Greek formula at the end, 'I have become an initiate of Attis', contains the result of the entire process, the Latin version says in effect: I have penetrated the mysteries of this cult. When he hands on this information, Firmicus Maternus' real intention is to make a confrontation between the mysteries and the Eucharist, in the context of the ritual of a meal: 'So do not fob yourselves off with the food from the hollow drum, you wretched mortals! Seek the grace of the food that brings salvation, and drink the immortal cup!' (18.8).

But what was eaten and drunk in the rite of admission? Here we can turn to Ovid, who has the following game of question and answer in his festal calendar *(Fasti* 4.367–73):

> I said: 'One feels no shame at placing a bunch of herbs on the table of the goddess? Is there a reason for this?' – 'It is said that those of old nourished themselves on pure milk, and ate herbs ... soft cheese is mixed with crushed herbs, an ancient food for the ancient goddess ...

Thus the initiate of Attis ate herbs from the hollow drum and drank milk from the bronze cymbal (as food appropriate to a newly-born or reborn child of the god, cf. Sallustius, *De Diis* 4.10?).

Firmicus Maternus tells us of another formula. Some scholars have attributed this to the mysteries of Attis, though recently there is an increasing tendency to attach it to the mysteries of Osiris; perhaps the author himself was not so sure about this. In any case, the text sheds important light on the mystery cults and on how an enthusiastic new convert saw them (22.1):

> We mention yet another symbol so that we may uncover the crimes committed by a tainted way of thinking. We shall set out the entire process, so that everyone who reads this may recognise that the law of the divine ordinance has been disfigured by the devil's perverted imitation. On a particular night, the image of the god is laid on its back on a bier and is mourned with lamentations in verse. After this, when they have had enough of these imaginary lamentations, light is brought in. Then the neck of the priest is anointed by all those who wept, and when this has been done, the priest whispers in slow murmurs:
> θαρρεῖτε μύσται τοῦ θεοῦ σεσωσμένου.
> ἔσται γὰρ ἡμῖν ἐκ πόνων σωτηρία.
> [Take comfort, O initiates of the god who has been saved:
> Out of suffering we shall have redemption].

The fate of the god, represented in the ritual, has the function of offering a model of the σωτηρία, the initiates' hope of salvation. The Christian author interprets this, en bloc and in detail, as a devilish parody of what Christians believe: 'So the devil too has his anointed ones' (22.4: *habet ergo diabolus christos suos*).

4. The taurobolium

List 48.
M. Beard et al., *Religions*, vol. 2 (L4) 160–62.
R. Duthoy, *The Taurobolium: Its Evolution and Terminology* (EPRO 10), Leiden 1969.

Taurobolium means literally the act of capturing a bull with a lasso; this term developed, via hunting as a sport and games in which beasts were goaded, to become the name of a particular sacrifice of bulls which is part of the cult of Attis. The most colourful description is provided by the Christian poet Prudentius in the fourth century CE in his *Peristephanon*, a collection of fourteen hymns in honour of martyrs:[35] the high priest puts on his full vestments and goes into a trench, above which a wooden stage has been erected, with boards pierced in the manner of a sieve. A mighty bull is led on to the stage and slaughtered in such a way that 'waves of hot blood gush out from the gaping wound' (1028f.). This blood rains down through the holes on to the priest, who does not flinch, but 'offers his ears, lips and nose ... until he has swallowed all the black blood' (1036–40). Dripping with blood, he then climbs back up, and all those present, far from fleeing in terror from the terrible sight, 'greet him and worship him at a distance [!]' (1048).

The blood contains the vital force (Lev 17:11), and to be covered in streams of blood need not necessarily mean that one becomes polluted (cf. the bold metaphor at Rev 7:14: 'they have washed their clothes and made them white in the blood of the Lamb'). The bull personifies primal, unfettered vitality. The high priest who undergoes this ritual needs this energy for his office, so that he in turn can transmit the energy to others. Besides this, pagan priests often submit to the *taurobolium* on behalf of others, viz. for the emperor and his well-being. An inscription from 367 CE tells us what they expected as a result of doing this:[36]

---

[35] Translation in C. K. Barrett, *Background* (L4) 96–7.
[36] CIL VI 510; ILS 4152; K. Latte, *Religion* (L4) 44f.

The most potent lord Sextilius Agesilaus Aedesius ... father of the unconquered sun god Mithras, hierophant of Hecate, chief shepherd of Dionysus, reborn for ever through sacrifices of bulls and rams [*taurobolio* ... *in aeternum renatus*] consecrated the altar to the great gods, to the mother of the gods and to Attis ...

It is interesting that this man was not only simultaneously an initiate of several mystery cults, but held high offices in them. Now he erected an altar to the mother of the gods and to Attis, in memory of the *taurobolium* to which he had submitted and which had resulted in his being 'reborn for ever'. This formulation is relatively isolated, especially in view of the fact that other inscriptions limit the effect of the *taurobolium* to twenty years. Duthoy concludes that the only ancient element is the sacrifice of a bull, without accompanying rites beyond those that were normal. The baptism in blood, linked to the idea of a rebirth, arose later as a reaction to more or less understood Christian ideas. This conclusion may perhaps help to explain the individual case of a 'rebirth for ever', but other scholars have questioned its universal applicability.[37]

E. The cult of Isis

List 49.

F. Cumont, *Religions* (L2) 73–102.

F. Dunand, *Le Culte d'Isis dans le bassin oriental de la Méditerranée*, vols. 1–3 (EPRO 26), Leiden 1973.

H. Gressmann, *Tod und Auferstehung des Osiris nach Festbräuchen und Umzügen* (AO 23.3), Leipzig 1923.

K. Koch, *Geschichte der ägyptischen Religion: Von den Pyramiden bis zu den Mysterien der Isis*, Stuttgart 1993, 556–609.

F. Le Corsu, *Isis: Mythe et Mystères* (CEMy), Paris 1977.

R. Merkelbach, *Isisfeste in griechisch-römischer Zeit* (BKP 5), Meisenheim 1963.

——*Isis regina – Zeus Sarapis: Die griechisch-ägyptische Religion nach den Quellen dargestellt*, Stuttgart 1995.

R. Turcan, *Cultes* (L2), 77–127.

[37] While W. Burkert, *Mystery Cults* (L30) 25, concedes for this a borrowing from Christianity, M. Giebel, *Geheimnis* (L30) 147, is unimpressed: 'without needing to borrow from Christian ideas'.

L. Vidman, *Sylloge inscriptionum religionis Isiacae et Sarapiacae* (RVV 28), Berlin 1969.

———*Isis und Sarapis bei den Griechen und Römern: Epigraphische Studien zur Verbreitung und zu den Trägern des ägyptischen Kultes* (RVV 29), Berlin 1970.

R. E. Witt, *Isis in the Graeco-Roman World*, Ithaca 1971.

With the cult of Isis we enter Egyptian territory, or, to put it more precisely, we follow the spread of Egyptian thinking in the Graeco-Roman Mediterranean world. There is no exaggeration involved in speaking of an 'Egyptomania' in the classical period in the last centuries BCE and the first centuries CE, comparable to the Egyptian romanticism spread by Free-masonry in the eighteenth century, to which we owe Mozart's *Magic Flute*, or to the *chinoiserie* in French rococo. People looked to the Egyptian spiritual world for ancient, hidden wisdom that would explain life's mysteries.

1. The myth

List 50.

J. Assmann, 'Die Zeugung des Sohnes: Bild, Spiel, Erzählung und das Problem des ägyptischen Mythos', in Idem, *Funktionen und Leistungen des Mythos: Drei altorientalische Beispiele* (OBO 48), Fribourg (Switzerland) and Göttingen 1982, 13–61.

J. Gwyn Griffiths, *Plutarch's De Iside et Osiride*, Cardiff 1970.

J. Hani, *La Religion égyptienne dans la pensée de Plutarche* (CEMy), Paris 1976.

W. Helck, 'Osiris', *PRE* Suppl. 9 (1962) 469–513.

T. Hopfner, *Plutarch: Über Isis und Osiris*, vols. 1–2 (MOU 9.1–2), Prague 1940, 1941.

G. Vandebeek, *De Interpretatio Graeca van de Isisfiguur* (StHell 4), Louvain 1946.

Isis and her consort Osiris increasingly occupy the centre of Egyptian religiosity in the late classical period, along with the antagonist Seth and their son, Horus (or Harsiese or, in another constellation, Harpocrates). We know of no finished, as it were canonical, form of the myth from Egypt; the scattered fragments can be seen in texts from the pyramids and inscriptions on temples and graves, in prayers and the Book of the Dead.

Significantly, it was the Greek Plutarch who created such a form at the beginning of the second century CE in his work *De Iside et Osiride*.

The final form is very complicated and displays many layers, but its original germ can be supposed to lie in the following simple story. A young shepherd is torn to pieces by wild animals while defending his herd against them. His beloved gathers the torn limbs together, weeps over the corpse and buries it. She is given the name Isis, which properly speaking denotes the throne of Pharaoh, which was personified and seen as the mother of the ruler. Thus the Pharaoh is already implicitly linked to the constellation 'living son (Horus) and dead father (Osiris)', and this was to be important for the further development. The wild animals are interpreted anthropomorphically, and replaced by the antagonist Seth. The Egyptians interpreted Isis' search for the corpse of Osiris and her lamentation over it as the ritual funeral which was so extraordinarily important in their culture. In concrete terms, this enabled Isis (together with her sister Nephthys) to ensure that Osiris would survive in the underworld.

A 'vegetational' layer was then superimposed on the fundamental core of the story, i.e. it was linked to the growth of the grain, which in Egypt depends on the water of the Nile and on the mud that the river deposits when it overflows its banks each year. The agricultural populace of the Nile valley created their own alternative explanation of Osiris' death: here, it is not by being torn to pieces that he dies, but by drowning in the Nile, and this is why he is at work with his power in the water that brings fruitfulness and in the corn that grows up from the mud. This is visually portrayed by means of the corn mummies: a figure is formed of soil and grains, or else a mould, with outlines representing Osiris, is filled with soil, and grains are sown in it. Water from the Nile is then poured over it, and the shooting upwards of the corn is observed. We also find such images among the objects placed in tombs (cf. UUC III nos. 229–32).

In the final version of the myth in Plutarch, the competing versions are simply placed alongside one another, without any apparent sense of their contradictoriness. Typhon (= Seth) entices Osiris to go into a precious coffin, which he then locks securely and sets afloat on the sea (death by drowning). Isis looks for him everywhere, as Demeter searches for Persephone (here Plutarch borrows from the Eleusinian myth). After many attempts, Isis finds the coffin and brings it back to Egypt. Once again, Seth finds it. He cuts the corpse into fourteen pieces (death by being torn apart) and scatters these abroad. Isis gathers them together and buries them, with a strange consequence (*Is. et Os.* 18 [358a–b]:

This is why there are so many graves of Osiris in Egypt, as one is told; for the goddess at once erected a tomb for each piece that she found. Others deny this, and say that Isis only made copies that she bestowed on the individual places, pretending that she was giving them the genuine corpse. The purpose was that he [Osiris] should be given more honour among mortals, and that Typhon, who was looking for the grave, should lose heart when he saw how many graves were identified and pointed out.

Thanks to his correct burial, Osiris can now grow into his most important role, that of lord and judge in the world of the dead. Initially, Osiris was used only as the prototype of the dead Pharaoh, but elements from the royal burial ritual penetrated the myth. In the course of a democratisation of the royal privilege, it was ultimately believed that each dead person became an Osiris, provided only that the rites concerning the corpse were carried out correctly.

The fate of Osiris also structures the course of the Egyptian festal year. The Egyptian services of worship had a special fascination for Greek visitors, thanks to their strangeness. This led them to see the Egyptian feasts as celebrations of the mysteries in the Hellenistic sense; we find this tendency as early as Herodotus, *Hist.* 2.71.1: 'At night, the Egyptians perform dramatic representations on the lake of the sufferings of Osiris. They call this "mysteries" [μυστήρια].' But what he calls 'mysteries' were dramatic representations of the sacred history in full public view; secret celebrations inside the temple were reserved to priests. This is not the same thing as the distinction between initiates and non-initiates in the mystery cults. The rites which were to bestow immortality were carried out on dead persons, perhaps with the exception of the Pharaoh, whereas they were carried out in Eleusis on living persons. The religion of Isis probably took on the typical structure of a mystery cult only when it was reshaped in Greece according to the well-proven pattern.

2. Cult and mysteries

List 51.
R. Baumgarten, *Heiliges Wort* (L43) 196–218.
J. Bergman, *Ich bin Isis: Studien zum memphitischen Hintergrund der griechischen Isis-Aretalogien* (HR[U] 3), Uppsala 1968.
Y. Grandjean, *Une Nouvelle arétalogie d'Isis à Maronée* (EPRO 49), Leiden 1975.

D. Müller, *Ägypten und die griechischen Isis-Aretalogien* (ASAW.PH 53.1), Berlin 1961.

W. Peek, *Der Isishymnus von Andros und verwandte Texte*, Berlin 1930.

F. Solmsen, *Isis among the Greeks and Romans* (Martin Classical Lectures 25), Cambridge, Mass. 1979.

M. Totti, *Texte* (L23) 1–84.

H. S. Versnel, 'Isis, una quae es omnia. Tyrants against Tyranny: Isis as a Paradigm of Hellenistic Rulership', in Idem, *Ter Unus* (L41) 39–95. Bibliography in L49.

(*a*) The cult

In the passage into the Graeco-Roman sphere, the goddess Isis moves more and more into the centre. She is exalted to the status of an all-embracing deity; for example, as the great healer, she possesses the medicine of immortality.[38] The aretalogies of Isis are significant here: these list the mighty deeds of the goddess in long litanies with self-descriptions. As an example, we take an excerpt from the Isis inscription from Kyme:[39]

> I am Isis, the mistress of the whole land ...
> I am she who discovered fruit on behalf of human beings ...
> I am she who separated the earth from heaven ...
> I discovered navigation ...
> I have shown mortals the initiations [μυήσεις].
> I have taught them to honour the images of the gods ...
> I have established language for Greeks and for barbarians ...
> I am she who is called the legislatrix.

We can follow the penetration of the cult of Isis into Athens from *c*.330 BCE. We find a private cultic association of worshippers of the Egyptian gods on the island of Delos *c*.220 BCE (cf. I/C, 3(*a*)). Those who promoted the worship of the goddess were merchants, soldiers, slaves, travellers, and officials; increasingly, a clergy of Isis was active in missionary work. Some

---

[38] Diodorus 1.25.6: τὸ τῆς ἀθανασίας φάρμακον. Cf. Ignatius, *Eph.* 20:2 on the Eucharist; on this, cf. L. Wehr, *Arznei der Unsterblichkeit* (L157).

[39] Following UUC II.96f.; also in M. W. Meyer, *Mysteries* (L30) 172–4; cf. NDIEC I.10–21; R. MacMullen and E. N. Lane, *Paganism* (L4) 50–4; A. J. Festugière, *Études* (L2) 138–69; Versnel summarises the secondary literature.

of the personnel for the newly erected sanctuaries of Isis were imported from Egypt; with their shaven heads and white vestments, the priests of Isis had a striking appearance. The cult of Isis obtained a foothold in Rome from 200 BCE onwards, but here it had to fight for a long time against strong opposition, due to its bad reputation as a religion of the *demi-monde* with loose morality. Josephus dwells with relish on the details of a scandalous story of the seduction of a respectable Roman matron by her despised wooer in the temple of Isis during the reign of Tiberius (*Ant.* 18.66–80). From the period of Caligula onwards, the cult of Isis began to make progress.

(b) The mysteries

We have evidence about the mysteries of Isis from the early imperial period onwards. Plutarch's treatise about Isis and Osiris is steeped in a remarkable atmosphere pertaining to the mysteries. It is dedicated to the priestess Clea, who served as the chief of the female devotees of Dionysus at Delphi and at the same time was initiated by her parents into the Egyptian mysteries. Plutarch intends to maintain silence about many things, since these belong to the secret doctrine of the mysteries; nevertheless, we find allusions to the mysteries in *Is. et Os.* 2–3 (351f–352b), where the unavoidable *cista mystica* is employed as a metaphor: 'Typhon cuts in pieces and destroys *the sacred teaching*, the goddess gathers it together again, recomposes it and entrusts it to those *who are initiated* ... These are the ones who bear the sacred doctrine about the gods in a pure manner in their soul as in a coffer [ὥσπερ ἐν κίστῃ].' A second passage is even more unambiguous (27 [361d–e]):

> The sister and wife of Osiris, as his helpmate, suffocated and put an end to the mad raving of Typhon. But she did not want her endeavour and the struggles in which she had engaged, her wanderings and the many deeds of her wisdom and her courage to be forgotten and to perish in silence. This is why she blended with the most sacred initiations of the mysteries representations, allusions and imitations of what she had suffered at that time. Thus she created something that gives both instruction in piety and consolation for men and women who experience similar misfortune.

The wanderings and struggles of Isis thus become a stable component of the mysteries. They are recalled by means of narratives, images, and rites, so that those who are in the midst of life's confusions may find in them strength and consolation.

3. Apuleius' book about Isis

List 52.

E. Brandt and W. Ehlers, *Apuleius: Der goldene Esel. Metamorphosen* (TuscBü), Munich and Zurich, 4th edn. 1989.

M. Dibelius, 'The Isis Initiation in Apuleius and Related Initiatory Rites', in F. O. Francis and W. A. Meeks (eds.), *Conflict at Colossae* (SBibSt 4), Missoula 1975, 61–121.

S. Eitrem, 'Elemente' (L37).

J. Gwyn Griffiths, *Apuleius of Madauros: The Isis-Book (Metamorphoses, Book XI)* (EPRO 39), Leiden 1975.

R. Helm, *Apuleius: Metamorphosen oder der Goldene Esel* (SQAW 1), Berlin and Darmstadt, 7th edn. 1978.

K. H. E. de Jong, *Mysterienwesen* (L30) 242–431.

R. Merkelbach, *Roman und Mysterium in der Antike*, Munich 1962.

A. D. Nock, *Conversion* (L3) 138–55.

D. Sänger, *Antikes Judentum und die Mysterien: Religionsgeschichtliche Untersuchungen zu Joseph und Asenath* (WUNT 2.5), Tübingen 1980, 118–47.

V. Tran Tam Timh, *Essai sur le culte d'Isis à Pompéi* (Images et Cultes), Paris 1964.

A. Wlosok, 'Zur Einheit der Metamorphosen des Apuleius', *Ph.* 113 (1969) 68–84.

Our chief informant about the mysteries of Isis is Apuleius, in the eleventh Book of his *Metamorphoses*. Apuleius was born in 125 CE in Madaura (northern Africa) and was a lawyer, orator and writer. He had the office of a provincial priest in the Roman cult of the emperor in Carthage, and testified before a court that he himself had 'taken part in numerous secret cults in Greece, out of a desire for the truth and out of veneration of the gods' (*Apol.* 55.4f.). The narrative thread holding together his burlesque novel of manners concerns the breathtaking wanderings of its protagonist Lucius, who is turned into an ass and gets to know the life of classical antiquity, in all its heights and depths, from this perspective. Apuleius borrows the narrative core from an older Greek model; the Book about Isis at the end is his own addition. It is only Apuleius – not his model – who has the transformation of Lucius back into a man take place at a procession in honour of Isis at Cenchreae, the port lying south of Corinth. But this puts the whole story in a new light: when one follows his own pleasures and lusts, one leads the life of a beast, until the conversion to the religion of Isis permits one to start anew a life that is genuinely worthy of a human being. The transformation of the human being through the ritual of the mysteries is already prefigured (in what is almost a caricature) in the transformation of Lucius from an ass into a human being.[40]

(a) The sequence as a whole

At the beginning of the Isis Book, Lucius, who is still in the form of an ass, addresses a fervent prayer to the heavenly queen, Isis (*Met.* 11.2.1: 'Regina caeli …'). The goddess appears to him in a dream and promises to rescue him, if he eats some of the roses that are borne on the following day in the procession which is held on the occasion of the *navigium Isidis*, the reopening of navigation. She speaks of herself in the style of the aretalogies of Isis (5.1–4), and her promises go beyond the immediate occasion to include also the assurance of her protection in this life and in the life beyond death (6.5):

> But you will lead a happy life, you will lead a life that is renowned under my protection, and when you have measured out the span of this earthly existence and depart to join those in the underworld, you will find … me, whom you now see, radiant in the darkness there in the vault under the earth. You yourself will dwell in the Elysian fields and will continuously adore in me your gracious protectress.

After his metamorphosis Lucius takes up residence in the temple precincts of Isis and takes part in the daily worship there, which is centred especially on the opening of the temple in the morning and its closing in the evening – one of the characteristic traits of the cult of Isis. He feels more and more intensely the wish to be initiated into the mysteries of Isis, but he must wait until a new dream reveals the right time for this. The high priest

---

[40] Merkelbach has supported the principle that classical novels are to be read as coded mystery texts. On the scholarly discussion of his suggestive theses (which however are too one-sided), cf. A. Geyer, 'Roman und Mysterienritual', in *Würzburger Jahrbücher für die Altertumswissenschaft* NF 3 (1977) 179–96; H. Gärtner, *PRE* II/9 (1967) 2074–80.

teaches him the meaning and the sequence of the ceremonies, using secret Egyptian books written in hieroglyphics and demotic characters. After a purifying bath and a ten-day fast, crowds come together on the vigil of the night of initiation and bring Lucius gifts; these are not to be understood as birthday presents (for such would be suitable only on the following morning), but as stylised funeral gifts or donations to the dead. We now move on to the events of the next morning (24.1–5):

> Then after the solemn ceremony was completed, I emerged, sanctified by the twelvefold garment, in what was certainly a very pious procession ... In the centre of the sacred temple, I mounted a wooden dais erected before the image of the goddess, conspicuous because of the garment, which was of fine linen, but with bright embroidery on it ... In my right hand I bore a burning torch, and a garland of palm encircled my head with stately splendour; the individual leaves stood out from it like rays. After I had been set up like a statue, decked out like the sun itself, the curtain was suddenly drawn aside and the mass of the people surged forward to see me. Then I celebrated my birthday feast as an initiate, and there was a delightful banquet and a merry drinking feast.

According to Egyptian beliefs, the twelvefold garment represents the twelve hours of the night, during which the sun-god passes in his barque until he emerges afresh in his splendour on the following morning. The initiate too appears shining like the sun god, or like the newly dawning day, to receive the homage of the crowd. Some days later Lucius addresses a concluding prayer to the goddess, moving and outstanding in its use of language (25.1–6). He leaves for Rome, where he has success as a lawyer. He undergoes two further initiations, but this is not to be understood as different degrees of consecration, but rather as an indication of the autonomous status of the local cultic centres, and of new psychological needs on Lucius' part. Finally, he is given a place among the priests of Isis.[41]

(b) The formulae of the mysteries

Although he has many expressions of the caution that was necessary (23.6: 'I would tell you, if I were allowed to do so; you would learn about it, if

---

[41] Cf. W. Burkert, *Mystery Cults* (L30) 17: 'Professional stress is alleviated by a religious hobby, with the mystery god taking the position of psychiatrist.'

you were allowed to do so'), Apuleius does in fact provide a summary of what happened in the initiation itself (23.8):

> accessi confinium mortis et calcato Proserpinae limine per omnia vectus elementa remeavi, nocte media vidi solem candido coruscantem lumine, deos inferos et deos superos accessi coram et adoravi de proximo.

> I have come to the borders of death and have set my foot on the threshold of Proserpina, I have travelled through all the elements and then returned, at midnight I have seen the sun shining in dazzling white light, I have come into the very presence of the gods below and the gods above, and I have adored them close at hand.

The use of the first person, the past tense, and the brief clauses suggest that here we have an example of the genre of *synthēma*. But there are differences too: this text does not intend to mention individual preparatory actions, as does the password from Eleusis. Rather, it clearly intends to recapitulate in veiled language everything that happens in the initiation, and to give it a symbolic interpretation. It seems perfectly possible that Apuleius has created this text autonomously, on the basis of the *synthēma* genre and employing genuine material from the mysteries of Isis that he himself had experienced. The 'borders of death' and the 'threshold of Proserpina' (goddess of the underworld) belong together. The initiand undertakes a journey to the entrance to the underworld. The 'elements' are the components of which the cosmos is constructed: the initiand comes into contact with these and now understands better what holds the world together. The intentional paradox of the sun shining in 'dazzling white light' at midnight recalls Eleusis, where the flames suddenly shoot up from the *anaktorōn* in the darkness of the night. The Egyptian provenance indicates that behind this lies the encounter between the sun god Re (as Ba) and Osiris (as his corpse). The entire range of the gods is included, from those in the underworld to those in heaven. When the initiand sees them face to face (which may mean that he has experienced the encounter between Re and Osiris), this can be linked to the *epoptia*, the secret vision which is the high point of the whole process.

Various opinions are held about how all of this was realised, and the degree of realism or abstraction that was involved. For example, de Jong attributes everything to suggestion and hallucination. He draws the comparison with occult phenomena, and assumes that mechanical means were employed to produce fraudulent manipulations on a massive scale. Eitrem suggests that perhaps the initiand was buried up to his neck in the earth: this would be the 'burial' and at the same time contact with the element, that is, with mother earth.[42] In Mozart's *Magic Flute* Tamino and Pamina walk over glowing fire and floods of water in the course of the initiation ritual (cf. the two men in armour, who sing: 'The one who takes this path with its many toils becomes pure through fire, water, air and earth; if he can overcome the terrors of death, he propels himself out of the earth to heaven'). Another suggestion is that the initiand was drugged and placed naked in a mummy-coffin, while his imagination played all kinds of tricks with him. A somewhat milder version of the same suggestion proposes that hints of the Egyptian funeral ritual were carried out on the initiand. Griffiths makes a proposal that is sober by comparison: the underground rooms, corridors and crypts in the temples of Isis (the existence of which is demonstrated by archaeology at Pompeii, cf. Tran Tam Tinh), were decorated with frescoes and statues of the gods, with scenes from the underworld and from the myth. The initiand wanders alone, or led by a guide, through these rooms and absorbs the impressions that they make, impressions strengthened by clever use of lighting, sounds, music, etc. If we dissect this suggestion analytically and descriptively, it sounds rather banal. But a sober eye would not have been able to discern much more than this in the reality itself; it was those strong symbolic and emotional values which we are no longer able to reconstruct, that ensured that many of those who submitted to the initiation received indelible impressions from it.

4. Sarapis

List 53.

H. Engelmann, *Aretalogy* (L23).

J. F. Gilliam, 'Invitations to the Kline of Sarapis', in *Collectanea Papyrologica I* (*Festschrift H. C. Youtie*), Bonn 1976, 315–24.

A. Höfler, *Der Sarapishymnus des Ailios Aristeides* (TBAW 27), Stuttgart 1935.

W. Hornbostel, *Sarapis: Studien zur Überlieferungsgeschichte, den Erscheinungsformen und Wandlungen der Gestalt eines Gottes* (EPRO 32), Leiden 1973.

J. E. Stambaugh, *Sarapis under the Early Ptolemies* (EPRO 25), Leiden 1972.

[42] It should however be noted that the Egyptian god of the earth (Geb) was masculine.

M. Vandoni, *Feste* (L22) nos. 125–47.
H. C. Youtie, 'The Kline of Sarapis', *HThR* 41 (1948) 9–29.

There also exist some indications of mysteries of Sarapis, who owes his existence as a god to the religious politics of the Ptolemies and whose cult spread beyond Egypt along with the cult of Isis. Among its characteristic traits were meals celebrated by the group of worshippers of Sarapis. In 143–4 CE Aristides praises Sarapis in his exuberant hymn as 'master of the feast and host', as 'himself both giver and receiver of donations', with whom alone human beings 'celebrate in an especial way the sacrificial fellowship in the true sense of the word', (*Or.* 45.27; cf. Höfler). With his customary sarcasm, Tertullian notes: 'The smoke rising up from the meal of Sarapis alarms the fire brigade' (*Apol.* 39.15). Tickets of invitation to these meals, preserved on papyri, give a very vivid illustration of what went on; these meals were held in private houses or in the sanctuary, and sometimes it was the god himself who issued the invitations (naturally enough, through a human intermediary), as in PKöln 57:[43]

καλεῖ σε ὁ θεός	The god invites you
εἰς κλείνην γεινο(μένην)	to the meal that will take place
ἐν τῷ θοηρείῳ	in the temple of Thoeris
αὔριον ἀπὸ ὥρ(ας) θ'.	tomorrow at the ninth hour.

F. The mysteries of Mithras

List 54.
R. Beck, 'Mithraism since Franz Cumont', *ANRW* II/17.4 (1984) 2002–2115.
——, 'The Mysteries of Mithra: A New Account of Their Genesis', *JRS* 88 (1998) 115–128.
U. Bianchi (ed.), *Mysteria Mithrae. Proceedings of the International Seminar* ... (EPRO 80), Leiden 1979.
CIMRM: see list of abbreviations.
M. Clauss, *Mithras, Kult und Mysterien*, Munich 1990.
——'Mithras und Christus', *HZ* 243 (1986) 265–85.

[43] In B. Krämer and R. Hübner, *Kölner Papyri*, vol. 1 (PapyCol 7), Opladen 1976, 175–7 (with bibliography); also SGUÄ 10496; a recent collection of comparable texts in Totti 124–7; Gilliam (L53); cf. also NDIEC I.5–9.

F. Cumont, *The Mysteries of Mithras*, New York 1956.
Études Mithriaques: Actes du 2e Congrès international Téhéran (Acta Iranica 17), Leiden 1978.
J. R. Hinnells (ed.), *Mithraic Studies: Proceedings of the First International Congress of Mithraic Studies*, vols. 1–2, Manchester 1975.
J. Leipoldt, *Die Religion des Mithra* (BARG 15), Leipzig 1930.
R. Turcan, *Mithras Platonicus: Recherches sur l'hellénisation philosophique de Mithra* (EPRO 47), Leiden 1975.
M. J. Vermaseren, *Mithras – The Secret God*, London 1963.
——'Mithras in der Römerzeit', in Idem, *Religionen* (L2) 96–120.

The name of the Persian god Mithra means 'contract' or 'mediator of a contract'. He has a special affinity to the leagues of men and hunters in ancient Iran. He protects the law of contracts and personifies the foundations of social order. It is not at all easy to grasp correctly the individual details of the myths about the god Mithra, since he does not play the pre-eminent role in the Iranian tradition that one would be inclined to attribute to him on the basis of the Roman mysteries of Mithras (one should note the slight transposition of the name from Mithra to Mithras). Besides this, we possess some of the Iranian sources only in a later written redaction from the Islamic period. These are the main episodes attached to the figure of Mithra: he is born from a rock, he pursues the primal bull, subdues it, drags it into his cave, and kills it, thereby creating the basis that allows the cultivated world to come into existence. In a period of drought, he shoots an arrow at a rock, and water streams forth. He fights against the sun god and is reconciled to him, they make a covenant with one another, eat a farewell meal and then return to heaven, whence Mithra is expected to return at the end of time.

1. The question of origin

List 55.
C. Colpe, 'Mithra-Verehrung, Mithras-Kult und die Existenz iranischer Mysterien', in J. R. Hinnells, *Studies* (L54) II.378–405.
R. Merkelbach, *Mithras*, Königstein 1984.
I. Roll, 'The Mysteries of Mithras in the Roman Orient: the Problem of Origin', *Journal of Mithraic Studies* 2 (1977) 53–68.
D. Ulansey, *The Origins of the Mithraic Mysteries: Cosmology and Salvation in the Ancient World*, New York and Oxford 1989.

A text in Plutarch has sometimes been considered the oldest piece of evidence for the mysteries of Mithras. Here he says of pirates from Asia Minor, against whom Pompey successfully fought: 'They offer foreign sacrifices on the [Lycian] Olympus, and celebrate certain hidden initiations, including those of Mithras, which exist up to the present day and were first founded by them' (*Pomp.* 24.5). Other evidence also points to Asia Minor, e.g. the worship of Mithra (as Apollo and Helios at one and the same time) in Commagene under a royal dynasty whose representatives bore the eloquent name 'Mithridates'. If we follow the dating to the period of Pompey, we come to the year 67 BCE, but it is possible that Plutarch, from his own perspective, has projected some things back in time, in the same way as Herodotus did with the Egyptian rites. A remark in Pliny the Elder also sounds 'Mithraic', although this name is not used: he writes that when King Tiridates journeyed to Rome in order to pay his homage to the emperor Nero, he brought with him in his suite some Persian magicians who 'initiated Nero into the magical meals' after the treaty of vassalage had been signed (*Hist. Nat.* 30.17). The oldest Mithraic inscription from Rome (if the attribution is correct) comes from the year 102 CE. The great wave of inscriptions begins only in the year 140 CE; this had three successive phases, and ebbed away in the fourth century.

The question of origin is increasingly explained by positing the conscious foundation of a cult at the beginning, for example by a consortium of Persian scholars and priests who were acquainted in their own milieu with the essential kernel of a Hellenistic mystery cult.[44] Scholars have paid particular attention to astrology; this certainly provides a key to unlock much of the interpretation of the mysteries, and possibly also provided terminology at the beginning of the cult (Ulansey). The place of origin is identified either as Asia Minor or as Rome (for the latter hypothesis, cf. e.g. Roll).

The mysteries of Mithras display some particularities that distinguish them from the phenotype of the other oriental-Hellenistic cults. Thus, Mithras has no female figure at his side, with the consequence that the Mithraic mysteries remained a religion exclusively for men. Nor is it easy to link Mithras to the type of the 'suffering god'. We have very few texts

---

[44] So Colpe; cf. also Merkelbach 77; M. P. Nilsson, *Geschichte* (L2) 675f.: 'A unique creation by an unknown religious genius.'

indeed that inform us about the Mithraic mysteries; much has to be deduced from sculptures and archaeological discoveries.

2. Grades and rites of initiation

List 56.

H. D. Betz, 'The Mithras Inscriptions of Santa Prisca and the New Testament', *NT* 10 (1968) 62–80, also in Idem, *Hellenismus* (L3) 72–91.

M. Clauss, 'Die sieben Grade des Mithras-Kultes', *ZPE* 82 (1990) 183–94.

J. P. Kane, 'The Mithraic Cult Meal in Its Greek and Roman Environment', in J. R. Hinnells, *Studies* (L54) II.313–51.

R. Merkelbach, 'Priestergrade in den Mithras-Mysterien?', *ZPE* 82 (1990) 195–7.

B. M. Metzger, 'The Second Grade of Mithraic Initiation', in Idem, *Historical and Literary Studies: Pagan, Jewish, and Christian* (NTTS 8), Leiden 1968, 25–33.

M. J. Vermaseren, *Mithraica I: The Mithraeum at S. Maria Capua Vetere* (EPRO 16), Leiden 1971.

——and C. van Essen, *The Excavations in the Mithraeum of the Church of Santa Prisca in Rome*, Leiden 1965.

(a) The grades

The Mithras cult had seven hierarchically ordered grades of initiation, which were considered as having a structure parallel to that of the seven planets. The ascent of the initiand via the various rungs of the ladder of the grades provides an image of the ascent of his soul through the heavenly spheres. Thus he overcomes the power of the heavenly bodies, no longer exposed to the coercion they exert and to the rule of blind chance. Their symbols, linked to the relevant planetary sign, adorn the mosaic floor of a Mithraeum in Ostia (CIMRM 299). Jerome gives a list of their names, assigning these to the corresponding images in a cave of Mithras (*Ep.* 107.2):

> Did not your neighbour Gracchus, when he was urban prefect a few years ago, destroy the cave of the Mithras and all the loathsome images before which the raven, the male bride [the larva of the bee?], the soldier, the lion, the Persian,

the sun as it runs, and the father (*corax, nymphus*,[45] *miles, leo, Perses, heliodromus, pater*) are initiated? He broke them into pieces and removed them.

1. The *raven* is assigned to the planet Mercury. It could be the task of the raven to wait on the other initiands at the festal meal.

2. The title of the second grade causes the greatest difficulties, because the word in this form is otherwise unattested either in Latin or in Greek; related words, however, denote a bride or bridegroom, or the larva of the bee. If one accepts the latter suggestion, this would mean that the initiands at the second stage are in a larval stage that is the transition to something higher. On the other hand, the choice of Venus as the associated planet would be evidence pointing to the 'male bride'. Firmicus Maternus records the acclamation employed here: 'All hail, *Nymphus*, all hail, new light!' (*Err. Prof. Rel.* 19.1).

3. The planet appropriate to the *soldier* is Mars, the god of war.

4. The planet corresponding to the *lion* is Jupiter. The wall of the Mithraeum of Santa Prisca in Rome (*c.*220 CE) depicts a procession of lions, with the inscription: 'Receive the incense-bearing lions, holy father, receive them' (CIMRM 485: 'Accipe thuricremos pater accipe sancte leones'). It may be presumed that most of the worshippers of Mithras reached this grade at the midpoint of the scale of seven. (Clauss takes a different view, seeing a distinction between the mass of the simple initiates on the one hand and those who had the seven priestly grades on the other; Merkelbach has argued against this.)

5. The fifth grade, that of the *Persian*, with the moon as the corresponding planetary symbol, signals more clearly the provenance of the mythical substratum.

6. As one would expect, the sun itself, as planet, corresponds to the *running sun* in the sixth position. Firmicus Maternus assigns to it the acclamation: 'Initiate of the theft of cattle, bound by a handshake to the venerable father' (*Err. Prof. Rel.* 5.2).

7. The *father*, spiritual head of a Mithraic community – the title also occurs in the intensified form *pater patrum*, 'father of fathers' – is under the protection of Saturn. In pictures he bears the headgear of a Persian priest.

---

[45] Despite the difficulties attaching to the second grade, modern scholars no longer follow the earlier conjectures of *cryphius* (the hidden one) or *gryphus* (vulture).

(b) The rites

Each of the seven grades had its own appropriate initiation rite, as we see from the mocking observation of an anonymous Christian author (Ambrosiaster, *Quaest. VNT* 114.11):

> What kind of a game are they playing with veiled eyes in the cave? For their eyes are bound so that they may not feel any disgust at being so shamefully dishonoured. Some flap with their arms like birds with their wings, imitating the voice of the raven. Others again actually roar like a lion. And finally, after their hands have been bound with the intestines of a chicken, some are thrown into pools full of water. Then one called the 'liberator' comes with a sword and cuts open the intestines.

It is no longer possible to reconstruct all the rites in their entire sequence, although we can discern central points, above all for the lower grades which were accessible to a larger number of initiates. In general, ceremonies of purification were involved: for the grades of lion and priest, honey was used (according to Porphyry, *Ant. Nymph.* 15f.; cf. the *leo melichrisus*, 'lion anointed with honey', CIMRM 2269), not water. Tertullian says (*Bapt.* 5) that water was used in general, and this is doubtless correct with regard to the other grades. Stylised tests of courage and ordeals can be guessed at, rather than distinctly recognised, in the frescoes of the Mithraeum in Capua.[46] Appropriate masks or headgear – for example, the garland with outspread rays in the case of the running sun – were set on the head of the initiand. But from then on, an initiate of Mithras will refuse to bear a garland in public, saying: 'Mithras is my garland' (so Tertullian, *De Corona* 15.3, basing on this an appeal to Christian soldiers to cease wearing pagan festal garlands). The Christian apologists were especially offended by certain ritual meals. In his *First Apology* (66.4) Justin proposes a demonological solution, not without its own elegance, to the problem of the similarities to the Eucharist which he himself notices: 'This too has been imitated by the evil demons. It is they who inspire the worshippers in the mysteries of Mithra to do this. For you know, or can now be told, that when they hold the initiations to admit a

---

[46]   UUC III nos. 124–6; cf. R. MacMullen, *Paganism* (L2) 125: a theatrical sword was discovered in a Mithraeum, its tip and handle bound by a bow which was passed around the wearer's body, creating the illusion that he had been pierced by the sword.

new member, they set out bread and a cup of water with a particular form of words.'

Bread and water are a frugal nourishment that well fits the rough life of soldiers, and it may be presumed that they played a role in the initiation into this grade. But more luxurious meals were also held, accompanying a more social phase of community life after the rites of initiation and sacrifice had been carried out. Excavations in Mithraea have brought to light sacrificial knives, sacrificial axes, drinking vessels, and clay tableware. Refuse middens have been found containing the remains of cattle and lambs, bones of fowl and of fish. Two bills for wine, fish, oil, wood, water, radishes, fish sauce, and other things were found scratched on a wall of the Mithraeum in Dura Europos (CIMRM 64f.), and the sum for wine and fish is relatively high in the context of the total sum involved. This shows that the Mithras cult also held festal meals.

The title 'Mithras liturgy' has been given to a section of the great Parisian Magical Papyrus (PGrM IV 475–834) in which the name 'Mithras' occurs and the words μυστήριον and μύστης are frequently employed.[47] But this text does not give a direct presentation of what was performed in the liturgy of the mysteries of Mithras, and a fortiori is this true of Egypt (the provenance of PGrM IV), where we have only very scanty evidence of Mithraean mysteries (cf. CIMRM 91–105: these texts are in part problematic). Rather, traces of concepts and ideas from mystery cults have been preserved as a kind of 'sunken matter' in these directions for the magical ascent of the soul.

3. Place of worship and cultic image

List 57.

L. A. Campbell, *Mithraic Iconography and Ideology* (EPRO 11), Leiden 1968.
J. R. Hinnells, 'Reflections on the Bull-slaying Scene', in Idem, *Studies* (L54) II.290–312.
R. Merkelbach, *Mithras* (L55).
L. M. White, *The Social Origins of Christian Architecture, vol. 2: Texts and Monuments for the Christian Domus Ecclesiae in its Environment* (HThS 43), Valley Forge 1997, 259–429.

[47] Cf. A. Dieterich, *Eine Mithrasliturgie*, ed. O. Weinrich, Leipzig 3rd edn. 1923; M. W. Meyer, *The 'Mithras Liturgy'* (SBLLT 10), Missoula 1976. In R. Merkelbach, *Abrasax* (L75) III.155–83, 233–49, this part of the text is now called the 'liturgy of Pschai and Aion'.

(a) Place of worship

The Christian writers tell us that the initiates of Mithras assembled in a grotto or cave. In the myth, Mithras himself lives in a cave which can be interpreted as an image of the cosmos; and this is why the walls and ceilings were painted with pictures of the planets and stars. The caves were artificially created in cellars or through the construction of closed rooms that admitted no daylight. All Mithraea are constructed in the following manner (as an example, cf. CIMRM 34; UUC III no. 107; see White's valuable catalogue): as long narrow rooms with a passage in the middle and with slightly inclined stone benches on either side reaching to half the height of the walls; the initiates reclined on these in the liturgy and at the meal. The furnishings also include a low altar. The cultic image (see below) had its place on the front wall, usually in relief, but sometimes also as a free-standing statue or a wall painting. A clever use of lighting could let this be seen in the way intended at particular points of the liturgy.[48] Such a Mithraeum had room for no more than between twenty and forty persons. By a conscious decision, larger Mithraea were not constructed; instead, if the need arose, an unlimited number of extra Mithraea could be set up in one and the same place, as was the case in Rome and Ostia.

(b) The iconography

The main cultic image follows a relatively rigid pattern (apart from the portion of CIMRM devoted to images, UUC III nos. 112f. suffice as an example): we see Mithras half kneeling, half standing, his head turned to the side, on the back of the bull which he has forced on to the ground. With his left hand he pulls the animal's head backwards, while his right hand thrusts the dagger into its flank. Ears of corn sprout from the tail of the bull. Besides this, we have varying combinations of a dog which springs at the wound in the bull, a serpent and a scorpion. The ultimate basis of this cultic image is the ambivalence of the sacrificial action: one must kill animals in order to remain alive. This chimes in with ancient creation myths which transpose the act of creation into a sacrifice performed before time began. Reluctantly, but under compulsion, Mithras in his sacrifice assumes the task of a demiurge: the killing of the bull generates life and

---

[48] Cf. R. MacMullen, *Paganism* (L2) 125f., with references to ceilings with openings in the shape of the half-moon and the stars and reliefs, and to reflecting materials and curtains that could be raised suddenly.

fruitfulness on earth. This is also the context of the much-discussed inscription on the wall of the Mithraeum in Santa Prisca (third century CE) which includes the words: '[nos] servasti eternali sanguine fuso', 'You have saved [us] by the shedding of eternal blood' (CIMRM 485).

Often we find the figures of two attendants nearby, one with a raised torch and the other with a lowered torch (Cautes and Cautopates, the morning star and the evening star). In the mosaic pavement in Ostia the raised torch is an attribute of the *heliodromus*. The attendant with the lowered torch is presumably a Persian. What this means (following Merkelbach) is that the various grades of initiation have found a place in the cultic image. The highest grade, that of *pater*, corresponds in the image to Mithras himself. The lion is either represented by the dog, or else directly depicted. The *miles* corresponds to the scorpion and the *nymphus* to the serpent, while the raven is frequently portrayed directly (e.g. CIMRM 35, in the upper left corner).

The scene of the killing of the bull can be framed by smaller pictures from the myth. The repertoire of these accompanying scenes includes one showing Mithras and the sun god eating a meal in the grotto. Some cultic reliefs are worked on both sides and can be turned on an axis; on the front there is the well-known canonical cultic image, and on the back a separate scene of a meal with a rich elaboration of detail (CIMRM 1896; UUC III no. 115). This surely reflects what was performed in the liturgy. In the first part of the celebration, the front of the relief, depicting the scene of the killing, recalled the great deed of Mithras, then the cultic image was reversed and the depiction of the meal accompanied the meal in the second part of the celebration.

4. Spread and significance of the Mithras mysteries

List 58.

R. Beck, 'The Mithras Cult as Association', *SR* 21 (1992) 3–13.

W. M. Brashear, *A Mithraic Catechism from Egypt* (Tyche.S 1), Vienna 1992.

M. Clauss, *Cultores Mithrae: Die Anhängerschaft des Mithras-Kultes* (Heidelberger Althistorische Beiträge und Epigraphische Studien 10), Stuttgart 1992.

C. M. Daniels, 'The Role of the Roman Army in the Spread and Practice of Mithraism', in J. R. Hinnells, *Studies* (L54) II.249–74.

R. Merkelbach, *Mithras* (L55).

A. D. Nock, 'The Genius of Mithraism', in Idem, *Essays* (L2) I, 452–8.

It is possible to state with relative precision the geographical spread of the Mithras mysteries. Greece remained inaccessible to the god of the ancient Persian enemy; the same is true of parts of Asia Minor, Palestine and Egypt. Most of the archaeological discoveries have been made in Rome and Ostia on the one hand, and in the military centres along the Roman border on the other. The field of excavations in Ostia, which encompasses something under half of the classical city, has brought seventeen or eighteen Mithraea to light. Merkelbach's model calculation for Ostia reckons that of the sixteen thousand adult men in the city about twelve hundred were worshippers of Mithras, distributed among thirty Mithraea. But this percentage (7.5%) is probably atypically high (cf. also Clauss 32–42).

The devotees of Mithras were recruited from the imperial bureaucracy and the Roman army. Essentially, they were civil servants and soldiers. Loyalty to the Roman imperial house was one of the fundamental traits of the cult, and this is why the emperors regarded it with favour and supported it.

Ernest Renan in the nineteenth century said that if late antiquity had not been Christianised, it would have been 'Mithraised'. This famous epigram is too simple, for the cult of Mithras had too many limitations of a social, ethnic, and geographical nature, which prevented it from spreading. First, women (with a few exceptions) were excluded, and the members were recruited from a relatively homogeneous social group; secondly, no matter where the cult became established, it always remained a kind of import, with no genuine rooting in the local populace; and thirdly, the geographical distribution, with Rome as its centre and the border territories, was uneven. Here, a remark of Adolf Harnack continues to be apposite: if one compares maps of the spread of Christianity and of the worship of Mithras, then one finds that, with the exception of Rome, 'what is white on the one map is black on the other, and vice versa'.[49]

Nevertheless, the comments of the Church fathers reveal that the Christians regarded the cult of Mithras as an especially dangerous enemy. We see this anew in the fourth century, when the worship of Mithras was coming to its end. Some Mithraean sanctuaries were systematically

[49] A. Harnack, *Die Mission und Ausbereitung des Christentums in den ersten drei Jahrhunderten*, vols. 1–2, Leipzig 4th edn. 1924, 939.

destroyed by Christians, but there was also a preference for building Christian churches over the ruins of Mithraea; San Clemente in Rome is an impressive example of this. Nor should we fail to mention 25 December, the day of the solstice, the feast of the *sol invictus* – the unconquered and unconquerable sun god closely associated with Mithras. This was the day on which the Christians located the celebration of the birth of Jesus.

G. Evaluation

List 59.

L. Alvar et al., *Cristianismo primitivo y religiones mistéricas*, Madrid 1995.

G. Anrich, *Das antike Mysterienwesen in seinem Einfluss auf das Christentum*, Göttingen 1894, reprint Hildesheim 1990.

W. Bousset, 'Christentum und Mysterienreligion', *ThR* 15 (1912) 41–61.

F. E. Brenk, 'A Gleaming Ray: Blessed Afterlife in the Mysteries', *Illinois Classical Studies* 18 (1993) 147–64.

M. Brückner, *Der sterbende und auferstehende Gottheiland in den orientalischen Religionen und ihr Verhältnis zum Christentum* (RV 1.16), Tübingen 1908.

O. Casel, *Die Liturgie als Mysterienfeier* (EcOra 9), Freiburg i.Br. 3rd–5th edn. 1923.

L. Cerfaux, 'Influence des Mystères sur le Judaisme Alexandrin avant Philon', in *Recueil Lucien Cerfaux*, vol. I (BETHL 6), Gembloux 1954, 65–112.

C. Colpe, 'Mysterienkult und Liturgie: Zum Vergleich heidnischer Rituale und christlicher Sakramente', in Idem et al. (eds.), *Spätantike und Christentum: Beiträge zur Religions- und Geistesgeschichte der griechisch-römischen Kultur und Zivilisation der Kaiserzeit*, Berlin 1992, 203–28.

E. R. Goodenough, *By Light, Light: The Mystic Gospel of Hellenistic Judaism*, New Haven 1935.

W. Heitmüller, *Taufe und Abendmahl im Urchristentum* (RV 1.22–23), Tübingen 1911.

H. J. Klauck, 'Die Sakramente und der historische Jesus', in Idem, *Gemeinde – Amt – Sakrament: Neutestamentliche Perspektiven*, Würzburg 1989, 273–85.

——*Herrenmahl* (L5).

G. Lease, 'Jewish Mystery Cults since Goodenough', *ANRW* II/20.2 (1987) 858–80.

B. M. Metzger, 'Methodology in the Study of the Mystery Religions and Early Christianity', in Idem, *Studies* (L56) 1–24.

A. D. Nock, 'Hellenistic Mysteries and Christian Sacraments', in *Essays* (L2) II.791–820.

J. Pascher, *Η ΒΑΣΙΛΙΚΗ ΟΔΟΣ: Der Königsweg zu Wiedergeburt und Vergottung bei Philon von Alexandreia* (SGKA 17.3–4), Paderborn 1931.

C. P. Price, 'Mysteries and Sacraments', in *Christ and His Communities* (Festschrift R. H. Fuller) (AThR.Suppl. 11), Evanston, Ill. 1990, 124–39.

D. Sänger, *Judentum* (L52).

A. J. M. Wedderburn, *Baptism* (L5).

D. H. Wiens, 'Mystery Concepts in Primitive Christianity and Its Environment', *ANRW* II/23.2 (1980) 1248–84.

G. Wobbermin, *Religionsgeschichtliche Studien zur Frage der Beeinflussung des Urchristentums durch das antike Mysterienwesen*, Berlin 1896.

D. Zeller, 'Die Mysterienkulte und die paulinische Soteriologie (Röm 6.1–11): Eine Fallstudie zum Synkretismus im Neuen Testament', in H. P. Siller (ed.), *Suchbewegungen: Synkretismus – Kulturelle Identität und kirchliches Bekenntnis*, Darmstadt 1991, 42–61.

As I mentioned at the beginning of this chapter, it would be possible to make several other additions to the list of lesser mystery cults. We should find particular interest in those cults which can be localised in some way in proximity to the New Testament, such as the mysteries of Artemis of Ephesus, known from Acts 19,[50] or the mysteries of a local hero (unimportant in himself) very close to Corinth.[51] We also have cases such as that of Adonis, where one would incline to assume the existence of a mystery cult of a divine personage, but with no convincing evidence of this.[52] But we must stop here in order to present some reflections on this topic as a whole.

---

[50] On this cf. R. Oster, 'The Ephesian Artemis as an Opponent of Early Christianity', *JAC* 19 (1976) 24–44, at 38.

[51] Cf. H. Köster, 'Melikertes at Isthmia: A Roman Mystery Cult', in *Greeks, Romans, and Christians* (Festschrift A. J. Malherbe), Minneapolis 1990, 355–66.

[52] R. Turcan, *Cultes* (L2) 146, rejects the existence of mysteries of Adonis.

The Hellenistic mystery cults play a decisive role in the argumentation of the representatives of the school of the history of religions (see the Introduction, above), in two ways. First, they postulate a genetic derivation of the Christian sacraments from the quasi-sacramental rites of the mystery cults (initiation, washings, anointings, sacred meals); they see the Christian sacraments as having no basis in the message of Jesus and in Palestinian biblical Judaism, but rather as the outcome of a process of Hellenisation which is evaluated as a lapse from the original purity of the gospel, whether this is dated (with Heitmüller) already before Paul, or (with Harnack: see p. 148, n. 49) only outside the New Testament itself, in the second century. Secondly, it is further argued (see Brückner) that the myth of the dying and rising again of a divinity, which lies at the centre of each cult, was a significant influence on earliest Christianity's image of Christ, which drifted off into myth.

Odo Casel, an important Catholic theologian and member of the Benedictine order in the first half of this century, developed very similar lines of thought, but with the opposite intention: he considers the classical mysteries as a kind of preparatory school for Christianity. These had a function to fulfil under divine providence, since they made ready models of thought and concepts that could not be found elsewhere, but were necessary for the development of the doctrine of the sacraments. He speaks also, in 'flowery' language, of the form of these cults, which needed to be redeemed: 'Right alongside the noblest movements of the soul, the dark forces of sensuality and self-seeking are at work, and only too often do they suffocate the striving for better things ... One feels like someone wandering in the tropics – he delights in the luxuriant fruitfulness, the colourful splendour of flowers and birds. But often his foot breaks the crust of rotten matter; sultry fragrances confuse his senses; in the thickets, the beast of prey lies in wait and the poisonous snake darts out its tongue' (43).

When scholars today speak of the dying and rising again of the divinities in the mystery cults, they do so as it were in quotation marks, with much more reserve than in the days of Brückner and Casel. One must see this 'type' in a more differentiated manner, since it does not apply to many divine figures, and there is nowhere anything exactly comparable to the Christian hope of resurrection (Wedderburn; Zeller). In the case of the sacraments, it is possible to demonstrate that they can be connected to actions of the earthly Jesus which had the character of eschatological signs, which become sacraments in the post-Easter transformation, no doubt also in intensified contact with Hellenistic thought (Klauck). The mediating function of Hellenistic Diaspora Judaism was also overlooked by earlier scholars. For reasons of apologetics and in the missionary hope of winning converts, with the intention of ensuring that its own tradition remained competitive and attractive, Diaspora Judaism adopted to a certain extent the language and the ideas of the mysteries,[53] without adopting the polytheistic mythology linked to these, and without substantially endangering its own faith. This tactic may have been successful, at least in regard to endangered members within its own ranks. But one must also bear in mind that despite a higher evaluation accorded to certain rites, Judaism did not develop any sacraments in the narrower sense of the word; it still does not have any sacraments, and tends to be critical of Christian sacramental praxis.

This means that no one today would wish to put up an unqualified defence of the main theses of the founders of the school of the history of religions. But this does not mean that the last word has been spoken on the subject of the relationship between the mystery cults and early Christianity. At any rate, the indisputable similarity of many phenomena remains interesting from an anthropological perspective. It is clear that certain modes of religious behaviour and forms of experience are deeply anchored in the human person, because they are closely linked with fundamental individual and societal experiences, and only limited potential resources of expression are available to deal with these – there are simply not unlimited numbers of gestures and actions that one might chance upon. This is true especially when a relatively homogeneous cultural background can be discerned, and this is the case in the Mediterranean world in the classical period, despite all its ethnic variety and political plurality. The mystery cults too are an intrinsic element of the non-Jewish horizon of the reception of the Christian message. They too are embraced by the process of the inculturation of Christianity in its initial phase, and they make their own contribution to this process. In my opinion, the Christian doctrine of the sacraments, in the form in which we know it, would not have arisen without this interaction; and Christology too understood how to 'take up' the mythical inheritance, purifying it and elevating it.

[53] Cf. *inter alios* Cerfaux; Sänger; Lease. I mention only in passing that here too exaggerations have occurred (e.g. thanks to Pascher and Goodenough; on this, see the bibliography, especially Riedweg [L30]).

Chapter III
Popular Belief: A Panorama – Astrology, Soothsaying, Miracles, Magic

List 60.

E. Ferguson, 'Personal Religion' in *Backgrounds* (L3) 165–97.

A. J. Festugière, *Personal Religion among the Greeks* (Sather Classical Lectures 26), Berkeley 1954.

A. Kehl, 'Antike Volksfrömmigkeit und das Christentum', in J. Martin and B. Quint, *Christentum* (L3) 103–42.

J. Leipoldt, *Von Epidauros bis Lourdes: Bilder aus der Geschichte volkstümlicher Frömmigkeit*, Hamburg and Bergstedt 1957.

G. Luck, *Magie und andere Geheimlehren in der Antike* (KTA 489), Stuttgart 1990.

J. D. Mikalson, *Athenian Popular Religion*, Chapel Hill and London 1983.

M. P. Nilsson, *Greek Popular Religion* (LHR NS 1), New York 1940.

E. des Places, 'Religion populaire et culte domestique' in *Religion* (L2) 147–53.

E. Stemplinger, *Antiker Volksglaube* (Sammlung Völkerglaube), Stuttgart 1948.

Popular religion, popular faith, popular piety – these and similar expressions are frequently used in the academic discussion of religion (as examples, see Kehl; Nilsson; Stemplinger, etc.), but it is not so easy to demarcate from other religious spheres the phenomena which these concepts are intended to identify. This can be seen, for example, in the fact that Ferguson subsumes the matters in question under the heading of 'personal religion', although this concept surely rather denotes a form of piety which is the object of conscious reflection on the part of the individual believer, and hence would be the exact opposite of 'popular religion' (cf. Festugière, although he too has two chapters on 'popular piety' [68–104]). One is tempted to agree with the following criticism: 'This concept, which the school of the history of religion liked to employ at the beginning of this century and which has once again become fashionable among Anglo-Saxon scholars, is exceedingly vague and does not correspond to any Greek concept.'[1]

Nevertheless, without making any exalted theoretical claims, we employ here the concept of 'popular faith' to embrace phenomena that partly converge upon and complement the exercise of religion in the city and the house, and partly act as a competitor and alternative to this (these phenomena are also covered by Luck in his valuable collection of material). We shall speak of miraculous healings, oracles, magic, and astrology; this order is suggested in part by the significance of these matters for a comparison with earliest Christianity.

We may recall here what was said in the Introduction about the Acts of the Apostles. Miraculous healings, some even with magical colouring (Acts 5:14; 19:12) accompany the working of the Christian missionaries, with the result that they are worshipped as gods (14:11–13; 28:6). The servant girl in Philippi has 'the spirit of a Pythia' (16:16), recalling the soothsaying Pythia in Delphi. Simon in Samaria and Barjesus on Cyprus are called magicians (8:9; 13:6); Barjesus may also have been an astrologer. We may also mention here the 'magi from the east' who have seen a star rising (Mt 2:1f.), and the 'seven stars in the right hand' of the one who appears in the opening vision of Revelation (1:16). As for the present, I mention only the fact that horoscopes enjoy immense popularity. Expressions such as the 'Pythia of Allensbach'[2] or the 'Lourdes of classical antiquity' (cf. Leipoldt) make clear how this transference works in both directions.

A. Miracles of healing

1. A place of healing: Epidauros

List 61.

S. B. Aleshire, *Asklepios at Athens: Epigraphic and Prosopographic Essays on the Athenian Healing Cults*, Amsterdam 1991.

E. J. and L. Edelstein, *Asclepius: A Collection and Interpretation of the Testimonies*, vols. 1–2 (Publications of the Institute of the History of

---

[1] L. Bruit Zaidman and P. Schmitt Pantel, *Religion* (L2) 66.
[2] [Translator's note: Allensbach in Germany is the seat of an institute for research into popular opinion and belief, which regularly publishes the results of its polls.]

Medicine 2.2), Baltimore 1945, reprints New York 1975, Baltimore 1998.

R. Herzog, *Die Wunderheilungen von Epidauros: Ein Beitrag zur Geschichte der Medizin und Religion* (Ph.S 22.3), Leipzig 1931.

A. Krug, *Heilkunst und Heilkult: Medizin in der Antike*, Munich 2nd edn. 1993.

F. Kutsch, *Attische Heilgötter und Heilheroen* (RVV 12.3), Giessen 1913.

M. Lang, *Cure and Cult in Ancient Corinth: A Guide to the Asklepieion* (American Excavations in Old Corinth. Corinth Notes No. 1), Princeton 1977.

L. R. LiDonnici, *The Epidaurian Miracle Inscriptions: Text, Translation and Commentary* (SBL.TT 36), Atlanta 1995.

G. Luck, *Magie* (L60) 171–204.

H. Müller, 'Ein Heilungsbericht aus dem Asklepieion von Pergamon', *Chiron* 17 (1987) 193–233.

W. Müri, *Der Arzt im Altertum* (TuscBü), Munich and Zurich 5th edn. 1986.

F. T. van Straten, 'Gifts for the Gods', in H. S. Versnel, *Worship* (L2) 65–151, esp. 105–51 with illustrations in the appendix.

O. Weinreich, *Antike Heilungswunder: Untersuchungen zum Wunderglauben der Griechen und Römer* (RVV 8.1), Giessen 1909, reprint Berlin 1969.

A. Weiser, *Was die Bibel Wunder nennt: Ein Sachbuch zu den Berichten der Evangelien*, Stuttgart 1975, 36–41, 164–67.

L. Wells, *The Greek Language of Healing from Homer to New Testament Times* (BZNW 83), Berlin 1998.

M. Wolter, 'Inschriftliche Heilungsberichte und neutestamentliche Wundererzählungen: Überlieferungs- und formgeschichtliche Betrachtungen', in K. Berger et al., *Studien und Texte zur Formgeschichte* (TANZ 7), Tübingen 1992, 135–75.

R. Wünsch, 'Ein Dankopfer an Asklepios', *ARW* 7 (1904) 95–116.

D. Zeller, *Christus* (L3) 58–65.

(*a*) The god Asclepius

The desire for bodily health and comfort, and the fear of illness, pain, and death are essential motivating factors of human conduct. In the classical period, a respectable medical science offered an answer to these concerns; it was based on empirical observations and developed startling insights (see

155

the selection of texts conveniently assembled by Müri). It is linked to the names of Hippocrates (fifth century BCE), the main representative of the medical school on the island of Cos, and of Galen of Pergamum (*c*.130–200 CE). But this was only one aspect; for gods, heroes, miracle workers and miraculous places also promised healing. It is not always easy to draw precise boundaries: 'In Greek and Roman culture, a medicine drawing on science and philosophy, and popular practices and cults of healing, stood side by side, without excluding one another, and indeed sometimes influencing each other' (Krug 7).

The god of healing, who emerged into greater prominence from among a number of older heroes and gods of healing and gradually came to occupy the centre of human hopes for healing, was Asclepius (Latinised as Aesculapius). The epics of Homer do not yet know this late arrival in the world of the Greek gods; here the god Apollo himself is one of those who perform healings. But a brief text of five lines in the so-called Homeric Hymns (no. 16, from the fifth century BCE) mentions him, presenting him as the son of Apollo and of the Thessalonian princess Koronis. Pindar describes his working as a mortal doctor among human beings, in an ode from 474/3 BCE:[3]

> All those who now came with a tumour on the body that grew by itself,
> or with limbs damaged by grey iron
> or by a stone flung from a distance,
> or with bodies scorched by the burning heat of summer or by winter,
> he set free from whatever torments each individual suffered,
> treating some with a mild magical spell,
> giving others a healing drink
> or binding dressings with ointment about their limbs.
> He restored others to health through amputation.

After his death Asclepius is raised to the rank of a hero, before finally attaining the status of a god, with an associated family. We should mention his daughter Hygieia, the personification of health and well-being, who was venerated together with him.

---

[3] *Pyth.* 3.47–56; text and German translation in O. Werner, *Pindar: Siegesgesänge und Fragmente* (TuscBü), Munich 1967; see also D. Bremer, *Pindar: Siegeslieder* (TuscBü), Munich and Zurich 1992; E. Dönt, *Pindar: Oden* (RecUB 8314), Stuttgart 1986; W. H. Race, *Pindar*, vols. 1–2 (LCL 56; 485), Cambridge, Mass. and London 1997.

After he had become a god, it was in principle possible for Asclepius to be worshipped everywhere. On the island of Cos, seat of the medical school, there was also a temple of Asclepius. The poet Hero(n)das, who came from Cos, describes the following scene about 250 BCE (*Mimiambi* 4):[4]

> Two women visit the temple of Asclepius with their female slave. Since they are poor, all they can sacrifice (instead of a bull or a pig) is a cockerel (12f.: 'Receive as a modest gift this cockerel, the herald of my household walls') and sacrificial loaves. They also wish to have a dedicatory tablet set up as thanksgiving for a healing that has been granted by the god (16–18: 'as a reward for the healing of illnesses that you, O Lord, have taken away by the laying on of your kind hands'). While they are looking at the works of art in the temple, the minister of the sanctuary sacrifices the cockerel on the altar. His salary is one leg of the bird, while the women take the rest home and eat it there. Besides this, they are given τῆς ὑγιίης for their journey, i.e. some of the barley bread that they had brought to the temple: now that it has been consecrated to the god, it has become health-giving bread.

There were, however, no therapeutic treatments, properly so called, in the temple on Cos; these were always reserved for the doctors. The distinguishing characteristic of the other centres of the cult of Asclepius was that they did provide therapy. I mention here only some of these sanctuaries, in cities we know from the New Testament, e.g. Athens and Corinth. The cult of Asclepius was introduced to Athens in 420 BCE in connection with a plague, and the tragedian Sophocles was a leading figure in its introduction. The sanctuary lies on the southern slope of the Acropolis. Excavations in Corinth have brought to light fine precincts of Asclepius, on two levels on the northern periphery of the city but still inside the walls (cf. Lang). Their dining rooms for visitors and patients make very vivid Paul's warning (1 Cor 8:10) not to eat meals in temples of the gods. The cult of Asclepius was introduced to Rome in 292/1 BCE. The god's temple was on an island in the Tiber (cf. the inscriptions in SIG 3/1173). But in the imperial period, it was the Asklepieion of Pergamum (cf. Müller) that took precedence over all others. It lay somewhat outside the city and comprised several buildings: a portico, a small theatre, two temples, a sacred spring, altars, and a library. We have especially good literary information about this sanctuary of Asclepius through the writings of the rhetor Aelius

---

[4] I. C. Cunningham, *Herodas: Mimes* (LCL 225), Cambridge, Mass. and London 1993; cf. Wünsch.

Aristides (b. 117 CE), who was driven by a lengthy illness to seek help in the Asklepieion of Pergamum in therapies that lasted for years and were sometimes a torment to him. During this period, he lived in the precincts of the sanctuary and composed 'sacred orations' in praise of the god. Here he relates, for example, how he smeared himself with mud in frosty weather at the god's command, then ran three times round the temple and bathed in a spring; on another occasion, he drank absinthe diluted with vinegar, and experienced a miraculous relief.[5]

(*b*) The sanctuary

From the sixth century BCE onwards Asclepius found his own dwelling near Epidaurus on the eastern coast of the Peleponnese. His myth was rewritten for local purposes, so that it was now said that Asclepius had been born in the sanctuary of Epidaurus and healed the sick and raised the dead there already in his boyhood. The sacred precincts present an impressive aspect even today, and not merely because of the well-preserved theatre with its excellent acoustics; the site includes principal and lesser temples, altars, a puzzling round building (as at Delphi) called a *tholos*,[6] as well as wells and baths for purification and for therapeutic treatment, storehouses, a gymnasium, and buildings where pilgrims could sleep; there is also a stadium for athletic competitions. But something characteristic of the sanctuaries of Asclepius is one or two rooms where the priests brought the sick in the evening, so that they could lie there: while they slept, a vision in a dream should bring relief to their suffering.

We can learn from Aristophanes what went on around this sleep (*incubatio*). His parody mocks the temple of Asclepius in Athens, but its fundamental lines can also be transposed to Epidaurus. The slave Karion

---

[5] Cf. extracts from the texts in Luck 189–94; K. Latte, *Religion* (L4) 3f.; also H. O. Schröder, *Publius Aelius Aristides: Heilige Berichte* (WKLGS), Heidelberg 1986; P. W. van der Horst, *Aelius Aristides and the New Testament* (SCHNT 6), Leiden 1980; C. Jones, 'Aelius Aristides and the Asklepieion', in H. Koester (ed.), *Pergamon* (L100) 63–76.

[6] On the supposition by earlier scholars that the cellar room was destined for the sacred serpents of Asclepius, cf. Krug 132: 'It is certain that the sacred serpents of the god were not kept in the labyrinthine, completely dark crypt, since snakes love warm and sunny places. Rather, the "snake pit" was created by the imagination of the nineteenth century!'

tells his mistress how it came about that Ploutos, the blind god of wealth, was healed of his blindness (*Pl.* 653–748):

KARION: The first thing we did on arriving at the temple
with our master ...
was to lead him to the sea
and wash him.
LADY: By Zeus, a bath in cold water –
not much fun for an old man!
KARION: Then we went back to the sanctuary
and placed our sacrifice, bread and cakes,
on the altar, 'to nourish Hephaistos' glow',
then, according to sacred custom, we brought Ploutos
to his bed, arranging our own straw mat beside him.
LADY: Were there others there, looking for healing?
KARION: Many others besides, with all kinds of ailments
afflicting them! – Well, the temple servant then extinguished
the lamps and told us to sleep calmly ...
I opened my eyes and saw – the priest!
He was stealing the cakes and figs from the table of sacrifice,
walking round the altar and sniffing,
to see if there might be a sacrificial loaf left over somewhere ...
he [the god] now went round from bed to bed
and examined and checked the sick ...
Then he sat beside Ploutos, touched all round his head
and took a clean cloth and wiped his eyelids;
Panakeia[7] covered his head and face all round
with a purple veil. Suddenly the god snapped his fingers,
and two enormous serpents shot forth from within ...
these crept gently up under the veil
and it seemed to me that they licked his eyelids,
and before you, my lady, could drink ten goblets of wine,
Ploutos stood on his feet and could see!
I clapped my lands loudly, for sheer joy
and woke my master. At once, the god with his serpents
vanished in the sanctuary ...
I sang hymns of praise to the god,
since he so quickly allowed Wealth to gain his sight.
LADY: O Lord and God, how great is your power!

[7] A daughter of Asclepius.

159

A further note on the history of the Asklepieion of Epidaurus: as I have already mentioned, this began before 500 BCE, and the inscriptions which we shall now discuss are dated between 350 and 300 BCE. The inscription of Apellas (SIG 3/1170; see below) belongs to the second century CE, and the latest extant votive inscription in Epidauros comes from the year 355 CE (IG IV 2/438).

(*c*) The accounts of miracles

Surviving texts

Pausanias visited this area *c.*170 CE, and describes Epidaurus as follows in the account of his travels (*Graec. Descr.* 2.27.3):

> In ancient times a greater number of inscriptions stood in the sacred precincts; six of these remain to the present day, with the names of the men and women who were healed by Asclepius, as well as the illness afflicting each one and the manner of the cure. These are written in the Doric tongue.

We know even less today than Pausanias; of these six columns, archaeologists have discovered three, with fragments of a fourth. This collection of inscriptions is the best known and most instructive bequest of Epidaurus.

The Greek text, with a German translation of the seventy items, complemented by other evidence (e.g. from the sanctuary of Asclepius in Lebena on Crete), is found most conveniently in Herzog's indispensable book (the enumeration here follows his: W1, etc.). In English we now have Li Donnici's valuable edition and translation. The full Greek text is in IG IV 2/1,121–4; for the first two columns, also SIG 3/1168–9; cf. also Edelstein I no. 423 (with English translation); some individual texts in two languages also in Müri 432–7; NDIEC II.21–3. Best German selection in M. P. Nilsson, *Religion* (L4) 88–91; also Luck 180–5; UUC II.68f. The inscription of Apellas (details below): IG IV 2/1,126; SIG 3/1170; Herzog 43–5; Luck 187–9; Müri 436–9; K. Latte, *Religion* (L4) 35f.

Titles

After a formulaic 'God! Good luck!', the inscriptions bear the title: 'Healings [ἰάματα] of Apollo and of Asclepius'. The title is in fact incorrect, since it is only Asclepius who works as the god of healing in the accounts; but in the myth Apollo is his father, and the de facto development changed an older sanctuary of Apollo into a sanctuary of

Asclepius, in which a small altar preserved Apollo's right of residence. But the title is misleading for a further reason: namely, that not only healings are involved, although these predominate. For example, a broken goblet is repaired (W10). Questions put to the oracle about lost gold (W46, 63) or a son who has gone missing (W24) are answered in a dream. We also find the opposite of miracles of healing, viz. miracles of punishment, in which illnesses and misfortunes come upon those who withhold from the temple a gift of money that was intended for it (W7, 47), or cheat the god in financial matters (W22, 55), make fun of his cures (W36), or break the prohibition against looking into the interior of the sanctuary with its sleeping room (W11).

Composition and transmission of the texts
How did these inscriptions come to be written? Who wrote them, and who was responsible for their contents? The very first text (W1) allows us to make extremely instructive observations about this matter:

> Cleo was pregnant for five years. After having been pregnant for five years, she turned to the god for help and slept in the healing-room. As soon as she emerged from this and was outside the sacred precincts, she gave birth to a son. Immediately after his birth, the child washed himself at the well and ran around with his mother. When she had attained this answer to her prayer, she had the following inscription made on her votive gift [ἄναθεμα]: 'Not the size of the tablet [*pinax*] is wonderful, but the god. For five years, Cleo had as it were (ὡς) carried a burden in her womb, until she slept here, and the god made her well.'

In thanksgiving for her cure, Cleo offers a votive gift: a *pinax*, a votive tablet with an inscription. Strabo confirms this when he notes that he has found such *pinakes* in many sanctuaries of Asclepius, with inscriptions on which those who sought help recorded how they had been healed (8.6.15). In their introduction, the inscriptions from the Asclepian sanctuary of Lebena are explicitly derived from older σανίδες (cf. Herzog 52), and we must picture these as wooden tablets with a coating of wax. These have not survived; similarly, the wooden votive tablets, like that of Cleo in Epidaurus, have not survived, because of the material used. This meant that a more permanent kind of collection was required.

When the *pinakes* were copied after a period of time on to the stone columns with their inscriptions, it was possible to produce a smoother text, to simplify the style, but also to intensify the miraculous element. We see this in our example too. According to the older votive tablet, Cleo had borne the burden for five years in her body ὡς ἐκύησε, 'as if she were pregnant', until the healing sleep freed her from this. To be precise, what is involved here is only a fantasy pregnancy, which may have psychological reasons; doctors in the classical period were perfectly familiar with this kind of illness. But this has become something else in the text of the later inscription, which precedes the text of the *pinax* – Cleo was in fact pregnant for five years, and the healing consisted in the ending of her pregnancy through the birth of a boy who was about five years old, a boy who was immediately able to run around and to wash himself in the well; and naturally, because of the prescriptions concerning ritual purity, this birth took place outside the temple area. Thus the initial simpler account of a healing which was intensely desired and then granted was intensified to become a mighty miracle performed by the god.

Construction and contents

This first text also permits us to identify the elements in the construction which Pausanias (see above) had already noted, when he specifies the contents of the inscription: 'the *names* of the men and women who were healed by Asclepius', 'the *illness* afflicting each one', and finally 'the *manner* of the cure'. The third point can be further subdivided into the description of what happens to the one who seeks healing, and the confirmation or demonstration that the healing has been successful (Wolter 142). Thus the genre has the following pattern:

1. The *name* and frequently also the *place of origin* (e.g., W4: 'Ambrosia from Athens'; W6: 'Pandaros from Thessaly') of the men and women who ask for healing. Indirectly, they are summoned as witnesses to the factuality of the miracle that has been performed on them, and as individuals, they offer subsequent individual visitors the possibility to identify with them (Wolter 146).

2. The diagnosis of the *illness* that brought them to Epidaurus. Pregnancy, childlessness and the desire for children are themes found from the first text onwards (W2, 31, 34, 39, 42). Many other sicknesses are mentioned too: a lame hand (W3), lame foot (W 16, 38, 64), lame body (W15, 35, 37, 57, 70), sight in only one eye (W4, 9, 69), blindness (W18, 20, 22, 55, 65), dumbness (W5, 44, 51), headaches (W29), wounds received in battle (W12, 30, 32, 40, 53, 58), ulcers (W17, 27, 45, 61, 66), dropsy (W21, 49), loss of hair (W19!), tapeworms (W23, 25, 41), lice (W28), epilepsy (W62).

3. As with Cleo, most of the *processes of healing* are connected with the healing sleep (*incubatio*) in the *abaton*, the inaccessible innermost room of the temple which was fitted out as a healing room. This is formulated using the following terms: he or she falls asleep, has a dream or sees a vision; the god Asclepius appears and either carries out the healing himself in a dream, or else gives an instruction that later leads to healing. Thus in W6: 'Pandaros of Thessaly with a birthmark on his forehead. In the healing sleep he saw a vision: he dreamed that the god bound a bandage around his birthmark and ordered him to take this off once he came out from the healing room.' W17 notes an incongruity between what is experienced in the dream and the reality itself: a man with a virulent ulcer on his toe falls asleep. A serpent comes creeping up to him, licks his toe with its tongue and thus heals him. But the sick man had seen in his dream 'a young man of beautiful form anointing his toe with ointment'.

4. In the case of Cleo, the obvious *demonstration* of the success is provided by the miraculous boy to whom she gives birth, as he runs about and (voluntarily!) washes himself. But often the healing is simply *noted* by means of expressions such as: 'he emerged healthy'. The demonstration can also assume an aetiological character, e.g. in the case of a cup that is one of the votive gifts in the sanctuary: the story is told of the broken vessel that the god 'made whole again' (W10) in analogy to his other acts of healing. W15 explains how a big stone came to lie before the temple: 'Hermodicus of Lampsacus was lame in his body. [The god] healed this as he lay in the healing room and commanded that when he came forth, he should bring into the sanctuary the largest stone that he could carry. So he brought the stone which now lies in front of the sanctuary' (cf. also the silver pig in W4).

5. The scene about Ploutos in Aristophanes ends with a transition to an act of thanksgiving and praise, i.e. with an acclamation (see above). There is no equivalent to this in the inscriptions from Epidaurus (unless the exceptional quotation from the *pinax* in W1 should be regarded as such; but this would still remain an exception). However, the inscriptions from Rome end with such remarks as: 'The crowd rejoiced together with him', 'He gave public thanks to the god' (SIG 3/1173; cf. Wolter 149f.).

Further examples

This structural outline does not include some particularities. For example, the payment of a modest fee after healing had been attained plays a role in more than the miracles inflicted as punishment (e.g. W22): the few texts preserved from the fourth column seem all to be concerned with this (W67–70), and this takes a humorous turn in W8:

> Euphanes, a boy from Epidaurus. He suffered from renal calculus and slept in the healing room. Then he dreamt that the god stood before him and said: 'What will you give me, if I make you well?' He said: 'I will click my fingers ten times.' The god laughed and said he would free him from his suffering. When day came, he emerged healed.

Lack of faith and mockery must often be overcome. In W3, a man whose fingers are lame does not believe (ἀπιστεῖ) the votive tablets (πίνακας) in the temple, indeed he jokes about them. Similarly, in W4 the one-eyed Ambrosia laughs at the idea that lame and blind persons can recover their health merely because of a dream (cf. also W9, 36). The god does indeed overcome this scepticism through his healing intervention, but the ideal picture of one seeking healing was certainly different from this. W37 confirms (surely against the will of the author of the text) how important for the success of the treatment was the will to attain healing and the belief in the healing powers that slumber within the human person:

> Cleimenes from Argus, lame in his body. He entered the healing room and slept, and saw a vision: he dreamt that the god wound a red woollen bandage round his body and led him a little way outside the sanctuary to bathe in a pool. The water of this pool was exceptionally cold. When he hung back in cowardice, Asclepius said that he would not heal people who were too cowardly for this, but only those who came into his sanctuary to him with the good hope that he would not do anything evil to them, but would send them away healthy. When he woke up, he bathed and emerged without any physical defect.

Operations of varying degrees of difficulty are performed in the dreams. We are still within the realm of what is medically possible, when fingers are forcibly straightened (W3) or an eye is cut open and drops of balsam are poured into it (W4, 9), when bandages are applied (W6), limbs are anointed (W17, 19), and medicinal drinks are given to the sick (W41). One source of what was done in the cultic healing was experiences from medical practice. But these possibilities are left behind, and we enter the sphere of the miraculous, through bold interventions such as that in W27: in the dream, Asclepius cuts open the stomach of a sick man, removes a tumour and sews up the abdominal wall again (cf. W25). This is even more true of W21: a mother sleeps in the sanctuary of Epidaurus, taking the place of her daughter who has dropsy. In her dream she sees the god cutting off the head of her daughter and hanging up the body neck downwards until the excess liquid has run out, then reattaching her head. The daughter, who also has the same dream (we note the motif of the double dream), is healed. The third example of healing is even more crass, involving the motif of the sorcerer's apprentice: it intends to say something about a competing temple. A woman seeks to be delivered from a tapeworm and has a dream in the Asklepieion in Troizen: she sees how the sons of the god (who is not himself there, but dwells in Epidaurus) cut off her head, but are then unable to reattach it to her body. They have to summon Asclepius, who comes on the following night and puts everything right. It follows that it is not a good idea to visit Troizen – it is better to stick to the original at Epidaurus (the same tendency can be seen in W48 too).

All that needs to be said about the Apellas inscription (SIG 3/1170), about five hundred years later, is that it keeps to the fundamental structure of mentioning the name (line 2: 'Marcus Julius Apellas, Idriaean from Mylasa'), the diagnosis (lines 3f.: 'I was frequently ill and had digestive problems'), the healing in a dream and the noting of the success. The prescriptions about what he should eat are very detailed (lines 7–12: 'to eat bread and cheese, celery and lettuce; to bathe alone; to practise the sport of running; to eat slices of lemon, soaked in water ... to smear myself with mud; to go for walks barefoot; to pour wine over myself before entering the warm water in the bath'). Apellas takes his leave, healthy and grateful (line 32: χάριν εἰδώς), after he has paid the fees (line 20). The text is composed in the first person throughout. Unlike the older collection, here we have the isolated *pinax*, so to speak, the individual votive tablet, but this was recorded on stone and therefore need not be copied into a subsequent collection; indeed, its length makes it inappropriate for such a collection.

Other votive gifts that have been found, as well as the inscriptions, are small-scale models of sick and healed limbs: ears, breasts, bodies, an oversize leg with a clearly visible varicose vein (cf. UUC III nos. 22f.; van Straten). These are not so common in Epidaurus, but more so in Corinth, Rome, and other places. There are also reliefs that record the process of healing. One such picture (see UUC III no. 25) with Amphiaraus, an older hero who bestowed healing, displays an astonishing complexity. We see first the sick man on his pallet in the temple; a snake creeps up to him and licks his sick shoulder. At the same time, in a dream, the healing god touches the painful place and uses a flat instrument to apply ointment to it.

Finally, on the extreme right of the picture, the healed man lifts his hands in gratitude and points to a tablet which represents either an inscription of thanks or this relief itself (Herzog 89–91).

Evaluation

We have not yet answered the question of the function of this collection of individual inscriptions on the six columns in Epidaurus (*pace* Pausanias, there were probably no more than this). Why did the officials of the cult collect them and make their style smoother, revising them so that the miraculous element was strongly emphasised, threatening penalties for unbelief and for a reluctance to pay? The spontaneous answer would be that this sought to increase the glory of the god Asclepius and to make propaganda for him; but this was not the primary aim. Even more than the god (who acted only in dreams), Epidaurus was to be praised as the place of healing, and the collection was addressed primarily to the pilgrims who sought healing and came to the temple of Asclepius and spent some time there. Reading these texts gave them the possibility of being strengthened in their hope; they were encouraged to submit to everything demanded of them. Above all, the editors of the collection consciously intended to emphasise, as a constructive element, the records of successful healings, and this was very reasonable on their part, since as a matter of fact those healed will have been fewer than those who left the sanctuary without having their prayer answered. The massive collection of accounts of healing, with its universalising effect attained through mentioning the names and places of origin of those who sought help, diverts the attention from the unfavourable statistics concerning healings.

What actually happened in Epidaurus and the other sanctuaries of Asclepius? No doubt it is easier to ask this question than to answer it. It has sometimes been supposed that the patients were put into a deep sleep through hypnosis or drugs, and that the priests operated on them during this time; but modern scholars have abandoned this hypothesis, since some of the operations experienced in the dreams cannot have been carried out, because of their difficulty. Even in the case of minor operations, one may wonder whether it would have been possible to carry them out at night without attracting attention; and no surgical instruments have been found at Epidaurus. The temple personnel will have restricted their activity to simpler things like bathing the sick, pouring water over them, anointing them, massaging them, straightening their limbs, and giving indications about diet.

No doubt the power of suggestion, autosuggestion, and psychosomatic elements made a substantial contribution to successful healing. Some of the illnesses, such as paralyses, disturbances of the senses of speech and sight, fantasy pregnancies and childlessness may have had psychological causes, and in such cases, healing may mean the removal of blockages in the psyche. There were spontaneous remissions of the symptoms of illness, thanks to the attitude of expectation, to the preceding journey, the initial visit to the splendid sanctuary, the accompanying rites, and the mysterious sleep in a holy place. It will also have been useful to enjoy treatment in a remote country district with many baths and well-planned nourishment. (Herzog 156f.: 'Treatment with water was doubtless carried out in all these places of healing, on the level of nature cures but not in opposition to the state of medical knowledge at that time. There can be no doubt that relaxation in the fresh summer weather, and a period spent in new surroundings and in the healthy forest air, made their own contribution to the improvement of health.')

There remain sufficient differences from academic medicine, with its empirical methodology, to permit us to speak of miraculous healings, or rather to account for the fact that people in the classical period saw miracles here. (Whether or not something is called a miracle often depends on the way those involved choose to interpret their own lives.) There was probably little rivalry between such places of healing and medical skill, since each had its own sector and knew that they depended on each other. But one cannot accept the generalisation that a temple of Asclepius would often have been the last hope for people who could not afford the high fees doctors asked: fees were paid at Epidaurus too, and an examination of the lists of names indicates a mixed public in terms of social background.

If we look briefly at the miracles of healing in the tradition about Jesus,[8] we do indeed note many parallels in the structure of the narrative, in the description of the illnesses and in other motifs, but they are found embedded in a different literary context. There are no catalogues of miracles in the New Testament; they are textual elements which have their place in a larger, overarching narrative. In Epidaurus, we see first the one who seeks help, then Asclepius in the dream; in the gospels, it is the coming of the miracle worker that begins the narrative, and he establishes a direct human relationship with those who are sick. Nor does he need a

---

[8] Cf. Wolter 170–5; M. Dibelius, *From Tradition to Gospel*, London 1934, 164–72.

clearly defined sacred area; the institutionalised practice of healing is replaced by the charismatic healing praxis. Fees are not required, and no miracles are inflicted on human beings as punishments. In Epidaurus there are no exorcisms, since the world is understood differently there, and no evil demons are known as yet; in the New Testament, exorcisms belong together with the healings as fundamental elements of the tradition about miracles.

2. A wonder worker: Apollonius of Tyana

(a) The sources

List 62.

G. Anderson, *Philostratus: Biography and Belles Lettres in the Third Century AD*, London etc. 1986.

E. L. Bowie, 'Apollonius of Tyana: Tradition and Reality', *ANRW* II/16.2 (1978) 1652–99.

F. C. Conybeare, *Philostratus: Life of Apollonius of Tyana*, vols. 1–2 (LCL 16; 17), Cambridge, Mass. and London 1912.

M. Dzielska, *Apollonios of Tyana in Legend and History* (PRSA 10), Rome 1986.

E. Koskenniemi, *Der philostrateische Apollonios* (Commentationes Humanarum Litterarum 94), Helsinki 1991.

——*Apollonios von Tyana in der neutestamentlichen Exegese: Forschungsbericht und Weiterführung der Diskussion* (WUNT 2.61), Tübingen 1994.

E. Meyer, 'Apollonios von Tyana und die Biographie des Philostratos', *Hermes* 52 (1917) 371–424, also in Idem, *Kleine Schriften*, vol. 2, Halle 1924, 131–91.

V. Mumprecht, *Philostratos: Das Leben des Apollonios von Tyana* (TuscBü), Munich and Zurich 1983.

R. J. Penella, *The Letters of Apollonius of Tyana: A Critical Text with Prolegomena, Translation and Commentary* (Mn.S 56), Leiden 1979.

G. Petzke, *Die Traditionen über Apollonius von Tyana und das Neue Testament* (SCHNT 1), Leiden 1970.

W. Speyer, 'Zum Bild des Apollonios von Tyana bei Heiden und Christen', *JAC* 17 (1974) 47–63, also in Idem, *Christentum* (L3) 176–92.

Apollonius of Tyana, a town in Asia Minor, lived in the first century CE (with 4 and 96 suggested as earliest and latest dates for his birth and death).

He was a Pythagorean philosopher (although some hold that he was a Middle Platonist too), an itinerant preacher, a religious reformer and miracle worker, at least in the eyes of those who had a positive opinion of him; Lucian, however, casts suspicion on him as a swindler, when he calls a pupil of Apollonius, who had a very close relationship to the master, 'one of those charlatans who employ magic, the invocation of spirits, and the art of kindling love or hate through magic means, in order to get hold of valuable goods and sneak their way into inheritances' and implies that this has been learned from Apollonius (*Alex.* 5). In some traditions he is seen as a magician, especially skilled in providing talismans that ward off serpents, scorpions, gnats and mice (Petzke 26). But this is not the view taken by our main source, which presents him rather as the divinely gifted worker of miracles and the philosopher who hands on secret wisdom from the East.

This main source is the fantastic biography of Apollonius by Flavius Philostratus (on the text and translation cf. Mumprecht), a sophist and rhetor who is to be dated between 170 and 245 CE; he is the second of several authors with this name. Julia Domna, the Syrian wife of the Roman emperor Septimius Severus, commissioned from him this lengthy account of the life of Apollonius (1.3). Her court took especial delight in wonder workers with an oriental colouring, something that Apollonius had acquired through his journeys, *inter alia* to Babylon, Egypt and India.

More than one hundred years separate the activity of the historical Apollonius and the writing of his biography, which Philostratus completed *c*.222 CE. Philostratus certainly relies on earlier sources for his work, including lost works by Apollonius himself, such as a *Life of Pythagoras* and a work on the bloody sacrifices of animals, which Apollonius decisively rejects, in keeping with Pythagorean thought. In his work Philostratus also quotes from letters of Apollonius. A corpus of about one hundred letters under his name survives (cf. Penella), although most of these are probably pseudepigraphical. Philostratus also knew local oral traditions as well as one or two older biographies, including one by Moiragenes; a note in Origen (*C. Cels.* 6.41) confirms the historical existence of this. But Philostratus takes a critical distance from those who had written before him, and from the traditions on which he draws, since he wishes at all costs to prevent Apollonius from being seen as a mere magician – something that had clearly been the case.

Philostratus himself asserts that he is using the writings of a certain Damis, one of the earliest and most faithful disciples of Apollonius, who recorded what he had experienced in the presence of the master (1.3):

'Under the guidance of Apollonius, he dedicated himself to philosophy and made a record of those journeys of his master in which he himself had taken part, as he assures us. Nor did he forget to mention the thoughts, speeches and prophecies of Apollonius.' But it is not difficult to perceive that this is a transparent fiction intended to make Philostratus' own book more credible (this is the view of the majority of scholars, at least since Meyer; cf. e.g. Bowie, Mumprecht, Dzielska and Koskenniemi; Anderson is confident of the existence of memoirs by Damis, while Speyer assumes a forgery, which would however be earlier than Philostratus himself). Caution seems indicated when one bears in mind the distance in time, the obvious tendential character of the work, and the uncertain state of the sources, but one need not exaggerate the scepticism to the point of doubting the existence of an historical Apollonius. At the same time, one must not simply accept the picture painted by Philostratus, which suits the second and third centuries CE better than the first; in the later period, belief in miracles became stronger among pagans (cf. Koskenniemi).

In the fourth century CE Apollonius was built up as a rival figure to Jesus Christ on the basis of Philostratus' book: the argument was that the classical religion too had its own saviours and healers. And in fact, much in Philostratus is reminiscent of the gospels, though more the apocryphal than the canonical texts. Thus the birth and the end of the hero are surrounded by miraculous events: an Egyptian god speaks to his mother in a dream (1.4), at his birth swans sing (a rather 'flowery' touch), and lightning falls from heaven to earth (1.5), so that those who dwell in the countryside declare that he is the son of Zeus (1.6: παῖδα τοῦ Διός). When he is old enough to go to school, all are astonished by the power of his memory and his beauty (1.5). His end remains an open question: Apollonius vanishes, but it is not quite certain how. No grave is found, and he appears (in a dream?) to an unbelieving disciple. A kind of ascension to heaven from a temple is described, while a choir of virgins sings: 'Leave the earth and come to heaven' (8.30f.). Likewise, there is a parallel to the gospels in the combination of an itinerant life, teaching, and the working of miracles, especially since these include exorcisms (see below). The existence of a loosely constituted group of disciples is also striking.

In view of the period of its composition, one must ask whether perhaps Philostratus himself intended to create an alternative to the Christian tradition about Jesus. This question was frequently answered in the affirmative in the nineteenth century, but more recent scholarship in general answers with a decisive negative. Even if Philostratus knew of the existence of Christianity, there is no evidence that he was interested in it; the related traits can be explained on the basis of narrative laws typical of this literary genre, the general mood of the period, and the general belief in miraculous powers. Koskenniemi (*Forschungsbericht* 193–206) is willing to make an exception only in the case of startlingly similar individual narratives such as that of the raising of the dead (see below) and the apparitions after Apollonius' death. He proposes that the Christian traditions had already had an effect on popular story telling and that it was the latter that was accessible to Philostratus, who did not know the original provenance of such materials. Koskenniemi himself concedes that these suggestions too are extremely hypothetical. Whatever one may wish to conclude here, methodological considerations mean that we must leave open the alternative that from the late second century CE onwards Christian motifs influenced the non-Christian sphere.

(*b*) The wonder worker

List 63.
S. Fischbach, *Totenerweckungen: Zur Geschichte einer Gattung* (FzB 69), Würzburg 1992, 113–54.
D. Trunk, *Der messianische Heiler: Eine redaktions- und religionsgeschicht- liche Studie zu den Exorzismen im Matthäusevangelium* (Herders Biblische Studien 3), Freiburg i.Br. 1994, 276–300.
Bibliography in L62.

In his early years Apollonius spent some time in the temple of Asclepius in Aegae (1.7). This indicates in advance that he is destined to be a healer (and provides a link to our preceding section). Indeed, his first patient, a young man with dropsy and an addiction to alcohol, is told by Asclepius in a dream to consult Apollonius. He cures the sick man, but through good counsels and appropriate warnings (1.9). The subsequent narrative contains some summaries of miracles, emphasising what Apollonius does to help the sick and the dead (e.g. 6.43 at the end); detailed accounts of miracles are however relatively rare in this lengthy book. The tradition concerning miracles occupies proportionally a much higher place in the gospels than in Philostratus. I present here two of these longer texts, which are given the structure of short stories: an exorcism and a raising of the dead.

An exorcism[9]

In Athens Apollonius speaks about the libations offered in sacrifice, and recommends that one should not drink out of the cup used for these, 'but should keep it pure and unstained for the gods'. A dissolute young dandy disturbs him with his rude laughter. One look suffices for Apollonius to make the diagnosis: 'It is not you who are mocking here, but the demon who has taken possession of you without your knowledge.' A narrative commentary is inserted here in confirmation of what Apollonius says: the young man laughs and weeps for no reason, and conducts soliloquies. Apollonius' sharp look has consequences:

> Then the demon cried out in fear and anger, as if he were being burned and tortured, and promised under oaths that he would let the young man go, and never again attack a human being. When Apollonius now spoke to him like a master to a wily, devious and impudent slave, ordering him to leave the young man in a visible fashion, the demon cried out: 'I will knock over that statue over there,' referring to a statue near the royal hall, where the entire scene took place. And this statue did indeed begin to move, and fell over. The noise that this produced, and the applause that followed the general astonishment, were indescribable.

Now a change takes place in the young man, as if he had taken some powerful medicine. He rubs his eyes, as if awaking from a deep sleep, abandons his dissolute way of life and, as a sign of this transformation, takes off his fine clothes and puts on the rough cloak of a philosopher.

One can discern clearly here the typical elements of a narrative of exorcism, as we know these from the New Testament, especially the *apopompē* (the command to the demon to depart) and the demonstration that the demon has left, through the overturning of the statue. One difference is that here the illness of demonic possession is not obvious, but must be diagnosed by the wonder worker. A struggle takes place, but it quickly leads to an unambiguous result: Apollonius is the master, the demon merely a disobedient slave. In this context, Philostratus interprets the older exorcism narrative, which may possibly be influenced also by belief in wonder working statues (cf. Lucian, *Philops.* 18–20), so that it becomes a paradigmatic conversion narrative which propagates the ideal image of the ascetic itinerant philosopher.

[9] *Vit. Ap.* 4.20 (other motifs of exorcism in 2.4; 3.8; 4.10, 25; 6.27). Cf. Trunk (who on 270–6 also deals with Lucian's account of an exorcism with his mocking commentaries, *Philops.* 16).

The raising of a dead person[10]

Apollonius is in Rome, where he incurs the disfavour of Nero and later proves to be a genuine foe of tyranny in his conflict with the emperor Domitian: it is especially his prophetic skill that is regarded as politically subversive. But because his enemies do not dare to arrest him, on account of his 'demonic, superhuman character' (4.44), the following event can take place:

> The following miracle is also related. A girl had died on the day of her wedding, or at least so it seemed, and the bridegroom was already following her bier, weeping and lamenting that his marriage remained so utterly unfulfilled. All of Rome joined in his mourning, since the girl came from a distinguished consular family. When Apollonius encountered the funeral procession, he said: 'Set the bier down! I will stop you weeping because of the girl.' At the same time, he asked what her name was. The crowd believed that he wished to hold a funeral speech, as is so common on such occasions, invoking and depicting the misery of the situation. But he only touched the dead woman, spoke a few incomprehensible words and thus awoke the girl from her apparent death. She began to speak again, and returned to the house of her parents like Alcestis, when she was brought back to life by Heracles. The parents wished to make him a present of one hundred and fifty thousand gold coins, but he told them to give it to the girl as her dowry. I cannot establish – nor would those present on the scene have been able to discover – whether he had discovered in her a spark of life that the doctors had not found (for it is said that Zeus had sent a dew down upon her and that a vapour had arisen from her face), or whether he had summoned the extinguished life back and rekindled it.

The methods of literary criticism permit us here to identify an older narrative which Philostratus has edited and reworked. The redactional layer includes the comparison with Alcestis and Heracles, the refusal of the present (since a true philosopher and genuine wonder worker does not accept money), and also the rationalistic explanation of the miracle in the overlong coda, which is already inserted into the beginning through the words 'at least so it seemed'. What remains in the text before Philostratus began to elaborate it is a popular story of the raising of the dead, transmitted by word of mouth; this may be a local Roman tradition. Typical motifs are the question about her name, the knowledge of which confers power over a person; the touching with his hand, which transmits

[10] *Vit. Ap.* 4.45; cf. Fischbach (also on parallel traditions such as Apuleius, *Flor.* 19).

power; and the reciting of incomprehensible words, which recalls magical formulae. The beginning of the traditional text describes a terrible situation: a young girl dies just as she is about to marry, and the bridegroom follows the bier weeping. The motivation lying behind this was also the incentive for the composition of the love novels of classical antiquity, viz. the forcible separation of two who love each other: and the greatest enemy of love is death. The wonder worker overturns the tragedy of this story, thereby showing that he is a benefactor of human beings.

Philostratus for his part adduces a parallel from Greek mythology, from the saga of Heracles (see Euripides, *Alc.* 1008–1152). Heracles is a guest of king Admetus, who mourns over his dead wife Alcestis, who had taken his death upon herself and descended into the realm of the shades. Heracles is moved by the hospitality which he has been shown despite the fact that it is the period of mourning, and decides to deprive death of its booty. He forces his way into the underworld and restores Admetus' wife to him.

The hypothesis of apparent death is the product of Philostratus' antimagical tendency: Apollonius employs none of the instruments of magic, but discovers a spark of life that the doctors had not been able to find. This implies a passing shot at the medical profession, since the wonder worker is superior to them. We have seen this ambivalent relationship already in the account of Asclepius' healings.

Ironically, Philostratus' rationalistic tendency may mean that he has achieved a more accurate picture of what actually happened than the popular narrative version of the oral tradition. When one examines them more closely, raisings of the dead prove to be intensified healings; they are developed versions of accounts of how life was saved at the very last minute (and one must remember that it is not always possible to define the boundary between life and death with total clarity). In their intensified form, the healings glorify the wonder worker who conquers even death, the greatest enemy. This intensification is also due to missionary and propagandistic aims: they serve to fascinate even more people and to convince them, at least in the world of the narrative.

(c) The 'divine man'

List 64.
G. Anderson, *Sage, Saint and Sophist: Holy Men and Their Associates in the Early Roman Empire*, London 1994.
H. D. Betz, art. 'Gottmensch' II, *RAC* 12 (1983) 234–312.

L. Bieler, *ΘΕΙΟΣ ΑΝΗΡ: Das Bild des 'Göttlichen Menschen' in Spätantike und Frühchristentum*, vols. 1–2, Vienna 1935, 1936, reprint Darmstadt 1967.

B. Blackburn, *Theios Aner and the Markan Miracle Traditions: A Critique of the Theios Aner Concept as an Interpretative Background of the Miracle Traditions Used by Mark* (WUNT 2.40), Tübingen 1991.

G. P. Corrington, *The 'Divine Man': His Origin and Function in Hellenistic Popular Religion* (AmUSt.TR 17), New York etc. 1986.

E. V. Gallagher, *Divine Man or Magician? Celsus and Origen on Jesus* (SBL.DS 64), Chico, Calif. 1982.

C. R. Holladay, Theios Aner *in Hellenistic Judaism: A Critique of the Use of this Category in New Testament Christology* (SBL.DS 40), Missoula, Mont. 1977.

E. Koskenniemi, *Forschungsbericht* (L62) 64–164.

D. L. Tiede, *The Charismatic Figure as Miracle Worker* (SBL.DS 1), Missoula, Mont. 1972.

D. S. du Toit, *Theios anthropos: Zur Verwendung von* θεῖος ἄνθρωπος *und sinnverwandten Ausdrücken in der Literatur der Kaiserzeit* (WUNT 2.91) Tübingen 1997.

H. Windisch, *Paulus und Christus: Ein biblisch-religionsgeschichtlicher Vergleich* (UNT 24), Leipzig 1934, 24–114.

D. Zeller, *Christus* (L3) 65–83.

Apollonius of Tyana is called a 'divine man' (θεῖος ἀνήρ) at *Vit. Ap.* 2.17 and 8.15. At 5.24 the crowd in Egypt look up to him 'as to a god' (θεός). The adjectives θεῖος and δαιμόνιος are frequently used of him (e.g. at 1.2, where we also find a remarkable list of names and instructive comparisons). Apollonius is related to Pythagoras, Empedocles, Democritus, Plato, Socrates and Anaxagoras, and linked to Babylonian magicians, Indian Brahmins and Egyptian gymnosophists. It is these contacts and the consequent accusation that Apollonius is a magician, as well as his gift of predicting the future, that link him to the great names who are mentioned first. But the fact that he 'draws close to wisdom in an even more divine manner' than Pythagoras himself exalts Apollonius above him, and thereby no doubt above all the others.

It cannot be disputed that the expression 'divine man' existed in the classical period (even Koskenniemi, the most recent and severest critic of this concept, himself notes [99f., n. 392] about twenty widely scattered pieces of textual evidence), nor that it was applied to Apollonius of Tyana and that it suits him better than anyone else. The bitter controversy which continues among scholars about this concept concerns above all the question of how widespread this category was. Can it be used to help grasp precisely the person and work of Jesus of Nazareth too? Was it applied to him by the first Christian theologians, at least in a secondary phase? Did Hellenistic Judaism make use of it to describe such figures as Moses and Elijah, thereby preparing the way for its adoption in earliest Christianity?

To some extent, these questions still receive a positive answer (Betz, Corrington), while other scholars cast doubt on the very existence of this *typos* of the 'divine man' (Koskenmemi) or question its applicability to Judaism (Holladay) and earliest Christianity (Blackburn). A more differentiated picture is demanded, e.g. between the teaching sage of the tradition of the philosophical schools, who works no miracles, and the charismatic miracle worker linked to more popular views (Tiede). It must be pointed out that Bieler's fundamental study is based on a very broad definition, viz. 'the great, outstanding man of genius', whose greatness was seen 'in the whole of antiquity as an emanation and an immediate proof of divine power' (I.1; cf. also Betz 236: 'The expression θεῖος ἀνήρ is applied especially to those persons who transcend the general human measure thanks to a particular charismatic gift'). Bieler himself calls his general *typos* a 'Platonic idea', the realisations of which 'never anywhere totally unite all its essential characteristics in an ultimate perfection' (I.4); a more serious methodological disadvantage is his failure to reflect sufficiently on the significance of the fact that some of the material with which he works is very late, and above all, that a Christian form has been imposed on parts of it (legends of saints, etc.). There is little value in adding to the work of Windisch (59–87) by compiling ever more complete lists of names of θεῖοι ἄνδρες, as several scholars have done, when fundamental questions can still be asked about the concept that undergirds all this work. In any case, such lists are regularly dominated by two of those mentioned above: Pythagoras, about whose historical career we know little, and Apollonius, for whose career we must rely on Philostratus. Among the philosophers, seers, thaumaturges, legislators, rulers, and others who are classified as 'divine men', Empedocles (485–425 BCE) deserves special attention,[11] because in the first book of his *Purifications* he says of himself, or rather of

---

[11] On this enigmatic figure cf. now P. Kingsley, *Ancient Philosophy, Mystery, and Magic: Empedocles and Pythagorean Tradition*, Oxford 1995.

his soul, a daimon of divine origin that is now fallen and banished into his body (FVS 31B112):

> I journey around as an immortal god, no longer mortal; as is fitting in my case, everyone bestows honours on me, binding me about with headbands and garlands of fresh flowers. I am honoured by all whose flourishing cities I visit, men and women alike. They follow me in their tens of thousands and ask where is the path that leads to success. Some demand that I foretell the future, others ask for information about illnesses of every kind, in order to hear a word that will bring healing, since they have now long suffered from piercing pains.

The critics are correct to object that too many disparate matters have been gathered together under the heading of 'divine man'. This concept has simply been taken for granted and then used to interpret the New Testament, so that for example Jesus has been compared to Apollonius, without reflecting that more than a century lies between the literary testimony to each, viz. the gospels on the one hand and Philostratus' biography of Apollonius on the other. A more nuanced view is required, one that takes due account of the phenomena in the context of their own period. Accordingly, we need not wholly abandon the hypothesis of the existence of the 'divine man', as far as the early imperial age is concerned; and the Apollonius of Philostratus (though not by any means the historical figure), who fills this role, can at the very least still indicate the horizons of reception and expectation encountered by the Christian proclamation of Jesus at this time. Archaic models like Empedocles, who may perhaps have been somewhat eclipsed in the interval since their death, likewise become more relevant in this period; apart from *Vit. Ap.* 1.2 (see above), we see this from the fact that the fragment quoted above was preserved by Diogenes Laertius (third century CE). Structurally speaking, this breathing of new life into older paradigms resembles the application to Jesus of the typology of Moses and Elijah.

B. Foretelling the future and interpreting signs

1. Clarification and general presentation of the concepts

List 65.
D. E. Aune, *Prophecy in Early Christianity and the Ancient Mediterranean World*, Grand Rapids 1983, 23–79.
R. Baumgarten, *Heiliges Wort* (L43) 15–69.

177

M. Beard, 'Cicero and Divination: the Formation of a Latin Discourse', *JRS* 76 (1986) 33–46.

——et al., *Religions*, vol. 2 (L4) 166–93.

C. Bergemann, *Politik* (L22) 89–113.

A. Bouché-Leclercq, *Histoire de la divination dans l'Antiquité*, vols. 1–4, Paris 1879–82, reprint New York 1975 and Aalen 1978.

R. Flacelière, *Greek Oracles*, London 1965.

C. Forbes, 'Early Christian Inspired Speech and Hellenistic Popular Religion', *NT* 28 (1986) 257–70.

J. H. W. G. Liebeschuetz, *Continuity* (L2) 7–29.

J. Linderski, 'The Augural Law', *ANRW* II/16.3 (1986) 2146–2312.

G. Luck, *Magie* (L60) 289–382.

B. MacBain, *Prodigy and Expiation: A Study in Religion and Politics in Republican Rome* (CollLat 177), Brussels 1982.

A. Motte (ed.), *Oracles et mantique en Grèce ancienne* = *Kernos* 3 (1990) 9-366.

J. North, 'Diviners and Divination at Rome', in M. Beard and J. North, *Pagan Priests* (L11) 49–71.

H. W. Parke, *Greek Oracles* (Classical History and Literature), London 1967.

P. Roesch, 'L'Amphiaraion d'Oropos', in G. Roux, *Temples* (L9) 173–84.

V. Rosenberger, *Gezähmte Götter. Das Prodigienwesen der römischen Republik* (Heidelberger Althistorische Beiträge und Epigraphische Studien 27), Stuttgart 1998.

M. Schofield, 'Cicero for and against Divination', *JRS* 76 (1986) 47–65.

J. P. Vernant (ed.), *Divination et rationalité* (Recherches anthropologiques), Paris 1974.

P. de Villiers, 'Oracles and Prophecies in the Graeco-Roman World and the Book of Revelation in the New Testament', in *Acta Patristica et Byzantina* 8 (1997) 79–96.

(*a*) Terminology

It has been noted in the preceding section that Asclepius, the god of healing, appeared in Epidaurus to the sick in dreams and gave them the instructions that would restore their health. In some cases, however, what was sought was not healing at all, but another matter: e.g., it was asked where a lost boy could be found (W24). This dual aspect emerges even more clearly in the case of the hero Amphiaraus, who had his main sanctuary in the territory of Oropus (Roesch 177: 'a sanctuary both oracular and medical'). People of all kinds sought counsel there, sleeping in the *incubatio* room on the fleece of a sacrificed ram and awaiting the word that would resolve their problem. In both cases, the cult of healing touches another wide field, that of *divination* or *soothsaying*, to which the acts of putting questions to an oracle and of interpreting dreams belong.

The Latin concept of *divination* may be connected to *divinus*, 'divine': sharing in the divine knowledge makes it possible to glimpse hidden future things and have some notion of them. The Greek equivalent, μαντεία, is most probably derived from μαίνομαι, 'to rave', and μανία, 'a fit of rage'. This is enough to indicate that such glimpses were often possible only in extreme emotional states, which often made the impression of madness on outsiders. In very general terms, the task of divination or soothsaying can be defined as the interpretation of premonitory signs and a look at the present and the future, in order to help people arrive at a decision in situations which are still open. As we shall see, it was by no means always the case that the utterance of an oracle demanded blind obedience, and was the sole decisive factor. Often enough, all the oracle did was to provide subsidiary help in processes of clarification that had already begun. It takes the sting from hard controversies, creates a climate of confidence for decisions that are inevitable, and gives courage in the face of difficult tasks that are imminent. Behind this general description, there shelters a multitude of individual phenomena that are not at all easy to classify.

Cicero attempted to create order in this field in his work *De Divinatione*,[12] a work that is centrally important for the present section of this book. He follows the teaching of the Stoics and distinguishes between 'natural' soothsaying and that which is the product of 'art': 'There are two kinds of soothsaying, one the product of art, the other the product of nature' (*Divin.* 1.11: 'duo sunt enim divinandi genera, quorum alterum artis est, alterum naturae'). He gives examples of this formal differentiation in a later text (2.27f.):

---

[12] Text: C. Schäublin, *Marcus Tullius Cicero: Über die Wahrsagung/De Divinatione* (TuscBü), Munich 1991; a valuable commentary in A. S. Pease, *M. Tulli Ciceronis De Divinatione libri duo* (University of Illinois Studies in Language and Literature 6 [1920] 161–500; 8 [1923] 153–474), reprint Darmstadt 1963; cf. also Beard; Schofield; J. Blänsdorf, '"Augurenlächeln" – Ciceros Kritik an der römischen Mantik', in: H. Wißmann (ed.), *Zur Erschließung von Zukunft in den Religionen*, Würzburg 1991, 45–65.

You wished to show that there exist two forms of soothsaying: one owed to 'art' and one that is 'natural'. The skilled form is based in part on interpretation, in part on lengthy observation; the natural form is based on what the soul draws to itself from the exterior, or receives from that divine sphere from which we assumed that souls were created or received. You said then that forms of soothsaying like the following were to be regarded as the work of human art: that of the people who inspect entrails and of those who deduce their predictions from lightning flashes and miracles, as well as those who look at birds and those who work with signs or premonitions; you also assign all that has to do with interpretations to this category. But with regard to the natural kind of soothsaying, you said that either it is generated and poured forth when the soul wells up within itself, or that the soul sees into the future in sleep, when it is free from the senses and those things that occupy the senses.

The criterion for the distinction is thus that, in natural cases, the insight that shows the future emerges from within the human person: the divine intervention passes by way of the states of his soul. In other words, what is involved here is soothsaying under divine inspiration, which includes the ecstasy in which the human person steps outside himself, dreams in which he hears the divine voice, and oracles that are the product of inspiration. Soothsaying on the basis of human skill can, however, be learned: it is based on the precise observation and competent interpretation of premonitory signs which exist in nature, or also on genuine 'experimental strategies' which are carried out, for example, by casting lots or throwing dice – this last point must be stated here more clearly than Cicero himself does.

Other categorisations are certainly possible. For example, soothsaying based on the observation of nature could be described as inductive or accidental, distinct from soothsaying 'by art' in the strict sense of the term, since the latter works with a prepared experiment; 'intuitive' soothsaying would be a better antithetical concept than 'natural'. Normally, it is not possible to apply these distinctions in a pure form to the material we have, since in practice they overlap. For example, Cicero classifies dreams under inspired soothsaying, but the interpretation of a dream is an art; oracles are not only communicated through inspired mediums, but also obtained by employing technological means.

Although Cicero himself belonged to the priestly college of augurs (those who looked at birds), he was sceptical about these practices. He asks in one place whether one should not simply admit 'that some of all this is based on error, some on superstition – and much on trickery' (2.83). But one must not suppose that this scepticism was a general phenomenon.

Among the philosophical schools, the Stoics were among those who vigorously defended the whole area of divination, whereas it was above all the Epicureans who spoke dismissively of it. Plato has Socrates say in his defence: 'The god [i.e. Apollo in Delphi] enjoined me to do this, by means of oracles and dreams [ἐκ μαντείων καὶ ἐξ ἐνυπνίων] and in every way that the divine guidance uses to enjoin a human being to do something' (*Apol.* 22 [33c]).

As this quotation confirms, the centre of this whole area is the oracle, with the dream alongside it. We shall examine oracles in greater detail in the further course of this section, and treat dreams and their interpretation in an appendix. First, we shall discuss in a rather summary manner non-inspired divination 'by art'. It is not difficult to guess where connections to the Jewish-Christian tradition lie. In his apologetically coloured presentation Karl Prümm has a long chapter about the oracles with the following formulation: 'The objective presentation of the individual facts relating to pagan seers shows us – quite without any specific intention on our part – how incomparably exalted the prophecy of the Old and New Testaments is.'[13] The wide-ranging study by David Aune (*Prophecy in Early Christianity and the Ancient Mediterranean World*), aiming at a more objective picture, avoids such full-bodied evaluations, but portrays the same state of affairs. Certain analogies can be seen in the way of looking at time, the interpretation of the present and the future; it should also be noted that some of those who interpreted signs in the sanctuaries of Greek oracles bore the name 'prophet'. Starting points for a structural comparison exist in the realm of the doctrine of inspiration also.

(*b*) Divination 'by art'

It seems that the Romans adopted their speciality, the interpretation of the future on the basis of the flight of birds, which Cicero mentions, from the Etruscans. One of the great priestly colleges, that of the augurs, was especially entrusted with this task. Particular rules allowed one to deduce the chances of success for particular undertakings (e.g. a battle on the following day) from the flight – whether the birds came from the left or from the right, whether they cawed loudly or not at all, whether they came

---

[13] *Handbuch* (L2) 427.

singly or in pairs or in a formation, whether they were tame birds or birds of prey. The undertaking should be carried out only if it stood under favourable 'auspices'. Another form of looking at birds consisted of looking at chickens while they ate; unlike wild birds, these were always available. If they did not come out of their cages, that was a bad omen; but if they greedily devoured the grains and fragments of cake that they were put down in front of them, the business in hand looked very good. However, the following episode is related from the first Punic War. When the sacred chickens refused to eat on the evening before a sea battle against the Carthaginians, the general Publius Claudius Pulcher had them thrown into the water with the laconic remark: 'vel bibant' ('Let them drink, then!': Cicero, *Nat. Deor.* 2.7 and many other texts). A passage in one of Cicero's letters also casts light on this: he communicates to a correspondent who is worried about his political future a prognosis which he derives, 'not from the flight of birds or the cry of the raven from the left – as is customary in our profession – nor from the way the chickens eat, or the way the grains fall to earth', but from 'other signs' which may indeed not be 'infallible, but at any rate are less obscure and misleading', viz, from the character of Caesar and the 'natural causal interconnection of the political events' (*Fam.* 6.5[6].7f.).

Among the forms of divination 'by art' listed by Cicero in the opening quotation was also the examination of entrails. In Seneca's tragedy *Oedipus* the future doom is announced in sequence by the flames of the sacrificial fire, the behaviour of the sacrificial animals, the way their blood flows, and the state of their entrails (*Oed.* 309–86). The Greeks likewise practised the examination of entrails when animals were slaughtered in sacrifice: when these were cut in pieces, the entrails were looked at, to ascertain whether they were in a healthy condition, or whether changes had taken place because of some disease. The former was a lucky premonitory sign, but the latter – obviously enough – was a bad one. Among the Romans a special form was practised, which also went back to the Etruscans: the central point was the examination of the liver, with specialists for this task who were called *haruspex*. In excavations in Piacenza a bronze image of a sheep's liver has been found, dating from *c.*100 BCE (illustration in North 68, et al.) and divided into various segments with Etruscan letters and signs. This served as a model for the *haruspex*, either to be consulted in his work or else retained in his memory after long practice. This praxis was not represented by a priestly college in the official state cult. Cicero criticises the misuse of this custom, quoting Cato the Elder to the effect that he always marvels that one *haruspex* can look another in the face without their both laughing aloud (*Divin.* 2.51). It cannot be denied that premonitory signs could be produced and manipulated in the service of political interests, e.g. by keeping the sacred chickens hungry for a period (Bergemann gives instructive examples).

It is impossible to gain an overview of the other premonitory signs, because everything in life could be drawn on here, both daily events and exceptional happenings, and also because the regulated interpretative techniques of the examination of birds and entrails no longer apply. Somewhat vaguely, Cicero spoke in his essay of flashes of lightning, miracles, signs and *omina* (premonitions). This can include meteorological and cosmological omens – storms of lightning and thunder, eclipses of sun and moon, earthquakes and floods – but trivialities of everyday life have their place here too: stumbling, twitches in the limbs, or sneezing could be interpreted as hints coming from a divine power. Finally, one must also mention a whole range of techniques that were developed in order to interpret the future, some of which however overlap with oracles in the more precise sense. Schooled interpreters – and charlatans too – promised that they could deduce the divine will from the way in which the incense clouds rose, the pattern formed by meal on the surface of water, how the dice fell, what lot a person drew, how a spindle turned, what one saw in a mirror, and many other things. Theophrastus in one of his character sketches describes how far this concern with premonitory signs could take over people's lives:[14]

> The superstitious person is one who after meeting a funeral procession washes his hands, sprinkles them with temple water, takes a laurel leaf in his mouth, and walks around all day like that. If a weasel crosses his path, he does not move a further step until another weasel has passed over the same spot, or until he has thrown three stones over the path along the tracks of the weasel. If he sees a snake while he is at home, and it is a common snake, he invokes Sabazios; but if it is a sacred snake, he at once erects a little temple to a hero ... If a mouse has eaten a sack of meal, he goes to the interpreter of signs [ἐξηγητήν] and asks what he should do; and if the interpreter replies that he should have the sack repaired by the saddler, then he does not pay any heed to this, but goes home

---

[14] *Char.* 16; cf. D. Klose, *Theophrast: Charaktere* (RecUB 619), Stuttgart 1970; J. Rusten, *Theophrastus: Characters* (LCL 225), Cambridge, Mass. and London 1993.

and offers a sacrifice ... If owls are startled as he passes by, he says: 'Athene is stronger', and only after saying this does he continue his journey ... If he has dreamt, he goes to the interpreters of dreams (ὀνειροκρίτας), the soothsayers [μάντεις], and those who examine birds [ὀρνιθοσκόπους], in order to ask which god or goddess he should pray to ... But if he sees one who is mad or an epileptic, he is terrified, and spits into the folds of his garment.

2. Delphi: the site of an oracle

List 66.
P. Amandry, *La Mantique apollinienne à Delphes: Essai sur le fonctionnement de l'Oracle* (BEFAR 170), Paris 1950.
M. Delcourt, *L'Oracle de Delphes* (BH), Paris 1981.
J. Fontenrose, *The Delphic Oracle: Its Responses and Operations with a Catalogue of Responses*, Berkeley 1978 (fundamental, especially for the questions posed to the oracle and the answers given).
S. Levin, 'The Old Greek Oracles in Decline', *ANRW* II/18.2 (1989) 1599–1649.
M. Maass, *Das antike Delphi: Orakel, Schätze und Monumente*, Darmstadt 1993.
H. W. Parke and D. E. W. Wormell, *The Delphic Oracles*, vols. 1–2, Oxford 1956.
G. Roux, *Delphes: Son oracle et ses dieux*, Paris 1976.
S. Schröder, *Plutarchs Schrift De Pythiae oraculis* (Beiträge zur Altertumskunde 8), Stuttgart 1990.

The sanctuary of the god Apollo in Delphi was the site of the most famous oracle of the classical period of Greek history. Its erstwhile dominance abruptly diminished in the Hellenistic period, a process that accelerated further in the early imperial period, partly because of altered political constellations: the Greek city states which had consulted Delphi had disappeared as political entities, and although the Romans did occasionally address inquiries to Delphi, they did not have the same interest in it (cf. Levin). Other forms of interpreting the future – simpler and above all cheaper – were developed, and these were found to be equally effective, prompting the question why anyone should still want to undertake the lengthy and expensive journey to Delphi. Plutarch complains about the decline of the Delphic oracle *c.*100 CE in his Delphic dialogues *De E apud Delphos* (about the mysterious letter 'E' which was on one of the pillars in the temple in Delphi), *De Pythiae Oraculis* and *De Defectu Oraculorum*.[15] These treatises were written out of a professional interest: Plutarch lived in Chaironeia, a day's journey from Delphi, and he was appointed one of the two high priests in the sanctuary of Apollo in Delphi in 95 CE. But this very fact itself shows that the Delphic oracle still existed at this date and that it still functioned to a modest extent. We will discuss below other sites of oracles which were still functioning; some of these experienced a new surge of life in the second and third centuries CE, robbing Delphi of its preeminence.

(a) The site

Delphi lies one hundred and sixty kilometres north-west of Athens on the slopes of Parnassus, in a rural situation which was often praised. According to the mythical prehistory (preserved for example in the third Homeric Hymn, 'To Apollo'), Delphi had a sanctuary of the earth goddess, which was protected by a large serpent which lived in a crevice of the earth and was called 'Python'. Apollo, who was born on the island of Delos, came to Delphi in the course of his wanderings and resolved to remain there (Homeric Hymn 3.287f.: 'This is where I intend to construct what will truly be the most beautiful temple: it will be a place of soothsaying for human beings'). He fought against the serpent Python, killed it, and took possession of the territory. The myth allows us to glimpse the fact that sites of oracles frequently go back to ancient earth cults and are located at caves, pits or crevices in the earth, where snakes (as representatives of the chthonic gods) feel at home.

Plutarch and Pausanias speak of extensive buildings at Delphi; in the classical period, these spread east and west of the Castalian spring, which flows from a crevice in the rock on the mountain slope. This literary testimony is essentially confirmed by the excavations which now allow modern visitors to have a good idea of how the ensemble as a whole looked. There were a temple site for Athene with a mysterious round construction, a gymnasium, and a stadium, but we concentrate here on the sanctuary of Apollo, which was enclosed by a wall. At the south-east corner there begins a serpentine path which leads up the ascent of the mountain to the temple, passing numerous small buildings which have names indicating the importance of the oracle for the Greek world, such as: the treasury of

---

[15] For texts and translations, cf. L 131.

the Sicyonians, the treasury of the Thebans, the treasury of the Athenians. The individual city states which consulted the oracle had furnished these buildings with votive gifts in the form of statues and booty of war. This has been (not unjustifiably) called carrying on war by other means, for here it was former enemies in war who now wanted to outshine one another by the display of wealth and booty. The mighty supporting wall on the south also deserves interest: this was covered with inscriptions, including documents about the sacral ransoming of slaves.

The temple itself lies on the platform which is thus constructed. It is a normal Greek temple, with the sacrificial altar outside before the entrance, the portico running around it, the antechamber, and the main room. It is in the main room that the central point of the entire site was located, namely the oracle. Only the Pythia, the one who sought counsel, and the priests entered this room, which was a typical *adyton*. It lies one and a half metres lower than the level of the main room, so that one had to go down several steps, ending on the bare earth. The client took his position in a narrow section on the right side, which was curtained off, and presented his questions there. In the other, larger section of the *adyton*, stood the *omphalos*, a conical stone portraying Delphi's claim to be the navel of the world, under a baldachin; then in clockwise direction, a golden statue of Apollo, the tomb of Dionysus, the opening for the oracle (which must have led very quickly to the naked rock), and a sacred laurel tree. The Pythia took her place on a tripod above the opening for the oracle, when she imparted the oracles.

(b) How oracles were imparted

This visionary called the Pythia had to be a virgin from the town of Delphi. It may be presumed that she originally uttered the oracles only once a year; later this happened once a month, and at the zenith of Delphi even more frequently, with the exception of certain days on which this was prohibited. At certain periods, two or three Pythias were held in readiness, since one on her own could not cope with the throngs who came. Before imparting the oracles, the Pythia had to fast. On the day itself, she purified herself by washing in the Castalian spring, then she was led in procession to the temple, where she threw sacrificial flour and laurel leaves into the fire of Hestia's hearth, which was in the main room. Finally she took her place on the tripod. Those seeking counsel had likewise offered a sacrifice earlier on. Cities and prominent persons enjoyed the right of *promanteia*, i.e.

precedence, but otherwise the sequence of suppliants was determined by casting lots.

We do not know for certain what happened in the midpoint of the action, since the veil of the mysterious is cast over so much. Delphi is a case of inspired soothsaying, which means that the Pythia answered in keeping with an inner suggestion. Some scholars assume that she was seized by wild contortions when this happened, and could only stammer almost incomprehensible fragments of words; others hold that she sat more or less calmly on her stool and worked in a rather routine manner.

The theory of ecstasy finds support in an impressive description in the *Pharsalia*, the Roman author Lucan's epic poem about the civil war (first century CE).[16] Appius, who has been charged by Pompey with the government of Greece, wants to learn more about how the war is going, and therefore goes to the Delphic oracle 'which had been shut down for many years now' (5.69f.). A detail of the prehistory is given: it was here that Apollo 'saw the giant crevice in the earth breathing the divine wisdom, and the earth blowing out winds that were gifted with speech' (82–4). He makes this power his own, and allows it to pass into the seeress. But this is not something desirable, from the perspective of the visionary herself (116–20):

> For when the god enters a mortal breast, a premature death is the penalty – or the reward? – for summoning the god. The structure of what it is to be a human being collapses under the waves of ecstasy that goad it, and the mighty impetus of the gods shatters the delicate soul.

At the request of this highly placed Roman, the Delphic high priest takes the first young woman he finds, and compels her to adopt the role of Pythia. She begins with an attempted deceit, merely pretending to fall into a trance, but this is not successful, since 'no confused and stammering words testified that her spirit was penetrated through and through by the spirit of sacred frenzy' (149f.). In a rage, Appius demands that she cease 'speaking with her own voice' (161). Now at last genuine inspiration occurs, and Lucan paints a dramatic picture of the accompanying phenomena (161–74, 190–7):

> In terror, the virgin finally fled to the tripod. She drew near to the enormous pit, stood there, and received for the very first time in her breast the divine

[16] Cf. G. Luck, *Lukan: Der Bürgerkrieg* (SQAW 34), Berlin 2nd edn. 1989; J. D. Duff, *Lucan: The Civil War* (LCL 220), Cambridge, Mass. and London 1928.

power that the spirit of the mountain, which was not yet exhausted even after so many centuries, breathed into the seeress. Now at last Apollo took possession of the soul of the girl from Delphi. Never before had he so powerfully stormed into the body of a priestess, excluding her normal consciousness and driving out all that was human in her heart, so that he could create there a place for himself. In ecstasy, she staggered through the cave; her neck no longer obeyed her; Apollo's fillet and the headband of the god quickly fell from her dishevelled hair; she reeled through the empty room of the temple, casting her head in all directions, overturning the tripods that stood in her path as she wandered around without any goal, with a mighty fire effervescing within her ... Only now does the madness flow over her foaming lips; she moans and cries aloud, and her breath wheezes. Now her sad cries ring muffled through the vast vaults, through which there echo the final words of the virgin who now has been overwhelmed: 'Roman! You have no share in this mighty decisive struggle; you escape the fearsome terrors of the war, and you will live in peace all by yourself in a broad valley on the shore of Euboea.' Apollo closed her throat, so that she could utter no more words.

But here we must bear in mind the literary stylisation in this text, which means that we cannot simply assume it reports things that genuinely happened. Lucan himself makes this clear when he says that Apollo 'had never before stormed so powerfully into the body of a priestess' (166f.). This account is therefore more dramatic than what actually took place; greater probability attaches to the alternative hypothesis, viz. that the Pythia remained sitting on her tripod and spoke calmly from that position. The classical period had developed an appropriate theory of inspiration to deal specifically with this phenomenon, something Lucan indicates when he says that the earth 'blew out winds that were gifted with speech' (83f.). Plutarch presents this theory in his Delphic dialogues: put briefly, it says that the tripod of the Pythia stood above a crevice in the earth, out of which there arose a fine vapour or steam (*pneuma* in Greek, which also means 'spirit'). When this *pneuma* entered the body of the Pythia, it took possession of her and 'inspired' her (in a very material sense of this word) to utter her prophecies (cf. e.g. Plutarch, *Def. Orac.* 40 [432d–e]: 'The prophetic stream and vapour [τὸ δὲ μαντικὸν ῥεῦμα καὶ πνεῦμα] is that which is most divine and sacred, whether it ascends in the form of air alone, or accompanied by a dampness. For when it enters the body, it produces in the soul an uncommon, rare state of being'). But this theory is untenable too. The excavations in Delphi have demonstrated that there was no crevice in the earth underneath the tripod, such that it would have been possible for vapours to arise (cf. Maass 7). Little can be said in favour of theories based on a prophetic power in the water from the Castalian spring, or the intoxicating effect of chewing laurel leaves.

How then can the genesis of the inspiration of the Pythia be explained? What was the source of her knowledge? We may begin by recalling that, according to Plato, every soul has a prophetic element (*Phaedr.* 20 [242c]), even if this is certainly not put into practice by every person. We may undoubtedly assume that the Pythia knew exceptional states of the soul, but these remained under control; an essential contributory factor in generating these and intensifying them was the accompanying phenomena of fasting, bathing, processions, special clothing, and the atmosphere of the place. Besides this, the original charismatic experience of each Pythia would become over time a matter of routine: she knew what was expected of her, and she half-consciously produced serviceable responses. Nor should we overlook the mediating activity of the priests and interpreters of the oracles, which could go as far as direct manipulation.

(*c*) Questions put to the oracle and its answers

The Pythia's answers were very varied. This variety begins with the form of language used and the degree of comprehensibility; both elements seem to have changed with the passing of time. Plutarch devotes one of his dialogues specifically to the question why the Pythia in his day speaks in prose, no longer in verse (*Pyth. Or.*) as clearly had been the rule earlier. In the same breath, he laments that people in earlier times had reproached the oracular utterances for their obscurity, whereas in his day they find fault with the excessive simplicity of the oracles. They 'yearn to see again the puzzling words, allegories and parables of the art of soothsaying, although these are only refractions of the truth' *(Pyth. Or.* 30 [409d]). The Presocratic Heraclitus locates the utterances of the oracle in a remarkable intermediary position: 'The Lord to whom the oracle in Delphi belongs [i.e. Apollo] does not speak [openly], does not conceal [totally], but gives indications (σημαίνει)' (FVS 22β93).

If we summarise the evidence presented hitherto, we can say that the verbal utterances range from incomprehensible stammers to the art of verse, including both statements coded in symbols and simple directives that were not open to misunderstanding. From the point of view of the temple personnel, the puzzling utterance had an advantage: it was necessary to turn to someone other than the Pythia for the interpretation, and professional exegetes of the oracles were available in the sacred precincts – for a fee.

Some of the ambiguous statements have become famous, and this brings us to a further aspect: what matters were brought to the oracle. In the specific case of Delphi, some of the questions that have been preserved concern far-reaching political decisions: ought one to begin a war or not? Ought one to make a truce? Ought one to enter an alliance? What ought one to do in face of the advancing army of the Persians? Such cases were most likely to be mentioned by writers; Herodotus quotes more than fifty oracular utterances from Delphi, as well as more than forty from seventeen other sites. Here however we have the problem that it is seldom possible to establish the authenticity of these oracles. It may be that they were recorded in an official way, but all such evidence is lost. This made it easier to fabricate *vaticinia ex eventu* when the oracles were written down by historians. Nevertheless, despite these reservations, we shall mention here two of the best-known episodes.[17]

The first of these (Herodotus, *Hist.* 1.46.2–53.3) concerns the Lydian king Croesus, who sent embassies with a trick question to various sites of oracles in Greece and Libya. The reply from Delphi convinced him. Accordingly, it was only to Delphi and to Amphiaraus (see above) that he directed the decisive question whether he should go into battle against the Persians or not. The reply was: if he did this, he would destroy a great kingdom. Croesus undertook the campaign against the Persians, but fell in the decisive battle. He did not destroy the Persian kingdom, as he had supposed, but his own. He ought to have paid more attention to the ambiguity of oracular utterances.

In the second case (Herodotus, *Hist.* 7.140.1–143.3), the Athenians enquired at Delphi when they were threatened by the army of Xerxes in 480 BCE. The first prophecy sounded a note of doom: all resistance was pointless, the disaster would not be averted. Despite their initial shock, the envoys of the city persisted, and a new response of the Pythia was accorded to their renewed question. This contained mysterious references to a 'wall of wood', which alone would remain unconquered, and concluded with the words: 'Salamis, divine island, you utterly destroy the children of women, whether at the sowing of Demeter or at the time of harvest' (141.3f.). Conflicting opinions clashed in the assembly. Professional

---

[17] Fontenrose classifies the first oracular directive of the following two as 'not genuine', the second as 'doubtful'.

interpreters of oracles, the so-called *chrēsmologoi*, interpreted the concluding verses to mean that Athens would suffer defeat if a sea battle was fought. Themistocles was decisive in persuading the majority to accept the alternative option, namely 'to employ the armour of ships in the battle, since these are the wooden walls' (143.2). As is well known, this resulted in victory in the Battle of Salamis. The oracular utterance seems here to be woven into complex processes whereby a political opinion is formed.

It was not always a matter of such far-reaching problems; often enough everyday matters, seemingly without any great significance, were involved, and Delphi did not disdain these. In Plutarch's time typical questions addressed to Apollo at Delphi were: whether one should marry, or put to sea, or engage in agriculture, or travel abroad (*E ap. Delph.* 5 [386c]; *Pyth. Or.* 28 [408c]). Small leaden tablets discovered at the oracle of Zeus in Dodona bring us even closer to this divine condescension to the concerns of daily life, because they preserve individual cases (SIG 2/793–8):

> The city state of the Mondaitai asks Zeus Naios and Dione about the money of Themistocles, whether it can afford this, and whether it is right to lend it to him.
>
> Heracleides asks Zeus and Dione to grant him good fortune, and he would like to hear from the god something about a child – will he receive a child from his wife Aigle, from the one who is his wife at present?
>
> Nikokrateia wishes to know to which god she should offer sacrifices in order to regain her health and be rid of her disease.
>
> Lysianos wishes Zeus and Dione to tell him whether the child that Annyla is bearing is his or not.
>
> Is it more advantageous and profitable to me to buy the house in the city and the piece of ground?

Luck appositely remarks, on the question put by Lysianos: 'It was not always easy for the oracle either. What should it say to a man who was not sure whether he was the father of the child his wife was expecting? Even a veiled reply in the traditional oracular style could have resulted in a family tragedy. In order to save the marriage, the oracle had no other choice than to say to the man: "It is your child."'[18]

We take a step even deeper into daily life when we read a book of oracles from late antiquity which was meant for domestic use. In the first part it contains a number of questions, out of which the reader should select the

---

[18] *Magie* (L60) 329.

appropriate one. In the second part ten answers were offered to each question, some of which were in fact useless. A complicated system of calculations, including also a generator of random possibilities, led the reader to the fitting answer. Here is a selection of questions put to the oracle (POxy 1477):[19]

72 Will I receive my wages?
73 Will I remain in the place to which I am travelling?
74 Will I be sold (as a slave)?
75 Will I get profit from my friend?
77 Will I be transferred to the inheritance (of my master)?
78 Will I get a holiday?
85 Will I be successful?
86 Ought I to run away?
89 Will my attempt at escape be hindered?
90 Will I be divorced from my wife?
91 Will I be poisoned?
92 Will I receive a bequest?

3. Further glimpses

List 67.

H. D. Betz, 'The Problem of Apocalyptic Genre in Greek and Hellenistic Literature: The Case of the Oracle of Trophonius', in Idem, *Hellenismus* (L3) 184–208.

P. and M. Bonnechère, 'Trophonios à Lébadèe: Histoire d'un oracle', *EtCl* 57 (1989) 289–302.

K. Buresch, *Klaros: Untersuchungen zum Orakelwesen des späteren Altertums*, Leipzig 1889, reprint Aalen 1973.

R. J. Clark, 'Trophonios: The Manner of His Revelation', *TPAPA* 99 (1968) 63–75.

J. Fontenrose, *Didyma: Apollo's Oracle, Cult, and Companions*, Berkeley 1988.

R. L. Fox, *Pagans* (L3) 168–261.

H. Hommel, 'Das Apollonorakel in Didyma', in Idem, *Sebasmata: Studien zur antiken Religionsgeschichte und zum frühen Christentum*, vol. 1 (WUNT 31), Tübingen 1983, 210–27.

[19] Text with German translation: J. Hengstl, *Papyri* (L4) 162f.; a collection of questions put to oracles on papyrus in M. Totti, *Texte* (L23) 130–48.

H. W. Parke, *The Oracles of Zeus: Dodona – Olympia – Ammon*, Oxford 1967.
——*The Oracles of Apollo in Asia Minor*, London etc. 1985.
T. L. Robinson, 'Oracles and Their Society: Social Realities as Reflected in the Oracles of Claros and Didyma', in L. M. White (ed.), *Social Networks in the Early Christian Environment: Issues and Methods for Social History* = *Semeia* 56 (1992) 59–77.

The last point has already brought us far from Delphi, and we will now deepen our knowledge of the sites and the praxis of oracles by further brief glimpses. The oracle of Apollo at Claros in Asia Minor was especially popular in the early imperial period (see e.g. Buresch). The medium who worked there was a priest who, according to Tacitus *(Ann.* 2.54.3), did no more than hear the names of the enquirers, then descended into a cave where he drank water from a mysterious spring. The result was that he could guess all the concerns that the enquirers had brought to the oracle, and supply absolutely appropriate answers. Apollo, who was also active in the Didymeion near Miletus (cf. Hommel and others), was the most popular oracular god, but by no means the only one; we have just mentioned the oracle of Zeus at Dodona. Here people listened to the rustling of the leaves of a mighty oak, and sometimes also the cooing of the doves (this latter point is disputed), and to the sounding of a gong that swung freely with its clapper moved by the wind. While we find soothsaying by inspiration at Claros and Delphi, we must include Dodona, strictly speaking, in the class of soothsaying 'by art', since what counted there was the employment of all the rules of art to decipher and explain the signs that happened naturally or were created by human means. But we will not examine in greater detail these and other oracles (among which Croesus was able to pick and choose). Instead, we shall present a few further illustrative individual examples.

(*a*) The oracle of Apollo at Korope

The longest inscription, with sixty-nine lines, that we possess on the theme of oracles comes from the period *c.*100 BCE and concerns the oracle of Apollo at Korope in Thessaly, for which the city of Demetrias, about thirty-five kilometres away, accepted the responsibility.[20] It is clear that a

---

[20] Text SIG 3/1157 = LSCG 83; cf. G. Luck, *Magie* (L60) 332f.

number of abuses existed, so that a reorganisation was necessary. This was promoted by a group of citizens (lines 1–8). An 'ideological prologue' (lines 8–17) recalls the venerable age of the oracle and the many blessings it has granted, with positive effects on health and well-being (ὑγίειαν καὶ σωτηρίαν).

The necessary personnel are listed in the decree proper (lines 17–63), which is followed by directives about how it is to be put into practice (lines 63–9); we find the priest of Apollo, one of the *stratēgoi* of the city and one of those who exercise vigilance over the laws, as well as a member of the council, a treasurer, the secretary (γραμματεύς) of the god, 'the prophet' (line 22), and three men paid to see to good order (these forfeit money if they do not appear for work). The proceedings take two days. On the first day, people go in procession the thirty-five kilometres from the city to the temple. They spend the night there and return home on the following day. After they have arrived in the temple and the offering of sacrifice is satisfactorily completed, the secretary notes on a white tablet the names of those who desire an oracle. Then he lines these persons up in front of the temple and calls them one by one, respecting the privilege of *promanteia* which some possess (lines 36f.: 'unless some have the right of entering first'). Unfortunately, it remains very unclear what happens next; translations and interpretations of the text diverge strongly. Lines 38–49 read:

> Those mentioned above [the officials, or those seeking counsel?] are to sit in the sanctuary with demure manners, clothed in white garments and wearing a garland of laurel leaves, pure and fasting, and they are to receive the small tablets παρὰ τῶν μαντευομένων [from those who impart oracles, or from those who seek an oracle?]. But when τὸ μαντεῖον [the process of giving the oracle] is finished, they are to cast the small tablets into a vessel and seal this with the seal of the *stratēgoi* and those who exercise vigilance over the laws, as well as with the seal of the priest, and they are to leave [the vessel] in the sanctuary. As soon as day breaks, the secretary of the god is to bring the vessel in. After he has shown the seals to those mentioned above, he is to break them, then summon in turn each one on the list and give him back his small tablet.

This much is certain: the questions posed to the oracle were scratched on small tablets of lead or wax, presumably in the simple form of a question about a decision: should I do this, or should I not? The oracle is imparted by the appearance of the answer yes/no on the tablet. We will hear how this was achieved technically, when we look below at the case of Alexander of Abonuteichos. The major problem concerns the time at which this was done: one possibility is that the answers were written on the tablets during the night, while they were in the sealed vessel, and that the oracles were imparted on the following morning, but it is equally possible that the tablets were already handed in on the evening of the first day, that perhaps lots were cast to take the decision and the answer written on the tablets, and that they were returned closed to those seeking counsel – the point of collecting them subsequently and then keeping them in the sealed vessel would have been to keep the tension alive until the following morning, a tension maintained by the crowd of visitors who remained demurely sitting in the temple precincts. The prescriptions about oaths which follow in the text (lines 51–63) were meant to supplement the employment of a variety of seals, and thus exclude the obvious suspicion of manipulation.

(*b*) The oracle of Trophonius at Lebadeia

Lebadeia is near Delphi, about thirty kilometres eastward of the city. Trophonius was an ancient hero of the country of Boeotia, according to the saga a son of Apollo or of Zeus or some other god. He is said to have died in the underground cave that serves as the site of the oracle; his oracle lasted from the archaic period into the Roman and Christian periods. Despite the geographical closeness to Delphi, no competition developed, and Delphi never suppressed Lebadeia, partly because the procedure of imparting oracles was completely different. At Lebadeia, each individual who put questions to the oracle himself became an inspired medium, although he had to pay a personal price for this. The information Pausanias gives about this (*Graec. Descr.* 9.39.5–14) is at the same time the most detailed description in classical literature of how an oracle was received; the other accounts (cf. Betz), especially Plutarch *(Gen. Socr.* 21–2 [589f–592e]), enrich the basic structures with further materials such as the journey to heaven of the one involved.

> The aspirant spends several days in preparation in a house that is dedicated to the *Agathos Daimōn* and *Tychē* (5). An examination of the entrails of the animals offered in sacrifice permits the identification of the favourable date; if all goes well, the nocturnal sacrifice of a ram over a pit gives the final signal that the visit of the cave may begin (6). Two thirteen-year-old boys wash the visitor in a river and anoint him (7). He must drink from two springs the water of forgetting, which erases all the past, and the water of remembering, which enables him to grasp what will happen next; he sees and venerates an ancient cultic image (8). The path taken to the place of the oracle, which resembles an

195

oven, is very complicated (9f.): a narrow ladder gives access to a raised marble platform with bronze latticework, in the middle of which an artificial chasm leads into the interior of the earth. With cakes of honey in his hand – no doubt intended for the chthonic snakes – the visitor slides down, and later returns by the same path, this time feet first (11). When this has been accomplished, the priests seat him on the throne of remembering and ask him what he has experienced; the answers will take individual forms. Relatives then take the visitor, who is still in a stupor over what he has experienced, into the house mentioned at the beginning of the text, where he comes back to his senses (13). He is to write down on a tablet what he has seen and heard in the cave, and set this tablet up in the sanctuary (14). Pausanias does not mention the duration of the stay in the cave; this could last from one day to a week.

Here it is impossible to avoid psychological explanations such as penetrating the womb of mother earth and being reborn; it is obvious that the oracle of Trophonius operated by administering massive shocks to the human psyche. One who submitted to these procedures would necessarily enter extreme psychological states. Hallucinations occurred, things suppressed or unconscious came to the surface, premonitions of death took place – the entire personality was exposed to a trial of strength, and if all went well, this will certainly have enriched the visitor to the oracle.

(c) Alexander of Abonuteichos

List 68.
H. D. Betz, *Lukian* (L3) 57–9, 224f. and frequently.
M. Caster, *Études sur Alexandre ou le faux prophète de Lucien* (CEA), Paris 1938, reprint New York and London 1987.
S. Eitrem, *Orakel und Mysterien am Ausgang der Antike* (AlVi NF 5), Zurich 1947, 73–86.
R. L. Fox, *Pagans* (L3) 241–50.
A. M. Hannon, *Lucian*, vol. 4 (LCL 162), Cambridge, Mass. and London 1925, reprint 1961, 173–253.
R. MacMullen and E. N. Lane, *Paganism* (L4) 119–37 (Eng. trans.).
H. R. Remus, *Pagan–Christian Conflict over Miracle in the Second Century* (PatMS 10), Philadelphia 1983, 159–81, 203f.
U. Victor, *Lukian von Samosata: Alexandros oder der Lügenprophet* (Religions in the Graeco-Roman World 132), Leiden 1997.
O. Weinreich, 'Alexandros der Lügenprophet und seine Stellung in der Religiosität des II. Jahrhunderts n.Chr.', *NJKA* 47 (1921) 129–51.

It is above all Lucian's polemical *Alexander, or the False Prophet* which informs us about Alexander of Abonuteichos. This was written after 180 CE, describes events that took place *c*.150, and is 'not in the least to be considered an objective historical narrative' (Weinreich 129). Lucian and Alexander were bitter personal enemies, and this is why Lucian portrays him as a swindler and charlatan who shamelessly tricks people with his private oracle. We must remove the element of satire and polemic from Lucian's description; what remains gives us valuable insights into a flourishing business dealing in oracles. Alexander's success with the public, which according to other testimony lasted even after his death, shows 'that the prophet and his god do have some significance and do communicate some religious values to their own period and the following time' (Weinreich 151). In his introductory paragraphs Lucian gives an acute analysis of the psychological and societal presuppositions on which the business of oracles was based (8):

> No particularly great effort of the understanding was required in order to discover that *fear* and *hope* are the two great tyrants that dominate human life and that one who knows how to make the proper use of these two has discovered the quickest way to wealth. They [i.e. Alexander and his companion] realised very well that nothing was more important for the one who hopes and the one who fears than to know the future in advance, and that there therefore are few things people desire more eagerly; and that it was only this desire that made Delphi and Delos and Claros and the Branchides [a reference to the oracle of Apollo at Didyma] rich and famous in olden times ...

With the intention of turning this situation of human need into a means of making money, Alexander returned after a long absence to his home town Abonuteichos on the southern coast of the Black Sea. He brought a very large tame snake with him from his wanderings, and he made of papier-mâché a figure resembling a human head, with a mouth worked by strings. But to begin with he hid both these, since he wanted to begin by staging the arrival of the god Asclepius in the city. To do this, he took a goose egg and blew the contents out. He then placed a new-born little snake in the egg, sealed it again with wax, and laid it in the mud of the diggings on a building site. Next morning, he ran like a madman in prophetic ecstasy through the city and discovered the egg (14):

> He held the egg aloft and cried: 'Here, here I have Asclepius!' The good people, who already were exceedingly astonished at the egg which had been discovered

in the water, looked up to him, full of expectation, to see what this would lead to. And when he broke the egg in the hollow of his hand and took hold of the tiny new-born snake, and they saw that it moved and wound itself around his finger, they cried aloud, welcomed the god and said that their city was blessed ...

A few days later, Alexander gave audience in a small, semi-dark room to the people who came running to see him: the tiny snake had in the meantime turned into an exceptionally large serpent which curled around Alexander's body in such a way that the head like that of a man, which Alexander had placed on the snake, emerged above his right shoulder. The snake was given the name Glykon. After this preparatory advertising campaign, Alexander could open his oracular praxis (19):

> Alexander told all those who visited him that the god [i.e. the snake Glykon in the role of Asclepius] would impart oracles, and he named a specific date for this. At the same time, he ordained that each one should write on a small tablet what he needed to know and most wished, and that this tablet should be given to Alexander, bound with twine and solidly sealed with wax, clay or something similar. When this was done, then he, the prophet, would enter the sanctuary of the temple – since this was now finished and thus the scene was set – bearing the tablet. When he came out, accompanied by a herald and a theologian, he would summon each one in order. Now each one would receive back his own writing tablet, unbroken and in the same state in which he had given it to Alexander. At the same time, he would find written on it in metrical form the god's answer to the question the tablet contained.

This reminds us of the oracle of Apollo at Korope (see above under (a)). Lucian leaves the reader in no doubt about what he believes really happened. Indeed, he is familiar with the precise instructions about how one can open a seal without breaking it (21): using a red-hot needle, a dough of plaster and bookbinder's glue, and similar methods. Lucian concedes that his adversary deserves respect as regards the contents of the oracular words, since Alexander was very clever at his work. He followed 'the circumstances and the rules of probability', gave 'oscillating and ambiguous answers to many questions, and indeed completely incomprehensible answers to many questions'; he frightened off some people from posing their questions but encouraged others to do so; he also prescribed 'medicines and a regimen of life, since he possessed a great deal of medical knowledge' (22).

The price for each oracle was one drachma and two oboloi, leading to a yearly income of between eighty and ninety thousand drachmas. But this was insufficient in the long term, so that Alexander had to discover new sources of income, since his business was in continual expansion and he needed more and more personnel: 'For he paid salaries to an endless mob of helpers, attendants, emissaries, oracle-smiths, registrars, setters of seals and exegetes, and he had to pay each in keeping with his office and his merits' (23). We need not examine here what precise functions are indicated by these terms, some of which are rather striking; it is enough that we discern the outlines of this oracle business.

In order to create an even greater impression and so make a greater profit, Alexander also had the snake with its human head proclaim oracles in direct speech (26). According to Lucian, this was done with the help of a hidden tube carrying the voice of a helper who spoke into it in an adjacent room. This form of oracular utterance has its own name: these are 'autophonic' oracles, i.e. the god speaks in his own voice, without making use of a medium.

Alexander attempted to win over to his side respected sites of oracles such as Claros and Didyma, by sending many of those who came to him with oracular utterances such as: 'Go to Claros, to hear the voice of my father' (this is how Glykon speaks of Apollo), or 'Listen to the utterance of the god in the sanctuary of the Branchides' (the dynasty of seers in Didyma) (29).

Since many of the questions posed to Alexander revealed a great deal about the questioners themselves and hence involved danger for them, Alexander widened his area of business to include blackmail, according to Lucian (32). Alexander considered his greatest enemies to be Epicureans (43–7) and Christians, since both groups refused to believe in his oracular arts. This is why they remained excluded from the three-day-long celebration of a mystery cult which Alexander founded and which included among other elements the dramatic portrayal of a sacred marriage (38f.). It is not surprising that Lucian accuses him of pederasty and adultery (41f.). Lucian won the implacable hostility of Alexander, which allegedly went as far as an attempt on his life (56), when he formulated anonymous questions and sealed them in such a way that it was not possible to break the seals. As he had expected, the answers he received were completely meaningless (53f.).

The sixty-one paragraphs of Lucian's polemic contain many other details that would enrich the picture given here. But we conclude by recalling only his clear-sighted grasp of the motives that could move people to seize the kind of help offered by an Alexander. In his introduction (8), Lucian states – almost in the categories of a modern functionalistic theory of religion – insights that are not so very far removed from Luck's summary observations on the oracles of antiquity: 'One must not forget that soothsaying was a form of psychotherapy. It helped people who believed in a multiplicity of supernatural powers to cope with their fears, and compelled them to take decisions when all possibilities of thought had been exhausted.'[21]

4. Collections of oracles: the Sibyllines

List 69.

J. J. Collins, 'Sibylline Oracles', *OTP* I, 317–472.

——'The Development of the Sibylline Tradition', *ANRW* II/20.1 (1987) 421–59.

J. D. Gauger, *Sybillinische Weissagungen* (TuscBü), Düsseldorf 1998.

J. Geffcken, *Die Oracula Sibyllina* (GCS 8), Leipzig 1902, reprint Berlin 1967.

V. Nikiprowetzky, *La Troisième Sibylle* (EtJ 9), Paris 1970.

H. W. Parke, *Sibyls and Sibylline Prophecy in Classical Antiquity*, ed. B. C. McGing, London and New York 2nd edn. 1992.

D. S. Potter, *Prophecy and History in the Crisis of the Roman Empire: A Historical Commentary on the* Thirteenth Sibylline Oracle (Oxford Classical Monographs), Oxford 1990 (with a valuable introduction).

R. J. Quiter, *Aeneas und die Sibylle: Die rituellen Motive im sechsten Buch der Aeneis* (BKP 162), Königstein 1984.

A. Rzach, 'Sibyllen, Sibyllinische Orakel', *PRE* II/2 (1923) 2073–2183.

G. Wissowa, *Religion* (L2) 536–49.

(a) The figure of the Sibyl

In the first strophe of the mediaeval rhymed sequence *Dies Irae*, which depicts the end of the world and the last judgement, we find the words: 'Teste David cum Sibylla', 'with David and the Sibyl as witnesses'. Who is this Sibyl, and why does she suddenly stand alongside King David, taking on the role of prophetess of the imminent doom? The *Dies Irae* shows us the final product of a long development to which Graeco-Roman, Jewish

---

[21] *Magie* (L60) 327.

and Christian traditions have made their successive, overlapping contributions, and in this context we encounter the literary genre of the collections of oracles, which in turn could also be used for the purpose of supplying new oracles.

The concept of 'Sibyl', which is virtually impossible to explain in etymological terms, has presumably developed from the proper name of a specific person to become the designation of a genre. The Sibyl is understood to be a woman of advanced age, with visionary gifts that break out from time to time. She is not linked to one site of oracles, nor are questions explicitly posed to her. In a condition of ecstasy, she prophesies calamitous premonitory signs and catastrophes. Her preferential dwelling is a cave in a cliff. It is not possible to determine exactly where the saying of Heraclitus quoted by Plutarch in *Pyth. Or.* 6 (397a) begins and ends, but at any rate it contains the name of the Sibyl and speaks of her special state of mind (FVS 22в92):[22]

> The Sibyl, who according to Heraclitus proclaims with raving (μαινομένῳ) mouth that which cannot be ridiculed, beautified or adorned, reaches with her voice across the centuries, through the god.

Homer's Cassandra, who predicts the destruction of the city of Troy, would fit this phenotype rather exactly, although she does not yet bear the name of 'Sibyl'. After Heraclitus, Plato is the next to show acquaintance with this name; he speaks in the *Phaedrus* of the prophesying Sibyl (22 [244b]). The god who according to the quotation from Heraclitus speaks through the mouth of the Sibyl is none other than Apollo, the god of oracles. Plutarch localises the activity of the first Sibyl in Delphi, where she sat and prophesied on a rock that allegedly could still be seen in Plutarch's day (*Pyth. Or.* 9 [398c]). Sibyls display clear affinities to the sites of oracles, although they acted as competitors to the institutionalised oracles. In the context of Delphi, Pausanias reproduces the statement of a Sibyl prophesying to the Athenians that they would be defeated in a battle caused by the treason of their generals *(Graec. Descr.* 10.9.11):

> And then Zeus who thunders from on high and whose might is greatest
> will make ready a pitiful song for the Athenians,

[22] On the question of the reconstruction of the exact words of Heraclitus cf. the standard work by G. S. Kirk, J. E. Raven and M. Schofield, *The Presocratic Philosophers*, Cambridge 2nd edn. 1983.

namely struggle and the turmoil of battle for the ships that bring war,
as they perish in a treacherous manner through the wickedness of their
    guardians.

The number of Sibyls mentioned by classical authors grew rapidly, so that
later writers endeavoured to order things by means of lists that included up
to ten names, although these were far from including all the representatives
of this group. It is not at all clear whether these Sibyls were genuinely
historical figures; it is also possible that the attempt was made to legitimate
existing collections of oracles by attributing them to a Sibyl as their
authoress. Among the most famous of these Sibyls (whether historical or
fictitious), we find among the Greeks the Sibyl of Erythrae and among the
Romans the Sibyl of Cumae. Vergil gives us a somewhat atypical
description of the appearance of the latter, which in turn became the
literary model of the description of the young Pythia at Delphi in Lucan's
Pharsalia (see above). Aeneas asks in Cumae for a word of the Sibyl that
will indicate his future. To obtain this word she visits an enormous cave in
the rock with hundreds of shafts, and predicts a perilous path for Aeneas
(*Aeneid* 6.98–101):[23]

> In such words the Cumaean Sibyl chants from the shrine
> her dread enigmas and echoes from the cavern,
> wrapping truth in darkness – so does Apollo shake the reins
> as she rages, and ply the spur beneath her breast.

The Sibyl then shows Aeneas the path into the underworld; only there does
he receive the decisive information. As in the *Nekya* of the *Odyssey*, another
form of putting questions to oracles is involved here, which we have not
discussed separately, viz. the summoning of the dead so that they may
impart oracles, so-called necromancy.

(*b*) The Sibylline prophecies

A legend relates that the Sibyl of Cumae offered King Tarquinus Priscus
nine books of oracles in the early days of Rome. After he refused to buy
these, she burnt three of them and then demanded the same price for the
remaining six. After his renewed refusal, she burnt a further three books.

---

[23] Translation by H. Rushton Fairclough, *Virgil*, vol. 1 (LCL 63), rev. edn.
    Cambridge, Mass. and London 1967; cf. Quiter.

The king became curious and bought the three last books for the full sum. Sibylline books were kept in the cellar vaults of the temple of Jupiter on the Capitol Hill, and perished along with this temple in the fire in 83 BCE. A Roman commission then visited various places where it was supposed that Sibyls had been active, and brought from these places copies of texts which formed the kernel of the new collection. This expedition must have been a powerful stimulus for the production of new Sibylline literature. Augustus had all the anonymous books of prophecies on which he could lay his hands, as well as a portion of the Sibyllines, burnt; he brought the purified collection into the temple of Apollo on the Palatine, where it was placed under the pedestal of the statue of the god (Suetonius, *Aug.* 31.1).

In spite of further restrictive measures under Tiberius, the Sibylline oracles continued in use until the beginning of the fifth century CE. They were the last to be consulted, when no other premonitory signs had given clear information, but a decision had to be taken. A formal decision of the Senate was required before they could be opened, and this task was entrusted from the period of the late republic onwards to the priestly college of the *quindecimviri* (cf. above, I/A, 4). Tibullus composed one of his elegies on the occasion of the nomination of a new member of this college, and he observes that since Apollo guides her, 'the Sibyl, who utters the hidden fate in hexameter verses, has never yet deceived the Romans' (2.5.15f.).

These oracles were most likely consulted by taking out at random one of the leaves of a book of oracles, which lay piled loosely one on top of the other, and regarding the text found there as binding information. The necessary accommodation of the text to the current situation gave the college sufficient scope for interpretation. After experts had been consulted, it was once again the Senate that had to take the decision about what should be done next. The result was frequently the introduction of new rites such as the *lectisternia* or new forms of religion such as the cult of the mother goddess from Asia Minor. The hope was that it would be possible to attain reconciliation to gods whose disfavour was held to be responsible for the crisis; at the same time, the anxious populace could be distracted and calmed.

Nothing of these Roman Sibylline books has been preserved. We do have a collection of Sibylline prophecies in fourteen or twelve books (Books 9 and 10 are doublets; see Geffcken, Gauger, English translation in Collins, *OTP*). But this body of texts in its present form comes from the fifth and sixth centuries CE. The final redaction and an earlier reworking were dictated by a Christian perspective, while the preceding older parts have a Jewish origin; at most, some non-Jewish texts which served as models can be discerned in the third book. From the second century BCE onwards, Judaism took over this literary genre and produced Sibylline oracles, in order to promote the cause of monotheism, to attack the Roman empire, to articulate its own messianic hope, and in this way to express apocalyptic expectations too. Christians who reworked the texts adopted and developed these tendencies; *inter alia*, confident of their victory, they proclaim through the mouth of the Sibyl the destruction of pagan Rome.

5. Dreams and their interpretation

List 70.

A. Bouché-Leclerq, *Histoire* (L65) I.277–329.

K. Brackertz, *Artemidor von Daldis: Das Traumbuch* (dtv 6111), Munich 1979.

D. del Corno, *Graecorum de re oneirocritica scriptorum reliquiae* (TDSA 26), Milan 1969.

———'I sogni e la loro interpretazione nell'età dell'impero', *ANRW* II/16.2 (1978) 1605–18.

G. Devereux, *Dreams in Greek Tragedy*, Oxford 1976.

E. R. Dodds, *Greeks* (L2) 102–34.

R. L. Fox, *Pagans* (L3) 150–67

S. Freud, *The Interpretation of Dreams*, Harmondsworth 1976.

J. S. Hanson, 'Dreams and Visions in the Graeco-Roman World and Early Christianity', *ANRW* II/23.2 (1980) 1395–1427.

C. G. Jung, *Traum und Traumdeutung* (dtv 15064), Munich 1990.

H. Klees, 'Griechisches und Römisches in der Traumdeutung Artemidors für Herren und Sklaven' in *Das antike Rom und der Osten (Festschrift K. Parlasca)* (ErF 56), Erlangen 1990, 53–76.

F. S. Krauss, G. Löwe, and F. Jürss, *Artemidor: Traumkunst* (Reclam-Bibliothek 1409), Leipzig 1991.

F. Kudlien, *Sklaven-Mentalität im Spiegel antiker Wahrsagerei* (FASK 23), Stuttgart 1991, 68–81.

R. G. van Lieshout, *Greeks on Dreams*, Utrecht 1980.

P. C. Miller, *Dreams in Late Antiquity: Studies in the Imagination of a Culture*, Princeton 1993.

C. Morgenthaler, *Der religiöse Traum: Erfahrung und Deutung*, Stuttgart 1992.

S. M. Oberhelman, 'Dreams in Graeco-Roman Medicine', *ANRW* II/37.1 (1993) 121–56.

A. Önnerfors, 'Traumerzählung und Traumtheorie beim älteren Plinius', *RMP* 119 (1976) 352–65.

S. R. F. Price, 'The Future of Dreams: From Freud to Artemidorus', *PaP* 113 (1986) 3–37.

A. Shankman, *Aristotle's* De Insomniis: *A Commentary* (PhA 5 5), Leiden 1994.

J. H. Waszink, 'Die sogenannte Fünfteilung der Träume bei Chalcidius und ihre Quellen', *Mn.* III.9 (1941) 65–85.

G. Weber, 'Traum und Alltag in hellenistischer Zeit', in *ZRGG* 50 (1998) 22–39.

(*a*) Oracles in dreams and theories about dreams

We have mentioned the *incubatio* dreams of the sick in the sleeping room of the sanctuary in the preceding section about miraculous healings, and affinities to oracles could already be glimpsed. Cicero composed a little book wholly concerned with dreams, with exemplary dreams and their interpretation, and integrated this into his treatise on soothsaying (*Divin.* 1.39–65), but only so that he might then take each of the categories applied to these dreams, and destroy them with polemical vigour (2.119–50). Plutarch, who abstained for a period from eating eggs because of a dream, exposing himself to the suspicion that he had joined the Orphites or Pythagoreans (*Quaest. Conv.* 2.3.1 [635e]), is full of respect for dreams and calls them our 'oldest, most venerable oracle' (*Sept. Sap. Conv.* 15 [159a]: πρεσβύτατον μαντεῖον). Here all he does is to take a position that was already familiar to the tragedians. A choral song in Aeschylus compares a dream to an unasked prophecy for which no money has been paid (*Ag.* 979–81); Prometheus is specifically identified as the one who discovered the interpretation of dreams (*Prom.* 485f.). In Euripides, the earth resists Apollo's usurpation of the Delphic oracle by sending human beings images in dreams while they sleep in the dark of the night, thereby rendering other forms of oracles superfluous (*Iph. Taur.* 1259–68).

As in the case of oracles, the attempt was made to develop criteria for the categorisation of dreams too (cf. Waszink for a model with a high degree of articulation). We limit ourselves here to a discussion of Artemidorus of Daldis (*c.*96–180 CE), who composed the only book about dreams that has survived from antiquity. He first makes a distinction between the simple dream (ἐνύπνιον) which merely works over fragments left over from the past day, and the dream in which something significant is seen (ὄνειρος). The latter are then subdivided into 'theorematic' and 'allegorical' dreams (*Oneirocr.* 1.1f.); theorematic dreams are immediately comprehensible, since the image and the matter involved correspond to one another, but allegorical dreams present what is meant only in a veiled manner, and therefore need interpretation. Artemidorus makes comparisons with ghostly apparitions (φάντασμα), visions (ὅραμα), and oracles (χρηματισμός).

The dominant conviction was that significant dreams were sent from heaven and therefore had the same rank as oracles. But even on this premise, dreams could be treacherous. The first dream related by Homer is a clear directive sent by Zeus to Agamemnon (*Il.* 2.8: 'Away with you, evil dream, to the fast ships of the Achaians'), and the dream appears to him in the form of Nestor (2.20f.: 'He stood above his head in the likeness of Nestor son of Neleus'). Thus the Greek army is directed astray, so that they attack too soon. In the *Odyssey*, Penelope has a symbolic dream that at first makes her afraid: an eagle swoops down and kills the twenty geese that she loves. She would like to believe the positive interpretation, viz. that the eagle represents the returning Odysseus who will get rid of the importunate suitors, but she is not sure to what category the dream and its interpretation belong (*Od.* 19.560–7):

> 'Dreams, my friend,' said the thoughtful Penelope, 'are awkward and confusing things: not all that people see in them comes true. For there are two gates through which these insubstantial visions reach us; one is of horn and the other of ivory. Those that come through the carved ivory gate cheat us with empty promises that never see fulfilment; whereas those that issue from the gate of burnished horn inform the dreamer what will really happen.'

Artemidorus departs from this predominant view in one passage, rather in the manner of an aside, when he defines what is seen in dreams as 'a movement of the soul, or a creating of multiple images by the soul' (*Oneirocr.* 1.2). Aristotle supplied the basis for this 'progressive' insight in three small treatises in the *Parva Naturalia*: *De Somno et Vigilia*, *De Insomniis* and *De Divinatione per Somnium*.[24] He gives a physiological and

---

[24] Cf. P. J. van de Eijk, *Aristoteles: Parva Naturalia* II: *De insomniis, De divinatione per somnium* (Werke 14.4–5), Berlin 1994; W. S. Hert, *Aristotle*, vol. 8: *On Soul. Parva Naturalia. On Breath* (LCL 288), Cambridge, Mass. and London 1936, reprint 1975; cf. Shankman.

psychological explanation of how dreams come about. They cannot be sent by a god, and they can be called demonic only in the sense that nature as a whole has a demonic dimension (463b13–15). In another manner, Aristotle holds that dreams retain their value for medical diagnosis (463a5f.) On the business of the interpretation of dreams, he notes: 'The most skilled interpreter of dreams is the one who is able to discover similarities' (464b7f.; similarly, Artemidorus, *Oneirocr.* 2.25). This is strikingly reminiscent of what Aristotle says in his writings on the theory of literature about the generation of metaphors: these likewise are based on surprising relationships of similarity. The narration of dreams and their interpretation also work with language; indeed, one can understand in a manner analogous to the metaphorical process the intensification of daily experience which dreams produce, and this opens up unsuspected possibil-ities in dealing with both realms (cf. for example Morgenthaler 174: dreams 'as acts, are metaphorical per se, linking different realms of meaning; they create meaning in an exemplary manner and are oriented towards meaning').

(b) The interpretation of dreams

The interpretation of dreams, when carried out as a profession, lives above all from the symbolic or allegorical dreams. The professional body found an early model in the old man in the *Iliad* who understood how to interpret dreams (5.149f.: ἐκρίνατ' ὀνείρους). Temples seem to have been one of their favourite places for work: the interpretation of dreams was one of the specialities of the exegetes in the sanctuary of Amphiaraus in Oropus, where oracles were sought: Amphiaraus himself seems to have preferred to impart oracles in dreams (Pausanias, *Graec. Descr.* 1.34.4f.). Written texts were available to help in this: a grandson of the great Athenian statesman Aristides, who had come down in the world, sat 'always near the so-called Iaccheion and earned his living with the help of a booklet about dreams' (Plutarch, *Aristid.* 27.3: ἐκ πινακίου τινος ὀνειροκριτικοῦ). Juvenal mocks a Jewish woman who earned modest sums by interpreting dreams, since 'the Jews give at a low price any interpretation of dreams that one desires' (*Sat.* 6.542–7).

Artemidorus of Daldis was a serious and successful representative of this profession. He mentions earlier writers whose works he has collected and studied, criticising them at the same time (e.g. 2.44f.). His own contribu-tion grew to encompass five volumes, the last two of which were intended only for his own son. This unique complete example of a once flourishing literary genre was to enjoy great success in the course of history; even Freud and Jung refer to Artemidorus more than once. His methodology is sometimes portrayed as very simple, but this is not correct. His book about dreams is not a mere lexicon in which fixed meanings for particular dream symbols can be consulted. On the contrary, Artemidorus recommends the most complete possible investigation of the special circumstances of the life of the dreamer; and the interpreter ought to acquire a comprehensive knowledge of the particularities of each culture, since identical images can signify very different matters in different situations. Artemidorus also gives some indications about how one should study dreams. He does not speak (like Jung) of archetypes, nor does he distinguish (like Freud) between the manifest contents of the dream and the latent idea behind it. A modern reader notes above all that Artemidorus does not speak of the free association of the dreamer, which alone is able to overcome the censorship of dreams and to open the path into the unconscious (and this reminds us to be cautious in assessing accounts of dreams which have only literary attestation). Artemidorus repays a lengthy study, since his interpretations often imply very instructive material for social and religious history.

A famous chapter concerns the so-called Oedipus dream (1.79). In the interpretation of dreams, one should treat with extreme caution everything that concerns mystery cults (2.37). Dreams about Demeter and Kore promise happiness, dreams about Sarapis and Isis promise mourning, because of the contents of the respective myths (2.39). A dream in which one eats books 'is positive for those who earn their daily bread by speaking and through books, but for everyone else it prophesies a sudden death' (2.45). If a slave dreams that he is being carried out to his grave, this signals that he will soon be set free, since 'the dead person is no longer subject to any master' (2.49). A dream involving a synagogue indicates sorrow, since normally only those full of cares enter a synagogue (3.53). A married woman who dreams that she enters the temple of Artemis in Ephesus and eats there, will die, because in reality she is forbidden to do this under penalty of death (4.4). Artemidorus dedicates a paragraph exclusively to dreams of healing (4.22) and another to recurrent dream visions (4.27). A dream in which one is crucified means that one will attain prestige and wealth, 'prestige, because the one crucified is raised above everyone else, and wealth because he feeds many birds' (4.49). If women dream that they will give birth to a dragon, their sons will become famous speakers, hierophants, excellent soothsayers, unbridled rascals, robbers on the streets of the city, slaves that escape, cripples (4.67). 'Nothing good is signified when one sees the food that is served at sacrifices for the dead and funeral meals, or when one eats from this food, or a funeral meal is served to one' (4.81). Someone dreamed that he ate bread dipped in honey. He studied philosophy at great depth and earned much money by imparting existential wisdom, since the honey 'quite naturally signified the power of wisdom to bring conviction, while the bread signified earning one's living' (5.83).

We must stop here, or our discussion of this fascinating work would take on the dimensions of a monograph. Let us conclude with an observation from the novel *Leukippe and Cleitophon* by Achilles Tatius, since it reflects on the difficulty involved in discerning the significance of dreams sent from heaven: according to a fatalist or Stoic world-view, these dreams cannot in any way alter the events that will de facto happen according to plan (1.3.2f.):[25]

> Often the demonic will predict the future to human beings while they sleep, not in order that they may protect themselves from misfortune – since they cannot conquer the fate that has once and for all been determined – but in order that they may the more easily bear it once they encounter it. For that which happens quickly, suddenly and unexpectedly numbs the soul by abruptly happening to it, and lowers the soul into the flood of unhappiness. But the vehemence of misfortune is reduced by the fact that one awaits the disaster before it strikes us, and already thinks of it beforehand.

C. Magic

1. Outward manifestations

List 71.
A. Abt, *Apuleius von Madaura und die antike Zauberei: Beiträge zur Erläuterung der Schrift de magia* (RVV 4.2), Giessen 1908, reprint Berlin 1967.

---

[25] J. J. Winkler in B. P. Reardon (ed.) *Collected Ancient Greek Novels*, Berkeley 1989, 170–284; S. Gaselee, *Achilles Tatius: Leucippe and Clitophon* (LCL 45), rev. edn. Cambridge, Mass. and London 1969.

P. S. Alexander, 'Incantations and Books of Magic', in E. Schürer, *The History of the Jewish People in the Age of Jesus Christ*, revised edn. vol. III/1, Edinburgh 1986, 342–79.

D. E. Aune, *Prophecy* (L65) 44–7.

J. Bidez and F. Cumont, *Les Mages hellénisés: Zoroastre, Ostanès et Hystaspe d'après la tradition grecque*, vols. 1–2 (1938), Paris 2nd edn. 1973.

F. Bömer, *Untersuchungen* (L2) III.101–38.

C. Daxelmüller, *Zauberpraktiken: Eine Ideegeschichte der Magie*, Zurich 1993.

F. Graf, *Magic in the Ancient World* (trans. F. Philipp), Cambridge, Mass. 1997.

T. Hopfner, *Griechisch-ägyptischer Offenbarungszauber*, vols. 1–2 (StPP 21, 23), Leipzig 1921, 1924 (handwritten), reprint (typed) Amsterdam 1974, 1983, 1990.

——art. 'Mageia', *PRE* 14 (1930) 301–93.

J. M. Hull, *Hellenistic Magic and the Synoptic Tradition* (SBT 2.28), London 1974.

G. Luck, *Magie* (L60) 1–170.

R. MacMullen, *Enemies of the Roman Order: Treason, Unrest, and Alienation in the Empire*, Cambridge, Mass. 1967, 95–127.

A. Önnerfors, 'Magische Formeln im Dienste römischer Medizin', *ANRW* II/37.1 (1993) 157–224.

P. Schäfer, 'Jewish Magic Literature in Late Antiquity and the Early Middle Ages', *JJS* 41 (1990) 75–91.

M. Smith, *Jesus the Magician*, New York 1978.

A. M. Tupet, 'Rites magiques dans l'Antiquité romaine', *ANRW* II/16.3 (1986) 2591–2675.

(a) Four types

The Greek magical papyri tell one how to produce an oracle in a dream (PGrM VII 1009: ὀνειρομαντεῖον) artificially, and how to request a dream in which instructions for one's behaviour are given (PGrM XII 14: ὀνείρου αἴτησις). No. II in this collection, which we will discuss in greater detail below (cf. 4), summons Apollo, the god of oracles, in the style of a hymn (PGrM II 2–4):

> Phoebus, you who help by means of oracles, come joyfully.
> Son of Leto, whose arrows strike distant targets,
> you who ward off disaster, come here, yes, come here!

Come here and predict the future; prophesy in the hour of night.

A 'friendly demon of soothsaying' should be 'compelled' to come (II 53f.), and the Delphic tripod is mentioned here too (III 192f.: 'And the god will come to you, making the whole house and the tripod shake before him; and then carry out the investigation of the future'). This shows us a connection between the world of oracles and magic; other links exist via 'medical magic' to the cult of healing and to medicine (cf. Önnerfors). Pliny the Elder inserts a small dissertation on magic into a book dealing with medicines; we learn here that Theophrastus knew a magic spell against sciatica, Cato a spell against dislocation of the limbs, and Varro a spell against gout in the feet (*Hist. Nat.* 28.21; but we must also mention here the vehement polemic against magic in 30.1–20).

Theodor Hopfner has proposed a useful subdivision of the broad realm of magic, in his richly documented studies which remain indispensable to scholars. He distinguishes:

1. *Prophylactic magic.* This serves to protect the human person from misfortune, illness, the traps set by enemies; last but not least, it is a defence against magical attacks of the following category.

2. *Magic that inflicts harm.* The magician carries out an attack in his own interests or at the request of a client. He intends through his manipulations to harm another person physically, even to kill him, or to harm his possessions, or at least to prevent a dangerous rival from winning a competition.

3. *Magic to do with love.* Our sources indicate that this was especially sought after. It was in its element wherever love, jealousy and hate were involved; or, more generally, wherever it was a question of winning power over others.

4. *Revelatory magic.* This brings us back to the examples mentioned at the beginning of this section. Here magic touches the world of oracles; in its own way, it seeks to bring the god to grant insights into hidden matters and into the uncertain future.

(*b*) Two varieties

Besides this, two varieties of magic existed in the classical period: 'white' and 'black' magic, the latter making a stronger impact on the general picture and evaluation of magic. Another word was available to speak of magic in its less respectable form, viz. γόης (cf. 2 Tim 3:13), translated by

211

dictionaries as 'magician' in the sense of 'conjurer', 'mountebank', 'swindler'. Etymologically, this word is connected to γοάω, 'to lament, howl' – something that points to the verbal form given to the spells that were uttered by the *goēs*. The ambiguity in the value attached to the other term μάγος, 'magician', can be explained by the provenance of the word, which comes from Persian and denotes a high priestly caste in Persia, to which respected, wise men skilled in knowledge of nature and the stars belonged (cf. Mt 2:1). Philo of Alexandria sets out this semantic ambivalence very clearly (*Spec. Leg.* 3.100f.):

> It is not only private persons, but also kings – even the greatest among them – and especially the Persian kings, who practise genuine magic, a science of seeing things which sheds light on the works of nature by means of clearer ideas, and deserves veneration and high esteem. Indeed, it is said that no one can attain the royal dignity among the Persians unless he has previously been an intimate of the magicians. But the magic practised by wandering beggars, jesters, the most disreputable women and slaves is a disfigurement of this art, nothing less than a perversion of it. They promise to achieve a purification or expiation by magical means, assuring that they can supply love potions and secret utterances that can bring lovers to a state of deadly hatred, and those who hate to a state of the most burning love. They lead astray and entice above all simple and harmless persons.

Apuleius argues very cleverly on the basis of this ambivalence, in the speech in his own defence which he had to make before the Roman proconsul in 158/9 CE.[26] He had married a rich widow who was considerably older than himself. His opponents, who considered that they had been cheated of their inheritance, brought a lawsuit against him accusing him of having been able to win over the widow only by means of forbidden love potions: everything in his behaviour resembled a wicked magician. At worst, the court could have sentenced Apuleius to death for this offence, but he defended himself successfully and refuted each point of the accusation. For example, he asked the 'most learned lawyers' what a magician was: 'For if it is true – as I read in most authors – that the word "magician" in Persian means what we in our language call a "priest", then how on earth is it a

---

[26] R. Helm, *Apuleius: Verteidigungsrede. Blütenlese* (SQAW 36), Berlin 1977; V. Hunink, *Apuleius of Madaura, Pro se de magia (Apologia)*, vols. 1–2, Amsterdam 1997; cf. Abt; MacMullen 121–6.

crime to be a priest and to be familiar with what is laid down in the sacred books, in the ordering of the sacrifices and the regulation of worship?' (*Apol.* 25.6f.). He supports this with two relevant passages from Plato, in which the philosopher speaks positively of the magicians Zoroaster and Zalmoxis (*Alcib.* 121E; *Charmid.* 157a). But if his opponents look on him as a magician in the usual sense of the word, i.e. as one who 'through speaking with the immortal gods is capable of attaining what he desires, thanks to a really incredible power in his magical formulae' (*Apol.* 26.3), then Apuleius can only be astonished at the foolhardiness with which they have brought him before the court, without reflecting on the terrible doom he (by definition) is able to inflict on them.

It was always supposed that the best magicians were in the East, not only in Persia but also in Egypt, source of most of the magical papyri. One should also recall here the *Jewish* magician on Cyprus (Acts 13:6). Judaism made its own contribution to magic in the classical period.[27] It was far from being utterly immune to the adoption of magical practices, and even without any activity on the part of Jews, the Hebrew and Aramaic divine names were widely employed among non-Jews as a well-tried magical instrument. Moses and Solomon were generally looked on as especially gifted magicians. The same thing happened in the case of Christian ideas. When the name of Jesus suddenly occurs in magical texts from the fourth century CE, this is not without further ado proof of the Christian provenance of such recipes, but rather of the profoundly syncretistic orientation of magic (cf. Luck 24: 'An Egyptian magician may well have considered Jesus – putting it rather crudely – as an exceptionally successful colleague from another culture, from whom one could learn quite a lot').

The accusation that Jesus of Nazareth practised magic was made very early, i.e. certainly in the second century CE, and probably already in the first. Morton Smith has recently collected the relevant data in his book *Jesus the Magician* and has proposed a global view of Jesus which in his opinion comes closer to the historical reality than the monochrome portrait in the canonical gospels: according to Smith, Jesus spent his early years in Egypt and learnt the basic tools of the magician's trade there. Thus

---

[27] Cf. Schäfer; Alexander; M. D. Swartz, *Scholastic Magic: Ritual and Revelation in Early Jewish Mysticism*, Princeton 1996; G. Veltri, *Magie und Halakha: Ansätze zu einem empirischen Wissenschaftsbegriff im spätantiken und frühmittelalterlichen Judentum* (TSAJ 62), Tübingen 1997.

he was able to impress people in Galilee and Judea with magic practices, which include not only miraculous healings and exorcisms,[28] but also (in Smith's view) the reception of the Spirit at baptism, which is a magical initiation, and the Eucharist as a magical participation, brought about with the aid of food on which a spell has been cast. However, the information from enemies of Christianity, on which Smith relies, is supplied not by primary sources, but by polemically distorted responses to the Christian tradition. The magical papyri are chronologically late (see above), so that one must make much more cautious use of them in drawing comparisons than does Smith; his treatment of the gospels often seems forced. Nevertheless, his book cannot simply be dismissed as frivolous: it must be confronted seriously. Such a confrontation leads to the problem which we must discuss in the next section: in the case of similar external phenomena, is it at all possible to distinguish between magic and non-magic? But before this, we must look briefly at the 'ideological' foundations of magic.

(c) Intellectual presuppositions

Magic does not per se require theoretical foundations, a kind of metaphysics or theology, but it is linked to certain intellectual presuppositions, two of which in particular can be heard behind the various statements: first, the conviction of the existence of transhuman beings, not only of gods (some of whom were thought of as too far removed from the human world), but above all of intermediary beings, the demons; and secondly, the hypothesis that everything in the universe is interconnected, linked together by the bond of sympathy which can also turn into antipathy. This is why it is possible to achieve the desired effects at one place by means of the direct application of particular means at another place. This conviction of cosmic sympathy finds points of contact with Stoic philosophy, but also with Neoplatonism, which further elaborated demonology. Ironically, it was representatives of the Neoplatonic school, especially Iamblichus with his work *De Mysteriis*,[29] who subsequently attempted to develop higher forms of magic called 'theurgy', a word denoting influence brought to bear on the god with the intention of uniting oneself with him. As the leader of the

---

[28]   Cf. P. G. Bolt, 'Jesus, the Daimons and the Dead', in A. N. S. Lane (ed.), *The Unseen World*, Grand Rapids 1996, 75–102.

[29]   Cf. E. des Places, *Jamblique: Les mystères d'Egypte* (CUFr), Paris 1966.

Neoplatonists, Plotinus formulated the theoretical bases of magic from his own perspective in a long passage (*Enn.* 4.4.40–5):[30]

(40.216) But how do we explain the magic effects? Through the sympathy [συμπάθεία] of the universe, through the existing harmony of that which is similar and the antithesis of that which is different, through the vivid fullness of the various powers which nevertheless collaborate so that the organism of the world is a unity ... For true magic is 'the friendship' and 'the conflict' in the universe, this is the highest magician and wizard. (217) Human beings know him very well and make use of his herbs and formulae against one another.

(42.225) Through the skills of doctors and of magicians, one thing is compelled to lend some of its power to another thing. In the same way, the universe too communicates powers to its parts, both spontaneously and also when moved to do so by one who directs the power to one particular part of the universe; since because the nature in question is one and the same, the universe is available to its parts, and this is why the one who makes the request is no alien.

(43.229) But how is the noble person influenced by magic spells and herbs? He is affected to the extent that an irrational element from the universe is in him ... (231) Further, the demons for their part are not immune to being affected by their irrational part. It is not meaningless to ascribe recollection and perception to them, nor to affirm that one can cast spells on them and summon them in a natural way; and that those who are closer to this world, to the extent that their attention is directed to this world, hear those who invoke them.

2. Problems of demarcation

List 72.

D. E. Aune, 'Magic in Early Christianity', *ANRW* II/23.3 (1980) 1507–57.

A. A. Barb, 'The Survival of Magic Arts', in A. Momigliano (ed.), *The Conflict between Paganism and Christianity in the Fourth Century* (Oxford Warburg Studies [7]), Oxford 1963, 100–25.

W. M. Brashear, *Magica Varia* (PapyBrux 25), Brussels 1991.

J. B. Clerc, *Homines Magici: Étude sur la sorcellerie et la magie dans la société romaine impériale* (EHS.G 673), Berne etc. 1995.

C. A. Faraone and D. Obbink (eds.), *Magika Hiera: Ancient Greek Magic and Religion*, New York and Oxford 1991.

---

[30] See A. H. Armstrong, *Plotinus*, vol. 4 (LCL 443), Cambridge, Mass. and London 1984.

W. Fauth, 'Götter- und Dämonenzwang in den griechischen Zauberpapyri. Über psychologische Eigentümlichkeiten der Magie im Vergleich zur Religion', *ZRGG* 50 (1998) 40–60.

W. J. Goode, 'Magic and Religion: A Continuum', *Ethnos* 14 (1949) 172–82.

H. G. Kippenberg and B. Luchesi (eds.), *Magie: Die sozialwissenschaftliche Kontroverse über das Verstehen fremden Denkens* (Theorie), Frankfurt a.M. 1978.

G. E. R. Lloyd, *Magic, Reason, and Experience: Studies in the Origin and Development of Greek Science*, Cambridge 1979.

M. Meyer and P. Mirecki, *Ancient Magic and Ritual Power* (Religions in the Graeco-Roman World 129), Leiden 1995.

J. Neusner et al. (eds.), *Religion, Science, and Magic: In Concert and in Conflict*, New York and Oxford 1991.

L. Petzold (ed.), *Magie und Religion: Beiträge zu einer Theorie der Magie* (WdF 337), Darmstadt 1978.

C. R. Philipps, 'The Sociology of Religious Knowledge in the Roman Empire to AD 284', *ANRW* II/16.3 (1986) 2677–2773, at 2711–32: Magic and Religion.

P. Schäfer and H. G. Kippenberg (eds.), *Envisioning Magic* (SHR 75), Leiden 1997.

A. F. Segal, 'Hellenistic Magic: Some Questions of Definition', in R. van den Broek and M. J. Vermaseren (eds.), *Studies in Gnosticism and Hellenistic Religions* (*Festschrift G. Quispel*) (EPRO 91), Leiden 1981, 349–75.

D. Trunk, *Heiler* (L63) 316–46.

It might have been thought that agreement about the definition of magic, e.g. as the control of supernatural powers for personal goals by means of secret means, and about the boundary separating magic from religion, would be relatively easy to achieve. But this ceased to be the case long ago: on the contrary, the demarcation between magic and religion is debated vigorously, and modern studies tend to speak of magic in a wholly value-free manner, denying that there is any essential difference from religious phenomena. We are told that only the standpoint of the individual scholar decides whether something is categorised as magic or as religion. Considered from the perspective of the theory of social deviance, magic appears as the obverse side of religion, as that manifestation of religion which is societally not fully accepted and integrated. The impression is given that the accusation of magic serves only to fight against socially deviant behaviour (see Aune as an example of this view). But it seems questionable whether one can prescind so completely from a consideration of the goals intended by those who engage in magical or religious practices.

A further difficulty is that a third dimension is also involved here, namely science. This may at first sight be surprising, but many scholars hold that science and magic are contiguous enterprises, since magic is carried out experimentally and with a strict orientation to results, accompanied by the conviction that specific results will be attained, with absolute certainty, through the construction of a specific experimental procedure. In the view of these authors, the common goal of science and magic is the domination of the forces of nature.

Ultimately, no brief definition will suffice; rather, one must picture magic and religion, the two great spheres on which we wish to concentrate our attention here, as antithetical poles within a continuum, or as the two end points joined by a common line. They can be characterised with the help of a number of antithetical conceptual pairs, though these describe the reality only to a varying extent; the realisation of the individual factors in specific cases determines whether we should identify the phenomenon more in terms of religion or more in terms of magic. Following Goode's model, as this has been accepted by Trunk, we can exemplify this in the following pattern:

Magic	Religion
1. oriented to concrete goals	oriented rather to general well-being and to eschatological events
2. tendency to manipulate the deity	tendency to use petitions to win the favour of the deity
3. relationship between expert and client	relationship between shepherd and flock or prophet and disciple
4. individual goals	group goals
5. the one carrying out the ritual is a private person	a group or its representative(s) carry out the ritual
6. the procedure includes vicarious actions or other techniques	less instrumental, more oriented to the inner significance of the ritual; the goals are attained less through vicarious actions than by the continuous relationship to the gods

217

7. impersonal and not very emotional	emotional (shame, veneration)
8. the one carrying out the ritual decides *whether* it should be set in motion	the ritual must be carried out, since it belongs to the structure of the universe
9. the one carrying out the ritual decides *when* the process begins	normally the ritual takes place at a determined time
10. at least potentially, magic is directed against society or its representatives	religion is integrative and leads to the formation of community
11. oriented to goals	bears its meaning in itself, is a goal in itself

If one wishes to reduce this to two slogans, then it is simplest to say that coercion is typical of magic, and petition typical of religion. In Ps 139:1 the petitioner says to God: 'Lord, you investigate me and know me'; in the magical papyri, the magician says: 'I know you' (e.g. PGrM VIII 8f.: 'I know your form too'; 20: 'I know also your exotic [βαρβαρικά] name'; 49: 'I know you, Hermes'). In the psalm we find the confident turning to God in prayer; in the magical texts we have the hidden threat: you cannot escape from me, because I know your name. It is undeniable that prayers of petition are also found in magical papyri – ideal types seldom occur in their pure forms in reality. The degree of realisation will vary, not only from group to group, but also from individual to individual and from one period to another.

3. Literary scenes involving magic

List 73.

S. Eitrem, 'La Magie comme motif littéraire chez les grecs et les romains', *SO* 21 (1941) 39–83.

M. Korenjak, *Die Erichthoszene in Lukans* Pharsalia (Studien zur klassischen Philologie 101), Frankfurt a.M. etc. 1996.

J. H. W. G. Liebeschuetz, *Continuity* (L2) 126–39 ('Magic in public life'), 140–5 (on Lucan).

G. Luck, *Hexen und Zauberei in der griechischen Dichtung* (Lebendige Antike), Zurich 1962.

H. Parry, *Thelxis: Magic and Imagination in Greek Myth and Poetry*, Lanham etc. 1992.
A. M. Tupet, *La Magie dans la poésie latine*, vol. 1: *Des origines à la fin du règne d'Auguste* (CEA), Paris 1976.

We have already mentioned the opinion expressed by Pliny the Elder about magic, in which the often-quoted words occur: 'There is in fact no one who is not afraid of being cursed by terrible imprecations' (*Hist. Nat.* 28.19; the use of the verb *defigi* makes it clear that the allusion here is to tablets on which curses were written [see below]). In the same passage, he looks briefly at poetry: 'This is why we find in Theocritus among the Greeks, and among ourselves in Catullus and most recently in Vergil the imitation of such formulae as amatory incantations' (ibid.). We begin with the literary texts, because many of them are much earlier than the magical papyri which will be discussed later. This makes possible a double check: corresponding passages in both groups of texts make it possible (*a*) to establish that the magical spells in the papyri are older, and (*b*) to show that despite all poetic licence and everything that must be attributed to the writers' specific intentions, they are working with elements drawn from reality.

From the earliest texts onwards, there appears to be more interest on the part of the writers in the young, beautiful sorceress and the old witch than in the μάγος, the male representative of this professional group. An early prototype is Circe, who transforms Odysseus' companions into swine by means of what are already the classical instruments of magic: 'terrible poisons' and a magic wand (*Od.* 10.234–40). The wretched swine, who retain their human consciousness, lie weeping in the pen (240f.) until Odysseus sets them free – but he is able to do this only because Hermes gives him a mysterious herb called 'moly' as antidote (302–6).

The second of the pastoral poems composed by Theocritus of Syracuse in Alexandria in the third century BCE bears the title φαρμακευτρία, i.e. 'the sorceress' who operates with φάρμακα, medicines and poisons. Not without irony, Theocritus puts the following words on the lips of the young Simaitha, who seeks to win back her faithless lover Delphis by means of a nocturnal ritual in which her maid Thestylis assists her:[31]

[31] Theocritus, 2.1–4,10–16; cf. F. P. Fritz, *Theokrit: Gedichte* (TuscBü), Munich 1970; J. M. Edmonds, *Greek Bucolic Poets* (LCL 28), Cambridge, Mass. and London 1912.

> Where is the laurel? Bring it here, Thestylis! Where are
> the implements of magic? Bind purple wool around the sacrificial bowl!
> For I want to bind my unloving beloved to me by magic.
> The wretched man has not even come here in the past twelve days ...
> Now I want to bind him by magic. Come now, moon,
> and give me a fair light! For now I want to sing softly to you, O goddess,
> and to the chthonic Hecate too, before whom the dogs tremble,
> when she passes among the graves of the dead and the dark blood.
> Hail, dreadful Hecate, guide me now to a happy end.
> Make this magic as effective for me as was the spell of Circe,
> effective as the magic of Medea and of the blonde Perimedes!
> Magical wheel, go into my house, to the man whom I love!
> First barley is melted in the fire. Come then, scatter it,
> scatter it with these words: 'I scatter the bones of Delphis.'
> Magical wheel, go into my house, to the man whom I love!
> Delphis brought me suffering. So I burn the laurel in his stead,
> and as this hisses vehemently in the fire and suddenly catches flame,
> without even leaving any ash behind it, so may the flesh of Delphis
> be reduced to powder in the flame.
> Magical wheel, go into my house, to the man whom I love!
> As I now melt the wax with the help of the goddess,
> so may Delphis melt from love ...
> Now I wish to sacrifice bran ...
> Delphis has lost this fringe from his cloak,
> which I now pull apart and throw into the fierce fire ...
> Magical wheel, go into my house, to the man whom I love!

This line – referring to the 'magical wheel', a kind of spindle (cf. Tupet 50–5) made of bronze (line 30) – recurs ten times in the poem as a refrain. The magical wheel was an important instrument in this ritual, and was meant to make the beloved literally 'whirl around' (line 31). Wax is melted in the fire, so that Delphis likewise may melt from love. A fringe from his mantle is thrown into the fire (lines 53f.), the maid rubs the sacrificial ash into the threshold of his house and whispers: 'I grind down the bones of Delphis' (line 62). It is clear how the transference is meant to function here, viz. on the basis of the principles of 'sympathy' and of representation. The second possibility, of magic that causes harm, can be seen here, and the poem ends with an unambiguous threat: if nothing else avails, Delphis will make his acquaintance with the dangerous poison that Simaitha keeps in a chest for him (lines 160f.). One understands readily why magic was not counted among the universally acceptable patterns for the resolution of social problems.

Apart from Circe, Theocritus mentions Medea (from the saga of the Argonauts) as a model for every sorceress (line 16). Ovid paints a lengthy portrait of her, showing her in full action (*Met.* 7.1–403). Vergil reworked Theocritus' second Idyll in his eighth Eclogue. In the refrain, he substitutes 'bewitching spells' for the magical wheel (8.68 and frequently), and the ritual is based on a magic of analogy, employing three woollen threads of different colours which visually symbolise the fetters of love (8.78: 'Just tie the knot and say: I tie the fetters of Venus'). The image of the beloved 'stands in' for him, so to speak, and is 'wrapped into' these threads (8.73f.). In a text by Horace, Vergil's contemporary, the garden god Priapus relates how he was the unwilling witness of a crazy magical spell by moonlight, in which (as in the modern voodoo cult) dolls were employed:[32]

Then I myself saw Canidia arrive, with her black mantle hitched high, her feet naked and her hair dishevelled, and the older Sagana accompanying her. A deadly pallor gave both of them a dreadful aspect. They began to scratch up the soil with their finger nails and to tear a black lamb asunder with their teeth. Blood flowed into the ditch, in order to entice the spirits of the dead, whose instruction they desired. They had a woollen doll and another doll of wax: the idea was that the woollen one, which was larger, should punish the other doll. The waxen doll stood in the position of a suppliant, as if it were about to suffer the death of a slave at any moment. One witch summoned Hecate, while the other summoned the cruel Tisiphone: I saw snakes creeping and the dogs of the underworld running, and so that it might not be the witness of these terrible things, the moon crept embarrassed behind high tombstones ... I will not go into the details of how the shades of the dead conversed with Sagana and gave their answers in horrid shrill tones, or how the two witches buried secretly in the earth the hairs from the beard of a wolf and the tooth of a brightly coloured viper, or how the fire flamed up more brightly thanks to the figure of wax, and how terror filled me as I heard the words of these two furies and saw what they were doing.

This pair of witches appear again in Horace's fifth Epode, in a yet more terrible scene. At night, they bury a young man in the earth so that only his

---

[32] *Sat.* 1.8.23–36, 40–5. Cf. K. Büchner, *Horaz: Sermones/Satiren* (RecUB 431), Stuttgart 1972; O. Schönberger, *Horaz: Satiren und Episteln* (SQAW 33), Berlin 2nd edn. 1991; H. R. Fairclough, *Horace: Satires, Epistles, Ars Poetica* (LCL 194), Cambridge, Mass. and London 1926.

head can be seen above the surface. Then they place food in front of his eyes and wait until he dies in full view of this nourishment which he cannot reach: only then are his marrow and liver suitable for use in making an especially effective, irresistible love potion.

Lucan displays an evocative power next only to Horace, when he follows the scene with the young Delphic Pythia in Book 5 of his epic about the civil war (see above) with a contrasting picture in the next book of a young witch in Thessaly called Erichtho (*Pharsalia* 6.419–830). Sextus Pompeius, the unworthy son of the great Pompey, consults her, since he does not trust the normal techniques of divination, but only the 'mysteries of black magic which the higher gods hate' (6.430f.). Even the dwellers in heaven are afraid of Erichtho, to whom Lucan attributes unbelievably horrible deeds, and she does not hesitate to threaten them in terrible terms, when the planned summoning of the dead does not immediately succeed (6.744–6: 'Are you willing to obey? Or must I summon up him whose call makes the earth shake and tremble every time?').

We can trace the continued use of many magical motifs, not only the 'voodoo' dolls, from classical literature into the modern period. Goethe's ballad about the sorcerer's apprentice is based on an anecdote related by Lucian in his 'Friend of Lies' (*Philops.* 33–6): an Egyptian wise man, who had spent twenty-three years in an inaccessible crypt under a temple of Isis, uses a magic spell to transform a broom into a human servant in each new lodging. When the master is absent, his companion tries to do the same, with the well-known fatal consequences. The ability of witches to transform themselves into animals with the aid of a magic ointment – a motif found as late as Goethe's *Faust* I – brings Lucius, the hero in Apuleius' novel, to his downfall. Full of curiosity about everything concerning magic, he peeps through a chink in the door and sees how his hostess turns into an owl and flies away. When the same procedure is to be carried out on Lucius, the maid picks the wrong ointment and Lucius takes on the form of an ass. He retains this form for the next seven books of the novel (Apuleius, *Met.* 3.21.1–25.4).

Tupet's excellent book provides a thorough examination of the relevant passages in poetry and narrative literature; all we have done here is to touch on some highlights. We conclude this section with a quotation from an historical work which shows something of the political importance of magic. In his *Annals* Tacitus describes the death of Germanicus in Antioch in 19 CE. Germanicus, the adoptive son of the emperor Tiberius, was very popular in the army and among the people, but he also had bitter enemies, including Piso, the Roman governor of Syria, and he believed that he had been poisoned by Piso, possibly correctly:[33]

> The raging violence of the illness was made even worse by his conviction that he had been poisoned by Piso. And as a matter of fact, a search in the floor and the walls revealed the presence of fragments of human corpses, magical spells containing curses and the name of Germanicus scratched on tablets of lead, the ashes of half-burnt parts of bodies smeared with dung, and other implements of magic. According to general belief, souls are consecrated to the gods of the underworld by such means.

Piso was accused, and committed suicide. The harmful magic practised against Germanicus brings us to our next point, the so-called curse tablets.

4. Magical texts

(a) Curse tablets

List 74.
P. S. Alexander, 'Incantations' (L71) 352–7.
A. M. H. Audollent, *Defixionum tabellae quotquot innotuerunt tam in Graecis orientis quam in totius occidentis partibus praeter Atticas in* Corpore Inscriptionum Atticarum *editas* ..., Paris 1904.
C. Bonner, *Studies in Magical Amulets, Chiefly Graeco-Egyptian* (UMS.H 49), Ann Arbor 1950.
C. A. Faraone, 'The Agonistic Context of the Early Greek Binding Spell', in Idem and D. Obbink, *Magika Hiera* (L72) 3–32.
——'Binding and Burying the Forces of Evil: The Defensive Use of "Voodoo Dolls" in Ancient Greece', *ClA* 10 (1991) 165–220.
J. G. Gager, *Curse Tablets and Binding Spells from the Ancient World*, New York and Oxford 1992.
F. Graf, *Gottesnähe* (L71) 108–57.
R. Kotansky, *Greek Magical Amulets: The Inscribed Gold, Silver, Copper, and Bronze Lamellae*. Part I: *Published Texts of Known Provenance* (PapyCol 22.1), Opladen 1994.
J. Naveh and S. Shaked, *Amulets and Magic Bowls: Aramaic Incantations of Late Antiquity*, Jerusalem 1985.
A. Önnerfors, *Antike Zaubersprüche* (RecUB 8686), Stuttgart 1991.

---

[33] *Ann.* 2.69.3.

K. Preisendanz, 'Fluchtafel (Defixion)', *RAC* 8 (1972) 1–29.

J. Schwartz, 'Papyri Magicae Graecae und Magische Gemmen', in M. J. Vermaseren, *Religionen* (L2) 485–509.

J. Trumpf, 'Fluchtafel und Rachepuppe', *MDAIA* 73 (1958) 94–102.

H. S. Versnel, 'Beyond Cursing: The Appeal to Justice in Judicial Prayers', in C. A. Faraone and D. Obbink, *Magika Hiera* (L72) 60–106.

D. Wortmann, 'Neue magische Gemmen', *BoJ* 175 (1975) 63–82.

R. Wünsch, *Antike Fluchtafeln* (KlT 20), Bonn 2nd edn. 1912.

Lead is a soft and durable material which can be worked into flat tablets and strips on which texts can be incised with a sharp instrument: they can then be rolled up. This is why most of the more than 1,500 curse tablets which survive are of lead. Their dates stretch from the fifth century BCE to the sixth century CE, and their literary attestation covers roughly the same period (cf. the list in Gager 245–64). New Testament exegesis draws on this group of texts to illuminate such passages as 1 Cor 5:5, where Paul says that he is handing over an evildoer to Satan for the destruction of his flesh, since many curse tablets hand over their victim to a demon in a very similar manner. In keeping with this, fourteen examples of this genre have been found in the sanctuary of Demeter in Corinth.[34]

The technical term for these tablets in Greek is καταδεσμός, a word that evokes the idea of binding. The Latin *tabellae defixionum*, from *defigere*, 'to pierce or push into', 'to rivet fast', has become the accepted term in scholarship (cf. Audollent), although it is actually rather rare in the sources. This is probably because it refers precisely to the fact that after the texts had been written on the strips of lead, they were often rolled up and pierced with a nail (illustration in Gager 19), symbolising not so much the pain that one wanted to inflict on one's enemy as the efficacy of 'fixing' the spell. The curse tablets were left at graves, the sanctuaries of underworld gods, battlefields, wells, cisterns and rivers, the circus and the racetrack. Our Greek example was found at Piraeus and dates from the fourth or third century BCE (SIG 3/1175):

> I have taken hold of Nikion and bound him by his hands, feet, tongue and soul. If he wants to speak contemptible words about Philon, then let his tongue turn to lead, and do you pierce his tongue through! And if he wants to undertake

---

[34] Cf. N. Bookidis and R. S. Stroud, *Demeter* (above, p. 105, n. 16)) 30f., with text and illustration.

anything, then let it be useless for him – indeed, may everything be pointless, ill-fated and uncertain for him!

I have taken hold of Hipponoides and Socrates and bound them by their hands, feet, tongues and souls. If they want to speak contemptible or evil words about Philon or do him any harm, then may their tongues and their souls turn to lead, and may they not be capable of saying or doing anything – even more, do you pierce their tongues and souls through!

I have taken hold of Ariston and bound him by his hands, feet, tongue and soul. May he not be capable of speaking evil of Philon, but rather may his tongue turn to lead! And do you pierce his tongue through!

The lead and the nail that holds the metal scroll together are employed here according to the principle of 'sympathy': the tongue is to turn to lead and be pierced through. The intention of the threefold formulation is to protect Philon, who is mentioned in the third person, from defamation, and also from other hostile actions on the part of his named enemies. It is probable that Philon also speaks in the first person (unless it is a professional magician who is undertaking the magic on his behalf), and a dark deity is addressed as 'you'.

A Latin counterpart from the first century BCE was discovered in a grave on the Via Latina near Rome. It contains a kind of magic directed against love (CIL I 1012; VI 140):

Just as the dead man buried here cannot speak nor converse [with anyone], so may Rhodine too be dead for Marcus Licinius Faustus, and be unable either to speak or to converse [with him]. As a dead person is welcome neither to gods nor to human beings, just so may Rhodine be unwelcome to Marcus Licinius: let her be worth just as much as the dead man who is buried here. Father Pluto, I hand over Rhodine to you, so that she may forever be hated by Marcus Licinius Faustus. In the same way, I hand over to you Marcus Hedius Amphion, Caius Popilius Apollonius, Vennonia Hermiona and Sergia Glycinna.

If one reads this text attentively, it is clear that it does not in the least wish that Rhodine were dead: the condition of death serves as a metaphor for the desired alienation between her and Marcus Licinius Faustus. This casts a different light on the harm intended by these curse tablets. In other examples, which have often been quoted,[35] the curse is directed against the horses and charioteers of the rival parties in the circus: a demon is to

---

[35] Cf. e.g. G. Luck, *Magie* (L60) 110f.; Gager has recently presented a representative selection of 134 texts.

torment the horses of the Greens and the Whites and kill them, as well as four charioteers who are mentioned by name, so that one's own party may win. The curse tablets deal mainly with the following spheres: love relationships, sporting contests, business life, political disputes, and the desire for justice when injustice has been committed (Versnel classifies this last category as a group on its own; on the contests cf. Faraone, 'Context').

The usefulness of such actions should not be sought one-sidedly in the way they affected other people; it is not the external world that is changed by magic, but the inner world of the one who practises it: emotional tensions, which would otherwise have been intolerable, are reduced, and this may permit one's social relationships to be shaped anew. This is why the fact that there is no external test proving success does not provoke any fundamental doubt about the effectiveness of the ritual – otherwise, it could scarcely have survived over so many centuries.

Fragments of pottery (*ostraka*) sometimes fulfilled similar functions to the lead tablets. We may give a brief list of some other objects that give us 'tangible' evidence that magic practices were carried out: the dolls that could be pierced with nails for purposes of cursing or revenge are not a creature of the imagination of Horace, but have been discovered by archaeologists in large numbers (illustrations in Gager 16f., 98, 102; cf. Trumpf; Faraone, 'Binding'). Those who wore *amulets* with magical inscriptions hoped for special powers and for protection against dangers of all kind (cf. Bonner); these were often worked in metal or in stone, and in the later case are called *gems* (cf. Schwartz; Wortmann). A further group are the '*incantation bowls*' (cf. Alexander; Naveh and Shaked), earthen bowls with protective and repellent magical inscriptions on the inside. These come from Mesopotamia in the third to fifth centuries CE, and the magical formulae are composed in Aramaic. Their Jewish origin is obvious in many cases, but one must also assume that they were used in non-Jewish circles.

(*b*) Magical papyri

List 75.
H. D. Betz (ed.), *The Greek Magical Papyri in Translation, Including the Demotic Spells*, vol. I: *Texts*, Chicago 1986, revised paperback edn. 1996.
——'Magic and Mystery in the Greek Magical Papyri', in C. A. Faraone and D. Obbink, *Magika Hiera* (L72) 244–76, also in Betz, *Hellenismus* (L3) 184–208.

——'Secrecy in the Greek Magical Papyri', 'The Changing Self of the Magician according to the Greek Magical Papyri', 'Jewish Magic in the Greek Magical Papyri', in Idem, *Antike und Christentum* (L3) 152–205.

W. M. Brashear, 'The Greek Magical Papyri: an Introduction and Survey. Annotated Bibliography (1928–1994)', *ANRW* II/18.5 (1995) 3380–3684.

R. W. Daniel and F. Maltomini (eds.), *Supplementum Magicum*, vols. 1–2 (PapyCol 16.1–2), Opladen 1990, 1992.

A. Dieterich, *Abraxas: Studien zur Religionsgeschichte des spätern Altertums*, Leipzig 1891, reprint Aalen 1973.

A. J. Festugière, 'La valeur religieuse des papyrus magiques' in *L'Idéal* (L3) 280–328.

E. Heitsch, 'Hymni e papyris magicis collecti', in *Die griechischen Dichterfragmente der römischen Kaiserzeit* (AAWG.PH 49), Göttingen 1961, 179–99.

R. Merkelbach and M. Totti (eds.), *Abrasax: Ausgewählte Papyri religiösen und magischen Inhalts*, vols. 1–4 (PapyCol 17.1–4), Opladen 1990–6.

M. P. Nilsson, 'Die Religion in den griechischen Zauberpapyri', in Idem, *Opuscula* III (L22) 129–66.

A. D. Nock, 'Greek Magical Papyri', in Idem, *Essays* (L2) I.176–94.

A. Önnerfors, *Zaubersprüche* (L74).

K. Preisendanz and A. Henrichs (eds.), *Papyri Graecae Magicae: Die griechischen Zauberpapyri*, vols 1–2 (Sammlung wissenschaftlicher Commentare), Stuttgart 2nd edn. 1973, 1974.

H. S. Versnel, 'Die Poetik der Zaubersprüche', *ErJb* NF 4 (1995) 233–97.

D. Wortmann, 'Neue magische Texte', *BoJ* 168 (1968) 56–111.

The Greek magical papyri (*Papyri Graecae Magicae*), presented in Greek and German by Preisendanz and Henrichs, and translated into English by Betz and others with additional material, are books of recipes that may have stood in the library of a magician. In their present form they come from the second to sixth centuries CE, especially from the third and fourth centuries; for example, the largest of them, the Parisian magical papyrus (PGrM IV), which comes from Thebes and has the character of an encyclopaedia with its 3,274 lines on 36 pages written on both sides, is dated to between 250 and 350 CE. One must suppose that the material has a lengthy prehistory, and this is confirmed in many points of detail by literary evidence (see 3 above).

One can discern from these texts the structure of a magical ritual grouped around the two main parts of the magical spell (λόγος) and the magical action (πρᾶξις), with a number of variable elements: invocation, petition, sacrifice, action, dismissal. This can be demonstrated in greater detail by means of excerpts from PGrM I 276–347:

Introduction	The magical action is as follows:
1. Action	Take a lamp that is not covered with red lead, and
– preparation	prepare it with a wick of fine linen and with oil of roses or of nard. Dress yourself in the garb of a prophet and take an ivory staff in your left hand and the amulet, i.e. the twig of laurel, in your right. But have the head of a wolf ready too, so that you can set the lamp on the wolf's head,
2. Sacrifice	and set up an altar of unscorched earth near the wolf's
– preparing it	head, so that you can offer a fragrant sacrifice to the god upon it. And at once the divine spirit enters.
– carrying it out	The fragrant sacrifice consists of the eye of a wolf, gum-resin, cinnamon, balsam and all other spices that are considered precious. Likewise, make a libation of wine, honey, milk and rain-water, and bake seven flat sacrificial cakes and seven other sacrificial cakes.
– ending it	You are to do all this near the lamp, clothed, abstaining from all that is impure and from eating any fish and from all sexual intercourse, so that you may kindle in the god a great desire for you ...
3. Spell	When you have performed all that is written
– introduction	here, call on the god with this song:
–epiclesis	'Apollo, Ruler, come with a paean and make known to me whatever I ask, Lord and Master. Leave Mount Parnassus and the Delphian Pytho, whenever our priestly mouth prays unutterable words. I call you, first angel of God, of the mighty Zeus, Jao,[36] and you, Michael who hold the heavenly world, and you, archangel Gabriel. Come down hither from Olympus, Abrasax ...

[36] Here and in the next lines, Jewish elements have been worked into the syncretistic context (the papyrus comes from the fourth/fifth century CE).

– petition	Send to my sacred magical songs this demon who moves at night compelled by you, in response to your commands: this comes from his tent,[37] and he is to tell me whatever I want in keeping with my desires.
– petition	And you, do not scorn my sacred song, but protect me, so that my form in its wholeness may emerge unharmed into the light of day.'
4. Action	And when he has come, ask him about whatever you wish, about soothsaying, verse oracles, the sending of dreams, the interpretation of dreams, about sicknesses, about everything found in the experience of magic. Cover a throne and an armchair with linen fabrics, but stand there and offer the above-mentioned fragrant sacrifice.
5. dismissal *– action*	And when the examination has been carried out and you wish to dismiss the god, then transfer to your right hand the above-mentioned ivory staff that you have in your left hand, and the twig of laurel that is in your right hand to your left. Put out the light that is burning, and turn away from the fragrant sacrifice with these words:
– words	'Be gracious to me, primal Father, early-born, who came into being from your own self. I call upon the fire that first appeared in the abyss, I call upon your power, which is the greatest for everyone, I call upon the one who destroys even in Hades, so that you may depart on to your own ship and may not harm me, but may always look with favour on me.'

This dismissal seems to be not without its risks: one does not always get rid of the spirits one has summoned up. In terms of substance, what we find in this text is oracular magic. The other types of magical action are found in the papyri as recipes also. PGrM IV 3014–18 describes how to make amulets for protection and to ward off demons. PGrM IV 1390–8 recommends the following powerful love potion: one should dip pieces of bread in the blood of a gladiator and throw them into the house of the

---

[37] The wolf's head or wolf's skin is meant here. The motif of the werewolf seems present in this text.

person one desires. PGrM II 1ff. (a detailed study of this text in Merkelbach and Totti I.81–102) describes the following harmful magic: the sorcerer drowns a male cat while saying to the 'god with the face of a cat' (line 3): 'See what my enemies [!] are doing to your likeness. Avenge yourself on them.' This ceremony, which is superior to all others, can be applied in various circumstances: 'as a spell for charioteers in the horse races, in order to cause dreams, as a love-potion that will captivate the desired person, or in order to cause strife and hatred' (lines 162–74). Many injunctions to keep silence about these actions and formulae occur in the texts, e.g. in PGrM 141: 'Keep secret, keep the action secret'; 130f.: 'Do not communicate it to anyone else, but keep . . . this high secret hidden.' The transmission takes place via family tradition, cf. ibid. 192f.: 'But hand this on to no one other than the son of your own body.'

We have still to consider the *voces mysticae*, semantically meaningless sequences of sounds which constitute an indispensable element of the magic spells. In translations, these are often only given a laconic representation by some such formula as 'magic words', but let us look more precisely at one case (PGrM I 222–31):

> An infallible means to become invisible: take the fat or the eye of a night-owl and the carapace of a ladybird and some oil from green berries, grind everything to a fine texture and anoint your whole body, saying these words while turned to the sun: 'I call on you by the great name *borke phoiour io zizia aparxeouch thythe lailam aaaaaa iiiii oooo ieo ieo ieo ieo ieo ieo ieo naunax aiai aeo aeo aeo.*' Make [the mixture] liquid and say over it: 'Make me invisible, Lord Helios *aeo oae eie eao*, to the eyes of every human being until sunset *io ioo phrix rizo eoa.*'

The groups of letters italicised here are the so-called *voces mysticae*. They have no genuine meaning in the original Greek, although one sometimes fancies that one can hear meaningful words echoing in them: in our text, the word *rizo* recalls *riza*, 'root'. But the effect is achieved through the tonal magic of the vowels which are piled up in this way, and through the continuous repetition. The idea was also that a new, superhuman, heavenly language was required when speaking to gods, and that these magical words supplied it. Exegetes often compare it to the glossolalia practised in Corinth, although the justification and intention of the praxis remain different in the two cases.

The *voces mysticae* are sometimes arranged graphically in the magical papyri to form particular geometric figures, e.g. in PGrM XIII (see Preisendanz and Henrichs II.124, 127; cf. also the lucid reproduction in

Merkelbach and Totti I.179–207; the first chart in Preisendanz and Henrichs; Betz 253–7). This brings us to the origin of a magical formula that is still popular among amateur magicians today. A book of medical prescriptions from *c*.200 CE describes how it is to be applied with skill as a means against fever. We read in the *Liber Medicinalis* of Quintus Serenus (935–40; cf. Önnerfors 25):

> How to cure malaria:
> Write the word ABRACADABRA on a leaf of papyrus and repeat it very often while coming down from above, but take the last letter [on each line] away, and one more element of the figures should be taken away for each line. You should keep on taking away the elements and writing down those that remain, until nothing more remains than one letter, which ends what you have written down in the form of a narrow cone [a conic tip]. Do not forget to tie this leaf of papyrus to the neck with a thread of linen.

Thus a powerful healing amulet is created, this time one made of papyrus. But how are we to visualise what is intended? How are the letters to be arranged? One possible realisation (cf. Önnerfors 62) would be the following:

ABRACADABRA
ABRACADABR
ABRACADAB
ABRACADA
ABRACAD
ABRACA
ABRAC
ABRA
ABR
AB
A

D. Astrology

1. Basic elements and history

List 76.

T. Barton, *Ancient Astrology*, London and New York 1994.
F. Boll, C. Bezold and W. Gundel, *Sternglaube und Sterndeutung: Die Geschichte und das Wesen der Astrologie*, Leipzig 4th edn. 1931, reprint Darmstadt 5th edn. 1966.

A. Bouché-Leclerq, *L'Astrologie grecque*, Paris 1899, reprint Aalen 1979.

W. Capelle, 'Älteste Spuren der Astrologie bei den Griechen', *Hermes* 60 (1925) 373–95.

F. H. Cramer, *Astrology in Roman Law and Politics* (Memoirs of the American Philosophical Society 37), Philadelphia 1954.

F. Cumont, *Astrology and Religion Among the Greeks and Romans*, Brussels 1912, reprint New York 1960.

F. J. Dölger, 'Die Planetenwoche der griechisch-römischen Antike und der christliche Sonntag', *AuC* 6 (1950) 202–38.

H. Gressmann, *Die hellenistische Gestirnreligion* (BAO 5), Leipzig 1925.

H. G. Gundel, *Weltbild und Astrologie in den griechischen Zauberpapyri* (MBPF 53), Munich 1968.

—— and R. Böker, art. 'Zodiakos: Der Tierkreis in der Antike', *PRE* II/10 (1972) 461–710.

W. Gundel, 'Astralreligion, Astrologie', *RAC* 1 (1950) 814–31.

W. Gundel and H.G. Gundel, 'Planeten', *PRE* 20 (1950) 2017–2185.

——*Astrologumena: Die astrologische Literatur in der Antike und ihre Geschichte* (SAGM.B 6), Wiesbaden 1966.

W. Hübner, *Die Begriffe 'Astrologie' und 'Astronomie' in der Antike: Wortgeschichte und Wissenschaftssystematik* ... (AAWML.G 1989,7), Stuttgart 1989.

J. H. W. G. Liebeschuetz, *Continuity* (L2) 119–26.

G. Luck, *Magie* (L60) 383–442.

P. Niehenke, *Astrologie: Eine Einführung* (RecUB 7296), Stuttgart 1994.

M. P. Nilsson, *Geschichte* (L2) I.841–3; II.268–81, 486–507.

W. Orth, 'Astrologie ind Öffentlichkeit in der frühen römischen Kaiserzeit', in G. Binder and K. Ehlich (eds.), *Kommunikation in politischen und kultischen Gemeinschaften* (Bochumer Altertumswissenschaftliches Colloquium 24), Trier 1996, 99–132.

(*a*) Initial observations

What awakens in us reverence before a higher power that is superior to ourselves? According to Immanuel Kant, there are above all two things that are capable of generating this feeling: the starry sky above us and the moral law within us. If the starry sky was still able to move the philosopher of German idealism to such an extent, we need not be surprised that classical antiquity gave it a religious consecration. It is not for nothing that the five planets known at that time bear the names of Roman gods, which were substituted for the older Greek divine names: Mercury, Venus, Mars, Jupiter and Saturn. It was usual to add the sun and the moon to this list, so that one arrived at a total of seven planets, which gave the seven days of the week their names (cf. Dölger). Tibullus (*c*.55–19 BCE) is the most ancient witness: 'I made the pretext of [an ill omen in] the flight of birds or evil premonitions, or else I asserted that I could not travel on *the sacred day of Saturn*' (1.3.17f.).

It is a matter of fact that the heavenly bodies affect the course of things in our world. It was very well known (see Cicero, *Divin.* 2.34) that the moon regulated the tides of the sea and the occurrences of ebb and flow; the alternation of day and night, and the rhythm of the seasons of the year, depends on the position of the sun. This prompted the question whether the stars directly cause these and similar effects, or merely send signals that accompany them. This question was never totally resolved in antiquity; even Plotinus, who devoted an entire treatise to the working of the stars *(Enn.* 2.3.1–18), discusses these two alternatives and concludes that they only 'indicate' (σημαίνειν), not 'bring about' (ποιεῖν). But even this restrictive view allowed the interpretation of the stars to remain a meaningful enterprise.

Belief in the stars is not, however, the same thing as astrology. We can still discern the older and broader phenomenon of an astral religion and piety which looked on the stars as living, divine beings, holding that the souls of the dead lived among the stars. This attained its zenith in the cult of Helios, with the adoration of the sun as the highest deity. But there is no great distance from this to the conviction that the position of the constellations allows one to deduce the destinies of human beings, both those of individuals and those of whole peoples and countries (Ptolemy [see below, 3(*c*)] differentiates between individual and universal astrology). Pliny the Elder assumes a simple synchronisation of events in the sky and on earth in his book on astronomy. Here he rebuts the apparently widespread postulate of this deeper kind of interconnection, which he sees as the human person's presumptuous attribution of too great importance to himself (*Hist. Nat.* 2.28f.):[38]

The stars ... are not, as the great multitude think, assigned to individuals among us, so that the bright stars would be assigned to the rich, the lesser stars

[38] Cf. R. König and G. Winkler, *C. Plinius Secundus d. Ä.: Naturkunde.* Buch II: *Kosmologie* (TuscBü), Munich 1974; H. Rackham, *Pliny: Natural History* vol. 1 (LCL 330), rev. edn. Cambridge, Mass. and London 1938.

to the poor, and the dark stars to the weak. Nor are they assigned to mortals with a degree of light appropriate to the destiny of each individual. They do not come into existence at the birth of the individual human beings to whom they would be assigned, nor does their fall indicate that someone is dying. We do not have so great a commonality with the sky that even the brightness of the stars up there would be something transient, as is the destiny of human beings.

But Pliny is also aware (cf. 2.23) that something more has developed from this initial position, viz. a specific branch of science, 'astrology', which was not linguistically distinguished in the classical period from 'astronomy'. Here we shall look primarily at astrology in the narrower sense, the individual astrology which interprets the character and destiny of a human being from the position of the stars in the hour of his birth, his 'horoscope'. This was carried out on various levels: as lay astrology which corresponds to what we find today in illustrated daily and weekly papers, and also as a serious undertaking which presupposed technical astronomical knowledge and demanded complicated calculations. Because it operated with tables, diagrams and numbers, genuine astrology was regarded as a high science, also known as *mathēsis*, 'science' or 'science of numbers'. *Mathematici* in antiquity were not mathematicians, but astrologers.

(*b*) Elements of the system

Various factors had to be considered when a horoscope was drawn up (cf. Niehenke). A fundamental significance is attributed to the planets which wander across the sky on seemingly irregular paths (hence their name 'planets', 'wandering stars', from πλανᾶν, 'to wander about'). The zodiac with its twelve signs is also important. These signs are derived from various constellations: Aries (ram), Taurus (bull), Gemini (twins), Cancer (crab), Leo (lion), Virgo (virgin), Libra (scales), Scorpio (scorpion), Sagittarius (archer), Capricorn (ibex), Aquarius (water-man), and Pisces (fish). The ascendant sign of a human person is that zodiac sign which, at the moment of his birth, is rising on the eastern horizon when seen from the place of birth. The position of the planets at this moment is also set in relation to this, using a further subdivision of the zodiac into sections, each with ten degrees. This produced thirty-six 'decans', and the rulers of these were thought of as personified divine beings. The angles between the planets in the sign of the zodiac were called 'aspects'. These went from the juxtaposition of two planets, or 'conjunction' (0°), to the 'opposition' (180°); the intermediary positions of 'sextile' (60°), 'quadrant' (90°), and 'trigon' (120°) were especially important here. In addition, twelve places or 'houses' were introduced, beginning at the point of intersection of the zodiac sign and the horizon. These cover various spheres of life: the first house concerns the personality, the second the guarantees of material well-being, the third education, the fourth the family of one's parents, the fifth one's own children and in general creative power, the sixth one's profession, the seventh partnership, the eighth death, the ninth one's intellectual activities, the tenth social relationships, the eleventh friendship and politics, the twelfth illness and other misfortunes. (Astrology also speaks of 'houses' in a different sense, denoting zodiac signs under the aspect of their subordination to a planet which preferentially 'dwells' in them. The two kinds of 'houses' should not be confused with one another.)

This basic knowledge is needed if we are to begin to understand what a man like Cicero writes about astrology (*Divin.* 2.89):

> This is how those who defend horoscopes of birth (*natalicia*) argue their case. They assert that the circle of signs, called 'zodiac' in Greek, possesses a determinative power, such that each individual section of this circle has its own specific influence upon the sky and changes it, depending on which stars would be found at any given point in time in the relevant sections, or in the adjacent sections. Likewise, those stars called 'planets' have their influence – in a different manner – upon the above-mentioned power, viz. by entering precisely that section of the circle in which the birth of the one who is entering the world occurs, or into a section which somehow stands near it or is in harmony with it (then they speak of triangles or quadrants) ... This permits them to determine for each person the natural inclination, the character, spirit, and body, the active conduct of life, and everything that may concern him.

Cicero is especially impatient in his treatment of astrology. He concludes his description with the exclamation: 'What incredible madness!' (2.90), thus continuing the tradition of academic scepticism which Carneades (second century BCE) before him had expressed. The sceptical objections to astrology are gathered together in the second century CE by Sextus Empiricus, a doctor who employed empirical methods, in his polemical work *Adversus Astrologos*, the fifth Book of his *Adversus Mathematicos*.[39]

Cicero discusses astrology under the category of divination 'by art'. This is not inappropriate, since that is where it belongs. Affinities to oracles can

---

[39] Cf. R. G. Bury, *Sextus Empiricus*, vol. 4: *Against the Professors* (LCL 382), Cambridge, Mass. and London 1949, reprint 1971.

be seen most directly in *katarkhēn* astrology, which sought to provide help when important decisions had to be taken, and therefore went beyond the horoscope to consider also the positions of the constellations at the actual moment. We find many other connections to the themes we have discussed above. The world-view of the magical papyri (cf. H. G. Gundel) betrays a strong astrological element. It suffices to compare only one passage from the 'Mithras liturgy': 'For first you will see the divine constellation of each day and each hour. You will see how some of the gods that wander around the pole ascend to heaven, while others descend' (PGrM IV 544–7; one should also recall the astrological substratum of the mysteries of Mithras, and the promise of salvation they made, viz. that one would be set free from the blind compulsion exercised by the constellations). A branch of astrology called *iatromathematics*, which diagnosed illnesses and recommended therapies on the basis of the zodiac signs, is related to the cult and the art of healing. Artemidorus has an entire chapter on the interpretation of astrological dreams in which the sleeper sees stars. He recommends that one should begin here 'from the method applied in the observation of the stars' (*Onirocr.* 2.36).

Cicero presents astrology as a subcategory. But that astrology is mainly presented on its own, above all in the later handbooks of the classical period (cf. 3 below), this is far from meaningless; not only because of its exceptional importance, but also in view of its history, which shows that it is a latecomer.

(c) Phases of development

Cicero often calls the astrologers (cf. *Divin.* 1.12: *astrologi*) 'Chaldaeans' (e.g. 1.2; 2.87, 88, 89, 91). This word denotes a provenance, and its first meaning is 'Babylonians'. The equation of 'Chaldaeans' and 'astrologers', which has virtually become an established fact (cf. e.g. Apuleius, *Met.* 2.12.2; 13.1; 14.1, 5) contains accurate information: Mesopotamia was an early home of astrology, which was used there *inter alia* to calculate the festal calendar. We need not follow all the intricate streams of tradition here. Astrology took on its essential form in Greek-speaking Egypt in the third and second centuries BCE. It was around this period that the indisputable authorities to whom the later technical literature appealed, such as the legendary king Nechepso and his priest Petosiris, or the thrice-great god Thoth (under the Hellenised name 'Hermes Trismegistos'), were established. It was along these circuitous paths that astrology reached the

Hellenistic-Roman world, where – despite some opposition – it quickly established its extraordinary victory from the second and first centuries BCE onwards. (Earlier mentions in Greek and Roman literature are either to be attributed to faith in the power of the stars or to be evaluated as a prelude to this victory.)

Significantly, King Antiochus of Commagene, who died in 34 BCE, had his horoscope depicted on his tomb in Nimrud-Dagh: the moon, Mars, Mercury and Jupiter in the zodiac sign of Leo (illustration: UUC III no. 118). A text in Seneca the Elder (father of the philosopher and statesman Seneca) shows us something of the transitional period in Rome, when astrology was beginning to enjoy success and to spread among the ordinary people. His *Suasoriae* is a collection of rhetorical exercises from his time as a student, written down from his memory, and here he speaks of the rhetor Arellius Fuscus, who was active in the period of Augustus. A subject is proposed for the speech: the interpreters of the stars attempted to prevent Alexander the Great, conqueror of the world, from entering Babylon, because of bad omens. What advice would we give him? The rhetor goes into great detail, using this occasion to describe the way astrology goes to work and attacking it:[40]

> But those who throw themselves into what they call the 'battle of human destinies' want to know your birthday and look on the first hour of your existence as the indicator of all the coming years. They observe the movement of the constellations, the directions in which they travel: whether the sun stood in threatening opposition or appeared favourable on the horoscope; whether the child received the light of the full moon, whether the moon was just beginning to wax, or whether the new moon hid its face in darkness, whether Saturn invited the newborn child to become a farmer, or Mars made him a soldier destined for war, Mercury a successful businessman, Venus graciously promised her favour, or Jupiter would bear the newborn child aloft from simple circumstances to dizzying heights. So many gods assembled around one head! ... It is quite simply the case that we share an uncertain destiny, and that all these things are mere illusions conceived by wily astrologers. There is no truth in any of this.

The important point to note here is first, the astrologers' view of themselves as struggling for their clients on the front line of the battle with destiny, and then the mocking exclamation: so many gods – in the form of

[40] *Suasoriae* 4.2f.; cf. M. Winterbottom, *The Elder Seneca: Declamations*, vol. 2 (LCL 464), Cambridge, Mass. and London 1974.

the planets, which bear the names of gods – assembled around the head of one newborn child.

(d) Political significance

But such objections were not strong enough to prevent astrology from having a powerful influence precisely on the political leadership of Rome. All the Roman emperors from Tiberius to Hadrian, with the exception of Trajan, were devotees of astrology. Tiberius himself drew up horoscopes, an art he had learned from Thrasyllus, one of his closest confidants, a very learned astrologer and scholar of the works of Plato. According to Suetonius, this meant that Tiberius neglected the gods and the exercise of religion, since he 'was devoted to astrology and convinced that all things were directed by fate' (*Tib.* 69; cf. Tacitus, *Ann.* 6.20.2). Nero's mother consulted 'Chaldaeans' about the prospects for her son's future (*Ann.* 14.9.3). Nero's court astrologer Balbillus, probably a son of Thrasyllus, is said to have advised the emperor to murder the most prominent Romans in order to neutralise the appearance of a comet which announced disaster (Suetonius, *Nero* 36.1). Tacitus laments the disastrous influence of the astrologers on Otho, the pretender to the throne, and makes the following jibe: 'There were not a few astrologers, the worst kind of accessories in the marriage of a prince, in Poppaea's private chamber' (*Hist.* 1.22.2).

It is easy to understand why Vitellius, Otho's rival, had no good opinion of the astrologers who prophesied his death, and that he expelled them from Rome by an edict and put recalcitrant astrologers to death (Suetonius, *Vitell.* 14.4). The behaviour of Tiberius may appear inconsistent – although he himself believed in astrology, he expelled the *mathematici* from Rome and Italy in 19 CE, with the exception of those who 'promised to give up their art' (Suetonius, *Tib.* 36) – but the contradiction is only apparent. His personal fascination and general political prudence were equally important. Astrologers could find themselves the victims of party politics, e.g. in the dispute between Augustus and Antony. In times of crisis, it was felt that they ought to be prevented from unsettling the people even further. The first expulsion of astrologers from Rome (for which however we have only one, not wholly unproblematic testimony) took place in 139 BCE. Augustus repeated this measure in 33 BCE and restricted the future activities of the astrologers in 11 BCE by forbidding people to consult them *inter alia* about the date of a person's death. In his work on *Astrology in Roman Law and Politics*, Frederick Cramer lists ten or eleven expulsions in the first century CE, as well as twelve judicial trials of clients of astrologers, often leading to the death sentence, and six trials of astrologers themselves (Cramer 232–81). But not even those who instigated such trials had any illusions about the effectiveness of their undertakings, for 'after every attack, astrology, the occult science which had become a world power, was rejuvenated and strengthened to face a new phase of its history and new struggles' (Gundel and Gundel, *Astrologumena* 135).

2. Reflections in literature

List 77.

J. Adamietz, *Juvenal: Satiren* (TuscBü), Munich 1993.

F. H. Cramer, *Astrology* (L76).

W. Gundel and H. G. Gundel, *Astrologumena* (L76, a fundamental work).

M. Heseltine, *Petronius: Satyricon*, rev. edn. (by E. H. Warmington) (LCL 15), Cambridge, Mass. and London 1969.

K. Müller and W. Ehlers, *Petronius: Satyrica/Schelmengeschichten* (TuscBü), Munich 2nd edn. 1978.

G. G. Ramsay, *Juvenal and Persius* (LCL 91), Cambridge, Mass. and London 1918, reprint 1979.

H. C. Schnur, *Juvenal: Satiren* (RecUB 8598), Stuttgart 1988.

O. Schönberger, *Petronius: Satyrgeschichten* (SQAW 40), Berlin 1992.

From the first century BCE onwards astrology in the narrower sense of the word begins to be reflected in literature, in a movement that parallels its diffusion in the Roman world. The poets make use of astrological *topoi* in their works and expect that their readers will possess sufficient knowledge to be able to decode these allusions. We have already spoken of Tibullus. His contemporary Propertius (*c.*50–15 BCE) provides a privately practising astrologer who was active near the Circus with a genealogy that naturally goes back as far as Babylon (4.1.77–86).[41] Horace and Ovid, Vergil and Lucan can all likewise be mentioned here, and Apuleius in the second century CE. We can also mention a brief work 'On astrology' from *c.*200

[41] On both poets, cf. G. Luck, *Properz und Tibull: Liebeselegien* (BAW), Zurich and Stuttgart 1964; G. P. Goold, *Propertius: Elegies* (LCL 18), Cambridge, Mass. and London 1990; J. P. Postgate, *Tibullus*, rev. edn. (by G. P. Goold) (LCL 6), Cambridge, Mass. and London 1988.

CE, which is included among the spurious works of Lucian. This creates a remarkable allegorical link between astrology and the oracles of earlier periods: the virginal Pythia in Delphi is a symbol of the zodiac sign of Virgo, and the very name of the oracle at Didyma shows that it is connected to the sign of Gemini (*Astrol.* 23; *didymos* in Greek = twin). The next two texts we shall consider are from Petronius (*d.*66 CE) and Juvenal (66–140 CE). They are representative of many other texts.

(*a*) Petronius

'Trimalchio's feast' from Petronius' *Satyricon* gives us 'valuable insights into the widespread popular belief in astrology and into the goings-on of lower-class astrologers' (Gundel and Gundel, *Astrologumena* 195). At the entrance to the dining room there hangs a painting which shows the paths of the moon and the images of the seven planets; a practical mechanism allows days of good and ill omen to be marked on this by means of stoppers (30.3f.). A round tray with the twelve signs of the zodiac is brought in. On the sign of Taurus (bull) lies a piece of beef, on the sign of Libra (scales) stand genuine scales with a pastry in the one bowl and a cake in the other, and so on. The high point of the evening is an explanatory astrological lecture given by the host, in which he exposes the total extent of his lack of education (39.5–15):

> 'The firmament here in which the twelve gods dwell turns into twelve images and becomes first of all a ram. Thus, everyone born under this sign possesses many sheep and much wool, as well as a thick skull, a shameless forehead and jutting horns. Great numbers of schoolmasters and quarrelsome people are born under this sign.' We paid him compliments on his astrological learning; then he continued: 'Then the entire firmament turns into a little bull ... Gluttons are born under Leo, as well as people who always want to command others; under Virgo womanisers and fugitives and chained slaves; under Libra grocers and apothecaries, and all those who add up sums; under Scorpio those who mix poisons and assassins ... under Aquarius owners of taverns and pumpkin-heads; under Pisces those who sell delicate foodstuffs and those skilled in speaking.[42] Thus the world turns around like a mill-wheel, and some evil cause brings it about again and again that a person is born or dies. But mother earth lies in the midpoint of it all, rounded like an egg.'

[42] One should note here that fish are dumb in classical astrology, as everywhere else!

The astrological view of the world which is put forward here does indeed still see the earth in the centre, but no longer as a flat disc under the vault of the firmament: now it is a freely floating sphere. The listeners react to Trimalchio's instruction with cries of: 'Ingenious!' and swear that Hipparchus and Aratus, both famous professional astrologers, are mere dabblers compared to him (40.1). It would scarcely have been possible for an author to formulate his contempt for vulgar astrology with greater clarity. Later, Trimalchio reveals that he keeps a 'fellow from Greece' who is 'intimate with the gods' as his domestic astrologer (76.10). He has told Trimalchio that he will live for a further thirty years, four months and two days (77.2).

(b) Juvenal

In his biting satire on ladies from higher urban society, Juvenal brings on the scene a priest of Isis, a Jewish woman who interprets dreams, and an Armenian who inspects entrails. He then introduces Babylonian astrologers (*Sat.* 6.553–62):

> But the Chaldaeans enjoy great confidence: they believe that whatever an astrologer says is information from the spring of Ammon,[43] since the oracle in Delphi is inactive, and the human race is punished by the darkness of the future. But the one who has been expelled more often enjoys a special position of honour among them. They have confidence in the skill of one on whose left and right hands iron chains have clanked, one who has lain for long in the prison of the Praetorian camp. No astrologer who has escaped judicial condemnation counts as gifted.

The ideal picture evoked by Juvenal is that of the 'martyr-astrologer' who has been caught up in the changing fortunes of the political evaluation of astrology, as discussed above. The conclusion drawn was that if the authorities were so much afraid of the astrologer, then there must be *something* of substance in his calculations. The satire is addressed to Postumus, whom Juvenal wishes to dissuade from marrying: his future wife will consult the astrologer about forbidden things: 'about her mother, who has jaundice and his taking far too long to die' (565), about the death of her sister, uncle, lover and husband. At least, one can say that she must consult a professional astrologer about these questions; in Juvenal's view,

---

[43] An allusion to the oracle of Zeus Ammon in the oasis of Siva in Libya.

much greater danger attaches to those women who have acquired some basic knowledge and practise astrology in their own homes (572–81):

> But be careful to avoid even meeting a woman in whose hands you see the worn-down *ephemerides*[44] like sticky amber spheres, a woman who consults no one but herself is consulted. When her husband wants to set out for the military camp or for his native land, she will not accompany him on the journey, because the numbers of Thrasyllus hold her back. If she resolves to travel as far as the first milestone, the hour propitious for this journey is deduced from the book; if she rubs the corner of her eye so that it itches, she checks in the book and then demands ointments; even when she lies sick in bed, no hour appears to her appropriate to take nourishment, unless it is indicated by Petosiris.

We have already met the names of Thrasyllus and Petosiris, and we return to the latter at 3 below. Juvenal's closing words show a case of *iatromathematics*, the employment of astrology for medicinal purposes.

3. Astrological handbooks

List 78.

F. Boll, *Kleine Schriften zur Sternkunde des Altertums*, ed. V. Stegemann, Leipzig 1950.

F. Cramer, *Astrology* (L76).

A. J. Festugière, *La Révélation d'Hermès Trismégiste*, vol. 1: *L'astrologie et les sciences occultes* (EtB), Paris 2nd edn. 1950, 89–186.

W. Gundel and H. G. Gundel, *Astrologumena* (L76, a fundamental work).

W. Hübner, 'Manilius als Astrologe und Dichter', *ANRW* II/32.1 (1984) 126–320.

G. Luck, *Magie* (L60) 383–442.

O. Neugebauer and H. B. van Hoesen, *Greek Horoscopes* (Memoirs of the American Philosophical Society 48), Philadelphia 1959.

The bases of the manuals of instruction in astrology in the imperial period were created in Egypt in the second and third centuries BCE and published pseudepigraphically. We possess only fragments of the works that were ascribed to Hermes Trismegistus (not to be confused with our Corpus

---

[44] Astrological calendars from which the position of the stars at a given time can be deduced.

Hermeticum, cf. also Festugière), or that circulated under the names of Pharaoh Nechepso and his high priest Petosiris. Fragments survive on papyrus of astrological works from the first to the fourth centuries CE;[45] but there is no edition that brings all these together. Inaccessible Greek manuscripts from the middle ages are described in the *Catalogus Codicum Astrologorum Graecorum*, published in twelve volumes at Brussels between 1898 and 1953, and excerpts given. One can also find some information in the individual horoscopes which were written down and collected (see Neugebauer and van Hoesen). As a minimum, they indicate the time of birth and the heavenly constellation that fitted this time.[46]

(*a*) Manilius

In the last years of the emperor Augustus' reign and the first years of Tiberius, an author named Manilius, about whom we have no biographical information, undertook the arduous task of recording in verse the astrological knowledge of his age, in the five Books of his didactic poem *Astronomica*.[47] However, the astrological system remains incomplete, since he does not deal with the planets. The close connection made in this work between traditional astrological ideas and Stoic philosophy is possibly Manilius' own achievement. This gives him the concept of the universal 'sympathy' in the universe as the basis of the correspondence between the movements of the stars and human destiny, e.g. at 2.60–66:

> For I declare in my song that God dominates nature in stillness,
> that he has utterly penetrated sky and lands and the sea,
> that he guides the enormous mass under the same conditions everywhere,
> that the entire cosmos lives in mutual harmony
> and that reason moves it, since one single breath dwells in all the parts
> and flies through everything, moving through the universe
> and giving life to it, giving it the form of bodies that breathe.

At the beginning of the fourth book he shows that he also has a 'pastoral' interest in astrology, when he asks: 'Why do we waste our lives year after

---

[45] An example is PTebt 276, in Luck 428.

[46] An example is POxy 2556, in J. Hengstl, *Papyri* (L4) 166.

[47] Text and German translation in W. Fels, *Marcus Manilius: Astronomica/ Astronomie* (RecUB 8634), Stuttgart 1990; text with an Eng. trans. in G. P. Goold, *Manilius: Astronomica* (LCL 469), Cambridge, Mass. and London 1977, rev. edn. 1992; among the secondary literature cf. Hübner.

year, full of fear, why do we torture ourselves with the blind desire for things?' (4.1f.). The insight into those regularities of life which stand written in the stars is meant to free human beings from slavery under their emotions and under the bustle of the world. Here we also find tenets derived from the Stoic belief in fate: 'Fate rules the world, everything is subject to stable laws' (4.14); 'From birth on, death threatens us, and the end is already poised in waiting at the beginning' (4.16) – in other words, the date of one's death is already fixed when the horoscope of birth is made.

In order to give astrology a solid foundation, Manilius argues that the sky influences the climate and the tides. He also adduces the reactions in the animal world (2.87–95). Trimalchio may have taken from Manilius his new picture of the world as a sphere that floats in the midpoint (1.173–235). Manilius gives heroes and important statesmen a place among the fixed stars of the sky (1.758–61). He makes astrological propaganda for the house of the Julian rulers, not only through the dedication of his work to Tiberius or Augustus (1.7–10), but also by his interpretation of Augustus' horoscope and his astrological deification: the emperor becomes a star in the heaven of the gods (1.926; cf. Cramer 96f.).

(b) Firmicus Maternus

One later writer who picks up the ideas of Manilius (though without naming him) is Firmicus Maternus in his 'Books of (exact) knowledge',[48] written in 335 CE. He is better known as the author of a refutation of the errors of the pagan cults from a Christian viewpoint, composed in 347 CE. His conversion to Christianity probably occurred between the writing of these two works. In his voluminous compendium, he speaks of the astrological preconditions for the profession of the astrologer: 'When Mercury stands in the third house, as seen from the position of the ascendant, he makes priests, magicians, famous doctors, astrologers and those who on their own discover and teach things not communicated to them by any other teaching authority' (3.6.1). Firmicus Maternus urges the astrologer at 2.30.1–15 to be very cautious in the exercise of his activity

[48] W. Kroll, F. Skutsch and K. Ziegler, *Julii Firmici Materni matheseos libri VIII* (BSGRT), Stuttgart 2nd edn. 1968; English translation by J. R. Bram, Park Ridge, NY 1975; extracts from this in R. MacMullen and E. N. Lane, *Paganism* (L4) 19–21.

and in his own conduct of life: he must avoid nocturnal sacrificial celebrations and suspicious secretiveness, and he must not give any information about the condition of the state or about the emperor's life expectation.

(c) Claudius Ptolemy

It was not Manilius, but Claudius Ptolemy (c.100–178 CE) who was the chief authority in Firmicus' eyes. Ptolemy wrote his main astrological work, the *Tetrabiblos* (= fourfold book) in Alexandria about the middle of the second century[49] as a continuation of his earlier *Syntaxis*, which had kept strictly to questions of astronomy. Ptolemy had proven his worth as a scholar in various fields of natural science, as well as in geography, the theory of numbers and the theory of harmony. A significant light is cast on the positive evaluation of astrology by the fact that such a scholar regarded astrology, when carried out seriously, as a natural complement to such fields. Thanks to his methodological clarity, his own contribution became a kind of 'bible' for all succeeding generations of astrologers until the modern period; Porphyry wrote an introduction to it, and Proclus composed a paraphrase of it. We quote only one passage of this work, which shows how he comes to list unpleasant personal qualities when he is describing the human characters produced by the constellations of the planets (3.13.14f.):

> When Saturn is united with Mars in an honourable position, he produces human beings who are neither good nor bad; they work with difficulty, they like to poke their noses into other people's business, they are boastful cowards, severe in their behaviour, merciless, arrogant, crude, fond of quarrels, they inflame others with no heed of the consequences, they engage in intrigues . . . In the opposite position, [Mars and Saturn] produce robbers, pirates, counterfeiters, persons who are the object of contempt, profiteers, atheists . . . thieves, perjurers, murderers, persons who eat forbidden foods, criminals, manslayers, poisoners, robbers of temples, desecrators of graves – in short, people who are utterly wicked.

---

[49] F. E. Robbins, *Ptolemy: Tetrabiblos* (LCL 435), Cambridge, Mass. and London 1940 (often reprinted). The quotation in our text is numbered in keeping with F. Boll and E. Boer, *Claudii Ptolemaei ΑΠΟΤΕΛΕΣΜΑΤΙΚΑ* (BSRGT), Leipzig 2nd edn. 1954.

245

The exegete will immediately be reminded here of the catalogues of vices in the New Testament, and this connection has in fact already been noted.[50] A beautiful epigram is also attributed to Ptolemy, summing up in two couplets the reserved pride of the astrologer who is able to free himself from earthly fetters through the continuous observation of the sky, and to rise up to the divine being:[51]

> I am indeed mortal – I know this, I who am a creature of the day.
>   Yet in my meditation I accompany the path of the stars,
>   as they circle the pole,
> and my foot no longer touches the earth: with Zeus himself at my side,
>   I feed on ambrosia at the divine meal.

(d) Vettius Valens

There is a comparable religious intensity in Vettius Valens, who compiled his *Anthologies* from older material, enriched with practical experiences and examples of horoscopes,[52] at roughly the same period as his superior rival Ptolemy, between 152 and 162 CE (with subsequent expansions). For him, astrology is like a mystery cult into which one must be initiated by a mystagogue before one can become an initiate of this science.[53] 'The one who reads his handbook with a pure heart takes his place in the immortal choir, sees the ranks of the gods and their mysteries, and attains a glory like that of the gods.'[54]

Otherwise, Vettius Valens writes on a less academic level than Ptolemy, more for praxis and on the basis of praxis. But he too discusses the

---

[50] Cf. A. Vögtle, *Die Tugend- und Lasterkataloge im Neuen Testament exegetisch, religions- und formgeschichtlich untersucht* (NTA 16.4–5), Münster 1936, 84–8.

[51] Critical text and translation in Boll 146, 155, 315.

[52] The older edition by W. Kroll, *Vettii Valentis anthologiarum libri*, Berlin 1908, reprint Zurich 1973, from which previous scholars have quoted, is now replaced by D. Pingree, *Vettii Valentis Antiocheni anthologiarum libri novem* (BSGRT), Leipzig 1986; a French translation of Book I (with text and commentary) is J. F. Bara, *Vettius Valens d'Antioche: Anthologies, Livre I* (EPRO 111), Leiden 1989; on the horoscopes in Vettius Valens cf. Neugebauer and van Hoesen 176–85.

[53] See the discussion by A. J. Festugière, *L'Idéal* (L3) 120–7; cf. the numerous entries in the index to Kroll or Pingree under μυστ–.

[54] Gundel and Gundel, *Astrologumena* 218.

fundamental question that has repeatedly accompanied astrology: in what sense is the human person free, if everything is predetermined by the position of the stars? Must not this idea – which has been illustrated by the picture of an enormous piece of clockwork, or a heavenly game of chess (Luck 394) – necessarily lead to fatalism and resignation? In his answer, Vettius Valens insists that destiny cannot be altered. Chance and hope act as its agents, in the manner of two gods; whoever is ignorant of astrology lies under their yoke. But the one who learns to understand his own horoscope achieves the minimum freedom that consists in accepting and bearing with courage that which is recognised to be unalterable:[55]

> But the one who strives for knowledge of the future and for the truth will be free in his soul from this servitude: he scorns chance and attaches no importance to hope, he does not fear death and lives without any inner disturbance, since he has educated his soul to have courage. He neither rejoices at good fortune nor lets himself become depressed by ill fortune, but is content with the present state of affairs. Since he does not desire impossible things, he bears with self-discipline that which is determined. Turning away from pleasure and flattery, he becomes a soldier in the service of fate. For it is impossible to employ prayer and sacrifice to gain mastery over the fate which has been determined from the very outset, and to create for oneself some other fate in keeping with one's own wishes. That which is accorded to us happens even without our prayer, and that which is not granted to us does not happen even when we pray. Just as the actors on the stage change their masks according to the works of the poets, calmly playing now kings and then robbers, peasants, simple persons or gods, so must we too play in the masks with which fate clothes us, and accommodate ourselves to the chances of passing time, even when we do not particularly care for them.

4. A look ahead

List 79.

F. Boll, *Aus der Offenbarung Johannis: Hellenistische Studien zum Weltbild der Apokalypse* (ΣΤΟΙΧΕΙΑ 1), Berlin 1914.

F. Cumont, *L'Égypte des astrologues*, Brussels 1937.

J. Freundorfer, *Die Apokalypse des Apostels Johannes und die hellenistische Kosmologie und Astrologie* (BSt[F] 23.1), Freiburg i.Br. 1929.

---

[55] 5.9 (220.19 = 221.5 Kroll) = 5.6.9–11 (209.34–210.14 Pingtree); cf. also Luck 429f.

W. Gundel and H. G. Gundel, *Astrologumena* (L76) 180–3 (on Philo), 190f. (on Josephus), 332–9 (on Christianity).

W. Hübner, *Zodiacus Christianus: Jüdisch-christliche Adaptationen des Tierkreises von der Antike bis zur Gegenwart* (BKP 144), Königstein 1983.

——'Religion und Wissenschaft in der antiken Astrologie', in J. F. Bergier (ed.), *Zwischen Wahn, Glaube und Wissenschaft: Magie, Astrologie, Alchemie und Wissenschaftsglaube*, Zurich 1988, 9–50.

F. Kudlien, 'Sklaven-Mentalität' (L70) 81–91.

R. MacMullen, 'Social History in Astrology', *AncSoc* 2 (1971) 105–16.

A. D. Nock, 'Astrology and Cultural History', in Idem, *Essays* (L2) I.493–502.

U. Riedinger, *Die Heilige Schrift im Kampf der griechischen Kirche gegen die Astrologie von Origenes bis Johannes von Damaskus: Studien zur Geschichte der Astrologie*, Innsbruck 1956.

The study of the astrological literature from the classical period is fruitful, not only for what it tells us directly about this one specific phenomenon from the border where religion and science meet, but also because it greatly enriches our knowledge of the history of religion and society in this period. Thus Cumont wrote a social and cultural history of late antiquity on the basis of astrological texts alone (*The Egypt of the Astrologers*), and Kudlien drew on them to reconstruct to some extent the mentality of slaves.

The controversy between Boll and Freundorfer about the significance of astrology in elucidating the astral symbolism of the Revelation of John was unsatisfactory, since Freundorfer's only intention was to defend the genuinely experiential character of the visions of the author of the Apocalypse (an untenable enterprise). We may venture to say that exegetes have not yet exhausted the potential contained in this group of texts, as this was briefly exemplified above in the case of the catalogues of vices.

A demanding programme of work is necessary here, because Judaism and Christianity too were compelled to take up the confrontation with the spiritual world power that astrology represented in late antiquity. They did this with the mixture – which we have already seen in the case of magic – of theoretical rejection and a partial coming to terms with the phenomenon in praxis. In an enigmatic note (*Bell.* 2.128), Josephus appears to say that the Essenes worshipped the sun; this may be a Hellenistic foreign influence on the Essenes, or a mere misunderstanding on Josephus' part. The community of Qumran was obliged to study astronomical data for the simple reason that these were necessary in order to calculate the calendar, which was very important for them. It is not always easy to evaluate how far this study went in the direction of astrology. 4Q186 consists of three horoscopes. According to the Jewish historian Ps.-Eupolemus, it was Abraham who invented the 'Chaldaean art', or else the original invention is transposed back to Enoch.[56] Apart from other astrological paraphernalia, Philo is acquainted with the seven planets and the twelve signs of the zodiac, and these are all the more welcome to him, since he is especially fond of contemplating these two sacred numbers seven and twelve. He makes his criticism of horoscopes clear in the case of Abraham, the model character who left Ur in Chaldaea (!) because his fellow countrymen 'liked to practise astrology and attributed everything to the movements of the stars', whereas he himself was no longer able to share this faith (*Abr.* 69f.). Philo's main concern here is to attack the fatalism that threatens faith in the divine providence (cf. his treatise *De Providentia*); it is improbable that he intended thereby to reject every theory involving the stars.

At a later date, the Church fathers drew above all on the Bible in their polemic against astrology (cf. Riedinger). The very fact that they continually had to fight a defensive battle is itself evidence of the abiding seductive power of their adversary. Adolf Harnack's verdict is surely too optimistic – or else, putting it differently, he shows only one side of the matter – when he cheerfully writes: 'One who is capable of assessing correctly what a power astrology represented in the imperial period – when the natural sciences as a whole were in decline – and how it succeeded in clothing itself in the garment of science, how it penetrated everywhere and suited the passive and weary mood of the period, will be able to appreciate the resistance put up by the Church (gnosticism was pretty helpless here too). Here we must say that the Church did something tremendous!'[57]

---

[56] Frag. 1.4 in N. Walter, JSHRZ I/2, 141f; R. Doran, *OTP* 11, 880.

[57] *Mission* (see above, p. 148, n. 49) 329.

Chapter IV
Divinised Human Beings: The Cult of Rulers and Emperors

List 80.

J .R. Fears, 'Herrscherkult', *RAC* 14 (1988) 1047–93.

M. Gilbert, *La critique des dieux dans le livre de la Sagesse (Sg 13–15)* (AnBib 53), Rome 1973, 130f.

M. E. Hoskins-Walbank, 'Evidence for the Imperial Cult in Julio-Claudian Corinth', in A. Small (ed.), *Subject and Ruler* (L81) 201–13.

H. J. Klauck, 'Das Sendschreiben nach Pergamon und der Kaiserkult in der Johannesoffenbarung', *Bib.* 73 (1992) 153–82, also in Idem, *Alte Welt und neuer Glaube: Beiträge zur Religionsgeschichte, Forschungsgeschichte und Theologie des Neuen Testaments* (NTOA 29), Fribourg (Switzerland) and Göttingen 1994, 115–43.

W. Schmithals, 'Die Weihnachtsgeschichte Lk 2.1–20', in *Festschrift für Ernst Fuchs*, Tübingen 1973, 281–97.

Å. von Ström, W. E. Pöhlmann, and A. Cameron, 'Herrscherkult', *TRE* 15 (1986) 244–55.

B. Wildhaber, *Paganisme populaire et prédication apostolique: D'après l'exégèse de quelques séquences des Actes* (Le Monde et la Bible), Geneva 1987, 69–74.

D. Zeller (ed.), *Menschwerdung Gottes – Vergöttlichung des Menschen* (NTOA 7), Fribourg (Switzerland) and Göttingen 1988.

The providence 'which orders all things in our life' has 'given us and our descendants the saviour who put an end to war' – a Christian who comes across such words for the first time will spontaneously feel that he or she is moving in the world of ideas found in Luke's nativity story. But every scholar will at once have recognised that these are some lines from the imperial inscription at Priene, to which we must return (see B, 2(*b*) below). It is none other than the Roman emperor Augustus who is called σωτήρ, 'saviour', in this text from the year 9 BCE. One may legitimately ask whether Luke, who wrote several decades later, knew this text and that this

250

is one reason why his Christmas story begins with a reference to the taxation edict of the emperor Augustus (Lk 2:1). There may be a 'subtle irony' in the point that 'Augustus, the imperial σωτὴρ τοῦ κόσμου [saviour of the world], is portrayed in the nativity story as the one who imposes the burden of the census *on the whole world* and that God makes use of this lordly command of the emperor in order to have the true saviour of the world born in the city of David' (Schmithals 290). Thus the New Testament itself poses the question of the significance of the Roman imperial cult, and it is not without reason that the theological encyclopaedias (see Fears, *RAC*; Ström et al., *TRE*) devote lengthy articles to this cult and to its predecessor, the Hellenistic cult of rulers.

As I have mentioned above in the Introduction, Wis 14.17–21 is also relevant to the study of the Hellenistic cult of rulers (cf. Gilbert). Here the Jewish author is especially critical of the significance of images for the genesis of the veneration of rulers, since he sees this as a transgression of the prohibition of images in the Old Testament, putting at risk the necessary distinction between God and human beings:

> (17) When people could not honour monarchs in their presence, since they lived at a distance, they imagined their appearance far away, and made a visible image of the king whom they honoured, so that by their zeal they might flatter the absent one as though present. (18) Then the ambition of the artisan impelled even those who did not know the king to intensify their worship. (19) For he, perhaps wishing to please his ruler, skilfully forced the likeness to take more beautiful form, (20) and the multitude, attracted by the charm of his work, now regarded as an object of worship the one whom shortly before they had honoured as a human being. (21) And this became a hidden trap for humankind, because people, in bondage to misfortune or to royal authority, bestowed on objects of stone or wood the name that ought not to be shared.

At Acts 12:20–3 Luke displays his reservations even more explicitly than in the nativity story. Here, the Jewish king Herod Agrippa I takes his place in sumptuous garments on the speaker's platform at Caesarea by the sea (cf. the parallel narrative in Josephus, *Ant.* 19.343f.), and the populace acclaim him: 'The voice of a god, and not of a human being!' But this touches already at the veneration of a ruler: therefore at once, an angel of God strikes him with a mortal illness, 'because he had not given the glory to God' (cf. Wildhaber). Exegetes often admit that it is impossible to interpret the Revelation of John without having recourse to the imperial cult (cf. Klauck). The terrible beast of Rev 13:1–4, which has blasphemous names written on its forehead and is adored by all the world, symbolises the Roman empire, represented by the figure of the *Imperator* at each point in time. (see further, e.g. for Corinth, Hoskins-Walbank)

Martin P. Nilsson has described the genesis of the cult of rulers as 'the most obscure and most highly disputed problem of Greek religion in the historical period'.[1] But we cannot avoid touching at least briefly on its beginnings, before we concentrate on the further development until the end of the first century CE. Apart from the differences in date, we must also pay heed to geographical differences. The phenomenon takes on very different forms in the various areas of the Mediterranean world – in Egypt otherwise than in Asia Minor, in Palestine otherwise than in Greece, and differently again in Rome and in the western half of the empire. Asia Minor, which is so important for the history of earliest Christianity, occupies a key position here. Once more, we shall attempt as far as possible to work with original texts. Apart from the literary sources, we are obliged in particular to study inscriptions and other archaeological discoveries such as coins, statues and temple precincts.

A. The Hellenistic cult of rulers

List 81 (standard works).

W. den Boer (ed.), *Le culte des souverains dans l'empire romain* (EnAC 19), Geneva 1973.

L. Cerfaux and J. Tondriau, *Un concurrent du christianisme: Le culte des souverains dans la civilisation gréco-romaine* (BT.B 5), Tournai 1957.

J. R. Fears, *Princeps a diis electus: The Divine Election of the Emperor as a Political Concept at Rome* (PMAAR 26), Rome 1977 (on this, cf. P. R. Brunt, 'Divine Elements in the Imperial Office', *JRS* 69 [1979] 168–75).

D. Fishwick, *The Imperial Cult in the Latin West*, vols. 1.1–2 and 2.1–2 (with continuous pagination) (EPRO 108), Leiden 1987–92.

C. Habicht, *Gottmenschentum und griechische Städte* (Zet. 14), Munich 2nd edn. 1970.

E. Kornemann, 'Zur Geschichte der antiken Herrscherkulte', *Klio* 1 (1901) 51–146.

S. R. F. Price, *Rituals and Power: The Roman Imperial Cult in Asia Minor*, Cambridge 1984, reprint 1987.

[1] *Geschichte* (L2) II.135.

A. Small (ed.), *Subject and Ruler: The Cult of the Ruling Power in Classical Antiquity* (Journal of Roman Archaeology. Supplementary Series 17), Ann Arbor 1996.

F. Taeger, *Charisma: Studien zur Geschichte des antiken Herrscherkultes*, vols. 1–2, Stuttgart 1957, 1960.

L. R. Taylor, *The Divinity of the Roman Emperor* (Philological Monographs of the American Philological Association 1), Middletown 1931.

A. Wlosok (ed.), *Römischer Kaiserkult* (WdF 372), Darmstadt 1978 (with a good Introduction by the editor, 1–52).

1. *The beginnings*

(*a*) Examples of texts

List 82.

V. Ehrenberg, 'Athenischer Hymnus auf Demetrios Poliorketes', *Antike* 7 (1931) 279–97, also in Idem, *Polis und Imperium*, Zurich and Stuttgart 1965, 503–19.

O. Immisch, 'Zum antiken Herrscherkult' (1931), in A. Wlosok, *Kaiserkult* (L81) 122–55.

O. Kern, *Religion* (L2) III.111–25.

M. Marcovich, 'Hermocles' Ithyphallus for Demetrius', in Idem, *Studies in Graeco-Roman Religions and Gnosticism* (SGRR 4), Leiden 1988, 8–19.

L. J. Sanders, 'Dionysius I of Syracuse and the Origins of the Ruler Cult in the Greek World', *Hist.* 40 (1991) 275–87.

Z. Stewart, *La religione* (L2) 562–77.

Bibliography in L81, especially Habicht and Taeger.

Lysander

It would be relatively easy for us to grasp the beginnings of the cult of rulers, if we accepted an ancient source which explicitly states how, when and why divine honours were paid to a living ruler *for the first time*. In a local history of the island and city of Samos written by Duris, who was ruler on the island from *c.*300 BCE, we find the following remarks:[2]

> For he [i.e. Lysander] was the first *Greek* to whom the cities erected altars and offered sacrifices *as to a god*, and also the first in whose honour religious hymns were sung. According to tradition, the first lines of one of these hymns run as follows:

[2] FGH 76F71, from Plutarch, *Lys.* 18.3f.

'Let us sing a solemn hymn
in praise of the general of sacred Hellas,
who came from spacious Sparta.
O! Io! Paean!'

The people of Samos also decided to change the name of their main feast, which was consecrated to the goddess Hera ('Ηραῖα) to the 'feast of Lysander' (Λυσάνδρεια).

If this account is reliable – and Habicht (3–6) has convincingly defended its correctness against the criticism by Taeger (162–4) – then it takes us back to the year 404 BCE. Setting up altars, offering sacrifices and singing paeans are rites that properly speaking are carried out only for the Olympian deities. According to this text, Lysander appears to have almost suppressed the goddess Hera. Her main yearly festival is replaced by his, or at the least, from now on his feast is celebrated each year along with hers.

Political reasons prompt these apparently excessive honours. In the final phase of the Peloponnesian War, Lysander, the general of the Spartans, had won important victories over Athens. In the course of his liquidation of the Attic maritime confederation, he also attacked Samos, expelled the supporters of Athens, and led back to their homeland the representatives of the ruling oligarchy, who had gone into exile. The foundation of his cult by these men can be explained 'as the expression of the personal gratitude of those who hitherto had been refugees, and who now received back their homeland, their sovereignty and their possessions' (Habicht 3f.). It can be understood as a reaction, expressing thanks for rescue and help to the power to whose intervention the surprising reversal of fortune was attributed. This specific constellation of factors helps to explain why the veneration of Lysander remained limited to one specific point in the year and one particular place. It is indeed possible that similar honours were paid to him at other places in Greece, but no evidence of this has been discovered as yet. It is certain that the veneration of Lysander did not encompass the whole of Greece.

This however allows us to perceive the fundamental structure of a phenomenon which is appropriately expressed in the title of Habicht's book: 'Greek cities and the phenomenon of the divine human being'. One can trace many further examples across a period of one hundred and fifty years, until c.240 BCE. Help and rescue are basic functions of the divine, and this seems to permit the inference that, where help and rescue are experienced, the one who brings these is acknowledged to be himself a manifestation of the divine power. These civic cults are freely offered acts of veneration, a demonstration of gratitude for concrete acts of help. They are limited to particular areas, frequently to one civic society alone, and in the nature of things they are often addressed to important political and military figures, since only these men possessed the power necessary to give genuine help when a city in Greece, in Asia Minor, or on the Aegean islands was in distress. One can illustrate this in greater detail by means of two examples from the available source material, which becomes ever more copious from the fourth century BCE onwards.

Antigonus I

Antigonus I, also known as Monophthalmos (the 'one-eyed'), was one of the Macedonian generals of Alexander the Great; on his death, Antigonus was given the sovereignty over a part of Asia Minor. In the year 311 the citizens of the city of Skepsis (near Troy in north-west Asia Minor) resolved to pay him various honours:[3]

> Resolution of the people [*dēmos*]: since Antigonus was the cause of so much good for the city and for the rest of the Greeks, one should praise Antigonus and congratulate him for what he has accomplished. Besides this, the city is to congratulate the Greeks on being free and autonomous, and because they can live in peace in the future. In order that Antigonus may be honoured in a manner worthy of his deeds, and that the *dēmos* may show that it is grateful for the benefits received, a sacred precinct is to be marked off for him, an altar set up and the most splendid cultic image possible erected. The sacrifice, the athletic contest, the bestowal of the garland and the other solemn ceremonies in his honour are to be held annually, as they have already been celebrated. He is to be garlanded with a golden wreath to the value of one hundred gold pieces. Likewise, [his sons] Demetrius and Philip are to be garlanded, each one to the value of fifty gold pieces. The bestowal of the garland is to be announced at the athletic contest during the celebrations. Besides this, the city is to offer thanksgiving sacrifices for the message [εὐαγγέλια] sent by Antigonus, and all the citizens are to wear festal garlands.

The good news mentioned in the final line of this text was contained in a letter from Antigonus (cf. OGIS 5) in which he told the city that he had made peace with Alexander's other generals and that, thanks to his initiative, 'all the parties to the treaty' guaranteed 'the freedom and autonomy of the Greek states' (Habicht 42). Although neither of these lasted very long, the peace treaty and the guarantee of freedom were due to

---

[3] OGIS 6.10–34.

Antigonus' good services, to which the inscription refers when it speaks of 'much good', 'what he has accomplished', and 'his deeds'. This is why he is honoured with thanksgiving sacrifices and athletic contests.

We do not find in this text the phrase 'as to a god', which we read in the text about Lysander, and one could attempt to explain these honours as purely non-religious. The possibility always existed in Greece of bestowing particular honours on well-deserving persons during their lifetime. Skilful diplomatic activity, successful discharge of high office, success in art or sport, the financing of public works are examples of works that could be rewarded by resolutions of the popular assembly, e.g. by the bestowal of a garland which was worn on the head of the person honoured, by the public reading of a *laudatio* which was then preserved on inscriptions, by the erection of a statue or the assigning of a particular place at performances in the theatre. But it is impossible to overlook the fact that the privileges accorded to Antigonus go further than what was customary in the case of one's fellow citizens: it was not normal to mark off sacred precincts and erect an altar for these (in the same way as a king like Antigonus was no longer a member of the *polis*, but stood above the *polis*). The veneration of Antigonus has traits resembling the cult of the gods.

Demetrius Poliorketēs

The elder of the two sons of Antigonus mentioned in OGIS 6.28f., Demetrius, had the sobriquet *Poliorketēs*, 'conqueror of cities'. For a time, he was a very successful general who exercised a great personal magnetism (cf. Immisch 130: 'a fairy-tale prince of genius'). He freed the city of Athens in 307 BCE from the rule of a tyrant and from occupation by the Macedonians. From then on, the Athenians heaped on him honours of a hitherto unheard-of variety. On his second visit in 304 BCE, the spot at which he alighted from his chariot was declared to be the sacred precincts of the 'descending god', and an altar was erected there (Plutarch, *Demetrius* 10.4). On a later occasion, an unknown poet composed a cultic hymn which is transmitted by Duris of Samos in his historical work (it is probable that the beginning and the conclusion are missing; for an explanation of this, cf. Ehrenberg):[4]

---

[4] FGH 76F13; from Athenaeus, *Deipnosoph.* 6 (253d–f); translations in M. P. Nilsson, *Religion* (L4) 85; UUC II.103; Immisch 126; Ehrenberg 279f. The text is composed in a difficult ithyphallic metre which cannot be imitated in translation.

The greatest among the gods have drawn close to our city
and shown us the greatest favour.
For the happy occasion has brought hither
both Demeter and Demetrius.
Behold, she comes to celebrate the exalted mysteries of the Korē,   5
while he, serene as befits the god,
has drawn near, beautiful and laughing.
The sight is exalted: all the friends in a circle,
and he himself in their midst –
just as if the friends were the stars, and he the sun.   10

Hail to you,
O Son of the mighty god Poseidon and of Aphrodite.
The other gods dwell so far away,
or else they have no ears,
or they do not exist, or do not care at all about us.   15
We see you in our midst,
not a wooden or stone presence, but bodily.
And so we pray to you.

First of all, Beloved one, bring about peace,
for you are the Lord [κύριος].   20
I am not able to fight against the Sphinx
which holds sway not only over Thebes,
but over the whole of Greece;
nor against the Aetolian who sits on the rock
(as she did in times gone by)   25
and robs and deports our people.
It was typical of the Aetolians to steal that which lay close at hand
– and now they also steal that which lies far off.
It is best that you yourself should inflict the punishment;
but if not, then find some Oedipus   30
who will either throw down this Sphinx from the rock
or else change it into stone.

The first two lines of this text speak of a 'parousia', a kind of entrance made by the gods into the city of Athens (the word πάρεισιν is used here, as also in lines 7 and 6). The external similarity of the names and of the season of the year prompts the association of Demetrius in line 4 with the goddess Demeter: it is September, and soon the celebration of the Eleusinian mysteries (cf. II/B), centred on the goddess Demeter and her daughter Persephone (called 'Korē', 'the Maiden', in this text), will begin. Thus a number of factors permit this time to be seen as a *kairos*, an especially favourable occasion. In Greek mythology, serenity, beauty and laughter (attributed to Demetrius in lines 6f.) are attributes accompanying the appearance of friendly divinities such as Dionysus, to whom a number of allusions are made elsewhere in the text. The comparison to the constellations in lines 9–10, with Demetrius as the radiant sun in the circle of his friends, may be nothing more than a metaphor; but it may also betray something of the belief in the stars that was to develop later (cf. III/D above), seeing human destiny as standing under the governance of the stars. In lines 11f. the poet gives Demetrius an 'honorary' pair of divine parents: Poseidon, the god of the sea, because Demetrius had just won important successes in naval encounters, and Aphrodite, the goddess of love, because his amatory exploits were on everyone's lips. Lines 13–15 display an extraordinary scepticism in relation to the traditional faith in the gods – we do indeed have a whole pantheon of gods, beginning with Zeus and his family, but do they really exist? If they do, do they hear us, are they concerned for us, or do they not remain much too far away? The last point especially recalls the Epicurean critique of the gods (see V/C, 2(a) below). Finally, the existence of wooden or stone statues of the gods in human form is turned against the gods (cf. Ps 135:15–17): is it not preferable to address a human being of flesh and blood, especially when one experiences vigorous help from him? The prayer which the Athenians address to their new god in the next strophe implores the peace which Demetrius, invoked as *kyrios*, could bring about thanks to the position of power which he has at the moment. The de facto political situation is contained in cipher language in the mythological comparison that follows: as the Sphinx once oppressed Thebes until Oedipus eliminated it, so now the Aetolians with their allies are threatening the sphere of influence of the city of Athens. The Athenians feel too weak in military terms (line 21) to be able to fight the 'thieving' Aetolians (lines 26f.). It is only Demetrius who can save the situation here, either in person or through a representative whom he designates.

Older scholarship tended to castigate the events involving Demetrius Poliorketēs and his cultic hymn as a symptom of decadence and of a falling-off from the gilded summits of the Olympian religiosity of the Greeks. Even reflective authors can express the verdict that this is the sign 'of the deepest degradation of religion and of the worst orgies of the cult of human beings'.[5] It is correct that even within the classical period voices

---

[5] M. P. Nilsson, *Geschichte* (L2) II.152.

were raised to criticise what the Athenians did as intolerable flattery (the evidence is preserved e.g. in Plutarch's biography of Demetrius). But here political motives often played a decisive role: the indignation was not caused by the veneration alone, but more by the fact that it was paid to one's political opponent. It is also correct that Demetrius himself appears to have reacted basically with irony to the veneration paid him. It soon became clear that this reaction was right, for his changing fortunes in war led the Athenians to turn away from him again in 288/7 BCE and to expunge all traces of the cultic honours that had hitherto been his. But the text of the cultic hymn allows us to perceive a serious problem of theodicy: how do people behave when they believe, not unreasonably, that they have been abandoned by their ancient gods? At any rate, an evaluation on moral terms alone fails to come to terms with the totality of the phenomenon, since it prevents us from inquiring about the function such a phenomenon had within the structure of religion and society as a whole.

(b) Attempts at an explanation

List 83.
M. P. Charlesworth, 'Einige Beobachtungen zum Herrscherkult, besonders in Rom', in A. Wlosok, *Kaiserkult* (L81) 163–200 = 'Some Observations on Ruler-Cult, especially in Rome', *HThR* 28 (1935) 5–44 (excerpts).

H. Dörrie, *Der Königskult des Antiochos von Kommagene im Lichte neuer Inschriften-Funde* (AAWG.PH 60), Göttingen 1964.

R. Gordon, 'The Veil of Power: Emperors, Sacrificers and Benefactors', in M. Beard and J. North, *Pagan Priests* (L11) 199–231.

A. F. Laurens (ed.), *Entre hommes et dieux: Le convive, le héros, le prophète* (CRHA 86 = ALUB 391), Paris 1989.

A. D. Nock, 'The Cult of Heroes', in Idem, *Essays* (L2) II, 575–602.

——'Notes on Ruler Cult' I-IV, ibid. 134–59.

F. Pfister, *Der Reliquienkult im Altertum*, vols. 1–2 (RVV 5.1–2), Giessen 1909, 1912, reprint Berlin 1974.

P. Veyne, *Bread and Circuses*, London 1990.

F. W. Walbank, 'Könige als Götter: Überlegungen zum Herrscherkult von Alexander bis Augustus', *Chiron* 17 (1987) 365–82.

Bibliography in L81.

Even if we leave open the strictly chronological questions concerning our first textual example (about Lysander on Samos), so that we do not claim that this shows the precise point in time when the cult of rulers began, this text nevertheless makes it clear that this was a new phenomenon in terms of the criteria of the classical world too, and that it required explanation. What had led to it?

There is nothing remarkable in the fact that political and especially kingly power should choose to clothe itself in a religious aura and that its subjects should exalt it in terms of religious transcendence; the ancient Orient already provided examples of this. This went furthest in Egypt, where the reigning Pharaoh was seen as a 'hieroglyph' of God;[6] the myths assign a divine father to him. A startlingly simple explanatory model takes this as its starting point, asserting that Alexander the Great had become acquainted with the divine kingship in Egypt, and that this had so impressed him and coincided to such an extent with his own self-understanding that he introduced it into the whole of his own realm, thereby consciously creating the cult of the ruler. However, this model collapses as soon as we take seriously the chronologically earlier information about the Spartan general Lysander and similar traditions. We shall return to this when we discuss the role of Alexander (see 2 below).

When it is proposed that the roots of the cult of rulers are to be found on Greek soil, the objection is often made that the Greeks made a careful distinction between the divine and the human. The famous expression 'Know yourself', which was inscribed on the temple of Apollo at Delphi, is in fact meant to be understood in this sense: recognise that you are a human being, not a god, and accept the boundaries that are laid down for you. Epic poetry and drama see hubris as a special transgression, the presumption that attempts to burst out of human boundaries and take hold of divine power for oneself.

All of this is perfectly true, but there are also trajectories running in the opposite direction, and these converge upon one another, as we shall see in what follows.

'Divine' human beings

It is precisely this attack upon hubris that reveals that a temptation to go beyond the boundaries did exist. Divine power could manifest itself in particular, favoured human beings, in philosophers, poets, seers, doctors

---

[6]   On this it suffices to read R. Gundlach, 'Der Pharao – eine Hieroglyphe Gottes: Zur "Göttlichkeit" des ägyptischen Königs', in D. Zeller, *Menschwerdung Gottes* (L80) 13–35.

and miracle workers. We need only recall Empedocles' (485–425 BCE) view of himself: 'I travel around as an immortal god, no longer mortal, and everyone heaps honours on me, as is appropriate in my case.'[7] Nevertheless, these honours paid to him do not include sacrifices, altars, statues, or athletic competitions; in other words, they are not yet assimilated to the ritual that is appropriate in the case of the gods of Olympus. Such expressions, to which presumably the immediate adherents of the speaker would have given the warmest assent, attest an exceedingly lofty self-consciousness linked to exceptional charismatic abilities.

Euhemeros

We should also pay heed to the simple fact that the Greeks imagined their gods in human form and that conduct in the world of their gods was very much human conduct. It became clear that this starting point could be developed in various ways. In his utopian vision of the state, presented in the form of a novel relating a journey, entitled the 'Sacred Inscription',[8] Euhemeros of Messene (*c.*340–260 BCE) turned the whole idea on its head. He claims to have discovered on the distant island of Panchaia a golden column with an inscription revealing that Uranos, Chronos and Zeus were prudent and energetic kings at the dawn of time. Because of their deeds, they were raised to the rank of gods. This was understood later as a critique of religion and of myth, as a hypothesis about the origin of the Greek belief in gods, but Euhemeros may also have meant something else: it may have been intended as a theoretical justification of the contemporary cult of rulers. He was in the service of King Cassandros from 311 to 298 BCE, and he supplied him and other aspirants with instructions on how they could attain divine honours through the correct performance of their role as rulers.

The cult of heroes

In yet another way, the boundaries between gods and human beings were somewhat porous: after their death, human beings could be declared 'heroes', i.e. they could ascend to become a kind of demigod (in individual cases, this path leads even further, to the status of a *daimōn* and ultimately of a god). What is a hero? Putting it in simple terms, and prescinding from

---

[7] FVS 31B112; cf. also III/A, 2(*c*) on the 'divine human being'.

[8] A selection from the text is given by M. P. Nilsson, *Religion* (L4) 80f.; on the influence of this work on the cult of rulers cf. Dörrie, esp. 218–24; see now R. Baumgarten, *Heiliges Wort* (L43) 182–96.

the other possibility of the 'descent' of those who had formerly been gods, heroes are men of an earlier age who performed exceptional deeds in their lifetimes, and it was believed that they still possessed some power after their death. The centre of their cult, which was often limited to one single city, was the tomb with the bones of the hero, and this has led Friedrich Pfister to speak of a genuine 'cult of relics'. Plutarch tells us about the help that the Athenians believed they had received from Theseus, the legendary founder of their democracy, and about the 'translation' of his bones as a consequence of the Peloponnesian War:[9]

> At a later period, a number of reasons led the Athenians to venerate Theseus as a hero, especially the fact that not a few of those who fought against the Persians at Marathon believed that they had seen how an apparition of Theseus in full armour led the attack on the barbarians before them. When the Athenians consulted the Delphic oracle after the Persian Wars, while Phaedon was archon [476/5 BCE], the Pythia replied that they should bring back the bones of Theseus and give them an honourable burial in Athens and watch over them ... When his mortal remains were brought back, the Athenians rejoiced and received them with splendid processions and sacrifices, just as if Theseus in person were returning to his own city. And now he lies buried in the heart of the city, beside the place where the gymnasium stands today,[10] and this place serves as a refuge for slaves and for all those among the common folk who are afraid of those more powerful than themselves – since Theseus too was a man who gave protection and assistance to the oppressed, and graciously received their petitions. They celebrate the main festival for him on the eighth of the month Pyanepsion ...

The founder of a city or a colony was almost always given heroic status after his death. Other candidates with good prospects of being declared heroes were lawgivers and those who murdered tyrants. Those who fell in war could be collectively declared heroes. Although the boundaries ought not always to be sharply drawn, one can say that the cult of heroes has some specific traits vis-à-vis the cult of the Olympian gods. Thus, the sacrifices in honour of heroes have retained clear traces of the sacrifices for the dead (see I/D, 3(a)): they are offered at the tomb. The sacrificial animal, commonly a black beast, is slaughtered over a pit in the earth, into which the blood flows as nourishment for the dead man. Everything that is

---

[9] *Thes.* 35.5–36.3; M. P. Nilsson, *Religion* (L4) 64.
[10] A special feature of the cult of heroes: normally, cemeteries had to be situated outside the city walls.

left over is burnt – a departure from the normal pattern whereby the sacrifices provide food for a subsequent meal on the part of those celebrating the ritual. The differences are too great to permit us to derive the cult of rulers directly from the cult of heroes. The cult of rulers is directed to a living human being, and the cultic forms resemble those of the Olympian gods, whereas the hero is always a dead person, whose veneration begins only after his death, and takes other forms. Nevertheless, one may not go to the other extreme and say that the two are not related at all. The cult of heroes certainly makes its contribution to the general framework within which the cult of rulers can be understood.

The cult of benefactors

Further light is given by a factor that has already been indicated in the discussion of the public honours paid to living persons, for here we found stereotyped concepts such as 'saviour' (σωτήρ) and 'benefactor' (εὐεργέτης) which were also employed in the cults of heroes and of rulers. Aristotle's observations in the *Rhetoric* (1.5.9 [1361a 28–37]) about benefactors and the honours paid to them are eloquent:

> Honours are rightly paid in most cases to those who have de facto provided benefits, although honours are also paid to the one who has the potential of providing benefits. This 'benefit' consists either in rescue [σωτηρία] or the preservation of life or wealth, or any of those other good things that are not so easily acquired, either now at this precise moment or in the past. It is the case that honours are paid to many persons on account of apparently trivial things, since the situation of time and place was favourable. The honours consist in sacrifices, [literary] monuments in verse and in prose, an honorary public office, first seats [in the theatre], tombs, statues, public banquets, a piece of land, or – as the barbarians do – prostrations to the ground [προσκυνήσεις] and ecstatic acclamations [ἐκστάσεις][11] – in short, gifts that the individuals concerned consider to be valuable.

When he begins his list of honours by speaking of sacrifices, Aristotle no doubt means that these are offered, not *to* the persons concerned, but rather *for* them and for their personal well-being. And the first items in what follows should be seen in connection primarily with living persons; there is nothing excessive here. The transition to another dimension begins

---

[11] One could also translate this word here as making way for someone, leaving the path clear, keeping a respectful distance (cf. Liddell and Scott s.v.).

with the tomb erected for the benefactor after his death. Analogously, his statue on its plinth and the public banquets held in memory of him are to be assigned to the period after his death. The custom that Aristotle ascribes to the barbarians is the one with the strongest religious overtones: *proskynēsis* and *ekstasis*. Not only did the relationship between 'benefits and honours' function well; it was something that held the structure of classical society together (on 'euergetism' cf. the detailed study by Veyne). It has been suggested that one should speak, not of a cult of rulers, but of a cult of benefactors (Charlesworth 163). But in that case, we would have to extend to living persons honours that Aristotle's account accords only after death, and accept that the 'barbarian' customs were found among the Greeks too.

Diodoros Pasparos

An example from the city of Pergamum shows a possible bridge between the cult of heroes and the attribution of honours to benefactors. The excavation of a complex of buildings and the interpretation of these discoveries with the aid of inscriptions from the gymnasium and of coins gives the following picture.[12] A wealthy and influential citizen of the city, Diodoros Pasparos, was paid numerous honours in the period after 70 BCE, after his meritorious service in successful negotiations with Rome which freed the city from heavy tax burdens; he had also paid out of his own pocket for extensive renovations to the gymnasium. The assembly of the citizens accordingly resolved on the foundation of a cultic site to be called the 'Diodoreion', while he was still alive. A priest was appointed to perform the cult there. Logically, this site did not contain a grave of Diodoros, and this distinguishes it from a genuine *herōon*.

The building consisted of a cultic room and an auditorium with about one hundred and twenty places. A niche for a marble statue of Diodoros was made in the front wall of the cultic room, and a votive inscription with his name may have been placed above this. The honorific inscriptions inform us that sacrifices of food and the decoration of the image with bands and garlands took place, as well as regular feasts with processions and athletic contests. The cultic room and vestibule would have been used for the sacrificial meals, while the auditorium would have been the suitable location for musical competitions at which hymns were sung in praise of

---

[12] On what follows cf. W. Radt, *Pergamon*, 1988 (L100) 279–85.

Diodoros and his deeds. Renovations were carried out *c*.17 CE, and the complex was still in use in the third century CE.

(*c*) Results

One difference between the cult of heroes and benefactors on the one hand and the cult of rulers on the other is that men like Lysander, Antigonus and Demetrius Poliorketēs do not belong to the *polis*, but intervene from without, as wielders of political power. Nevertheless, it is possible to discern various phases, which can almost be brought into a logical sequence. We find the bestowal of secular honours for living persons, thanks to their especial merits; and the cultic veneration of dead persons, again because of their deeds, through the declaration after their death that they are heroes. If one combines the two and develops the trajectories, one arrives at the cultic veneration of living human beings because of their exceptional achievements. The specific point of this final step (which cannot be explained in terms of linear development alone) is that the forms of veneration are now taken over from the cult of the Olympic deities and thus lead beyond the stage at which a human being is declared to be a hero.

In the initial phase we must be cautious in assessing what this means for the 'divinity' of those who are honoured in this way; we do not find such expressions as θεὸν ποιεῖν, 'to make someone a god', or *apotheōsis*, 'deification'. In the strict sense of the word, no new gods are created: rather, the divine quality which is already present and has manifested itself in mighty acts of deliverance, is officially acknowledged for what it is. 'However, a divinity that depends on human assessment cannot be absolute in the manner of the divinity of the Olympians. It is not immanent to the person of the "god", but appears only in particular places and on particular occasions, and is therefore neither universal nor eternal.'[13] Nor was it possible to remain indifferent forever to the glaring contradiction between divinity and mortality. The death of the one honoured in the cult must necessarily prompt the question – to some extent posed also in mockery – of what kind of divinity this was, if it did not involve eternal duration. An elegant reply might be the suggestion that divinised human beings did not die, but were caught up into the heaven of the gods.

[13]   C. Habicht, *Gottmenschentum* (L81) 198.

Although the cult of heroes and benefactors allows us to identify some explanatory frameworks, the question still remains why this transition occurred precisely between c.400 and 300 BCE. Other factors must have been involved, including major societal and political transformations. In the long term, the city state as a self-sufficient entity was no longer capable of existence; when it is breached, it looks to external powers to provide the help and protection which it needs. A very significant psychological element surely lies in the fact that this can no longer be provided by the citizens of the city, but only by the intervention of outsiders; this makes it easier to link such events to the intervention of gods who stand over the *polis*, appear 'from above' and intervene with power.

2. Alexander the Great

List 84.

J. P. V. D. Balsdon, 'Die "Göttlichkeit" Alexanders', *Hist.* 1 (1950) 363–88, also in A. Wlosok, *Kaiserkult* (L81) 254–90.

M. Giebel, *Plutarch: Alexander. Caesar* (RecUB 2495), Stuttgart 1980.

C. Habicht, *Gottmenschentum* (L81) 17–41, 225–29, 245–52, 272–74.

J. R. Hamilton, *Plutarch: Alexander. A Commentary*, Oxford 1969.

G. Hölbl, *Geschichte des Ptolemäerreiches: Politik, Ideologie und religiöse Kultur von Alexander dem Grossem bis zur römischen Eroberung*, Darmstadt 1994.

D. Kienast, 'Alexander, Zeus und Ammon', in *Zu Alexander dem Grossen* (*Festschrift G. Wirth*), Amsterdam 1987, 309–33.

E. Meyer, 'Alexander der Grosse und die absolute Monarchie' (1905), in A. Wlosok, *Kaiserkult* (L81) 203–17.

J. Seibert, *Alexander der Grosse* (EdF 10), Darmstadt 3rd edn. 1990 (with bibliography).

F. Taeger, *Charisma* (L81) I, 171–233.

W. W. Tarn, *Alexander the Great*, Cambridge 1948.

U. Wilcken, 'Zur Entstehung des hellenistischen Königskultes' (1938), in A. Wlosok, *Kaiserkult* (L81) 218–53, at 218–33.

(*a*) The present state of scholarship

It is not a matter of dispute that the figure of Alexander the Great made a lasting impression on his contemporaries and on those who came after him. The breathtaking conquests which he began at the age of twenty, the destruction of the apparently invincible Persian world empire, and his early death – all this belongs to the stuff from which his legend was woven. The most appropriate concept to apply to him is no doubt that of the charismatic personality which Taeger seeks to use in general in his two-volume work. However, a lively scholarly discussion finds no consensus on whether the deification took place already in his lifetime, as a necessary consequence of these already existing elements, and whether Alexander consciously aimed at this.

No less a man than Aristotle was the tutor of the young Alexander. W. W. Tarn therefore takes as his starting point a passage in Aristotle's *Politics*, in a description of the true king which includes the following affirmation: 'For such a one seems to be counted as a god among human beings' (*Pol.* 3.8.1 [1284a10f.]); Tarn argues that Alexander learned this from his tutor and applied it consistently to himself. But this does seem to be an exceptionally narrow basis for such a broad enterprise (cf. the criticism in Balsdon's essay). We must also point out that this extravagant praise (similar to that used much earlier of Hector in the *Iliad* [24.258f.]) is introduced by the comparative particle 'as', and must therefore be seen as a metaphorical statement. There is no indication at all in this text of de facto cultic honours paid to such a king; and precisely this is the *specific difference*.

Eduard Meyer proposes another explanation. He maintains the thesis, mentioned above, that Alexander became acquainted in the East, especially in Egypt, with the divine monarchy and saw this as the exact category for his own person. Thus he discovered a suitable instrument for his power politics, something that would allow him to reconcile the Greek city states, which valued their autonomy and were therefore still putting up resistance, to the new form of absolute monarchy. Finally, Alexander saw the position of a godlike supreme ruler, on whom cultic honours from all parts of the world converged, as a fitting framework for his far-flung world empire with its different peoples, cultures and religions. This model, however, requires us to play down the chronologically earlier examples of a cult of rulers, and this calls into question its ability to solve the question of the origins of this cult. To establish how far it corresponds to Alexander's own plans, one would first have to evaluate the meaning of several ambiguous episodes in his life. Our investigation proceeds in two steps. First we recall some traits of Alexander's biography in the form given by Plutarch, and then we discuss the three most disputed points from an historical perspective, so that we can arrive at a concluding evaluation.

(b) Plutarch's *Life of Alexander*[14]

The fact that Plutarch wrote *c.*100 CE, centuries after the events he is relating, can be an advantage, since it makes clear how the figure of Alexander was still seen even after the lapse of a considerable period of time. This gives us a better grasp of a number of topoi which have taken on a fixed place in his biography. Besides this, Plutarch is reckoned as a critic of the cult of rulers.[15] Thus one cannot suspect him of having gone too far in adapting the figure of Alexander to the role of a divine ruler: on the contrary, as we shall see, he occasionally deletes elements from the already existing tradition about Alexander, which sometimes goes much further in this direction.

Birth and childhood

Plutarch already surrounds Alexander's conception and birth with the aura of the numinous. His conception is framed between two dreams, one bestowed on his mother Olympias before their wedding night and the other on his father Philip of Macedon afterwards (2.2):

> Now before the night on which they were to be united in the bridal chamber, the bride dreamed that it was thundering and that a flash of lightning penetrated her body. This flash kindled a mighty fire which blazed up with many flames and spread on all sides. Some time later, after the wedding, Philip for his part had a dream in which he pressed a seal upon the body of his wife, and it seemed to him that the engraving on the seal bore the image of a lion.

An interpreter of dreams explains the seal in the form of a lion as a sign that a son who is 'passionate and courageous like a lion' will be conceived (2.3). There is no difficulty in understanding the conflagration which spread on all sides: it signals the future conqueror of the world. Plutarch restricts himself to cautious hints when he continues his narrative (2.4):

> Once, while Olympias was sleeping, a snake was seen, stretching out beside her; it is said that this caused Philip's love and devotion to her to cool off, so that he no longer went so often to her that he might rest with her. Perhaps he was afraid that his wife practised witchcraft, or that she might give him poisoned potions;

[14] Cf. B. Perrin, *Plutarch: The Parallel Lives*, vol. 7 (LCL 99), Cambridge, Mass. and London 1919, reprint 1958, 223–439, and Hamilton's commentary.

[15] Cf. K. Scott, 'Plutarch and the Ruler Cult', *TPAPA* 60 (1929) 117–35; a more reserved judgement in G. W. Bowersock, *Intellectuals* (L95) 187–91.

but perhaps he was also averse to intercourse with her because he thought that she was linked to one more powerful than himself.

We pay especial attention a little later, when we are told that this situation leads Philip to send messengers to consult the oracle at Delphi, and he is told that he must offer sacrifice to Ammon (an Egyptian god whom the Greeks identified with Zeus), and pay special veneration to him (3.1); and when we read that he 'lost the sight of one eye, when he put it to the chink in the door and saw how the god, in the form of a snake, had intercourse with his wife' (ibid.). We are then told that Olympias 'revealed the mystery of his conception' to Alexander, when he was a grown man and set out on his great military campaign, 'commanding him to display a disposition worthy of his origin' (3.2). There is historical evidence that Philip did indeed lose the sight of one eye, but this happened in a battle. The tradition has invented a new aetiological legend here. Taken as a whole, the hints in Plutarch give the impression that possibly it is not Philip who is the father of Alexander, but rather a deity, Zeus-Ammon, who comes in the form of a serpent and has intercourse with the mother. Only the mother knows the truth of this mystery, and she entrusts it to Alexander as an appeal to him to show by his deeds that he is the son of a god. Plutarch's language, especially the insertion of terms like 'it is said', betrays his scepticism. This is also seen in the inconsistent narrative: the serpent is mentioned only after the wedding night, i.e. after Alexander has already been conceived. There is in fact an alternative narrative, which Plutarch passes over in silence, about the Egyptian king and priest Nektanebo. He deceives Olympias and wins her confidence, disguises himself as the god Ammon, and in this form begets Alexander with her.[16]

According to Plutarch, the temple at Ephesus burns down on the day of Alexander's birth (3.3). Magicians who happen to be there become very excited, and prophesy that a great disaster will befall Asia (3.4). Philip, however, who has just conquered a hostile city, receives the news of the birth along with news of two further victories, and this leads the seers in his entourage to predict that this boy will be invincible (3.5). When he speaks of Alexander's outward appearance, Plutarch informs us that his entire body diffused a most delightful fragrance (4.2: εὐωδία), something that is sometimes said about the epiphanies of deities. While yet a boy, Alexander

---

[16] Cf. the detailed version from the Alexander Romance (1.1.1–13.2) in H. van Thiel, *Leben und Taten Alexanders von Makedonien: Der griechische Alexanderroman nach der Handschrift L* (TzF 13), Darmstadt 1974, 3–19.

receives ambassadors in the absence of Philip and holds discussions with them, impressing them with his questions, which are not in the least boyish, but rather intelligent and businesslike, so that they are astonished (5.1).

There are obvious links to the Gospel narratives about the birth and childhood of Jesus. All we need to note here is that the tradition of Jesus too is carried out in already-existing literary forms and selects motifs from a stable repertoire. It is above all Luke, in the way in which he presents his narrative in Lk 1–2, who goes the furthest in taking account of specific expectations of a Graeco-Roman readership.

The march through the wilderness

We now leap ahead in Plutarch's biography and accompany Alexander on his perilous journey to the oracle of Zeus-Ammon in the oasis of Siva in the Libyan wilderness. After founding the city of Alexandria, the general resolves to visit this celebrated oracle site, which the Greeks too held to be infallible (cf. III/B, 2–3). He and his companions experience miraculous help en route (27.2f.):

> After the signs which were there for the guides had disappeared, a great confusion arose and the caravan broke up in uncertainty. Then ravens appeared and took over the guidance of the march. These flew ahead, when the caravan followed them, and urged them to greater speed; when it hung back and moved more slowly, the ravens waited for them. But the most marvellous thing of all was this: at night, the ravens ... with their harsh cries brought them back to the right path, when they were going astray.

When they reach their goal and the priest of the oracle receives them, Plutarch notes that he greets Alexander in the name of the god ὡς ἀπὸ πατρός, 'as from a father', an expression that remains rather vague in Greek. Then Plutarch goes on to report another version of Alexander's arrival in Siva (27.5):

> Others, however, relate that the prophet wanted to salute Alexander in Greek with the friendly address παιδίον, 'dear child'. But since he was not a Greek, he made a mistake at the end of the word, putting an 's' in place of the 'n' and thus saying παιδίος, *Paidios*. Alexander is said to have taken great pleasure in this slip of the tongue. And this is said to have started the rumour that Alexander had been addressed by the god as παῖ Διός, 'son of Zeus'.

The construction of this strange phonetic misunderstanding contains what can only be called rationalistic reservations, and it is obvious that Plutarch is happy to include these in his account. This passage is immediately followed by an observation about the reasons of propaganda that led Alexander to make a differentiated usage of his alleged divinity before different audiences. It was only vis-à-vis barbarians that 'he presented himself as if he were totally permeated by his divine origin', whereas he showed 'more moderation and reservation in his claim to divinity' vis-à-vis the Greeks (28.1). When he was wounded by an arrow, he said to those around him: 'What is flowing there, my friends, is blood, not ichor' (28.2), i.e. the colourless liquid that according to *Il.* 5.340 flows in the veins of the gods.

A case of conflict

As time passes, Plutarch notes in his hero an increasing tendency to accept assimilation to his new oriental-Persian environment. This included the custom of the *proskynēsis*, falling to one's knees and prostrating oneself in reverence before the king, which was customary in the Persian court ceremonial and which Alexander ultimately demanded of his Macedonian soldiers and officers too. A significant incident occurred at a feast. One of Alexander's friends received a goblet of wine from his hand, turned to the house altar, drank, performed the *proskynēsis*, and kissed Alexander, before returning to his place on the couch (54.3). The altar was certainly not dedicated to Alexander, but probably to the *Agathos Daimōn*, one of the patronal deities of the drinking feast, and the *proskynēsis* may originally have been directed to this deity, although Plutarch presents it as directed to Alexander. The others follow the example of this first guest, but the philosopher Callisthenes attempts to avoid performing the *proskynēsis*. However, he attracts attention and leaves the feast without receiving a kiss. Plutarch makes the following approving comment: 'He refused, in a decisive manner worthy of a philosopher, to prostrate himself and he was the only one to state openly something that caused indignation in all the most prominent and senior Macedonians. Thereby he preserved the Greeks from a dreadful disgrace' (54.2).

The declaration of heroic status

The closest friend of Alexander's youth and his companion in arms was Hephaistion. When he died of a raging fever in Ecbatana, Alexander's grief knew no bounds (72.2):

> He gave orders that, as a sign of mourning, the manes of the horses and mules should at once be shorn, and he had the battlements removed from the walls of the neighbouring cities. He had the wretched doctor crucified; he forbade the playing of flutes and all kinds of music in the camp for a long time, until an

oracle came from Ammon with the directive that honours should be paid to Hephaistion and sacrifices offered to him as a hero.

What we have here is an unspectacular case of the attribution of heroic status after death, as happened later to Alexander himself in various places. It makes good sense, psychologically speaking, that this should be used to help ease the process of mourning. Unfortunately, Plutarch does not tell us much about what happened after Alexander's death; it is possible that some pages have disappeared from the end of the manuscript. Despite all the coded hints at a divine origin, and other indications, we basically do not find in Plutarch the specific essence of the cult of rulers, viz. the ritual veneration of Alexander while he was still alive.

(c) The points of controversy

The oracle of Ammon and the proskynēsis

It is historically certain that Alexander went to the temple of Ammon in Siva in 331 BCE. The reason why he consulted this oracle site, and not any of the others which existed at that time in Egypt, is that only Siva was known in the Greek world and enjoyed high prestige. But does this of itself suffice to indicate (as Meyer argues) that Alexander expected to hear a message in Siva that would meet with universal acceptance in Greece? Was he looking for his real father – did he want to have his divine sonship authenticated? To put it in these general terms is surely to read too much out of these events. Perhaps all Alexander intended, in view of his audacious plans, was to get reliable information about his future from an acknowledged source; one indication of this may be that he preserved the contents of most of the oracles as a secret until the end of his life. No problem is involved for Egyptian thinking in the fact that he is addressed as son of the god, and there is no need to invoke a phonetic misunderstanding. As liberator and ruler of Egypt, he was greeted with the title which the prevalent royal ideology attributed to the pharaoh (see above, p. 260, n. 6). Only when this is translated does it take on other, much more explosive connotations for Greek readers.

The *proskynēsis* involves primarily a cultural misunderstanding. This was indeed accorded to the Persian Great King and to the high Persian court officials in general, but this does not in the least mean that the king was looked on as a god. Unlike Egypt, the Persian empire does not show evidence of a divine kingship. Thus the motivation for the prostration was not religious, but political and social. The Greeks and Macedonians, on the other hand, never accorded the *proskynēsis* to an earthly ruler. It was performed only in the cult of the gods, and even there was a rare occurrence. It is probable that all Alexander wished to achieve was a uniform court ceremonial both for the Persians, among whom this custom was too deeply rooted for him to be able to abolish it, and for the Greeks in his entourage, but that he underestimated the importance of the specific emphases of each tradition.

Deification in the last year of his life?
A third and final point of controversy concerns a deification of Alexander which he is said to have required from the Greek cities of his fatherland in the last year of his life. Let us begin by noting that it is relatively certain that the cultic veneration of Alexander as a god existed in a number of Greek cities in Asia Minor. This should not be interpreted, as some scholars assume, as the post-mortem declaration of heroic status; these cults were founded while Alexander was still alive, more specifically, in the years of his campaign in Asia Minor (334–333 BCE), when Alexander freed the Greeks of Asia Minor from the crushing yoke of the Persians. The honours paid to him as expressions of gratitude for what he had done remain within the framework of the cult of benefactors, which has been discussed above. Some of these localised cults survived for a very long time. There is evidence that a temple of Alexander with priest and cult of Alexander existed in Ephesus as late as 102–16 CE (Habicht 18f.).

The situation in the cities of Greece is somewhat different. It is historically certain that intense discussions raged in Sparta and Athens in 324 BCE about whether Alexander should be deified. It is likewise certain that the outcome of these discussions was the arrival in Babylon of an embassy from Greece with the intention of according Alexander divine honours. Some scholars (e.g. Meyer) account for this by saying that when a decree about the reintegration of political refugees was read aloud to the assembled Greeks at the Olympic Games in 324 BCE Alexander used this occasion to demand his own deification, with the intention of suffocating all opposition before it could properly take form. We have no sources that directly attest this demand, so that its very existence has been called into question (e.g. by Balsdon).

A self-correction in Habicht's book shows how difficult it is to decide this question. First he argued as follows (28–36 in the first edition): on another occasion, not in connection with the decree about the refugees, Alexander demanded that the Greek cities declare his friend Hephaistion

273

to be a hero, and specifically as πάρεδρος, i.e. 'the subordinate who shares his throne'. Thereby Alexander hinted that he himself was the superior in this pair of friends, and that even now, while he was still alive, greater honours should be paid to him – and the knowledgeable Greeks would immediately have grasped the point. After some initial hesitation, the cities followed this discreet hint. When objections were raised, Habicht withdrew his argumentation based on the role of Hephaistion (246–50, in the postscript to the second addition: here he says that πάρεδρος simply means 'assistant' or 'protector', and that one cannot place so much weight upon this term). It remains 'an open question, in what form Alexander communicated to the Greek cities his wish that divine honours be paid to him' (250). Habicht insists that this did in fact take place, and that the decisive motivation was not power politics. Rather, the clearly superhuman tasks which Alexander had already carried out, and his sovereign position led him to believe that he now had a general right to such honours. Taken together, the expressions of thanks which he had already received, and the model of the post-mortem declaration of heroic status, which had recently taken concrete form on the death of Hephaistion, as well perhaps as the greeting at the oracle of Ammon, may all have contributed to set Alexander thinking along these new lines.

If this constellation of ideas is correctly defined, it contains some new elements which point forward in time to the period of the successor kings to Alexander. The initiative is taken by the ruler, not by his subjects, and there is no longer a direct relationship between the experience of concrete benefits and the spontaneous reaction of gratitude. It is no longer only one city that is affected, but the cities of an entire country. We do not know how things would have developed, if Alexander had not died within the year, and it is pointless to speculate on this. In the final analysis, Alexander's role as founder of the cult of rulers appears modest. Nevertheless, one can call him a precursor of the Hellenistic-Roman cult of rulers and emperors, less because of what he himself did in this direction than because of the myths and legends which quickly formed around his person and served later rulers as a model for the way in which they portrayed themselves.

3. The period after Alexander

List 85.

E. Bikerman, 'Le culte monarchique', in *Institutions des Séleucides* (BAH 26), Paris 1938, 236–57.

B. Funck, 'Herrscherkult der Seleukiden – Religion einer Elite oder Reichsideologie? Einige Bemerkungen zur Fragestellung', *Klio* 73 (1991) 402–7.

G. Grimm, 'Die Vergöttlichung Alexanders des Grossen in Ägypten und ihre Bedeutung für den ptolemäischen Königskult', in H. Machler and V. M. Strocka (eds.), *Das ptolemäische Ägypten: Akten des internationalen Symposions 27.–29. September 1976 in Berlin*, Mainz 1978, 103–12.

C. Habicht, *Gottmenschentum* (L81), esp. 42–126.

H. Hauben, 'Aspects du culte des souverains à l'époque des Lagides', in L. Criscuolo and G. Geraci (eds.), *Egitto e storia antica dall'Ellenismo all'età araba: Bilancio di un confronto*, Bologna 1989, 441–67.

H. Heinen, 'Vorstufen und Anfänge des Herrscherkultes im römischen Ägypten', in *ANRW* II/18.5 (1995) 3144–80.

A. D. Nock, 'Sunnaos Theos', in Idem, *Essays* (L2) 202–51.

U. Wilcken, 'Entstehung' (L84) 229–53.

E. Winter, 'Der Herrscherkult in den ägyptischen Ptolemäertempeln', in H. Machler and V. M. Strocka, *Ägypten* (see above, under Grimm) 147–60.

It was very difficult to fill the power vacuum that resulted upon Alexander's early death. His Macedonian generals divided the world empire among themselves in the lengthy and complicated 'wars of the successors', so that there arose the dynasties of the Lagides or Ptolemies in Egypt, the Seleucids in Syria, the Antigonids in Asia Minor and Greece, and the Attalids in Pergamum. The titles in the names borne by various rulers of the Lagides and Seleucid dynasties have themselves religious implications. Among the Lagides, we may mention Ptolemy I Sōtēr ('the deliverer'), Ptolemy III Euergetēs ('the bestower of benefits'), Ptolemy XII Neos Dionysos ('the new Dionysus'); among the Seleucids, Antiochus II Theos ('the god'), Antiochus IV Epiphanes ('the manifestation' of divine power), and Antiochus VI Epiphanes Dionysos ('the apparition of Dionysus'). It seems that Dionysus was preferred when a direct identification was desired, not least because of the vitality, the joyful celebration, and the display of pomp which the cult of the god of wine allowed. Other factors were the association between the myth of Dionysus and the biography of Alexander as a result of his Indian conquests, and the endeavour to secure a divine origin for the family of the rulers. The city of Miletus bestowed the especially far-reaching title of 'god' on Antiochus II, after he had freed it from the lordship of tyrants. This means that what we have here is another example of the civic cults, which must be distinguished from the imperial cults properly so called.

(a) The civic cults

Most of these rulers received specific divine honours from individual cities on specific occasions. In the case of the Antigonids we have already seen two examples at the beginning of this section: Antigonus I in Skepsis and Demetrius Poliorketēs in Athens (cf. 1(a) above). One could fill many pages with the texts of the inscriptions which are our pimary sources for this practice. We limit ourselves to one example which allows us to indicate the importance of the Attalids, who otherwise stand somewhat in the background in this book. The last representative of this dynasty was Attalos III, king in Pergamum from 138 to 133 BCE, who bequeathed his state to the Romans in his will. An inscription from the city of Elaia in the south or from Pergamum itself dates from his reign. The first lines are fragmentary, but it seems that they described a successful military action:[17]

> ... hostile country, which he was the first to ... since no one exceeds the king in benevolence ... to resolve that the fitting honours be paid to him, so that the citizens may show the king their recognition of all the good that they have received from his hands, by thanking him for his successes and for the benefits he has bestowed on them: May success attend us! Resolution of the council and of the assembled people: The king is to be crowned with a golden garland of victory. A cultic image five ells high is also to be dedicated to him, showing him in his armour as he tramples upon the booty of war: this is to be set up in the temple of Asclepius Sōtēr, so that he may be a temple companion of the god. A golden equestrian statue of the king is also to be erected on a marble plinth beside the altar of Zeus Sōtēr, so that the statue may stand in the most prominent position in the market place. Each day, the bearer of the garland and the priest of the king and the one responsible for organising the athletic contests are to offer incense in sacrifice to the king upon the altar of Zeus Sōtēr. The eighth day of the month on which he entered Pergamum is to be sacred for all time, and each year the priest of Asclepius is to organise a splendid procession on this day, from the town hall to the temple precinct of Asclepius and of the king, with the customary persons taking part ... Inscriptions are also to be made. On the cultic image the inscription is to read: 'The assembled people [honours] King Attalos Philomētōr Euergetēs, son of the divine king [this was said only of a dead ruler] Eumenēs Sōtēr, because of his skill and bravery in war, because he overcame our enemies.' On the equestrian statue, the inscription is

[17] OGIS 332 (excerpts).

to read: 'The assembled people [honours] Attalos Philomētōr Euergetēs, son of the divine king Eumenēs Sōtēr, because of his skill and prudence, so advantageous in matters of state, and because of his generosity to the people.' When he enters our city, each single garland bearer of the twelve gods[18] and of the god-king Eumenēs is to bear a garland, and the men and women priests are to open the temples of the gods, and pray while they offer incense that the gods may now and for all time bestow on King Attalos Philomētōr Euergetēs health, deliverance, and victory both on land and on sea, when he attacks and when he repulses those who attack him, and that his kingship may endure inviolate for ever in complete safety. The priests and priestesses mentioned above are to go out and meet him, together with the stratēgoi, the archons, the victors in the sacred athletic contests with their wreaths of victory, those in charge of the gymnasium with the ephebes and the young people, the educators of boys with the children, the citizens, all women and girls. The inhabitants of the city are to wear white garments and garlands ... But in order that the success which the king has won in the struggles against his foe may remain visible for all times, and that all may be able to see the generosity he has shown, this resolution is to be written on a marble pillar which is to be erected in the sanctuary of Asclepius in front of the temple; the stratēgoi are to see that this is done. And this resolution is to remain valid for all time, and is to be included among the sacred laws.

The original text also includes regulations about sacrifices and sacrificial meals, and technical indications about how the resolution is to be drawn up and made known. The text closes with directives about the publication of the resolution in the form of an inscription. Attalos III is not directly addressed as a god in this text, and one can discuss whether the incense mentioned in lines 12f. is offered *for* the king or – more probably – *to* the king himself. As we know from other testimonies (cf. III/A, 1), Asclepius the god of healing had made his special dwelling place in Pergamum. The integration of the king into the cult of Asclepius is achieved by declaring Attalos to be the συννάος, 'temple companion', of the god (see Nock). Lines 33ff. give the choreography for a typical welcome of the ruler, who is met in a procession that appears appropriate to the celebration of his *parousia*, i.e. his entrance into the city.

(*b*) The state cult

A dynastic cult centred on the ruling family was developed with the greatest consistency by the Ptolemies. While the primary addressee was the

---

[18] On these cf. I/A, 3 above.

Graeco-Macedonian element among the people, this also made it easier to integrate the new dynasty into the ancient Egyptian royal ideology. We must suppose that a mutual interaction occurred here, but it is difficult to grasp the details of this process. From *c.*290 BCE onwards, the development took place in several stages. Up to this date, only Alexander the Great, as the founder of the capital city, had been given the status of a hero in Alexandria. In a first step, Ptolemy I Sōtēr created a new state cult for Alexander as god: one indicator of the exceptional rank of this cult is the fact that from now on the name of the priest of Alexander is mentioned alongside the name of the king in the formulae used to date official documents. Next, Ptolemy II Philadelphos, the son of Ptolemy I Sōtēr, divinised his deceased father and, later, his father's wife Berenice: as *theoi sōteres*, they were accorded temples and priests. Ptolemy II also instituted festivals in remembrance of Ptolemy I, to be held at four-yearly intervals. The Alexandrian poet Theocritus speaks of these in the seventeenth of his Idylls, a song in praise of Ptolemy:[19]

> Only Ptolemy – no one before him, nor any of those
> whose still warm footprints are reflected in the path through desert sand –
> has founded fragrant temples for his mother and father.
> There he has placed them, shining in gold and ivory,
> as helpers for all mankind.
> In the course of the moon's cycle he burns many fat shanks of bulls
> upon altars reddened by blood,
> he and his noble consort; nor has ever a better
> wife embraced her betrothed in the bridal chamber.
> For she loves him who is both brother and spouse to her.

The concluding line of our quotation reveals that Ptolemy II, following the Egyptian custom, took his sister Arsinoe as his wife. This is the source of his sobriquet 'Philadelphos', which does not refer here to 'brotherly love', but means 'the lover of his sister'. In lines 131–4, Theocritus compares this marital union to the sacred wedding of Zeus and Hera, possibly intending to hint that he already knew what was to happen in the future – for Ptolemy II divinised his sister-wife. It is unclear whether this happened shortly after her death, or while she was still alive; at any rate he himself, while still alive, gave himself a place in this cult soon afterwards. Under the name θεοὶ ἀδελφοί, 'sibling deities', he had himself and his sister assumed

---

[19]   Lines 121–30; for edition and translation of above p. 219, n. 31.

as 'temple companions' into the imperial cult of Alexander the Great. The succeeding generations of the Ptolemies continued this practice until the end of the dynasty. The best way to classify the model thus created would be to call it a genuine ruler cult. It is decreed and imposed from above, with the aim of providing a sacral foundation for political power, translating the earthly ruler in the whole of his domains into the heavenly realms.

In Syria, where the earlier history and the political structure were different from those in Egypt, the parallel processes in the case of the Seleucids took much longer. The only argument in support of the hypothesis that Antiochus I had already founded the dynastic cult of the Seleucids is that his rivalry with the Lagides left him no other choice (Wilcken 253); the only unambiguous piece of evidence in the sources is an inscription giving the text of a decree of Antiochus III Megas from the year 204 BCE,[20] composed on the occasion of the appointment of high priests in the individual satrapies for his consort Laodike. A comparison made in passing (lines 26–8 or 10–12: 'as high priests are appointed for us in the whole realm') indicates that there already existed a cult for him, the living king, and his deceased ancestors.

All we have in the case of the Antigonids and Attalids are the local cults; these dynasties did not found a state cult in the strict sense of the word. Nevertheless, the dynastic cult too is 'a part of the general religious context in which the cult of rulers participated. It is against this background that it must be understood.'[21]

(c) Reactions within Judaism

List 86.

J. J. Collins, 'Sibylline Oracles', in *OTP* 1.317–472.

C. Elsas, 'Argumente zur Ablehnung des Herrscherkultes in jüdischer und gnostischer Tradition', in *Loyalitätskonflikte in der Religionsgeschichte* (*Festschrift C. Colpe*), Würzburg 1990, 269–81.

C. Habicht, *2. Makkabäerbuch* (JSHRZ I/3), Gütersloh 1976.

J. Kügler, 'Die Windeln Jesu als Zeichen', *BN* 77 (1995) 20–8 (on the Book of Wisdom).

[20] OGIS 224, better in C. B. Welles, *Royal Correspondence in the Hellenistic Period: A Study in Greek Epigraphy*, New Haven 1934, reprint Chicago 1974, as no. 36, with commentary 158–63.

[21] F. W. Walbank, 'Könige' (L83) 380.

H. Merkel, *Sibyllinen* (JSHRZ V/8), Gütersloh 1998.
V. Nikiprowetzky, *La Troisième Sibylle* (EtJ 9), Paris 1970.
K. D. Schunk, *1. Makkabäerbuch* (JSHRZ I/4), Gütersloh 1980.

A considerable portion of the Jewish population in the Hellenistic period lived within the domains of the Seleucid and Ptolemaic dynasties and in the sphere of influence of the civic *sōtēr* cults of Asia Minor and Greece. The cult of rulers, in both these forms, does not seem to have posed any particular problem for Judaism, since there are very few reflections of it in Jewish literature. This warns us against overestimating the importance of this cult, which certainly did not continually generate situations in which the fundamental profession of faith in the one God of Israel was at stake and martyrdom threatened. Specific conflicts such as that with Antiochus Epiphanes IV were kindled, not directly by the cult of the ruler, but by the attempts to promote Hellenisation and cultural alienation in general. A theoretically based critique of the cult of rulers occurs within the broader context of polemic against Gentile polytheism and the worship of idols. We can discern most clearly the tendency to accuse those who persecuted the Jewish people of transgressing the limits set for human beings and usurping the power of God, e.g. in 2 Maccabees, when the author gleefully relates the terrible death of Antiochus IV (2 Macc 9:8–12):

> Thus he who only a little while before had thought in his *superhuman* arrogance that he could command the waves of the sea, and had imagined that he could weigh the high mountains in a balance [Is 40:12], was brought down to earth and carried in a litter, making the power of God manifest to all. And so the ungodly man's body swarmed with worms, and while he was still living in anguish and pain, his flesh rotted away, and because of the stench the whole army felt revulsion at his decay. Because of his intolerable stench no one was able to carry the man who a little while before had thought that he could *touch the stars of heaven*. Thus it was that, broken in spirit, he began to lose much of *his arrogance* and to come to his senses under the scourge of God, for he was tortured with pain every moment. And when he could not endure his own stench, he uttered these words, 'It is right *to be subject to God; mortals should not think that they are equal to God.*'

The fictional *mise-en-scène* of the Book of Judith refers in reality, like 2 Maccabees, to the Seleucid period. Here the Assyrian general Holofernes boasts of the power of his king: 'What god is there except Nebuchadnezzar?' (Jdt 6:2), who is 'lord (κύριος) of the whole earth' (6:4). Likewise, the Book of Daniel reflects the alien Seleucid sovereignty.

Dan 3:3ff. relates how the three young men are thrown into the fire because they refuse to fall down before a golden statue that King Nebuchadnezzar has erected and to worship this. The author does not state that this was a statue of the king himself; it may have been a statue of any one of the gods. But this does not exclude the possibility, when the passage is read afresh in the light of new circumstances, that it takes on a significance with regard to the role that images of the king played in the cult of rulers. In the case of the Book of Wisdom, apart from the critique of the images of rulers (Wis 14:17–21) mentioned at the beginning of this section, one should also note the passage Wis 7:1–6, which can be read 'as a sweeping polemic against the Hellenistic royal ideology which spoke of the divine provenance and miraculous birth of the ruler' (Kügler 23): the author affirms that no king has any other entrance into existence than that of humankind as a whole. Besides this, it is to the pious Jews, faithful to the law, that divine childhood and royal dignity are attributed.

The Psalms of Solomon attack the Roman Pompey, who died in 48 BCE: 'He did not bear in mind that he was a human being, nor did he bear in mind his end. He said: "I will be lord over earth and sea," and he did not acknowledge that God is great.'[22] The kernel of the third book of Sibylline prophecies comes from Jewish circles in Egypt under the Ptolemies in the second century BCE (cf. III/B, 4). The following lines display a critique – although in rather vague terms – of the cult of rulers (Sib 3.545–9):

> Hellas, I ask you: why did you trust mortal rulers
> who do not have the power to escape their end in death?
> Why do you bring votive gifts in vain to dead human beings?
> Why do you sacrifice to idols? Who has inspired in you the error
> of doing such things while abandoning the face of the great God?

Lines 551ff. contain an 'euhemeristic' explanation of the pagan belief in gods, which is said to come from an early veneration of deceased human beings (cf. Wis 14:15f.). This makes it probable that the primary concern in the text quoted here is likewise the attribution to dead men of the status of hero; but the confidence which according to the opening line is placed in the mortal ruler opens the path to a genuine cult of rulers. The inexorable fact of death is the decisive argument against every form of the cultic veneration of human beings. In the same third book of the

---

[22] Ps Sol 2:28f.; cf. S. Holm-Nielsen, JSHRZ IV/2.66; R. B. Wright, *OTP* 11, 653.

Sibyllines, however, the same literary hand surprisingly builds up a king of the Ptolemaic dynasty as a saviour figure, attributing messianic characteristics to him (Sib 3.652–6):

> Then God will send from the rising of the sun the king
> who frees the whole earth from the scourge of war;
> he will kill some and fulfil his oath to others.
> But in all this, he will not act according to his own ideas,
> but will obey the noble counsels of the great God.

Scholars are broadly in agreement that these lines use the Egyptian title 'king from the rising of the sun' to refer to Ptolemy VI Philomētōr (180–145 BCE). We have other evidence of his good relations with the Jews of Egypt, who here raise a literary monument to him (cf. 2 Macc 1:10; Josephus, *Ap.* 2.49). Jewish circles placed great hopes in him. This non-Jewish king is to be God's chosen instrument, like the Persian king Cyrus in Deutero-Isaiah: 'Thus speaks the Lord to Cyrus, his *anointed one*' (Is 45:1). Christian readers should not immediately think in christological categories when they read such language: they must rather bear in mind that a messiah in Judaism was not a divine figure, or one like God, but 'only' an earthly human figure who had received a commission from God. Thus, the terms used here about Ptolemy do not mean that Egyptian Judaism had succumbed to the cult of rulers. They are entirely in keeping with the usage in Deutero-Isaiah.

4. The integration of Roman power

List 87.

G. W. Bowersock, 'Augustus und der Kaiserkult im Osten' (1965), in A. Wlosok, *Kaiserkult* (L81) 389–402.

M. P. Charlesworth, 'Observations' (L83).

C. Classen, 'Gottmenschentum in der römischen Republik', *Gym.* 70 (1963) 312–38.

G. Devallet, 'Apothéoses romaines: Romulus à corps perdu', in A. F. Laurens, *Entre hommes et dieux* (L83) 107–23.

D. Fishwick, *Cult* (L81) 46–55.

R. Mellor, *ΘΕΑ POMH: The Worship of the Goddess Roma in the Greek World* (Hyp. 42), Göttingen 1975.

——'The Goddess Roma', *ANRW* II/17.2 (1981) 950–1030.

S. R. F. Price, *Rituals* (L81) 23–52.

F. Taeger, *Charisma* (L81) II.3–49.
L. R. Taylor, *Divinity* (L81) 35–57.
K. Thraede, 'Die Poesie und der Kaiserkult', in W. den Boer, *Culte* (L81) 271–308.

(a) The development in the East

From 220 BCE on, the Romans put out their feelers into the eastern half of the Mediterranean area and began to bring one territory after another under their rule. The inhabitants of Greece and Asia Minor reacted to the new rulers in their accustomed manner: they transposed the varied cult of rulers, which by now had a lengthy tradition, to the Romans. No individual central authority existed continuously in the Roman republic, but there were two other possibilities, both of which were utilised. The first was the veneration of the *Dea Roma*, the goddess Rome, conceived as the personification of the power of the Roman state and of the virtues of the Roman people (cf. Mellor). It was only in the Greek world, as a consequence of the Roman penetration of East and West, that this concept was developed – or perhaps one should rather say, invented. In the competition to see which of the cities of Asia Minor would be permitted to build a new temple for Tiberius, his mother Livia and the Senate in 26 CE, the envoys from the city of Smyrna boast in Rome in the presence of the emperor that they were the first to erect a temple to the city of Rome, represented by its goddess (Tacitus, *Ann.* 4.56.1). This had happened in the year 195 BCE (cf. Mellor 14f.). The second possibility was the attribution of honours to individual representatives of Rome, i.e. governors, high officials and legates. One of the first to receive such honours was the proconsul Titus Quinctius Flaminius, who nominally restored their freedom to the cities of Greece in 196 BCE. The inhabitants of Chalcis, who were especially grateful to him because of an incident that had occurred, founded in 191 BCE a cult to him which survived into the time of Plutarch, who not only relates this event, but also quotes parts of a cultic song which had been composed at that time (*Tit.* 16.3f.):

> After the inhabitants of Chalcis had been rescued by him in this manner, they dedicated to him the finest and greatest monuments in their city, on which one can to this very day read inscriptions such as: 'The people [dedicates] the gymnasium to Titus and to Heracles', or in another place: 'The people [dedicates] the Delphinium to Titus and to Apollo.' Besides this, the people of Chalcis have continued into our own days to choose a priest of Titus, and after

the sacrifice and the libations in his honour, they sing a hymn of praise which was specially composed for the occasion. It is too long to be quoted in full here, but let us present the concluding verses of the song:

In filial piety we honour the fidelity (πίστιν) of the Romans –
may our prayers and our oaths protect them.
Sing, O girls, to the great Zeus,
praise Rome and Titus and the fidelity of the Romans:
'Hail to you, paean! O Titus, saviour!'

The list of Roman administrators in the East whose names are preserved in inscriptions or in literary testimony includes more than twenty names (cf. Bowersock 401f.). Cicero had performed outstanding service in Asia Minor as a consul, and had been a model administrator (although unwilling) as governor of the province of Cilicia in 51/50 BCE. He rejected the temples and monuments that the grateful cities wished to erect in his honour, as he notes in his Letters, not without a touch of pride.[23] The last such instances come from the years 2/3 CE, and it is easy to see why this custom dies out at this period. From thenceforward, in the person of Augustus there existed a central authority, making the payment of honours to officials dependent on him superfluous, if not indeed possibly dangerous.

The behaviour of the Greek populace vis-à-vis the Roman power has been judged negatively, both at the time and subsequently. For example, Tacitus spoke of 'Greek flattery', Nilsson of 'servility'. Price has suggested a new approach to the interpretation of this phenomenon, recommending that it be understood as a form of reaction to the experience of power. The Greeks had to cope with a new situation which required them to integrate the political and military superiority of Rome into their own image of the world and to make sense of their own identity in relation to Rome. The strategy which allowed them do this successfully was the transposition to the Roman power of the well-tried categories of the Hellenistic cult of benefactors and rulers. This established an order in the world and restored the existential framework with which they were familiar.

---

[23] *Quint. Fratr.* 1.1.26; *Att.* 5.21.7: 'In return for such benefits, which strike the people here rigid with amazement, the only attestations of honour that I will accept are words: I reject statues, dedications and carriages. In this way, I do not impose any burdens on the municipalities – but perhaps I impose a burden on you, when I boast like this. But please let me have my way.'

(b) Repercussions on Rome

The title '*repercussions* on Rome' is intentionally chosen for the following
reflections, since scholars agree that Rome's own political and religious
traditions provided nothing that could have furnished a pretext for the
development of a cult of rulers.[24] Not even the Greek attribution of heroic
status to especially meritorious deceased persons was known at Rome
initially. It is wrong to claim that the Roman cult of ancestors focused on
the *Di(vi) Parentum*, the Manes and Lares (cf. I/C, 2(b)), was parallel to
the Greek practice; it must be judged to be fundamentally different, since it
is not addressed individually to a pre-eminent single personality. One
might, at most, expect that Romulus, the mythical founder of the city,
would be raised to divine status, and this does indeed happen, e.g. by
means of the later narrative of his translation to heaven, and the equation
of Romulus with the ancient Roman god Quirinus. But it is striking that
this happens at a very late date, towards 100 BCE, or even only *c.*60 BCE in
the time of Caesar. In the latter case, the divinisation of Romulus would be
due to Caesar's own interest in creating a model for the way in which he
wished his own person to be treated.

The repercussions from the East, without which it is impossible to
understand how the Roman imperial cult came into existence, have many
dimensions and aspects. The Greek influence on educated persons is
exercised by means of the reception of literature and philosophy; many
teachers in Rome were Greek slaves or freedmen. Eastern forms of religion
obtained a foothold in the city and made their attraction felt. The
indigenous population of the city came increasingly to be leavened by
strong contingents of immigrants from the eastern half of the empire.
Roman officials and officers experienced at first hand the culture in eastern
lands, which included the phenomena described above. This converges
with a tendency on the part of the Roman plebs in the late republican
period to shower praises on their especial favourites such as the Gracchi or
Marius. These praises can be formulated in very exuberant terms, but they
stop short of divinisation. Finally, gratitude to benefactors is found in the
entire classical period, and is indeed something common to humanity as a

---

[24] Taeger's language (39) is very definite, but his views are typical: 'Thus it is
absolutely certain that at the turn of the first century, and still later, Rome
completely lacked the presuppositions, in terms of the history of religion and of
ideas, necessary for the development of a cult of the king in line with what
happened in the Hellenistic sphere.'

whole. It can take on very intense verbal forms, as in one of Plautus' comedies, where a character who hopes for a meal cries out to the potential benefactor: *O mi Iuppiter terrestris*, 'O my Jupiter here on earth!' (*Persa* 99f.).

It is in this way that the posthumous attribution of heroic status makes its entry into the spiritual world of the Romans. After the death of his beloved daughter Tullia, Cicero wanted to erect for her a sanctuary that would be accessible to the public, and he himself uses the Greek word when he speaks of her 'apotheosis' (*Att.* 12.35.1 and frequently). When the first sharp pain of mourning was past, he abandoned this idea. But he had given theoretical formulation to the possibility of a posthumous deification, and given this a mystical form in the 'Somnium Scipionis' (*Rep.* 6.13):[25]

> A sure place is destined in heaven for all who have assured the safety of their native land, have helped it and promoted its welfare, so that they may enjoy eternal life in bliss in heaven. For nothing is more agreeable to the divine ruler [principi deo] who governs the whole world – nothing, that is, of those things that are done upon earth – than those assemblies and fellowships of human beings, united by law, that we call states. After they have departed hence, those who govern and protect the states return hither.

Thanks to the intervention of Octavian, Vergil had regained possession of properties which he had lost in the confusion after the Battle of Philippi (42 BCE). He shows how intense the verbal formulation of gratitude could become (cf. Thraede 276–8): it is none other than Vergil who praises Octavian in his first Eclogue with the words: 'Indeed, it was a god [deus] who bestowed on us the delight of *otium*, for I shall always look on him as a god, and the blood of a lamb from our flocks will often bedew his altar' (*Ecl.* 1.6–8). He gives space to a comparable evaluation of Octavian in his 'national epic', the *Aeneid*, too: 'And this one is the hero who was so often promised to you, Augustus Caesar, offspring of the divine one.[26] He brings back to the fields of Latium the golden age of the world' (*Aen.* 6.791–3). Vergil's interpretation of time reaches its high point in the celebrated fourth Eclogue, composed in 40 BCE. The Christian tradition wrongly

---

[25] Cf. K. Büchner, *Cicero: Der Staat* (TuscBü), Munich 5th edn. 1993; C. W. Keyes, *Cicero*, vol. 16 (LCL 213), Cambridge, Mass. and London 1928.

[26] Latin: 'divi genus'. The reference is to the divinised Julius Caesar as the adoptive father of Octavian.

interpreted this as a pagan prophecy of Jesus Christ; many points in it
remain obscure, and it has not yet yielded up all its secrets (*Ecl.* 4):[27]

> Now is come the last age of the song of Cumae;
> the great line of the centuries begins anew.
> Now the Virgin returns, the reign of Saturn returns;
> now a new generation descends from heaven on high.
> Only do thou, pure Lucina,[28] smile on the birth of the child,
> under whom the iron brood shall first cease,
> and a golden race spring up throughout the world!
> Thine own Apollo now is king!
> And in thy consulship, Pollio,[29] yea in thine,
> shall this glorious age begin,
> and the mighty months commence their march.
>
> But for thee, child, shall the earth untilled pour forth
> as her first pretty gifts, straggling ivy with foxglove everywhere,
> and the Egyptian bean blended with the smiling acanthus.
> Uncalled, the goats shall bring home their udders swollen with milk,
> and the herds shall fear not huge lions;
> unasked, thy cradle shall pour forth flowers for thy delight.
> The serpent, too, shall perish, and the false poison-plant shall perish;
> Assyrian spice shall spring up on every soil.

[27] Translation: H. R. Fairclough, *Virgil*, vol. 1 (LCL 63), Cambridge, Mass. and London 1916, rev. edn. 1967, 29f. Cf. J. and M. Götte, *Vergil: Landleben* (TuscBü), Munich 5th edn. 1987, 44–9; commentaries and bibliography, ibid. 362–5, 532–5; on Vergil in general, *ANRW* II/31.1–2 (1980, 1981). I do not wish to discuss in greater detail here the use that has been made of this text in the discussion of how the virginal conception is to be understood in terms of the history of religions; on this point cf. the excursus by R. E. Brown, *The Birth of the Messiah: A Commentary on the Infancy Narratives in the Gospels of Matthew and Luke* (The Anchor Bible Reference Library), New York 2nd edn. 1993, 564–70.

[28] 'Goddess of light': she was regarded as the protectress of birth and of new-born children.

[29] The reference is to C. Asinius Pollio, consul of the year in question, negotiator in the peace treaty between Octavian and Antony in Brundisium, a man who took an interest in literature and was a benefactor of the young Vergil. The similarity between his name and that of the god means that the reference to Apollo's lordship in the previous line is an allusion to Pollio's consulship.

Begin, baby boy, to know thy mother with a smile –
to thy mother ten[30] months have brought the weariness of travail.
Begin, baby boy! Him on whom his parents have not smiled,
no god honours with his table, no goddess with her bed! (4–12; 18–25;
60–3)

Other sections of this poem emphasise with even greater intensity the
peace in the animal world, the harmony of nature and the abundant
fertility of the earth. The description has paradisal and apocalyptic traits; in
the figure of the boy, it has almost a messianic character. One suggestion
that has been made is that Vergil knew Sibylline texts from Egypt which
bore the imprint of Jewish apocalyptic traditions. It remains uncertain
whether it is possible to identify the awaited child in terms of temporal
history, e.g. as a newly born son of Pollio to whom the poem is addressed,
who was the repository of great hopes, or ultimately as Octavian himself. A
purely allegorical reading of the poem is also possible: the Virgin represents
Dikē, the goddess of justice, and the child personifies the peace for which
all so passionately longed. One must certainly warn against the danger of a
Christian overinterpretation;[31] but even a symbolic interpretation of the
poet's intention does not exclude the possibility of a subsequent application to the figure of a living ruler, especially since Vergil uses at least
somewhat similar terms in speaking of Octavian in other places (see above;
also *Georg.* 1.24–42).

B. The Roman imperial cult: persons

List 88.
R. Etienne, *Le Culte impérial dans la Péninsule ibérique d'Auguste à
Dioclétien* (BEFAR 191), Paris 1958.
J. Gagé, 'Psychologie du culte impérial romain', *Diogène* 34 (1961)
47–68.
W. Günther, 'Zu den Anfängen des Kaiserkults in Milet', *MDAI* 39
(1989) 173–8.

---

[30] Here the period of pregnancy is reckoned according to lunar months, as at Wis
7:2.

[31] It seems to me that Götte in fact succumbs to this danger (see above, n. 27)
365: 'An atmosphere of the expectation of salvation and the promise of peace
clothes this poem and shimmers around it, kindling a yearning and an
anticipation ... One who looks for the concretisation of these words all too

H. Heinen, 'Zur Begründung des römischen Kaiserkultes: Chronologische Uebersicht von 48 v. bis 14 n.Chr.', *Klio* 11 (1911) 129–77.

P. Herz, 'Bibliographie zum römischen Kaiserkult (1955–1975)', *ANRW* II/16.2 (1980) 853–910.

——'Der römische Kaiser und der Kaiserkult: Gott oder primus inter pares?', in D. Zeller, *Menschwerdung* (L80) 115–40.

H. von Hesberg, 'Archäologische Denkmäler zum römischen Kaiserkult', *ANRW* II/16.2 (1980) 911–95.

K. Latte, *Religionsgeschichte* (L02) 294–326.

J.-P. Martin, *Providentia deorum: Recherches sur certains aspects religieux du pouvoir impérial romain* (BEFAR 61), Paris 1982.

The bibliography in L81, esp. Fishwick, Price, Taeger vol. 2, Taylor.

At the meeting point between the Roman republic and the Roman principate stand Julius Caesar and Octavian, subsequently the emperor Augustus, on whom Vergil's hopes were concentrated. Both men had decisive significance for the history of the Roman imperial cult, although the precise definition of Caesar's role here is the object of vigorous scholarly debate. We cannot avoid treating Caesar and Augustus separately, before going on to a briefer discussion of the other members of the Julio-Claudian and the Flavian dynasties up to the end of the first century CE. A separate section then summarises material concerning the external order of service, the feasts and rites, in the case of both the cult of rulers and the imperial cult.

1. Julius Caesar

List 89.

M. Beard et al., *Religions*, vol. 2 (L4), 140–49.

K. Christ, *Caesar: Annäherungen an einen Diktator*, Munich 1994, esp. 302–4 (a good sketch of the history of scholarship; bibliography on further questions).

H. Gesche, *Die Vergottung Caesars* (Frankfurter Althistorische Studien 1), Kallmünz 1968; summary in A. Wlosok, *Kaiserkult* (L81) 368–74.

——*Caesar* (EdF 51), Darmstadt 1976, 154–76.

C. Meyer, *Caesar* (dtv 4596), Munich 3rd edn. 1993.

---

literally in the daily life of earth, and more specifically in the daily life of the empire of Augustus, need not be surprised when he turns back from this poem with an empty heart, full of disappointment. The realm of the poet of the

S. R. F. Price, 'Gods and Emperors: The Greek Language of the Roman Imperial Cult', *JHS* 104 (1984) 79–95 (on the predicate θεός).
S. Weinstock, *Divus Julius*, Oxford 1971 (fundamental).
A. Wlosok, *Kaiserkult* (L81) 329–74 (eight essays).

(*a*) Cultic honours or the official declaration of divinity?

Our only interest here is to determine to what extent, and from what date onwards, divine honours were paid to the person of Caesar. Helga Gesche has proposed that we should operate with a distinction between 'divinisation' and 'deification', the former understood as the attribution of a great many cultic honours, the latter an official elevation to a position among the civic gods in keeping with sacred law. It seems at first sight that we should make a clear distinction between the lifetime of Caesar, to which 'divinisation' would apply, and the time after his death, when the formal 'deification' took place. But things are more complicated in the case of Caesar, and if we wish to work with this distinction at all, we must recognise the presence of a sliding scale, rather than of direct antitheses. The study of this question directs us to Caesar's last years, when it appeared that he had essentially succeeded in grasping absolute power. We begin with an inscription from Ephesus, from the year 49 BCE (SIG 3/760):

> αἱ πόλεις αἱ ἐν τῆι 'Ασίαι καὶ οἱ [δῆμοι]
> καὶ τὰ ἔθνη Γάιον 'Ιούλιον Γαίο[υ υἱ-]
> ὸν Καίσαρα, τὸν ἀρχιερέα καὶ αὐτο-
> κράτορα καὶ τὸν δεύτερον ὕπα-
> τον, τὸν ἀπὸ ῎Αρεως καὶ 'Αφροδε[ί-]
> τῆς θεὸν ἐπιφανῆ καὶ κοινὸν τοῦ
> ἀνθρωπίνου βίου σωτῆρα.

The cities in Asia and the [communities] and the country districts (honour) Gaius Julius, son of Gaius, Caesar, Pontifex Maximus, Imperator and consul for the second time, descendant of Ares and Aphrodite, the god who has appeared visibly [θεὸν ἐπιφανῆ] and universal saviour of the life of human beings.

Eclogue and of the *Aeneid* is a kingdom of promise, a kingdom that is not of this world: all those of good will must have as their abiding goal the intense desire that this kingdom may descend from heaven.'

A contemporary inscription from Demetrias in Thessaly puts it in even more lapidary fashion: 'Gaius Julius Caesar, Imperator, god'.[32] This is an unambiguous use of words, and there is little point in arguing that Greek was unfortunately incapable of retaining the distinction between *divus* ('deified') and *deus* ('god'), a distinction which in any case was not so sharp (see Price's justified criticism). It is not by chance that these inscriptions come from the eastern half of the empire. What began many years previously with Demetrius Poliorketēs is now transferred to Julius Caesar, the most powerful Roman in his day. The external occasion in Ephesus was Caesar's new regulation of the crushing system of taxes; in Demetrias, it was probably the victory of Pharsalus. Caesar had long since united in his person in Rome the offices which are listed in these inscriptions, thereby continuously increasing the importance of his own position. One further point seems noteworthy here, viz. the attribution to him of a mythical genealogy: he is said to be a descendant of Ares and Aphrodite (Mars and Venus in Latin). We do not hear such words in Rome as yet. It is only some resolutions from the years 46 to 44 BCE, after important victories over Pompey in northern Africa and Spain, that go beyond the piling-up of offices on Caesar's part and honours such as triumphal processions after a military success: the erection of his statue in the sanctuary of Quirinus makes Caesar a 'temple companion' of this god (Cicero, *Att.* 12.45.3). A month – 'July' – is named after him. A temple is to be built for him, and a priest is appointed specifically to this temple, namely Mark Antony. The most important (because contemporary) document concerning this question is found in the second Philippic address of Cicero, which he delivered after Caesar's death. Here he attacks Mark Antony directly (*Phil.* 2.110):[33]

And you pretend to preserve a genuine memory of Caesar, to love him even after his death? What greater honour did he receive than when he was given a cultic couch, a statue, a gable of the temple, a priest? This means that a priest has the responsibility for worship – as with Jupiter, as with Mars, as with

---

[32] SEG XIV 474; also in G. Pfohl, *Inschriften* (L4) 64f.

[33] Cf. M. Giebel, *M. Tullius Cicero: Philippische Reden gegen M. Antonius. Erste und zweite Rede* (RecUB 2233), Stuttgart 1989; W. C. A. Ker, *Cicero: Orations*, vol. 15 (LCL 189), Cambridge, Mass. and London 1926. A later text in Dio Cassius, 44.6.4 is a partial parallel to this text.

Quirinus, so also in the case of the divine Julius. And that priest is Mark Antony!

In retrospect, Suetonius will describe these as 'honours too great for a mortal man' (*Div. Jul.* 76.1). It is not very easy to discern the motivations of those involved here. Did Caesar himself plan and intentionally pursue a sacral elevation of his own position of power? Did he want to acquire the royal dignity, and if so, did he want to shape this kingship in keeping with the idealised figure of Alexander the Great, following the model of the dynastic cults of rulers? It is in fact possible to discern in Caesar some traits of the conscious imitation of Alexander, but equally traits of an imitation of Romulus. Does this mean that he thought of a revitalisation of the ancient Roman kingship in the manner of Romulus, who had recently – perhaps thanks to Caesar's own vigorous contribution – come to be seen as a god? Or did he want to create a synthesis of various elements? Finally, we must bear in mind the possibility that Caesar himself was not at all the driving force, but that a servile and excessively zealous Senate, and the Roman populace with its many foreign elements, forced the divine honours on him. Many scholars have rejected Helga Gesche's harmonising suggestion that it was resolved during Caesar's lifetime that divine honours were to be paid him, but the intention was that these should come into force only after his death (Wlosok 30). One reason why we do not have clear answers to these questions is that the period of time was too short to allow the outlines of the further development to emerge with greater clarity. Caesar's murder in 44 BCE marks an irreversible caesura.

(*b*) The *consecratio*

List 90.
E. Bickermann, 'Die römische Kaiserapotheose', in A. Wlosok, *Kaiserkult* (L81) 82–121; from *ARW* 27 (1929) 1–31.
——'Consecratio', in W. den Boer, *Culte* (L81) 1–37.
L. Kreitzer, 'Apotheosis of the Roman Emperor', *BA* 53 (1990) 211–17.
S. R. F. Price, 'From Noble Funerals to Divine Cult: The Consecration of Roman Emperors', in D. Cannadine and Idem (eds.), *Rituals of Royalty: Power and Ceremonial in Traditional Societies* (PaP.S), Cambridge 1987, 56–105.
J. C. Richard, 'Recherches sur certains aspects du culte impérial: Les funérailles des empereurs Romains aux deux premiers siècles de notre ère', *ANRW* II/16.2 (1980) 1121–34.

There is no doubt about the fact of the posthumous divinisation of Caesar; only about its date is there a certain amount of disagreement. According to the traditional view, Caesar as *Divus Julius* was numbered among the gods of the state in the first days of January in 42 BCE at the prompting of Octavian, and was given a temple with a statue, cultic personnel, and regular sacrifices. One slight difficulty, however, is that this temple was not dedicated until 29 BCE. From now on, Octavian himself, as Caesar's adopted son, was called *Divi filius*, a title which could be translated into Greek only as υἱὸς τοῦ θεοῦ. This relationship of adoption leads in some texts from Egypt to the attribution to Octavian of the extraordinary title θεὸς ἐκ θεοῦ, literally 'god from god' or better, in a paraphrase 'a god himself, and the son of a god', e.g. in a papyrus with an oath from the first year of Octavian's government 30/29 BCE (POxy 1453.11) and an inscription from the year 24 BCE (OGIS 655.2).

What happened for the first time in the case of the deceased Caesar shows us in exemplary fashion what was to remain the standard model for the deification of Roman emperors, in the forms established at the death of Augustus. Unless they had made themselves particularly unpopular, resolutions of the people and the Senate included them after their death in the list of the civic gods. The technical term for this in Greek is ἀποθείωσις (apotheosis), with *consecratio* as the Latin equivalent. The Alexandrian historian Appian notes in the second century CE: 'Every holder of the imperial office, unless he has been a tyrant or a blameworthy man, is paid divine honours by the Romans after his death, although these same people once upon a time could not even endure to give them the title 'kings' during their lifetime' *(Bell. Civil.* 2.148). The act of *consecratio* required a witness to arise in the assembled Senate and to swear that he had seen the soul of the Imperator ascend to heaven from the pyre, for example in the flight of an eagle up to heaven out of the flames. This 'ascension' of members of the imperial family – including wives, siblings and children of the emperor – became a popular motif on coins and in other works of visual art.

In the case of Caesar, another event had convinced the people that Caesar had been given a place among the gods in heaven. Suetonius relates that during the first athletic competition which Augustus held in his honour, a comet arose at the eleventh hour and lit up the sky for seven days; people believed that 'this was the soul of Caesar, who had been taken up into heaven' *(Div. Jul.* 88). A belief in astrological immortality (see

I/D, 4) is here pressed into the service of the apotheosis. Ovid joins in the chorus in the final passage of his *Metamorphoses*, which he dedicates to Caesar, but already looking to Octavian Augustus (*Met.* 15.745–51):[34]

> He has come hither as a foreigner to our temples:
> Caesar is a god in his own city. He was a man of importance
> in armour and toga, but it is no less thanks to the wars
> which he brought to a triumphal conclusion of victory
> that he has become a star with a blazing tail.
> It is not so much what he did at home that constitutes his glory –
> which so quickly spreads abroad – but rather his progeny.
> For none of all Caesar's great deeds was greater than this:
> that he was the father of this progeny.

This illustrious 'progeny', which constitutes the true glory of Caesar, is Octavian, his great-nephew and adopted son. It is he who sees to it that Caesar 'arises to heaven as a god and is venerated in temples' (818). In mythical language, however, it is Venus, Caesar's divine mother, who snatches the soul out of the murdered body of her son and brings it to the heavenly stars (844–6). From now on, he looks for ever down upon the Capitol and the Forum (841f.).

2. Augustus

List 91.
A. Alföldi, *Die zwei Lorbeerbäume des Augustus* (Ant. 3.14), Bonn 1973; more briefly in A. Wlosok, *Kaiserkult* (L81) 403–22.
J. Bleicken, *Augustus: Eine Biographie*, Berlin 2nd edn. 1998.
J. Deininger, *Die Provinziallandtage der römischen Kaiserzeit von Augustus bis zum Ende des dritten Jahrhunderts n.Chr.* (Vestigia 6), Munich 1965.
D. Fishwick, 'Prudentius and the Cult of Divus Augustus', *Hist.* 39 (1990) 475–86.
——'Ovid and Divus Augustus', *CPh* 86 (1991) 36–41.
C. Habicht, 'Die augusteische Zeit und das erste Jahrhundert nach Christi Geburt', in W. den Boer, *Culte* (L81) 39–88.
H. von Hesberg and S. Panciera, *Das Mausoleum des Augustus: Der Bau und seine Inschriften* (ABAW.PH 108), Munich 1994.

[34] Cf. M. von Albrecht, *Ovid: Metamorphosen* (RecUB 1360), Stuttgart 1994; F. J. Miller, *Ovid*, vol. 4, rev. edn. (by G. P. Goold) (LCL 43), Cambridge, Mass. and London 1984.

O. Immisch, 'Herrscherkult' (L82).

U. Laffi, 'Le iscrizioni relative all'introduzione nel 9 a. C. del nuovo calendario della Provincia d'Asia', *SCO* 16 (1967) 5–98.

A. D. Nock, 'Die Einrichtung des Herrscherkultes' (1934), in A. Wlosok, *Kaiserkult* (L81) 377–88.

W. Pötscher, '"Numen" und "Numen Augusti"', *ANRW* II/16.1 (1978) 355–92.

W. Speyer, 'Das Verhältnis des Augustus zur Religion', *ANRW* II/16.3 (1978) 1777–1805.

We can anticipate the results of our investigation by summarising Octavian's attitude to the imperial cult as follows: although he may initially have had other plans, desiring to develop further the outlines of a sacrally elevated absolutist kingship which Caesar had sketched, he imposed on himself a prudent reservation – not least in view of Caesar's fate. The outcome, in Habicht's words, is 'a mixture of reservation and imperious urgency' (51) in regard to the imperial cult; other scholars speak more directly of a 'disguise' or an 'intentional lack of uniformity' (Wlosok 32). Augustus did not allow things in Rome to go so far as a formal veneration with cultic images, a temple and priests, but he exploited to the uttermost the remaining possibilities of a numinous elevation of his own position. He accepted in a somewhat reduced form cultic honours that were offered him in the East; and during Augustus' lifetime, forms of cultic veneration going further than those tolerated in Rome were introduced in those western provinces which had only recently become part of the Roman empire. After his death, he was definitively given a place among the civic gods by a resolution of the Senate on 17 September 14 CE. His ashes were not laid to rest in his temple, but in his mausoleum, where the visual works of art contain a political-religious programme.

(a) The conflict with Mark Antony

Octavian's first years were marked above all by the political and military confrontations with Mark Antony, until the latter committed suicide in 30 BCE. Antony, who had become the partner of the Egyptian queen Cleopatra, increasingly adopted the Hellenistic model of divine kingship. He elevated himself to the role of the new Dionysus-Osiris, while Cleopatra took on the part of Aphrodite-Isis (cf. Immisch). We see this in legendary form in a macabre scene in Plutarch's biography of Antony: we are told that during the final night before Octavian's troops began their assault, music and cries of exultation were suddenly heard in the city, making towards the outermost gate, 'as if some cultic organisation were making its exit from the city, and making as much noise as possible'. This was interpreted as a sign 'that the god whom Antony always most resembled, and on whom he depended, was now abandoning him to his own resources' (75.3f.). Considerations of propaganda also played a role when Octavian developed his well-known reserve about the payment of divine honours to his own person. He chose as his own guiding star the god Apollo, who represented not intoxication and ecstasy, but clarity, measure and sobriety, and he avoided an excessively close association of his person with the god.

(*b*) Honours paid in the East

The cities of Asia Minor paid their customary honours in the case of the liberator Octavian, as in other cases, and he had to make his position clear on this. In the year 29 BCE, he permitted the construction of a temple for *Dea Roma* and *Divus Julius* in Ephesus, and at the same time he allowed the construction in Pergamum of a temple for the goddess Rome and for himself. The inhabitants of Mytilene celebrated the birthday of the emperor *c*.25 BCE (OGIS 456). This is the *Sitz-im-Leben* of inscriptions from Asia Minor which address Augustus as the divine saviour of the human race and as the author of peace. It is unfortunately not possible to date precisely the few surviving lines of an inscription from Halicarnassus, which present in a brief space the entire array of formulae:[35]

> ... Since the eternal and immortal nature of the universe, out of overflowing kindness, has bestowed on human beings the greatest of all goods by bringing forth Caesar Augustus, the father who gives us a happy life and father of his own native goddess Roma,[36] the native Zeus and saviour of the human race. Providence not only granted all his wishes, but went far beyond them, for land and sea live in peace, cities are resplendent with the order of law, in harmony and abundance; now is the favourable zenith for all good things – good hopes for the future, solid courage for the present state of human beings, who with feasts, statues, sacrifices and songs ...

[35] Text CAGI IV/1 no. 894; V. Ehrenberg and A. H. M. Jones, *Documents* (L4) no. 98*a*; translation in H. Freis, *Inschriften* (L4) 17; cf. also UUC II.107.

[36] This phrase requires an explanation. It employs personification to paraphrase Octavian's honorific title *pater patriae*, 'father of the fatherland'.

The inscription breaks off at the point where the rites for the new salvific deity are laid down. We must come back here to the calendar decree of 9 BCE, which has been best preserved on an inscription from the city of Priene in Ionia (further fragments come from Apameia, Dorylaeum and Eumeneia). The Julian calendar is to be introduced into Asia Minor, and now the year is to begin on 23 September, in climatic terms the beginning of autumn. The first part of the text points out the happy coincidence that this is also the birthday of Augustus. The proconsul Paullus Fabius Maximus communicates this in a document to the κοινόν, the assembly of the cities in the province of Asia (cf. Deininger). While the Latin original of his letters remains within the categories of Roman legal thinking, the Greek translation introduces much more strongly Hellenistic conceptions of the *sōtēr*. We begin with a quotation from the letter of the proconsul (lines 3–30), the first part of which is missing:[37]

[It is difficult to say] whether the birthday of the divine emperor has caused more joy, or more benefit. We may rightly set it at the beginning of all things; not indeed in terms of the order of nature, but because of the advantage (accruing to us). He has re-established all that had decayed and turned to disaster. Thanks to him, the whole world presents a different aspect. Had not the emperor, who is the common happiness of all the human race, been born, then the world would have fallen victim to corruption. This is why one may rightly regard that event as the beginning of life and existence: the event of his birth set an end and a limit to whatever regrets people had at the fact of their existence. Since there is no other day with which one could more happily make a beginning, to public and private advantage, than this date, and since it is in any case at this time that the public officials in the cities of Asia enter upon their offices – and it is clear that the divine will has ordered things in this way, so that we might have an occasion to pay honour to Augustus – and also since it is difficult to repay him in kind for his numerous benefactions, unless we are to invent some completely new form of thanksgiving; and finally, since people are all the more happy to celebrate the birthday which they all share in common, when they also experience a personal joy at entering upon public office, then it

---

[37] Text: OGIS 458; emended by Laffi; trans. UUC II.106f.; K. Latte, *Religion* (L4) 24; F. W. Danker, *Benefactor* (L103) 215–22; a portion also in G. Pfohl, *Inschriften* (L4) 134f; cf. C. Ettl, 'Der "Anfang der ... Evangelien". Die Kalenderinschrift von Priene und ihre Relevanz für die Geschichte des Begriffs εὐαγγέλιον', in S. H. Brandenburger and T. Hieke (eds.), *Wenn drei das gleiche sagen: Studien zu den ersten drei Evangelien* (Theologie 14), Münster 1998, 121–51.

is my opinion that all the cities should have one and the same New Year's Day: the birthday of the divine emperor ...

The proconsul submits this proposal to the provincial assembly, which assuredly had no other option than to agree. Nevertheless, the provincial high priest formally moves that this measure be accepted, and the assembled 'Greeks in Asia' give their assent. Their resolution, which ends with numerous individual regulations, begins with the following programmatic passage (lines 32–41):

> Since providence, which governs all things in our life in a divine manner, has with eager generosity bestowed the most beautiful ornament on our life by bringing forth Augustus, whom it has filled with virtue to the good of the human race, as the saviour for us and for our descendants, the man who ends war and creates peace; and since by his appearing the emperor has now superabundantly fulfilled the hopes of all earlier times, in that he has not only towered over all the benefactors who lived before him, but has also robbed all future benefactors of the hope of doing more than he has done; and since finally the birthday of the god meant for the world the beginning of the message of peace (εὐαγγελίων) which has him as its author ...

The sense requires that we complete the end of this complicated sentence (which has further clauses) as follows: 'therefore the proposal of the proconsul, that Augustus be honoured in the above-mentioned manner, is accepted'. We note the concept εὐαγγέλια (in the plural) in the last line quoted above. This belongs to the established repertoire of the imperial cult, and is applied to the birthday of the emperor, his coming of age, his ascent of the throne, and his recovery of health.

(c) Developments in the city of Rome

In his account of what he had done, the posthumously published *Res Gestae*, Augustus does not speak of these matters. He avoids all that is shrill and ostentatious. With diplomatic skill, he conceals his position of power behind the official designation of *princeps*, and with similar reserve he merely indicates a sacral elevation of his person: 'For my merits, the Senate bestowed on me by a resolution the title "Augustus", the doorposts of my house were publicly decorated with laurel, the civic garland was set above my door, and the Senate and the people of Rome set up a golden shield in the Curia Julia, dedicated to me in return for my courage, clemency, uprightness and devotion to duty' (34).

This encapsulates the situation in the city of Rome: Augustus was not officially declared to be a god during his lifetime, but every possibility stopping short of such a declaration was exploited. Augustus was not the direct object of religious veneration, but his 'genius' was venerated, i.e. his benevolent protector spirit, or in abstract terms the genius that guided him. The fact that two laurel trees were set up at his doorposts indicates that a separate object of veneration was his 'numen', the divine power which dwelt in him (see Alföldi). At all private and public banquets, toasts were made to Augustus under this linguistic covering. The Senate chose the designation 'Augustus', which comes from the sacral vocabulary, as his honorific name in the year 27 BCE. According to the dictionary *augustus* means 'sanctified', 'inviolable', 'venerable', 'exalted', and the Greeks translated it as σεβαστός. In 17 BCE, the Secular Games were held,[38] celebrating the dawn of a new age which would once more be governed by ancient values such as *fides, pax, honor, pudor* and *virtus*. The Roman tendency to deify abstract concepts favoured the veneration of such entities as *concordia, victoria* and *pax Augusta*.

Peace was indeed an exceptionally significant topic, and not only on the inscriptions from Asia Minor. In 25 BCE, the temple of Janus was closed, indicating that there were no longer any wars (or at least no civil wars). In 11 BCE the *ara pacis*, the altar of peace, was erected. The *pax Romana* was seen as the great achievement of the Augustan age; and it was precisely this state of peace, so long unknown until then, that earned Augustus genuine gratitude and veneration. It undeniably had its negative aspects,[39] yet it impressed so many people that it led to the mythical exaltation of Augustus as the creator of peace and the ruler over a peaceful realm. An anecdote in Suetonius captures this mood well: towards the end of his life, when Augustus passed by the bay of Puteoli, passengers and sailors from a ship which had just arrived from Alexandria overwhelmed him, 'clothed in white robes and garlands, and burning incense, with wishes that he might live a happy life and with boundless acclamations of praise: it was thanks to

---

[38] The relevant documents from ILS 5050 are translated in K. Latte, *Religion* (L4) 27–9.

[39] Cf. the critical and destructive dissection of this 'peace' by K. Wengst, *Pax Romana and the Peace of Christ*, London 1987; see the discussion of this book (itself no less critical) by G. Lüdemann and H. Botermann, ' "Pax christiana" versus "Pax Romana" ', *ThR* 53 (1988) 388–98.

him that they lived, thanks to him that they put out to sea, and thanks to him that they enjoyed freedom and prosperity'.[40]

(d) The formation of legends

Myths and legends comparable to those of the biography of Alexander very soon formed around the life of Augustus, especially around his birth and his death (cf. Speyer 1783f.). If we restrict ourselves once again to Suetonius, we learn the following about the premonitory signs and the accompanying circumstances of his birth (94.4):

> It is said that Atia (his mother) went by night to the feast of Apollo, where she had her litter set down in the temple. After the other women already slept, she too fell asleep. Then suddenly a snake crept up to her, and soon left her again. When she awoke, she purified herself as women do after sexual union with a man ... Augustus was born in the tenth month and was accordingly regarded as the son of Apollo. Before the birth, the same Atia dreamt that her body was carried to the stars and was spread out over the entire breadth of heaven and earth. His father Octavius likewise dreamt that a ray of sunlight came forth from Atia's body.

According to Suetonius, comparable omens and prodigious signs accompany the growing years of the boy and the public activity of Octavian the man. Shortly before his death, premonitory signs announce his imminent deification. One of these signs presupposes considerable linguistic knowledge: a statue of Augustus was struck by lightning, so that the first letter of his full name 'Caesar Imperator Augustus', the 'C' which denotes the number 100, melted away, leaving only *aesar*. This was interpreted to mean that Augustus now had only one hundred days to life, but would then be taken up among the gods, since the word *aesar* in Etruscan meant 'god' (97.2). The necessary pretext for his apotheosis was provided when one of the witnesses of his cremation, a former praetor, swore that he had seen Augustus' figure ascending into heaven (100.4).

---

[40] *Aug.* 98.2; on this and on the following section cf. O. Wittstock, *Sueton: Kaiserbiographie* (SQAW 39), Berlin 1993; J. C. Rolfe, *Suetonius*, vol. 1, rev. edn. (introd. by by K. R. Bradley) (LCL 31), Cambridge, Mass. and London 1998; on Augustus alone cf. also D. Schmitz, *C. Suetonius Tranquillus: Augustus* (RecUB 6693), Stuttgart 1988.

Another tradition, full of inimitable understatements, may come closer to the historical Augustus. We are told that as he lay dying, he asked his friends 'whether he had played the comedy of life in a respectable manner', closing with the Greek formula used by actors at the close of a performance in the theatre: 'If the play has been excellently played, then give your applause, and all of you accompany us with joy [as we exit]' (99.1).

3. The Julio-Claudian emperors

List 92.

M. Altman, 'Ruler Cult in Seneca', *CP* 33 (1938) 198–204.

J. R. Fears, *Princeps* (L81).

D. Fishwick, *Cult* (L81).

——'The Development of Provincial Ruler Worship in the Western Roman Empire', *ANRW* II/16.2 (1980) 1201–53.

C. Habicht, 'Die augusteische Zeit' (L91).

P. Herrmann, 'Ein Tempel für Caligula in Milet?', *MDALI* 39 (1989) 191–6.

E. G. Huzar, 'Emperor Worship in Julio-Claudian Egypt', *ANRW* II/18.5 (1995) 3092–3143.

E. Köberlein, *Caligula und die ägyptischen Kulte* (BKP 3), Meisenheim am Glan 1962.

S. R. F. Price, *Rituals* (L81).

D. R. Schwartz, *Agrippa I: The Last King of Judaea* (TSAJ 23), Tübingen 1990.

F. Taeger, *Charisma* (L81) II.226–407.

A. Wlosok, *Kaiserkult* (L81).

We could simply bring the discussion to an end at this point, contenting ourselves with the summary remark by Fritz Taeger: 'The model provided by Augustus remained determinative for the external form given to the imperial cult for about three hundred years' (226). He himself, however, continues his own presentation up to the emperor Constantine, and the collection of essays edited by Wlosok goes even further, to Julian the Apostate (361–3 CE). Such studies often conclude with reflections on what elements of this ideology of the imperial cult may have survived in the western 'kingship by the grace of God', in the Byzantine Caesaropapism and in the papacy (e.g. Taeger 694). We continue our own sketch, which will be briefer than hitherto, up to the beginning of the second century CE, since this corresponds to the period in which the New Testament texts were written.

(a) Tiberius

Tiberius, who reigned from 14 to 37 CE, contributed to a stable organisation of the imperial cult above all by seeing to the *consecratio* of his predecessor and to the spread and performance of his cult. Evidence of a temple dedicated to Tiberius, with priests and a cult, is found in at least eleven cities in Asia Minor. It is possible that some of these were erected only after his death, but at least some of them go back to his lifetime. One example of the latter group must suffice here, an honorific inscription from the city of Myra in Lycia: 'The people of Myra (honours) the emperor Tiberius, the exalted god, son of exalted gods, lord of land and sea, the benefactor and saviour of the entire world.'[41]

In the case of Tiberius, discussion centres primarily on the fact that he reacted negatively when the city of Gytheion in Asia Minor addressed to him the request that they might put into practice a resolution concerning his cultic veneration.[42] He replies politely that such honours are not appropriate to him; Caesar and Augustus are more fitting objects of such veneration. The emperor Claudius reacted in the same way in two subsequent cases. Scholars have tended to interpret this as a clear sign that these two emperors rejected their divinisation, but Habicht (47f.) objected some time ago that the reply does not formulate an explicit prohibition. Nor did the cities in fact seek such an answer as such; their main objective was to present themselves to the emperor in a good light, and they could certainly interpret his reaction as a sign of personal favour. Price too has recently maintained that these rejections have been 'traditionally over-emphasized' (72). A specific strategy is involved here. When the question was put directly, the only path open to the emperors was to express their contentment with more modest honours, such as were appropriate to human beings, since they always had to take Rome into consideration, where – according to the legal fiction – the emperor during his lifetime had the status only of a simple fellow citizen. With diplomatic finesse, things

---

[41] IGRR III no. 721; in G. Pfohl, *Inschriften* (L4) 68 as no. 75.

[42] The document can be found e.g. in SEG Xl 922f.; V. Ehrenberg and A. H. M. Jones, *Documents* (L4) no. 102; trans. in R. MacMullen and E. N. Lane, *Paganism* (L4) 74–6.

are left in the air so that an equilibrium between the different systems can be achieved.

(b) Caligula

Caligula, who had an unparalleled reputation for arbitrary despotism, was greeted with exceedingly high expectations when he took office. On his way to Rome, he passed 'amidst altars, sacrificial beasts and burning torches through a crowd of people who thronged around him, full of exultation. They came out to meet him and continually acclaimed him with words of good fortune, calling him their "star", their "little chick", their "little boy", their "schoolboy"' (Suetonius, *Calig.* 13). This is confirmed by Philo too, when he writes in his *Legatio ad Gaium* that 'all the world rejoiced over Gaius, more than over any ruler since human memory began' (*Leg. Gai.* 11). This initial rejoicing then increased all the more, after he recovered from an illness that had threatened his life.[43] Now it was believed that 'he would pour out new streams of blessings on Asia and Europe as saviour and benefactor [σωτὴρ καὶ εὐεργέτης], bringing lasting good fortune to all in common and to each one individually'.[44]

In keeping with the scheme of contrasts, the reverse follows at once. In Philo, Caligula turns into a brute beast (*Leg. Gai.* 22). Suetonius promises that from this point onwards, he will relate his career as a monster (*Calig.* 22.1: 'reliqua ut de monstro narranda sunt'). One element of this monstrous quality is that Caligula is the first emperor to compete directly with the ancient traditional gods. Here we follow Suetonius once again (22.2f.):

> So he gave orders that statues of the gods famous for their sacredness and their artistic perfection, including the statue of Olympian Zeus, should be brought from Greece. The heads were to be knocked off these statues and a copy of his

---

[43] Cf. also the resolution of the people in Cyzicus in 37 CE (SIG 3/98): 'Since the new sun, Gaius Caesar Augustus Germanicus, deigned to give light with its rays also to those realms which are subject to the imperial dominion, so that the splendour of its immortality demands of us an even greater veneration ... although the kings were unable to find an expression of thanksgiving suitable to the benefits bestowed by such a god ... Now they enjoy the superabundance of the divine favour.'

[44] *Leg. Gai.* 22; cf. E. M. Smallwood, *Philonis Alexandrini Legatio ad Gaium*, Leiden 2nd edn. 1970.

own head put there instead. Then he extended a part of the palace as far as the Forum, changed the temple of Castor and Pollux into a vestibule and often stood between the pair of divine brothers, presenting himself as an object of adoration to those who entered. And some in fact greeted him with the title 'Jupiter of Latium'. He also set up a temple dedicated to his own divine person, with priests and exquisite sacrificial beasts. A golden statue of him, true to life, stood in this temple, and day by day it was clothed in the garments that he happened to be wearing that day.

When Philo appeared before Caligula to present in person the concerns of the Jews of Alexandria, the emperor engaged him in a hair-splitting theological disputation. He greeted Philo with a mocking laugh and the observation: 'So you are the ones who despise god, those who do not believe that I am a god' (*Leg. Gai.* 353). Philo and his companions protested that this was a calumny: they had already offered sacrifice for him three times, on his ascent to the throne, when he recovered health, and when he marched to battle against Germany. 'It may be true that you have offered sacrifice,' replied Caligula. 'But that was to another god, even if it was for my person. That does not help because you did not offer sacrifice to *me*' (357).

Another measure taken by Caligula touches the historical period of the New Testament directly. The non-Jewish population of the city of Jamnia in Palestine had set up an altar for Caligula, which was at once torn down by the Jewish inhabitants. When Caligula was informed of this, he ordered that 'an enormous gold-plated statue of himself be set up in the temple of the Jewish capital'.[45] It is scarcely necessary to state in detail what this meant for Judaism, and what an appalling catastrophe could have resulted. The Syrian legate Petronius did all he could to delay the execution of this command, and the Jewish King Agrippa I obtained a temporary postponement. But it seems that only Caligula's murder in 41 CE genuinely put an end to the threat. He was not deified after his death, although this had happened in the case of his predecessor Tiberius.

(c) Claudius

After Caligula's death the praetorian guard acclaimed Claudius, nephew of Tiberius and uncle of Caligula, as emperor. In general, Claudius followed

[45]   *Leg. Gai.* 203; the sources for this event are *Leg. Gai.* 197–347 and Josephus, *Ant.* 18.256–309; detailed discussion in Schwartz 18–23, 77–89.

the reserved policy of Augustus and Tiberius in questions of the imperial cult. A number of problems of interpretation in individual cases exist, but these cannot be discussed in greater detail here. (Fishwick 195–218 provides an instructive example: contrary to what has usually been assumed, the altar and temple of Divus Claudius in Camulodunum in Great Britain were built only after Claudius' death, when it was easier to venerate him as a god; before this, there stood on this site only an altar to the goddess Rome and Divus Augustus.)

Seneca, whom Claudius had banished to Corsica for several years (cf. V/B, 2), took vengeance on the emperor after his death by means of the satire *Apocolocyntosis*, i.e. the 'Pumpkinification' or 'Leg-pulling'. This work is relevant here because it satirises the institution of *consecratio* with the oath that was sworn by a witness to the heavenly ascent. I quote only some lines from the Introduction (1.1f.):

> I wish to transmit to posterity, so that it may not be forgotten, what took place on 13 October,[46] in the first year of a new chronology, at the beginning of the age most rich in blessings[47] . . . If anyone asks how I know these things, then my first response will be not to answer at all, if I do not wish to do so – for who would want to force me to answer? . . . But if it is necessary to present a guarantor, then one should ask the man who earlier saw Drusilla ascend to heaven,[48] and he will then affirm that he saw Claudius 'limping along'[49] on his journey to heaven. For whether or not he wants to, he is obliged to see everything that happens in heaven, since he is the chief inspector of the Via Appia, and as we know, it was along this road that the divine Augustus and the emperor Tiberius already passed on their way into the realm of the gods.[50]

[46] The date of Claudius' death. Cf. W. H. D. Rouse, *Seneca: Apocolocyntosis* (LCL 15), Cambridge, Mass. and London 1969, 431–83.

[47] A reference to the beginning of the reign of Nero, from whom again wonderful things were expected.

[48] The senator Livius Geminus made possible the deification of Caligula's deceased sister Drusilla by his oath in the Senate. The emperor rewarded him with a large sum of money for this. It appears that he had a post in the administration of the roads at the time of Claudius' death (see below).

[49] A double allusion to Vergil, *Aen.* 2.724, and to the fact that Claudius limped (hence his sobriquet).

[50] Augustus and Tiberius died outside Rome, and their corpses were brought along the Via Appia into the city for burial; for the satire, this was the first part of their 'ascension into heaven'.

(d) Nero

Whatever else may be said about Nero, it appears that – unlike Caligula – he did not see it as a point of personal honour to compete with the gods. This means that his contribution to the praxis of the imperial cult remains within the customary boundaries. (It has been alleged that Nero made claims to divinisation by means of the coins which he had struck; such assertions are critically analysed by Fears 325–8.) But in retrospect the figure of Nero took on a mysterious dimension, beginning with his early death at the age of thirty-one and his burial in the presence of only a very few persons. In the East, Nero's rule was not experienced as especially oppressive, and he even maintained good relationships with the Parthian people. The legend based on this says that Nero did not commit suicide at all, or that he survived the attempt; he then fled to the Parthians in the East, where he remained in hiding until he would return with a mighty army to reconquer his power. The rather sober accounts in Tacitus and Suetonius already show traces of this legend. According to Tacitus, the first false Nero appeared on the scene as early as 69 CE:[51]

> At this time, Achaia and Asia were struck with terror – for which of course there was no rational cause – through the belief that Nero would soon return. For various rumours about his death ran around, so that people spun fables about this continually, and believed that he was still alive. I shall speak about what happened to the other pseudo-Neros, and what they did, in the subsequent course of my narrative. In this case, a slave was involved . . .

According to Suetonius, for a long period there were those who bore statues of Nero on to the speakers' platform and set up tablets with his edicts 'as if he were still alive and would shortly return to destroy his enemies'. An unknown man appeared twenty years after Nero's death, claiming to be Nero: he had great success among the Parthians (*Nero* 57.1f.). This idea is taken up in Jewish/Christian apocalyptic, given a negative colour, and raised to the status of myth. The Sibylline Oracles inflate Nero so that he becomes God's satanic opposite number, appearing in the end time and bringing war and destruction on the final generation of mankind (Sib 5.361–5):

> At the close of the age, towards the end of the moon's shining, a war rages and lays waste the world. The deceiver full of cunning comes from the end of the

---

[51] *Hist.* 2.8.1; cf. C. H. Moore, *Tacitus: Histories I–III* (LCL 111), Cambridge, Mass. and London 1925.

earth, the man who murdered his mother, appearing in the form of a fugitive. In his head he conceives evil plans, he hurls down the universe, bringing all to subjection under his rule.

This idea of *Nero redivivus* is also the basis of some enigmatic hints that the Revelation of John makes about the Antichrist, e.g. when we are told at 13:3 that one of the heads of the beast that rises out of the sea 'had been slain, but its mortal wound was healed', or at 17:8, 'The beast that you saw was and is not, and will ascend from the abyss and go to destruction.' Nero's return is depicted as his ascent from the underworld: this intensification of the imagery is probably due to the apocalyptic writer who put the final touches to the work and who contrasts with it the image of the parousia of the risen Christ who returns to earth from heaven.

4. The Flavian emperors

List 93.

J. R. Fears, *Princeps* (L81).

D. Fishwick, *Cult* (L81) 295–300.

S. J. Friesen, *Twice Neokoros: Ephesus, Asia and the Cult of the Flavian Imperial Family* (Religions in the Graeco-Roman World 116), Leiden 1993.

A. Henrichs, 'Vespasian's Visit to Alexandria', *ZPE* 3 (1968) 51–80.

T. W. Hillard, 'Vespasian's Death-Bed Attitude to his Impending Deification', in M. P. J. Dillon (ed.), *Religion in the Ancient World* (L2) 193–215.

B. W. Jones, *The Emperor Domitian*, London and New York 1992.

F. Millar, 'The Imperial Cult and the Persecutions', in W. den Boer, *Culte* (L81) 143–75.

F. Sauter, *Der römische Kaiserkult bei Martial und Statius* (TBAW 21), Stuttgart 1934.

M. G. Schmidt, 'Claudius und Vespasian: Eine neue Interpretation des Wortes "vae, puto, deus fio" (Suet. Vesp. 23.4)', *Chiron* 18 (1988) 83–9.

R. Schütz, *Die Offenbarung des Johannes und Kaiser Domitian* (FRLANT 50), Göttingen 1933.

K. Scott, *The Imperial Cult under the Flavians*, Stuttgart 1935, reprint New York 1975.

E. Stauffer, *Christ and the Caesars: Historical Sketches*, London 1955, 147–91.

L. L. Thompson, *The Book of Revelation: Apocalypse and Empire*, New York and Oxford 1990, 95–115.

M. H. Williams, 'Domitian, the Jews and the "Judaizers": a Simple Matter of Cupiditas and Maiestas?', *Hist.* 39 (1990) 196–211.

(a) Vespasian

We pass over the other competitors for the highest office of state in 68–9 CE (the year of the four emperors), Otho, Vitellius and Galba, and turn our attention to the victor, Titus Flavius Vespasian. At the time of Nero's death, he was commander of the Roman troops outside Jerusalem in the Jewish War, and his soldiers acclaimed him as emperor in Alexandria in July 69. He is said to have worked miracles, including acts of healing, precisely in this decisive hour:[52]

> He was an emperor whom no one had expected and was still new in this position, so that he lacked authority; but this was bestowed on him. A blind man from among the people and another with a lame leg appeared before him together, as he sat on the judgement seat, and asked him for the healing of their illness, which Sarapis had foretold them in a dream: he would restore sight to the one, if he spat on his eye, and strengthen the leg of the other, if he deigned to touch it with his own heel. Although it was scarcely credible that this could come about in any way, so that he did not dare even to try it, his friends persuaded him and he finally undertook the attempt in both cases, in full view of the assembled crowd, and this was crowned with success.

The introduction to this narration makes it perfectly plain that these miracles, which exalt Vespasian above normal human stature, serve the ideological legitimation of his power base, which was still fragile (see Fears 171f.). Recent scholarship has shown that Vespasian made a determinative contribution to the further development of the imperial cult. Not only did he allow it to take its course in the East; it was he who first truly introduced it into the western provinces. This policy is due to his endeavours to secure legitimation, and it contributed more than the scanty accounts of miracles to the consolidation of the rule of his dynasty. Vespasian was well aware that he came from an undistinguished family, and that he had attained the

---

[52] Suetonius, *Vesp.* 7.2f.; cf. H. Martinet, *C. Suetonius Tranquillus: Vespasian, Titus, Domitian* (RecUB 6694), Stuttgart 1991; J. C. Rolfe, *Suetonius*, vol. 2, rev. edn. (LCL 38), Cambridge, Mass. and London 1997; the longer source text is in Tacitus, *Hist.* 4.81.1–3.

imperial dignity only by an indirect route. The imperial cult offered him the possibility of overcoming this obstacle and establishing continuity with his Julio-Claudian predecessors, including the 'divine' Augustus, thereby at the same time overcoming the crisis in which the principate found itself. It is also illuminating to see how Pliny the Elder interrupts a sceptical tirade against belief in the gods to 'elevate' Vespasian literally 'into heaven'; and one can easily recognise in his words the fundamental structure of the cult of benefactors, as well as something that points in the direction of an euhemeristic explanation of myths:[53]

> To be a god means that a mortal human being helps another mortal, and this is the path to eternal glory. This was the path taken by the most noble of the Romans, and now Vespasian Augustus, the greatest ruler of all times, takes this path along with his children, coming to the help of the enfeebled world. The oldest custom whereby gratitude is shown to highly meritorious men is to give such helpers a place among the gods. For the names of other gods too, and the above-mentioned names of the constellations, have arisen from the meritorious deeds of human beings.

At first sight there seems to be a tension between this and some words that, according to Suetonius, Vespasian said as he was dying (23.4): 'Vae, puto deus fio' ('Alas! I think that I am becoming a god'). Fishwick, who devotes a section specifically to the study of these words, comes to the conclusion that Vespasian's character displays a strange mixture of credulity, scepticism and cynical common sense. This means that we cannot be entirely certain what his last words meant. In view of all that he did in other contexts to promote the imperial cult, it is hardly likely that he intended open mockery of the apotheosis as a naive ritual; rather, his words should be understood 'as the ironic legacy of a hard-boiled administrator who realised clearly that his eternal reward would consist in being caught posthumously in his own trap' (300; Schmidt, however, rejects these words as inauthentic; see now Hillard).

(b) Domitian

All that we need note about Vespasian's son Titus (79–81 CE) is that his brother Domitian saw to his *consecratio*. Domitian himself did not receive this rite, since his fate was the *damnatio memoriae*. A resolute hostility held sway between him and the Senate from the outset, and this is why the

---

[53] Pliny the Elder, *Hist. Nat.* 2.18f.

historians and writers who shared the Senate's view are against Domitian; likewise, the Jewish-Christian tradition mistrusted him because of a number of events which have been evaluated in very different ways (see Williams). Historical scholarship has long been working on a revision of the very sombre picture of Domitian which these sources provide, a picture which owes much too much to New Testament scholarship;[54] Domitian had considerable achievements in the fields of administration, organisation, and the legal system.

There can be no dispute about the fact that Domitian also promoted the imperial cult; but it remains very questionable whether he was the first emperor since Caligula to broach boundaries that were otherwise respected. It would be necessary to investigate this matter thoroughly. In general, the point is made that, according to Suetonius, he made use of the expression *Dominus et deus noster* ('Our lord and god') when referring to himself as the author of letters and edicts (*Dom.* 13.2), and also let himself be addressed in this way. This is reflected in texts of the poet Martial (cf. Sauter), but not, as far as is known, in inscriptions and coins. The first imperial temple in Ephesus was built in his lifetime, dedicated to the *Sebastoi*, i.e. the ruling Flavian dynasty including Domitian's own person (cf. Friesen 41–9). Excavations have unearthed the head and the left forearm of his statue, which stood in the *cella* within the temple; these fragments allow us to estimate that his statue had the considerable height of between five and seven metres. After Domitian was murdered in 96 CE, the Ephesians changed the dedication of the temple and the statues by eliminating his name from the inscriptions and replacing it with that of Vespasian. It is still possible to see clearly some of the traces of this activity.

5. Trajan

List 94.

J. Beaujeu, *La Religion romaine à l'apogée de l'empire*, I: *La politique religieuse des Antonins (96–102)* (CEA), Paris 1955, 58–278 (Trajan and Hadrian).

J. R. Fears, 'The Cult of Jupiter and Roman Imperial Ideology', *ANRW* II/ 17.1 (1981) 3–141.

---

[54] An extreme example is provided by the relevant passages in Stauffer's problematic book; Schütz is more reserved; Thompson now takes a wholly different view.

A. Giovannini, 'Pline et les délateurs de Domitien', in Idem and D. van Berchem (eds.), *Opposition et résistance à l'Empire d'Auguste à Trajan* (EnAC 33), Geneva 1987, 219–48.

W. Kühn, *Plinius der Jüngere: Panegyrikus. Lobrede auf den Kaiser Trajan* (TzF 51), Darmstadt 1985.

B. Radice, *Pliny the Younger: Letters and Panegyricus*, vol. 2 (LCL 58), Cambridge, Mass. and London 1969, 317–547.

D. N. Schowalter, *The Emperor and the Gods: Images from the Time of Trajan* (HDR 28), Minneapolis 1993.

Pliny the Younger (cf. Giovannini) made a powerful contribution to blackening the image of Domitian in a work which can be understood correctly only if due attention is paid to its *Sitz-im-Leben* and to the rules governing its genre. After the brief interlude of Nerva (96–8 CE), Trajan began his long reign (98–117 CE). He appointed Pliny to succeed to the office of consul from 1 September 100, and Pliny made the customary speech of thanks in the Senate, which he later published in an expanded form as his *Panegyric* on the emperor Trajan. If one reads this text with sober precision, without being deflected by the optical illusion of its rhetorical exaggerations, one will see what Pliny's intention was (cf. Schowalter): as the Senate's representative, he wanted to induce the new ruler to adopt a moderate style of government that would be friendly to the Senate. Thus he has the same intention as Dio Chrysostom in his four discourses on the royal sovereignty (*Or.* 1–4), which are likewise addressed to Trajan. By putting Domitian in a bad light, he is enabled to present Trajan, the object of hope, in the most glorious light possible. One of the things he attacks is Domitian's *divinitas*, his divine status, during his lifetime (49.1). Pliny suggests that Domitian 'as it were captured mighty herds of sacrificial beasts on their way to the Capitol, and forced them to take a different path', so that his own statue, 'the hideous image of a brutal tyrant, might be honoured with as much sacrificial blood as he himself had shed human blood' (52,7). Trajan is utterly different: he does not even permit the invocation of his 'genius' (52.6), and enters the temple only in order that he himself may pray, without aiming at a place among the gods (52.2). Pliny writes programmatically in his Introduction that this must remain so (2.3f.):

> Let us nowhere flatter him as a god, as a higher being – for we are not speaking here of a tyrant, but of a citizen; not of a lord, but of our father. 'I am only one

of you' – and it is precisely this that gives him still greater pre-eminence, namely the fact that he looks on himself as one of us, and is aware both that he himself is a human being and that he is placed at the head of human beings!

Posthumous divinisation poses no problem; quite the contrary. Pliny gives a list at 11.1–3: Augustus, Claudius, Vespasian, Titus and Nerva, who had adopted Trajan in order to hand on power to him. The consequence of the *consecratio* of his father Nerva is that Trajan can be called not only 'son of an immortal father' (11.4), but directly 'son of a god' (14.1: here *dei filius*, not *divi filius*; cf. also 23.4). Pliny promises Trajan that he will receive divinisation as his future heavenly reward (35.4).

Pliny is very generous with his comparisons: a *princeps* of irreproachable moral purity resembles the gods (1.3). He was given his office with the assistance of the gods, and chosen by Jupiter himself (1.4f.). He has the same fullness of power as the immortal gods (4.4). Jupiter, who is father and governor of the world, is completely relieved of this burdensome task and can devote all his attention to heaven, since he has the emperor on earth as his vicar in relation to the human race (80.4f.). Those who need help find healing and rescue through the simple fact that the emperor comes to know of their plight (30.5). The most compact statement is at 80.3, with a rhetorical exaggeration that threatens to burst out of the linguistic rules governing the use of metaphor:

> In truth, this is how a *princeps*, indeed a god cares for those who belong to him: he reconciles cities that are torn apart by disputes, he calms down peoples in revolt, less by means of his stern command than by means of reasonable arguments; he takes action when the authorities fail to respect the rule of law, and abolishes measures that ought never to have been taken; finally, like the sun, swiftest of all the stars, he sees everything and hears everything. And wherever he is invoked, he is immediately present with his help, like a deity.

It scarcely needs to be emphasised that Pliny's reservations had no effect on the cultic veneration of Trajan in the provinces. As proconsul in Bithynia, Pliny would have had the chance to reduce the imperial cult there, but, on the evidence of his famous letter concerning the Christians (see below), he did not do so. On the contrary, he continued to practise the established forms, as we shall see in a special section below. A brief look into subsequent years shows that Trajan's successor Hadrian (117–38 CE) was honoured *inter alia* as the new Dionysus and as an Olympian, or as the Olympian Zeus, in this specific case by the island of Chios.[55]

C. The imperial cult: forms and diffusion

1. Forms

(*a*) Sacrifices and prayers

List 95.

G. W. Bowersock, 'Greek Intellectuals and the Imperial Cult', in W. den Boer, *Culte* (L81) 177–212.

D. Fishwick, 'Votive Offerings to the Emperor?', *ZPE* 80 (1990) 121–30.

S. J. Friesen, *Twice Neokoros* (L93) 151f.

R. Klein, *Die Romrede des Aelius Aristides* (TzF 45), Darmstadt 1983.

A. D. Nock, 'Deification and Julian', in *Essays* (L2) 833–46.

S. R. F. Price, 'Between Man and God: Sacrifice in the Roman Imperial Cult', *JRS* 70 (1980) 28–43.

The ritual forms practised in the imperial cult correspond to those found in the exercise of religion in general in the classical world: sacrifices, temples with images and priests, processions, feasts, athletic contests (see I/A), but with one or other particularity. This begins with the sacrifices: although there are some indications to the contrary, it seems (cf. Price) that sacrifices in the imperial cult were not offered directly to the emperor during his lifetime, but that he was their beneficiary. This means that Caligula would have been correct in the accusation he made to Philo (see above) that sacrifice was offered, not *to* the emperor, but *for* the emperor. Since the dative case can be used in Greek for both these situations, it is difficult to determine this precisely. Where it is unmistakably clear that the living emperor is one of the direct addressees of the sacrifice, he makes his appearance in temple fellowship either with other gods who have a secure place in ancient tradition (and it is these who are mentioned first) or else together with his deified (but already deceased) predecessors and family members. Quite apart from the debate about whether the living emperor could be the exclusive and direct addressee of a sacrifice, it remains sig-

[55] Cf. SEG XV 530; also in G. Pfohl, *Inschriften* (L4) 72 as no. 79; cf. Beaujeu 200–3.

nificant that, whatever the answer to this question may be, sacrifices were offered for his well-being at all: for such sacrifices found no place in the cult of the Olympian gods, nor in the cult of the deceased and deified emperors. Thus the living emperor has a strange, structurally defined intermediary position between mortality and divinity. In the following paragraphs, the antithesis between 'living' and 'deceased and divinised' must always be borne in mind, although this cannot be mentioned explicitly each time.

We also find gaps immanent to the system in matters of oaths and prayers. One of the fundamental actions of religious praxis in the classical period was the taking of an oath in a situation of distress or with the aim of attaining a goal, and then, after things turned out well, making good one's promise by a sacrifice to the deity. In his careful analysis Fishwick concludes that the living emperor was not chosen as the addressee of oaths, and that consequently there was no need to offer him votive sacrifices. In the case of the divinised and deceased members of the imperial families, it appears that oaths were taken to them only in conjunction with other Roman civic gods. In view of the great importance attached to oaths, the fact that prayers were not addressed to the living emperor is almost equally significant. One must in any case warn against overestimating prayer as an act of interior spirituality and personal relationship to the divine – as scholars have repeatedly tended to do, under Jewish-Christian influence. Besides this, Aelius Aristides makes a small, but precise distinction in his discourse about Rome (*Or.* 26.32):

> No one is so arrogant that he could remain unmoved when he hears even only the name of the ruler. He stands up, praises and honours him and speaks two prayers [διπλῆν εὐχήν], one to the gods for the ruler [ὑπὲρ αὐτοῦ] and one to the ruler himself for his own well-being [περὶ τῶν ἑαυτοῦ].

Not only the double prayer per se, but also the change of prepositions from ὑπέρ to περί is eloquent, for the περί used with reference to the emperor implies 'societal negotiation and a diplomatic request', conferring a 'much more neutral sense' on the prayer (Bowersock 201; against this see Friesen).

(*b*) Mysteries and associations

List 96.
P. A. Harland, 'Honours and Worship: Emperors, Imperial Cults and Associations at Ephesus', *SR* 25 (1996) 319–34.

M. P. Nilsson, *Geschichte* (L2) II.357, 370f.
E. Olshausen, '"Über die römischen Ackerbrüder": Geschichte eines Kultes', *ANRW* II/16.1 (1978) 820–32.
H. W. Pleket, 'An Aspect of the Emperor Cult: Imperial Mysteries', *HThR* 58 (1965) 331–47.

To a small extent the veneration of the emperor also took on the external form of a mystery cult. An inscription from Ephesus from the year 88/9 BCE mentions mysteries and initiates in connection with Demeter, the goddess of the Eleusinian mysteries (cf. II/B), and with the *Augusti*, i.e. members of the imperial house:[56]

Μυστήρια καὶ θυσίαι, κύριε, καθ' ἔκαστον
ἐνιαυτὸν ἐπιτελοῦνται ἐν 'Εφέσῳ Δήμητρι
Καρποφόρῳ καὶ Θεσμοφόρῳ καὶ θεοῖς
Σεβαστοῖς ὑπὸ μυστῶν ...

Mysteries and sacrifices, Lord, are offered year by year
by the initiates to Demeter who brings fruit,
(goddess of the) Thesmophoria,
and to the august gods ...

We do not know much more about these imperial mysteries than the mere fact of their existence. The form of a mystery cult, already established through Eleusis, will have been filled out with a substance related to the imperial house. Thus, an image of the emperor will doubtless have played a role in the ritual: like the statues of the gods and sacred objects in other mystery cults, it will have been shown by the hierophants (cf. Pleket). It is also possible that particular emphasis was laid on the immortality of the emperor, thanks to his apotheosis. The divinisation of the human person and hope for a better life after death are the two elements of the mystery cults which take on especial prominence precisely in the imperial period. The few pieces of evidence available do not allow us to conclude that the imperial mysteries, like other mystery cults, sometimes took on the form of associations, but at any rate the association (cf. I/B) was the obvious form for the imperial cult too (see Harland). In Egypt we hear of a σύνοδος

---

[56] *Die Inschriften von Ephesus II* (Inschriften griechischer Städte aus Kleinasien 11.2), Bonn 1979, no. 213.3–6; cf. also SIG 3/820; NDIEC IV, 94 as no. 22; the κύριε in the first line apostrophises the addressee of the text, the Roman proconsul Lucius Maestrius Florus.

Σεβαστὴ τοῦ θεοῦ αὐτοκράτορος Καίσαρος (BGU 1137.137: 'venerable association of the god, the Imperator Caesar'), and in Italy of *cultores Larum et imaginum Augusti* (ILS 6778: 'venerators of the Lares and of the images of Augustus'), as well as a *collegium magnum*, a 'great association' for the same purpose (ILS 7120); here one need only refer to Tacitus, who speaks of venerators of Augustus who 'have fellowships after the manner of *collegia* in all their houses' (*Ann.* 1.73.2). In the case of the Arval Brothers, a very ancient Roman priestly college organised like an association, from the time of the reorganisation under Augustus onwards the imperial cult overlays the old rites, parts of which were no longer understood.[57]

(*c*) Images

List 97.

R. Freudenberger, *Das Verhalten der römischen Behörden gegen die Christen im 2. Jahrhundert dargestellt am Brief des Plinius an Trajan und den Reskripten Trajans und Hadrians* (MBPF 52), Munich 1967.

H. von Hesberg, 'Denkmäler' (L88).

H. P. Kuhnen, *Palästina in der griechisch-römischen Zeit* (Handbuch der Archäologie. Vorderasien 2.2), Munich 1990, 178–81.

T. Pekáry, *Das römische Kaiserbildnis in Staat, Kult und Gesellschaft, dargestellt anhand der Schriftquellen* (Das römische Herrscherbild 3.5), Berlin 1985, esp. 116–29: 'Das Bildnis im Kaiserkult'.

S. J. Scherer, 'Signs and Wonders in the Imperial Cult: A New Look at a Roman Religious Institution in the Light of Rev. 13:13–15', *JBL* 103 (1984) 599–610.

P. Zanker, *The Power of Images in the Age of Augustus*, Ann Arbor 1988.

We have just mentioned once again, in connection with the mysteries and the associations, the images of the emperor. Wis 14:17–21 had already cast a polemical light on the role of such images; and we have also heard of Caligula's attempt to have his own statue set up in the temple at Jerusalem, as well as of Domitian's larger-than-lifesize statue in the temple at Ephesus. The image of the emperor, usually a statue, was the central point of reference for the imperial cult. Sacrifices and feasts were held before this image; it was crowned with garlands and carried around in festal

---

[57] Cf. Olshausen; excerpts from the Acts of the Arval Brothers in translation in K. Latte, *Religion* (L4) 15–18; H. Freis, *Inschriften* (L4) 6–9; cf. M. Beard et al., *Religions*, vol. 1 (L2), 194–6.

processions. Precisely in the case of the conflict with Caligula, one must note that statues of the emperor were erected in Palestine too; not indeed in Jerusalem and its temple, but certainly in the harbour city of Caesarea by the sea, built by Herod the Great, who founded there an imperial temple in which initially statues of Augustus and of the goddess Rome stood (see Kuhnen, also on the Herodian temple of Augustus in Samaria). Josephus pays particular attention to the image of the emperor in his description of this site (*Bell.* 1.414):

> On a hill opposite the harbour entrance stood a temple of Caesar, distinguished by its beauty and size, in which there was a 'colossal' [κολοσσός] statue of Caesar, every bit the equal of its model, that of Zeus in Olympia, and a second statue of Roma, which was like the Hera of Argos.

The Revelation of John sees in the imperial image a means of satanic seduction (Rev 13:14ff.). The beast that arises from the earth causes the dwellers on earth to make an image of the beast that arises from the sea, 'and it was allowed to give breath to the image of the beast so that the image of the beast could even speak, and cause those who would not worship the image of the beast to be killed'. (The technical means required to stage the magic here described existed in classical temples: cf. Scherer.) Despite the in any case brief distance in time, we may link this passage to the Younger Pliny's letter about the Christians (*Ep.* 10.96.1–97.2; cf. Freudenberger). He applies a 'sacrificial test' in order to convict suspects of their Christian faith. This test is passed successfully by all who 'followed my example in invoking the gods and offering a petitionary sacrifice with incense and wine to your image, which I had had fetched for this purpose along with the images of the gods; besides this, they cursed Christ' (96.5). Trajan does not mention his own image when he replies, contenting himself with speaking of 'an act of worship of our gods' (97.1), but one may well ask whether he could indeed have done anything else, in a letter emanating from Rome. It would at any rate be over-hasty to conclude from Trajan's formulation that the image of the emperor played no role whatever in this controversy. According to the concluding evaluation of Pekáry (154), the image of the emperor did not have the primary function of representing the emperor or of expressing the omnipresence of the ruler. Rather, it served as 'a symbol of the unity of the state composed of many peoples, a symbol visible to all and binding the various ethnic groups, communities, political and social organisations to the emperor, expressing their loyalty to him'. This means that while the imperial image did not

317

become 'a genuine statue of a god', it nevertheless took on 'a religious aura that one should not altogether deny'. We can mention only in very summary fashion the numerous coins stamped with the portrait of the emperor. In two cases, there is an indisputable link to the imperial cult: when an imperial temple is depicted, recognisable as such through the inscription; and when the coin depicts the apotheosis, the ascension to heaven which was an element of the divinisation of the emperor.

(*d*) Priests

List 98.
J. Deininger, *Provinziallandtage* (L91) 37–50, 141–54 and frequently.
S. J. Friesen, *Twice Neokoros* (L93) 76–113, 167–214.
R. Gordon, 'Veil' (L83) 224–31.

An entire apparatus was necessary for the performance of the sacrifices. Above all, priests were needed to oversee the correct observance of the rites. As we know (cf. I/A, 4), priestly offices were exercised only as a supplementary activity, often by persons who had achieved success in other fields. Through the allocation of priestly offices, the imperial cult fulfilled an important societal function: it offered local families in the provinces the possibility of making a name for themselves and increasing their public prestige, while also thereby binding the rich and distinguished provincials more closely to the imperial house and to the Roman imperial ideology. It was a desirable goal to be high priest in the imperial cult for an entire province, because the high priest had a most outstanding religious and political position. Apuleius, the author of the *Metamorphoses* and a highly educated man, became *sacerdos provinciae*, high priest in the imperial cult in his land of origin, northern Africa, in the second century CE, and this was a high point in the changeable fortunes of his career. Reasons of health obliged the rhetor Aelius Aristides to decline this same office, which was offered him in Asia Minor.

Women too had the possibility of attaining the office of high priestess, not (as earlier scholars thought) as the spouses of male high priests, but in their own right (see Friesen). The earliest example of an inscription dealing with this comes from the period between 40 and 59 CE:[58]

---

[58] O. Kern, *Die Inschriften von Magnesia am Maeander*, Berlin 1900, no. 158; the lacunae in the text can be indicated only approximately in the translation.

The council [and the people honour]
Juliane, daughter of [Eus]stra[tos, the son of Pha-]
nostratos, the wife [of Al-]
kiphronos, who (was) for A[sia high pri-]
est. She [became] high priestess
of Asia as the first of the [women,]
wearer of the garland, [president of the gymnasium],
priestess of Aphrodite and of the [divine Agrip-]
pina, the mother,[59] for [life, prieste-]
ss also in Ephesus for De[meter for]
life be[cause of] her universal capability.

(e) Feasts

List 99.

P. Herz, 'Kaiserfeste der Prinzipatszeit', *ANRW* II/16.2 (1980) 1135–1200.
S. MacCormack, 'Change and Continuity in Late Antiquity: The Ceremony of Adventus', *Hist.* 21 (1972) 721–52.

In its civic centres, the imperial cult culminated once a year, or more frequently, in festival days with sacrifices, processions, banquets, and athletic and musical competitions. These could take place on the emperor's birthday, or less often on the anniversary of his ascent of the throne, or the date on which the imperial cult had been founded in the city in question. Tertullian reacts against this when he attacks with his customary sarcasm what he sees as 'meaningless, mendacious and frivolous' honours paid to the emperor:[60]

> It is of course a service that bestows great honour, to carry out fire-pots and couches on to the street, to hold banquets the length of an entire lane, to let the city disappear behind the façade of a public house, to turn the earth under one's feet into clay through the wine that runs down, to run in gangs to crimes, shameless acts and the enticements of sexual lust! For it is indeed a source of glory, when a feast of the state demands it, to make one's house take on the appearance of a newly opened brothel.

---

[59] I.e. mother of the emperor Nero.
[60] *Apol.* 35.2–4; cf. C. Becker, *Tertullian: Apologeticum. Verteidigung des Christentums*, Munich 2nd edn. 1961; T. R. Glover, *Tertullian: Apology and De Spectaculis* (LCL 250), Cambridge, Mass. and London 1931.

The imperial ceremonial took on especial intensity at irregular intervals, when the ruler was due to visit a city in person: this was his parousia or *adventus*. Susan MacCormack has synthesised a typical description from the sources. The citizens decorated their city. On the day of the emperor's arrival, a procession with the leading citizens at its head went outside the city walls at a specific hour to meet the ruler with his cortège and to receive him solemnly. The participants bore branches of olive and palm, candles and incense. Solemn greetings were exchanged at the meeting place, and continued inside the city. An encounter between the ruler and the local authorities was part of the programme, and on this occasion urgent requests and matters of business could be laid before him. The programme also included the sacrifices and games which were held at the yearly festival in honour of the emperor, but these took on a new dignity through the presence of the ruler in person.

As well as these seasonal high points, the imperial temples also possessed a calendar that envisaged regular cultic events throughout the course of the whole year. We quote from the festal calendar of a temple of Augustus in Italy. This came into force between 3 and 14 CE, and one should note both the early date – while Augustus was still alive – and the location, viz. Italy, although outside Rome itself. Only Julius Caesar is directly called *divus*, under 12 July; otherwise, the name of Caesar *tout court* always refers to Augustus. Other family members mentioned in this calendar are Drusus, Tiberius and Germanicus. We do not know whether this calendar remained in full force after the death of Augustus, nor, if so, for how long this was the case:[61]

19 Aug. On this day, Caesar became consul for the first time. Prayer . . .

3 Sept. On this day, the army of Lepidus surrendered to Caesar. Prayer.

23 Sept. Birthday of Caesar. A sacrifice is offered to Caesar.[62] Prayer.

7 Oct. Birthday of Drusus Caesar. Prayer to Vesta.

18 Oct. On this day, Caesar put on the toga of the adult man. Prayer to Hope and Youth.

16 Nov. Birthday of Tiberius Caesar. Prayer to Vesta.

15 Dec. On this day, the altar of the returning Fortuna, whom Caesar Augustus brought back from the provinces beyond the sea, was dedicated. Prayer to the returning Fortuna.

[61] Text: ILS 108; the so-called Feriale Cumanum; other examples (Fasti Amiterni, Praenestini and Ostienses) in H. Freis, *Inschriften* (L4) 1–6; cf. the literature in L12.

[62] The dative has several meanings both in Latin and in Greek: see above.

7 Jan.	On this day, Caesar was first given a cortège of lictors. Prayer to the eternal Jupiter.
15 Jan.	On this day, Caesar was given the name Augustus. Prayer to Augustus.
30 Jan.	On this day, the Altar of Peace was dedicated. Prayer to the lordship of Caesar Augustus, the protector of the Roman citizens and of the whole earth.
6 Mar.	On this day, Caesar was elected Pontifex Maximus. Prayer to Vesta and to the civic gods of the Roman people.
14 Apr.	On this day, Caesar won his first victory. Prayer to Victoria Augusta.
15 Apr.	On this day, Caesar was acclaimed for the first time as Imperator. Prayer to the good luck of his supreme military command.
12 May	On this day, the temple of Mars was dedicated. Prayer to the toil of Mars.
24 May	Birthday of Germanicus Caesar. Prayer to Vesta.
12 July	Birthday of the god Julius. Prayer to Jupiter, to Mars the avenger and to Venus his ancestor ...

(*f*) Temples and sanctuaries

List 100.

H. Hänlein-Schäfer, *VENERATIO AUGUSTI: Eine Studie zu den Tempeln des ersten römischen Kaisers* (Archaeologica 39), Rome 1985.

H. Koester (ed.), *Pergamon: Citadel of the Gods. Archaeological Record, Literary Description, and Religious Development* (HThS 46), Harrisburg 1998.

E. Ohlemutz, *Die Kulte und Heiligtümer der Götter in Pergamon* [1940], Darmstadt 2nd edn. 1968.

S. R. F. Price, *Ritual* (L81) 252f. (bibliography).

W. Radt, *Pergamon: Geschichte und Bauten, Funde und Erforschung einer antiken Metropole* (DuMont Dokumente), Cologne 1988.

——*Pergamon: Geschichte und Bauten einer antiken Metropole*, Darmstadt 1999.

Finally, we must discuss the temples (cf. I/A, 2) which were employed in the imperial cult – some given a new use alongside an older dedication, some with a change of dedication, some newly founded. Instead of furnishing a catalogue, we prefer to exemplify by means of one single place the way in which the public architecture was structured by the cult of rulers and emperors. Our choice falls on the city of Pergamum in Asia Minor, to which the third of the letters in the Revelation of John is addressed (Rev 2:12–17).

A chronological study must begin with the *temenos*, the sanctuary of the ruler cult (Radt (1988) 275–9), which goes back to the time of the Attalids. From the second century BCE onwards there existed a cult association specifically dedicated to the Attalids, which made use of a building with a cultic niche beside the theatre for its assemblies and feasts (ibid. 222–4). This is evidence of a coalescence (attested elsewhere too) of the cult of Dionysus (as god of the theatre) and the cult of the ruler. The mighty altar of Zeus, now in the Museum of Pergamum in Berlin, has nothing directly to do with the ruler cult; its construction probably began in 181 BCE on the occasion of a victory in the battle of Magnesia. In the excavations in the city, the *heröon* for Diodoros Pasparos deserves special attention; this has already been mentioned above, in the discussion of attempts at an explanation of the genesis of the cult of rulers (cf. A, 1(*b*)).

The oldest surviving sanctuary of Pergamum is the temple of Athene. The celebrated library of Pergamum was housed on its site. A statue of the goddess stood on a round plinth in the temple courtyard; this was demolished in 20 BCE and replaced by a statue of the emperor Augustus (Radt (1988) 182f.). An honorific inscription from this period runs as follows:[63]

[Αὐτοκράτ]ορ[α Κ]αίσαρα [θ]εοῦ υἱὸν θεὸν Σεβαστὸ[ν]
[πάσης] γῆ[ς κ]αὶ θ[α]λάσσης [ἐ]π[όπ]τ[ην.]

[We honour] the Imperator, Caesar, son of a god, the god Augustus,
who has the oversight over the entire earth and sea.

Statues of the *Theoi Sebastoi* (i.e. the emperor Augustus and his consort Livia) stood on the middle terrace of the largest gymnasium of the city, and the cult of these two also found its way into the sanctuary of Demeter. As early as 29 BCE the city was given permission to erect the first temple for Augustus and the goddess Rome in the province of Asia. It has unfortunately not yet been possible to determine precisely where this temple stood; one suggestion is that it stood on the site of the later Trajaneum, the temple for Zeus Philios and the emperor Trajan or the emperor Hadrian, which literally dominated the city of Pergamum after it was constructed

---

[63] *Inschriften von Pergamon* no. 381; text with illustration in A. Deissmann, *Light from the Ancient East* (L3) 347.

early in the second century CE, set into the summit of the mountain on which the citadel stood, with mighty buttresses that fell steeply downwards (Radt (1988) 239–250). It remains a matter of scholarly dispute whether the two emperors were worshipped as Zeus Philios and Zeus Olympios (Radt), or whether they merely entered a temple fellowship with the Olympian deity which was superior to them (Price).

Outside the city, to the south-west, lies a sanctuary of Asclepius with a fame as a place of healing and convalescence that scarcely fell short of that of Epidaurus. At the portico which leads to this sanctuary there is a genuine *herōon* with a tomb chamber, perhaps dedicated to the legendary founder of Pergamum. On the base of a statue of the emperor Hadrian, from a room on the north-east corner, there is the votive inscription: 'to the god Hadrian'.

2. Diffusion

List 101.
R. Etienne, *Culte* (L88).
D. Fishwick, *Cult* (L81).
C. Habicht, 'Die augusteische Zeit' (L91).
S. R. F. Price, *Rituals* (L81) xxi–xxvi (maps), 249–74 (catalogue).

Generalised affirmations about the diffusion of the imperial cult in the Roman empire presuppose numerous specialised investigations (cf. Etienne; Fishwick) which differentiate carefully between the different geographical, political and social levels. Habicht has proposed a programme for this in his excellent study of the Augustan period, in which he distinguishes the sphere of the individual, the autonomous cities, the capital Rome, the provinces in the East, the provinces in the West, the Roman army, and the independent border states.

It is obvious that one cannot adequately perform this task in a brief sketch; but we choose to go into greater detail only in the case of the diffusion of the imperial cult in Asia Minor in relation to the New Testament writings. From the catalogue and maps in Price, we list here those places in Asia Minor that are mentioned also in the New Testament, indicating the biblical passage and the number of the catalogue or map in Price. The criteria for the existence of the imperial cult in any particular place are traces of altars, temples, or priests of the imperial cult mentioned in inscriptions. In order to prevent the list from becoming too complicated, we do not include the temporal duration. Here then are the places in the catalogue:

Antioch in Pisidia (Acts 14:19; Price no. 123)
Assos (Acts 20:13; Price no. 13)
Chios (Acts 20:13; Price no. 2)
Ephesus (Rev 2:1; Price nos. 27–36)
Hierapolis (Col 4:13; Price nos. 85f.)
Cos (Acts 21:1; Price no. 3f.)
Laodicea (Rev 3:14; Price nos. 87f.)
Miletus (Acts 20:14; Price nos. 38–42)
Mitylene (Acts 20:14; Price nos. 7f.)
Pergamum (Rev 2:12; Price nos. 19–23)
Perge (Acts 13:13; Price no. 140)
Philadelphia (Rev 3:7; Price no. 55)
Rhodes (Acts 21:1; Price no. 9)
Samos (Acts 20:15; Price no. 10)
Sardis (Rev 3:1; Price nos. 56f.)
Smyrna (Rev 2:8; Price nos. 45–6)
Tarsus (Acts 9:30; Price nos. 154–6)
Thyatira (Rev 2:18; Price no. 59)

In addition, the following cities are mentioned only on the maps: Adramyttium (Acts 27:2; no. 7); Derbe (Acts 14:6; no. 163); Iconium (Acts 13:51; no. 162); Colossae (Col 1:2; no. 93); and Patara (Acts 21:1; no. 118). It will be seen at once that this list includes all the seven communities to which the letters in the Revelation of John are addressed, and that it accords at many points with the itinerary of the apostle Paul.

The picture changes somewhat when we inquire about the geographical and demographic spread. The sites of the imperial cult are found above all along the coast to the west and the south; things look different in central Asia Minor, and different again on the northern coast. The area with the highest concentration of imperial cultic sites is at the same time the most densely populated area and the area of early Greek immigration, where Greek culture and language had long been dominant. In the other, less populous areas, the local inhabitants continue to some extent to speak their own language (Acts 14:11) and to practise their own ancient cults. A certain amount of Hellenistic civilisation provided a good soil not only for the cult of rulers, but later for the imperial cult too, whereas it made its way only slowly among the local inhabitants.

We may assume that the situation in the western provinces was similar. The imperial cult was spread by soldiers, officials, merchants and immigrants, in cooperation with groups of prominent local citizens who aimed at a positive relationship with the Roman power. This path permitted a wide diffusion, in purely geographical terms, but a profound penetration of all layers of the population took much longer.

D. Concluding observations

1. The imperial cult as 'institutional metaphor'

List 102.

G. W. Bowersock, 'Intellectuals' (L95).

G. F. Chesnut, 'The Ruler and the Logos in Neopythagorean, Middle Platonic, and Late Stoic Philosophy', *ANRW* II/16.2 (1980) 1310–32.

C. Habicht, 'Die augusteische Zeit' (L91).

S. R. F. Price, *Rituals* (L81).

It is possible to interpret texts, decipher inscriptions, and evaluate the results of excavations without thereby necessarily arriving at a genuine understanding of the phenomena that have been discovered. One wishes that it were possible to ask the people of the classical age directly what they thought about the imperial cult, what it meant for them; it is however far from certain that this would really help us, for perhaps we would already employ the wrong categories when we drew up our questionnaire. The understanding of 'religion' with which Christianity has equipped us even before we set out to understand the imperial cult, essentially involves faith, spirituality, an orientation given to the entirety of one's existence, the practice of the contents of faith in daily life. But it is not possible to presuppose the existence of these things as immutable elements of every religion; or putting it differently, as soon as one has said this, one is confronted with the question of how 'religion' is to be defined at all. Religion can be described, using approaches inspired by sociology, as a kind of sign system which formulates matters important to a society, not by naming these directly but rather in a symbolic manner, and in such a way that the participants in this linguistic game are not even conscious of the exact significance (see the Introduction to Part I). Thus we have not advanced very far in our investigation if we say, for example, that the imperial cult involved no genuine faith. All we would say thereby is that the imperial cult does not correspond to what Christians understand as 'piety'. This does not affect in the slightest the position of the imperial cult in the world outside Christianity.

Earlier scholars repeatedly employed the argument that educated persons criticised the imperial cult and that no hesitation was felt about making jokes (sometimes gross) at the expense of the divinised emperors. What is the significance of such evidence (see Bowersock)? Apuleius of Madaura, one of the most highly educated men of his age, did not think it below his dignity to take on the post of the provincial priest of the imperial cult in northern Africa. Philosophical attempts at a justification of the position of the ruler were made by means of the concept of the *logos* (see Chesnut). We ought at least since the time of Sigmund Freud to be aware that unconscious mechanisms lead people to make jokes even about things whose high value is unquestioned.

Rather too much importance has also been attached to the question of the consciousness of the rulers who found themselves the objects of this veneration. One can say in general that, with a few exceptions (e.g. Caligula), they looked on themselves as human beings, not as gods (cf. Habicht). This is well caught in the case of Tiberius, who had an exceptionally well-developed scepticism in this area, in an address to the Senate which Tacitus places on his lips:[64]

> It would be a sign of vanity and arrogance to let oneself be honoured as a living deity; and the veneration of Augustus would cease, if indiscriminate flatteries made it a matter of daily occurrence. In my own case, senators, I attest before you that I am mortal and that I fulfil human duties, and I am content when I do all that is required by my position as *princeps*. It is my wish that those who come after me may bear this in mind ... Those are my temples in your hearts, those are the most beautiful statues – and statues that last, too ...

Originally, the cult of rulers and emperors was not something *demanded*, but something freely *offered*, as a reaction to the experience of being helped. At other periods there was a stronger social pressure to set up such cults, and they were also promoted by the imperial court itself. Nevertheless, the imperial cult never made any exclusive claims for itself, nor did

---

[64]   *Ann.* 4.37.3 and 38.1f; cf. J. Jackson, *Tacitus: Annals IV–VI, XI–XII* (LCL 312), Cambridge, Mass. and London 1937.

it become a genuine competitor to the traditional belief in the gods; it was something added on to everything else. This meant that, as a rule, conflicts of loyalty did not arise – the participants did not face a decision *either* to sacrifice to Zeus and Dionysus *or* to take part in the cult of the emperor. There was nothing problematic about doing both, and indeed the two could sometimes merge, in that the emperor was given cultic fellowship with Zeus or was presented as a 'new Dionysus'. This integration into already existing cults was a useful means of offering a unified super-structure as a common element in face of the fragmentation and the many forms of belief in the gods found in the various parts of the empire.

Differences between the new gods and the old are signalled by many particularities in the ritual, such as the rarity of sacrifices offered to the living emperor when compared with the frequently attested sacrifices to the gods; and the divinised emperors, whether living or dead, take on an intermediary position between gods and human beings. Their final state sets them closer to the gods, while their origin sets them closer to human beings. The first result of a structural analysis is that we discern a fundamental antithesis between gods and human beings – fundamental indeed, yet neither utterly absolute nor completely unbridgeable. From a structural perspective, it is the role of myth to mediate between contrasting concepts such as 'god/human being', 'life/death'. The person of the mythically exalted emperor provides a successful mediation of the antithesis between the heaven of the gods and the world of mortals.

From a purely pragmatic point of view, the imperial cult was not least a factor making for good order in the classical world. It channelled loyalty vis-à-vis the Roman empire and gave it a stable orientation. Its symbolism also mirrors the structure of power, in which the ruler and his subjects had their established positions. This is why it can very suitably be called an 'institutional metaphor', supplying a brief formula for the fundamental structure of the social system, which otherwise could not be put into words, and working actively to transmit this system to future generations: 'The imperial cult, along with politics and diplomacy, constructed the reality of the Roman Empire' (Price 248).

2. Points of contact with early Christianity

List 103.
J. Beaujeu, 'Les apologistes et le culte des souverains', in W. den Boer, *Culte* (L81) 101–42.

A. Brent, 'Luke-Acts and the Imperial Cult in Asia Minor', *JThS* 48 (1997) 411–38.

D. Cuss, *Imperial Cult and Honorary Terms in the New Testament* (Par. 23), Fribourg (Switzerland) 1974.

F. W. Danker, *Benefactor: Epigraphic Study of a Graeco-Roman and New Testament Semantic Field*, St Louis 1982.

A. Deissmann, 'Christ and the Caesars: Parallelism in the Technical Language of their Cults', in *Light from the Ancient East* (L3) 287–324.

E. Faust, *Pax Christi et Pax Caesaris: Religionsgeschichtliche, traditionsgeschichtliche und sozialgeschichtliche Studien zum Epheserbrief* (NTOA 24), Fribourg (Switzerland) and Göttingen 1993.

D. L. Jones, 'Christianity and the Roman Imperial Cult', *ANRW* II/23.2 (1980) 1023–54.

H.-J. Klauck, 'Sendschreiben' (L80).

E. Lohmeyer, *Christuskult und Kaiserkult* (SGV 90), Tübingen 1919.

F. Millar, 'Persecutions' (L93).

D. Zeller, 'Die Menschwerdung des Sohnes Gottes im Neuen Testament und die antike Religionsgeschichte', in Idem, *Menschwerdung* (L80) 141–76.

When Luke has Jesus say 'The kings of the Gentiles rule over them, and those who have power over them are called benefactors (εὐεργέται)' (Lk 22:25), he reveals that he is very well acquainted with the basic structure of the Hellenistic cult of benefactors. He reserves for God (1:47) and for Jesus Christ (2:11) the title *sōtēr*, which was linked to this cult. In our review of the cult of rulers and emperors, we have encountered other christological titles of honour, viz. the sobriquet 'son of (a) god' and the title *kyrios* (one need only compare such phrases as: 'Nero, lord of all the world'[65] or 'Caesar, lord of all'),[66] to say nothing of the direct address with the title θεός, 'God', which the New Testament applies to Jesus only in borderline cases, if at all. We have also noted the concept of *euangelion*, which takes on a rudimentary narrative dimension through its use in the plural to designate striking events in the biography of an emperor. The fact that Jewish authors such as Philo and Josephus likewise use related terms in this sense shows how closely they were linked to the imperial cult. Philo uses the verb for the joyful news of Caligula's ascent to the throne and of his

---

[65] SIG 3/814,31: ὁ τοῦ παντὸς κόσμου κύριος Νέρων.
[66] Epictetus, *Diss.* 4.1.12: ὁ πάντων κύριος Καῖσαρ.

recovery from a serious illness *(Leg. Gai.* 18 and 231), Josephus employs the noun for the news that Vespasian has seized power *(Bell.* 4.618: 'Swifter than the flight of thought, rumour proclaimed the news of the new ruler over the East, and every city celebrated the good tidings [εὐαγγελία] and offered sacrifices for him'). The linguistic style used to speak of the parousia of the *Kyrios* in the New Testament traditions recalls the arrival of the ruler in his city. Even more fundamentally, one may ask whether the incarnation of the Son of God and his role as mediator have any connection with the proven fact of the attribution of divine status to human beings in the non-Jewish classical world.

Adolf Deissmann's study of the cult of Christ and that of Caesar (in *Light from the Ancient East*) is a pioneering work of great value. Here he has shown us a viable path for scholarly assessment of these phenomena, when he writes: 'Thus there arises a polemical parallelism between the cult of the emperor and the cult of Christ, which makes itself felt where ancient words derived by Christianity from the treasury of the Septuagint and the Gospels happen to coincide with solemn concepts of the imperial cult which sounded the same or similar' (342). No scholar would wish to postulate simple adoptions and derivations from one cult to the other. Rather, one must tackle the question in terms of the history of the reception of these terms. How are specific concepts understood in a new context? What contribution did this intellectual horizon make to the evaluation, accentuation, and elaboration of these concepts? Where must antagonisms necessarily be generated? On the basic level, we have the indispensable task of determining critically the relationship between the Christological models supplied by the New Testament and two concepts: the idea of the epiphany of heavenly powers in human form, and the apotheosis of earthly human beings either during their lifetime or after their death. Here, of course, the imperial cult is only one partial aspect of a much larger complex of ideas.

One must warn against a one-sided exaggeration of the significance of the imperial cult for the New Testament. For example, Paul could scarcely have spoken so straightforwardly of the God-given authority of rulers as he does in Rom 13:1–7 if he had seen the emperor as posing a problem that dominated every other concern; and in the case of the persecutions of Christians too much importance is usually attributed to the imperial cult, which does not appear in isolation, but as part of the entire polytheistic system. Within the New Testament, this applies also to the persecution in the background to the Revelation of John (see Klauck). It is a gross

329

anachronism to suppose that Christians were always and everywhere at risk of being dragged in front of an image of the emperor to be tested to see if they would sacrifice, with martyrdom as the necessary result of their failure to do so. The author of Revelation is not really struggling against this 'hard' form of the imperial cult. In his eyes, a much greater danger is presented by the 'soft' imperial cult, understood as an especially prominent example of pagan religious praxis in general. In liberal Christian circles, which he attacks in the letters of Rev 2–3 as heretical, it could happen that someone went along with a festal crowd or took part in a companionable meal of an association which had superficial religious overtones, because he believed that professional considerations forbade him to hold aloof, without seeing questions of religious belief as affected in any way. The many forms of the imperial cult which our investigation has disclosed suggest that this idea of a 'soft' cult which provoked disputes within Christian groups lies close to the social reality.

Chapter V
In Search of Happiness: Philosophy and Religion

A. Introduction

List 104.

J. M. André, 'Les Écoles philosophiques aux deux premiers siècles de l'Empire', *ANRW* II/36.1 (1987) 5–27.

H. W. Attridge, 'The Philosophical Critique of Religion under the Early Empire', *ANRW* II/16.1 (1978) 45–78.

D. Babut, *La religion des philosophes grecs de Thalès aux Stoiciens* (Littératures anciennes 4), Paris 1974.

J. Brunschwig and M. C. Nussbaum (eds.), *Passions and Perceptions: Studies in Hellenistic Philosophy of Mind*, Cambridge 1993.

H. Flashar (ed.), *Die Philosophie der Antike*, vol. 4: *Die hellenistische Philosophie* (Grundriss der Geschichte der Philosophie), Basle 1994.

H. Flashar and O. Gigon (eds.), *Aspects de la philosophie hellénistique* (EnAC 32), Geneva 1986.

H. B. Gottschalk, 'Aristotelian Philosophy in the Roman World from the Time of Cicero to the End of the Second Century AD', *ANRW* II/36.2 (1987) 1079–1174.

A. Graeser, *Interpretationen: Hauptwerke der Philosophie der Antike* (RecUB 8740), Stuttgart 1992.

M. Hossenfelder, *Die Philosophie der Antike 3: Stoa, Epikureismus und Skepsis* (Geschichte der Philosophie 3), Munich 1985.

A. A. Long and D. N. Sedley, *The Hellenistic Philosophers*, vols. 1–2, Cambridge 1987 (selected texts with commentary).

A. J. Malherbe, *Moral Exhortation: A Greco-Roman Sourcebook* (LEC 4), Philadelphia 1986.

——*Paul and the Popular Philosophers*, Minneapolis 1989.

G. Maurach, *Geschichte der römischen Philosophie: Eine Einführung* (Die Altertumswissenschaft), Darmstadt 1989.

P. A. Meijer, 'Philosophers, Intellectuals and Religion in Hellas', in H. S. Versnel, *Faith* (L2) 216–62.

M. C. Nussbaum, *The Therapy of Desire: Theory and Practice in Hellenistic Ethics* (Martin Classical Lectures NS 2), Princeton 1994.

K. Praechter, *Die Philosophie des Altertums* (Friedrich Ueberwegs Grundriss der Geschichte der Philosophie 1), Berlin 12th edn. 1926, reprint Tübingen 1953 and frequently.

G. Reale, *A History of Ancient Philosophy*, vol. IV: *The Schools of the Imperial Age*, ed. and trans. J. R. Catan, New York 1990.

F. Ricken, *Philosophie der Antike* (Grundkurs Philosophie 6) (UB 350), Stuttgart 3rd edn. 1999 (with basic bibliography).

——(ed.), *Philosophen der Antike* II (UB 459), Stuttgart 1996.

R. W. Sharples, *Stoics, Epicureans and Sceptics: An Introduction to Hellenistic Philosophy*, London and New York 1996.

C. Stead, *Philosophy in Christian Antiquity*, Cambridge 1994.

W. Wieland, *Antike* (Geschichte der Philosophie in Text und Darstellung 1) (RecUB 9911), Stuttgart 1978.

E. Zeller, *Die Philosophie der Griechen in ihrer geschichtlichen Entwicklung*, vols. 1–6, Leipzig 4th to 6th edns. 1919–23, reprint Darmstadt 1963 (vol. 5 translated as *The Stoics, Epicureans and Sceptics*, London 1870).

One may wonder what philosophy is doing in a book about the religious milieu of earliest Christianity. But let us recall that, according to Acts 17:18, Paul met Epicurean and Stoic philosophers in the Agora at Athens, and that they reacted differently to his preaching: the Epicureans dismissed it, while the Stoics were more open. Parts of his speech in the Areopagus employ a Stoic diction, going as far as a quotation from a Stoic didactic poem in verse 28. Did only these two philosophical schools exist at the time of Paul? If not, why does Luke select precisely these two, and why does he not evaluate them in exactly the same terms?

The reply leads us into the heart of our new subject. In the early imperial period, the classical philosophical schools continued to exist, with some modifications, and indeed even experienced in part a new momentum. In the chronological order of their coming into existence, these schools are: the Academy, the Peripatetics, Epicureanism (also called *Kēpos*, 'Garden'), and roughly contemporary with this, the Stoa. The Academy, as representative of Plato's philosophy, yields place in the Common Era to Middle Platonism, before the great Neoplatonic synthesis comes into being in the third century CE, with Plotinus as its founder, and develops into the universally dominant form of late classical philosophy. This, however, lies outside the period which concerns us (for an overview, see e.g. Reale 293–449). In the Peripatetic school the inheritance of Aristotle is conserved and handed on. Thanks to the first edition in the first century BCE by Andronicus of Rhodes of Aristotle's didactic writings for internal use in the school, there is a definite renaissance of Aristotelianism at this time (see Gottschalk). We should also mention other tendencies such as Scepticism; Neopythagoreanism, formed anew at the turn of the first century BCE to the first century CE, though without any recognisable historical continuity with the mysterious ancient teaching of Pythagoras (sixth century BCE); and Cynicism, which arose as an imitation of Socrates, underwent a symbiosis with Stoicism, and then had prominent representatives of its own school once again in the first and second centuries CE.

It goes virtually without saying that exchanges and overlaps between the various schools took place, and that it is therefore not always very easy to determine exactly the philosophical correlatives of a particular idea or author. Cicero's works as a whole offer a representative cross-section of the philosophical thinking in Rome in the first century BCE.[1] He had Epicurean, Academic, and Stoic teachers and friends, and was also familiar with Peripatetic thought. He understood himself primarily as an Academician who incorporated Sceptic elements into his thinking, but he makes space for an account of other systems of thought in his writings, which take the form of dialogues. His ethics are not essentially different from those of Stoicism. Above all, he gives philosophy the task of guidance in coping with life. His prayer to philosophy (in the *Tusculan Disputations*) is eloquent here:[2]

> O philosophy, guide of life, discoverer of virtue, victress over the vices! What would we be without you – indeed, what would human life at all be without you? You have given birth to states, you have called together scattered mortals

[1] Cf. Maurach 53–78; G. Gawlick and W. Görler, 'Cicero', in Flashar 991–1168; on Stoicism in Cicero, M. L. Colish, 'Tradition' (L106) I.61–157; M. V. Ronnick, *Cicero's Paradoxa Stoicorum: A Commentary, an Interpretation and a Study of its Influence* (Studien zur klassischen Philologie 62), Frankfurt a.M. 1991.

[2] *Tusc.* 5.5: on the text and translation cf. O. Gigon, *Marcus Tullius Cicero: Gespräche in Tusculum* (TuscBü), Munich 6th edn. 1992; J. E. King, *Cicero: Tusculan Disputations* (LCL 141), Cambridge, Mass. and London, rev. edn. 1945.

into the fellowship of life. We take our refuge in you, we ask you for help and we entrust ourselves to you ... Whose help should we seek rather than yours? For it is you who have given us rest in our life, and taken away from us the fear of death.

Against this background, let us ask once again: why does Luke concentrate on the Epicureans and Stoics in the Acts of the Apostles? It may be presumed that he saw these two schools as having the widest influence. They were concerned with the individual and sought to provide help so that the individual could attain a successful life (*eudaimonia* is the technical term in Greek) and cope with the blows of fate. It is not entirely wrong to call their activities pastoral care or spiritual direction,[3] or even psychotherapy.[4] We should bear in mind that no other providers of pastoral care or therapists existed in the classical period; this task had to be taken on by the philosophers. This meant that while they did become competitors of Christianity as it strove to establish itself, they also provided welcome points of contact for Christians.

There is thus no cause for surprise that philosophy served educated circles as a guideline for a religiously based conduct of life. If one speaks of a conversion experience in the classical period outside the Jewish/Christian sphere, what is meant is the adoption of one particular philosophical world-view with all its consequences for existential praxis. No one needed to 'convert' in this sense to a belief in the gods or to a mystery cult. One should also bear in mind that the question of the existence of a divinity was discussed in antiquity in the framework of philosophy; no other locus than that of metaphysical and cosmological reflection was available for theological discourse. This also means that the critique of religion was one of philosophy's concerns, and that recourse was also had to philosophy in justifying atheism (see Attridge; Meijer). Atheism, however, was less widespread than our experiences of modern atheism incline us to assume.

All these observations find additional confirmation in the fact that the handbooks on the history of religion in the classical period normally see the necessity of including a chapter devoted specifically to philosophy. This is

---

[3] Cf. P. Rabbow, *Seelenführung: Methodik der Exerzitien in der Antike*, Munich 1954.

[4] This is indeed conceded by modern psychology: cf. the instructive essay by B. Hoellen and J. Laux, 'Antike Seelenführung und Kognitive Verhaltenstherapie im Vergleich', *Zeitschrift für Klinische Psychologie, Psychopathologie und Psychotherapie* 38 (1988) 255–67.

the case, e.g. with O. Kern, *Religion* (L2) III.12–37; M. P. Nilsson, *Geschichte* (L2) II.249–68, 295–466; E. des Places, *Religion* (L2) 260–81 and frequently; and J. Ferguson, *Religions* (L2) 190–210. From a philosophical perspective, Babut deals programmatically with religious questions, as does Reale in the framework of his broader presentation (cf. for example 39–41: Epicureanism as a 'secular religion'). Religious values in Hellenistic-Roman philosophy are considered more from an exegetical perspective by UUC I.346–70; Malherbe; E. Ferguson, *Backgrounds* (L3) 255–314.

The sheer volume of the material forces us to make a drastic selection. We treat Stoicism in somewhat greater detail, since this is accepted generally as the most important point of comparison for Christianity in its earliest development; we also touch on Neopythagoreanism and Cynicism. We discuss Epicureanism more briefly (and we will see why Luke found its adherents unpromising). We take Plutarch as our representative of Middle Platonism (cf. Reale 494 n. 28: 'Plutarch is one of the most important Middle Platonists').

B. Stoicism in the imperial period

List 105 (texts).
J. von Arnim, *Stoicorum veterum fragmenta* (Sammlung wissenschaftlicher Commentare), vols. 1–3, Stuttgart 1903–5, reprint 1978–9, with vol. 4: *Indices*, ed. M. Adler, 1925/1978 (abbreviated as SVF).
K. Hülser, *Die Fragmente zur Dialektik der Stoa*, vols. 1–4, Stuttgart and Bad Cannstatt 1987–8.
A. A. Long and D. N. Sedley, *Philosophers* (L104) I.158–437; II.163–431.
W. Weinkauf, *Die Stoa: Kommentierte Werkausgabe* (Bibliothek der Philosophie), Augsburg 1994.

1. Overview

List 106.
ANRW II/36.3 (1989) 1365–1543 (six essays on Stoicism in the imperial period).
M. L. Colish, *The Stoic Tradition from Antiquity to the Early Middle Ages*, vols. 1–2 (SHCT 34/35), Leiden 1985.

R. H. Epp (ed.), *Spindel Conference 1984: Recovering the Stoics = The Southern Journal of Philosophy* 23 (1985) Supplement (with extensive bibliography, which unfortunately is full of errors).

M. Forschner, 'Das Gute und die Güter: Zur Aktualität der stoischen Ethik', in H. Flashar and O. Gigon, *Aspects* (L104) 325–50.

M. Pohlenz, *Stoicism*, New York 1987.

H. Reiner, 'Die ethische Weisheit der Stoiker heute', *Gym.* 76 (1969) 330–57.

J. M. Rist, *Stoic Philosophy*, Cambridge 1969.

F. H. Sandbach, *Die Stoa. Geschichte einer geistigen Bewegung*, vols. 1–2, Göttingen 6th edn. 1984; Engl. trans. as *The Stoics* (Ancient Culture and Society), London 1975.

P. Steinmetz, 'Die Stoa', in H. Flashar, *Philosophie* (L104) 491–716.

The name 'Stoa' comes from a long colonnade in the Agora in Athens, which was called στοὰ ποικιλή (the 'colourful hall') because of its frescoes. About 300 BCE, Zeno of Kition, founder of the school, began to teach there. He had come to Athens *c*.311 BCE. One of his teachers was the Cynic Crates, and Cynicism, which traced its intellectual ancestry back to Socrates, would be a kind of shadow continuously accompanying Stoicism, with an influence reaching as far as Seneca and Epictetus (see 6 below). It is probably from his Cynic teacher that Zeno adopted the orientation to Socrates in questions of ethics. For the Stoics too, knowledge means action: it suffices to know the good, in order to put it into action. From Xenocrates, head of the school of the Platonic Academy, Zeno borrowed the division of philosophy into logic (including the philosophy of knowledge and of language), physics (including the whole field from cosmology to theology), and ethics. From the outset, a special interest in ethics was characteristic of the Stoa; this is due in part to the fact that the school came into being at a time when established external order was breaking down. The disappearance of the classical *polis* led to the isolation of the individual and to a feeling of being left unprotected. It was here that Stoic ethics endeavoured to indicate a path to an inner happiness that could not be influenced and endangered by external circumstances.

Zeno's successor at the head of the school was his pupil Cleanthes of Assos, the author of the great hymn to Zeus, to which we shall return (cf. 4 below); his successor was Chrysippus of Soloi in Asia Minor, who began his studies under Cleanthes *c*.260 BCE. He became the third head of the school after Cleanthes' death in 232/1 BCE. Chrysippus was regarded in the classical period not as a renewer, but as a consolidator who systematised the body of Stoic knowledge which had been gathered in the course of several decades, and made a synthesis of it for the future. His death in 208 or 204 BCE marks the end of three generations of Stoic philosophy. Original works from this period have not been preserved, but since these three heads of the school are quoted frequently, it is possible to reconstruct an extensive collection of fragments from citations in other authors (cf. SVF [L105]).

We have spoken hitherto of the older Stoa. We mention only two names from the middle or younger Stoa: Panetios of Rhodes (*c*.185–109 BCE) and Poseidonius of Apameia (*c*.135–50 BCE). Both worked in Rome, Panetios for a longer period, Poseidonius more briefly, and thus made essential contributions to the birth of Roman Stoicism. The sources available in their case are perhaps even fewer than in the case of the older Stoa. Their works have not survived, and it remains uncertain whether – as has sometimes been suggested – long passages from Cicero or from Philo of Alexandria may be attributed to them (cf. now Steinmetz).

The late Stoa of the imperial period forms the conclusion. In this final phase, it cannot point to its most original and significant thinkers, but it is at the zenith of its influence and its diffusion. Apart from this, a great advantage is that we have lengthy works by three of its main representatives, viz. Lucius Annaeus Seneca, for a time the most powerful man in the Roman empire; as a contrast to him, Epictetus, who had been a slave and then obtained his liberty; and finally in the second century CE Marcus Aurelius, the philosopher on the imperial throne. It is worth emphasising the social breadth within this trio. We shall turn in the next two sections to specific consideration of Seneca and Epictetus, who are of general interest for the history of the New Testament period. Marcus Aurelius has left us his autobiographical reflections in twelve books,[5] written during his period as Roman emperor and not destined for publication. The substance of these reflections is essentially influenced by Epictetus; these personal notes

---

[5] W. Theiler, *Kaiser Marc Aurel: Wege zu sich selbst* (BAW), Darmstadt 3rd edn. 1984; R. Nickel, *Marc Aurel: Wege zu sich selbst* (TuscBü), Munich 1990; C. R. Haines, *Marcus Aurelius* (LCL 58), Cambridge, Mass. and London rev. edn. 1930; cf. J. M. Rist, 'Are You a Stoic? The Case of Marcus Aurelius', in B. F. Meyer and E. P. Sanders, *Self-Definition* (L3) III.190–2; G. Maurach, *Geschichte* (L104) 131–41; P. Hadot, *Die innere Burg: Anleitung zu einer Lektüre Marc Aurels*, Frankfurt a.M. 1997.

are not entirely set in order, and the high value placed on them is due not least to the political position held by their author.

The history of the Stoa ends in the second century CE, because – as it has been observed in a joke that is nevertheless not entirely off the mark – by then everyone was a Stoic. In other words, certain essential Stoic ideas had become commonplaces and had entered the underlying structure of ethical thought. Not a little of this thinking had already made its mark felt on Middle Platonism (see D below) and was absorbed by the Neoplatonic synthesis.

2. Seneca

(a) His life

List 107.

K. Abel, 'Seneca: Leben und Leistung', *ANRW* II/32.2 (1985) 653–775 (with bibliography).

M. Fuhrmann, *Seneca und Kaiser Nero. Eine Biographie*, Darmstadt 1997.

M. T. Griffin, *Seneca: A Philosopher in Politics*, Oxford 1976.

P. Grimal, *Seneca: Macht und Ohnmacht des Geistes* (Impulse der Forschung 24), Darmstadt 1978.

I. Hadot, *Seneca und die griechisch-römische Tradition der Seelenleitung* (QSPG 13), Berlin 1969.

L. Herrmann, *Sénèque et les premiers chrétiens* (CollLat 167), Brussels 1979.

G. Maurach, *Seneca: Leben und Werk*, Darmstadt 1991 (an introduction that can be highly recommended).

M. Rozelaar, *Seneca: Eine Gesamtdarstellung*, Amsterdam 1976.

J. N. Sevenster, *Paul and Seneca* (NT.S 4), Leiden 1961.

V. Sörensen, *Seneca: Ein Humanist an Neros Hof*, Munich 2nd edn. 1985.

W. Trillitzsch, *Seneca im literarischen Urteil der Antike: Darstellung und Sammlung der Zeugnisse*, vols. 1–2, Amsterdam 1971.

Cf. also L109 below.

Lucius Annaeus Seneca was born about the beginning of the first century CE in Cordoba in Spain. His father Seneca the Elder won his place in Roman literary history with two rhetorical works (*Controversiae*; *Suasoriae*). Seneca had two brothers, the older named Lucius Annaeus Novatus, and the younger named Marcus Annaeus Mela who was the father of the poet Lucan, author of the *Pharsalia*. The fundamental attitude in this epic about the civil war is unmistakably Stoic.[6] The older brother was adopted by the orator Lucius Junius Gallio, and bore his name from then onwards. He went to Greece *c*.52 CE as proconsul of the province of Achaea. In this capacity, the city of Corinth was subject to his authority, and it is there that we meet him in Acts 18:12–17.

His father moved at an early date in Seneca's life to Rome with his three sons, and there he received instruction in rhetoric and philosophy. We know scarcely more than the names of his teachers: Sextius, Attalus, Fabianus, Sotion. To some extent, they imparted Stoic thought to him. Another influence was Pythagoreanism, which gained a foothold in Rome in the first century BCE;[7] its influence on Seneca can be seen in two typical points, daily self-examination (cf. 5(*b*) below) and vegetarianism (cf. *Ep.* 108.20–2: as a young man Seneca lived as a vegetarian for a whole year, and abandoned this practice only under pressure from his father, who was motivated by considerations of political prudence – the vegetarian lifestyle could cause suspicions that Seneca followed one of those foreign cults whose adherents had recently yet again been expelled from Rome by the emperor Tiberius).

After an education on which great care had been expended, Seneca began the *cursus honorum*, the career of public offices. This plan was rudely ended by a grave chronic illness which is described in terms that suggest pneumonia, feverish bronchitis, and severe asthma. For the rest of his life, Seneca, who was troubled for a period by serious ideas of taking his own life because of this illness, had a precarious state of health, and it was often only thanks to extreme self-discipline and asceticism that he was able to keep going. A direct remedy was brought by a stay of several years in the dry and warm climate of Egypt, where one of his relatives had been nominated to the office of prefect. It seems doubtful whether Seneca became acquainted in this period with Philo of Alexandria and oriental syncretism (suggested by Grimal 57; Maurach 27f. is sceptical).

---

[6]   Cf. M. Billerbeck, 'Stoizismus in der römischen Epik neronischer und flavischer Zeit', *ANRW* II/32.5 (1986) 3116–51.

[7]   For a general introduction cf. G. Maurach, *Geschichte* (L104) 79–82; G. Reale, *History* (L104) 235–72; B. L. van der Waerden, *Die Pythagoräer: Religiöse Bruderschaft und Schule der Wissenschaft* (BAW), Zurich and Munich 1979, 260–93.

On his return to Rome in 31 CE Seneca played his role in the confused final years of the emperor Tiberius, experiencing the fall of the omnipotent Prefect of the Guard, Sejanus, and continuing the career in public office which had been interrupted. He proved to be an outstanding orator, and it is said that this put his life at danger by provoking the jealousy of the emperor Caligula (an alternative explanation looks to Seneca's relationships with women of the imperial household). After Caligula's murder in 41 Seneca, as a representative of the senatorial party, stood in the path of Messalina, the consort of the emperor Claudius. He was sentenced to death, but Claudius commuted this to banishment to Corsica. Seneca went there as an exile, and it is probable that he wrote his first works there. (We may mention here that Seneca was married twice. His first wife seems to have died before his exile.)

In the meantime Messalina was convicted in Rome of a conspiracy against the emperor, and executed. Her place was taken by Agrippina, the mother of Nero, who brought about Seneca's recall from exile in 49 and appointed him tutor of her twelve-year-old son. In 54 she poisoned her husband Claudius, hoping that now she could use her son Nero to take the government of the Roman empire into her own hands. This plot was foiled by Seneca, in alliance with the second most powerful man in the state, Sextus Afranius Burrus, the prefect of the Praetorian Guard. Initially Nero followed these two teachers as if he had no will of his own, and they held the reins of the world empire in their hands for about five or six years. This did not remain hidden from outsiders: in the classical period, people spoke of the *quinquennium Neronis*, the first five years of Nero's reign, in which Seneca and Burrus governed. Even the severest critics and enemies of Seneca find praise for these years. The state was guided prudently, and skilful decisions were taken in domestic, financial and foreign politics.

But the seeds of Seneca's downfall had already been sown, in the person of Nero himself. In some points his tutors felt the need to loosen the reins, in the case of his early sexual adventures, which they directed into specific channels, and in the case of his inclination to appear on stage as an actor, which they tolerated within the society of the court.

In 55 Nero's stepbrother Britannicus, who could have posed a threat to his rule, died at the age of fourteen, possibly poisoned by Nero. But the great crisis began only in 58, when Nero became the lover of Sabina Poppaea, whose first step was to intrigue against Nero's wife Octavia and his mother Agrippina. Nero's clumsy plan was to have his mother killed in a pretended disaster at sea, but she escaped and was alerted to the danger.

She wanted to gather her followers together, so that a civil war threatened. In this situation, Nero threw himself upon the mercy of Seneca and Burrus and confessed his mistake. Both agreed in their evaluation of the matter: Agrippina was convicted of high treason and sentenced to death, and this sentence was carried out on the spot by the troops from the ranks of the Praetorian guards who arrested her. There is no doubt that Seneca paid a high tribute here to sheer power politics.

It is clear that Nero suffered under a pathological maternal fixation, which had even caused incestuous situations. He saw his mother's death as the emancipation from authorities that controlled his life. In the background, a new woman pulled the strings, while new dubious friends obtained high offices of state. Burrus died in 62, most likely by poison, and Octavia, Nero's first wife, died in the same year. Seneca offered Nero his retirement from politics and from court life, undertaking to hand over to the emperor his entire fortune, which had grown to incalculable dimensions, not least thanks to Nero's favour, but Nero declined this offer in a well-measured speech. Nevertheless, Seneca withdrew from public life, under the pretext of illness and other commitments. His retirement took place in small individual steps.

Looking back on his time as tutor of the prince, Seneca saw it as utterly worthless and a completely wasted period of his life. In the few years left to him, he devoted himself to intense literary activity, and he produced voluminous works in this period; at times, he must have worked night and day. In public affairs, his programme was one of reserve, so that he said nothing for example about the fire in Rome in 64 or about Nero's persecution of the Christians. It seems doubtful whether he even became aware of the existence of Christians; he is certainly not influenced by Christian thought (although this is asserted by Herrmann).

His end came as a consequence of the Pisonian plot. Nero's development into an intolerable tyrant inevitably provoked resistance, and a group of plotters formed with the aim of killing Nero and putting the senator Piso on the throne. The question is whether their genuine aim was to have Piso as emperor, or whether their underlying wish was in fact to confer the imperial dignity on Seneca; the further question is whether Seneca himself knew of this, and if so, whether he had signalled his assent. Whatever may have been the case, he fell a victim to the great purge after the plot was discovered. He was ordered to commit suicide in 65 CE, and he did so with great dignity, although it was not easy for him to die, and Nero's soldiers may have helped to finish him off (cf. Maurach 46f.).

(*b*) Seneca's work

List 108 (texts).

J. W. Basore, *Seneca, vols. 1–3: Moral Essays* (LCL 214, 254, 310), Cambridge, Mass. and London 1928, 1932, 1935 (several reprints).

M. Billerbeck, *Seneca: Hercules Furens* (Mn.S 187), Leiden 1999.

M. F. A. Brok, *L. Annaeus Seneca: Naturales Quaestiones/Naturwissenschaftliche Untersuchungen*, Darmstadt 1995.

K. Büchner, *L. Annaeus Seneca: De clementia/Über die Güte* (RecUB 8385), Stuttgart 1970, reprint 1981.

T. H. Corcoran, *Seneca, vols. 7 and 10: Naturales Quaestiones* (LCL 450, 457), Cambridge, Mass. and London 1971, 1972.

J. Feix, *L. Annaeus Seneca: De brevitate vitae/Von der Kürze des Lebens* (RecUB 1847), Stuttgart 1977, reprint 1994.

G. Fink, *L. Annaeus Seneca: Die kleinen Dialoge*, vols. 1–2 (TuscBü), Munich 1992.

R. M. Gummere, *Seneca, vols. 4–6: Epistles* (LCL 75, 76, 77), Cambridge, Mass. and London 1917, 1920, 1925 (several reprints).

H. Gunermann, *L. Annaeus Seneca: De tranquillitate animi/Über die Ausgeglichenheit der Seele* (RecUB 1846), Stuttgart 1984.

F. Haase, *L. Annaei Senecae opera quae supersunt*, III: *Fragmenta*, Leipzig 1853 (no better edition of the fragments has been published since then).

F. Loretto and R. Rauthe, *L. Annaeus Seneca: Epistulae morales ad Lucilium/Briefe an Lucilius über die Ethik*, so far Books 1–18 (RecUB 2132–7, 2139–43, 9370–3), Stuttgart 1977ff., often reprinted.

F. J. Miller, *Seneca, vols. 8–9: Tragedies* (LCL 62, 68), Cambridge, Mass. and London 1917 (several reprints).

F. H. Mutschler, *L. Annaeus Seneca: De vita beata/Vom glücklichen Leben* (RecUB 1849), Stuttgart 1990.

M. Rosenbach, *L. Annaeus Seneca: Philosophische Schriften*, vols. 1–5, Darmstadt 1980–9.

T. Thomann, *Seneca: Sämtliche Tragödien*, vols. 1–2 (BAW), Zurich 2nd edn. 1978, 1979.

List 109.

K. Abel, 'Die Taciteische Seneca-Rezeption', *ANRW* II/33.4 (1991) 3155–81.

ANRW II/36.3 (1989) 1545–2012 (ten essays on Seneca's philosophical work).

A. Bäumer, *Die Bestie Mensch: Senecas Aggressionstheorie, ihre philosophischen Vorstufen und ihre literarischen Auswirkungen* (Studien zur klassischen Philologie 4), Frankfurt a.M. 1982.

M. Lausberg, *Untersuchungen zu Senecas Fragmenten* (UaLG 7), Berlin 1970.

——'Senecae operum fragmenta: Überblick und Forschungsbericht', *ANRW* II/36.3 (1989) 1879–1961.

G. Maurach (ed.), *Seneca als Philosoph* (WdF 414), Darmstadt 1975.

A. L. Motto and J. R. Clark, *Essays on Seneca* (Studien zur klassichen Philologie 79), Frankfurt a.M. 1993.

R. G. Tanner, 'Stoic Philosophy and Roman Tradition in Senecan Tragedy', *ANRW* II/32.2 (1985) 1100–33.

P. Veyne, *Weisheit und Altruismus: Eine Einführung in die Philosophie Senecas* (Fischer Taschenbuch 11473), Frankfurt a.M. 1993.

Bibliography in L107.

Scholars face virtually insoluble problems in tracing the genesis and dating of Seneca's numerous literary works. We may mention in passing that Seneca wrote a large number of tragedies in which he adapts the classical material of the Greek dramatists. Here he analyses extreme human situations with great acuteness and puts psychological studies of human characters on the stage. A well-developed psychological analysis was indeed one of Seneca's strengths (cf. Bäumer; Tanner). Much is lost and survives only in quotations by other authors (cf. Lausberg), including the *De Superstitione* ('On superstition'), which surprised Augustine by the inexorable severity of its critique of religious phenomena. At the beginning of Nero's reign, Seneca dedicated the *De Clementia* to him, a treatise 'On leniency' which belongs to the genre of 'mirrors for princes'. The treatise *De Beneficiis* ('On benefactions'), in which Seneca defines the mutual bestowal of aid as a factor of cohesion within the societal structure, can be considered as a piece of social philosophy. He also wrote books on questions of natural science (*Naturales Quaestiones*).

The dialogues and letters are the most significant for our present purpose. The dialogues encompass twelve Books, with individual treatises on philosophical questions with an existential significance that is already seen in their titles: *Ad Marciam de Consolatione* (addressed to Marcia to offer her consolation on the occasion of her son's death), *De Ira* I–III ('On wrath'), *De Constantia Sapientis* ('On the constancy of the wise person'), *De Brevitate Vitae* ('On the shortness of life'), *De Vita*

343

Beata ('On the blessed life'), *De Tranquillitate Animi* ('On the repose of the human spirit'), *De Otio* ('On leisure'), *De Providentia* ('On providence'). In terms of their form, these are composed in the style of diatribes, i.e. a fictitious dialogue-partner repeatedly intervenes with questions and objections; this is why they have been given the name 'dialogue'. Their selection and collection may perhaps have been made by Seneca himself.

Seneca's most mature work, written in the last years of his life after he had retired from politics, is the *Ad Lucilium Epistulae Morales*, the 'moral letters' to his friend Lucilius: 124 letters in twenty Books. In a loose form, these take positions on many existential questions from a Stoic perspective. There is still discussion today about whether these are genuine or fictitious letters. They sound remarkably true to life and repeatedly refer to concrete situations in the communication between Seneca and Lucilius, an historical person, who is quoted in the form of questions and objections from the letters he sends in reply to Seneca. All of this still leads some prominent scholars to believe that we have here a genuine exchange of correspondence; nevertheless, it is probable that the epistolary form is fictitious. In favour of this hypothesis is the carefully planned construction of the letters, both singly and as a collection. Close inspection is required if one is to notice this construction, for it must be admitted that the fiction has been carried through in masterly fashion. And this is more than a mere imitation of an external form: in the mode of presentation which Seneca has chosen, we see the dialogic and communicative character which is typical of his philosophical thinking as a whole, a character that was already present in his dialogues and clearly determined Seneca's entire approach to intellectual questions. In the conversation, philosophical truth is to be communicated as the basis for the conduct of life. This is stated programmatically in the eighth letter at the beginning of the collection, which also sheds light on Seneca's last years (*Ep.* 8.1–3):

I have concealed myself and closed the doors – as I sometimes appeared to be advising you to do – in order that I may be useful to more people. I do not spend any of my days in idleness, and I reserve a part of my nights for intellectual work ... I have not only withdrawn from human beings, but also from things, above all from my business. Now I dedicate myself to the concerns of those who will come after me: it is for them that I am writing something that can be useful. I entrust to the written letters salutary admonitions, as it were collections of useful medicines. I have experienced the effectiveness of these medicines in my own ulcers. Although these are not yet fully healed, they have at any rate ceased to grow. I show to others the right path, which I myself discovered late in life, weary as I was from my wanderings.

These sentences display something of Seneca's literary style, his predilection for similes and comparisons, the typical staccato of short sentences. Maurach speaks of his 'nervously aggressive' style; it has also been called a 'dynamic style, the living style of someone who is excited and who excites the reader, a style that attacks the reader, wishing to address him, take hold of him and shake him; the style of a missionary who seeks to proclaim his good news with the greatest possible emphasis'.[8]

(c) Evaluation

Tertullian calls Seneca *saepe noster*, 'often one of us'. Jerome saw him as the perfect example of an *anima naturaliter christiana* ('a naturally Christian soul'). Augustine wondered whether he might not have been a crypto-Christian. Indeed, an early Christian went to the trouble of fabricating an exchange of letters between Seneca and the apostle Paul; their content is regrettably of a less high quality than the genuine texts, but the very fact of their existence makes them interesting.[9] This high evaluation of Seneca continued until the time of Erasmus, Zwingli and Calvin, reformers with a humanistic education.

Things changed in the sixteenth century, thanks to a transformation in historical consciousness and in the evaluation of the relationship between politics and morality, and above all thanks to the rediscovery of the works of Tacitus, which were not known until then. Seneca made enemies among his contemporaries because of his exposed position and of many of the decisions he had to take, and these enemies worked eagerly to blacken the picture of his character; and the Roman historian Tacitus gives a negative assessment of his person in his historical writings a few decades after Seneca's death (see, however, Abel's arguments against this widespread theory). This view became even less nuanced in later historiographers like Cassius Dio, where Seneca appears as an intriguer at court, greedy for power and money, servile, cowardly, corrupt and without a conscience.[10]

---

[8] B. Kytzler, 'Die nachklassische Prosa Roms', in M. Fuhrmann (ed.), *Römische Literatur* (NHL 3), Frankfurt a.M. 1974, 291–322, at 298.

[9] Translation of the fourteen Letters in *New Testament Apocrypha* (ed. E. Hennecke and W. Schneemelcher), London 1965, II.133–41.

[10] Unfortunately, this picture is adopted in a completely uncritical manner by the former Professor of New Testament at Erlangen, E. Stauffer, *Christ* (L93) 139–40.

It is not our main goal to rehabilitate Seneca in the face of this evaluation, which reached its lowest point in the nineteenth century, since this has essentially been done already in new studies by authors such as Grimal and Maurach, who once again sketch a very differentiated picture of Seneca which puts him in a much more favourable light, without however falling into the opposite error of an uncritical glorification. Our aim is to grasp Seneca's thought in its historical conditioning and its human limitation. Besides this, irrespective of his character, his writings remain a contemporary document of irreplaceable value for the study of the first century CE.

3. Epictetus

List 110.

A. Bonhöffer, *Epictet und die Stoa: Untersuchungen zur stoischen Philosophie*, Stuttgart 1890, reprint 1968.

——*The Ethic of the Stoic Epictetus* (trans. by W. D. Stephens), New York 1996.

——*Epiktet und das Neue Testament* (RVV 10), Giessen 1911, reprint Berlin 1964.

J. J. Duhot, *Épictète et la sagesse stoïcienne*, Paris 1996.

J. P. Hershbell, 'The Stoicism of Epictetus: Twentieth Century Perspectives', *ANRW* II/36.3 (1989) 2148–63.

B. L. Humans Jr., *ΑΣΚΗΣΙΣ: Notes on Epictetus' Educational System* (WTS 2), Assen 1959.

A. Jagu, 'La Morale d'Epictète et le christianisme', *ANRW* II/36.3 (1989) 2164–99.

R. Laurenti, 'Musonio, maestro d'Epitteto', *ANRW* II/36.3 (1989) 2105–46.

F. Millar, 'Epictetus and the Imperial Court', *JRS* 55 (1965) 141–8.

R. Radice, *La concezione di dio e del divino in Epitteto* (Collana di filosofia 2), Milan 1982.

M. Spanneut, 'Epiktet', *RAC* 5 (1962) 599–681.

P. R. C. Weaver, 'Epaphroditus, Josephus, and Epictetus', *CQ* 44 (1994) 468–79.

J. Xenakis, *Epictetus: Philosopher – Therapist*, The Hague 1969.

(a) His life

The name 'Epictetus' is derived from ἐπι-κτᾶσθαι and means literally 'obtained in addition' or 'purchased additionally', indicating that the one who bears it is a slave. Presumably, he was added as a child to the personnel of slaves in a great household, and received his eloquent name on this occasion.

It is not possible to determine Epictetus' biographical dates with precision. He was born *c.*50 CE in the city of Hierapolis in Asia Minor (cf. Col 4:13), and his death is assigned by some to the year 120, by others to 130 or even later. He was a slave in Rome in the household of Epaphroditus, a rich freedman of Nero, who had a high position at the imperial court but fell into disfavour under Domitian and committed suicide. This is probably the same man whom Josephus mentions several times as the object of dedications (*Ant.* 1.8, *Ap.* 1.1, *Vit.* 430). In the three passages in which Epictetus speaks of Epaphroditus (*Diss.* 1.1.20, 19.17–23, 26.11f.), he is described as very rich, completely integrated into society, opportunistic, familiar with the rules of play in the centre of power, and one who submitted to these rules to the point of losing all dignity. Epictetus limped, and a tradition in late antiquity says that this handicap was the result of physical torture performed at the orders of his master; one may, however, question the veracity of this tradition. At any rate, Epaphroditus gave his slave access to a good scholastic education, granting him the possibility of studying philosophy and emancipating him.

We know the identity of Epictetus' most important philosophical teacher from mentions in his works and from a number of fragments which are transmitted elsewhere: this was Musonius Rufus (*c.*30–100 CE; cf. Laurenti), a Roman knight and Stoic philosopher. He was exiled by Nero in 65/6, recalled in 69 by Galba, soon after exiled anew by Vespasian, and finally recalled by Titus – an eventful external fate suffered by other philosophers too (inluding Epictetus: see below) and caused by the fact that Stoic thinkers were the only serious local critics of the imperial government in Rome in the second half of the first century CE.[11] According to the evidence of fragments, Musonius Rufus (whose pupils included the celebrated orator Dion of Prusa as well as Epictetus) specialised in questions of ethics and the practical conduct of life. For example, he composed treatises on clothes, on styles of hair and beard, and on marriage.[12] We quote one of the six passages in which Epictetus speaks of his teacher (*Diss.* 3.23.29):

[11] On the 'philosophers' opposition', cf. R. MacMullen, *Enemies of the Roman Order: Treason, Unrest and Alienation in the Empire,* Cambridge, Mass. 1967, 46–94.

[12] Selected texts in R. Nickel, *Epiktet, Teles, Musonius* (L111) 399–537.

> Rufus was accustomed to say [to his pupils]: 'If you have the time to bestow praises on me, then my discourses have no effect.' For he held such discourses that each one of us who sat there had the feeling he would have had if someone had been accusing him – so vigorously did he attack the things one is accustomed to do, so clearly did he reveal his errors to each one. The schoolroom of a philosopher is a doctor's surgery: you must not leave it in a spirit of merriment, but rather downcast.

It is without doubt that Epictetus never mentions Seneca with so much as one single syllable: this is most likely a reflection of Epictetus' reservations vis-à-vis the person of Seneca, in view of their respective social and political positions.

Epictetus began his own career as teacher of philosophy in Rome, so that he too was affected when Domitian expelled all the philosophers from the city in 89 or 94. Thereafter, he lived in Nicopolis (cf. Tit 3:12), a city on the western coast of Greece with the main harbour for the ships that plied between Greece and Rome. This nodal communication point meant that he could expect to continue to have an audience coming from Rome, the capital of the world. He lived from what his hearers gave him, and this appears to have sufficed only for a modest lifestyle. We may mention a further biographical detail: Epictetus remained unmarried. Instruction in his school took the form of reading with commentary of Stoic classics such as Zeno and Chrysippus. The pupils had to prepare essays on these subjects, which Epictetus discussed critically with them. Epictetus presupposed a knowledge of logic and physics, and this framework also allowed a more detailed treatment of these topics. His own didactic lectures, in which he concentrated almost exclusively on ethics, were the high point. People travelled from distant places to hear him. His pupils, properly so called, remained over a period of years and then took up various professions. Other visitors remained only for a few weeks, or took advantage of a stop on their journey to hear the famous teacher or to seek his advice.

For Epictetus, even more than in the case of Seneca, we must ask about a possible acquaintance with Christianity. This must be affirmed, because he speaks in one passage of his works about Christians, though not exactly in flattering terms. In *Diss.* 4.7 he argues that the Stoic must know no fear in the presence of a tyrant who threatens him with death, and he gives the following example at 4.7.6: while some people display indifference to death out of foolishness, 'the Galileans do it out of custom'. Thus he grants that the Christians, whom he calls 'Galileans' (i.e. a kind of Jewish sect), show courage in the face of martyrdom and death, although he does not acknowledge their motives positively. Other passages which scholars have adduced in this context speak rather of Judaism, such as *Diss.* 2.9.20: 'But as soon as he has taken on the inner disposition of one who is baptised and consecrated, then he is de facto a Jew' (an allusion to Jewish proselyte baptism). Against positions taken in older scholarship, it must be affirmed that Epictetus is not substantially touched by Christianity.

(*b*) Works

List 111 (texts).

G. Boter, *The Encheiridion of Epictetus and its Three Christian Adaptations* (PhA 82), Leiden 1999.

R. F. Dobbin, *Epictetus: Discourses. Book I* (Clarendon Later Ancient Philosophers), Oxford 1998.

R. Mücke, *Epiktet: Was von ihm erhalten ist nach den Aufzeichnungen Arrians*, Heidelberg 1924 (German trans.).

R. Nickel, *Epiktet, Teles, Musonius: Ausgewählte Schriften* (TuscBü), Zurich and Munich 1994.

W. A. Oldfather, *Epictetus: The Discourses as Reported by Arrian, the Manual and Fragments*, vols. 1–2 (LCL 131, 218), Cambridge, Mass. and London 1925, 1928, often reprinted.

H. Schenkl, *Epicteti Dissertationes ab Arriano digestae* (BiTeu), Leipzig 2nd edn. 1916, reprint Stuttgart 1967 (fundamental Greek edition).

J. Souilhé and A. Jagu, *Epictète: Entretiens*, vols. 1–4 (CUFr), Paris 1943–65.

K. Steinmann, *Epiktet: Handbüchlein der Moral* (RecUB 8788), Stuttgart 1992.

List 112.

P. A. Brunt, 'From Epictetus to Arrian', *Ath.* 55 (1977) 19–48.

I. Hadot, *Simplicius: Commentaire sur le manuel d'Epictète* (PhAnt 66), Leiden 1994.

K. Hartmann, 'Arrian und Epiktet', *NKJA* 15 (1905) 248–75.

T. Wirth, 'Arrians Erinnerungen an Epiktet', *MH* 24 (1967) 149–89, 197–216.

Bibliography in L110.

Epictetus himself published nothing for future generations, but there exists a work bearing his name: the *Dissertations*, in Greek Διατρῖβαι, i.e.

didactic lectures or dissertations, which have come down to us in four books, although this is probably only half of the original length. They were written down by Flavius Arrian, who was one of Epictetus' pupils from 117 to 120. Arrian was general, statesman, historian, and consul in Rome in 130 CE. He composed works of his own, including a history of Alexander the Great for which he took Xenophon and Thucydides as his models. The stylistic difference between these works and the *Dissertations*, composed in a much simpler Greek, is considerable, and although it is not easy to determine his contribution to their final linguistic form, this difference does make it appear plausible that what we have in these didactic lectures are notes taken by Arrian, rather than his own free compositions. It remains an open question to what extent they give us the *ipsissima vox* of Epictetus, and how far Arrian's editorial work goes (cf. the opposite positions taken by Hartmann and Wirth). Arrian himself informs us about his method of work in a foreword which at least defines precisely the stylistic aim of his text, viz. its orientation to the spoken word:

> I have not composed Epictetus' discourses in the way one might indeed compose something of this sort ... All I have done is to endeavour as far as possible to write down in his own words what I heard from Epictetus' lips, so that I myself might have some recollections of his clear spirit and his frankness. Accordingly, as is natural, the dominant mode of speech in them is somewhat approximate, the mode that is common when one enters a conversation with another person, and not at all that mode which one employs when one is writing for future readers.

He goes on to say that he has been impelled to publication by 'thieving publications', i.e. the surreptitious diffusion of the notes he had taken. Besides this, we possess under the name of Epictetus the *Encheiridion* ('little handbook', or 'little hand-weapon' in a metaphorical sense), a synthesis of the basic Stoic attitude of the *Dissertations* in a few compact, pithy aphorisms. It is possible that this too was produced by Arrian. The *Handbook* contains matter not found in the longer work, and it is possible that this comes from the lost four books of the *Dissertations*; the same is true of a number of fragments transmitted under the name of Epictetus (collected by Schenkl). The *Handbook* had a great influence up to the modern period. The Neoplatonist Simplicius wrote a commentary on it (cf. Hadot), and it passed for a long time as an original Christian work under the name of the monastic father Nilus, so that it was found in every monastic library (see now Boter).

4. Characteristics of the system

List 113.

A. Bonhöffer, *Epictet* (L110).

B. Effe, *Hellenismus* (Die griechische Literatur in Text und Darstellung 4) (RecUB 8064), Stuttgart 1985, 156–59.

T. Engberg-Pedersen, *The Stoic Theory of Oikeiosis: Moral Development and Social Interaction in Early Stoic Philosophy* (Studies in Hellenistic Civilization 2), Aarhus 1990.

M. Forschner, *Die stoische Ethik: Über den Zusammenhang von Natur-, Sprach- und Moralphilosophie im altstoischen System*, Darmstadt 2nd edn. 1995.

G. W. Most, 'Cornutus and Stoic Allegoresis: A Preliminary Report', *ANRW* II/36.3 (1989) 2014–65.

M. Pohlenz, *Stoa* (L106).

R. Radice, *Concezione* (L110).

J. M. Rist, 'Seneca and Stoic Orthodoxy', *ANRW* II/36.3 (1989) 1193–2012.

Bibliography in L106.

(a) Cleanthes' hymn to Zeus

Before we turn to individual topics, after presenting a historical outline and biographical sketches, we must set out, even if only very briefly, some basic points and coordinates of the Stoic system which must be known if the point of the individual observations is to be grasped. We choose as our basis one of the most famous texts of this school, Cleanthes' hymn to Zeus. The text is transmitted by Stobaeus, *Ecl.* 1.1.12, and is printed in Arnim's collection as SVF I. 537 (cf. P. Steinmetz [L106] 577f., with bibliography):

> Most exalted of the immortals, with many names, always ruling all,
> Zeus, prime mover of nature, you who govern all things according to law,
> all hail! For it is fitting for all mortals to call on you.
> For it is from you that we have our origin, we alone – among
> everything mortal that lives and moves on earth –   5
> have attained the likeness of the god.[13]
> Therefore I will praise you and always sing of your power.

[13] θεοῦ μίμημα λαχόντες. This may mean reason or language (thus Pohlenz and others); Steinmetz follows another reading: 'the likeness of the sun'.

All this world obeys you as it turns about the earth,
wherever you lead it, and freely lets itself be ruled by you.
In invincible hands you hold your assistant,   10
the double-edged, fiery, ever-living thunderbolt
under whose strokes all the works of nature are brought to completion.
By means of it you guide the universal reason which passes
through everything and mingles with the great and small lights.
[Through it you are so powerful, the highest king of the universe.][14]   15
No work is done on earth without you, O deity,
neither in the divine ethereal sphere nor in the sea,
apart from what the wicked do in their own foolishness.
But you know how to make straight that which is crooked
and to order that which is disordered, you love that which is unlovely.   20
For thus you have brought all into a unity, the noble with the wretched,
so that one reason, eternally existing, comes into being out of all things.
In their flight, all those among mortals who are wicked, unhappy ones,
abandon these things. They do indeed ever yearn to acquire good things,
but neither see nor hear the god's universal law, which would give them   25
a good life, if they listened to it with understanding.
Instead, they cast themselves foolishly upon that which is evil,
each finding his own evil: some provoke evil strife causing eagerness
for honour, others set their disordered thoughts only on their profits,
others again on idleness and lustful bodily actions [...].[15]   30
Therefore, O Zeus who gives all things, surrounded by dark clouds,
sending bright lightning flashes, preserve human beings
from destructive lack of experience – banish it, Father, from the soul.
Let us find knowledge, the basis of your righteous governance of all things,
so that we may be honoured and pay you honour in return,   35
by praising your works without cease, as is fitting for a mortal.
For there is no greater gift of honour for mortals or for gods
than to praise the universal law, as is right.

If we simply let this hymn, in which 'Stoic religious feeling has found its
most individual expression',[16] have its effect on us, without asking detailed
questions about its meaning and correlating it with the entire body of

---

[14] Text uncertain.
[15] The text is corrupt in lines 30–1. Pohlenz renders these lines: 'Each one yearns
      for that which is good, but they all go astray and strive precisely to attain that
      which is opposed to the true good.'
[16] Pohlenz, I.108; cf. also what he goes on to say: 'The hymn was assuredly meant
      to be recited at the common celebration of the school.'

Stoic thought, we may arrive at the conviction that the Stoa upheld a clear monotheism and professed faith in a personal god. This is not the case.

On this question, we pick up the following perspectives from the hymn (line numbers as given above in the translation):

Line 1 speaks of the 'most exalted of the immortals', who at the same time possesses 'many names', before he is called 'Zeus' in line 2. This signals to the informed reader that this bestowal of a name is somewhat arbitrary. Ultimately, in the background there stands the Stoic pan-divinity, or put in more abstract terms, the world-principle which can be given other names in other contexts: *heimarmenē* (fate), *pronoia* (provi-dence), *logos* (reason), or *physis* (nature). The mythological image of the Zeus who hurls thunderbolts is employed in lines 10 and 32, while line 14 alludes to the sun and the stars ('the great and small lights'). Here one should recall that for the Stoa the divine primal matter consists of a subtle fire which is also called *pneuma*. An important concept is found in line 13: κοινὸς λόγος, 'universal reason'. Logos is the preferred name in the Stoa for the world-principle. We find it again in our text in line 22. A sharp critique of the human person begins in line 17 and continues to line 30: all the evil that human beings do is derived from their foolishness (line 18), which is due to their ignorance of the universal law (νόμος) – though all they need to do is to use their understanding (νοῦς, lines 25f.). The criticism of such wrong dispositions as seeking honour, greed for profits and the pursuit of sensual lust in lines 28–30 allows us to infer that the Stoa demanded an ascetic attitude to life. The overarching divine plan for the world is not seriously called into question by the phenomenon of evil, which according to lines 19–22 belongs to the great cosmic harmony that embraces all things. But this in turn implies far-reaching questions to which the Stoa gave only unsatisfactory answers. We can already sense an inherent contradiction in the text: if we take line 18 seriously in connection with lines 16f., then the evil that human beings do out of their own impulse would be the only thing that remained outside the grip of the deity – a weighty plea for the human freedom to make decisions. But this becomes much less clear when we are told that evil must serve the great totality and make its own contribution to this. This does indeed mean that the question of theodicy – how the image of god found here permits us to make intellectual sense of evil – no longer exists; but it seems doubtful whether it is quite so easy to find the solution. In the final section (lines 31–8), the language of prayer ascends to moving heights. But we should also note that the prayer requests above all true knowledge (γνώμη, line 34) – something intellectual. The final line says that human beings and gods stand together under a common law. It may perhaps not be so obvious, but this is a first indication that the divine is not thought of as transcendent, but as immanent.

(b) Building-bricks of theory

Max Pohlenz has described 'the fundamental attitude of Stoic theology' as a 'monistic pantheism which recognises the divinity in the entire world filled with life, both in the macrocosm and in the lowest form of existence' (I.108). If we add two other terms to the keywords 'monism' and 'pantheism', we arrive at four concepts which permit us to summarise (in a somewhat pointed and undifferentiated manner) Stoic cosmology: monism, materialism, pantheism and immanence. *Monism* means that Being is thought of as a unity. The Stoa does indeed recognise two first principles (ἀρχαί), viz. the active (τὸ ποιοῦν) and the passive (τὸ πάσχον), but the specifically Stoic view brings these two together again by postulating a material substratum for both. A subtle fire which infuses everything is the material bearer of the formative principle too. This is the *materialism* of the Stoa, which according to its own conviction permits a unified explanation of the world: there exists nothing beyond the world and its material principles, no world of ideas, no transcendent creator god. At the same time, this is the Stoic *immanence*, and when this is applied to theology it must necessarily lead to a *pantheism*. While it is possible to speak of gods, and even of a highest god, as Stoicism in fact does, this god does not stand over against the world, but is an immanent component of it.

This can also be seen in the Stoic doctrine of *ekpyrōsis*, i.e. the teaching that the world periodically perishes in a mighty fire and then arises anew. Everything falls a victim to the fire – gods, human beings, and nature. Only Zeus, the highest god, will survive this catastrophe. Does this perhaps mean that at least the highest god is thought of as transcendent? The answer must be negative, if one follows this idea to its roots. The fire which consumes everything in the final catastrophe is identical to the fire which works as 'the active' factor when the world comes into being. The highest god is equated with this operative fire (πῦρ τεχνικόν). 'Zeus' serves as a metaphorical or mythological designation that can be employed in the framework of a religious world-view instead of the specialist philosophical terminology.

What abstract concepts are available? The vitalising, creative power which penetrates the universe with its fiery warmth is also called *pneuma* in Stoicism. *Pneuma* consists of a subtle matter and is thus to be thought of as a substance. This becomes concentrated in the Logos. The Logos is the central concept, to which are orientated the world-reason, natural law, providence, and fate. All that exists shares to varying degrees in the Logos. The human being has a privileged position thanks to the endowment of reason.

The Logos structures reality. This gives the Stoa a model for the descriptive explanation of the world; however, this goes beyond a mere description to become the normative interpretation. The same Logos determines also our knowledge of reality and the language we use to speak of reality, and this means that he must also determine our behaviour in relation to reality and our conduct. Thus epistemology, linguistic theory, and ethics found a unified ontological basis in Stoicism.

The linguistic theory led to a methodological preference for an allegorical interpretation in dealing with ancient texts. For example, when we read in the *Iliad* that the gods come into conflict with one another, this must be understood either as the portrayal of a battle of the natural elements in a storm or else as the coded description of the conflicts of various forces within the human person. It is not so much apologetic interests that lead to the use of this allegorical reading in the Stoa – i.e. because a genuine conflict among gods would have been considered theologically intolerable – but rather the doctrine of the Logos. Since the one Logos works in all things, it must be possible to recognise its traces on the different levels, and this means that one can perceive the course of events of nature and intrapsychical processes in the narration of the myth.[17]

The basic ethical principles of the Stoa have been condensed in a so-called *telos* formula (from τέλος, 'goal'): τέλος ἐστὶ τὸ ὁμολογουμένως τῇ φύσει ζῆν, 'The goal is to live in agreement with nature' (SVF I.552). This is not meant in the same sense as a modern ecological programme. One could perfectly well omit τῇ φύσει and say only: ὁμολογουμένως, 'to live in agreement', for this word itself contains the λόγος. Thus the fundamental idea is: to live in harmony with the Logos. The Logos is the divine will of the totality of nature, and as such is also *nomos*. Φύσις can

---

[17] A *chef d'œuvre* of Stoic allegory from the first century CE is Cornutus, *Theologiae graecae compendium*, ed. C. Lang (BiTeu), Leipzig 1881; further references in Most.

also be introduced into the formula, so that it takes on its final form. An unchangeable and constraining regularity holds sway in the world, but the Stoic does not understand this as a blind and meaningless coercion: rather, he accepts it as a benevolent providence, as an order that provides meaning and protection. And this provides him with the starting point from which he can cope with all of life's problems.

(c) Eclecticism and theism?

We must face one other objection: now that the outlines of this system have been sketched, may we simply presuppose it in the cases of Seneca and Epictetus? Was not Seneca an eclectic thinker who borrowed everywhere; and does not Epictetus speak of a warmth coming from God that demands a personal, transcendent image of God, so that (as Radice proposes) Epictetus would take his place in the history of philosophy as a thinker influenced by Middle Platonism? In the case of Epictetus, Adolf Bonhöffer has shown in a number of studies that there are no essential doctrinal differences between the founding fathers of the school and their followers in later generations: on the contrary, Epictetus consciously turns back to the older Stoa. In his first thirty letters to Lucilius, Seneca repeatedly quotes fundamental propositions of Epicurus with approval, so that one wonders whether he has silently changed sides. But it is Seneca himself who gives the answer: 'I am accustomed to go over into the camp of the enemy – not as a deserter, but as a spy' (*Ep.* 2.5). He summarises as follows: 'One finds in a synthesis among our people [i.e. the Stoics] what is found only as isolated, selected themes among others' (*Ep.* 33.3). Borrowings of very various kinds do not stand in antithesis to this, since it is this organising centre that gives the borrowings their function (cf. Rist).

Nevertheless, the theistic-sounding language in both writers is very striking. One can certainly go so far as to say that a religious ferment in the general atmosphere of the period lent their thinking and feeling on a more intuitive level accents that, of necessity, almost broke out of the Stoic framework. But in neither of these thinkers do such accents contribute to a reflection on the bases of the system. This means that no means were available to promote the speculative development of the obscure new presentiments.[18] The consequence for our evaluation is that we must deal very cautiously with the religious elements in Seneca and Epictetus. In

[18] This is roughly the position also of G. Reale, *History* (L104) 59, 62, 83, 87; K. Praechter, *Philosophie* (L104) 494, 495f.

order not to go wrong, we take as our point of comparison relatively reliable knowledge of the Stoa, refusing to introduce Christian coordinates surreptitiously.

5. Individual topics

(a) Stoic eschatology

List 114.

E. Benz, *Das Todesproblem in der stoischen Philosophie* (TBAW 7), Stuttgart 1929.

D. Elsässer, ' "Omnia ferenda sunt?" Seneca und das Problem des Selbstmordes', in *Schola Anatolica (Festschrift H. Steinthal)*, Tübingen 1989, 97–120.

R. Hoven, *Stoicisme et Stoiciens face au problème de l'au-delà* (BFPUL 197), Paris 1971.

H. J. Klauck, 'Dankbar leben, dankbar sterben: Εὐχαριστεῖν bei Epiktet', in Idem, *Gemeinde* (L59) 373–90.

A. A. Long, 'The Stoics on World-Conflagration and Everlasting Recurrence', in R. H. Epp, *Conference* (L106) 13–37.

C. E. Manning, *On Seneca's 'Ad Marciam'* (Mn.S 69), Leiden 1981.

J. M. Rist, *Philosophy* (L106) 233–5.

J. N. Sevenster, *Paul* (L107) 52–62, 218–40.

A life that continues after death?

Our starting point is provided by the cosmological parameters, i.e. the *ekpyrōsis*, the periodical destruction of the world and its subsequent reconstruction. This reconstruction of the world is defined in Stoicism as a numerically identical new edition: everything is repeated exactly as it was the previous time and in all previous cycles. The consequence is that all individuals must repeat their appearance on the scene; the result would be a cyclical rebirth which could be termed a constant continuance of individual existence. But it is clear that this doctrinal theme, which in itself is already problematic, and which poses far-reaching problems about the underlying understanding of time (cf. Long), was not developed by Stoic thinkers in this direction; Seneca affirms in *Ep.* 36.10 that the cyclic recurrence takes place without the memory of earlier events. It would be misleading to postulate on this basis that the Stoa believed in a doctrine of rebirth or had a hope in immortality (as Hoven argues).

According to the dominant view among the Stoics, the soul parts company with the body at death and lives on. But this continued existence has temporal limits. For Cleanthes it lives until the next *ekpyrōsis*, when the soul meets its end along with the entire cosmos. It seems that Chrysippus introduced a distinction here: only the souls of the wise Stoics survive until the *ekpyrōsis*, while the souls of all other human beings continue in existence for a period but are then dissolved during that period of the world. It is clear that it is their especial 'strength of soul', acquired through unwearying exercise during the course of their lives, that bestows this particular capacity on the wise.

The souls dwell, not in the underworld of Greek mythology, but in the air; one could also say, in 'heaven', understanding thereby the entire sphere of the air from the earth to the stars. The Stoics engage in polemics against customary ideas of the underworld, or else interpret the relevant myths allegorically, e.g. by equating the name 'Hades' with the dark air that becomes bright only when fire is added to it. In physical terms, this is only logical, since the soul consists of a subtler matter than the body and thus ascends upwards at death, when it is freed from the fetters of the body. Here too, a distinction is sometimes made, when it is said that the souls of the wise dwell closer to the moon and the souls of the foolish nearer to the earth, since they cannot detach themselves completely from their milieu; but other sources say that even after their death, the souls of the wise engage in teaching and take on for a time tasks as mediators between gods and human beings.

Seneca
We should expect to find an explicit treatment of hopes in an existence beyond death in one of Seneca's treatises, viz. his *Consolatio ad Marciam*, written to console a mother whose promising son had died early. The first form of a continued life of which Seneca speaks is the *memoria*, the memory of subsequent generations who praise the deceased person. It is not by accident that Seneca puts this programme on the lips of an Epicurean philosopher (cf. e.g. 5.2: 'When we are among ourselves and have gathered, we celebrate his deeds and words'). He goes on to knock down the myths about the underworld that we may presume were widespread in popular belief (19.4):

> Bear this in mind: nothing that is evil affects the deceased person; what makes the underworld frightening is fairy stories [*fabula*]. No darkness threatens the dead, no prison; neither rivers burning with fire nor the stream of 'forgetting'

[i.e. Lethe], nor court chambers and the status of being accused ... The poets have invented all this in a frivolous manner and have frightened us with dreadful images lacking all reality.

The continuation (19.5) has likewise an Epicurean ring: 'Death is the resolution of all pains. Our sufferings do not go beyond this end.' In the next passage, Seneca seems to be borrowing from Plato when he states that the death of Marcia's son in his youth was an advantage to him, since those souls that separate themselves very early from dealings with human beings and from the burden of the body have an easier path to the gods. The description of the soul's further path is also interesting. After a brief phase of purification near the earth, it takes up its dwelling in the world of the stars, where it meets the souls of other outstanding personalities, and Marcia's father, who takes his grandson to himself and 'gladly introduces him into the mysteries of nature; and just as the guest is happy to find a signpost in a city that he does not know, so the grandfather serves him as a native interpreter when he inquires about the causes of the heavenly phenomena' (25.2; cf. the *angelus interpres* of Jewish apocalyptic). The general impression which has gradually been built up is, however, shattered abruptly by the final lines of the treatise, in which Seneca paints a dramatic picture of the *ekpyrōsis* and makes an inference from it about the existence of the souls (26.6f.):

> And when the time has come for the world to extinguish itself, so that it may renew itself, all of this will destroy itself through its own power. Stars will collide with each other, and that which now shines in a careful order will burn in a conflagration, when all matter catches fire. And we too, happy souls who have attained eternity – when it pleases the god to undertake this work again and everything is set in motion, we ourselves as a small part of the immense collapse will be transformed into the old constituent elements [*in antiqua elementa*]. Happy is your son, Marcia, who already knows this.

According to the laws of the genre this work closes with a macarism of the deceased boy. But now Seneca has defined eternity in keeping with the Stoic position: there is indeed a continued existence of the soul after death, but this has a time limit, reaching at most to the next end of the world, which is already programmed. Within these boundaries, Seneca sometimes allows his eclectic inclinations free rein. We hear echoes of Epicureanism and of Plato (Platonic dualism, e.g. also 24.5). In *Ep.* 108.19 he also betrays knowledge of the Pythagorean doctrine of the transmigration of souls, without favouring it as an attempted solution. The thematically relevant *Ep.* 102, claiming to react to a sceptical question posed by Lucilius, takes us further (102.2):

> I delighted in reflecting upon the immortality of the soul, indeed – by the god! – in believing in this. For I was willing to accept the views of significant men, although they promise, rather than demonstrate, a most welcome thing. I adopted this great hope; I was already wearied by myself, already looked on the remainder of my fragile life as something of small value, since I was on the point of crossing over into that immeasurable time where I would possess all of eternity. Then I received your letter, and suddenly I awoke. The beautiful dream was gone.

It may be that Seneca gives us a glimpse of his own heart here, when he speaks of the immortality of the soul as a beautiful dream. He would dearly like to believe more than is permitted by the orthodox Stoic doctrine, but he cannot defend this and justify it intellectually. These words show us how to read other 'dreamings' in the body of the letter (cf. 102.21–8; especially 26: 'This day [of death], before which you shrink in horror as if it were the last day, is the birthday of your eternal life'). The final words (102.30) are like a slap in the face for such dreams, since Seneca accepts the correctness of a position which holds that 'the soul exists only as long as it is held captive in the prison of the body; as soon as it is separated from the body, it dissolves'. But even this view allows something positive to remain, viz. that good models can always be useful for us and that the memory of significant men can be just as valuable to us as their presence among us.

Epictetus

Epictetus is surer of his position than is Seneca, and is more radical than the earlier Stoa. His straightforward definition runs as follows: all that happens at death 'is that the wretched body [σωμάτιον] and the soul part company' (*Diss.* 3.22.33). He abandons the idea of a temporally limited continuing life of the soul and localises its dissolution, which other Stoics see as taking place at a later point, at the moment of death:

> What do you mean [by saying:] 'dying'? At all costs, one must avoid talking about this matter in the style of the tragedians. Speak in keeping with simple reality: now the moment has come when the matter is once again to be dissolved into the elements of which it is composed (4.7.15).

> It does not go to any terrible place, but to its source, joining its friends and relatives, the primal elements. That which was fire in you, returns into the fire;

that which was of earth, into the earth; that which was air, into the air; that which was water, into the water (3.13.14f.).

What takes place is a kind of cosmic recycling. Each of the material components of the human person is reduced to its most elementary structure – the body to water and earth, the soul to fire and air – and is utilised as components for something new. This is all that Epictetus can promise in terms of a continued existence after death. He explicitly denies a continuing personal existence: as an individual, 'You will no longer exist, but there will exist something else that the world now needs' (3.24.94).

This fundamental statement provides the key to the interpretation of other passages which take a different line and seem to contradict this. A well-known image of eschatological hopes both in Jewish apocalyptic and among the Greeks is the sharing in a heavenly meal, where the blessed have fellowship with God or (in the pagan mythology) recline side by side with the gods at table. In *Ench.* 15 Epictetus promises the one who endeavours to attain moral perfection in all of life's situations: 'Not only will you be a worthy table companion of the gods, but you will also share in their lordship.' This, however, is not intended in an eschatological, but in an innerworldly sense, in keeping with the principle that the wise man is a king who participates in the divine lordship over the world. The eschatological metaphor illustrates the consciousness of perfection which the Stoic wise man has here and now.

Making sense of death

On such a basis, is it at all possible to attempt to make sense of the problem of death? Will it not end in a defeatism that makes a principle of meaninglessness? Both Seneca and Epictetus were convinced that the former is possible and the latter is not the case. We can begin with the following brief summary of their central idea: this is how life in fact is, fate has determined things in this way, we must make the best of it. This takes very different nuances in each author, sometimes very positive. We hear a rather negative note in a frequently quoted passage from the *Consolatio ad Marciam*, where Seneca presents dying as an immutable definition of what it is to be human, and sketches a disturbing portrait of the *conditio humana* (11.1–5):

> You are born mortal, you have given birth to mortal beings – and have you yourself, a decaying and slack body filled with illnesses, hoped that you had borne something stable and eternal in such a weak material? . . . The saying

inscribed at the site of the Pythian oracle [in Delphi], 'Know yourself', means this: what is a human being? A vessel that can be broken in pieces by any shock at all, by any blow at all. No great storm is required to make you crack; you break up whenever you bump into anything at all. What is a human being? A weak and fragile body, naked, provided by nature with no weapons, needing the help of others, exposed to all the ill-treatments of fate ... Woven out of weak and flabby elements, handsome only in the external outlines of the figure; incapable of bearing cold, heat and exertions ... Do we then find death something surprising, the death that is the work of one single sobbing breath? ... [The human being] considers undying and eternal things in his heart and makes plans for grandchildren and great-grandchildren, but sometimes death overcomes him while he is yet sketching his wide-reaching schemes. And what we call a 'great age' is the course of only a few years.

Seneca employs the pregnant words *cotidie morimur*, 'we die each day' (*Ep.* 24.20), to describe this immutable situation which confronts the human person. Consequently, he appeals to us to make the best use of the time that remains (*Ep.* 1.2). All of life serves the one task of practising death and undergoing death with composure: 'A whole life is needed in order to learn how to live. And you may perhaps be even more surprised at this: a whole life is needed in order to learn how to die' (*Brev. Vit.* 7.3). It is easy to understand that Seneca often dreams the dream of a life that continues after death and of the immortality of the human person, which he equates with the soul. But he never fully accepted this position. He always took seriously the much more sceptical possibility which harmonises better with Stoicism, and attempted to justify living and dying in this 'hopeless' perspective.

Epictetus is even more startling. He does not hold any metaphysical escape hatch open, but he finds very impressive words when he speaks of dying. Without great emotions, *Ench.* 7 uses an image to capture the law to which life is subject: life is like the anchoring of a ship during a sea voyage. We can go on shore, but without straying too far from the landing stage and encumbering ourselves too much with 'souvenirs'. When the helmsman calls, we will lose no time in hastening to the ship. Behind the helmsman, theologically speaking, stands the god who 'is like a good general giving me the signal for retreat'. The human person will react to this as follows (*Diss.* 3.26.29f.): 'Then I am obedient and follow, I cry out in praise of my general and eulogise his deeds. I came when it pleased him to call me forth; in the same way, I now depart as he sees fit. And as long as I lived, my work was to praise the god.'

All life is a great feast which the philosophically inclined human being experiences as participant and observer, with his task that of giving thanks by singing hymns of praise. Dying means nothing other than taking one's leave with thanks, obedient to the god, and with a prayer on one's lips.

At first sight, these themes in Epictetus stand so close to Christian beliefs that we must feel surprise; and these texts were in fact read with Christian spectacles in the Middle Ages, as marginal notes by the Christian copyists indicate. It cannot be doubted that the existential programme which we encounter here is impressive in its own way, and deserves high respect; it would be just as wrong to condemn it arrogantly as it is to rush to claim it as Christian. But once again, we must recall the foundations of the Stoic system, which provide the framework for thanksgiving and praise in Epictetus' theology. Despite everything, Epictetus' god remains the Logos of the Stoa, immanent to the world; behind the human person's planning and execution there still stands the undeviating unfolding of the cosmic process. When we give thanks, we activate our own logos so that it becomes something active, thereby achieving harmony with our own selves. We take on our role in the great play. We make sense of something that exists a priori, by giving our consent and making it our own deed, instead of letting ourselves be overwhelmed by it: and this in turn gives us the possibility of encountering our own death.

Suicide

Here we must mention a further particularity of the Stoa, something it does indeed share to a certain extent with the mentality of the classical period in general, but has made its own in an emphatic manner, namely the positive attitude of the Stoic to freely chosen death. Suicide is seen as morally allowed, and in some cases even as obligatory. The collection of evidence in SVF III.757–68 under the title *De rationali e vita excessu* ('On the rational departure from life') attests to this attitude in the earlier representatives of the school, and Seneca for his part speaks very frequently of suicide. This frequency reflects not least the biographical relevance of this theme to his own life. There is no reason to lament about the intolerable harshness of life, since destiny has always left an escape hatch open to the human person, and it is entirely up to him whether he chooses it. Seneca states this bluntly enough in the *De Ira* 3.15.4:

> Why do you groan, you foolish man? ... Wherever you look, you see the end of your wretchedness. Do you see that place that plunges down steeply? That is where one steps down to freedom. Do you see that sea, that river, that cistern?

363

> Freedom dwells in the depths there. Do you see that tree, stunted, dried up, bereft of fruit? Freedom hangs on it. Do you see your neck, your throat, your heart? They are escape routes from servitude. Do you think that these exits are too strenuous, demanding too much courage and strength? Do you ask which path leads to freedom? Any vein in your body at all!

Seneca is aware that this Stoic view is not without its opponents (*Ep.* 70.14: 'You will also find teachers of philosophy who do not accept that one is permitted to do violence to one's own life') and that it is necessary to define the conditions precisely, for otherwise one may give encouragement to the *libido moriendi* (*Ep.* 24.25), what Horace calls the *famosae mortis amor* (*Ars Poet.* 369), i.e. a yearning for death caused by a diffuse weariness with life. It must be possible to sense powerful signals of fate which cannot be interpreted otherwise than as a summons to end one's life.

On this point in particular there is no difference between the views of Epictetus and Seneca. Epictetus' advice has almost a frivolous ring to it (*Diss.* 1.24.20): 'You should never forget that the door is always open for you. Do not be more stupid than little children. When they tire of a game, they say: "I'm not playing any more." You should do the same, when something seems intolerable to you. Say, "I'm not playing any more," and go away.' But Epictetus too incorporates conditions. When one of his pupils wants to starve to death for no particular reason, he employs arguments to dissuade him from this resolve (2.15.4–12). The basic principle is: 'Wait for the god, mortals! As soon as he gives you the sign and dismisses you from this service, you have the freedom to return to him. But for the moment, endure patiently at the post to which he has assigned you' (1.9.16).

The following observation helps us to understand better the often-criticised attitude of the Stoa to suicide: in this context, Seneca and Epictetus often envisage an early and violent death as a genuine possibility. They adduce everything that can happen to a person: life-threatening illness and the torments caused by the cruel treatment of one's doctors; attacks by robbers when one is on a journey; piracy at sea; tyrannical rulers who inflict torture and execution. In general, peace had reigned since the emperor Augustus, but this did not mean that the life of the individual was so very safe. Even a man like Seneca had to reckon with the worst, and that not only at the end of his life. It suffices to quote from *Cons. Marc.* 20.4:

> There I see the wooden stakes on which people are tormented; of course, these are not uniform, but the tormentors set them up in various ways. Some crucify

head-downwards, others drive a stake through the body, others stretch out the arms on the cross. I see ropes used to rack people, I see scourges; and they have invented instruments of torture for the limbs, and others for the joints. But I also see death ... It is not intolerable to be a slave, where it is possible in one single step to cross over into freedom.

Seneca possesses a genuine Stoic martyrology: again and again he lists the names of those men and women who have met a violent death with an exemplary attitude. This may be suicide, execution, or death at the hands of torturers; the roll includes Socrates, Mucius Scaevola from the early Roman period who thrust his hand into the fire and kept it there immovably, Cato the Elder, Scipio, and others. In one passage, Seneca goes so far as to speak ironically of the obsession that leads him to refer repeatedly to these examples. After he has listed three examples, he places the following objection on the lips of his dialogue-partner (*Ep.* 24.6): 'These stories were recited by rote in every school. Since we are speaking of contempt for death, you will doubtless tell me next about Cato.' Why not?, says Seneca, and proceeds calmly to speak of Cato's death.

It is important here, with regard to the Stoic attitude to death and to life, to note that this teaching is elaborated in view of similarly extreme situations. Even such a sombre conclusion is not intended, nor allowed, to call into question the meaningfulness of the life that has been lived. What is the connection with daily life? The fundamental philosophical attitude must be practised day by day, in order that it may stand firm at some future point, under this final test. The Stoic indifference has been much reviled, but if one bears in mind that it is formulated with this goal directly in view, then it loses something of its severity.

(*b*) The autonomy of the conscience

List 115.
H. Böhlig, 'Das Gewissen bei Seneca und Paulus: Religionsgeschichtliche Untersuchung', *ThStKr* 87 (1914) 1–24.
H. Cancik-Lindemaier, 'Gewissen', *HRWG* 3 (1993) 17–31.
H. J. Eckstein, *Der Begriff Syneidesis bei Paulus: Eine neutestamentlich-exegetische Untersuchung zum 'Gewissensbegriff'* (WUNT II/10), Tübingen 1983, 72–104.
I. Hadot, *Seneca* (L107) 66–71.
H. J. Klauck, '"Der Gott in dir" (Ep 41.1): Autonomie des Gewissens bei Seneca und Paulus', in Idem, *Alte Welt* (L80) 11–31.

——'Ein Richter im eigenen Innern: Das Gewissen bei Philo von Alexandrien', ibid. 33–58 (with bibliography). Cf. Idem, 'Accuser, Judge and Paraclete: On Conscience in Philo of Alexandria', *Skrif en Kerk* 20 (1999) 107–118.

D. E. Marietta, 'Conscience in Greek Stoicism', *Numen* 17 (1970) 176–87.

G. Molenaar, 'Seneca's Use of the Term *conscientia*', *Mn.* 22 (1969) 170–80.

G. Rudberg, 'Cicero und das Gewissen', *SO* 31 (1955) 96–104.

P. W. Schönlein, 'Zur Entstehung des Gewissensbegriffes bei Griechen und Römern', *RMP* NF 112 (1969) 289–305.

J. N. Sevenster, *Paul* (L107) 84–102.

On the terminology
In Greek, the verb σύν-οιδα means 'I know with', 'I share in knowledge'. Used reflexively, it means 'I know with myself', 'I am aware of myself', and from the classical period onwards this is used also in the sense of a moral self-evaluation. From this verb derive the two related terms for the conscience, τὸ συν-ειδός and 'συν-είδησις. Initially these occur only very seldom, with the broader meaning of shared knowledge or self-awareness, but from the first century BCE onwards they are attested also in the sense of an evaluative self-assessment about one's own (usually negative) deeds. The corresponding Latin word-formation, *con-scientia*, probably came into being independently, but the two terms later interacted. It is interesting that the two authors in the Greek sphere who most frequently employ συνειδός or συνείδησις in the first century CE are Philo of Alexandria and Paul (cf. Klauck, 'Richter'). Epictetus employs τὸ συνειδός only once, in the Cynic diatribe (cf. 6(*b*) below). Among Latin authors, the concept is employed with striking frequency by Cicero and Seneca. This evidence does not allow us to assert that the concept of conscience comes from the Stoa, or that it was Stoicism that attached a new value to this concept. Nor do our texts give more than scanty support to the alternative hypothesis that this concept derives from the philosophy of Epicurus or from Pythagoreanism. Many modern scholars maintain that the concept was based on universally accessible anthropological experiences, and that it was first used in popular daily speech; this was elevated to the level of philosophical reflection only at a relatively late date, and only to a limited extent. One should, however, also take seriously the suggestion (cf. Schönlein) that the original *Sitz-im-Leben* of the terms referring to the

conscience is the rhetoric of the courtroom. One of the earliest Latin attestations is in the *Rhetorica ad Herennium* (2.5.8), and the metaphorical scene evoked by descriptions of the conscience (as in Paul, at 1 Cor 4:4f. and Rom 2:15) always includes the picture of the judgement of a court.

'The god in you'

It is significant in this context to note how Seneca gives the theme of conscience a place within the Stoic framework of his thought. We take an indirect route here, beginning with *Ep.* 41.1–3, a text that is often (and rightly) quoted, since this allows us to clarify further aspects of his idea of the divine:

> (1) ... One need not raise one's hands to heaven, nor beseech the guardian of the temple to give us admittance to the ear of the divine image, as if that would mean that our prayer would have a greater likelihood of being heard. The god is near to you, he is with you, he is within you [*prope est a te deus, tecum est, intus est*]. (2) So I say, Lucilius: a holy spirit dwells in us [*sacer intra nos spiritus sedet*], observing and watching over [*observator et custos*] our evil and good deeds. As we treat him, so he himself treats us ... (3) If you find a grove which consists of ancient trees that have reached a greater height than usual ... the sublime character of the wood, the mysteriousness of the place and your surprise at finding such a deep and unbroken shade in the open countryside will kindle in you belief in the divine governance. When a cave, created out of rock by the motion of the waters, holds up the mountain above itself ... it will make your soul tremble by a perception of what the fear of god is. We venerate the springs of important rivers; altars are built to honour the very spot where a mighty stream breaks forth from its hidden origin; the springs of sacred waters are venerated, and many lakes are consecrated either by shadowy darkness or by their unfathomable depths.

Although the term *conscientia* is not employed here, we sense that this passage is related to the phenomenon of the conscience. But we shall first reflect on this text in three steps, in relation first to the anthropological immanence of the divine, secondly to the doctrine of the protective spirit, and thirdly to the knowledge of the divine which is provided by nature.

1. When Seneca says that the god dwells in the human being (41.1), this is in keeping with the line from Cleanthes' hymn to Zeus which Luke quotes in an approximate manner at Acts 17:28, 'For we are of his stock'. This can be put in other terms, viz. that 'God comes into human beings' and 'divine seeds are scattered abroad into the bodies of human beings' (*Ep.* 73.76: '*semina ... divina dispersa sunt*', the Stoic doctrine of the *logos spermatikos*).

God in the human being is the portion of logos or *pneuma* (cf. the *sacer spiritus*, 41.2) which is assigned to him and allows him to share in the divinity of nature as a whole. Epictetus argues in exactly the same way here, when he says for example: 'You are a portion of God, you have a small part of him in yourself... You carry around a god with you, you wretched man, and do not know it' (*Diss.* 2.8.11f.).

2. The spirit, as representative of the divine within us, takes on the task of watching over us and guarding us. Seneca describes this activity in very visual terms in *Ep.* 94.55: 'Thus there must be a guardian, and his task is to tug us by the ear again and again, to keep idle chatter far from us and to contradict the people when they offer us hypocritical praise.' Seneca here takes another, older tradition and presses it into the service of Stoic thought, viz. the doctrine of the personal protective spirit, the δαίμων or δαιμόνιον or *genius*. Plutarch and Apuleius composed dissertations on the *daimōn* of Socrates which Plato mentions. Some modern scholars have wished to interpret this Socratic *daimōn* as the conscience, but this is incorrect in the case of the original context, since the *daimōn* in Socrates does not make any evaluative judgements. But it is difficult to dispute the thesis that when Seneca takes over this concept, it comes very close to what we know as 'conscience'. Epictetus, who likewise avoids using the concept of conscience, is in substantial agreement here, though making a sharper distinction than Seneca between the god and the internal guardian who represents him (*Diss.* 1.14.12–14):

> [Zeus] has assigned to each one a guardian [ἐπίτροπον], namely the protective spirit [δαίμονα] of each one, and he has charged this spirit to observe the human person, without slumbering or letting itself be deceived ... Thus, even if you close the doors and make everything dark within, do not think you may say that you are alone. For you are not alone: rather, the god is within [in the room, or in the human person?], and so is your protective spirit.

3. Let us remain by way of an epilogue with *Ep.* 41.3, where one must ask whether our enlightened Stoic has suddenly been unmasked as the adherent of an animistic nature religion, since he is willing to pay the tribute of divine veneration to trees, caves and springs. We have already seen the same thing in the case of the *genius*: a brief consultation of a standard work of reference suffices to confirm that remnants of an older Roman nature religion underlie this text. 'The concept of sacredness attaches first to the earth; the form of the cultic site located on this sacred earth has only secondary significance. This can be a grove, a spring, a ditch

[*mundus*], a cave (Lupercus), a gate (Janus), a covered hearth (Vesta) ...,
depending on the particular character of the deity worshipped there.'[19]
Seneca understands such ideas in keeping with a demythologisation that
sees them as a reference to the gradated governance of the one divine
principle in the totality of animate and inanimate nature, and this allows
him to continue to employ such ideas with what one might call a
pedagogical intention. Nature is God, and God is in nature, and the
human person, thanks to the specific endowment with reason, is capable of
penetrating nature to see that it follows a divine regulation. Immediately
after saying this, Seneca goes on in *Ep.* 41.4f. to state that the *vis divina* can
be even more clearly perceived in a human being who calmly holds out
under stormy times, thanks to his *animus:* must not the sight of such a
person overwhelm us with an even more powerful sense of religious awe?

Analysis of the phenomenon of conscience
We may summarise what has been said as follows: the divine component in
the human person is to be identified with rationality. Where the reason
appears in the special function of guardian, seeing to it that the human
person is in harmony with the natural law in what he does, it comes close
to what we are accustomed to call the conscience. Seneca employs the
concept of *conscientia* with relative frequency, not indeed exclusively in the
sense of 'conscience', but often with this meaning. If he does not always do
so wherever we recognise the presence of phenomena related to the
conscience, this is not least because of the history of the tradition, i.e.
because the materials he uses are of various provenance.

Well-known topoi are found in the description of the activity of the
conscience. Seneca was not the first to say that the conscience 'bites': this is
already found in Cicero (*Tusc.* 4.45: 'It is better to be bitten [*morderi*] by
one's conscience'). But Seneca goes further than Cicero, reflecting on our
proverbial experience that a good conscience allows one to sleep well: 'Even
when one has a bad conscience, some circumstance or other may allow one
to have an exterior safety, but never an interior tranquillity. For even if one
is not caught out, one thinks that one could be caught out, and one is
uneasy as one sleeps' (*Ep.* 105.8). Even when crimes remain undiscovered,
the conscience torments those who are guilty, convicting them in their
own internal courtroom, so that they tremble (*Ep.* 97.15f.). A bad
conscience cannot stand the light of the sun (*Ep.* 122.14), it torments and

[19]   G. Wissowa, *Religion* (L2) 468.

weighs one down (*Ben.* 3.17.3), whereas a good conscience is a good thing that is easily attained (*Tranq. An.* 3.4). The conscience is the highest authority against which one's own actions must be measured (*Vit. Beat.* 20.4): 'I would not do anything for the sake of a good reputation, but I would do everything for the sake of a good conscience. And when I do something that is known only to myself, I will nevertheless do it as if the entire populace were watching.'

The 'examination of conscience'

What must be done if one seriously wishes to improve one's conduct? Seneca replies to this question in *Ep.* 28.10: 'As far as possible, argue with yourself, cross-examine yourself. Take on first the task of the prosecutor, then of the judge, and finally that of the defending counsel.' The human person assumes in relation to his own self these three functions of *accusator* (prosecutor), *iudex* (judge) and *deprecator* (advocate); we may note in an aside that these roles are assigned in the biblical-Christian tradition to Satan as accuser, God as judge, and Jesus Christ or the Spirit as advocate. The place where this occurs is provided by the conscience (which is not mentioned explicitly here), and de facto this demands that the examination of conscience be systematised. The Pythagoreans practised daily self-examination, which was not yet called 'examination of conscience' since the concept of conscience was not initially available. On this, Epictetus quotes verbatim from the *Golden Verses* ascribed to Pythagoras:[20] 'Do not accord your weary eyes any sleep before you have given yourself an account of the deeds of the day' (*Diss.* 3.10.2), and Seneca adopted this custom, according to his own account, from his teacher Sextius, who was influenced by Pythagoreanism (*De Ira* 3.36.1–3):

> Sextius was wont to do as follows. At the end of a day, when he had retired to rest for the night, he asked himself: 'Which of your weaknesses have you healed today? Which error have you resisted? In what point have you improved?' Anger will cease, and the one who knows that he must appear each day before the judge will be more moderate in his conduct. So what is finer than this custom of submitting the whole day to a thorough examination? The sleep that ensues on a self-examination is calm, deep and free, when the soul has been commended or reproved and, as its own observer and judge, has secretly acquired knowledge

[20] On this cf. J. C. Thom, *The Pythagorean Golden Verses: With Introduction and Commentary* (Religions in the Graeco-Roman World 123), Leiden 1995.

of its own character. I make use of this possibility and give an account of myself to myself each day. When there is no more light to be seen, and my wife, who is already familiar with this custom of mine, has fallen silent, then I examine my entire day and evaluate my actions and words; I conceal nothing from myself and pass over nothing.

The voice of God?

It is not necessary to adduce any detailed evidence for the claim that – leaving aside the necessary differentiations due to the history of tradition, and assuming a unified concept of the conscience – Seneca's analyses and advice could be adopted virtually word for word by Christian asceticism. This makes it all the more important to investigate the structural position of the concept of conscience in Seneca's ethics. Does there exist a still higher authority, before which the conscience in turn would have to give an account of itself? This is the view held by Max Pohlenz, who writes that the human person 'possesses in his conscience the unerring guide for his conduct. But above this conscience there stands in turn the divinity as the final authority. It is the divinity that has given us the conscience as a guardian that accompanies us; it is to the divinity that we owe our life, to which we must give an account of ourselves. Nothing of all that happens escapes the divinity' (*Stoa* [L106] I.320). Thus Pohlenz implicitly dissociates the *observator et custos* of the second verse of *Ep.* 41.1f. from the 'near' god of the first verse, interpreting the latter in the sense of a transcendental, personal image of God. This image, however, is not found in Seneca, despite many verbal formulations which come astonishingly close to it.

What Pohlenz writes here is open to misunderstanding, if not indeed downright wrong. The passages quoted here have not given the impression that there would exist a transcendent or eschatological forum beyond the conscience for the conscientious responsibility of the human person. In Seneca, it is precisely the ethical autonomy of the Stoic that is expressed by the entire complex of concepts which converge upon the idea of the conscience, so that an exact expression is created for the philosopher's self-consciousness. The Christian tradition would later define the conscience as *vox Dei*, the 'voice of God' within the human person. This cannot appeal for support to Paul, but it can certainly be compared to Seneca's teaching on the conscience, if one eliminates the pantheistic implications of this doctrine and allows the conscience to embody the voice of the transcendent god.

(c) The freedom of the Stoic wise man

List 116.

H. Braun, 'Die Indifferenz gegenüber der Welt bei Paulus und bei Epiktet', in Idem, *Gesammelte Studien zum Neuen Testament und seiner Umwelt*, Tübingen 1962, 159–67.

H. Cancik and H. Cancik-Lindemaier, 'Senecas Konstruktion des Sapiens: Zur Sakralisierung der Rolle des Weisen im 1. Jh. n.Chr.', in A. Assmann (ed.), *Weisheit* (Archäologie der literarischen Kommunikation 3), Munich 1991, 205–22.

K. Döring, *Exemplum Socratis: Studien zur Sokratesnachwirkung in der kynisch-stoischen Popularphilosophie der frühen Kaiserzeit und im frühen Christentum* (Hermes.E 42), Wiesbaden 1979, esp. 43–9.

M. Forschner, *Ethik* (L113) 104–13.

J. C. Gretenkord, *Der Freiheitsbegriff Epiktets*, Bochum 1981.

D. Nestle, *Eleutheria: Studien zum Wesen der Freiheit bei den Griechen und im Neuen Testament*, I: *Die Griechen* (HUTh 6), Tübingen 1967, 120–35.

O. Schmitz, *Der Freiheitsgedanke bei Epiktet und das Freiheitszeugnis des Paulus: Ein religionsgeschichtlicher Vergleich* (NTF I/1), Gütersloh 1923.

S. Vollenweider, *Freiheit als neue Schöpfung: Eine Untersuchung zur Eleutheria bei Paulus und in seiner Umwelt* (FRLANT 147), Göttingen 1989, 23–104 (an admirable presentation).

The Greeks were always preoccupied by the question of the freedom of the human person. The answer given by the Stoa met much criticism and was accused of an inherent contradictoriness. Stoic thought bears the traits of determinism: everything is laid down by fate and follows its course in keeping with immutable regularities. What is left for the human person to do? Where does he have any possibilities of action? The Stoa responded by an attack of its own, meeting its opponents with the slogan that only the Stoic wise man is truly free (cf. the early testimonies in SVF III.589–603: 'Sapiens est dives, formosus, liber [The wise man is rich, handsome and free]').

Definitions
One can see the importance of this theme for Epictetus from the simple fact that he dedicates by far the longest of his individual diatribes to it in *Diss.* 4.1: Περὶ ἐλευθερίας. The initial definition runs as follows: 'The

free man is the one who lives as he wills, one who cannot be coerced, prevented or overpowered. Nothing stands in the way of what he wills. His endeavours attain their goal. If he rejects something, this decision is not overturned' (1). This sounds like a demand for a total freedom from all ties, and Epictetus does in fact intend to produce this impression: he takes up a popular definition of freedom which was common at the time, in apparent agreement with this – but only in order to refute it and to give 'freedom' another meaning. He begins with this redefinition in the very first paragraphs, since 'willing', 'endeavours' and 'rejections' are already technical terms in Stoic philosophy for movements which have their origin in the human person and are oriented to things outside him. The all-important point here is that these movements should be employed correctly.

In a number of *exempla* Epictetus criticises the common view which measures freedom in terms of social position, possibilities of bringing political influence to bear, etc. Even a Roman senator has the emperor as lord above him, and is therefore nothing other than 'a slave in a large household' (13). Even if he is spared this fate, it might happen that he was tyrannised by a demanding lover, perhaps even by a young slave-girl (17: 'Have you never spoken flattering words to your little slave-girl? Have you never kissed her feet?'). People may assert as loudly as they like that they have freedom – but Epictetus asks indignantly where this freedom is genuinely to be found in such a situation. Do not passions lead directly into a loss of freedom, unless one fights against them in keeping with Stoic doctrine?

Identifying the problem

Epictetus defines as follows the basic problem which can be seen in these and other *exempla*: 'The source of all ills for human beings is their inability to apply to the individual things those fundamental concepts [προλήψεις] which are common to all' (42). Nature supplies the human person with the προλήψεις which tell him what he must prefer and what he must avoid. Difficulties always arise in their application: often we do not truly know what is good and what is bad for us. We go astray in the evaluation of our goals, and hence also when we assess the difficulties involved in attaining them.

All this culminates in the question: if even kings and their friends remain subject to certain forms of coercion, 'who is then still free?' (51). Epictetus begins a new line of argument in order to find an answer, and now at last he introduces a distinction already found in Aristotle, which is fundamentally important for his ethics and is connected with the basic concepts and the categories of willing, desiring and avoiding. We must learn to distinguish between what is at our disposal (τὰ ἐφ' ἡμῖν) and that which is not at our disposal (τὰ οὐκ ἐφ' ἡμῖν). In principle, nothing external – whether family, possessions, health or body – is at our disposal. We can behave for a time as if this were indeed the case, but we soon encounter our limitations. We have control only of our assessment and evaluation of things, of the importance that we allow them to have for us. Freedom is transposed into the internal dimension and becomes a question of my attitude to given facts that I cannot essentially alter.

Consequences

A first consequence is that one must be able to let things go, without clinging to them – not even to one's own body and life. Such an attitude of detachment must be practised. It demands 'asceticism', as we read in §81, a passage full of philosophical technical terms:

> When you have established yourself in such an interior disposition and have practised a way of thinking that distinguishes between the alien and that which is one's own, between that which can be refused admittance and that which cannot be refused admittance, regarding the latter as something that concerns you and the former as something that does not concern you; and when you pay attention in the one case to what you desire and in the other to what you reject, whom will you then fear?

In a subsequent passage Epictetus raises these ideas to the level of religious language. Now the goal is defined as assenting to the will of the god, bringing one's own will into harmony with the divine will (cf. 89, 99f.). This requires one to study precisely what the divine intentions are, by asking what the god has placed at our disposal (the inner goods) and what he has not placed at our disposal (the external goods). In §§103–10 Epictetus discusses death, which he sees (to borrow Dietrich Bonhoeffer's language) as the greatest feast on the path to freedom, and not as a definitive limitation set upon human freedom. Provided that one does not let one's heart become attached to the things of this world, one will not cling to them when the time has come to take one's leave. To depart life with thankfulness is also to put freedom into practice. This can be learned from philosophy, when this is correctly understood and practised; but philosophy demands an iron discipline (111–13).

In the centre
The heart of this text is formed by the four paragraphs 128–31, which sum up what has been said hitherto, compress it into a few very pregnant sentences, and conclude with a prayer: 'This, then, is the path to freedom, this alone signifies that servitude is abolished: namely, that one is able one day to say the following words with all one's heart, "Lead me, O Zeus, and you my destiny, to the place where I am to stand in accordance with your counsel and will".' The introduction here comes from Epictetus, but not the prayer itself, which is taken from a hymn by Cleanthes quoted by Epictetus in four other passages, some of which give longer extracts from it (cf. SVF I.527). Seneca gives us the longest version, with five lines, the last of which acquired proverbial status (*Ep.* 107.11):

> Lead on, O father and lord of high heaven,
> wherever you will: I do not delay to obey.
> Here I am, unflagging. Even did I not wish to do so, I would follow you with
>   groans
> and endure against my will what your goodness would permit me to
>   experience.
> Fate leads one, if one assents to it – otherwise it drags one away, if one refuses
>   [*ducunt volentem fata, nolentem trahunt*].

A provocative parable attributed to Chrysippus (SVF II.975) can illustrate the dimensions of this concept of freedom: we should picture a dog tied to a wagon. The wagon begins to move, and sets off. The dog has only one choice: either he runs freely with the wagon, or else, if he does not wish to do so, it drags him off. Thus the human person too can freely do that which is unavoidable, thereby reconciling himself with his destiny. If he refuses to do so, he does not alter the course of events. All he does is to inflict grave harm on himself (on the exegesis of this parable cf. Forschner 110–12).

Living examples?
The lengthy concluding passage in Epictetus does not attain the concentrated argumentation and sublimity of the preceding passages, but belongs rather to the category of *paraenesis*. This always includes *exempla*. In other words, we need concrete persons who have realised the Stoic ideal. It ought to be possible, after four hundred years of the scholastic tradition, to give a list of some exemplary Stoic wise men. Epictetus says that he himself does

not yet feel truly free, since he is as yet too much concerned about his lame leg (151). While this modesty does him honour, it draws our attention to a certain dilemma: it is clear that genuine Stoics occur in real life only very seldom, and the situation always becomes critical when concrete names are to be named. Once again, Diogenes and Socrates must serve as models (152–69), although neither was a Stoic (Socrates lived before the Stoa came into being, and Diogenes was a Cynic).

It appears that the Stoic ideal in its pure form exists only in theory: in praxis, only differing degrees of approximation to this ideal are found. The Stoics do not, however, infer from this that they must abandon their ideal and cease to strive towards it. On the contrary, they infer that they must never relax their efforts: their own deficiency is translated into an intensified imperative. The corresponding image of the human person is theoretically very optimistic, but in practice rather sceptical and gloomy.

Conclusion

The concluding remarks (170–7) intensify the appeal. The price of true freedom is high, because 'freedom does not come into being through the fulfilment of the most keenly desired wishes, but through the abolition of desires' (175). It can however be attained with the help of philosophy: therefore 'stay awake throughout the nights, so that you may acquire the attitude that can make you free [δόγμα ἐλευθεροποιόν]' (176). It would certainly be anachronistic and inappropriate to translate this phrase as 'the dogma that makes you free'; but the underlying theological structure in the heart of this dissertation about the freedom of the Stoic wise man also makes it clear that what we find in Epictetus is a promise of salvation.

There can be no doubt that the Stoa generated scarcely soluble tensions immanent to its own system by both declaring the human person to be lord over his conduct and asserting a strict determinism in its metaphysics. The solution it offers involves transposing freedom almost exclusively into the inner realm, into the consciousness of the thinking human person, so that freedom is 'a condition of the internal disposition, not primarily an objective legal status or a quality of conduct in the world' (Forschner 111). This can provide a limited help in the praxis of life, although it lacks an ultimate justification. One may compare – not in terms of substance, but of structure – what Karl Rahner has written about Christian freedom as the ability to give one's assent: freedom is precisely not 'the capacity to realise ever new and various possibilities, the capacity of an endless revision, but rather the capacity to realise something unique and definitive, something that is definitively valid precisely because it is done in freedom'.[21]

6. Cynicism and the Stoa

(*a*) General coordinates

List 117.

H. W. Attridge, *First Century Cynicism in the Epistles of Heraclitus* (HThS 29), Missoula 1976.

H. D. Betz, 'Jesus and the Cynics: Survey and Analysis of a Hypothesis', *JR* 74 (1994) 453–75; also in Idem, *Antike und Christentum* (L3) 32–56.

M. Billerbeck, *Der Kyniker Demetrius: Ein Beitrag zur Geschichte der frühkaiserzeitlichen Philosophie* (PhAnt 36), Leiden 1979.

——(ed.), *Die Kyniker in der modernen Forschung: Aufsätze mit Einführung und Bibliographie* (BSPh 15), Amsterdam 1991.

R. B. Branham and M. O. Goulet-Cazé (eds.), *The Cynics: The Cynic Movement in Antiquity and Its Legacy* (Hellenistic Culture and Society 23), Berkeley 1996.

A. Delatte, 'Le sage-témoin dans la philosophie stoico-cynique', *BAB.L* 39 (1953) 166–86.

F.G. Downing, *Christ and the Cynics: Jesus and other Radical Preachers in First-Century Tradition* (JSOT Manuals 4), Sheffield 1988.

——*Cynics and Christian Origins*, Edinburgh 1992.

——*Cynics, Paul and the Pauline Churches*, London 1998.

D. R. Dudley, *A History of Cynicism: From Diogenes to the 6th Century AD*, London 1937, reprint Hildesheim 1967.

M. O. Goulet-Cazé, 'Le cynisme à l'époque impériale', *ANRW* II/36.4 (1990) 2720–2833.

——and R. Goulet (eds.), *Le Cynisme ancien et ses prolongements* (Actes du colloque international du CNRS. Paris, 22–5 juillet 1991), Paris 1993.

R. F. Hock, 'Cynics', *AncBDict* I (1992) 1221–6.

R. Höistad, *Cynic Hero and Cynic King: Studies in the Cynic Conception of Man*, Uppsala 1948.

G. Luck, *Die Weisheit der Hunde. Texte der antiken Kyniker* (KTA 484), Stuttgart 1997.

A. J. Malherbe, *The Cynic Epistles: A Study Edition* (SBibSt 12), Missoula 1977.

---

[21]   K. Rahner, *Gnade als Freiheit*, Freiburg i.Br. 1968, 42; cf. Gretenkord 180f.

———'Self-Definition among the Cynics', in Idem, *Paul* (L104) 11–24.
L. E. Navia, *Classical Cynism: A Critical Study* (CPh 58), Westport 1996.
H. Niehues-Pröbsting, *Der Kynismus des Diogenes und der Begriff des Kynismus* (stw 713), Frankfurt a.M. 2nd edn. 1988.
L. Paquet, *Les Cyniques grecs: Fragments et témoignages* (Philosophica 35), Ottawa 2nd edn. 1988 (collection of texts).
C. M. Tuckett, 'A Cynic Q?', *Bib.* 70 (1989) 349–76.

The tradition in antiquity attributed the formation of Cynicism to Socrates' pupil Antisthenes (*c*.455–360 BCE) or even to Socrates himself, but the real progenitor of this movement is most probably Diogenes of Sinope (*c*.350 BCE), who is also its prototypical representative. He was given the mocking nickname κύων, 'dog', because he led 'a dog's life' characterised by the proverbial shamelessness of a dog. The name of the movement should be seen as derived from this nickname (and not from a gymnasium called 'Kynosargēs' in Athens, where Antisthenes is said to have taught). An inexhaustible wealth of anecdotes (see, for instance, Diogenes Laertius, *Vit. Phil.* 6.20–81) tell us, e.g., that Diogenes spent his life in a large storage vessel and that when Alexander the Great offered to grant him a wish, he asked him only to move out of the sun. This suffices to show that Cynics lead a poor life as wanderers who have no needs. Their nonconformist and provocative behaviour is a critique of 'bourgeois' values. They seek their *eudaimonia*, their freedom and happiness, in a conscious self-marginalisation. In short, Cynicism was and remained more a form of life than a doctrine or school. Nevertheless, the Cynics did address other people by word or pen, in vivid and rousing moral sermons in the style of diatribes.[22]

One of Diogenes' pupils was Crates of Thebes, who attained the zenith of his success as teacher at Athens *c*.328–25 BCE; one of his pupils was Zeno, the founder of Stoicism. From this time on, close mutual influences between Cynicism and Stoicism can be seen, something reflected in common modern formulations such as 'Cynic-Stoic popular philosophy' or 'Cynic-Stoic diatribe'.

It is not possible to state with certainty whether independent Cynics were active in the second and first centuries BCE, but at any rate Cynicism took on a new momentum in the early imperial period. Seneca had friendly

---

[22] More details in T. Schmeller, *Paulus und die 'Diatribe': Eine vergleichende Stilinterpretation* (NTA NF 19), Münster 1987.

relations with a Cynic called Demetrius who was active in Rome (cf. Billerbeck, *Demetrius*). Under the Flavian emperors, the great orator Dion of Prusa[23] was compelled for a time by external circumstances to practise the Cynic way of life. Oinomaos of Gadara probably belongs to the period of Hadrian's reign. Other Cynics of the second century CE known to us are Demonax of Cyprus, to whom Lucian dedicated an idealised portrait study, [24] and Peregrinus Proteus, who was close to the Christians for a time and died by setting fire to himself; he is commemorated in a bitter polemical text by Lucian.[25]

The Cynicism of the imperial period created a literary instrument of propaganda for itself in the pseudepigraphical Cynic letters (cf. Malherbe; Attridge) which find their inspiration in the genuine letters of the philosophers (see below, on Epicurus) and in an exercise in the training of orators, the *sermocinatio*, which involved the composition of fictitious speeches of historical personalities in particular situations. These letters allow the heroes of the Cynic movement to speak of their ideals and teachings. We quote here two examples chosen at random, which reveal something about the definition of Cynicism and about the outward appearance of a prototypical Cynic, which we shall encounter again below in the essay of Epictetus:

> The Cynic philosophy is that of Diogenes. The Cynic is one who strives to live in accordance with it. But to be a Cynic [κυνίζειν] means choosing the short path to philosophical activity. Do not be ashamed of the name on this account; do not for this reason flee from the cloak and the beggar's bag, which are the weapons of gods ... (Ps.-Crates, *Ep.* 16; to students).
>
> After I [i.e. 'Diogenes'] had chosen this [Cynic, short] path, he [the Socratic teacher] removed my cloak and tunic and clothed me in a double, rough cloak

---

[23] On his person and his significance for the New Testament, cf. G. Mussies, *Dio Chrysostom and the New Testament* (SCHNT 2), Leiden 1972; C. P. Jones, *The Roman World of Dio Chrysostom* (Loeb Classical Monographs), Cambridge, Mass. 1978.

[24] Cf. H. Cancik, 'Bios und Logos: Formengeschichtliche Untersuchungen zu Lukians "Leben des Demonax"', in Idem (ed.), *Markus-Philologie: Historische, literargeschichtliche und stilistische Untersuchungen zum zweiten Evangelium* (WUNT 33), Tübingen 1984, 115–30.

[25] Text and translation in A. M. Harmon, *Lucian*, vol. 1 (LCL 14), Cambridge, Mass. and London 1913, 141–73 (Demonax), and vol. 5 (LCL 302), Cambridge, Mass. and London 1936, 1–51 (Peregrinus).

of wool. He hung on my shoulder a traveller's bag in which he put bread, a drink, a cup and a bowl. On the outside of the bag he fastened a bottle of oil and a vegetable-peeler and also gave me a wanderer's staff. Thus equipped, I asked him why he had clothed me with a double, rough cloak of wool. He told me: 'In order to help you to train yourself for both possibilities, for heat in summer and for cold in winter . . .' – 'And why have you hung the traveller's bag [or beggar's bag] on my shoulder?' His answer was: 'So that you may carry your house with you everywhere' (Ps.-Diogenes, *Ep.* 30.3f.).

The Cynicism of the imperial period was not a unified movement. There existed, for example, both a more radical and a milder tendency, a distinction which applied also to the attitude taken to religion and belief in the gods. Nor should the points of contact with Stoic thought make us forget that Cynicism and Stoicism remained distinct realities, although the outlines of genuine Cynicism threaten to be obscured in the Stoic perspective. Despite these reservations, it is helpful for us to study Epictetus' Cynic diatribe in greater detail. We shall immediately see parallels to the early Christian Jesus movement, although reservations (cf. Tuckett, Betz) are appropriate vis-à-vis a modern tendency to take Cynicism as the primary background against which to understand Jesus and those who first proclaimed him (cf. Downing).

(*b*) Epictetus' Cynic diatribe

List 118.
M. Billerbeck, *Epiktet: Vom Kynismus* (PhAnt 34), Leiden 1978.
R. F. Hock, *The Social Context of Paul's Ministry: Tentmaking and Apostleship*, Philadelphia 1980.
A. J. Malherbe, *Paul* (L104).
H. Niehues-Pröbsting, *Kynismus* (L117) 229–39.
H. Rahn, 'Die Frömmigkeit der Kyniker' (1959/61), in M. Billerbeck, *Die Kyniker* (L117) 241–57.
G. Theissen, *Studien zur Soziologie des Urchristentums* (WUNT 19), Tübingen 3rd edn. 1989; Eng. trans.: *The Social Setting of Pauline Christianity*, Minneapolis and Edinburgh 1982; *Social Reality and the Early Christians*, Minneapolis 1992 and Edinburgh 1993.
L. E. Vaage, 'Q and Cynicism: On Comparison and Social Identity', in R. A. Piper (ed.), *The Gospel Behind the Gospels: Current Studies on Q* (NT.S 75), Leiden 1995, 199–229.

Epictetus devotes an entire long essay to the discussion of Cynicism at *Diss.* 3.22.1–109 (edited, translated and commented upon by Margarethe Billerbeck). Here he continuously emphasises the function which the Cynic way of life has for other people. Thus he presses the older Cynicism, with its pronouncedly individualistic traits, into service by binding it into the fabric of society.

The vocation to become a Cynic
The text begins with a dialogue. One of Epictetus' students sympathises with Cynicism, presumably because he has in mind the definition of Cynicism as an abbreviated path to ethical perfection (cf. the letter of Ps.-Crates above): the break with conventions would make it possible to live with fewer compromises to such Stoic ideals as self-sufficiency and imperturbability. Epictetus' first comment is: 'One who ventures upon such a path of action without the divine will is deeply hated by the god, and is only looking for a pretext for unseemly behaviour' (2). With regard to the divine vocation to Cynic existence, we recall that in other texts it is destiny or nature that indicates one's place in life. Inherent dangers can already be seen: Cynicism can also be misused as a mere pretext for shameless public behaviour. Epictetus puts the following reflection on the lips of a 'false' Cynic (10):

> I already wear a shabby cloak now, and I will do it then [as a Cynic] too. I already sleep on a hard bed now, and I will do it then [as a Cynic] too. I will get hold of a little leather bag and a staff, I will begin to roam around as a beggar, and to insult the people who encounter me.

The standard equipment of the Cynic includes a cloak of rough wool which serves as a blanket at night, a leather bag slung around his neck for the daily ration of food which he begged, and a wanderer's staff which could also be used in self-defence. These 'props' were his trademark (cf. the even harder regulations when Jesus sends out his disciples at Mk 6:8f.; Lk 10:4). We see from his subsequent rebuke that Epictetus is not completely happy with this Cynic vagabond life: 'But no – instead of that, a little bag, a staff and big jaws; swallowing greedily down everything that people give, or else hoarding it, or making a nuisance of oneself by insulting those who encounter one' (50; cf. 2 Cor 11:20).

Messenger and herald

Epictetus goes on to explain that the Cynic must always lead an ethically irreproachable life. He is continuously exposed to public view, and this means that other people are always subjecting him to their examining gaze (14–17). One who cannot stand up to this will himself provide a priori the refutation of his moral sermon. In Epictetus' opinion it is especially important that the Cynic should be aware of the task that is laid upon him vis-à-vis other people (23–5):

> The true Cynic ... must be aware that he is sent to people as a messenger [ἄγγελος] of Zeus, in order that he may show them that they are caught fast in error with regard to what is good and what is evil, and that they seek the essence of good and evil where it is not to be found ... In reality, the Cynic is a spy [κατάσκοπος] sent to discover what is good for human beings, and what is harmful for them. And when he has investigated this carefully, he must return and relate the truth about this [ἀπαγγεῖλαι].

A fundamental Socratic principle remains valid here, viz. that if people behave badly, this is because they do not know any better. All that the Cynic has to do is to bring their errors to light; but lofty titles are given him in this function. He is messenger and spy, and §69 calls him a 'herald' (κῆρυξ) in the service (διακονία) of the divinity. The term 'witness' (μάρτυς) is also found (in §88 for Diogenes; cf. 3.24.112f.). Understandably enough, the question arises how the Cynic thinks that he can lead a happy life under these circumstances (45). Epictetus has the great hero of the school, Diogenes, give the answer. He has no house, no native land, no possessions, no slaves, neither wife nor child. Under him, he has only the earth as his sleeping place, above him only the sky and his shabby cloak (47), yet he can ask: 'What do I lack? ... Am I not free? [cf. 1 Cor 9:1] ... Would not anyone who saw me believe that he was looking at his own king and lord?' (48f.).

Love of one's enemies

The Cynic existence has unquestionably its price, however. One who takes his profession seriously will be exposed to blows from all sides. But he bears ill treatment and insults with the impassiveness of a stone. More than this, he will even love those who torment him:

> Naturally, the Cynic's ability to endure must be so great that he appears in the eyes of most people to be devoid of feeling, and like a stone. No insult, no ill

treatment, no mockery affects him; indeed, he himself has handed over his wretched body to whoever may want to abuse him, in any way such a person may desire (100).

For this too is woven exceptionally closely into the profession of Cynic: he must allow himself to be oppressed like a donkey, and when he is oppressed he must even love [φιλεῖν] his oppressors like a universal father, like a brother (54).

Margarethe Billerbeck comments on this passage: 'The demand that Epictetus here makes of the true Cynic goes beyond the Stoic standard. The idea that the one tormented should love his tormentors lies closer to the paradoxical spirit of the Sermon on the Mount ... than even to Cynic philanthropy' (Billerbeck 119). Exegetes have not overlooked the parallels to the command in the synoptic tradition about Jesus that one should love one's enemies (cf. Theissen, *Reality*, 128f., 146–8). These can be explained in part by the similarity, indeed the identity of the *Sitz-im-Leben* in the two cases. This demand was preserved and handed on in a group of homeless itinerant preachers without possessions, for whom ill treatment was a fact of daily life; in this context, it is particularly apposite to demand that one love, not only an 'enemy' in abstract terms, but even more concretely, the tormentor at whose hands one must endure the ill treatment. Resistance and feelings of hatred would reveal that the message one preached was not genuine. It is, of course, necessary to have a very strong motivation, if one is to succeed in maintaining such a disposition, and this motivation is derived by Epictetus in various ways from the Stoic attitude to life, the two most important components of which are the belief that all human persons are related (so that none may be shut out) and the ideal of *apatheia*.

Abstinence from society

In sections 62–85 Epictetus discusses the themes of friendship, marriage, children and civic life. An essential aspect of the character of the Stoic wise man is that he knows himself to be a member of human society and carries out his social obligations. The origins of Cynicism, however, lead it to reject social ties, since these contradict the autarchy of the individual. Epictetus endeavours to reconcile these by acknowledging the exceptional role of the Cynic but without attributing any absolute value to it. He defines it in terms of its functional orientation to human society. Were the world to consist of nothing but wise men, then we should not need any Cynics; but in that case, nothing would prevent the Cynic from getting married. However (69):

Since things are in fact the way they are, so that we are as it were on the front line of battle, must not the Cynic be free of distracting ties [ἀπερίσπαστον, cf. 1 Cor 7:35], wholly at the service of the deity, capable of moving around among people without being fettered by civic duties, and free from personal relationships? For if he inflicts harm on such relationships, he no longer retains the character of a man of honour, while if he observes them, he destroys the messenger, the spy and herald of the gods.

This then is the dilemma: if the Cynic establishes his own family and takes on the concomitant obligations, he must do this in an exemplary fashion. Epictetus describes very vividly and amusingly what would then await the Cynic. He must, for example, get clothes for his children, send them to school armed with writing tablets and stylus, and prepare a bed for them, since the poor children 'cannot be Cynics from their mother's womb' (74). But if he does do all this in an exemplary fashion, he will have no time left to carry out his task as Cynic, viz. to go among people as their living conscience, observing them, criticising them, and seeing to it that they hear the Stoic message of salvation. His radical philosophical commitment in the service of the community presupposes that the Cynic abstains from personal ties.

Personality ideal
We quote only one passage from the concluding section, which formulates various demands on the personality of the Cynic. This passage deals with the ethical self-consciousness of the Cynic (94–6):

Bodyguards and weapons give kings and tyrants their power to rebuke people and to punish those who commit crimes, even when these kings and tyrants themselves are scoundrels. But the Cynic has neither weapons nor bodyguards. All that can give him this power is τὸ συνειδός [conscience, or consciousness]. When he sees that he has remained alert for the salvation of human beings, and has accepted the burden of hard work, when he sees that he has fallen asleep with a pure heart and awakened even purer still, and that he has thought his thoughts as a friend of the gods, as their servant, as one who shares in the lordship of Zeus ... why should he not then have the confidence to speak candidly to his brothers, to his children, indeed to all his relatives?

Whence then does the Cynic derive his authority? We can begin by saying: from his divine mission; but Epictetus explains here somewhat more clearly how the Cynic becomes conscious of this mission. Once again, we encounter here the conscience, of which Epictetus otherwise does not speak, or else the ethical self-consciousness of the human person, as the final authority and the embodiment of personal autonomy. The Cynic must ask himself sincerely what motivations lead him to act as he does. If he is certain that he does everything only in the interests of those whom he addresses and at the service of the philosophical ideas which guide him, without self-seeking motives, he can set his mind at rest. This conviction gives him his personal identity, and it is this alone that equips him with authority vis-à-vis other people, who note that they are in the presence of a mature personality. Only this can lead them to accept that this uncomfortable admonishing voice should speak to them.

In conclusion, we should not forget that Epictetus is sketching an ideal picture, not simply giving an account of existing reality. The latter was certainly rather different – polemical eruptions in Epictetus himself show that reality was more sobering at many points. But the parallel early Christian missionary movement was likewise not pure light. It too had many dark shadows.

In earliest Christianity, comparisons with Cynicism can be suggested by the radical itinerant way of life of the early movement of followers of Jesus in Palestine, which still finds its echo in logia in Q (see Theissen, *Reality*, 33–59; Vaage), and by the double strategy followed by Paul (see Hock; Malherbe). On the one hand, Paul wishes to avoid the risk that the Christian missionaries in a Graeco-Roman civic culture may be confused with the itinerant Cynic philosophers, whose reputation was not very good; but at the same time, one of the weapons he can employ to discredit his own opponents within the communities is to attribute Cynic traits to them (see Theissen, *Setting*, 27–67).

C. Epicurus and his school

1. Epicurus: personality and influence

List 119.

N. W. De Witt, *St. Paul and Epicurus*, Minneapolis 1954 (very unreliable).

M. Erler, 'Epikur', 'Die Schule Epikurs', 'Lukrez', in H. Flashar, *Philosophie* (L104) 29–202, 203–80, 381–490 (the most recent summary presentation; a basic work).

M. Hossenfelder, *Epikur* (Beck'sche Reihe 520: Grosse Denker), Munich 1991.

H.-J. Klauck, *Die antike Briefliteratur und das Neue Testament, Ein Lehr- und Arbeitsbuch* (UTB 2022), Paderborn 1998, 121–47 (on the letters of Epicurus, and of Cicero, Seneca and the Cynics).

A. A. Long, 'Pleasure and Social Utility – The Virtues of Being Epicurean', in H. Flashar and O. Gigon, *Aspects* (L104) 283–316.

P. Mitsis, *Epicurus' Ethical Theory: The Pleasures of Invulnerability* (CSCP 48), Ithaca 1988.

R. Philippson, *Studien zu Epikur und den Epikureern*, ed. by W. Schmid and C. J. Classen (Olms Studien 17), Hildesheim 1983.

J. M. Rist, *Epicurus: An Introduction*, Cambridge 2nd edn. 1977.

W. Schmid, 'Epikur', *RAC* 5 (1962) 681–819.

H. Steckel, 'Epikuros', *PRE* Suppl. 11 (1968) 579–652.

(*a*) His life

Epicurus was born in 341 BCE and grew up on the island of Samos as the son of an Athenian citizen who had emigrated there as a colonial settler. Years of many wanderings took him to the city of Teos in Ionia, where he studied philosophy under Nausiphanes, an adherent of Democritus, to Athens, where he did his two-year military service, to Colophon in Lydia, and finally to Mytilene on Lesbos and to Lampsacus on the Hellespont. Here Epicurus, by now thirty years old, began his own activity as teacher of philosophy and found his first enthusiastic disciples, some of whom accompanied him to Athens and remained faithful to him to the end of their lives. In 306 BCE Epicurus settled definitively in Athens in a house of his own with a schoolroom in the garden (this is the source of the term κῆπος, 'garden', which was often used to refer to his school). Apart from two or three visits to groups of adherents of his teaching in Asia Minor and on the islands, he lived and worked there, surrounded by the group of his disciples and friends, until his death in 271/70 BCE. Besides this, he wrote letters in order to maintain contacts within his school, which was in the process of speedy formation. Externally considered, his life in Athens was withdrawn and quiet, as if he himself wanted to illustrate the fundamental principle that he entrusted to his disciples: λάθε βιώσας, 'Lead a hidden life' (Fr. 551 Usener). This means that the philosopher is not to get entangled in political affairs, nor to seek public notice or fame (in modern terms, one would say that he should avoid the 'media'). But Epicurus recommended that political responsibility should be accepted, especially when this was in the interests of the Epicurean circle of friends which needed ordered circumstances and a certain standard of life, if it was to survive (see Long).

(*b*) His work

List 120.

G. Arrighetti, *Epicuro: Opere* (BCR 41), Turin 2nd edn. 1973.

O. Gigon, *Epikur: Von der Überwindung der Furcht. Katechismus, Lehrbriefe, Spruchsammlung, Fragmente* (BAW), Zurich and Munich 3rd edn. 1983.

F. Jürss, R. Müller and E. G. Schmidt, *Griechische Atomisten: Texte und Kommentare zum materialistischen Denken der Antike* (Reclam-Bibliothek 409), Leipzig 4th edn. 1991, 203–361.

H. W. Krautz, *Epikur: Briefe – Sprüche – Werkfragmente* (RecUB 9984), Stuttgart 2nd edn. 1985.

H. Usener, *Epicurea* (Sammlung wissenschaftlicher Commentare), Leipzig 1887, reprint Stuttgart 1966 (my enumeration follows Usener).

Only a little of Epicurus' voluminous literary work has survived. The most important materials are preserved by Diogenes Laertius (third century CE), who devoted the entire tenth book of his *Lives of the Philosophers* to Epicurus. Among the sources he employed was valuable biographical material, including a testament (probably authentic) in which Epicurus provides for the continuing institutional and organisational existence of his school (*Vit. Phil.* 10.16–22). In a lengthy list, Diogenes lists forty-one titles of works by Epicurus which have disappeared, and he quotes at full length three didactic letters by Epicurus and a kind of catechism in forty propositions. The first of the three letters, addressed to Herodotus, draws on the thirty-seven books of Epicurus' *chef d'œuvre* Περὶ φύσεως to sketch a compressed (though still very difficult) outline of his system of natural philosophy. The second letter, to Pythocles, is not accepted as genuine by all, it deals with questions of astronomy and meteorology. We shall return to the third letter to Menoikeus, as well as to the collection of propositions called Κύριαι Δόξαι (a parallel textual transmission of part of this work is found in the *Gnomologium Vaticanum*). Fragments of works of Epicurus from two further sources complete the textual dossier: quotations from Epicurus in later authors (collected in exemplary manner by Usener) and papyrus discoveries in the city of Herculaneum in Lower Italy, one of the towns hit by the eruption of Vesuvius in 79 CE (found e.g. in Arrighetti).

(c) Subsequent influence

List 121.

C. J. Castner, *Prosopography of Roman Epicureans from the Second Century BC to the Second Century AD* (Studien zur klassischen Philologie 34), Frankfurt a.M. 1988.

C. W. Chilton, *Diogenes of Oenoanda: The Fragments*, Oxford 1971.

D. Clay, 'A Lost Epicurean Community', *GRBS* 30 (1989) 313–35.

——'The Philosophical Inscription of Diogenes of Oenoanda: New Discoveries 1969–1983', *ANRW* II/36.4 (1990) 2446–2559.

J. Ferguson, 'Epicureanism under the Roman Empire', *ANRW* II/36.4 (1990) 2257–2327.

H. Jones, *The Epicurean Tradition*, London and New York 1992.

D. Kimmich, *Epikureische Aufklärungen: Philosophische und poetische Konzepte der Selbstsorge*, Darmstadt 1993.

A. A. Long and D. N. Sedley, *Hellenistic Philosophers* (L104) I.25–157, II.18–162.

M. F. Smith, *Diogenes of Oinoanda: The Epicurean Inscription* (La Scuola di Epicuro, Suppl. 1), Naples 1993.

K. Summers, 'Lucretius and the Epicurean Tradition of Piety', *CP* 90 (1995) 32–57.

The discoveries at Herculaneum brought more to light about Philodemus of Gadara, an Epicurean of the first century BCE who worked in Italy and Rome, than about Epicurus himself. This brings us to the further history of Epicurean philosophy, of which we can mention only a few points. Cicero gives relatively ample space to the Epicurean position in the discussions he presents in the *De Finibus* and the *De Natura Deorum*, although he himself rejects this position. The poet Horace displays unmistakable affinities to Epicureanrism and makes his own contribution to the development of a stereotypical negative image of the Epicureans (see below). The greatest influence in the Latin sphere was exercised by Lucretius (*c.*96–55 BCE) with his great didactic poem *De Rerum Natura*, a title that imitates Epicurus' main work Περὶ φύσεως. We have already mentioned that Seneca frequently includes quotations from Epicurus (cf., for example, the remarkable requirement that Epicurus makes of a student, in Seneca, *Ep.* 25.5: 'Do everything as if Epicurus were looking on'). We may mention as a curiosity Diogenes of Oenoanda, who had a monumental inscription with Epicurean texts set up on a wall in a city in Asia Minor for purposes of propaganda.[26] We lose trace of the Epicureans as an independent body in the third and fourth centuries CE. They are characterised especially by great constancy in the views they held and in their faithfulness in holding on to the original impulses. In their case, even more than with other schools, this justifies our turning back continually to the founder himself.

(*d*) The school

List 122.
W. Crönert, *Kolotes und Menedemos: Texte und Untersuchungen zur Philosophen- und Literaturgeschichte* (StPP 6), Leipzig 1906; reprint Amsterdam 1965.
R. A. Culpepper, *The Johannine School: An Evaluation of the Johannine-School Hypothesis Based on an Investigation of the Nature of Ancient Schools* (SBLDS 26), Missoula 1975, 101–21.
N. W. De Witt, *Epicurus and His Philosophy*, Minneapolis 1954.
B. Frischer, *The Sculpted Word: Epicureanism and Philosophical Recruitment in Ancient Greece*, Berkeley 1982.

The characteristic traits of a philosophical school in antiquity can be seen with particular clarity in the case of the Epicureans. These include a founding personality, concern to preserve the tradition, life in common, an ideal of friendship, and the establishing of the school's own identity vis-à-vis the external world (cf. Culpepper). Although the Epicureans did not (as is sometimes supposed) acquire for themselves the legal status of a cultic association (θίασος), religious practices are not lacking. For example, Epicurus lays down in his testament that his birthday is to be celebrated each year and that memorial meals are to be held on the twentieth of each month 'in memory of myself and of Metrodorus of Lampsacus' (the latter was one of the earliest disciples and companions of Epicurus, along with Colotes). The celebration of this meal served even centuries later to define the identity of the Epicureans. One of their highest ideals was friendship among the like-minded, with corresponding behaviour. This friendship is,

[26] Cf. Chilton; Clay; Smith. German translation also in the useful collection by F. Jürss et al., *Atomisten* (L120) 427–50.

however, also considered from the viewpoint of mutual benefit, and holding all things in common, otherwise a common ideal in similar contexts, was not practised among the Epicureans.

During his lifetime, and even more after his death, Epicurus grew into the role of a σωτήρ, a rescuer and 'saviour' of human beings. Cultic veneration was paid to his image, which was first set up as a statue in Athens and often copied; this image was also used for missionary purposes. In iconographic terms, it combines traits of a father, philosopher, cultic hero, rescuer, guide of the soul, indeed of a god. In psychodynamic terms, it evokes the archetype of the wise old man. Its impressive stylisation is intended to kindle in outsiders the wish to learn more about this man and his teaching (cf. Frischer).

No special prior study was expected of adepts of the Epicurean mode of life, and access was open to women and slaves too. Especial characteristics of life within the group were *askēsis* and *therapeia*, the former understood as a training in that way of life which was based on philosophy, the latter understood as the healing and helping guidance of the soul which was carried out by means of individual conversations in which one gave account of oneself and received intensive counselling (modern scholars go so far as to speak of a 'confessional praxis').[27] There can be no question that Epicurean schools had a well-developed group charisma, and that it was this that made them especially attractive.

2. Epicurus' letter to Menoikeus

List 123.
A. Graeser, *Hauptwerke* (L104) 151–69.
K. Held, 'Entpolitisierte Verwirklichung des Glücks: Epikurs Brief an Menoikeus', in P. Engelhardt (ed.), *Glück und geglücktes Leben: Philosophische und theologische Untersuchungen zur Bestimmung des Lebensziels* (WSAMA.P 7), Mainz 1985, 77–127.
H. W. Krautz, *Epikur* (L120) 40–51.

We shall attempt to present central substantial positions of the Epicurean doctrine in areas that concern us in this book, viz. the idea of the divine, the problematic of death, and ethics, first using the letter to Menoikeus and then confirming this further with some quotations from the doctrinal propositions. The text, as has been said, is found in Diogenes Laertius, *Vit.*

---

[27] Cf. e.g. S. Sudhaus, 'Epikur als Beichtvater', *ARW* 14 (1911) 647f.

Phil. 10.122–35. It has the form of a letter, as the brief address at the beginning shows: 'Epicurus sends greetings to Menoikeus'; in terms of its contents, it is a protreptic didactic text, inspired probably by Aristotle's *Protreptikos Logos*. 'Protreptic' means 'making propaganda, providing an introduction, making an invitation', and in the case of Epicurus we could perfectly well say: 'missionary'. It is meant to explain effectively the new existential wisdom to its addressee – not only the historical person Menoikeus, who first received the letter, but every potential reader. Thus the text begins by observing that philosophy knows no distinctions of age, but offers to all the stages of life the indispensable aid to attain health of soul; and *eudaimonia*, 'the happy life', is introduced as the ultimate concept, the goal at which everything aims, for 'one must be concerned to acquire everything that achieves happiness (εὐδαιμονία)' (122).

(*a*) The idea of God

List 124.
A. J. Festugière, *Épicure et ses dieux* (MR 19), Paris 3rd edn. 1985.
F. Jürss, *Die epikureische Erkenntnistheorie* (SGKA[B] 33), Berlin 1991.
D. Lemke, *Die Theologie Epikurs: Versuch einer Rekonstruktion* (Zet. 57), Munich 1973.
D. Obbink, 'The Atheism of Epicurus', *GRBS* 30 (1989) 187–223.
W. Schmid, 'Götter und Menschen in der Theologie Epikurs', *RMP* NF 94 (1951) 97–156.

The first large topic which Epicurus discusses is the idea of the divine. Possession of a correct concept of the divine is an essential precondition for success in life. It is not easy to understand Epicurus' teaching on this point; even in antiquity it was exposed to a variety of misunderstandings and mistaken interpretations. We begin by reading the text itself (123):

> First of all, take the god to be an imperishable and blessed being, as we are assured by the general idea of god, but do not attribute to him anything that would be incompatible with his imperishability and blessedness ... Thus gods do in fact exist, and the knowledge of them is immediately obvious. But they are not as the mass of people imagines them to be ... The atheist is not the one who does away with the gods of the masses, but rather the one who accepts the ideas about the gods which the masses hold.

Let us attempt to set out in greater detail what these concise affirmations mean. The fundamental thesis is that gods exist. The proof is derived from epistemology, and here it is important to know that Epicurus' epistemological starting point is a sensualism which accords absolute primacy to sense impressions; in metaphysics, although not uninfluenced by Aristotle, he goes back further into the past and has recourse to the atomic theory of the Presocratic Democritus. All that exists consists of atoms and of the empty space in which the atoms meet one another. Small atomic-material particles (εἴδωλα) continually detach themselves from objects and penetrate our senses, creating in them exact copies of the objects and collaborating with certain antecedent concepts (προλήψεις) – we may leave aside here the question whether these concepts are congenital, or acquired through reception by the individual – to make possible the structuring of the reality that is experienced. However, the continuous irradiation of particles of matter means that all that exists must ultimately at some point cease to exist. We carry around with us particular ideas of deities, which have for example impressed themselves on people in dreams. These images can have been created only by de facto realities that exist outside the human being. The logic can be inverted to affirm that there must exist gods who are the origin of the little images that show us these gods in a form similar to that of human beings.

One of the virtually irresolvable questions in this area is the extent to which Epicurus himself thought along these lines, and the extent to which later pupils and successors did so. In any case, there is no escaping the fact that intellectual difficulties arise at this point. Does what has been said mean that the gods too are subject to the universal law that everything passes away? The answer is negative, since the gods are imperishable and immutable. This is presumably because they have their existence in a continuous flow and exchange of matter, in a finely balanced process of filtering out and transmitting. Epicurean thought locates the place where this is possible, and hence where the gods dwell, in so-called intermediary worlds. The decisive mistake which human beings commit is to identify the images of the gods which they have received with phenomena and experiences of nature which frighten them, so that they develop a fear of the gods and look for means to appease them or to put them in a favourable mood. But according to Epicurus, the gods lead a blessed life outside time and are not in the least concerned about what happens on earth. The prayers and sacrifices addressed to them do not reach them at all. In other words, there is no divine providence, nor does world history follow a course directed towards any goal. The widespread contrary idea of the divine, held by the masses or the common people, is not only false, but directly atheistic, since its mythical narratives attribute to the gods all kinds of things that are utterly foreign to their dignity and their being.

Various reactions to this emphatically stated position are possible. The Epicureans were accused of atheism in the classical period (cf. Obbink), despite the fact that they also recommended prayers to the gods and even sacrifices, indeed participation in general in the cult and care for religious customs (with exceptions – oracles were rejected, for example). The critics dismissed all this as mere hypocrisy, an external façade behind which the Epicureans could cultivate their own godless philosophy safe from disturbance. There are indeed discrepancies here, which we too perceive, but it is clear that Epicurus combined both elements in his thought: the unattainable remoteness of the gods and the sensory character of their veneration. The gods with their blessed, incorruptible life that is untouched by the business of the world embody the ideal which the wise man strives to attain and attempts to realise through philosophy. When we venerate the gods, this goal is kept continuously before our eyes, so that we ourselves become better persons. Thus the exercise of religion is given a function in terms of psychological health, perhaps even of social health too.

We encounter the other potential reaction in Lucretius, who celebrates Epicurus as the great hero who has freed human beings from an unutterable oppression caused by religion:[28]

> When life on earth appeared shameful in human eyes,
> bowed down by the burden of terribly heavy religion,
> which stretches out its head from the exalted heights of heaven
> and threatens human beings with a dreadful grimace,
> it was *a Greek* who first dared to raise his mortal eye
> against the monster and oppose it boldly.
> The fables about gods, lightning and thunder from heaven,
> did not frighten him with their menace. No, his courage only
> grew stronger and reached higher heights. So he was the first
> who dared to break open the gates of mother nature in a mighty assault.
> And so it happened. His brave spirit bore off the victory . . .

---

[28]   *Rer. Nat.* 1.62–72; cf. K. Büchner, *Titus Lucretius Carus: De rerum natura/Welt aus Atomen* (RecUB 4257), Stuttgart 1973, reprint 1986; W. M. D. Rouse, *Lucretius*, rev. edn. by M. F. Smith (LCL 181), Cambridge, Mass. and London 1992.

In other words, the kind of god portrayed by Epicurus can no longer be used to threaten anyone. Such a god can no longer inspire fear in anyone, no one need fear his judgement; and according to Lucretius, who writes against the background of the Roman belief in demons and is therefore more critical of religion than Epicurus himself, this is all to the good. People will be rescued from a gloomy superstition and given the possibility of leading a life worthy of human beings, in which they bear responsibility for their own lives.

(b) The problem of death

Death too has a particular capacity to inspire fear in human beings, and this is the next subject that Epicurus takes up. It must be clear from the outset that after death there is no kind of continuing existence of the human being, or even only of his soul (which consists of round and delicate atoms), except – as has been indicated in the discussion of the *Consolatio ad Marciam* above – in the memory of later generations. This means that there is no place for any anxious obsession with the punishments of the underworld. Death means the beginning of a total lack of sensation. The human person ceases to exist at the moment of death, which therefore no longer affects him in any way (Letter to Menoikeus, 124f.):

> Become accustomed likewise to the idea that death is nothing that affects you. For all that is good and all that is bad is a matter of sensation alone, while death involves the cessation of sensation. This is why the correct knowledge of the fact that death is nothing that affects us makes even the mortality of life something that we can enjoy. This fact means that we are no longer confronted with the vista of an endless future time; it puts an end to the yearning for immortality ... Thus, death – allegedly the worst of all ills – does not affect us in any way. For as long as we exist, death does not exist, and when death ensues, we no longer exist.

Epicurus replies to the objection that death does at any rate shorten the time available for the enjoyment of life, by arguing that what matters is not the temporal length of life, but the intensity and quality that characterise it. The quantitative distribution of his material here reveals that Epicurus himself nevertheless felt this to be problematic: he devotes fourteen lines to the gods, but thirty-one to the subject of death. One cannot avoid the impression that his intention is simply that death will disappear under an avalanche of words. It appears that his adherents found his attempted solution more or less sound. In the following passage, Epicurus defines somewhat in the manner of an aside the goal (τέλος) of a happy life as health of body and unshakability (ἀταραξία) of soul (128), thereby ultimately coming very close, though from a completely different direction, to the Stoic ἀπάθεια. (In point of fact, while the two schools are clearly distinct in the structures of their systems, they converge in an astonishing fashion in the advice they give for the practical conduct of life. This is no doubt due to the general spectrum of problems that existed in the period of their birth and their prime.) Drawing on an older metaphorical tradition, Epicurus employs the image of a storm at sea that abates, so that the sea becomes calm, to speak of the attainment of inner peace. This paragraph closes with the words: 'Precisely for this reason, as has been said, pleasure [ἡδονή] is the origin and goal [ἀρχὴ καὶ τέλος] of the happy life' (one should note how close this comes to the Stoic *telos* formula).

(*c*) The principle of pleasure

List 125.
H. J. Krämer, 'Epikur und die hedonistische Tradition', *Gym.* 87 (1980) 294–326.
R. Müller, *Die epikureische Ethik* (SGKA[B] 32), Berlin 1991.
A. Rehn, 'Vomunt ut edant, edunt ut vomant: Beobachtungen zur Epikurpolemik in der römischen Literatur', in R. Feldmeier and U. Heckel (eds.), *Die Heiden: Juden, Christen und das Problem des Fremden* (WUNT 70), Tübingen 1994, 381–99.
G. Striker, 'Epicurean Hedonism', in J. Brunschwig and M. C. Nussbaum, *Passions and Perceptions* (L104) 3–17.
K. Zacher, *Plutarchs Kritik an der Lustlehre Epikurs: Ein Kommentar zu 'Non posse suaviter vivi secundum Epicurum' Kap. 1–8* (BKP 124), Königstein 1982.

This new *telos*, pleasure, brings us to the famous (or infamous) principal point of Epicurus' ethics, namely the thesis that the highest goal must always be the endeavour to achieve pleasure, and linked with this, that pain must be avoided. Epicurus takes this over from Aristippus of Cyrene, a pupil of Socrates, who maintained an unconditional principle of pleasure along with the school of the Cyrenaeans which was named after him.

Epicurus does not follow him in this, although he does provide a justification for his teaching on pleasure based in ethnological and developmental history, when he claims that this iron law can be seen already in the behaviour of small children. There is no doubt that Epicurus understands 'pleasure' to mean sensual and bodily satisfaction; he understands the chief cause of intellectual pleasure to be the recollection of bodily pleasures experienced in the past. In one much-discussed passage he speaks of the 'holy body' (Fr. 130 Usener: ἱερὸν σῶμα). This does not refer (as some scholars hold) to the venerable person of the founder of the school, nor does it intend (in keeping with the usage in 1 Cor 12) to give a metaphorical description of the Epicurean community; rather, it pays tribute to the human body as an instrument for the attainment of pleasure.[29]

Epicurus does however introduce a number of differentiations and limitations, for example when he distinguishes between an active pleasure which allows the desires to have full play in passion, and a passive pleasure which consists of the absence of pain. He declares that the most desirable condition is this latter state, when one has a calm life free of pain. (We ourselves can easily grasp what he means, and indeed agree with him to a considerable extent, if we take the example of acute toothache.) Epicurus develops strategies that will make possible the achievement of the greatest degree of pleasure, but not at all in the way that the somewhat discredited concept of 'pleasure' might lead us to suspect. Let us hear his own words (129):

> For we have recognised [pleasure] as our first good, something that we are born with. We choose it as the starting point for all that we choose or avoid. We return to it when we evaluate every good thing with our sensations, as with a plumbline. And precisely because it is the first good, something that we are born with, we do not simply choose any old pleasure: we pass by a whole number of sensations of pleasure, because they would only lead to even greater unpleasantnesses. Indeed, we hold that many kinds of pain are more important than sensations of pleasure, if the fact of enduring these pains for a long period means that a correspondingly greater pleasure is the result.

It is easy to find examples of what is meant here. Eating and drinking can be very pleasant, even when done to excess, but already the hangover on the next morning is unpleasant, and in the long term one ruins one's own

---

[29] Cf. W. Schmid, 'Epikur' (L119) 721.

health thereby. One who is prudent will prefer a more modest intake of nourishment, in his own interests. Athletic training can be painful, but we undertake it in the hope that we will thereby improve our expectation of life as a whole. This is how the further argumentation runs in Epicurus (130–2):

> We also hold self-sufficiency [αὐτάρκεια] to be a great good ... Even bread and water furnish the highest degree of pleasure, if one consumes them out of hunger. To become accustomed in this way to a simple, unextravagant lifestyle bestows on one the capacity for perfect health. It relieves the human person of worry when faced with the necessary demands that life makes. It enables us even to accept invitations to more sumptuous banquets from time to time, and it frees us of fear in relation to the dictates of chance ... For a life full of pleasure does not consist in drinking parties followed by carousing processions, nor in intercourse with boys and women, nor in eating fish and everything else one finds on a richly laid table, but rather a sober manner of thought [λογισμός] which investigates the reasons why particular things should be chosen or rejected and which refutes the erroneous ideas which are the ultimate cause of the most violent disturbance of our souls. Insight [φρόνησις] is the basis of all this, and the highest good.

The highest good is redefined yet again at the end as insight into precisely these matters, and philosophy is the handmaid that guides one to attain this insight. This has taken us a long, but fully logical, way from the starting point of an absolute principle of pleasure to the ideal of a reflective, rational way of life that almost offers the vision of a veiled asceticism with the permission to kick over the traces, in a cautious manner, by way of exception. This shows that the picture of the Epicureans as noisy (or even only as quiet) bons-viveurs is one-sided, and must be corrected. It is nevertheless easy to understand how such a picture could be formed, since some of the formulations employed sound very provocative and make the hearer suspect that they envisaged a very different praxis. This is how a popular negative image of the Epicureans could be generated. It is no doubt also true that this high level of speculative development of the principles of Epicurus was not always and everywhere maintained – there were also Epicureans who spent all their energies in living in accordance with the traditional image. The Roman poet Horace reflects in self-irony the stereotypes of anti-Epicurean polemics, when he posits the basic principle *Carpe diem*, 'Pluck the day', and sketches the following self-portrait in a letter: 'If you want to enjoy a good laugh some time, then come and visit me. You will find me corpulent and placid, taking good care of my body, a real pig in Epicurus' herd [*Epicuri de grege porcum*]' (*Ep.* 1.4.15f.).

The final appeal in §135 promises that everyone who is willing to devote himself to the correct way of life based on philosophy will become like the divine: 'You will live like a god among human beings. For the human person who lives in the midst of immortal goods no longer resembles any mortal thing.' Such a one has overcome, as far as is possible, the parameters of earthly and bodily existence, and resembles the unattainably remote gods who lead their blessed life. This text also shows us the starting point for the genuinely religious veneration which was paid to Epicurus himself, as well as for the quasi-religious traits in the community life and in the Epicurean school's care to preserve its tradition. We have seen a similarly high self-awareness in the Stoa, but this tended rather to take the form among the Stoics of such propositions as: 'Only the wise man is free, only the wise man is king.' The Epicureans emphasise more strongly the similarity to the gods of the thinking human person who knows how to translate his insight into existential praxis. Probably one will have to conclude that both schools overestimated the cognitive abilities of the human person – both the Stoics with their very strong orientation to reason, and also the Epicureans, despite their basic thesis of the irrationality of existence. This also involves an overestimation of the possibilities of motivating and guiding the human being by means of cognitive insights alone. Although the Epicureans begin with the principle of pleasure, they do not take sufficient account of the entire complexity of the structure of human instincts and the significance of the emotions. But we must not forget that two thousand years were to pass before psychology brought us these insights.

3. The 'decisive propositions'

List 126.

O. Gigon, *Epikur* (L120) 106–13.

H. W. Krautz, *Epikur* (L120) 65–97.

R. Müller, in *Atomisten* (L120) 284–305.

H. Usener, *Epicurea* (L120) 67–81.

Diogenes Laertius concludes his portrait of Epicurus in *Vit. Phil.* 10.139–54 with forty numbered paragraphs, relatively short, with the title Κύριαι Δόξαι, in Latin *Ratae Sententiae*. This is a collection of aphorisms or pithy propositions. Some of these may have been formulated by pupils and then included in the collection, but essentially it comes from the hand of Epicurus himself. They were meant to be learned by heart in the manner of catechism answers, so that beginners could get a quick overview of the system of teaching. A pointed expression was always available for use in controversies, and they could be recalled when help was urgently needed in any of life's situations. The first propositions are given this position because of their centrality to the teaching. When we read them, it is not difficult to recognise that we have the same lines of thought here that we have already seen in the letter to Menoikeus:

1. A happy and imperishable being has no cares of its own, nor does it cause concern to others. Thus neither outbreaks of anger nor the bestowal of favours can make any impact on it; for such things are found only in a weak being.
2. Death does not affect us. For that which is dissolved has no sensations. And that which is without sensations does not affect us.
3. The limit set to the extent of the sensations of pleasure is the removal of all that causes pain. Wherever a source of pleasure is present, then as long as it lasts, there is nothing that causes pain or suffering, nor both of these together.
4. That which causes pain does not remain uninterruptedly in the flesh. The extremity of pain is present only for a very short time. That which is only just stronger than the source of pleasure in the flesh does not remain many days with us. But those maladies that remain a long time contain a larger element of that which causes pleasure than that which causes pain.

From the following sentences we quote only no. 8, which is parallel to the argumentative development of the principle of pleasure in the letter to Menoikeus: 'No pleasure is a bad thing per se. But some of those things that generate particular sensations of pleasure also cause disturbances rather greater than the sensations of pleasure themselves', and no. 27 which praises the ideal of friendship: 'Gaining friends is by far the greatest of all those things that wisdom supplies to help us attain blessedness in the totality of our lives.' The first four propositions are found again in a brief form, compressed into one sentence with four clauses: 'One need not be afraid in the presence of God; one need not encounter death with fear; it is easy to acquire the good; and it is easy to bear what is ill' (p. 69 Usener). This sentence was given the title *Tetrapharmakos*, 'fourfold medicine': it was to be used as first aid in all of life's disasters.

4. On the reception of Epicurus' thought

List 127.

F. Bornmann, 'Nietzsches Epikur', *NS* 13 (1984) 177–88.

C. E. Glad, *Paul and Philodemus: Adaptability in Epicurean and Early Christian Psychagogy* (NT.S 81), Leiden 1995.

E. G. Schmidt, 'Zu Karl Marx' Epikurstudien', *Ph.* 113 (1969) 129–49.

A. Schmitt, *Das Buch der Weisheit: Ein Kommentar*, Würzburg 1986, 44–47.

It is easy to grasp why the Jewish and Christian traditions found little that was positive in Epicureanism, especially since they took over without deeper reflection the distorted image of the anti-Epicurean polemic. Thus it may be the case that we find polemic against the stereotypical Epicurean attitude to life in the picture of the wicked men who deny the existence of God in Wis 2:1–9 (cf. Schmitt), or in Paul when he quotes the slogan: 'Let us eat and drink, since tomorrow we die' (1 Cor 15:32). All that could be drawn on, at least to some extent, was the Epicurean critique of religion, as far as the common mythical narratives about the gods were concerned. But this remained an isolated matter. Scholars have as yet only begun to investigate the structural analogies between Epicurean and early Christian 'pastoral care' (cf. Glad).

We conclude with two brief glances at the history of the reception of Epicurus in the modern period. First, Karl Marx devoted his early philosophical dissertation to two materialists and atomists of classical antiquity, namely Democritus and Epicurus. Friedrich Nietzsche speaks of Epicurus relatively often, initially always in positive terms of assent, and makes acute differentiations, as one sees in the following observation from *Die fröhliche Wissenschaft*:[30]

> Yes, I am proud to say that I react to Epicurus' character in a way that may perhaps be different from anyone else, and I am proud to enjoy the happiness of the afternoon of antiquity in all that I hear and read about him ... Only one who suffers uninterruptedly can have such a happiness, the happiness of an eye that has reduced the sea of existence to calmness ... never before did lust know such modesty.

[30] *Kritische Studienausgabe*, ed. G. Colli and M. Montanari, vol. 3, Munich and Berlin 2nd edn. 1988, 411.

D. A Middle Platonist: Plutarch of Chaironeia

1. The context in the history of philosophy

List 128 (on Middle Platonism in general).

R. M. Berchman, *From Philo to Origen: Middle Platonism in Transition* (BJST 69), Chico, Calif. 1984.

L. Deitz, 'Bibliographie du platonisme impérial antérieur à Plotin: 1926–1986', *ANRW* II/36.1 (1987) 124–82.

J. Dillon, *The Middle Platonists: A Study of Platonism 80 BC to AD 220*, London 1977.

H. Dörrie and M. Baltes, *Der Platonismus in der Antike: Grundlagen – System – Entwicklung*, vols. 1–3, Stuttgart–Bad Cannstatt 1987–93 (further volumes are planned).

H. J. Krämer, *Der Ursprung der Geistmetaphysik: Untersuchungen zur Geschichte des Platonismus zwischen Platon und Plotin*, Amsterdam 1964.

G. Reale, *History* (L104) 205–34.

D. T. Runia, *Philo of Alexandria and the Timaeus of Plato* (PhAnt 54), Leiden 1986.

R. E. Witt, *Albinus and the History of Middle Platonism* (Cambridge Classical Studies), Cambridge 1937, reprint Amsterdam 1971.

J. Wittaker, 'Platonic Philosophy in the Early Centuries of the Empire', *ANRW* II/36.1 (1987) 81–123.

C. Zintzen (ed.), *Der Mittelplatonismus* (WdF 70), Darmstadt 1981.

List 129 (on Plutarch's philosophical orientation).

ANRW II/36.1 (1987) 184–393 (five essays).

D. Babut, *Plutarque et le stoicisme* (Publications de l'Université de Lyon), Paris 1969.

H. D. Betz, 'Observations on Some Gnosticizing Passages in Plutarch', in Idem, *Hellenismus* (L3) 135–46.

J. Dillon, *Platonists* (L128) 84–230.

H. Dörrie, 'Gnostische Spuren bei Plutarch', in R. van den Broek and M. J. Vermaseren, *Studies* (L2) 92–117.

C. Froidefond, 'Plutarque et le platonisme', *ANRW* II/36.1 (1987) 184–233.

I. Gallo (ed.), *Aspetti dello stoicismo e dell'epicureismo in Plutarco* (Quaderni del Giornale Filologico Ferrarese 9), Ferrara 1988.

R. M. Jones, *The Platonism of Plutarch* [1916] *and Selected Papers*, New York 1980.

H.-J. Klauck, 'Mittelplatonismus und Neues Testament: Plutarch von Chaironeia über Aberglaube, Dämonenfurcht und göttliche Vergeltung', in Idem, *Alte Welt* (L80) 59–81.

The eventful history of the Platonic Academy with its various phases and its temporary turn to scepticism reached its end in the first century BCE. The renewal of Platonism begins outside the context in which the school of Plato transmitted the traditional teaching, and those who follow his philosophy now call themselves 'Platonists', not 'Academicians'. This is the beginning of the Middle Platonist period, which lasts from *c.*80 or 50 BCE to 220 CE. The phenomenon of Middle Platonism can be identified through the following minimum of ideas held in common: divine transcendence, existence of the ideas, immortality of the soul; and Middle Platonism is more open to the other schools, with the exception of the Epicureans. The Peripatetic logic, to some degree the concept of logos, and other philosophical concepts are adopted from Stoicism, as well as the mystical attitude and numerology of the Neopythagoreans. Religious and theological interests come into the foreground. Especial weight is also attached to exegetical work on Plato's writings. Middle Platonism is not only important as a forerunner of Neoplatonism; recent scholarship (see Dillon) allows it to be seen in its own right as a body of thought with its own clearly defined profile. Its importance for the history of theology lies in the fact that it provided essential intellectual presuppositions for the Jewish philosopher of religion Philo of Alexandria and for the early Christian apologists Justin, Tatian and Athenagoras, although both Philo and the apologists lie outside the thematic framework that interests us in this book.

An early representative of Middle Platonism was Eudorus of Alexandria (*c.*25 BCE), to whom a new *telos* formula, borrowed from Plato, is ascribed: the goal is the ὁμοίωσις θεῷ κατὰ τὸ δυνατόν, 'becoming like god as far as is possible' (cf. *Theaetetus* 176b). One of the Middle Platonists in the second century CE was Apuleius of Madaura, usually much better known as the author of the novel *Metamorphoses* with its concluding book about Isis.[31] By far the best-known Middle Platonist, however, is Plutarch of Chaironeia. There can be no doubt of his basic philosophical orientation, which can be seen in the education he had received and is documented in

---

[31]   Cf. II/D; on his philosophical writings cf. J. Beaujeu, *Apulée: Opuscules philosophiques (Du dieu de Socrate, Platon et sa doctrine, Du monde) et fragments* (CUFr), Paris 1973.

his writings, for example in his contributions to the exegesis of Platonic works, of which the *Platonicae Quaestiones* (999c–1011e: 'Platonic Questions') and *De Animae Procreatione in Timaeo* (1012a–1030c: 'On the Creation of the Soul in the *Timaeus*') survive. He engaged in critical dialogue with the Stoics: *De Stoicorum Repugnantiis* (1033a–1057c: 'On the Self-contradictions of the Stoics') and *De Communibus Notitiis adversum Stoicos* (1057c–1086b: 'Against the Stoic Doctrine of Universal Concepts'), and he also composed some polemical writings against the Epicureans: *Non Posse Suaviter Vivi secundum Epicurum* (1086c–1107c: 'One cannot be Happy if one Lives in accordance with Epicurus'), *Adversus Colotem* (1107d–1127e: 'Against Colotes', a pupil of Epicurus), and *An Recte Dictum sit Latenter esse Vivendum* (1128a–1130e: 'Whether it is Good Advice [that Epicurus gives when he says:] Lead a Hidden Life'). This did not prevent Plutarch from following a trend that is found everywhere in Middle Platonism, by adopting a whole number of Stoic doctrines as his own. He also borrows from Neopythagoreanism in his early discourses about eating meat, which is to be avoided (*De Esu Carnium Orationes II* [993a–999b]). But apart from the philosophical context in which he wrote, it must be affirmed that Plutarch is possibly the most important of the writers of antiquity, when we wish to shed light on the early imperial period from the perspective of the history of religions, and when we wish to make comparisons with earliest Christianity.[32]

2. Life and work

(a) His life

List 130.

R. H. Barrow, *Plutarch and His Times*, London 1967.

F. E. Brenk, 'An Imperial Heritage: The Religious Spirit of Plutarch of Chaironeia', *ANRW* II/36.1 (1987) 248–349.

R. Hirzel, *Plutarch* (Das Erbe der Alten 4), Leipzig 1912.

C. P. Jones, *Plutarch and Rome*, Oxford 1971.

D. A. Russell, *Plutarch* (Classical Life and Letters), London 1973.

K. Ziegler, 'Plutarchos', *PRE* 21.1 (1951) 636–92, also published as a book, Stuttgart 2nd edn. 1964.

---

[32] Plutarch is the single most frequently quoted author in K. Berger and C. Colpe, *Textbuch* (L4); and M. E. Boring et al., *Hellenistic Commentary* (L4); see also Betz (L132).

Plutarch was born a short time before 50 CE and died soon after 120 CE. He was born in the city of Chaironeia in Boeotia, about thirty kilometres east of Delphi, and came from a respected family that had lived there for many generations. Apart from the period of his education and from journeys he undertook, Plutarch was to remain all his life in Chaironeia. He was clearly happily married to his wife Timoxena, and at least four sons and a daughter were born of this marriage; only two of the sons survived their parents.

As a young man Plutarch studied in Athens under the Platonist Ammonios, whose name suggests that he came from Egypt. In his later life Plutarch made many journeys for the purpose of study, to give lectures, or in political service, by clarifying legal questions and negotiating treaties on behalf of his native city. He visited Rome frequently and won high esteem there. It seems that a conflict arose under Domitian, who turned against the philosophers, but Plutarch became friendly with highly placed persons at the court of the emperor Trajan. An inscription at Delphi informs us that Plutarch also had the rights of a Roman citizen and bore the Roman name Mestrius, after one of his friends in Rome.

About 95 CE, at the age of roughly fifty, Plutarch took on the office of one of the two high priests at the sanctuary of the oracles of the god Apollo at Delphi, a day's journey from Chaironeia. He worked actively to improve the condition of the sanctuary, which was in decline, and to promote the consultation of the oracles. He speaks of the theoretical and mythological questions connected to this in the so-called Pythian dialogues which form a group among his writings.

Plutarch can be called a teacher only in a limited sense. The main *Sitz-im-Leben* of his study and teaching was something that has rightly been termed a 'private and family Academy'. In other words, Plutarch discussed a great variety of questions in the large circle of his friends, which also included members of his family. More than one hundred names of members of this group can be found in his writings; many are attested elsewhere in inscriptions or literature.

(*b*) His writings

List 131 (texts).
F. C. Babbitt et al., *Plutarch's Moralia*, vols. 1–15 (LCL 197, 222, 245, 305f., 321, 337, 405f., 424–9, 470), Cambridge, Mass. and London 1927–76, often reprinted.

H.-J. Klauck, *Plutarch von Chaironeia: Moralphilosophische Schriften* (RecUB 2976), Stuttgart 1997.

B. Perrin, *Plutarch's Lives*, vols. 1–11 (LCL 46f, 65, 80, 87, 98–103), Cambridge, Mass. and London 1914–21, often reprinted.

B. Snell, *Plutarch: Von der Ruhe des Gemüts und andere philosophische Schriften* (BAW), Zurich and Munich 1948.

K. Ziegler, *Plutarch: Grosse Griechen und Römer. Gesamtausgabe der vergleichenden Lebensbeschreibungen*, vols. 1–6 (BAW), Zurich and Munich 1954–65.

——*Plutarch: Über Gott und Vorsehung, Dämonen und Weissagung. Religionsphilosophische Schriften* (BAW), Zurich and Munich 1952.

——W. Wuhrmann and M. Fuhrmann, *Plutarch: Fünf Doppelbiographien* (TuscBü), Zurich 1994.

The Greek text has been published in numerous volumes of the Bibliotheca Teubneriana and in the Collection Budé (with French translation).

Abbreviations, where used, follow the *TDNT*.

List 132.

H. Almqvist, *Plutarch und das Neue Testament* (ASNU 15), Uppsala 1946.

ANRW II/33.6 (1992) 3963–4915 (22 essays on Plutarch's works, primarily on the *Vitae*).

H. D. Betz (ed.), *Plutarch's Theological Writings and Early Christian Literature* (SCHNT 3), Leiden 1975.

——(ed.), *Plutarch's Ethical Writings and Early Christian Literature* (SCHNT 4), Leiden 1978.

F. E. Brenk, *In Mist Apparelled: Religious Themes in Plutarch's Moralia and Lives* (Mn.S 48), Leiden 1977.

——*Relighting the Souls: Studies in Plutarch, in Greek Literature, Religion, and Philosophy, and in the New Testament Background*, Stuttgart 1998.

J. Hani, *La Religion égyptienne dans la pensée de Plutarque* (CEMy), Paris 1976.

H. G. Ingenkamp, *Plutarchs Schriften über die Heilung der Seele* (Hyp. 34), Göttingen 1971.

H.-J. Klauck, 'Die Bruderliebe bei Plutarch und im vierten Makkabäerbuch', in Idem, *Alte Welt* (L80) 83–98.

L. van der Stockt (ed.), *Plutarchea Lovaniensia: A Miscellany of Essays on Plutarch* (StHell 32), Louvain 1996.

A library catalogue from the third or fourth century CE, allegedly composed by Plutarch's (fictitious) son Lamprias, lists two hundred and twenty-seven works by Plutarch; eighty-three of these survive. But many of the titles given in this list do not come from his pen, and other works that we ascribe to Plutarch are not mentioned here. Scholars hold that Plutarch composed two hundred and fifty writings of very various length, and that we have about half of these.

His works can be divided into two groups: (1) the parallel biographies and (2) the *Moralia*. In the parallel biographies, Plutarch brings together a Greek and a Roman who for some reason appear comparable figures: Theseus and Romulus, mythical founders of cities; Lycurgus and Numa, legislators of the earliest periods; Alexander and Caesar, conquerors of the world; Demosthenes and Cicero, orators. He concludes with a well-known rhetorical device, the *synkrisis* or evaluative comparison. One of Plutarch's aims here is political: he wishes to bring Greeks and Romans closer to one another by emphasising their common historical inheritance. He explicitly disavows any historiographical claims: 'For I am not writing history. I paint images of human lives, and outstanding ability or corruption does not always reveal itself in those actions which attract most attention. Often it is a small event, a word or a joke, that casts a more significant light upon a character than battles with thousands slain and the greatest military enterprises and sieges of cities' (*Alex.* 1.2).

The *Moralia*, treatises with various contents, are so called because topics of moral philosophy are very prominent in them. It is clear that such themes were dear to those Byzantine scholars who preserved and transmitted a selection of Plutarch's works, and it must be said that moral philosophy was one of Plutarch's strengths. He wanted to guide friends and pupils to a right life by forming their intellect. It is exceedingly difficult to date the individual treatises in the sense of a relative chronology, and we shall discuss this only in specific cases (see below on the *De Superstitione*). An initial orientation is provided by the division of the corpus into groups. The œuvre as a whole contains:

1. *Writings with a popular-philosophical and pedagogical* character. Examples are: 'How an Adolescent should Hear or Read the Poets' (17d–37b); 'How one can Perceive one's own Progress in Virtue' (75a–86a); 'On the Avoidance of Anger' (452e–464d); 'On Fraternal Love' (478a–492d).

2. *Political writings*, e.g. 'Whether an Old Man should still Continue to Engage in Politics' (783a–97f).

3. *Philosophical writings*, most of which have been mentioned above in connection with Plutarch's philosophical orientation.

4. *Theological writings*, including the dissertation 'On Isis and Osiris' (351c–385c), a hermeneutically instructive discussion of the Egyptian Isis mythology which ends in a Platonic allegorical exposition of the mythical narrative, and the Pythian dialogues.

5. *Writings on natural science*, the best known of which is 'On the Face that Appears in the Sphere of the Moon' (920a–945d).

6. A few *writings on rhetoric*.

7. *Antiquarian writings*, such as the 'Roman' and the 'Greek Questions' (263d–304f) with explanations of unusual customs. The authenticity is disputed, but it is informative for the history of religions.

8. *Conversations at banquets or at table*, following the genre of symposium literature which finds its model in Plato's account of Socrates' symposium. The external framework gives occasion for many conversations on various questions. We find here *inter alia* a curiously distorted discussion of Judaism which draws on half-truths and false information. Because of remotely similar rites such as the feast of booths and the custom of drinking wine on the sabbath, Plutarch reckons Judaism as a form of the cult of Dionysos.[33] In another passage he accuses Judaism of superstition, and this brings us to the first individual topic which we shall discuss.

3. Individual topics

(a) On superstition

List 133.

G. Abernetty, *De Plutarchi qui fertur de superstitione libello*, Diss. phil., Königsberg 1911.

E. Berardi, 'Plutarco e la religione, l'εὐσέβεια come giusto mezzo fra δεισιδαιμονία e ἀθεότης', *CClCr* 11 (1990) 141–70.

H. Braun, 'Plutarchs Kritik am Aberglauben im Lichte des Neuen Testaments', in Idem, *Studien* (L116) 120–35.

F. E. Brenk, *Themes* (L132) 9–84.

H. Erbse, 'Plutarchs Schrift Peri Deisidaimonias', *Hermes* 70 (1952) 296–314.

---

[33] *Quaest. Conv.* 4.5.1–3; 6.1f. (669e–672c); cf. M. Stern, *Greek and Latin Authors on Jews and Judaism*, vol. I: *From Herodotus to Plutarch*, Jerusalem 2nd edn. 1976, 545–76.

H.-J. Klauck, 'Religion without Fear: Plutarch on Superstition and Early Christian Literature', *Skrif en Kerk* 18 (1997) 111–26.

P. J. Koets, Δεισιδαιμονία: *A Contribution to the Knowledge of Religious Terminology in Greek* (Diss. phil. Utrecht 1929), Purmerend 1929, esp. 68–83.

G. Lozza, *Plutarco: De superstitione*, Milan 1989 (revised version; previously as TDSA 68, 1980).

H. Moellering, *Plutarch on Superstition: Plutarch's De Superstitione, its Place in the Changing Meaning of Deisidaimonia and in the Context of His Theological Writings*, Boston 2nd edn. 1963.

A. Pérez Jiménez, 'ΔΕΙΣΙΔΑΙΜΟΝΙΑ: El Medio a los Dioses en Plutarco', in L. van der Stockt, *Plutarchea* (L132) 195–225.

M. Smith, in H. D. Betz, *Theological Writings* (L132) 1–35.

M. Theobald, 'Angstfreie Religiosität: Röm 8, 15 und 1 Joh 4.17f im Licht der Schrift Plutarchs über den Aberglauben', in *Lebendige Überlieferung: Prozesse der Annäherung und Auslegung* (Festschrift H. J. Vogt), Beirut and Ostfildern 1992, 321–43.

The guiding concept of δεισιδαιμονία

One of the treatises in Plutarch's *Moralia* (165e–171f) is entitled Περὶ δεισιδαιμονίας, in Latin *De Superstitione*. Our word 'superstition', which we must retain for the sake of simplicity, does not have quite the same meaning as this guiding concept. Behind the word δεισιδαιμονία (found in the New Testament at Acts 17:22; 25:19) lie δείδω, 'I fear', and δαίμων, which means not only 'demon', but more generally a transhuman power (cf. 3(*d*) below). 'Fear of demons' would, however, be an equally imprecise translation, since one and the same term is used to cover both a fear of the divine that is legitimate per se and a reprehensible superstition. Δεισιδαιμονία enters the negative sector of the spectrum of meanings in the character portraits of Theophrastus,[34] where the description of the superstitious person includes the following lines (*Char.* 16.6f., 11f.):

> When a mouse has nibbled at a sack of flour, he goes to the interpreter of signs and asks what he should do. If the interpreter replies that he should get the harness-maker to mend it, he does not pay any heed to this, but goes back home and offers a sacrifice ...

[34] D. Klose, *Theophrast: Charaktere* (RecUB 619), Stuttgart 2nd edn. 1981; J. Rusten, *Theophrastus: Characters* (LCL 225), Cambridge, Mass. and London 1993.

If he has had a dream, he goes to the interpreters of dreams, the soothsayers, and those who study the flight of birds, to ask them which god or goddess he should pray to ... And he seems to be one of those who often stand by the sea and sprinkle water on themselves.

The best translation of δεισιδαιμονία in Plutarch, not in terms of the basic meaning of the word but in terms of its context in his writings, would be: faith generated by fear, a pious neurotic fear in all its forms, religion as a compulsive obsession born of fear and as compulsive ritual.

Plutarch begins *De Superstitione* 1 with a definition that brings atheism and superstition into a mutual relationship, but from the outset he refuses to see ἀθεότης and δεισιδαιμονία as equivalent terms. He insists on a clear asymmetry: atheism (which he illustrates by means of the Epicurean theory of atoms) is indeed false, but superstition is even more dangerous, because it involves not only an erroneous judgement, but also πάθος, 'passion', which in turn arouses fear, aptly described as 'gnawing at the soul, depriving one of all sense, holding sleep far away, restricting and throttling' (165a).

The development of Plutarch's theme
The following paragraphs present an impressive, fascinating, and also horrifying description of religiously motivated fear, which superstitious practices aim to keep in check. Along the way, we also learn a great deal about forms of popular piety and about the inroads made by oriental cults: superstitious people who are tormented even in their sleep by terrifying images of the gods fall victim by day to charlatans and cheats, getting an old woman to carry out magical rites of purification, rolling in mud, calling on foreign names of gods and making use of 'barbarian' (i.e., for example, Egyptian, Syrian, or Aramaic) incantatory formulae (166a–b). This section concludes with the appeal: 'The gods have given us sleep, so that we may forget our misery and find rest. Why do you turn it into an unadulterated torture chamber that inflicts torments on your wretched soul which does not have any *other* sleep where it may find refuge?'

Plutarch equally disapproves of the frightening images which superstition paints of the punishments of hell (167a: 'The deep gates of the underworld open, streams of fire mingle with the secondary branches of the Styx, darkness is filled with bizarre spectres taking many forms, showing hideous faces and howling piteously; there are also judges and torturers and abysses and deep pits filled with many thousands who sigh'). This negative picture leads him to call the gods our saviours (166d:

409

σωτῆρας), from whom 'we ask for wealth, prosperity, freedom, harmony and success in our best words and works' (166e). In other words, the gods act to stabilise personal and societal harmony, and the error of atheism consists in denying this by evidencing indifference (ἀπάθεια) vis-à-vis the divine and by refusing to perceive the good things provided by the divine (167e). Through its share of pathos, superstition leads to an even worse emotional confusion (πολυπάθεια), which has a clearly ambiguous character: superstitious people 'fear the gods and seek refuge with the gods, flatter them and heap scorn on them, pray to them and accuse them' (167f).

In §§7f. Plutarch discusses the various reactions of the atheist and the superstitious person to the blows of fate. His basic affirmation, illustrated in ever new examples, is that superstition prevents the activity which is demanded by the concrete situation. Superstitious people throw in the towel and accept everything fatalistically, or else they react by increasing the number of their compulsive rituals, instead of taking up arms energetically against disaster and at least salvaging what can still be salvaged, if an all-out effort is made. One of Plutarch's examples concerns Judaism, with a theme that lies strikingly close to 2 Macc 3:32–8.

After speaking of behaviour at times of disaster, he goes on to speak of behaviour at happier hours – more precisely, at the joyful feasts of the gods, since 'Nothing is more pleasant for human beings than feasts and sacrificial meals in the temples, initiations and mystical rites and prayers, and the veneration of the gods' (169d). The atheist deserves punishment for laughing at this; but the superstitious too is prevented from taking his part with joy in the celebration. He 'prays with a stuttering voice, and scatters his incense with trembling hands'; he draws near 'to the halls and sanctuaries of the gods as if these were dens of bears or holes of serpents, or hiding places of sea monsters' (169e). In this way superstition supplies ammunition to atheism, and this is its worst crime. For one who sees superstitious behaviour must necessarily ask himself whether it would not 'be better for no gods to exist than such gods as delight in these forms of veneration, gods that are so tyrannical, so petty, so easily moved to irritation' (171b).

Plutarch reserves his heavy artillery for the concluding section, in which he describes with intentional vividness and horror the Carthaginians' sacrifices of children (171c–d). One may wonder slightly why, despite the asymmetry which characterises this treatise, true piety (εὐσέβεια) is presented in the concluding lines in true Peripatetic manner as the correct middle path between the two extremes of superstition and atheism (171f). This probably reflects Plutarch's own view. He himself aimed at this midpoint, although the material in Cynic or Epicurean sources with which he was working saw superstition as representative of all belief in the gods, and recommended atheism as the only meaningful option.

Problems of authenticity
This brings us abruptly to the question of the authenticity of the *De Superstitione*. Some scholars dispute Plutarch's authorship, despite his personal testimony at 169f–170a, where he employs his own person to illustrate what he is discussing (in the case of non-authenticity, one would have to declare this, in an excessively subtle manner, as a mark of consciously pseudepigraphical character). The doubts are based primarily on contradictions that can be discerned between this text and other statements of Plutarch about demonology, the veneration of the gods, foreign religions and expectations of life after death; we shall return to some of these below. Does he not accept in other texts things that he rejects in the *De Superstitione*?

Although these objections must be taken seriously, their force should not be overestimated. Apart from theories about the sources used, which draw our attention to the wealth of divergent material that Plutarch has worked on without smoothing out all the inconsistencies in it, it is important to note the place that *De Superstitione* has in Plutarch's biography. Stylistic grounds likewise suggest that this work belongs to an early period of his literary activity. In its crudest form, the 'developmental' thesis goes so far as to say that the *De Superstitione* is a product of Plutarch's rebellious early manhood: in subsequent years (and at the latest, when he became high priest of the sanctuary of the oracles in Delphi), he receded tacitly or explicitly from the radical positions taken in his early writing, and became more open to things that he had initially, in the enthusiasm of youth, condemned as superstition. Doubts about the validity of this thesis arise when one observes that the late dissertation *De Iside et Osiride* argues in the same way as the conclusion to *De Superstitione*, thereby as it were setting significant brackets around the whole of Plutarch's œuvre (*Is. et Os.* 67 [378a]):

> Thus human beings employ sacred symbols. Some of these are dark, while others are brighter, but common to them all is that they lead human thought to the divine. This, however, is not without danger, for some have gone wholly astray and fallen victims to superstition [δεισιδαιμονία], while others, fleeing

411

from superstition as from a quagmire, rushed down without noticing it into an abyss, namely into atheism [ἀθεότης].

For this reason, while not entirely denying the existence of various phases of development in Plutarch's thought, Frederik Brenk assumes a greater continuity between his early and his late works, and shows that the early work too has a less rationalistic and sceptical orientation than scholars have often assumed; rather, it tends to a mysticism of a Pythagorean hue. Brenk argues that it is far from certain that Plutarch's position in the later works has always been correctly expounded: the interpreters have taken literally things that Plutarch meant in a more ironic sense. One must also take account of the literary character of the dialogues, in which a variety of speakers put forward different viewpoints, and investigate in each individual case which of these views is Plutarch's own, or in other words, which of the characters in the text serves as his mouthpiece. If due attention is paid to these factors, then it can be seen that even the late Plutarch is less superstitious and less inclined to believe in demons than is often supposed.

(b) The doctrine of retribution

List 134.
H. D. Betz, *Theological Writings* (L132) 181–235.
F. E. Brenk, *Themes* (L132) 265–75.
G. Méautis, *Du délais de la justice divine par Plutarque* (Visages de la Grèce), Lausanne 1935.

The dialogue *De Sera Numinis Vindicta*, 'On Tardy Retribution by the Deity' (548a–568a), may be regarded as Plutarch's most mature work. Its subject is the question of atonement for criminal acts, a question which is also prominent in the parallel biographies (see Brenk), and the inherent reasons for the blows of fate. This broadens imperceptibly to embrace the entire problem of theodicy: how is divine justice realised in a world that often seems empty of the divine presence?

Starting point
In the first section (§§1–21), Plutarch attempts a rational and argumentative development of the doctrine of retribution. The dialogue is conducted between Plutarch himself and his brother Timon; it is occasioned, within the context of the text itself, by the attacks which an Epicurean makes on

faith in a divine providence. The most impressive attack is his mocking question why the divinity which is alleged to exist often takes so long to punish evildoers (548d). He argues that a punishment which ensues only after a great delay in time is no longer recognised as a *punishment*, but is accounted merely as one of the unfortunate things that happen in the course of human life. There is no longer any awareness of the inter-connection between action and its consequence, between what one does and what one suffers, so that the punishment cannot have any educational effect. Here it is worth reading the well-observed example in *Ser. Num. Vind.* 3 (549c), drawn from behavioural research. If a horse is hit with the rod immediately after making a mistake, this has the effect of correcting its behaviour, but if one lets some time go by before using the whip, this no longer makes any contribution to training the animal, but looks like a mere infliction of pain without any educational effect. The speaker closes with the remark that he can discern no value in the proverb that the mills of God grind slowly (549d–e).

Plutarch himself offers an initial reply by defining in §4 his Platonic starting point from an epistemological perspective: we wish 'to start with the circumspection (εὐλάβεια) of the philosophers of the Academy with regard to the divine, and to take care not to speak of these matters as if we actually knew anything about them' (549e). He then gives the example of a doctor whose decisions are not always fully understood by us lay people, and draws the conclusion that the goal here is always the healing of the soul: punishment is not an end in itself, but must be employed with therapeutic intention, in order to improve the human person.

Converging arguments
The discussion continues with converging arguments that achieve persua-sive force only through their cumulative effect. By delaying punishment, the deity gives us an example: we too should not act out of our initial anger, but should calculate the emollient effect of time, thereby imitating the divine forbearance (§5). God sees the totality of the human person, discovering in his soul good elements that may perhaps be hidden. Where this is the case, he gives the evildoer time to change his conduct (§6). Many persons who have done evil are destined to achieve great things for humanity in their later life, or they are themselves the instrument of the punishment that the god inflicts on others (§7). Besides this, a punishment has stronger effect if it is carried out in an impressive manner, and this takes time (§8). In the text these points are greatly enriched by means of

413

examples from history, from mythology, and from daily life, which we cannot present in detail here; we should have to spend too much time in the detailed exposition of many passages that would otherwise be difficult for us to grasp.

In §§9–11 Plutarch takes up a line of argument that can be summarised as follows: the evil deed bears its punishment in itself. Vice 'has a mysterious ability to inflict woe on human life, producing all kinds of fears mingled with shame, moods of repentance and disturbing emotions, with convulsions that never cease' (554b). Most criminals 'pay the price not *after* a long time, but *for* a long time' (554c). They 'do not have to wait until old age before they are punished, but have reached old age accompanied by continuous punishment' (554d). They enjoy the dissipations of life 'only as prisoners engage in games of dice and chess, while the noose dangles above their heads' (554d).

Punishment of their descendants?

Plutarch's brother Timon now joins in the conversation (§12) and introduces a new point of view. According to a passage of Euripides (Fr. 980 Nauck), the gods burden 'the head of the children with the sins of the parents' (556e). Is it not unjust to delay negligently to punish the evildoers, but then – when it is too late to reach these people themselves – demand that innocent persons pay this debt?

Plutarch's first reaction in §13 is only a hasty *argumentum ad hominem*: the examples adduced here are inadmissible inventions of poets. Besides this, it happens that descendants receive honours and rewards that their ancestors had merited. Why should this be different in principle in the case of evil deeds (557f–558c)? But then he seeks to make a more fundamental response, which we could term a cross-generational solidarity in blessing and curse. It is often enough the case in the *polis* that all must bear the consequences of the error of an individual (§15). Essential components derived from their ancestors may be present from their birth onwards in the children of criminals, with an effect on their future conduct (§16).

Immortality of the soul?

A critical objection is made somewhat abruptly at §17. This is centrally important for the subsequent course of the argument, and Plutarch takes it up at once (560a–d):

> While I was still speaking, Olympichos interrupted me and said: 'It seems that you base the evidence you present on a very substantial hypothesis, namely the

continuing existence of the soul.' – 'That is indeed so,' I replied, 'and you will assent to this, if you have not already done so ... Is the god truly so petty ... that he sows short-lived souls in corruptible flesh which cannot accept the root of a durable life, souls that sprout and then pass away for the slightest cause? ... Do you believe that he [i.e. Apollo, the god in Delphi, where the dialogue is set] would order so many expiatory sacrifices for the dead and so great gifts and honours for the departed, if he knew that the souls of the dying immediately cease to exist, when they ascend like a mist or smoke from the bodies? Would he not be practising a deceitful swindle on those who trust him? I for my part do not wish to abandon the immortality of the soul.'

The argument in §18 explains what is meant here: the punishment of living descendants also includes a punishment of the ancestor who performed the evil deeds and who now dwells among the dead, since his soul sees from beyond this world the suffering which he has caused his family, and this is a source of torment for him too. This does however involve the danger of shifting the level of the discussion completely. A question which was treated up to this point in terms of innerworldly realities, and which should have been brought to a harmonious conclusion on this level, is suddenly enriched by a transcendent component. But Plutarch parries this potential objection with a parenthetic observation that attempts to define the relationship between logos and myth: 'Let me first finish the presentation of that which is rational and probable [τῷ λόγῳ τῷ εἰκός], and then, if you wish, we shall turn to the myth (μῦθος), if it is indeed a myth' (561b). The logos embraces the rational process of argumentation, and remains in the sphere of empirical causalities, while the myth relates stories and belongs in the realm of poetry; the myth can also be suspected of lying. These two realms must be separated, yet the logos cannot do without the myth, since it comes to a limit where insoluble residues remain. The only possibility of getting any further here lies in clothing the matter in the forms of myth.

Prophylaxis
But first, in §§19–21, Plutarch brings the interrupted logos to its conclusion, taking up an affirmation by Bion of Borysthenes, a Cynic itinerant philosopher of the third century BCE, who allegedly said that 'the god who punishes the children of the wicked acts even more ridiculously than a doctor who treats the grandson or son for the illness of the grandfather' (561c). This is both true and false. It is true in the medical sphere, since it is obviously the sick man himself who needs treatment. But Bion has completely overlooked

415

the far wider implications of his comparison. For it may be that a particular illness is inherited, so that the doctor begins prophylactic treatments of the children too; and this is the situation with the natural predisposition to future crimes. Even if such an hereditary taint leaps over several generations in a family, it remains latent and can break out in the third or fourth generation. Only the god sees the total situation, and intervenes prophylactically. Since we do not see so far, we often have the impression that there is no reason whatever for the god's pedagogical action.

Dilemmas

Plutarch admits one exception, however, as a concession to a minimal sense of justice. An upright son descended from a wicked father is absolved from bearing a share in the family penance (562f). There must also exist a link between the evil predisposition and actual evil deeds, in order to justify the punishment of the children for the sins of their fathers, whether this takes place at a subsequent point in time or as a prophylactic measure; thus, one who passes the ethical test can escape from this nexus of woe. The problem that remains is the very heart of the question of theodicy: what is happening, when hard blows of fate are inflicted on a righteous person who has no share in wrongdoing? A neurotic search for hidden guilt does not measure up to the seriousness of this situation, but no other exit from the dilemma is in sight. The logos, the rational presentation of arguments, encounters an *aporia* where it is unable to offer a coherent explanation of the question of punishment and guilt, free of contradictions and, above all, existentially satisfactory. This *aporia*, however, is a birthplace of eschatology, and it is precisely here that the thought occurs: if there is no way to balance the accounts in innerworldly terms, then there must be more than this life alone.

The myth of the immortality of the soul and of life after death had already been mentioned by Plutarch, and the last third of *Ser. Num. Vind.* (§§22–33) is devoted to this. One need not necessarily keep silent about things that go beyond the possibility of rational discussion. One can also attempt to clothe these matters in narratives, and this is our next topic.

(c) Eschatological myths

List 135.
P. R. Hardie, 'Plutarch and the Interpretation of Myth', *ANRW* II/33.6 (1992) 4743–87.

Y. Vernière, *Symboles et mythes dans la pensée de Plutarque: Essai d'interprétation philosophique et religieuse des Moralia* (CEMy), Paris 1977. Cf. also L134.

Plato as model
There are three eschatological myths in Plato. The shortest of these concludes the *Gorgias* at 79–80 (523a–525a; cf. the introduction: 'Listen now – for that is how one begins to tell a fable – to a very lovely story that I expect you will take to be a legend'). The corresponding piece in the *Phaedo* is somewhat longer. Here the myth is at 61–3 (112f–115a), not at the very end, because the narrative of Socrates' death follows at 63–7. Much the most detailed narrative is found in the concluding chapters of the *Republic*, at 10.13–16 (614a–621d), presented as the account of the visionary experiences of a man who was left for dead on the field of battle, but woke to life again twelve days later on the funeral pyre and tells the tale of his wanderings in the other world.

Plato was the model who provided the standard for Plutarch so decisively in terms of number, literary form, position and contents, that we really ought to compare his texts synoptically with those of Plato, but here we content ourselves with the question of number. Plutarch too has three eschatological myths. The shortest is found in *De Genio Socratis* 21–4 (590b–594a), incorporated into a more detailed narrative preceded by a hermeneutical programme that may also be considered as applying to the other versions too: 'For that which is mythical touches the truth, not indeed very exactly, but nevertheless in its own way' (589f). The concluding myth in the natural-scientific discussion of the face in the moon is longer (*Fac. Orb. Lun.* 26–30 [941b–945d]), while the most ample eschatological myth, in *Ser. Num. Vind.* 22–33 (563b–568a) must, as has been said, provide us with some answers to questions about the doctrine of retribution which the logos could not supply.

The narrative framework
We take up the thread here from the previous paragraph. The dialogue partners insist that Plutarch tell them the myth he has promised. Plutarch makes it clear that he himself knows the story only indirectly, employing a literary device opposite to a fictional authentication. The story concerns a man of Soli called Thespesius, who led a debauched life. After suffering a heavy fall, he was thought for three days to be dead, but he returned to consciousness, changed his life completely, and from now on proved to be

a paragon of piety and honesty. Asked the reason for this transformation of his character, he reluctantly revealed what he had experienced during a journey to heaven which his soul had undertaken while his body lay on the earth. To say 'his soul' here is imprecise, for it is only the highest part of the soul, the power of thought (νοῦς), that goes on the journey, while the other parts remain in the body as an anchor. When Thespesius later looks round, he sees behind himself the line of a dark shadow which is like a cable linking his intellect with his body (24 [564d]). It prevents him from asending into the highest regions of heaven, but at the same time it also makes possible his return to earth and his revivification.

The place of purification
In heaven Thespesius encounters a relative, a guide (or *angelus interpres*) who takes him on a *tour d'horizon*. Enlightening information is given about the fate of the souls, or parts of souls, of the dead. Thespesius sees how their souls

> ascending from below, formed fiery bubbles in the air that they dislodged. When these bubbles burst, they emerged in a shape like that of human beings, but softer and lighter. Their movements were not identical – some sprang out with a marvellous agility and positively shot upwards, while others turned in circles like spinning tops, making now downwards and now upwards, moving in an unequal, disordered spiral which, even after a good space of time had passed, came to rest only with difficulty (23 [563f–564a]).

We already sense the meaning of this variety of movements: the good ascend immediately, while the others initially lack orientation. In addition, some souls emit a clear light like the full moon, while there are other souls covered in weals and scars (24 [564d–e]). This is a consequence of their purification. Dikē, the personified justice, rips every vice out of their souls, and this painful process leaves traces behind (26 [565b]). But these are not 'the punishments of hell'; as yet, we are in 'purgatory'.

The place of punishment
After several intermediary stages, we come to the true place of punishment, which lies not in the underworld, but in the heavenly regions. §30 relates a profoundly moving encounter, with descriptions that need no further commentary:

> Finally, he [i.e. Thespesius] saw his own father ascending from a pit, covered with scars and wounds. He stretched out his arms to his son and was not

allowed to keep silence: those charged with punishing him compelled him to confess that once, in his depravity, he had poisoned guests who were carrying gold on their persons. On earth, he had remained undetected, but here he had been convicted of his deed. He had already suffered a part of his penalty, but he was now being led to further punishments (566f).

Some lakes lay close to one another here, one consisting of boiling gold, another consisting of ice-cold lead, a third of unyielding iron. Alongside these stood some demons who acted like smiths, using their tools to draw out of the lakes and then once again to immerse in them the souls of those who had committed crimes out of insatiability and covetousness. When the souls had become glowing and transparent because of the molten gold, the demons threw them into the lead and thus extinguished them; when they had become rigid there and hard like hailstones, they dropped them once again into the sea of iron, where they became completely black, and were ground down and crushed because of their hardness (567c).

Return to the topic of discussion

This brings us closer to the main theme. According to §31, the worst-off are those who have already paid the penalty of their guilt and have been set free, for then there appear their descendants, who have to bear terrible woes because of their ancestors, in keeping with the principle that the gods burden the heads of the children with the sins of their parents. These descendants swoop down on those who were responsible for their sufferings, and bring them once again before the judgement seat. 'At once, whole swarms of their descendants had fastened on some of them, clinging to them like bees or bats, crying out in shrill voices, recalling angrily the suffering that they had endured because of their ancestors' (567e). This is the last piece of information that we are given about this problematic: when children and grandchildren are punished for the errors of their ancestors, this takes place in view of the punishment after death of those who are really guilty. For them, the penalties are increased every time they are discovered by a new group of their descendants, who have experienced suffering.

The humorous tone in which the terrible picture closes entitles us to ask whether Plutarch himself found this convincing. In §32 Thespesius sees how souls are made ready for their rebirth in the form of animals. One of these is the soul of Nero, which has undergone very harsh treatment; but since he was a benefactor of the Greeks, he is not transformed into a serpent (the animal which symbolised one who murdered his own mother), but 'into another, tamer being, into a singing animal that lives in marshes

419

and lakes' (567f), i.e. into a swan (as Ziegler holds: L131) or, more probably, into a frog. When we hear that the emperor is turned into a singing frog, this prompts us to look back over the myth and to ask whether it too does not contain a playful element, and is born of the delight in literary composition.

We need mention only one aspect of the variant form of the myth in *Fac. Orb. Lun.*, viz. that on the point of death the three components of the human person return to their place of origin. The body remains on the earth, the soul on the moon, and only the intellect makes for the sun in order to be fused with it (28 [943a], 30 [944e]). This also shows how the eschatological myths are interwoven with the theme of each individual work. Here Plutarch succeeds in providing a mythical explanation for the face in the moon: its contours are formed by indentations and caves on the surface of the moon, in which the souls receive their punishments (29 [944c]).

Reflection

Yvonne Vernière (214f.) draws on the developmental thesis to explain the discrepancy between these colourful myths and the critique to which they are exposed: it is in his old age that Plutarch composes the myths. In support of this she makes a clever quotation from Plato, who states at *Rep.* 1.5 (330d–e): 'When someone feels death drawing near, he falls victim to fear and anxiety about things that did not concern him before. For he has often heard the stories about the underworld, where one who has been unjust on earth will be punished; but until now, he has laughed at these. But now they preoccupy his mind – is it possible that they are true, after all?'

How much 'reality' does Plutarch attribute to the mythical dimension? One may not wish to go so far as Brenk, who asserts that the souls are in principle incapable of suffering, for this would void the 'punishments of hell' of all meaning; but one must certainly relativise what Plutarch says. He discusses the eschatological themes in a more considered manner in his anti-Epicurean treatises, where he must confront the thesis that death is the absolute end point. Against Epicurus, Plutarch energetically defends the immortality of the soul. He argues that Epicurus, while affirming a doctrine of pleasure, paradoxically robs human beings of one of their greatest joys, viz. the certainty of a better life after death, and of the hope that we shall one day see our deceased friends and relatives again. In order to be able to hold on to the idea of a continued existence after death, the human person accepts the price of the possibility of punishments in the next life. Epicurus is quite wrong, for the human person thinks that torments lasting for a while are preferable to total non-existence. Plutarch also holds that we must not underestimate the pedagogical effect of such pictures of the afterlife, for without them, some people could not be motivated to lead an upright life (*Suav. Viv. Epic.* 25 [1104a–b]). If they follow Epicurus' teaching,

> the unrighteous and the crooks, who fear punishment and torment in the underworld and who refrain from committing acts of cruelty because of this fear, will have a pleasanter and more tranquil life here on earth too. Epicurus himself knows of no other deterrent from wicked deeds than the fear of penalties. It follows then that we ought to infuse superstition directly into such people, letting the whole terror of heaven and earth, their abysses, their mechanisms that produce fear and their horrors cascade down upon them. The shock would motivate them to a more peaceful and moral life.

Many contradictions remain, and it is possible to systematise the whole material only up to a point. Plutarch engages in several language games: a theological (in *Ser. Num. Vind.*), a natural-scientific (in *Fac. Orb. Lun.*), a political (in *Gen. Socr.*), a philosophical (in the debate with the Epicureans), and a mythological language game which is integrated in varying degrees into the others. The material on which he works and the specific situations bring their own weight to bear, and this results in statements that are not harmonised with each other. The common basis of all these passages is the immortality of the soul, a concept owed to Platonic philosophy. Plutarch affirms a fundamentally optimistic idea of gods and human beings; he considers the doctrine of immortality to be a message of hope, and he says this clearly. This means that he cannot attach so much importance in reality to the images of terror from the other world, even if his portrait of the joyful future expectations does not reach the intensity and concentration of the negative images (it may be observed that in Dante too, the *Inferno* makes more exciting reading than the description of paradise).

The pedagogical-political motivation of the punishments in the afterlife remains especially remarkable. Plutarch wishes to employ these for an 'education of the human race' which seems to him otherwise scarcely possible, and at this point he comes surprisingly close to Polybius, who had earlier diagnosed precisely this intention as the real driving power behind the religious praxis of the Romans, though his analysis and interpretation were made from the Greek perspective. Because of their simple directness, Polybius' observations on this question deserve to be recorded here.[35]

> But it seems to me that the greatest advantage of (their) society lies in their view of the gods. Something that exists only in its outlines among other peoples seems to me to form the very basis of the Roman state: namely, an almost superstitious fear of the gods. It is scarcely possible to imagine how important a role is played by religion both in private and in public life there, and how much is made of it. Many will think what I am saying odd, but I am convinced that this is done for the sake of the masses; for if it were possible to construct a state consisting only of wise persons, then such methods would surely be superfluous. But since the multitude is always frivolous and full of desires for things forbidden by the law, inclined to meaningless wrath and to passions that explode in acts of violence, nothing else remains than to bridle them by means of sombre fantasies born of fear and by a skilfully invented mythology. In my view, accordingly, those of old did not act without due reflection, but rather with prudent consideration when they imbued the multitude with ideas of the gods and belief in the underworld. On the contrary, it seems to me exceedingly vapid and foolish, when people now root out this faith from the multitude.

(d) Demonology

List 136.

D. Babut, *Plutarque* (L129) 388–440.

F. E. Brenk, 'In the Light of the Moon: Demonology in the Early Imperial Period', *ANRW* II/16.3 (1986) 2068–2145.

H. Dörrie, 'Der "Weise vom Roten Meer": Eine okkulte Offenbarung durch Plutarch als Plagiat entlarvt', in P. Händel and W. Meid (eds.), *Festschrift für Robert Muth* (IBKW 22), Innsbruck 1983, 95–110.

J. Holzhausen, 'Zur Inspirationslehre Plutarchs in De Pythiae oraculis', *Ph.* 137 (1993) 72–91.

G. Soury, *La Démonologie de Plutarque: Essai sur les idées religieuses et les mythes d'un platonicien éclectique* (CEA), Paris 1942.

E. Valgiglio, *Divinità e religione in Plutarco*, Genoa 1988, 79–88.

Linguistic observations

We find a relatively fully developed demonology in Plutarch, but unfortunately this is also a problematic sphere where clarification is at its most

---

[35] Polybius, 6.56.6–12; cf. W. R. Paton, *Polybius: The Histories*, vol. 3 (LCL 138), Cambridge, Mass. and London 1923.

difficult. Scarcely at any point is Plutarch's own opinion more a matter of scholarly dispute than here, and one reason for this is the plurality of phenomena covered by the conceptual field of δαίμων. Even the etymological root is unclear. Most scholars derive this word from δαίω, δαίομαι (= 'to apportion', 'to divide in parts', but also 'to tear asunder'). This would mean that a *daimōn* was an apportioner, one who quite concretely handed out to people the portions of meat in the sacrificial meal, or, less concretely, one who assigned them their destinies. The following are very frequently identified as archaic starting points for belief in demons: fear of the activity of spirits of the dead, i.e. of the souls of the deceased who find no rest and go around as ghosts, and the personification of natural forces and powers; but a demon can also be the personal protective spirit of a human being. We find demons in *Ser. Num. Vind.* as spirits who inflict punishment in the heavenly dwelling place of the souls. Sometimes *daimōn* is close to *tychē* (blind chance, destiny, disposition of providence), or is a synonym for a numinous heavenly power.

Platonic elements

Plutarch cannot simply dispense with demons, not least because he is faithful to his great model Plato, who speaks of the demons in the *Symposium*, in the course of a discussion of the status of Eros, the god of love. This passage already contains most of the motifs of Middle Platonic demonology (*Symp.* 23 [202d–e]):

> For all that is demonic is something lying between the god and the human being ... It functions as interpreter and messenger from human beings to the gods, and from the gods to human beings. It brings prayers and sacrifices from human beings, from the gods it brings commands and rewards for the sacrifices. The demonic is the link that maintains the connection between the two, so that the universe is a firmly-established entity. Thanks to this demonic power, all visionary power too is kept in being, as well as the art of priests, both of those who have to do with sacrifices and initiation into the mysteries and of those who are skilled in consultations and magical arts of all kinds.

Accounts of journeys

According to *Ser. Num. Vind.* 30 and *Symp.* 23, demons are at work in visionary power and oracles. Plutarch speaks of this topic at greatest detail in *De Defectu Oraculorum* (409e–483e), the longest of his Pythian dialogues, in which, as priest at Delphi, he discusses questions concerning oracles in a conversation with his brother Lamprias, his teacher Ammonios, and others, who include the Spartan Kleombrotos, who has travelled round the world collecting religious knowledge, above all from the East. In *Def. Orac.* 10, he introduces the demons into a debate about the ways in which the god works, and presents a classification:

> It seems to me that a great dilemma was solved by those thinkers who posited the race of the demons between gods and human beings, thereby discovering a power that in a certain sense establishes and maintains a fellowship [κοινωνία] between us and them ... Hesiod was the first to list in clear and specific terms four classes of rational beings: gods, then demons, then heroes, and finally human beings. It is clear that he also assumes the possibility of a transformation ... As one sees water come into being out of earth, air out of water, and fire out of air, when the substance moves upwards, so the better souls accomplish a transformation from human beings into heroes, from heroes into demons. A very few of the demons, thanks to their great ability, have been purified and have become wholly sharers in the divinity.

Thus it is possible in individual cases for a human being to become a god, passing through the intermediary stages of hero and demon. But it is also possible for demons to sink back down into mortal bodies, and finally to die, even if only after millennia have passed.[36] Kleombrotos supports his assertions, which the others contest, by appealing to Plato's successor Xenocrates. Tradition says that he was the first to introduce evil demons into demonology, for a plausible apologetic reason: one need no longer attribute responsibility to the gods for all the raw cruelty in the myths and rites, for adultery, human sacrifice, and the dismembering of living animals, since this can be ascribed to demons whose character is inferior. This is what Kleombrotos does at *Def. Orac.* 13–15:

> As we find with human beings, so too there are differing measures of perfection among the demons. In some there dwells only a weak and insignificant remnant of passion and irrationality, like a kind of dregs, whereas in others there is a concentration of passion and irrationality, leaving traces that are difficult to erase. The sacrifices, the mysteries and the myths preserve many images and symbols of this, scattered in their performance and in their narrative (417b).

---

[36] An additional proof of this at *Def. Orac.* 17 (419a–e) is the singular narrative of the death of the great Pan. On this, cf. P. Borgeaud, 'La Mort du grand Pan: Problèmes d'interprétation', *RHR* 200 (1983) 3–39; G. A. Gerhard, *Der Tod des grossen Pan* (SHAW 1915, 5), Heidelberg 1915.

The things related and sung in myths and hymns – abductions, helpless wanderings of the gods, who conceal themselves and escape and are reduced to servitude – are not actual experiences and fates of gods, but rather of demons. They were not forgotten, thanks to the ability and power of those beings (417e).

If we return to the initial question, viz. why oracles are in decline at present, the conclusion is that the demons who perform the service of oracles have departed. Only when they return 'will the oracles sound forth again, like musical instruments when the artists come and play on them' (418d). Kleombrotos quotes at *Def. Orac.* 21 yet another exotic authority for his demonology, a wise man whom he himself had met at the Red Sea, a 'guru' from the East. The Greeks, grown pale and sick through intellectual work, will not be able to put up any resistance to his wisdom.

Alternative models
Now, however, Plutarch's brother Lamprias intervenes, observing in lapidary fashion that everything Kleombrotos has put forward is Greek thought, borrowed from Plato and Pythagoras. It has been presented as an exotic sapiential teaching, but he unmasks it as a plagiarism from Plato. Ammonios supports him. At §38, following Hesiod (*Op.* 125), he is willing to accept as 'demons' only 'souls [of the dead] that wander round cloaked in mist' (431b). Lamprias takes up this idea and develops at §§39–44 an alternative explanation of the silence of the oracles, linked to a theory of inspiration. If demons are nothing other than bodiless souls, then one may wonder why the soul in the body still has need of them. Does it not share in the prophetic power on its own account? Certainly, differences of degree do exist: the soul sits imprisoned in the body, and its powers of perception are dimmed. But a human soul can develop the prophetic power that has been bestowed on it, if favourable external circumstances exist. The soul provides the *pneuma*, which Lamprias defines as air, moisture and warmth. A stream of air and warmth floods the soul and causes orifices in it to open, so that images of future things can enter it. Vapour of this kind arises from a crevice in the earth in Delphi and inspires the soul of the Pythia for her activity. When these factors are altered by an event such as an earthquake, the oracle ceases to function.

Lamprias' ideas sound very materialistic and rationalistic; but when Ammonios laments at §46 that he has severed all connection between the gods and the oracles, and that even the demons, who did at any rate maintain a connection to the divine, have been eliminated, Lamprias says that this is a misunderstanding, and offers a compromise suggestion

425

(47–52). The inspiring vapours are generated by the earth and the sun, both of which are considered deities. The demons direct these vapours and ensure the correct mixture of warmth, dryness and moisture. Primary and secondary causes collaborate here. Natural predispositions, innerworldly factors and the control of these by the demons produce the oracle, which is rightly understood to be a divine utterance.

Plutarch's own position
Earlier scholars (e.g. Soury) quite straightforwardly understood Kleombrotos' lengthy statements as a normative doctrine which they ascribed to Plutarch himself. This then became a key to the correct understanding of other passages in his voluminous writings, so that they presented a broad panorama of popular belief in demons, supported by intellectual concepts from the Platonic tradition. Against this, a more convincing recent interpretation (Dörrie; Brenk) begins with the literary form of the dialogue and the persons who conduct it. If we assume (not implausibly) that Plutarch's brother Lamprias and his teacher Ammonios are putting their own positions forward, what then becomes of Kleombrotos? What Plutarch does when he portrays this personality is nothing less than a caricature, and at the same time a critique of second- and third-class revelation literature of his age. What offers itself as sapiential teaching from the far East is nothing more than Platonism dressed up with a dash of sensationalism, and it should be classed as literary rubbish. Kleombrotos is a 'charlatan on the periphery of Pythagoreanism' (Dörrie 105).

For Plutarch himself, the centre of demonology remains faith in the immortality of the soul, which can be transformed into a demonic being (in the neutral or the positive sense of this term), and ultimately even into the sphere of the divine. The attempt at a reconciliation between rationalism and exclusive transcendence in the conclusion to *Def. Orac.* reveals Plutarch to be a 'mediatory theologian', with all the strengths and with all the weaknesses that are characteristic of this position.

E. Retrospective

List 137.
D. L. Balch, 'Neopythagorean Moralists and the New Testament Household Codes', *ANRW* II/26.1 (1992) 380–411.

K. Berger, 'Hellenistische Gattungen im Neuen Testament', *ANRW* II/ 25.2 (1984) 1031–42.

H. Chadwick, *The Sentences of Sextus: A Contribution to the History of Early Christian Ethics* (TaS NS 5), Cambridge 1959.

M. L. Colish, 'Stoicism and the New Testament: An Essay in Historiography', *ANRW* II/26.1 (1992) 334–79.

C. E. Glad, *Paul and Philodemus* (L127).

A. J. Malherbe, 'Hellenistic Moralists and the New Testament', *ANRW* II/ 26.1 (1992) 267–333.

C. Markschies, 'Die platonische Metapher vom "inneren Menschen": eine Brücke zwischen antiker Philosophie und altkirchlicher Theologie', *ZKG* 105 (1994) 1–17.

A look back over the last pages confirms our initial supposition that the philosophy of the Hellenistic imperial period provides the most important and wide-reaching body of comparative material to help identify the position of early Christianity in intellectual and religious history. Possible points of contact go far beyond what we have been able to indicate above. Many of the literary forms employed in the New Testament, such as the apophthegmata, the catalogues of vices and virtues, and the household codes, could be investigated in terms of their antecedent history in philosophy, taking into account the possibility of a mediation by Hellenistic Judaism. Especially in the field of ethics, many scholarly works on the Graeco-Roman moral philosophers have already shown the existence of broad agreements, as well as contrasts (cf. Malherbe; Balch; Glad). It is, for example, a remarkable fact that Pythagorean material could be adapted for a rigorist Christian instruction *c*.200 CE in the *Sentences of Sextus* (Rufinus and Jerome disputed whether the author was the Roman Pope Sixtus II or a non-Christian Pythagorean with the same name). Much of early Christian reflection was carried on within the framework of Middle and Neoplatonism, and this permits us to glimpse a bridge that leads us to our last theme, viz. gnosis, for the question arises whether this phenomenon draws on a Platonic or (more accurately) a vulgar-Platonic inheritance.

It is necessary to make a nuanced judgement in the evaluation and explanation of the agreements. Conscious borrowings are probably the exception rather than the rule. A total reconstruction of the new Christian view of the world could not be the work of an instant; in the daily life of the newly converted Christians, codes that they had brought with them and that were presupposed as something taken for granted continued in force, thanks to their inherent plausibility. One must also reckon with the possibility of convergences that are due to the shared horizon of the period: 'In the milieu of early Christianity, often only half-educated, it is often precisely these *inherent convergences* that are a contributory factor to the legendary rise of Christianity in late antiquity. They are the reason why the pagan and the Christian worlds often lie so astonishingly close to one another; historically speaking, we shall never be able to explain this closeness completely' (Markschies 17).

Chapter VI
Return to the Divine Origin: The Gnostic Transformation

List 138 (collections of essays, congress volumes, Festschriften).

B. Aland (ed.), *Gnosis* (FS H. Jonas), Göttingen 1978.

ANRW II/22.1–2: Gnostizismus und Verwandtes (awaiting publication; contains about 40 essays).

U. Bianchi (ed.), *The Origins of Gnosticism: Colloquium of Messina, 13–18 April 1966* (SHR 12), Leiden 1967.

A. Böhlig, *Mysterion und Wahrheit: Gesammelte Beiträge zur spätantiken Religionsgeschichte* (AGSU 6), Leiden 1968.

——*Gnosis und Synkretismus: Gesammelte Aufsätze zur spätantiken Religionsgeschichte*, vols. 1–2 (WUNT 47/48), Tübingen 1989.

P. Koslowski (ed.), *Gnosis und Mystik in der Geschichte der Philosophie*, Munich 1988.

M. Krause (ed.), *Gnosis and Gnosticism* (NHS 8/17), Leiden 1977, 1981.

H. Langerbeck, *Aufsätze zur Gnosis*, ed. H. Dörrie (AAWG.PH 3.69), Göttingen 1967.

B. Layton (ed.), *The Rediscovery of Gnosticism*, vols. 1–2 (SHR 41), Leiden 1980, 1981.

A. H. B. Logan and A. J. M. Wedderburn (eds.), *The New Testament and Gnosis* (FS R. McL. Wilson), Edinburgh 1983.

B. A. Pearson, *Gnosticism, Judaism, and Egyptian Christianity* (Studies in Antiquity and Christianity), Minneapolis 1990.

J. Ries, Y. Janssens and J. M. Sevrin (eds.), *Gnosticisme et monde hellénistique: Actes du Colloque de Louvain-la-Neuve (11–14 mars 1980)* (PIOL 27), Louvain-la-Neuve 1982.

K. Rudolph (ed.), *Gnosis und Gnostizismus* (WdF 262), Darmstadt 1975 (the breadth and wealth of material in this one book is the equivalent of a small library).

——*Gnosis und spätantike Religionsgeschichte: Gesammelte Aufsätze* (NHS 42), Leiden 1996.

D. M. Scholer (ed.), *Studies in Early Christianity: A Collection of Scholarly Essays*, vol. 5: *Gnosticism in the Early Church*, New York and London 1993.

A. The question at issue

1. On the relevance of this topic

List 139.

N. Brox, *Erleuchtung und Wiedergeburt: Aktualität der Gnosis*, Munich 1989.

M. Brumlik, *Die Gnostiker: Der Traum von der Selbsterlösung des Menschen*, Frankfurt a.M. 1992.

K. Dietzfelbinger, *Apokryphe Evangelien aus Nag Hammadi* (Edition Argo. Weisheit im Abendland), Andechs 1988.

W. Jaeschke, 'Gnostizismus – Ein Schlagwort zwischen geschichtlicher Aufklärung und Häresiomachie', *ABG* 28 (1984) 269–80.

H.-J. Klauck, 'Gnosis als Weltanschauung in der Antike', *WiWei* 56 (1993) 3–15, also in Idem, *Alte Welt* (L80) 163–79.

E. Pagels, *The Gnostic Gospels*, New York 1979.

P. Sloterdijk and T. H. Macho (eds.), *Weltrevolution der Seele: Ein Lese- und Arbeitsbuch der Gnosis von der Spätantike bis zur Gegenwart*, Zurich 1993.

J. Taubes (ed.), *Religionstheorie und Politische Theologie*, vol. 2: *Gnosis und Politik*, Munich and Paderborn 1984.

The collection of studies of gnosis by the American scholar Elaine Pagels mentioned in List 139 appeared in a paperback edition in German translation under the title 'Versuchung durch Erkenntnis', i.e. 'Temptation by means of knowledge' (st 1456, Frankfurt a.M. 1987). This was an apt title, since the Greek word γνῶσις means precisely 'knowledge'. But since the knowledge of God is a desirable goal in life for the Bible too, there must be something more than this, before gnosis can be distinguished from Judaism and Christianity in the classical period as a specific form of religious world-view. Our first question will be the identification of this specific element. We introduce this section with another observation, namely that gnosis appears to be still (or once again) relevant today, as one may see from the paperbacks that are published on gnostic themes, journalistic attempts at a panoramic presentation drawing on Heidegger,

Bultmann and Jung (cf. Brumlik), the publication of texts from Nag Hammadi in a collection that has an esoteric flair about it (cf. Dietzfelbinger), and last but not least the existence of a popular reader which employs selected texts to cast a bridge across the span separating late antiquity from the present day (cf. Sloterdijk and Macho). What is the source of this sudden interest? Instead of answering this question directly, let us begin with two texts, one from classical antiquity, the other from the twentieth century:

> Who are we?
> Where do we come from?
> Where are we going?
> What are we waiting for?
> What awaits us?

> Who were we?
> What have we become?
> Where were we?
> Whither have we been thrown?
> Whither are we hastening?
> Whence have we been set free?
> What is birth, what is rebirth?

Both texts pose the question of the being of human persons, their origin and future, their expectation from life, subjectively and objectively considered; and both sound very modern, each in its own way. The first quotation is from the introduction to Ernst Bloch's philosophical *chef d'œuvre*, *The Principle of Hope*,[1] the second from Clement of Alexandria (*c*.200 CE), in his *Excerpta ex Theodoto*, a collection of statements by various gnostic teachers.[2] The interest of this second text for us lies in the fact that it is identified in context as a definition of gnosis: the knowledge that confers freedom consists in knowing the answer to these seven questions.

The agreement with fundamental themes of modern philosophy is certainly striking, and prompts the following question: do we have here the continued vigour of gnostic ideas (in a hidden manner) in modern thinking, or are the similar questions and answers generated by similarities

---

[1] E. Bloch, *The Principle of Hope*, Oxford 1986, 3.

[2] Clement of Alexandria, *Exc. Theod.* 78.2 (131.17–19 GCS 17, 2nd edn. Stählin-Früchtel): τίνες ἦμεν, τί γεγόναμεν, ποῦ ἦμεν, [ἢ] ποῦ ἐνεβλήθημεν, ποῦ σπεύδομξν, πόθεν λυτρούμεθα, τί γέννησις, τί ἀναγέννησις.

between the way in which the gnostics in the classical period and people today experience the world and their own selves? Bloch continues in the passage quoted above: 'The only feeling many people have is one of confusion. The earth shakes under their feet, but they do not know the reason, or what moves it. This state is anxiety, and if it becomes more specific, it is fear.' The feeling of anxiety and of being threatened in the world as it exists is extremely strong in gnosis, which affirms that it experiences this world as a prison. This shows us that the study of gnosis has also an element relevant to today, and can help us to understand our own period. Much of what is marketed today under the slogans of esoterica, self-experience, dropping-out, and the return to mythical thinking would certainly deserve to be labelled 'gnostic' if considered under the categories of the history of religions, although one may well agree with Jaeschke's warning that one should not extend this concept too vigorously.

2. A description of the phenomenon

Let us remain with the *Excerpta ex Theodoto* for a little longer, and attempt to employ this text to determine more precisely the contours of the phenomenon of 'gnosis'. We can discern three temporal stages in the quotation in Clement of Alexandria. The questions, 'Who were we?', 'Where were we?', are addressed to a distant past. The questions, 'What have we become?', 'Whither have we been thrown?', likewise look to a point in the past, but to a point with immediate impact on the present life of those who put the questions: we are now what we have become; it is into this existence that we have been thrown. But there is also a way out, and a future: 'Whither are we hastening?' And for those who put the questions, this future already reaches into the present: 'Whence have we been set free?' In individual terms, being 'thrown' concerns birth, while being freed correspondingly concerns rebirth. Thus a path is outlined which can be described as follows: once there existed an ideal primal state, out of which we have been thrown into this existence. The present state is indeed wretched, looked at from the outside, but not completely without hope: liberation is a reality, there is a goal and the possibility of regaining the lost primal state. The path to this goal is called gnosis, knowledge, insight into the true state of affairs and into the true essence of things.

Up to this point, it all sounds fairly unproblematic. One could perfectly well summarise the path of the fallen human being too, in the Bible's perspective, like this: paradise, fall, redemption through Christ, return into heaven after death, end of the world with the restoration of the original perfection. Why do all the Church fathers agree in portraying gnosis as a heresy? The answer is to be found in a special element in this 'knowing' that has given the whole movement its name. Knowing has exclusive soteriological significance. Soteriological, because the possession and acquiring of knowledge are salvific per se: this knowledge is all that is required for salvation, everything else is inessential trimmings. And exclusive, because whoever possesses this knowledge is saved, while all who lack it are damned. This divides the human race into two categories, the gnostics and the non-gnostics. Thus knowledge has a sharply defined esoteric character. Finally, we can note another perspective. The question, 'Whither have we been thrown?', indicates a negative evaluation of the present state. It is not, however, the present state of the world, nor human existence in its bodiliness and historicity, that is capable of redemption and that needs redemption, but only an intellectual substratum of the gnostic, the kernel of his being in which he possesses and acquires knowledge. This is sometimes called the 'soul', but strictly speaking, even this says too much, since gnosis is characterised by a rigorous dualism that devalues all that is material and bodily. All this must be overcome, since the primal state to which we wish to return was immaterial and bodiless, characterised by pure intellectuality.

Behind the apparently simple questions of the *Excerpta ex Theodoto*, we gradually discern the outlines of a cosmic drama of the fall and rise of the soul. The gnostic writings portray this drama with the help of an exuberant mythology. The simplicity of the questions quoted above is deceptive, since they cannot be taken as a criterion for gnostic thought as a whole. The first time one reads original gnostic texts, the usual effect is a strong feeling of being on alien territory. Gnostic texts are especially in need of laborious and patient interpretation, if they are to be understood aright, and this is quite apart from the linguistic barriers – the scholar of gnosis ought at least to know Coptic, in addition to Greek and Latin.

3. Relationship to the New Testament

List 140.

R. Bultmann, 'Die Bedeutung der neuerschlossenen mandäischen und manichäischen Quellen für das Verständnis des Johannesevangeliums',

ZNW 24 (1925) 100–46, also in Idem, *Exegetica: Aufsätze zur Erforschung des Neuen Testaments*, Tübingen 1967, 55–104.

——'Johanneische Schriften und Gnosis', *OLZ* 43 (1940) 150–75, also in *Exegetica* (see above) 230–54.

C. Colpe, *Die religionsgeschichtliche Schule: Darstellung und Kritik ihres Bildes vom gnostischen Erlösermythus* (FRLANT 78), Göttingen 1961.

G. Haufe, 'Gnostische Irrlehre und ihre Abwehr in den Pastoralbriefen', in K. W. Tröger, *Gnosis und NT* (see below) 325–39.

P. Perkins, *Gnosticism and the New Testament*, Minneapolis 1993.

J. Roloff, *Der erste Brief an Timotheus* (EKK 15), Zurich and Neukirchen-Vluyn 1988, 230–9.

W. Schmithals, *Gnosticism in Corinth: An Investigation of the Letters to the Corinthians*, Nashville 1971.

——'Gnosis und Neues Testament', *VuF* 21 (1976) Heft 2, 22–46.

——*Neues Testament und Gnosis* (EdF 208), Darmstadt 1984.

K. W. Tröger (ed.), *Gnosis und Neues Testament: Studien aus Religionswissenschaft und Theologie*, Gütersloh 1973.

——*Altes Testament – Frühjudentum – Gnosis: Neue Studien zu 'Gnosis und Bibel'*, Gütersloh 1980.

What has been said above has not yet answered the question why one studying the New Testament should be concerned with the study of gnosis. Let us begin with the late, deutero-Pauline Pastoral Letters.

At 1 Tim 6:20 we read: 'Timothy, guard what has been entrusted to you. Avoid the profane chatter and contradictions of what is falsely called knowledge [γνῶσις]; by professing it some have missed the mark as regards the faith.' The three Letters attack an erroneous doctrine which the author calls 'gnosis'; this has gained a foothold in the Christian communities which he knows. At Tit 1:16 (a passage drawing on stereotypical elements of the polemic against heretics), we are told that: 'They profess to know God, but they deny him by their actions. They are detestable, disobedient, unfit for any good work.' Further indications of the substance of their teaching are given. There is doubtless a Jewish element, even if one should not overestimate its significance, cf. above all, apart from Tit 1:10f., the fatal interest in 'Jewish myths' (μῦθοι) noted by the author at Tit 1:14. We find the same word 'myths' at 1 Tim 1:3f.: 'Instruct certain people not to teach any different doctrine, and not to occupy themselves with myths [μῦθοι] and endless genealogies [γενεαλογίαι] that promote speculations rather than the divine training that is known by faith.' These myths and genealogies may perhaps have been speculations about the origin and destiny of humanity and of the cosmos, no doubt with their starting point in the corresponding Old Testament traditions, but unmistakably developed in a direction of their own. These heretics reject marriage and other things: 'They forbid marriage and demand abstinence from foods, which God created to be received with thanksgiving by those who believe and know the truth' (1 Tim 4:3). Knowledge of the truth is here reserved pointedly for the genuine believers. The taboos on food probably concern primarily meat and wine. The presupposition of both forms of this ascetic tendency, the sexual and the 'gastronomic', is a devaluation of created reality. According to 2 Tim 2:18, Hymenaeus and Philetus, two representatives of this group, 'claim that the resurrection has already taken place'. The point of this may be a denial of bodily resurrection, which a dualistic world-view could not find a desirable goal. These words may also reflect a consciousness of perfection, which no longer awaited the fulfilment of redemption as something belonging to the future, but saw it as something already realised in the present.

Thus we find in the Pastoral Letters $c.100-10$ CE representatives of an early form of Christian gnosis (cf. Haufe; Roloff). But how far back may one trace its presence? Was, for example, Simon Magus in Acts 8 really already the first head of a gnostic school, something later Christian writers made him out to be (see below B, 2(*a*))? Rudolf Bultmann's writings have given the theme of gnosis a particular significance for Johannine exegesis, since he holds that the writer of St John's gospel projected on to the historical Jesus of Nazareth a fully fledged gnostic redeemer-myth in which the heavenly revealer descends to earth, takes on human form for a period and then returns above. This would confront the modern interpreter with the hermeneutical task of cutting back the remnants of mythical language to free the existential contents, which would be the evangelist's true intention. Bultmann's pupil Walter Schmithals has made this task his own, defending in numerous publications the thesis that the enemies of Paul in Corinth and elsewhere were likewise genuine gnostics with a Jewish past. This means that the interpreter of the Letters to the Corinthians is suddenly confronted with the same challenge to take gnosis into account.

While it is true that these far-reaching hypotheses have not withstood the test of a thorough examination (cf. Colpe), it is also true that one senses in the attitude of the Corinthian enthusiasts with whom Paul debates a number of traits that recall the later gnosis, and it remains at the very least worth asking whether the Johannine writings in their final phase are involved in a defensive fight against gnostic tendencies. Thus, New Testament exegesis cannot avoid gnosis, especially since scholarly discussion makes it clear that the contrary assertion (equally radical in its own way), viz. that there is no reflection at all of gnosticism in the New Testament, cannot simply be put forward, but must be backed by genuine competence in this field. The meagre amount of agreement reached on such an important point reflects the state of our sources, and the problems of origins which these pose.

B. State of the sources and problems of origins

List 141 (panoramic presentations, scholarly reports, collections of texts).

K. Berger and R. McL. Wilson, 'Gnosis/Gnostizismus', *TRE* 13 (1984) 519–50.

R. van den Broek, 'The Present State of Gnostic Studies', *VigChr* 37 (1983) 41–71.

C. Colpe, 'Gnosis II (Gnostizismus)', *RAC* 11 (1981) 537–659.

G. Filoramo, *A History of Gnosticism*, Oxford 1990.

W. Foerster (ed.), *Gnosis*, vols. 1–2, Oxford 1972, 1974.

R. Haardt, *Gnosis: Character and Testimony*, Leiden 1971.

W. Hörmann, *Gnosis: Das Buch der verborgenen Evangelien*, Augsburg 1989.

H. Jonas, *The Gnostic Religion: The Message of the Alien God and the Beginnings of Christianity*, Boston 3rd edn. 1970.

K. Latte, *Religion* (L4) 56–85.

B. Layton, *The Gnostic Scriptures: A New Translation with Annotations and Introductions*, Garden City, NY 1987.

H. Leisegang, *Die Gnosis* [1924] (KTA 32), Stuttgart 5th edn. 1985.

A. H. B. Logan, *Gnostic Truth and Christian Heresy: A Study in the History of Gnosticism*, Edinburgh 1996.

G. Quispel, *Gnosis als Weltreligion: Die Bedeutung der Gnosis in der Antike*, Zurich 2nd edn. 1972.

K. Rudolph, *Gnosis: The Nature and History of an Ancient Religion*, Edinburgh 1983 (standard work).

H. M. Schenke, 'Die Gnosis', *UUC* I.371–415; II.350–470.

W. Schultz, *Dokumente der Gnosis*, Jena 1910, reprint (with additional essays) Munich 1986.

See also L149 and L150.

1. The sources

(a) Church fathers

List 142.

B. Aland, 'Gnosis und Kirchenväter: Ihre Auseinandersetzung um die Interpretation des Evangeliums', in Idem, *Gnosis* (L138) 158–215.

N. Brox, *Irenäus von Lyon: Adversus Haereses/Gegen die Häresien* (FC 8.1–5), Freiburg i.Br. 1993ff. (Greek text with German trans.; Eng. trans. *The Ante-Nicene Fathers*, vol. 1, reprint Grand Rapids 1973).

H. Cancik, 'Gnostiker in Rom: Zur Religionsgeschichte der Stadt Rom im 2. Jahrhundert nach Christus', in: J. Taubes, *Gnosis* (L139) 163–84.

W. Foerster, *Gnosis* (L141), I: *Patristic Evidence*.

J. Mansfeld, *Heresiography in Context: Hippolytos' Elenchos as a Source for Greek Philosophy* (PhAnt 56), Leiden 1992.

M. Marcovich, *Hippolytus: Refutatio omnium haeresium* (PTS 25), Berlin 1986.

W. Völker, *Quellen zur Geschichte der christlichen Gnosis* (SQS NF 5), Tübingen 1932.

F. Williams, *The Panarion of Epiphanius of Salamis, Book I (Sects 1–46)* (NHS 35), Leiden 1987.

A. Wlosok, *Laktanz und die philosophische Gnosis: Untersuchungen zu Geschichte und Terminologie der gnostischen Erlösungsvorstellung* (SHAW.PH 1960,2), Heidelberg 1960.

The definition of gnosis in the *Excerpta ex Theodoto* which formed our starting point was not available to us in the original: we took it from a work by Clement of Alexandria. This state of affairs is symptomatic: for a long period, access to gnostic thinkers was possible virtually only via the accounts which the Church fathers gave of them. The most important of these here are Irenaeus of Lyons and Hippolytus of Rome. Irenaeus composed his work *Adversus Haereses c.*180–85 CE, aiming in his own words to 'unmask and refute the gnosis which is falsely given this name'. In his first book he presents the gnostic schools with their teachings and attempts to bring order into this whole area. Shortly after 222 CE Hippolytus composed his *Refutatio Omnium Haeresium*, which likewise is chiefly concerned with the refutation of gnosis; his authorship of this work seems not entirely certain. He derives the gnostic systems from pagan, i.e. Greek, philosophy. In the fourth century these two writers were joined by Epiphanius of Salamis, who composed an ample history of heresies. We also find scattered quotations and polemical passages to a lesser extent in other fathers, especially in Tertullian, Clement and Origen; and in the case of the Manichaeans, in Augustine. Taken together, the original gnostic texts which this indirect path makes available to us amount to no more than about one hundred printed pages (they are collected, e.g. by Völker and Foerster).

The problem involved in working with the Church fathers is obvious: their intention is not to deliver a neutral observation of facts, but to fight polemically against heretics, and this is why they blacken their opponents completely, not even shying away from personal insinuations. The result is necessarily a distorted image, and this means that one must study the patristic testimonies in the light of the authors' tendencies: when allowance is made for the polemical intention, what usable substantial information remains? Read in this way, the patristic texts remain an indispensable source for gnosis, and the discoveries at Nag Hammadi (see below) have confirmed anew that much of what Irenaeus says is correct. A further point is that we can also discern from the Church fathers' discussion of gnosis what they themselves, as representatives of orthodoxy, took to be the specific distinction between their own position and gnosis. Besides this, one must examine the Christian tradition to see how much gnostic thought it adopted despite its own intention, and despite every attempt to contradict gnosis – and how much became a part of the fundamental structure of Christian thought, especially in the sphere of hostility to the body and rejection of the world.

(b) Apocryphal texts

List 143.

G. Bornkamm, *Mythos und Legende in den apokryphen Thomas-Akten: Beiträge zur Geschichte der Gnosis und zur Vorgeschichte des Manichäismus* (FRLANT 49), Göttingen 1993.

F. Bovon et al., *Les Actes apocryphes des Apôtres: Christianisme et monde païen* (PFTUG 4), Geneva 1981.

E. Hennecke and W. Schneemelcher, *New Testament Apocrypha*, vols. 1–2, London 1963.

E. Junod and J. D. Kaestli, *Acta Johannis*, vols. 1–2 (CChr.SA 1–2), Turnhout 1981.

A. F. J. Klijn, *The Acts of Thomas: Introduction – Text – Commentary* (NT.S 5), Leiden 1962.

M. Lattke, *Die Oden Salomos in ihrer Bedeutung für Neues Testament und Gnosis*, vols. 1–3 (OBO 25.1–3), Fribourg (Switzerland) and Göttingen 1979–86.

R. A. Lipsius, *Die apokryphen Apostelgeschichten und Apostellegenden: Ein Beitrag zur altchristlichen Literaturgeschichte*, vols. I–II/1.2, Brunswick 1883–1890.

R. A. Lipsius and M. Bonnet, *Acta Apostolorum Apocrypha*, vols. I–II/2, Leipzig 1891–1903, reprint Hildesheim 1972.

D. R. MacDonald (ed.), *The Apocryphal Acts of Apostles* = Semeia 38, Decatur, Ga. 1986.

If we prescind from the discovery at Nag Hammadi of works attributed to apostles, and simply take the earlier state of knowledge as our starting point, we see that many of the often very vivid narratives collected by Hennecke and Schneemelcher as *New Testament Apocrypha* display a gnostic colouring. They were read, used, and handed on in gnostic groups, and it is clear that they also served as a vehicle to bring gnostic ideas to a wider circle of Christian readers. This classification is exemplified above all in two texts from the second or third century CE, viz. (1) the Acts of John, above all the hymn of Christ and the passage about the cross of light (ActJoh 94–102), and (2) the Acts of Thomas with the celebrated Song of the Pearl (see D below; both Acts are translated in Hennecke and Schneemelcher, II). When the text of the forty-two poems from the second century CE called the 'Odes of Solomon' was discovered in 1909 (see Lattke; Eng. trans.: J. H. Charlesworth, *The Odes of Solomon*, Oxford 1973), they were thought to be the hymnal of a gnostic community in Asia Minor. The poetic language, rich in images, remains however open to various interpretations, and is only of limited value in the attempt to reconstruct the underlying theology; a fortiori, it gives very little information about ritual practices.

(*c*) Hermetic writings

List 144.

H. D. Betz, 'Hermetism and Gnosticism: The Question of the *Poimandres*', in Idem, *Antike und Christentum* (L3), 206–21.

R. van den Broek and W. J. Hanegraaff (eds.), *Gnosis and Hermeticism from Antiquity to Modern Times*, Albana 1998.

J. Büchli, *Der Poimandres, ein paganisiertes Evangelium: Sprachliche und begriffliche Untersuchungen zum 1. Traktat des Corpus Hermeneuticum* (WUNT 2.27), Tübingen 1987.

A. J. Festugière, *La Révélation d'Hermès Trismégiste*, vols. 1–4 (EtB), Paris 1949–54.

A. Gonzales Blanco, 'Hermetism: A Bibliographical Approach', *ANRW* II/ 17.4 (1984) 2240–81.

W. C. Grese, *Corpus Hermeticum XIII and Early Christian Literature* (SCHNT 5), Leiden 1979.

G. F. G. Heinrici, *Die Hermes-Mystik und das Neue Testament* (Arbeiten zur Religionsgeschichte des Urchristentums 1.1), Leipzig 1918.

J. Holzhausen and C. Colpe, *Das Corpus Hermeticum Deutsch*, vols. 1–2, (Clavis Pansophiae 7.1–2), Stuttgart-Bad Canstatt 1997 (vol. 3 in preparation).

J. P. Mahé, *Hermès en Haute-Égypte*, vols. 1–2 (BCNH.T 3 and 7), Québec 1978 and 1982.

G. van Moorsel, *The Mysteries of Hermes Trismegistus: A phenomenologic study in the process of spiritualisation in the Corpus Hermeticum and Latin Asclepius* (STRT 1), Utrecht 1955.

A. D. Nock and A. J. Festugière, *Corpus Hermeticum*, vols. 1–4 (CUFr), Paris 2nd–4th edn. 1972–78, often reprinted.

B. A. Pearson, 'Jewish Elements in Corpus Hermeticum I (Poimandres)', in R. van den Broek and M. J. Vermaseren, *Studies* (L2) 336–48.

R. Reitzenstein, *Poimandres: Studien zur griechisch-ägyptischen und früh-christlichen Literatur*, Leipzig 1904, reprint Darmstadt 1966.

K. W. Tröger, *Mysterienglaube und Gnosis im Corpus Hermeticum XIII* (TU 110), Berlin 1971.

Another group of writings, likewise from the second or more probably the third century CE, had long been available to scholars; these writings enjoyed great respect, especially in the period of the Renaissance. They are called the 'Corpus Hermeticum' after the god Hermes who imparts secret revelations in these writings to selected pupils (our word 'hermetic' – as in 'hermetically sealed' – is derived from this). Closer examination shows that the name Hermes is only an alternative term for Thoth, the Egyptian god of wisdom. The Hermetica are an Egyptian work, probably written in Alexandria. They represent a particular type of pagan revelation literature with a basis in vulgar Platonism, which promises to communicate a knowledge surrounded by mysteries. Formally speaking, this brings it close to gnosis. An explicitly dualistic orientation can be seen above all in the first tractate, the *Poimandres* (a word interpreted in popular etymology as 'pastor of human beings'). The Nag Hammadi discoveries also include a Coptic translation of some portions of the Hermetic writings, which were originally composed in Greek (see Mahé).

It has often been claimed that *Poimandres* is an example of a purely pagan, or even a pre-Christian gnosis; at most, it has been admitted that the text borrows from the Septuagint. Büchli has recently rejected this thesis, arguing that while the author of *Poimandres* knows the Gospel of John and other writings, and the gnostic elements were mediated to him by Alexandrian theologians like Clement and Origen, he writes consciously as a pagan, from a Platonic philosophical standpoint, in order to get the better of a Christianity that increasingly made use of Platonic intellectual models for the elaboration of its own theology. This thesis cannot yet be called certain; but in view of the date of the Hermetica, it does not seem impossible. At any rate, the Hermetic writings cannot serve as principal witness to a gnosis exterior to or chronologically antecedent to Christianity.

This brings us to other groups of texts, some newly discovered, others already known but interpreted linguistically only in our century: Mandaean and Manichaean original texts and the discovery of texts at Nag Hammadi. These have provided a new basis for the study of gnosticism.

(d) Mandaeans

List 145.
E. S. Drower, *The Canonical Prayerbook of the Mandaeans*, Leiden 1959.
M. Lidzbarski, *Mandäische Liturgien* (AGWG.PH 17.1), Berlin 1920, reprint Göttingen 1970.
——*Ginza: Der Schatz oder das grosse Buch der Mandäer* (QRG 13.4), Göttingen 1925, reprint 1978.
——*Das Johannesbuch der Mandäer*, Giessen 1915, reprint Berlin 1966.
E. Lupieri, *I Mandei: Gli ultimi gnostici* (BCR 61), Brescia 1993.
K. Rudolph, *Die Mandäer*, vols. 1–2 (FRLANT 74/75), Göttingen 1960/61.
——'Mandean Sources', in W. Foerster, *Gnosis* (L141) II.

The Mandaeans form an ancient religious community which still exists today, although it is threatened with extinction. Between five thousand and fifteen thousand adherents – the numbers given vary – live in southern Iraq. They employ a language of their own – Mandaean, a dialect of

441

eastern Aramaic – for their sacred writings. Their self-designation 'Man-daean' is derived from a root that means 'gnostic', 'one possessing knowledge'. Scholars see the Mandaeans as the last surviving witnesses of gnosticism to preserve a continuity with its origins (cf. Lupieri).

The oldest Mandaean texts received their written form in the third or fourth century CE; a longer oral prehistory of the material is possible, but difficult to establish. After the pioneering translation work by Mark Lidzbarski, it is above all Kurt Rudolph who has opened up their writings in terms both of content and of the history of tradition; Lady Drower studied their religious praxis in detail. These show that the Mandaeans are a cultic fellowship with baptism at its centre. This is celebrated repeatedly and with great solemnity in flowing water, i.e. in a river or the branch of a river. Their cultic language always calls this river 'Jordan'. This may permit us to deduce that the Mandaeans derive from the pluriform baptist movement in the Jordan area in the first century CE; they would then have settled in Mesopotamia in the second century, and have come into contact with Syriac Christianity at a secondary stage; later still, they would have come into contact with Islam.

(e) Manichaeans

List 146.

A. Adam, *Texte zum Manichäismus* (KIT 175), Berlin 2nd edn. 1969.

A. Böhlig, *Die Gnosis*, Vol. III: *Der Manichäismus* (BAW), Zurich and Munich 1980, reprint 1995.

———and C. Markschies, *Gnosis und Manichäismus: Forschungen und Studien zu Texten von Valentin und Mani sowie zu den Bibliotheken von Nag Hammadi und Medinet Madi* (BZNW 72), Berlin 1994, esp. 243–82.

R. Cameron and A. J. Dewey, *The Cologne Mani Codex 'Concerning the Origin of His Body'* (SBL.TT 15), Missoula 1979.

I. Gardner, *The Kephalaia of the Teacher: The Edited Coptic Manichaean Texts in Translation with Commentary* (NHS 37), Leiden 1995.

A. Henrichs and L. Koenen (eds.), *Der Kölner Mani-Kodex: Über das Werden seines Leibes* (PapyCol 14), Opladen 1988.

R. Jolivet and M. Jouron, *Augustin: Six traités anti-manichéens* (BAug: Oeuvres 17), Paris 1961.

S. N. C. Lieu, *Manichaeism in the Later Roman Empire and Medieval China* (WUNT 63), Tübingen 2nd edn. 1993.

G. Widengren (ed.), *Der Manichäismus* (WdF 168), Darmstadt 1977.

We are better informed about the origin of the Manichaeans, because we know their founder Mani. He was born in Mesopotamia in 216 CE and died in prison as a martyr for his faith in 276/7. His father was a member of the Jewish-Christian baptist sect of the Elchasaites, in which Mani grew up. Already in his early years, a prophetic self-consciousness nourished on visions made Mani the successful founder of a new religion. He himself composed several books in order to define precisely the foundations of the new faith, but unfortunately none of these has survived. We do however have original writings from the later community, which became accessible only in the twentieth century. They were discovered in excavations in widely separated areas, e.g. in the oasis of Turfan in eastern Turkistan and in Medinet Madi in Egypt, and in languages that are unrelated to one another (e.g. Coptic, Iranian, Old Turkish, Chinese), and this fact suffices to show the broad diffusion of Manichaeism. It was also found in north Africa, where Augustine was an adherent for almost twenty years. Manichaeism is an example of how church organisation and practical living could look when everything was interpreted in gnostic terms.

(f) Nag Hammadi

List 147 (texts and translations).

ARE–UNESCO, *The Facsimile Edition of the Nag Hammadi Codices*, ed. J. M. Robinson, vols. 1–12, Leiden 1972–84.

R. Kasser et al., *Tractatus Tripartitus*, vols. 1–2, Berne 1973, 1975 (the so-called Codex Jung).

M. Krause, 'Coptic Sources', in W. Foerster, *Gnosis* (L141) II.

J. Leipoldt and H. M. Schenke, *Koptisch-gnostische Schriften aus den Papyrus-Codices von Nag Hammadi* (ThF 20), Hamburg and Bergstedt 1960.

M. Malinine et al., *Evangelium Veritatis* (SJI 6), Zurich 1956, with supplement 1961 (the so-called Codex Jung).

J. M. Robinson (ed.), *The Nag Hammadi Library in English*, Leiden and San Francisco 3rd edn. 1988 (hereafter: *NHLibrary*).

C. Schmidt, W. C. Till and H. M. Schenke, *Koptisch-gnostische Schriften*, I: *Die Pistis Sophia. Die beiden Bücher des Jeû. Unbekanntes altgnostisches Werk* [1905] (GCS 45), Berlin 4th edn. 1981.

C. Schmidt and V. MacDermot, *Pistis Sophia* (NHS 9), Leiden 1978 (with Eng. tr.).

——*The Books of Jeû and the Untitled Text in the Bruce Codex* (NHS 13), Leiden 1978 (with Eng. trans.).

443

W. C. Till and H. M. Schenke, *Die gnostischen Schriften des koptischen Papyrus Berolinensis 8502* (TU 60/2), Berlin 2nd edn. 1972. A selection in Eng. trans. also in Hennecke and Schneemelcher, *NT Apocrypha* (L143).

Bilingual editions of the individual treatises in the as yet incomplete collection *Nag Hammadi Studies: The Coptic Gnostic Library* and *Bibliothèque Copte de Nag Hammadi: Textes*. A complete German translation is planned for the collection *Griechisch-christliche Schriftsteller*. Preliminary studies can be found in *Texte und Untersuchungen*.

More detailed bibliographies are given below for some individual texts *(AJ* in L152; StelSeth in L156; EvPhil in L157). Because it is so well known, there is no individual discussion of EvThom here; see Fieger and Scholer in L148.

List 148 (secondary literature).

B. Barc (ed.), *Colloque international sur les Textes de Nag Hammadi (Québec, 22–25 août 1978)* (BCNH 1), Québec and Louvain 1981.

O. Betz, 'Das Problem der Gnosis seit der Entdeckung der Texte von Nag Hammadi', *VuF* 21 (1976) Heft 2, 46–80.

M. Fieger, *Das Thomasevangelium: Einleitung, Kommentar und Systematik* (NTA NF 22), Münster 1991.

C. W. Hedrick and R. Hodgson, Jr. (eds.), *Nag Hammadi, Gnosticism, and Early Christinity*, Peabody, Mass. 1986.

H. J. Klauck, 'Die Himmelfahrt des Paulus (2 Kor 12,2–4) in der koptischen Paulusapokalypse aus Nag Hammadi (NHC V/2)', in Idem, *Gemeinde* (L59) 391–429.

——'Die dreifache Maria: Zur Rezeption von Joh 19,25 in EvPhil 32', in Idem, *Alte Welt* (L80) 145–62.

B. A. Pearson, 'Nag Hammadi', *ABD* 4 (1992) 982–93.

H. W. Schenke, 'Nag Hammadi', *TRE* 23 (1994) 731–6.

D. M. Scholer, *Nag Hammadi Bibliography 1948–1969* (NHS 1), Leiden 1972; *1970–1994* (NHS 32), Leiden 1997, with yearly continuations covering the entire field of gnosis in the periodical *Novum Testamentum*.

C. Scholten, *Martyrium und Sophiamythos im Gnostizismus nach den Texten von Nag Hammadi* (JAC.E 14), Münster 1987.

——'Die Nag-Hammadi-Texte als Buchbesitz der Pachomianer', *JAC* 31 (1988) 144–72.

Numerous individual volumes in the series *Nag Hammadi Studies*.

Gnostic writings in the Egyptian Coptic language were already discovered in the first half of our century, and made accessible to a wide readership by C. Schmidt and W. C. Till. These include the *Pistis Sophia*, the *Books of Jeû* and the four tractates of the so-called Papyrus Berolinensis Gnosticus (BG; see above in L147 under Till). These texts are linked to the sensational discovery at Nag Hammadi by the Coptic language, the fact of their discovery in Egypt and the substantial overlaps in their contents.

Nag Hammadi is the name of an insignificant place on the upper reaches of the Nile, about one hundred kilometres north of Luxor. About ten kilometres from here, on the opposite bank of the Nile, fellahin discovered by chance a hidden pottery jug in 1945, which contained a large store of manuscripts. When conservation had been carried out and the contents examined, the following picture resulted. The discovery comprised thirteen codices with a total of about fifty-two individual texts (the number depends on the method of counting them) on about twelve hundred pages. Some of the codices are in a very poor condition; it is reckoned that about 10 per cent of the contents is lost. The texts were written in Coptic on papyrus. The writing of the codices can be dated rather exactly to the period around 350 CE, but this does not indicate any judgement about the date of the individual texts, most (and perhaps all) of which were translated from Greek and were composed in the second and third centuries CE. Parts of this material were already known in another version or at least under another name, but more than forty of these texts present completely new material that was previously unknown.

In terms of their contents the Nag Hammadi writings are religious treatises which to a considerable extent (though not exclusively) proclaim gnostic ideas. In many cases this is either a Christian gnosis or a gnosis that has been Christianised at a later stage; in some cases it is relatively easy to detach the layer of Christianisation. The Old Testament is extensively employed and expounded in some texts, but seems completely unknown in other tractates. Besides this, Homer and Greek philosophy are quoted and utilised.

How does such a complete library come into existence? Why was it hidden in a cemetery? It is probable that the codices belonged to the library of a Christian community of monks, either because these writings were collected there to provide a better basis to study and fight against gnosticism (although it is not so easy in this case to explain why they were concealed), or because they were employed in the monastery as theological reading and edifying literature, so that they would attest the existence of a heterodox, gnostic tendency in Egyptian Christianity. On this second view, the monastic librarian would have brought his treasures to a safe place when the signal was given from the episcopal see in Alexandria for a new anti-gnostic campaign that would have led to the confiscation and destruction of these texts because of their suspect character. In this context, it is natural to recall the Paschal Letter of Athanasius in 367 CE, which defines the limits of the New Testament canon for Egypt.

The critical edition of these writings took a long time. The first codex was initially known as 'Codex Jung' (cf. in L147 under Kasser; Malinine), because it was given as a present to the psychologist Carl Gustav Jung before finding its final location with the other codices in the Coptic Museum in Old Cairo. Work on its edition, translation and commentary is not yet complete, but we can be glad that it has come so far, through bilingual editions and the practical one-volume edition in English (*NHLibrary*). For the sake of a convenient overview and orientation, the tractates, including BG, are listed here with details of the place of discovery, abbreviation and title:

NHC	Column/lines	Abbreviation	Title
I/1	A.1–B.10	PrecPl	Prayer of the Apostle Paul
I/2	1.1–16.30	EpJac	Apocryphon of James
I/3	16.31–43.24	EV	Gospel of Truth
I/4	43.25–50.18	Rheg	Treatise on Resurrection
I/5	51.1–138.27	TractTrip	Tripartite Tractate
II/1	1.1–32.9	AJ	Apocryphon of John
II/2	32.10–51.28	EvThom	Gospel of Thomas
II/3	51.29–86.19	EvPhil	Gospel of Philip
II/4	86.20–97.23	HA	Hypostasis of the Archons
II/5	97.24–127.17	OW	On the Origin of the World
II/6	127.18–137.27	ExAn	Exegesis on the Soul
II/7	138.1–145.19	LibThom	Book of Thomas the Contender
III/1	1.1–40.11	AJ	Apocryphon of John
III/2	40.12–69.20	EvEg	Gospel of the Egyptians
III/3	70.1–90.13	Eug	Eugnostos
III/4	90.14–119.18	SJC	Sophia of Jesus Christ
III/5	120.1–147.23	Dial	Dialogue of the Saviour
IV/1	1.1–49.28	AJ	Apocryphon of John
IV/2	50.1–81.2	EvEg	Gospel of the Egyptians
V/1	1.1–17.18	Eug	Eugnostos
V/2	17.19–24.9	ApcPl	Apocalypse of Paul

V/3	24.10–44.10	1ApcJac	First Apocalypse of James
V/4	44.11–63.32	2ApcJac	Second Apocalypse of James
V/5	64.1–85.32	ApcAd	Apocalypse of Adam
VI/1	1.1–12.22	ActPt	Acts of Peter and the Twelve Apostles
VI/2	13.1–21.32	Bronte	Thunder, Perfect Mind
VI/3	22.1–35.24	AuthLog	Authoritative Teaching
VI/4	36.1–48.15	Noema	Concept of our Great Power
VI/5	48.16–51.23		Plato, *Republic* 588b–589b
VI/6	52.1–63.32	OgdEnn	Discourse on Eighth and Ninth
VI/7	63.33–65.7	PrecHerm	Prayer of Thanksgiving
VI/8	65.15–78.43	Ascl	Asclepius 21–29
VII/1	1.1–49.9	ParSem	Paraphrase of Shem
VII/2	49.10–70.12	2LogSeth	Second Treatise of Great Seth
VII/3	70.13–84.14	ApcPetr	Apocalypse of Peter
VII/4	84.15–118.7	Silv	Teachings of Silvanus
VII/5	118.10–127.27	StelSeth	Three Steles of Seth
VIII/1	1.1–132.6	Zostr	Zostrianos
VIII/2	132.10–140.27	EpPet	Letter of Peter to Philip
IX/1	1.1–27.10	Melch	Melchizedek
IX/2	27.11–29.5	OdNor	Thought of Norea
IX/3	29.6–74.30	TestVer	Testimony of Truth
X/1	1.1–68.18	Mar	Marsanes
XI/1	1.1–21.35	Interpr	Interpretation of Knowledge
XI/2	22.1–39.39	ExpVal	Valentinian Exposition
XI/2a	40.1–44.37	PrecVal	Anointing, Baptism, Eucharist
XI/3	45.1–69.20	Allog	Allogenes
XI/4	69.21–72.33	Hyps	Hypsiphrone
XII/1	15.1–34.28	Sextus	Sentences of Sextus
XII/2	53.19–60.30	EV	Gospel of Truth
XII/3			Fragments
XIII/1	35.1–50.24	Protennoia	Trimorphic Protennoia
XIII/2	59.25ff.	OW	On the Origin of the World (fragments)
BG			
8502/1	7.1–19.5	EvMar	Gospel of Mary
8502/2	15.6–77.7	AJ	Apocryphon of John
8502/3	77.8–127.12	SJC	Sophia of Jesus Christ
8502/4	128.1–141.7	ActumPt	Act of Peter

We shall return to some of this material below in the discussion of the contents of the gnostic systems. We draw attention here only to some more formal points, for example, the fact that a number of writings are found more than once, e.g. AJ four times (NHC II/1; III/1; IV/1; BG 2), and the following twice: SJC (NHC III/4; BG 3), EV (NHC I/3; XII/2); EvEg (NHC III/2; IV/2), OW (NHC II/5; XIII/2), Eug (NHC III/3; V/1). A number of different literary genres are found, including all the main genres of the New Testament: gospels, though here only in name (EvThom NHC II/2; EvPhil NHC II/3), letters (EpJac NHC I/2; Rheg NHC I/4; EpPt NHC VIII/2), acts of the apostles (ActPt NHC VI/1), and apocalypses (ApcPl NHC V/2; 1 and 2 ApcJk V/3–4, etc.). In the Gospel of Thomas, which from the very beginning attracted the greatest attention and also found a place in the appendix to Aland's *Synopsis*, we have a collection of logia, and the letters in NHC are more like camouflaged treatises and homilies. We should also mention the prayers (PrecPl NHC I/1; PrecVal NHC XI/2a) and dialogues (Dial NHC III/5; OgdEnn NHC VI/6), nor should we forget the sapiential writings with their popular-philosophical, non-gnostic paraenesis (Sextus NHC XII/1; Silvanus NHC VII/4). Other texts are to be reckoned as apocalypses, or more generally as revelation literature, although the titles do not indicate this clearly, e.g. ParSem NHC VII/1, Zostr NHC VIII/1 and Mar NHC X/1.

2. Founders of the schools and teachers

List 149.

G. Bardy, 'Cérinthe', *RB* 30 (1921) 344–73.

C. Barth, *Die Interpretation des Neuen Testamentes in der valentinianischen Gnosis* (TU 37.3), Leipzig 1911.

K. Beyschlag, *Simon Magus und die christliche Gnosis* (WUNT 16), Tübingen 1974.

R. J. Hoffmann, *Marcion: On the Restitution of Christianity. An Essay on the Development of Radical Paulinist Theology in the Second Century* (AAR.AS 46), Chico, Calif. 1984.

J. Holzhausen, 'Ein gnostischer Psalm? Zu Valentins Psalm … ', *JAC* 36 (1993) 67–80.

H. Langerbeck, *Aufsätze* (L138) 38–82.

W. A. Löhr, *Basilides und seine Schule: Eine Studie zur Theologie- und Kirchengeschichte des zweiten Jahrhunderts* (WUNT 73), Tübingen 1996.

G. Lüdemann, *Untersuchungen zur simonianischen Gnosis* (GTA 1), Göttingen 1975.

C. Markschies, *Valentinus Gnosticus? Untersuchungen zur valentinianischen*

Gnosis mit einem Kommentar zu den Fragmenten Valentins (WUNT 65), Tübingen 1992.

E. H. Pagels, *The Johannine Gospel in Gnostic Exegesis: Heracleon's Commentary on John* (SBL.MS 17), Missoula 1973.

K. Rudolph, 'Simon – Magus oder Gnosticus? Zum Stand der Debatte', *ThR* NF 42 (1977) 279–359.

Cf. also the editions of texts in L142.

We complement our overview of the available sources with some remarks on founders and teachers of gnostic schools who are known by name. (In recent research into Church history these are increasingly coming to be seen as genuinely Christian thinkers who put forward their own attempts at the resolution of theological problems; cf. Löhr and Markschies. In our own context, we can only bear in mind the questions this new tendency prompts.) We must begin with a problematic case, that of Simon Magus (Acts 8).

(*a*) Simon Magus

Luke describes in Acts 8 a Samaritan magician named Simon who says of himself that 'he was something great' (8:9, a hidden divine predicate), and whom the people praise for his magical tricks with the words: 'This man is that power of God which is called great' (8:10). Some of the Church fathers, who attest the existence of a Simonian gnosis in their own period, and the Acts of Peter present Simon Magus as the first gnostic and the founder of the entire gnostic heresy. It suffices here to read Irenaeus (*Adv. Haer.* 1.23, 2.4):

> Simon from Samaria, the ultimate ancestor of all the heresies, maintained a system which had the following basic affirmation. He led around with him a woman called Helena, a prostitute from the Phoenician city of Tyre whom he had purchased, and he named her the first *Ennoia* [thought] of his spirit,[3] the mother of all, through whom he resolved at the beginning in the spirit to create angels and archangels ... They [i.e. his later disciples] have fashioned an image of Simon, copying the figure of Zeus, and an image of Helena in the form of Minerva, and they adore these. They also have a name: in keeping with the inventor of their abominable doctrine, Simon, they call themselves Simonians.

[3] Cf. the treatise *Protennoia* in NHC XIII/1.

One may accept their own assertions and say that the gnosis falsely so called had its beginning with them.

Has Luke, writing at a later date than Simon, degraded a proto-gnostic in Acts 8 to the rank of a mere magician? That would be very significant for the problem of dating, since if we follow the time he indicates in Acts 8, with Philip and the apostles in Samaria shortly after the resurrection of Jesus, we would arrive at roughly 35 CE, and this would make gnosis just as old as Christianity, and originally uninfluenced by it. It would be possible to trace a trajectory via pupils and followers of Simon such as Dositheus, Menander and Saturnilus to the Simonian gnosis of the second century. But Acts 8 is no more able to support such a construction than are the patristic testimonies. The Church fathers and the gnostics themselves searched in the New Testament for a possible head of the school of the gnostic movement, identified Simon Magus as their candidate and attributed this significance to him. In the case of Luke, all that seems possible is that he uses the figure of Simon to portray and project backwards in time proto-gnostic tendencies of his own period (i.e. *c.*80–90 CE).

(*b*) Cerinthus

Cerinthus worked *c.*100–20 CE in Asia Minor, and seems to stand at the point of transition from Jewish Christianity to pure gnosis. The traditional material gives a contradictory picture, presenting him also as a Judaist who held fast, against Paul, to the requirement of circumcision and as a chiliast with a very materialistic eschatological expectation. A doctrine which Irenaeus ascribes to him identifies him as a gnostic, viz. that 'the world was not made by the first God, but by a particular power that is separated by a wide distance from the highest power that rules over all', and that this power 'does not know the God who is above all' (*Adv. Haer.* 1.26.1). Cerinthus is linked in various ways to the Johannine writings. There is something almost charming about an anecdote related *inter alia* by Eusebius (*Hist. Eccl.* 4.14.6): once, when John wanted to visit the baths in Ephesus, he saw Cerinthus inside and immediately fled from the house without bathing, crying that he feared the building would collapse because of the presence in it of Cerinthus, the enemy of the truth. According to Irenaeus, the Gospel of John was written against Cerinthus; those in the early Church who disapproved of the fourth Gospel turned this assertion on its head and claimed that Cerinthus was the real author of the Gospel, which thus was a heretical work and not one of the fundamental elements of Christian tradition. Thus particular affinities or antagonisms between gnosis and the Johannine writings were certainly noticed even in antiquity.

(c) Marcion

In chronological terms, Marcion would belong at this point, but there is no agreement about the extent to which he may be called gnostic. The sharp antithesis he posits between the Old Testament God of law and the redeeming God of Jesus Christ, who has no connection with the first God, certainly sounds gnostic, but we do not find in Marcion the elaboration of a mythological system such as we find in most of the gnostic schools, nor does he know of an essential relatedness of the inner human being to the higher, divine sphere. Even Kurt Rudolph, who includes Marcion among the founders of gnostic schools, admits that he 'stands as it were with only one foot in the gnostic tradition': it was only Marcion's 'Church' that became more open to gnosis.[4]

(d) Basilides

Basilides lived and taught in Alexandria between 117 and 160 CE, and founded a school that became important in Egypt. We mention three topoi from his teaching, each of which shows us something typical of gnosis.

Esoteric teaching

When Irenaeus tells us about Basilides, he quotes the following statement: 'But there are not many who are able to know this, but only one out of a thousand and two out of ten thousand ... One must at all costs avoid blurting out the contents of their mysteries. These must be kept hidden through silence' (*Adv. Haer.* 1.24.6). This confirms in a vivid way the elitist and esoteric character of gnosis. The true teaching is to be communicated only within the group. The proportions in the numbers given speak for themselves – it is obvious that there exist only a few

---

[4]   *Gnosis* (L141) 313.

gnostics, and they are solitary figures in human society, alien to the business of the world.

Secret tradition

Basilides traced his esoteric teaching to the interpreter of Peter or to the apostle Matthew. This served as the explanation why his special views were not to be found in the tradition of the worldwide church, or at least did not claim the same centrality within that tradition. This is an essential component of the gnostic formation and justification of tradition. The contents of their own revelation literature are presented as a secret instruction imparted by the risen Christ to selected disciples who now function as bearers of the tradition, such as Thomas in EvThom or Philip in EvPhil or James in 1 and 2 ApcJac. This makes the period of forty days between the resurrection and the ascension (Acts 1) very important; where this seems too brief for such a quantity of instruction, it is extended, e.g. to eighteen months (cf. *Adv. Haer.* 1.30.14) or in one case even to eleven or twelve years (in the *Pistis Sophia*).

Exegesis

But what is the real source of the contents of this instruction? The *chef d'œuvre* attributed to Basilides is his *Exegetica* in twenty-four books, i.e. expositions of the New Testament, and possibly also the Old. This was in fact the major means by which gnosis found the teaching revealed by the risen Christ, viz. through the speculative exegesis of the testimonies of Scripture; the same technique was applied to texts of poets and philosophers, and to pagan myths. The allegorical exegesis applied here could make these texts yield the most surprising information, and scholars have spoken here of a downright 'protest-exegesis', done in conscious opposition to the way in which other Christians were using the scriptures. Typical here is the gnostic groups' choice of biblical characters as models and patrons whose names they took: there was a sect of Cainites who venerated as their hero Cain, who murdered his brother (Gen 4), and also 'professed their relatedness to Esau, to Korah, to the men of Sodom and to all those like them' (*Adv. Haer.* 1.13.1). Judas Iscariot too arrived at unexpected honours along this path (ibid.):

> And they say that the traitor Judas likewise knew this very well. And since he alone among all [the disciples] knew the truth, he also carried out the mystery of betrayal. He was the cause of the redemption of everything in heaven and on

earth. They issue a scurrilous concoction which they call the 'Gospel of Judas', with these contents.

(e) Valentinus

The most important school to be founded within gnosis in the second century CE was that of Valentinus, who converted in Egypt to a Christianity that probably already bore a gnostic imprint. He worked in Rome between 140 and 160, and is said to have enjoyed such high prestige initially in the Roman community that he was even put forward as candidate for the office of bishop, until the inevitable rupture came. We do not know what happened to him subsequently.

Valentinus had significant pupils, including Ptolemaeus and Heracleon, the earliest commentator on the Gospel of John (cf. Pagels). All the Church fathers who are genuinely acquainted with gnosis discuss Valentinus, and modern scholarship attributes a considerable amount of the Nag Hammadi texts to the Valentinian tendency. (It has been claimed by some that the really new discovery made possible by Nag Hammadi is Sethian gnosis, but since fundamental questions concerning this are not yet clarified, we do not discuss it in greater detail here.) Valentinus was also a poet, and he concentrated the outlines of his doctrine with supreme skill into a psalm of seven lines which is preserved by Hippolytus (in *Ref.* 6.37.7; cf. Holzhausen):

> *Harvest*
> I see everything set in suspension by the spirit,
> I understand that everything is borne up by the spirit,
> the flesh depends on the soul,
> the soul linked to the air,
> the air dependent on the ether.
> [I see] fruits emerging from the depths
> and a child from the womb.

What Valentinus is describing in this poem is ultimately 'the harvest of gnostic knowledge' (Holzhausen 79), but the language he uses to express this idea remains obscure and puzzling at individual points. We can offer the following indications as a help in understanding the text: according to the two opening lines, the divine spirit is the source of the interconnected order of all things in the cosmos which the speaker ('I') grasps when he looks at it and reflects upon it. One would expect the four elements (earth, water, air and fire) to be listed in the intermediary lines 3–5 as the building bricks of the cosmos, but the poet has given this an anthropological twist by introducing flesh and soul, since his real concern is with the human person, and more precisely with the indestructible inner kernel of the human person. The two concluding lines, if understood literally, speak of the continuous miracle of new life, of the growth of the fruits from the depths of the earth and of newborn children; read allegorically, however, they speak of the supreme male–female deity, from whom there proceed the world of ideas (as 'fruit') and the logos which unites these (the 'child'). Despite the Platonic provenance, this allows another point of contact with the Christian tradition, which sees the eternal divine Logos in the child in the crib.

3. On the subsequent history

The list of names suffices to show that the zenith of the gnostic movement was attained in the second century CE and lasted just into the third century. In the West we find only late forms of the older gnostic schools in the third and fourth centuries, elaborating the system of ideas which they have inherited; the picture is somewhat different in the East, thanks to the church which Mani had founded.

One must ask why gnosis apparently lost its initial impetus at some point. One factor was external pressure from the worldwide Church or, in the East, from other religions which to some extent enjoyed the favour of the political authorities. With the exception of the Manichaeans, the gnostics lacked an efficient organisation and a unified structure of leadership: they were split into too many competing groups. Another factor is certainly the fact that gnostic ideas were integrated as much as possible into Christian popular piety, also becoming a standard component of theological systems. This allowed the worldwide Church to give a partial answer to the question that gnosis posed: it accepted what seemed acceptable, and thus cut away the ground on which gnosis stood.

Nevertheless, one can trace the existence of gnosis into the Christian Middle Ages. Very roughly speaking, the trajectories run from the Manichaeans via the gnostic sect of the Paulicians, which reached Macedonia in the eighth century, to the Bogomils, who were influenced by the Paulicians and spread in the Balkans. In the eleventh century, their ideas penetrated Italy and southern France, where the church of the Cathars came into being and was able to survive from c.1150 to 1300.

(The word *Cathar*, via the Italian *gazzari*, is the origin of the German word for heretic, *Ketzer*.) Elements in modern thought that could be termed gnostic or Manichaean from a structural perspective have no demonstrable historical contact with the gnosis of classical antiquity.

4. The question of origins

(*a*) Classification of the models of a solution

List 150.

W. Anz, *Zur Frage nach dem Ursprung des Gnostizismus: Ein religionsgeschichtlicher Versuch* (TU 15.4), Leipzig 1897.

R. Bergmeier, 'Quellen vorchristlicher Gnosis?', in *Tradition und Glaube: Das frühe Christentum in seiner Umwelt* (Festschrift K. G. Kuhn), Göttingen 1971, 200–20.

U. Bianchi (ed.), *Origins* (L138); various essays from this volume are also found in K. Rudolph, *Gnosis und Gnostizismus* (L138) 626–748.

W. Bousset, *Hauptprobleme der Gnosis* (FRLANT 10), Göttingen 1907, reprint 1973.

E. Haenchen, 'Gab es eine vorchristliche Gnosis?', *ZThK* 49 (1952) 316–49, also in Idem, *Gott und Mensch*, Tübingen 1965, 265–98.

A. Harnack, *History of Dogma*, London and Edinburgh 1894; excerpts (in German) also in K. Rudolph, *Gnosis und Gnostizismus* (L138) 142–73.

H. Jonas, *Gnosis und spätantiker Geist*, Teil I: *Die mythologische Gnosis* [1934] (FRLANT 51), Göttingen 4th edn. 1988; Teil 2: *Von der Mythologie zur mystischen Philosophie. Erste Hälfte* [1954] (FRLANT 63), Göttingen 2nd edn. 1966; *Erste und zweite Hälfte*, ed. K. Rudolph (FRLANT 159), Göttingen 1993.

S. Pétrement, *A Separate God: The Christian Origins of Gnosticism*, San Francisco 1990.

R. Reitzenstein and H. H. Schaeder, *Studien zum antiken Synkretismus aus Iran und Griechenland* (SBW 7), Leipzig and Berlin 1926, reprint Darmstadt 1965.

H. M. Schenke, 'Hauptprobleme der Gnosis: Gesichtspunkte zu einer neuen Darstellung des Gesamtphänomens', *Kairos* 7 (1965) 114–23; also in K. Rudolph, *Gnosis und Gnostizismus* (L138) 585–600.

E. Yamauchi, *Pre-Christian Gnosticism: A Survey of the Proposed Evidences*, Grand Rapids 1973.

The search for the origin of gnosis remains one of the unsolved fundamental problems of the study of gnosis. It is, of course, sometimes forgotten that the origin and the essence of a phenomenon are two distinct things; nevertheless, knowledge of the origin is a decisive contribution to the understanding of the phenomenon. Another important factor in our context is that the definition of the relationship between gnosis and the New Testament, or more generally between gnosis and Christianity, also depends on the answer to the question of origins. Three basic types of attempted solutions, which have led the field for a long period and are still dominant in one way or another, can be identified.

Church history

The influential Church historian Adolf Harnack presented a derivative model in terms of 'Church history'; Simone Pétrement has recently presented a new justification of this in great detail. Harnack defines gnosis as the acute secularisation or Hellenisation of Christianity. In chronological terms, therefore, Christianity would be the older and gnosis the younger phenomenon – without Christianity, there would be no gnosis. According to Harnack, the gnostics' primary interpretative categories for the New Testament tradition were derived from Greek, and especially Platonic philosophy. Thus they falsified the Christian faith from the very outset, even if they were thereby enabled to present themselves as the first systematic thinkers of the early Church. As a Christian heresy, gnosis belongs to Church history, and more specifically to the special section of the history of heresy.

History of religions

A location of gnosis within the history of religions, in its essential points maintained today by Kurt Rudolph, was already proposed by the New Testament scholar Wilhelm Bousset, who saw gnosis as an independent phenomenon of the history of religions in the classical period, with its roots lying in the non-Christian sphere as far as its contents were concerned, and earlier than Christianity. The fundamental dualistic pattern comes from Iran; and Bousset sees other mythological themes from the general history of religions as contributing to the birth of gnosis. Gnosis does not mean the Hellenisation of Christianity, but rather its reorientalisation. Those who handed on the New Testament traditions made use of the already existing gnostic redeemer myth. It is easy to see how the path leads from this point to Bultmann's commentary on John (see A, 3 above). Harnack's reaction was to dismiss Bousset's form of gnosis as 'utterly antiquated, a weird collection of fossils, a junk room and a rubbish heap', classifying it, with its unmistakable tendency to elitism, among the 'inferior, superstitious and miserable phenomena that had survived from past stages of religion and . . . ascend anew like bubbles from the deep'.[5]

Existential phenomenology

The two-volume work by the philosopher Hans Jonas is a milestone in the history of the treatment of gnosis. He prescinds from all the endless ramifications of the attempts to establish the provenance of gnosis, and instead seeks to break through to a contemplation of the essence of this phenomenon with the aid of an existentialist analysis inspired by Heidegger. What is the unmistakable character of gnosis, given expression in the numerous myths and images? How does the movement understand existence and its own self? Jonas identifies as the most basic characteristics a remarkably pessimistic world-view and the retreat to the interior sphere; these distinguish gnosis from two other great intellectual tendencies, viz. the Judaism of the Old Testament with its belief in a creator God and the Stoic philosophy which is 'at home in the world' (141), 'in harmony with the cosmos' (142), 'very certain of existence within the world' (143). For Jonas, gnosis is the spirit of late antiquity (cf. the title of his book). This has significant consequences when one seeks to identify the actual boundaries of the phenomenon; among those Jonas includes under gnosis are Philo of Alexandria, Origen and Plotinus. At this point, the concept which has been defined on the basis of a systematic approach loses all historical precision.

Factors producing uncertainty

Why cannot a greater degree of unity be achieved in so central a question? The answer certainly does not lie in the terminology alone, and this is why the Congress of Messina (cf. the volume of essays edited by Bianchi) did not achieve any genuine clarification with its proposal to make a distinction between 'gnosis', understood as a particular intellectual attitude which can be articulated in many different ways, and 'gnosticism', using only the latter term for the systems of the second and third centuries CE. More help is found in Rudolph's observation that gnosis should be classified as a 'parasitic' phenomenon: i.e. it has only a very limited number of views that

---

[5] A. Harnack, review of W. Bousset, *Hauptprobleme* [1908], in K. Rudolph, *Gnosis und Gnostizismus* (L138) 231–7 at 232, 237.

are unmistakably its own, and since it needs material in order to illustrate these, it adopts this material indiscriminately from every available source – from Judaism, Christianity, the pagan religions, and Greek philosophy.

The fundamental problem, however, is connected with the sources available to scholars. We have no literary testimonies to a developed gnosis that can be dated *indubitably* to the first century CE or even earlier. The *unambiguous* attestation of gnosis by means of quotations by non-gnostic authors or of original documents begins, at the earliest, at the start of the second century CE; this fact would speak in favour of the Church history hypothesis. The only loophole remaining to other models is opened by the words 'indisputably' and 'unambiguous' which we have used above. It is possible that the literary testimonies have a longer prehistory, and that these, taken together with many hints in early texts, permit us to postulate an earlier date for the beginnings of gnosis.

(*b*) Results and perspectives

List 151.

K. Alt, *Philosophie gegen Gnosis: Plotins Polemik in seiner Schrift II 9* (AAWLM.G 1990.7), Stuttgart 1990.

C. Elsas, *Neuplatonische und gnostische Weltablehnung in der Schule Plotins* (RVV 34), Berlin 1975.

G. Filoramo, 'Sulle origini dello gnosticismo', *RSLR* 29 (1993) 493–510.

H. A. Green, *The Economic and Social Origins of Gnosticism* (SBL.DS 77), Atlanta 1985.

H. G. Kippenberg, *Die vorderasiatischen Erlösungsreligionen in ihrem Zusammenhang mit der antiken Stadtherrschaft* (stw 917), Frankfurt a.M. 1991, 369–425.

H. J. Krämer, *Ursprung* (L128) 223–63.

J. Maier, 'Jüdische Faktoren bei der Entstehung der Gnosis?', in K. W. Tröger, *Altes Testament* (L140) 239–58.

B. A. Pearson, 'Philo and Gnosticism', *ANRW* II/21.1 (1984) 295–342.

K. Rudolph, 'Randerscheinungen des Judentums und das Problem der Entstehung des Gnostizismus', *Kairos* 9 (1967) 105–22, also in Idem, *Gnosis und Gnostizismus* (L138) 768–97.

H. M. Schenke, 'Die Tendenz der Weisheit zur Gnosis', in B. Aland, *Gnosis* (L138) 351–72.

A. F. Segal, *Two Powers in Heaven: Early Rabbinic Reports about Christianity and Gnosticism* (SJLA 25), Leiden 1977.

R. T. Wallis and J. Bregman (eds.), *Neoplatonism and Gnosticism* (Studies in Neoplatonism: Ancient and Modern 6), Albany, NY 1992.
W. Wink, *Cracking the Gnostic Code: The Powers in Gnosticism* (SBL.MS 46), Atlanta, Ga. 1993.

Pre-Christian and non-Christian

We may consider some of the results of the discussion up to this point as relatively certain. The first distinction to be made with regard to gnosis is that between pre-Christian and non-Christian. There did not exist the kind of pre-Christian gnosis that the older school of the history of religions posited, chronologically antecedent to the New Testament and providing one of its intellectual presuppositions. Neither Philo (see Pearson) nor the Book of Wisdom can be appealed to in support of such a hypothesis. All that remains possible is to speak of a non-Christian gnosis, which is to say that gnosis does not originally depend directly on Christianity. It developed contemporaneously with Christianity, with the same intellectual and societal presuppositions, and very quickly came to interact with Christianity – but the fundamental structure of its thought cannot be derived from Christianity. Further debate among scholars will make it clearer whether, and to what extent, the idea of contemporary, parallel origins is plausible.

Philosophy

The contribution of philosophy to the birth of gnosis must be estimated as relatively significant. Dualistic explanatory models already lay to hand in Middle and Neoplatonism, as well as the idea of emanations, which is typical of gnostic thought. As will be shown below, the anthropological conception of gnosis too owes much to Platonism. On the other hand, we must warn against a simplistic equation of gnosis and Neoplatonism; not for nothing did Plotinus compose an entire treatise against the gnostics, since he could not share their pessimistic world-view. One of the ideas he attacks is the view that an unhappy accident took place in the course of the emanation (see below), and that the world soul has sunk down into matter, against its own will and knowledge:[6]

> And if they [the gnostics] say that it [the world soul] has committed an error, then let them declare the cause of this error. And when is it supposed to have

---

[6] *Enn.* 2.9.4; cf. A. H. Armstrong, *Plotinus*, vol. 2 (LCL 441), Cambridge, Mass. and London 1966.

committed the error? From all eternity? ... We on our part deny that the creative soul sinks down. Rather, we affirm that it is not allowed to sink down. For if it sinks down, this is because it has forgotten that which lies above, but if it has forgotten this, how can it then be the artificer of the world?

Apocalyptic and wisdom

In the course of our discussion we have already found traces that point to Judaism (in the widest sense). Scholars in recent decades have paid increasing attention to Jewish components in gnosis, which was able to borrow essential building bricks from Jewish apocalyptic and Jewish sapiential literature. Apocalyptic displays a pessimistic view of the world and works with a dualistic construction of history. It has an esoteric orientation, making known secret knowledge to a selected few. The personified power of evil is multiplied, and the distance to God in the highest heaven seems to grow beyond all measure. The interest of the sapiential tradition for the gnostics lies not so much in the scepticism into which its world-view, per se positive, could turn under the pressure of negative experiences, but rather in the speculations about Sophia, who appears in the later texts as a personified female figure who seeks a dwelling on the earth among human beings (Sir 24:7f.). Sometimes we are told that things go wrong, and she does not find a dwelling, but returns to heaven (Ethiopian Enoch 42.1f.). Gnosis constructed entire mythical systems around the figure of Sophia.

Syncretism

Like Platonic philosophy, sapiential literature and apocalyptic do not simply provide material on which gnosis then worked; they belong to the basic intellectual presuppositions without which gnosis could not have been elaborated. We may leave open the question of the extent to which factors from other religions also play a role. In the case of the Iranian dualism which is often mentioned in this context – incidentally, a religion that had a positive view of the world and was optimistic – we should note that we know much less about the early history of Iranian religion than we do about the history of gnosis. At any rate, the centres of gnosis, such as Syrian Antioch, Egyptian Alexandria, and the capital Rome, were meeting places where exchanges took place between the world-views of late antiquity. All in all, the 'parasitic' character of gnosis (see above) means that it should be classified as a syncretistic form of religion, as a product of the preference for mixed religious forms in late antiquity.

Location in society

The perspective of social history has given a new impulse to the study of gnosis (cf. Green; Kippenberg). We may leave open the question whether it is correct to go as far as the categorical assertion that Jewish intellectuals in Egypt were the initiators of gnosis (Green); but it is correct to state that gnosis is a phenomenon of the city culture of the imperial period, that its protagonists had a very high level of education, and that gnosis is nourished by a deep discontent with the state of things as they were. Gnosis displays traits critical of society and of rulers. The escape route it recommends is that of interior emigration, thereby offering the possibility of a new identity to *déracinés* who felt alien and lost in the world. We may use the language of Berger and Luckmann and say that gnosis attempts the construction of social reality from within.

C. An outline of the doctrinal system

List 152 (on AJ).

R. van den Broek, 'The Creation of Adam's Psychic Body in the Apocryphon of John', in Idem and M. J. Vermaseren, *Studies* (L2) 38–57.

S. Giversen, *Apocryphon Johannis: The Coptic Text of the Apocryphon Johannis in the Nag Hammadi Codex II* (AThD 5), Copenhagen 1963.

R. Haardt, *Gnosis* (L141), 180–206.

M. Krause, 'The Apokryphon of John', in W. Foerster, *Gnosis* (L141), I, 105–20.

——and P. Labib, *Die drei Versionen des Apokryphon des Johannes im Koptischen Museum zu Alt-Kairo* (ADAI.K 1), Wiesbaden 1962.

B. Layton, *Scriptures* (L141) 23–51.

T. Onuki, *Gnosis und Stoa: Eine Untersuchung zum Apokryphon des Johannes* (NTOA 9), Fribourg (Switzerland) and Göttingen 1989.

G. Quispel, 'Valentinian Gnosis and the Apocryphon of John', in B. Layton, *Rediscovery* (L138) I, 118–32.

M. Tardieu, *Écrits Gnostiques: Codex de Berlin* (Sources Gnostiques et Manichéennes 1), Paris 1984, 83–166.

W. C. Till and H. M. Schenke, *Papyrus Berolinensis* (L147) 78–195.

M. Waldstein and F. Wisse (eds.), *The Apocryphon of John: Synopsis of Nag Hamadi Codices II.1, III.1 and IV.1 with BG 8502.2* (NHS 33), Leiden 1995.

F. E. Williams, 'NHC I,2: The Apocryphon of James', in H. W. Attridge (ed.), *Nag Hammadi Codex 1 (The Jung Codex)*, vols. 1–2 (NHS 22–3), Leiden 1985, I.13–53, II.7–37.

F. Wisse, 'The Apocryphon of John', in *NHLibrary* 104–23.

Despite the indisputable variety of gnostic groups and tendencies which did not acknowledge any ultimately binding teaching authority, it ought to be possible to identify some constant elements which make it possible to grasp the existence of gnosis as an autonomous entity. We turn in the following pages to the task of discerning some of these constitutive ideas. We study the fields of cosmology, anthropology, soteriology, eschatology, ecclesiology and ethics, and look for those elements in gnosis that serve the construction of a system. Apart from other selected texts, we base our investigations as far as possible on the Apocryphon of John (in the version from BG 8502/2), aware that this means that we are dealing primarily with Valentinian ideas. The basic document antecedent to the four Coptic versions was probably written in the second century CE. Its teaching is presented within the framework of the revelation of mysteries by the risen Lord to his disciple John (hence the title: 'hidden writing of John').

1. Cosmology

(a) On the concept of God

If we return to our opening quotation from the *Excerpta ex Theodoto*, we find that the cosmology of AJ gives an answer to the question: 'Where were we? Whither have we been thrown?' In order to understand this answer, however, we must begin with the concept of God. In Eugnostos (NHC III/3), a treatise about the God of truth in epistolary form, the author begins by citing three alternative hypotheses which Greek philosophy discussed about how the world came into being, and rejects them as erroneous. Then he develops his own concept of God, which consists almost exclusively of negations (70.6–73.11):[7]

> Inquiring about God, who he is, and what he is like, they have not found him. The wisest among them have speculated about the truth from the ordering of the world ... (of) the three opinions that I have just described, none is true ... The one who is, is ineffable. No sovereignty knew him, no authority, no

---

[7] Eng. trans. of Nag Hammadi texts: *NHLibrary* (here, 208ff.).

subjection, nor did any creature from the foundation of the world, except himself. For he is immortal. He is eternal, having no birth ... He is unbegotten, having no beginning ... He is unnameable. He has no human form ... He is without end; he is incomprehensible. He is ever imperishable, (and) has no likeness (to anything) ... He is unknowable, while he (nonetheless) knows himself. He is immeasurable. He is perfect, having no defect ... For he is all mind, thought and reflecting, thinking, rationality, and power.

While this kind of negative theology (cf. also the parallel in AJ 22.19–26.13) can sometimes be a salutary corrective to an all too self-assured way of speaking about God, what we find here goes beyond such a corrective, to make definitive affirmations. When the unknown God is exalted to such an extent, he is transposed to an insuperable distance from the world, and the conclusion is that he can no longer be its creator. But what is the next step, theologically speaking? How does the world in fact come into being? Within its general dualist framework, gnosis gives two different answers to this question. We could characterise these as *metaphysical dualism* and the *devolution of the divine*.

(*b*) Metaphysical dualism

One tendency, with Manichaeism as its most decided main representative, postulates the existence of an evil principle which from the very outset stands alongside the highest God, who is the representative of the good; in metaphorical language, we hear of the armed struggle between the kingdom of darkness and the kingdom of light. The world comes into being in connection with plans devised by the powers of darkness in their fight against the kingdom of light, and with the strategies which the kingdom of light devises to counter these plans. Psalm 233 in the Coptic Manichaean Psalter states that the Holy Spirit[8]

> taught us two natures, that of light and that of darkness, separated from one another since the beginning. The kingdom of light consisted of five magnitudes ... The kingdom of darkness consists of five chambers ... They dared to wage war on each other, and to attack the land of light, thinking that they could conquer it ... When the first human being had ended his struggle, the Father sent his second Son, who *set up this entire world out of the mixture* of light and darkness that had come into being.

[8] In A. Böhlig, *Gnosis* (L146) III.118–20.

Thus the world is a mixed reality. Apparently it is the darkness that dominates, since without the attack by the darkness, it would not have been necessary for the world to come into being. But the world also contains particles of light. In a hidden dimension of the reality of the world, the struggle between light and darkness rages continuously.

(*c*) Devolution of the divine

More frequently, however, we find another model, which works with a devolution of the divine ('devolution' is understood here as the opposite concept to 'evolution', i.e. as a movement downwards rather than upwards or forwards). Although the dualism remains fundamentally present, it is pressed into the service of a general monistic framework. Within the divinity itself there takes place a development and a rupture, and the world and human beings are born of this rupture: a kind of cosmic accident or fall is projected into the divine principle itself. EvPhil 99a says it apodictically (NHC II/3 75.2–6): 'The world came about through a mistake. For he who created it wanted to create it imperishable and immortal. He fell short of attaining his desire.'

AJ describes these events in detail. The process begins with a series of emanations. The highest God recognises himself in the light that he is, that he irradiates, and that surrounds him. He sees his image reflected in this light. This mirror image takes on autonomous existence and becomes a new being, which stands one degree lower than the highest God, yet also constitutes an aspect of him. This process can also be described in other, more intellectual terms; then it is the thought of the highest Being that emerges from itself and in this way brings something new into existence. To employ the words of AJ (26.15–27.15):[9]

> He has told this to us, he who understands himself in his own light, which is around him ... The source of the Pneuma flowed out of the living water of Light ... He understood the image of himself when he saw it in the pure water of light which surrounds him. And his Thought became operative. It revealed itself ... the perfect Providence of the All, the Light, the Image of the Light, the picture of the Invisible, that is the perfect Power, the Barbelo, the Perfect Aeon of Glory.

The name 'Barbelo' has not yet been explained satisfactorily. This is an artificial word which designates a gnostic mother goddess. The name

[9] Haardt, *Gnosis* (L141) 182ff.

Sophia (wisdom) can also be employed, often explicitly equated with Barbelo; in the system which we are studying here, this name occurs only at a later stage. The various beings which emanate from Barbelo in a sequence of gradations are related to one another as pairs. The entire process remains in the sphere of the *plērōma*, i.e. within the divine fullness. The highest God takes on differentiations within his own divine reality. These differentiations do not bring into existence anything that would be utterly different from him; above all, they do not bring the world into existence.

(*d*) The world comes into being

AJ gives a long account of the various emanations, covering many pages. The term common to the powers that thus come into existence is 'aeons'. They are given the names of abstract concepts or of angels: 'Charis is with the first light Harmozel, which is the angel of light in the first aeon, three Aeons being with it, namely Charis, Truth and Morphe [form]' (33.7–12). It is only the following passages that bring us close to the crisis (36.16–37.16):

> Our sister, the Sophia, being an Aeon, conceived a thought, and through the thought of the Pneuma and Prognosis, attempted to project from herself the Image. The Pneuma had not approved and had not given her permission, nor her Partner and Consort, the male Virginal Pneuma ... Her thought could not remain ineffective, and her work emerged imperfect, and ugly in appearance, since she had produced it without her Consort.

The fatal accident has occurred: a momentary lack of harmony in the *plērōma* brings something unforeseen into existence. Precisely because of the enormous intellectual energies which are at work within the *plērōma*, this cannot remain without consequences. The result of this deviant way of acting on the part of Sophia cannot simply be erased, although she attempts to do so (37.18–38.14):

> She saw that it was different in form, having the appearance of a snake and a lion. Its eyes streamed fire. She cast it away from her, outside of those areas, so that none of the Immortals might see it, because she had borne it in Ignorance. She bound it in a cloud of light and set a throne in the midst of the cloud ... She gave it the name *Ialdabaoth*.

'Ialdabaoth' includes the Semitic roots *jalad*, 'to beget or give birth', and *sebaōth*, an Old Testament designation of the heavenly powers, and also an attribute of God, who is the Lord Sabaoth, Lord of the heavenly hosts. It is very obvious that both this name and the description of the dwelling place with the bright cloud and the throne are an allusion to the creator God of the Old Testament. And that is precisely what Ialdabaoth does: he creates his own world. A negative view of belief in a creation can be clearly seen in this text, as well as a rejection of the Old Testament concept of God. No matter how much material gnosis may take over from the Old Testament, the fundamental dissension cannot be bridged. To call the Lord Sabaoth the product of an error by Sophia implies a sharp polemic against biblical Judaism. (It is obvious, when we use the word 'error', that the narrative pattern here was itself borrowed from a myth that spoke much more drastically and directly of the procreation and birth of an illegitimate divine child, which had to be hidden after birth. This already existing narrative was read allegorically by the gnostics and interpreted as speaking of events that happened in the spiritual realm.)

(e) The elaboration of the world

We now have a demiurge who makes himself independent and begins to set up his own world. The powers which now come into existence are called aeons or archons, sometimes also angels or kings. Ialdabaoth installs seven kings as rulers over the seven lower heavens. (This picture of the world contains altogether ten heavens, with the *plērōma* in the ninth and tenth heavens, the eighth heaven as a transitional realm, and the seven lower heavens, which are identical with the planetary sphere, as the playground of the demonic creatures of the creator of the world.)[10] Most of the names of the lords over the seven lower planetary spheres recall attributes of the biblical God (41.17–42.10):

> The first is Iaoth, the face of a lion; the second, Eloaios, the face of an ass; the third, Astaphaios, the face of a hyena; the fourth is Iao, the face of the snake with seven heads; the fifth, Adonaios, the face of a dragon; the sixth, Adoni, the face of an ape; the seventh, Sabbataios, the face of shining flames of fire. This is Hebdomas [Seventh] of the Week, [and] these are the rulers of the world.

The text tells us that these lords came into being in the following way: Ialdabaoth 'gave them some of his own fire and power. He did not give them any of the pure light of the Power which he had taken from his

[10] On this cf. the diagram of the Ophites in K. Rudolph, *Gnosis* (L141) 68.

Mother, however' (42.13–19). This is important for us, since it reveals the starting point of all that is to come. There is more in Ialdabaoth than the wild, degenerate fire that he breathes into his creatures: since he is descended from Sophia, he also bears pure light in himself, components of energy or particles of spirit from the *plērōma*, which yearn to return to the *plērōma*. A direct line leads from here to the coming into existence of human beings and into soteriology.

2. Anthropology

(a) The creation of the human being

Up to this point, we have a world without human beings. Whence do they come? How did they come into being, where do they find their place in the universe? We still have the following questions from our initial definition: 'Who were we?', 'What have we become?' We have seen the first acts of the cosmic drama unfold, and in general terms, the coming into being of the human person must have some connection to this drama. Most of the narratives of the coming into being of the human person in the gnostic sources work on the paradise story from Gen 2–3, though in a way that distorts its original intention. AJ is no exception: the error committed by Sophia must be put right, and the highest God himself takes the initiative. He reflects himself in human form in the waters of the lower heavens. The demiurge and his archons see this mirror image, without knowing what it means. They are fascinated by it; or else, according to another textual reading, they feel themselves threatened by it. In any case, they decide to create such a being, employing the words of Gen 1:26 (48.4–14):

> The Blessed One revealed his appearance to them, and the entire group of Archons of the seven Authorities accepted this with pleasure [*or:* they were dejected]. They saw the form of the Image in the water and said to one another: 'Let us make a man in the Image and Likeness of God.'

Each of the seven powers makes a contribution to the soul of the human being that is created; behind this lies the idea found in classical antiquity, that the planets were involved in the creation of the human soul. What is created is a spiritual or psychical being. But this enterprise does not meet with great success, for: 'he (Adam) remained for a long time motionless, since neither the seven Authorities nor the three hundred and sixty angels who put his body together, could raise him up' (50.15–19).

467

The highest God of light now employs a stratagem in this situation. His four agents come in disguise to Ialdabaoth, who will believe that they are his own angels. These counsel him to impart to the lifeless creature some of the pure light that he had received from Sophia and had hitherto withheld from his own creatures. From his point of view, this is wrong advice, but now he allows himself to be persuaded and breathes this light into Adam, who at once awakens to life (51.8–20):

> By holy decree he [the Light-God] dispatched Autogenes [i.e. the one born of his own self], together with the four Lights in the form of the Angels of the First Archon. They gave him [Ialdabaoth] advice, to remove from him the Power of the Mother. They said to him: 'Breathe the Pneuma that is in you into his face and the creature will raise itself up.' So he breathed into him some of his Pneuma, from the Power of the Mother, and he [Adam] moved ...

The point of this becomes clear: the demiurge is no longer the only one to possess those particles of light which he had stolen from the heavenly kingdom through his mother Sophia. Now a different possibility exists: viz. this potential energy can be brought back to its place of origin via an indirect route, through the human being. Now a real struggle breaks out, centred on Adam. The human being was initially endowed only with a soul, but now he is also equipped with trace elements of the divine spirit, which guarantee his vitality. This makes him superior to the powers that hold sway over the world: 'And the Man shone forth because of the Shadow of the Light in him and his Thought dominated those who had created him' (54.5–8). The powers of the world resolve to do something about this (55.3–13):

> They created another creature then, out of earth, water, fire and Pneuma [here: wind], which means: out of Hylē [matter], Darkness, Epithymia [Desire] and the Antikeimenon Pneuma [the Opposed Pneuma]. This is the Fetter, this is the Tomb of the physical Creature, which they cast over Man to bind him in Hylē.

The four archons use the four elements of the world, the building blocks of matter, as well as passions and instincts, here represented by 'desire', to form the body into which they then imprison the being that is soul-spirit. The body is fetters, prison, a tomb for soul and spirit – an idea borrowed from the well-known Platonic play on words σῶμα – σῆμα. In addition, a rebellious hostile spirit is implanted in the human person, as a counterweight to the trace elements of the divine spirit which he bears in himself. AJ integrates the creation of woman from the rib of man into this perspective too: all that the demiurge seeks to do through the creation of woman is to get hold once again of Sophia's power. He has put human beings at a serious disadvantage by implanting in them the desire for procreation (63.2–9).

(b) The concept of the human being

The result of this is the tripartite concept of the human being which is typical of the majority of gnostics, especially of Valentinian gnosis. The myth relates in a narrative how this comes into existence. The evil powers of the world create a soul; through the stratagem of the highest God, it is possible to breathe a spirit into this being; the archons imprison it in a body. Thus the human person consists not only of body and soul, but of body, soul and spirit. All that is of value in the human person is the spark of light, the particle of spirit, that he has received. Only this substratum is destined for salvation, only this is worthy of salvation. In more abstract terms, this can also be called the 'I' of the human person, his self or the kernel of his being.

The surprising point here is the devaluation of the soul. This can be explained to some extent in psychological terms: the soul in the human person is the source of those passions, desires, and instincts which keep him bound to his body and to the world. The history of philosophy shows that the reason was isolated from the Platonic model of the soul as the only valuable part, and acquired an autonomy of its own. All that remains to the soul are the desires and the driving power. We find traces of such a disintegration of the Platonic concept of soul already in Plutarch (cf. Dörrie, L129).

The three components have not been brought into the same relationship in everyone, and this means that human beings can be divided into three classes, depending on what is dominant or else completely lacking: the 'pneumatic', the 'psychic', and the 'fleshly' (from σάρξ, 'flesh'; they are also called 'earthly', from χοικός, 'earthly', at Gen 2:7 Septuagint, or 'material', from ὑλή, 'matter'). Irenaeus confirms this in the case of the Valentinians: 'There are three kinds of human beings, the pneumatics, the psychics and the material, like Cain, Abel and Seth; they use these three biblical figures to demonstrate the three natures, not in the individual human being, but in the human race as a whole' (*Adv. Haer.* 1.7.5).

The pneumatics are destined for salvation, and the earthly will perish. The destiny of the psychics is as yet undecided; it depends on the direction in which they develop. It is possible that Christian gnostics understood 'the mass of ordinary Christians' in the communities as psychics; they 'stood between the heathen and the gnostics and were the target for missionary effort'.[11] EvPhil 85 (NHC II/3 72.1–4) expresses the pneumatics' feeling of superiority in very drastic terms: 'That is the way it is in the world – men make gods and worship their creation. It would be fitting for the gods to worship men!' The gods created by human beings are the idols of the pagans, whom the gnostics considered to be the progeny of the evil demiurge, i.e. beings belonging to the innerworldly order. The gnostic looked to his relatedness to the highest God and knew that this relationship placed him on a higher level than all the gods of this world.

3. Soteriology

The definition of gnosis in the *Excerpta ex Theodoto* contains the theme of soteriology in the two questions: 'Whence have we been set free?', 'What is rebirth?' We have already said that the movement as a whole derives its name from the excessively high evaluation of knowledge. Accordingly, we begin our reflections on soteriology with a consideration of this salvific knowledge.

(a) Redemption through knowledge

Naturally enough, the texts that speak of the process of acquiring knowledge as the event of salvation are legion. In Irenaeus knowledge is presented in relationship to the tripartite anthropology. Knowledge does not affect body and soul, but only the *pneuma*, which is identical to the inner human being (*Adv. Haer.* 1.21.4):

> The perfect redemption is the knowledge of the unutterable greatness. For whereas ignorance produces deficiency and sufferings, the entire condition that caused the ignorance is dissolved by knowledge. This is why gnosis is the redemption of the inner human being. It is neither bodily (since the body is perishable) nor psychic (since the soul too has its origin in deficiency, and is merely a dwelling for the *pneuma*). It follows that redemption must be pneumatic. For it is through gnosis that the inner, pneumatic human being is redeemed.

[11] K. Rudolph, *Gnosis* (L141) 92.

The process of acquiring knowledge is linked in this quotation to the mythical primal history. Knowledge cures the 'fall' of ignorance, which was the cause of deficiency and sufferings. The Gospel of Truth speaks likewise of the overcoming of the deficiency, employing a number of comparisons and images (EV NHC I/3 24.28–25.19):

> Since the deficiency came into being because the Father was not known, therefore when the Father is known, from that moment on the deficiency will no longer exist. As with the ignorance of a person, when he comes to have knowledge his ignorance vanishes of itself, as the darkness vanishes when light appears, so also the deficiency vanishes in the perfection. So from that moment on the form is not apparent, but it will vanish in the fusion of Unity, for now their works lie scattered. In time Unity will perfect the spaces. It is within Unity that each one will attain himself; within knowledge he will purify himself from multiplicity into Unity, consuming matter within himself like fire, and darkness by light, death by life.

Light blazes up where darkness reigns, and the state of perfection replaces deficiency. The material façade of the world becomes transparent, and disappears. Things are brought together out of dispersion and isolation. The plurality of the phenomena that we experience here on earth is the result of a fatal split in the original unity, that unity to which all the gnostics seek to return. A final example brings the apostle Thomas, a bearer of special gnostic revelations, into the centre of the process of knowledge. He owes his special position to the fact that his name can be interpreted to mean 'twin', and thereby, as in the following text, 'twin brother' of Christ. At the beginning of the 'Book of Thomas the Contender' (i.e., the model ascetic), the risen Lord speaks to him (NHC II/7 138.4–18):

> Brother Thomas, while you have time in the world, listen to me and I will reveal to you the things you have pondered in your mind. Now since it has been said that you are my twin and true companion, examine yourself that you may understand who you are, in what way you exist, and how you will come to be. Since you are called my brother, it is not fitting that you be ignorant of yourself. And I know that you have understood, because you had already understood that I am the knowledge of the truth ... You will be called the one who knows himself. For he who has not known himself has known nothing, but he who has known himself has at the same time achieved knowledge about the Depth of the All.

These texts allow us to identify the position of the process of acquiring knowledge in the myth that we have studied up to this point through AJ.

Through a momentary ignorance on the part of Sophia, the world came into being; it now contains sparks of light and particles of *pneuma* imprisoned within human beings. Thus redemption must mean that these sparks of light are freed from their imprisonment in the world, that they are collected together and brought back into the upper world of light. This, however, is possible only if those who bear these sparks of light come to awareness of their own selves and recognise what a treasure they bear in themselves; otherwise, it is not possible for the sparks of light to return into their native realm. Although much still remains for the gnostic to do, redemption is already largely achieved in the present through the acquisition of knowledge. From now on, the gnostic feels himself redeemed, in the genuine sense of this word.

(*b*) Forgetfulness and call

It is not, however, so easy and natural to come to knowledge as it may have seemed up to this point. The process must triumph over obstacles, and can also incur failure. The powers of evil try everything to neutralise the communication of *pneuma* (which had happened by mistake): their intention is that the human person should not notice anything of this, nor become aware of this treasure. No yearning for the heavenly world is to take hold of him, and this is why the body is imposed on him as chains, this is why he is entangled in passion and desires. This is the state in which human beings, including the potential gnostics, discover that they exist: tyrannised by sleep and drunkenness, wholly preoccupied with the business of the world, forgetful of their true being, and forgetful of their own selves. They must first be shaken out of this self-forgetfulness, as happens impressively in the Corpus Hermeticum (CH 7.1–3):[12]

> You men, where are you rushing in your drunkenness, you who have drained the undiluted doctrine of ignorance, which you cannot contain, but are already spewing out? Be sober and stop, look up with the eyes of your heart! And if all of you cannot, then at least those who can. For the evil of ignorance is flooding the whole earth and corrupting also the soul imprisoned in the body, and not letting it reach port in the havens of salvation. Therefore do not let yourselves be swept on by the great flood, but use an eddy, you who can reach the haven of salvation, make port there, seek a guide who will lead you to the gates of knowledge, where the bright light is, uncontaminated by darkness ... But first

[12] W. Foerster, *Gnosis* (L141) I.335f.

you [singular] must tear up the garment you are wearing, the fabric of ignorance, the base of evil, the bond of corruption, the dark wall, the living death, the perceptible corpse, the grave you carry around with you, the robber within you ... Such is the enemy whom you have put on as a robe, who drags you by the throat downwards towards himself, so that you may not look up and see the beauty of the truth ... he who makes insensitive the organs of sense, which are such but are not held to be such, blocking them with much matter and filling them with filthy desire, so that you neither hear what you ought to hear nor see what you ought to see.

The mildest form of this impulse *ab extra* can be stated thus: a call is necessary. A voice must be heard, waking the human person from his sleep and opening his eyes. Such a summoning call in one form or another belongs to the constitutive elements of the various gnostic systems (we take only one example, Gospel of Truth, NHC I/3 21.5–30: 'Those whose name he knew in advance were called at the end, so that the one who has knowledge is the one whose name the Father has uttered'; 22.2–7: 'If he is called, he hears, he answers, and he turns to him who is calling him, and ascends to him'). Messengers from the heavenly realm of light appear with this call, revealers who communicate the secret knowledge. The call can take on a form and be personified; the way lies open for saviour and redeemer figures.

(c) Redeemer figures

Tour d'horizon

The various gnostic systems display a considerable plurality of such redeemer figures. This is a heterogeneous gallery in which historical personages stand alongside purely mythical figures and pagan gods. We mention only a few names: Simon Magus from Acts 8; the Greek god Hermes as the equivalent of the Egyptian Thoth; Poimandres, a name interpreted in popular etymology as the 'pastor of human beings', in the Hermetic writings; Zoroaster, the legendary Persian religious founder (as Zostrianus in NHC VIII/1); Seth, the third son of Adam and Eve; and among the Mandaeans, Manda d-Haiyē, the messenger of light and of life, who says of himself in the *Right Ginza* (2.3 [58f. Lidzbarski]):

I give light to the dark hearts. With my voice and my proclamation, I sent out a call into the world ... I am the messenger of the light, whom the Great One sent into this world ... I fill with light the eyes of all who accept his words in

473

themselves ... I am the messenger of life, the truthful One in whom there is no lie.

The obvious question is: what is the relationship of such redeemer figures to history? In general, we can affirm that gnosis attaches no particular weight to a unique, historically datable appearance of such messengers. Rather, their actions have an atemporal quality. What they do can be repeated at any time and any place. Ultimately, this is because the redemption which takes place at specific points in history is always intimately connected to the mythical primal event, as a prolongation of the primal struggle into the present time.

Salvator salvandus?

An older generation of scholars was firmly accustomed to reducing gnostic soteriology to the formula *salvator salvandus*, i.e. the 'redeemed redeemer', or more precisely, 'the redeemer who himself is in need of redemption'.

This formula synthesises the following mythical narrative. A being from the world of light, e.g. a primal human being, loses parts of himself to the power of darkness. These parts are imprisoned in matter. This is why the primal human being must descend into the world and gather together these particles of light in a wearisome process, so that he himself may once again be made whole and may return to the perfection he had at the outset. By liberating the particles of light that are in the world, he redeems himself from a profound deficiency which gives him no rest.

The redeemer myth in this special form is, however, found first in Manichaeism and cannot simply be extended to all the gnostic systems. This is why modern scholars handle the 'redeemed redeemer' more cautiously. Another formulation has become more central, viz. that of the consubstantiality of the redeemer and that which he redeems. Both share in a common spiritual substance, so that they are essentially related to each other. This consubstantiality is not brought about by an event such as the incarnation of the redeemer, but is antecedent to his appearing on earth, and has its origin in the primal event, when the devolution of the divine and the splitting of the pneumatic particles occurred.

Female redeemer figures

According to AJ, when the initial error is to be made good, this concerns above all Sophia herself, or else her male consort. In theory, it is also possible for Sophia to take on the role of the heavenly messenger in gnosis, so that the redeemer figure is given female attributes. One example is found in the treatise *Protennoia* (NHC XIII/1). Protennoia means 'first thought' in the feminine. She is the first thought of the father God who exists before time and above the world, and she contains the female aspects of his being. Her own first word, her logos, is also accounted her son. This results in the trinity of Father, Mother and Son which is not uncommon in gnosis. The text describes the successive threefold revelation (this is the source of the title: *Tripartite Protennoia*)[13] of the one primal power as father, as woman, and as son. In the revelatory discourse of the middle, female Protennoia, we are told: 'It is I who lift up the Sound of the Voice to the ears of those who have known me, that is, the Sons of the Light. Now I have come the second time in the likeness of a female and have spoken with them' (AJ 42.14–18).

Motif of the cloak of invisibility
We quote one idea found in the revelatory discourse of the third figure, the Logos, which likewise belongs to the stereotyped motifs of gnostic soteriology, and can be classified as the motif of the cloak of invisibility. The redeemer figure must take care, while descending into the world, that the hostile troops in the seven lower heavens do not block his path. To thwart them, he puts on a disguise. The redeemer appears to the hostile powers in their own form, thus deceiving them (AJ 47.13–24):

> The third time I revealed myself to them [in] their tents as the Word and I revealed myself in the likeness of their shape. And I wore everyone's garment and I hid myself within them, and [they] did not know the one who empowers me ... And I hid myself with them until I revealed myself to my [brethren]. And none of them [the Powers] knew me.

The final affirmation which the Logos makes about himself in this document brings us directly to our next point: 'I put on Jesus. I bore him from the cursed wood, and established him in the dwelling places of his Father' (50.12–15).

(*d*) Docetic christology

List 153.
M. Franzmann, *Jesus in the Nag Hammadi Writings*, Edinburgh 1996.

[13] Cf. G. Schenke, *Die dreigestaltige Protennoia* (Nag-Hammadi-Codex XIII) (TU 132), Berlin 1984.

U. B. Müller, *Die Menschwerdung des Gottessohnes: Frühchristliche In-karnationsvorstellungen und die Anfänge des Doketismus* (SBS 140), Stuttgart 1990.

E. Rose, *Die manichäische Christologie* (StOR 5), Wiesbaden 1979.

M. Slusser, 'Docetism: A Historical Definition', *SecCen* 1 (1991) 163–72.

K. W. Tröger, 'Doketistische Christologie in Nag-Hammadi-Texten: Ein Beitrag zum Doketismus in frühchristlicher Zeit', *Kairos* 19 (1977) 45–52.

D. Voorgang, *Die Passion Jesu und Christi in der Gnosis* (EHS.T 432), Frankfurt a.M. 1991.

P. Weigandt, *Der Doketismus im Urchristentum und in der theologischen Entwicklung des zweiten Jahrhunderts*, theological dissertation, Heidelberg 1961.

The role of redeemer was often atttibuted to Jesus Christ by Christian gnostics. All they needed to do was to adopt the Christian soteriology with gratitude and give it a gnostic twist. The result of this, in terms of dogmatic theology, is docetism in Christology, in a strict version and also in a form of 'separation Christology'. Strict docetism concedes that Christ had only the semblance of a body, made of a pneumatic substance. 'Separation Christology' speaks of an external unification of the heavenly spiritual being Christ with the human being Jesus of Nazareth for the time that elapsed between the baptism and the crucifixion, but not including the latter. These christologies are different, but ultimately they converge: not only is the incarnation eliminated, but also – by means of various artifices – the death on the cross.

Such Christologies were already known from the patristic accounts. Irenaeus tells us that Satornilus (before 150 CE) taught that the redeemer was 'not born, nor embodied, and without form; it was only in outward appearance that he became visible as a human being' (*Adv. Haer.* 1.24.2). His contemporary Cerdo denied 'that Christ was in the flesh', asserting that 'he was present only in a deceptive image. He did not suffer at all, in reality; it was only thought that he suffered' (Ps.-Tertullian, *Adv. Omn. Haer.* 6.1). Cerinthus favoured a Christology of indwelling and separation (*Adv. Haer.* 1.26.3). Basilides operated with a switch of characters at the crucifixion: it was not Jesus who suffered, 'but a certain Simon of Cyrene, who was forced to carry the cross for him. This man was crucified out of error and ignorance, after he had been transformed by him [i.e. Jesus] so that he was taken to be Jesus. But Jesus took on the form of the Son and stood there, laughing them to scorn' (*Adv. Haer.* 1.24.4). The Acts of John combine the idea that the redeemer takes on many forms (ActJoh 93: 'Sometimes, when I made to touch him, I encountered a material, firm body; another time, when I touched him, the substance was immaterial and unbodily, as if it did not exist') with his self-distancing from the event of the cross: 'John, as far as the crowd down there in Jerusalem are concerned, I was crucified and pierced with lances and reeds, and given vinegar and gall to drink. But now I am talking to you ... I am not the one on the cross ... thus I have not suffered any of those things that they will say about me' (ActJoh 97–101; from the point of view of literary criticism, this combination may be a sign of a secondary stage).

Here the Nag Hammadi texts have surprised us with new textual evidence. The *Second Treatise of the Great Seth* (NHC VII/2) also knows of the confusion of Simon of Cyrene with Jesus: 'I did not die in reality, but in appearance' (55.18f.); 'it was another, Simon, who bore the cross on his shoulder. It was another upon whom they placed the crown of thorns. But I was rejoicing in the height ... And I was laughing at their ignorance' (56.9–14, 18–20). In the Apocalypse of Peter (NHC VII/3), Peter is led step by step to the knowledge that only the fleshly element of the redeemer suffers, not the pneumatic element: 'He whom you saw on the tree, glad and laughing, this is the living Jesus. But this one into whose hands and feet they drive the nails is his fleshly (σαρκικόν) part, which is the substitute [the Coptic has the word for 'exchange'] being put to shame, the one who came into being in his likeness' (81.15–23).

There can be no question that this point reveals the greatest difference between gnosis and the faith that has established itself as orthodox Christianity. This, however, does not alter the fact that shared roots in Jewish adoptionist theology of the Messiah and in an 'angelic' Christology influenced by Judaism can still be discerned. It suffices here to recall the angel Raphael in the Book of Tobit, who takes his leave, after having been present in a very direct and living manner as Tobias' travelling companion, with the words: 'Although you were watching me, I really did not really eat or drink anything – but what you saw was a vision' (Tob 12:19f.). At the same time, there is a point of convergence here with Graeco-Hellenistic thinking, which operated against the background of a dualistic view of spirit and matter and thus was confronted with a dilemma by incarnational Christology. It was also accustomed to the idea that deities and heroes from time to time *appeared* on earth in human form, or let themselves be represented by a shadowy image. Striking examples of this are the shadowy image of Heracles in the underworld in Homer, *Od.* 11.601f.; the sentient image of Helena, which Paris possessed only to outward appearances (Euripides, *Hel.* 33–6: Hera 'wove my image from the air of heaven for Paris, who thought that this image was my own self, and who possessed me only in blind madness'); and the empty image (*simulacrum nudum*) or mere shadow (*umbra*) of Caesar, which was all that the daggers of those who attacked him were able to reach, since the goddess Vesta had carried off Caesar himself beforehand (in Ovid, *Fasti* 3.696–702). The convergence of these lines of thought is surely a basic reason for the attractiveness and the success of a Christology with docetic tones.

4. Eschatology

One last question from the *Excerpta ex Theodoto* remains: 'Whither are we hastening?' This addresses the eschatology which finds its main emphasis in gnosis in the ascent of the individual soul, although we also find traces of a universal eschatology that reflects on the end of the world.

(a) The ascent of the soul

The ascent of the soul to the highest heaven after death is a central theological tenet of gnosis, affirmed with varying intensity. For the Mandaeans, it is the very heart of their faith and their cultic praxis; but it is not wholly lacking in any of the gnostic systems, as far as we can tell. Its place within the mythical event can be defined as follows. Redemption does indeed take place already in the act of knowledge, but it is admitted that even the gnostic who has discovered his own self has not yet returned to the heavenly realm of light. This can happen only in the moment of death.

Dangers and means of protection

The path by which the soul ascends was made ready in advance by the redeemer, through his descent. But it is not without its dangers, for here there is a final confrontation with the opposing forces. The soul which leaves its body behind on earth must pass through all the seven heavens, in which demons, powers, authorities, and ultimately the demiurge, have their dwelling. These attempt to block the path before the soul. Once again, it is knowledge that helps the soul here. For example, if it knows the names of the lords of the seven heavens, it can use this knowledge to shatter their resistance. When the individual eschatology is clothed in narrative form, the texts usually speak of these difficulties and of how they can be overcome. The soul needs special means of protection, incantatory formulae, or magical signs and amulets that it displays to the watchers at the gates of each heavenly sphere. Origen relates in his debate with Celsus that the gnostic Ophites are given a special epigram for each of the seven heavens when they set out on their journey. This epigram permits them to continue their journey (*C. Cels.* 6.31):

> They are also instructed that when they pass through the one whom they call Ialdabaoth, they are to say: 'But as for you, archon Ialdabaoth, to whom lordship was given as the first and the seventh, I pass as a free man once again through your authority, as a sovereign logos of the pure Nous, as a perfect work for the Son and the Father, bearing the sign [σύμβολον] of life marked with the blow, opening for the world the door that you have closed by means of your aeon.

The same process can be recognised easily in the First Apocalypse of James (NHC V/3), because this text links the ascent of the soul to the fundamental questions of gnosis. The risen Jesus gives his brother James, who is still on earth, secret teachings which include directives for the time of James' death (33.4–34.20):

> A multitude will arm themselves against you that [they] may seize you. And in particular three of them will seize you – they who sit [there] as toll collectors. Not only do they demand toll, but they also take away souls by theft. When you come into their power, one of them who is their guard will say to you, 'Who are you or where are you from?' You are to say to him, 'I am a son, and I am from the Father.' ... When he also says to you, 'Where will you go?', you are to say to him, 'To the place from which I have come, there shall I return.' And if you say these things, you will escape their attacks.

As has been indicated, the Mandaeans are especially concerned about the ascent of the soul. The purpose of the repeated baptisms during life on earth is to equip the soul for its journeying after death. The ascent will take forty-two days, and during this time the community accompanies the soul with prayers and sacrifices. The good works that it performed here on earth are also a source of protection against the attacks of the hostile powers. Besides this, troops are sent from the highest heaven to protect the soul. It suffices to quote one text from the *Left Ginza* here (3.9f., 15 [519, 522, 533 Lidzbarski]):

Soul, arm yourself with the donation that is your reward, with your works and your alms. For the path you are to take is broad and endless. No miles are marked off on that path, no milestones measured off along it. Guardhouses have been set up along that path, and bailiffs and customs officers stand along it ... From the very beginning I have been marked with the sign. The demons stand along the street. As soon as the Seven saw me, the Seven took up their positions and armed themselves ... The demons surround my body, and the Seven stand there and make evil plans. The Seven plot against me and form secret plans against me: 'When he departs from us, we will bind him in the house of the customs officers. If he calls, who will answer him, and who will be a redeemer for him?' ... A great Uthra was sent to me, a man who is to be my helper. He broke down their guardhouses and made a breach in their fortress, and the Seven fled away out of his path. He brought splendour and clothed me with it, bringing me out of the world with pomp.

Judgement

The path of ascent also means that the soul is judged, and it appears to some extent that a purification is possible. Unworthy souls are not permitted to continue along the path; sooner or later, the point arrives where they must stop. Where the gnostics reflected on the destiny of these souls, they offered various answers. For example, when we are told that the soul is sent back into a new body, thus receiving a new possibility of proving its worth, there lies behind this the doctrine of the transmigration of souls, popularised by Pythagoreanism (although this school was not especially prized by the gnostics). We also find various descriptions of how the souls of the unworthy are tormented by the demonic powers in the lower heavens. Here the traditional concept of the underworld with its hellish penalties is taken over, now transposed into the realm between the earth and the highest heaven (as we have already seen in Plutarch). Once again, we find a vivid statement of this in the *Left Ginza* (1.4 [444 Lidzbarski]):

Then the soul went on and came upon a guardhouse in which were the instrument of torture, stocks for the feet, torment and pain. Here the guilty souls are judged by a law that knows no law. Magicians and witches are whipped with a fiery scourge, and they are thrown like worms into the mouths of the ovens. When the soul sees these in the place assigned to them, it shivers and trembles, and its whole figure trembles in its garment. It calls to the great, exalted Life ... and it receives this reply: 'O soul! You are ascending to the place of light. Why are you calling upon the great, exalted Life? State your name and your sign ...'

It is also possible for souls to perish definitively: 'For he who is ignorant to the end is a creature of oblivion, and he will vanish along with it' (Gospel of Truth, NHC I/3, 21.34–8). One may presume that this is first of all the destiny of the 'material' human beings; in the case of the 'psychics', the pendulum can swing in either direction. AJ reckons with the possibility that even gnostics can lose their salvation (70.8–71.2):

> I said to him: 'Lord, how is it then with the souls of those who have attained Gnosis, but then turned away?' He said to me: 'They shall reach the place at which the angels of poverty, who have not been converted, will withdraw, and they shall all be preserved until the day on which they are punished. Everyone who has blasphemed against the Sacred Pneuma shall be tormented in everlasting punishment.'

The unforgivable sin against the Holy Spirit (familiar from Mk 3:28f.) is the conscious decision to refuse the knowledge that has been granted. Does this mean that the gnostics accept that some particles of light are lost, so that the realm of light will not contain the full number when the final reckoning is drawn up? Perhaps this inconsistency is tolerated, in order to intensify the exhortation; it is also possible that the universal eschatology can somehow balance the books.

Resurrection

A classical topos of eschatology in the Jewish-Christian tradition is the resurrection of the dead. Gnosis treats this theme in two ways. First, resurrection is understood metaphorically, as an image of the process of acquiring knowledge. In Christian gnosis, resurrection is seen as already brought about by baptism; only against this background can one understand two logia from the Gospel of Philip (NHC II/3) which otherwise seem meaningless, viz. 21*a* (56.15–18): 'Those who say that the Lord died first and (then) rose up are in error, for he rose up first and (then) he died', and 90*a* (73.1–4): 'Those who say that they will die first and then rise are in error. If they do not first receive the resurrection while they live, when they die they will receive nothing.' Secondly, resurrection can also be identified with the ascent of the soul, as in the *Exegesis on the Soul* (NHC II/6): 'This is the resurrection that is from the dead. This is the ransom from captivity. This is the upward journey of ascent to heaven. This is the way of ascent to the Father' (134.11–15).

One final problem still remains open. The soul too is a product of the seven lower planetary spheres; only the spirit returns into the *plērōma*.

What happens then to the soul in the framework of a tripartite anthropology? The answer is that the first event is reversed in the ascent of the soul. The soul leaves behind in each of the seven heavens the building brick that it received from there (a detailed description can be found in *Poimandres*). At the end of this path the soul has dissolved itself. All that remains is the hard core, the spark of the soul, the gnostic self. It has now been completely detached from the world. Nothing now stands in the way of the return of the pure spirit into the realm of spirit.

(b) The end of the world

The last remarks on individual eschatology above open the way to a consideration of universal eschatology. A spiritual particle returns into the realm of light, purified from every last element of the earth. One fragment of that which was broken into pieces and shattered is restored to its original place. When this has happened to the totality of the particles of light and spirit, then the realm of light must be once again complete. In any case, the earthly world, as the creation of the demiurge, lived only from the power that its creator had stolen from above; when this power is totally withdrawn from the world, then it must disintegrate and vanish. This is the completion of the circle; the world has reached its end, in the usual sense of this term. Despite this circular movement, the orientation as a whole must be called linear; it is not established cyclically. A programme unfolds resolutely from the devolution of the divine to its total restitution: 'It is a matter of a "process of separation" with its own inner dynamic which eventually comes to a standstill when the alienation of the "spirit" is annulled.'[14] This abolition is irrevocable – no new alienation is envisaged.

Gnosis remains dependent on the common, already existing myths when it wishes to elaborate the eschatological events. One of these is the *ekpyrōsis*, the conflagration in which the world perishes at the end of time. A text of Irenaeus agrees here with a treatise from Nag Hammadi called *The Concept of our Great Power* (NHC VI/4):

> Then the pyschics, who have divested themselves of their souls and have become pure spirits, enter the *plērōma* invisibly, without any hindrance ... But after this, the fire that is hidden in the world will break forth, catch light,

---

[14] K. Rudolph, *Gnosis* (L141) 195.

destroy all matter, and perish together with this matter and be reduced to nothing (*Adv. Haer.* 1.7.1).

When the fire has consumed them all, and when it does not find anything else to burn, then it will perish by its own hand ... Then the firmaments [will fall] down to the depth. Then [the] sons of matter will perish; they will not be, henceforth' (46.29–47.8).

This world conflagration may offer a last possibility of liberation for the remaining particles of light, which the fire will melt out of matter, before everything else is reduced to nothing. One may also wonder whether it is ultimately possible for the demiurge too to be saved in this way, since he too has particles of spirit in himself. This would come close to the (Origenist) doctrine of *apokatastasis*, with the difference that here the ideal is not a renewed and redeemed world, but rather a dematerialised realm of pure spirit.

Manichaeism, in which dualism found its strongest metaphysical expression, took a different view. According to Manichaean doctrine, there will be a world conflagration lasting 1,468 years. The wretched remnant that survives when the fire is extinguished – darkness, particles of matter, demons, and sinful souls – will be squashed into a lump (βόλος in Greek) and shut up in a pit. This is the definitive victory over evil, which can never be dangerous again: it has been cleared away like rubbish and stored away for ever.

5. Ecclesiology

Up to this point, we have been able to link our overview to particular questions from the definition of gnosis in the *Excerpta ex Theodoto*, but no such question is available for the gnostic view of community and Church. At most, one could take the first person plural form of the first six questions as an indication that it is not an isolated individual who speaks here, and that there must exist an awareness of a solidarity which unites those who ask these questions. It can scarcely be denied that gnosis has a fundamental tendency towards individualisation. Its writings employ wide-reaching mythical narratives to speak of the destiny of the individual soul, apparently with virtually no place for a discussion of the problems involved in the formation of community. Nevertheless, we know from the Church fathers that there existed a multiplicity of gnostic schools which could be identified in some way. The existence of the gnostic writings likewise demands an explanation; there must have been groups behind these texts. The question can be put in other terms: how did one realise that one was a chosen gnostic? In practice, this presumably came about only through membership of a gnostic community.

(a) The concept of *ekklēsia*

The concept of *ekklēsia* is found *tout court* in gnostic texts, but it is supplied with a specifically new interpretation. The exclusive primary meaning of *ekklēsia* is a 'higher', pre-existent Church which itself belongs to the emanations of the highest God and is a personified aeon. Other spiritual beings in the realm of light belong to this true Church. Its earthly image is the totality of the pneumatics who bear the spirit in themselves, have attained knowledge and are awaiting the ascent of their souls, which will unite them definitively with the *ekklēsia*. The Tripartite Treatise (NHC 1/5) speaks of this higher Church (57.33–40; 58.29–33):

> Not only does the Son exist from the beginning, but the Church, too, exists from the beginning. Now he who thinks that the discovery that the Son is an only son opposes the word [about the Church] – because of the mysterious quality of the matter it is not so ... Such is the Church consisting of many men, which exists before the aeons, and which is called, in the proper sense, 'the aeon of the aeons'.

Even as the earthly image of the heavenly *ekklēsia*, the *ekklēsia* of the pneumatics remains a theoretical or, better, a mythological construct. It need not appear actively as a visible organisation. Gnosis knows of the Church in this general sense only as an entity belonging purely to the sphere of consciousness and knowledge; the exception to this rule is Manichaeism, and we shall therefore begin by discussing this on its own.

(b) Forms of organisation

List 154.
G. Koffmane, 'Die Gnosis nach ihrer Tendenz und Organisation: 12 Thesen', Breslau 1881, reprinted in K. Rudolph, *Gnosis und Gnostizismus* (L138) 120–41.
K. Koschorke, *Die Polemik der Gnostiker gegen das kirchliche Christentum* (NHS 12), Leiden 1978.

————'Eine neugefundene gnostische Gemeindeordnung: Zum Thema Geist und Amt im frühen Christentum', *ZThK* 76 (1979) 30–60.

H. Kraft, *Gnostisches Gemeinschaftsleben*, theological dissertation, Heidelberg 1950.

Church structure

In our discussion of the sources we have already drawn attention to the astonishing geographical diffusion of the Manichaeans, especially in the East, a fact that justifies the classification of Manichaeism as a world religion. One contributory factor here is certainly the fact that the Manichaeans created the most stable Church structures of any gnostic group, which permitted them to maintain the unity of their community (which they themselves called the 'holy Church') across territorial boundaries. The most striking trait of the Manichaean Church structure is the strict division of the believers into two distinct classes, the *electi* (perfect) and *auditores* (hearers). 'For they wanted their Church to consist of these two groups, the *electi* and the *auditores*.'[15] This division is reproduced in each individual community. Only the *electi* can move upwards into the hierarchy, which borrows from models current in the worldwide Church and consists of a supreme leader who is the direct successor of Mani, twelve *magistri*, seventy-two bishops and deacons, and three hundred priests (cf. Augustine, loc. cit.: 'From among the number of the *electi* they have twelve as teachers and a thirteenth as leader. But they also have seventy-two bishops, who are installed by the teachers, and presbyters who are installed by the bishops. The bishops also have deacons').

The strict dualism leads to demands for an exceptionally severe lifestyle: the harshest asceticism including a vegetarian life without wine and meat, renunciation of marriage and private property. Physical labour was not permitted, since it could damage the particles of light which the Manichaeans believed were enclosed not only in the human person, but in nature too. These requirements were addressed in full only to the *electi*, who depended on the collaboration of the *auditores*, if they were to have any chance of observing them. The *auditores* provided financial support for the life of the *electi*, and it was they who did all the work, since the observance of the ascetic guidelines forbade many things that were simply necessary in life. A catalogue of other, less severe commandments was

[15] Augustine, *De Haeresibus* 46.

drawn up for the *auditores*. Significantly, its ten fundamental principles include the obligation to care indefatigably for the *electi*.

While the *electi* are saved and enter the realm of light, the *auditores* are initially not damned. They incur guilt, but this can be forgiven. In their case, there is a justified hope that their souls will at some later point be reborn in one of the *electi*, or will come afresh to the world in a plant that contains light and that will then be eaten by one of the *electi* (cucumbers and melons are prominent in the list of such plants): 'They believe that the souls of their *auditores* will be changed into *electi*, or else, in a happier fashion, into the food of their *electi*, so that they may be purified there and may avoid returning into a body' (Augustine, loc. cit.). It is clear that this involves a compromise between the gnostic ideal and the demands made by real life. A high price was paid for the consistent asceticism of the *electi*, viz. the division of the community into an elite and foot-soldiers.

The formation of fractions

As Koschorke has shown, Christian gnostics attempted to find and maintain their place in the worldwide Church. They formed an inner circle within a local community. They did not simply give up the 'ordinary' Christians in community and Church as lost, but rather classified them as psychics who had not yet gone beyond the initial basic elements of true doctrine, but whose situation could still be changed. To the extent that one can speak of missionary endeavours on the part of gnostics, their preferred addressee was the average Christian believer, who was to be transformed from a psychic into a pneumatic.

It is obvious enough that such conduct would necessarily provoke a conflict within the Church. Concrete reasons of Church politics led a man like Irenaeus, bishop of Lyons, to devote such intensive study to gnosis. The gnostics saw the kind of polemic in which Irenaeus engaged in a rather different light: in their view, the ecclesiastical authorities wanted to expel them unjustifiably from the Church. They felt that they were the victims of persecution, not by pagans, but by their own fellow Christians – something much harder to take. A passage in the *Second Treatise of the Great Seth* (NHC VII/2) alludes to this situation (59.19–32):

> After we went forth from our home, and came down to this world, and came into being in the world in bodies, we were hated and persecuted, not only by those who are ignorant, but also by those who think that they are advancing the name of Christ, since they were unknowingly empty, not knowing who they

are, like dumb animals. They persecuted those who have been liberated by me, since they hate them.

Independent groups

Gnostics also availed themselves of the possibility of forming independent groups. Two main models were available to guide the gnostics here (cf. Koffmane, whose study is still relevant), viz. the cultic and mystery associations and the philosophical schools. Ritual practices such as memorial meals, ceremonies of initiation, and the *disciplina arcani* could be adopted from these, as well as the internal self-organisation according to particular rules (cf. in greater detail I/B). The technical term in Greek for such associations, *thiasos*, is also attested as a name applied to gnostic groups both by themselves and by outsiders. The interest in intellectual activity and in the care of particular traditions was a further factor promoting an inherent closeness to the philosophical schools.

The model of the associations and schools offered many advantages. It permitted loose gatherings according to specific needs and situations, making it easier (where this was desired) for them to isolate themselves vis-à-vis the outer world, and it also gave freedom to decide what ministries were needed and how these should be assigned. However, it prevented an overarching organisation from coming into existence, and provoked a succession of new processes of division. The Church fathers were angered above all by the lack of discipline in the question of Church ministry. Tertullian wrote polemically against this, sarcastic and sharp-tongued as ever. The passage most likely comes from his Catholic period *(Praescr. Haer. 41)*:

> Nor will I omit a description of the manner of life of the heretics, portraying it in all its looseness, its worldliness, its low human character, without dignity, without authority, without Church discipline, and utterly in keeping with their own faith. To begin with, one does not even know who is a catechumen and who is a believer. They go in together, they listen together, they pray together ... All are puffed up, all promise knowledge. The catechumens are already *perfecti*, even before they have received any instruction. And then, the heretical women – how impertinent and presumptuous they are! They take it upon themselves to teach, to engage in disputes, to carry out exorcisms, to promise healings, perhaps even to baptise too ... Nowhere is promotion easier than in the camp of the rebels, where mere physical presence counts as a virtue. So one of them is bishop today, another tomorrow; someone is a deacon today and a lector tomorrow; or else, a priest today and a layman tomorrow. For they entrust the priestly functions to laymen too.

(c) The role of women

List 155.

R. H. Arthur, *The Wisdom Goddess: Feminine Motifs in Eight Nag Hammadi Documents*, Lanham, Md. 1984.

J. J. Buckley, *Female Fault and Fulfilment in Gnosticism* (Studies in Religion), Chapel Hill and London 1986.

D. L. Hoffmann, *The Status of Women and Gnosticism in Irenaeus and Tertullian* (SWR 36), Lewiston etc. 1995.

K. L. King (ed.), *Images of the Feminine in Gnosticism* (Studies in Antiquity and Christianity), Philadelphia 1988.

A. Marjanen, *The Woman Jesus Loved: Mary Magdalene in the Nag Hammadi Library and Related Documents* (NHS 40), Leiden 1996.

M. W. Meyer, 'Making Mary Male: The Categories "Male" and "Female" in the Gospel of Thomas', *NTS* 31 (1985) 554–70.

Tertullian appears to have been stirred to extreme wrath by the activity of women in gnostic communities. Other Church fathers too seize the opportunity offered by precisely this point to pour scorn on the community life of the gnostics and to express the gravest suspicions. Kurt Rudolph has expressed as follows the substantial issue that is involved here: 'The percentage of women was evidently very high and reveals that Gnosis held out prospects otherwise barred to them, especially in the official Church. They frequently occupied leading positions [in gnostic groups] either as teachers, prophetesses, missionaries, or played a leading role in cultic ceremonies (baptism, eucharist) and magical practices (exorcisms).'[16]

Testimonies from the gnostic writings offer us little direct information, since they do not speak of community forms. But we can collect a number of pointers. The Coptic gnostic texts include a 'Gospel of Mary' (i.e. of Mary Magdalene: BG 8502/1), who consoles the desolate disciples after Jesus' departure. At Peter's request, she holds a revelatory discourse about things the Lord had entrusted to her (and to no one else) in a vision (10.1–11):[17]

> Peter said to Mary: 'Sister, we know that the Saviour loved you more than the rest of women. Tell us the words of the Saviour which you remember – which you know [but] we do not nor have we heard them.' Mary answered and said,

[16] *Gnosis* (L141) 211.

[17] Eng. trans. *NHLibrary* 471ff.

'What is hidden from you I will proclaim to you.' And she began to speak to them these words: 'I', she said, 'saw the Lord in a vision ...'

The apocryphal Acts of the Apostles, which to some extent display a gnostic colouring, are likewise familiar with the participation of women in the activity of preaching and in community tasks. Nor should we underestimate the significance of the integration of a female figure into the redeemer myth, whether she is called Barbelo, Sophia, Ennoia, Helena (among the Simonians), etc. It is of course true that doubts are reawakened when we hear the final logion of the Gospel of Thomas (114):

> Simon Peter said to them, 'Let Mary leave us, for women are not worthy of Life.' Jesus said, 'I myself shall lead her in order to make her male, so that she too may become a living spirit resembling you males. For every woman who will make herself male will enter the Kingdom of Heaven.'

To understand this, however, we must return to the gnostic mythology and recall the ideal of androgyny, i.e. of the dual gender or of the total overcoming of sexuality. The fact that two genders exist is a sign of division. This fact does indeed govern the earthly world, but it contradicts the perfection of the eternal *plērōma*. One can also draw here on the idea of the pairs of consorts, e.g. Christ and Sophia: such syzygies normally consist of a male and a female half. Their separation corresponds to a defective state of affairs, their uniting in a male-female, virginal being signifies that unity and perfection have been re-established. This is expressed in logion 22 of the Gospel of Thomas:

> When you make the two one, and when you make the inside like the outside and the outside like the inside, and the above like the below, and when you make the male and the female one and the same, so that the male not be male nor the female female ... then will you enter [the Kingdom].

One must certainly admit that androcentric categories often play a leading role when the separation and the reuniting are described, as in EvThom 114, though this is less the case in EvThom 22, where the idea is a genuine integration, without excessive emphasis on the one pole. Such relics of traditional patterns of speech and thought seem not to have had any profound effect on the de facto activity of women within the gnostic groups. It must be said, however, that the committed activity of women within these gnostic groups proved to be an additional burden, in terms of their role in the worldwide Church: in addition to all the other reservations

489

that already existed, the fact that this was now seen as a typical trait of gnostic heresies was a totally negative factor.

(d) Worship, I: prayers

List 156.

P. Claude, *Les Trois Stèles de Seth: Hymne gnostique à la Triade* (BCNH.T 8), Québec 1983.

M. Krause and V. Girgis, 'Die drei Stelen des Seth', in F. Altheim and R. Stiehl, *Christentum am Roten Meer*, vol. 2, Berlin 1973, 180–99.

B. Layton, *Scriptures* (L141) 149–58.

H. M. Schenke and K. Wekel, '"Die drei Stelen des Seth": Die fünfte Schrift aus Nag-Hammadi-Codex VII', *ThLZ* 100 (1975) 571–80.

E. Segelberg, 'Prayer among the Gnostics? The Evidence of Some Nag Hammadi Documents', in M. Krause, *Gnosis* (L138) 55–89.

M. Tardieu, 'Les Trois Stèles de Seth', *RSPhTh* 57 (1973) 545–75.

Where communities exist, they also engage in common activities, elaborating forms of worship and cult. Here too, it would have been more consistent if the gnostics had rejected all external actions, and withdrawn in a radical manner into the internal spiritual realm; but even gnostics were seldom so consistent. Thus, the Mandaeans gave their existence the shape of a cultic community centred on baptism. We are told that the Manichaeans gave cultic veneration to the portrait of Mani, which occupied an honoured place in their assemblies. They placed votive gifts in front of this image. We shall discuss this question in two stages. First, there are relatively few problems about the hymns and prayers, i.e. the verbal actions. Secondly, more problems arise with the gnostic sacraments, to which we shall devote a specific section.

Prayers were spoken when the gnostic groups came together, and our sources contain a number of relevant texts, including entire collections of prayers such as the Manichaean Psalter, the Mandaean liturgies, and perhaps also the Odes of Solomon (cf. B, 1(*b*)). Much of this material could have been used without any reservation by Christians of the worldwide Church at that period, but sometimes what we might call gnostic fish hooks and traps for the feet are concealed in the texts.

Out of this ample material, we choose as our example the *Three Steles of Seth* (NHC VIP5). This is a relatively short text, occupying ten columns in the manuscript, complete in itself and well preserved. The three steles or pillars contain three texts of prayers that are to be recited in the community, preceded by a brief text that sets the scene (118.10–19):

> The revelation of Dositheos about the three steles of Seth, the Father of the living and unshakeable race, which he [Dositheos] saw and understood. And after he had read them, he remembered them. And he gave them to the elect, just as they were inscribed there.

Josephus tells us that Seth, the son born to Adam after the fall, bequeathed esoteric knowledge on two stone tablets to those who would come after him (*Ant.* 1.70f.). Here he is called the ancestor of the gnostics ('the living and unshakeable race'). He inscribed the prayers on the pillars. A seer called Dositheos (the name of a pupil and successor of Simon Magus, according to patristic testimony) saw the pillars in a vision and memorised the texts of the prayers, and now hands them on to the gnostic community. This fictitious framework is admirably suited to increase the value of the following prayers in cultic practice. Here are some excerpts from the second Stele (121.19–26; 122.4f.; 123.15–124.15):

> The Second Stele of Seth: Great is the first aeon, male virginal Barbelo, the first glory of the invisible Father, she who is called 'perfect'. Thou [fem.] hast seen first him who really pre-exists ... [We] bless thee, producer [fem.] of perfection, aeon-giver [fem.] ... Salvation has come to us, from thee is salvation. Thou art wisdom, thou knowledge; thou art truthfulness. On account of thee is life; from thee is life. On account of thee is mind, from thee is mind. Thou art a mind, thou a world of truthfulness, thou a triple power ... Unite us as thou hast been united. Teach us [those] things which thou dost see. Empower [us] that we may be saved to eternal life. For [we] are [each] a shadow of thee as thou art a shadow [of that] first pre-existent one. Hear us first. We are eternal ones. Hear us as the perfect individuals. Thou art the aeon of aeons, the all-perfect one who is established. Thou hast heard! Thou hast heard! Thou hast saved! Thou hast saved! We give thanks! We bless always! We shall glorify thee! The Second Stele of Seth.

The prayer is addressed to Barbelo, the gnostic mother goddess, and recapitulates essential stages of the myth, with emphasis on the theme of knowledge. Petitions are made in the middle section, *inter alia* that unity may be achieved, that the state of division and scattering may be overcome. It is not however petitionary prayer that dominates, still less lamentation, but rather thanksgiving and praise for the redemption which has already taken place. After the prayer text of the third stele, the treatise concludes with these words (127.6–21):

He who will remember these and give glory always will become perfect among those who are perfect and unattainable from any quarter. For they all bless these individually and together. And afterwards they shall be silent. And just as they were ordained, they ascend. After the silence, they descend. From the third they bless the second, after these the first. The way of ascent is the way of descent.

This is nothing other than a liturgical rubric. The three prayers on the three pillars are intended for the worship of the community. There are precentors who speak alone; there are parts that are recited together; there are phases of meditative silence. The sequence of the prayers is laid down: first they ascend from the first prayer on the first pillar, via the second, to the conclusion of the third, and this is the way of ascent. Then the path leads downwards, from the end of the third pillar back to the beginning of the first pillar, and this is the path of descent. When the three texts have been read aloud individually and in common, forwards and backwards, the act of worship is at its end.

(e) Worship, II: sacraments

List 157.

W. Bousset, *Hauptprobleme* (L150) 276–319.

L. Fendt, *Gnostische Mysterien: Ein Beitrag zur Geschichte des christlichen Gottesdienstes*, Munich 1922.

H. G. Gaffron, *Studien zum koptischen Philippusevangelium mit besonderer Berücksichtigung der Sakramente*, theological dissertation, Bonn 1969.

W. W. Isenberg, 'The Gospel of Philip', in *NHLibrary* 139–60.

H.-J. Klauck, *Herrenmahl* (L5) 205–33 (with bibliography).

K. Koschorke, *Polemik* (L154) 142–8.

M. Krause, 'Das Philippusevangelium', in W. Foerster, *Gnosis* (L141) II.76–101.

——'Die Sakramente in der *Exegese über die Seele*', in J. E. Ménard (ed.), *Les Textes de Nag Hammadi* (NHS 7), Leiden 1975, 47–55.

B. Layton, 'The Gospel According to Philip', in Idem, *Scriptures* (L141) 325–53.

—— and W. W. Isenberg, 'The Gospel According to Philip', in B. Layton (ed.), *Nag Hammadi Codex II,2–7 ... vol. 1* (NHS 20), Leiden 1989, 129–217.

H. M. Schenke, 'The Gospel of Philip', in Hennecke and Schneemelcher, *New Testament Apocrypha* (L143), I.271–8.

J. M. Sevrin, *Le Dossier baptismal séthien* (BCNH 2), Québec 1986.

W. C. Till, *Das Evangelium nach Philippus* (PTS 2), Berlin 1963.
M. L. Turner, *The Gospel According to Philip: The Sources and Coherence of an Early Christian Collection* (NHS 38), Leiden 1996.
L. Wehr, *Arznei der Unsterblichkeit: Die Eucharistie bei Ignatius von Antiochien und im Johannesevangelium* (NTA NF 18), Münster 1987, 280–314.

Sacraments not only presuppose a community; they also involve material signs. How does this agree with the gnostic rejection of created matter? Would not the only consistent attitude be the one summarised as follows by Irenaeus: 'Others again reject all these practices and say that one must not represent the mystery of the ineffable and invisible power by means of visible and perishable created things, nor the mystery of the unthinkable and bodiless beings by means of sensuous and material things' (*Adv. Haer.* 1.21.4)? But those whose assertions are reported here are in fact attacking their fellow gnostics, who differed from them by acknowledging and celebrating sacraments. This is why Wilhelm Bousset could go so far as to say that: 'Just as in them [i.e. the mystery cults] the centre of practical piety is everywhere the belief in sacred actions, mysteries, and sacraments which are effective *ex opere operato*, so it is here too [i.e., in gnosis]' (227). In praxis, the sacramental action and the gnostic knowledge of substantial realities did not cancel one another out, but were mutually complementary. Bousset argues that the gnostics borrowed the sacramental rites themselves from the mystery cults (see our Chapter II above) and from the worldwide Church. They inherited one rite, namely baptism, and also developed a number of rites of their own.

We shall use the Gospel of Philip (NHC II/3) as our guideline in studying the gnostic sacraments. The key text is EvPhil 68 (67.27–30):

> The Lord [did] everything in a mystery [μυστήριον]:
> a baptism [βάπτισμα]
> and a chrism [χρῖσμα]
> and a Eucharist [εὐχαριστία]
> and a redemption [ἀπολύτρωσις][18]
> and a bridal chamber [νυμφών].

We know three of these mysteries from the praxis of the worldwide Church, viz. baptism, anointing with oil, and the Eucharist, but two are

---

[18] A Coptic word is used in the original text, not a Greek loanword as in the other cases.

new: the redemption and the bridal chamber. All five are attested in other gnostic texts, and are mentioned in numerous further logia in the Gospel of Philip. The evaluation of these mysteries, which we shall now carry out, reveals a double structure of the list of five in EvPhil 68, with regard both to the chronological sequence and to their order of precedence.

Baptism

The Gospel of Philip has some daring images for baptism, which is doubtless something the gnostics (like others) inherited from the Jewish baptist movement in the Jordan valley, e.g. in 43 (61.12f.): 'God is a dyer', or in 54 (63.25–30):

> The Lord went into the dye works of Levi. He took seventy-two different colours and threw them into the vat. He took them out all white. And he said, 'Even so has the Son of Man come [as] a dyer.'

To understand this image, one must recall the possibility of a play on words in Greek. Both βαπτίζειν, 'to baptise', and βάπτειν, 'to colour', can be derived from the root βαπτ–. The seventy-two colours, an allusion either to the seventy-two disciples in Lk 10:1 or to the seventy-two peoples in the table of the nations in Gen 10, serve here as a symbol of the multiplicity of phenomena which are to be brought back to unity. All that remains is the colour white, and this recalls the garment of light which will be received in the future.

Anointing with oil

Together with baptism, the anointing with oil forms the sacrament of the beginnings, the initiation into the Christian-gnostic community. We can find indications of how this was understood in EvPhil 95 (74.12–2.1), where we are reminded that the root χρίω, 'to anoint', lies behind the name 'Christ' and the term 'Christian':

> The chrism is superior to baptism, for it is from the word 'chrism' that we have been called 'Christians', certainly not because of the word 'baptism'. And it is because of the chrism that 'the Christ' has his name. For the Father anointed the Son, and the Son anointed the apostles, and the apostles anointed us. He who has been anointed possesses everything. He possesses the resurrection, the light, the cross, the Holy Spirit.

In another passage, the Gospel of Philip says: 'You saw Christ, you became Christ' (44 [61.30f.]). Not only does the gnostic become a Christian, he also becomes a Christ. Symbolically, this happens not through baptism alone, but only through the subsequent anointing with oil. Presumably the forehead was anointed, but possibly the whole body received the anointing.

Eucharist

Some form of sacred meal is a constant element in the numerous types of religion in classical antiquity, and thus in gnosis too. The Gospel of Philip designates it with the term common in the vocabulary of the worldwide Church. Unlike baptism and chrism, it is often repeated, and accompanies the life of the believers. EvPhil 26b (58.10–14) tells us what happens to them when it is celebrated: 'He [Jesus or Philip?] said on that day in the Thanksgiving, "You who have joined the perfect, the light, with the Holy Spirit, unite the angels with us also, the images".' The hoped-for salvation consists in the uniting of the earthly image with the heavenly archetype, and this is shown forth in the Eucharistic celebration of the community (one should note the plural form: 'Unite the angels with us'; cf. also EvPhil 100 and 108).

Redemption

We know very little about the ritual and meaning of the two last sacraments, the redemption and the bridal chamber. It is possible to grasp their place in the life of the believer if we take them together as a pair, a double rite corresponding to baptism and chrism. Baptism and chrism stand at the beginning of the path, redemption and bridal chamber at its close, and this means that they would be gnostic rites for the dying. It is possible to extend this hypothesis of a correspondence, on the supposition that the ritual too was parallel, i.e. that the external form of the sacrament of redemption was an anointing with oil and that of the sacrament of the bridal chamber a washing with water, or vice versa (in support of this, one may mention that the bath of the bride is found as a wedding ritual both in Judaism and among the Greeks). We do not know the substance of the sacrament of redemption, since there is no explanatory text in the Gospel of Philip. As a substitute for such a text, we may adduce a passage from Irenaeus (*Adv. Haer.* 1.21.3):

> Others again speak about the redemption as follows: 'The name that is hidden ...' The one who is perfected makes this response: 'I have become strong and am redeemed, and I free my soul from this world and from all that

belongs to it ...', and then they anoint the perfect one with oil of balsam, since they hold that this oil expresses the fragrance that lies over the universe.

In the hour of death, therefore, the anointing gives the dying person the certainty that he will come victoriously through the perilous ascent of the soul. He can leave his body, relinquishing the particles of the soul in the individual stages through which he will pass, and thus can enter into the *plērōma* as a spiritual being. The ritual act depicts the process of redemption.

Bridal chamber

The *Sitz-im-Leben* and ritual practice of the bridal chamber were probably not very different from this; the same is true of the interpretation given to this sacrament. The expression 'bridal chamber' was chosen in order to recall the uniting of that which was separated; the background for this interpretation is supplied by the ideas of androgyny (the male–female unity) and syzygy (the heavenly pairs of consorts). The consummation of marriage in the nuptial chamber is the conceptual material behind the religious-sacramental metaphors. EvPhil 76 (69.27f.) says that the bridal chamber is more exalted than baptism and even than the redemption, thereby confirming that the list of five mysteries in EvPhil 68 is structured to lead up to the bridal chamber as its high point. The final logion, EvPhil 127 (86.4–13), is once again devoted to the bridal chamber, and this position at the close of the entire work is an indication of its significance:

> If anyone becomes a son of the bridal chamber, he will receive the light. If anyone does not receive it while he is in these places, he will not be able to receive it in the other place. He who will receive that light will not be seen, nor can he be detained ... when he leaves the world, he has already received the truth in the images.

Like the other sacraments, only to a higher degree, the bridal chamber permits the proleptic experience of the future perfection of salvation, which lies closer than ever before at the hour of death. We maintain, therefore, that despite the erotic language, the sacrament of the bridal chamber, as we find it in the Gospel of Philip, signifies a wholly spiritual event, not a bodily action (nor a spiritual betrothal celebrated in real life between a man and a woman, as some scholars hold). It is unsurprising that this sacrament was exposed to distortions and misunderstandings; the

Church fathers portrayed it as a sexual act, seeking thereby to discredit the gnostics in ethical terms – what the gnostics call sacraments are merely a pretext for adultery and fornication. If we prescind from what we are told in the Gospel of Philip, it is of course possible that the fathers' views did find some support in the de facto conduct of gnostics.

6. Ethics

List 158.
S. Benko, 'The Libertine Gnostic Sect of the Phibionites according to Epiphanius', *VigChr* 21 (1967) 103–19.
M. R. Desjardins, *Sin in Valentinianism* (SBL.DS 108), Atlanta, Ga. 1990.
M. J. Edwards, 'Some Early Christian Immoralities', *AncSoc* 23 (1992) 71–82.
R. M. Grant, 'Charges of "Immorality" against Various Religious Groups in Antiquity', in R. van den Brock and M. J. Vermaseren, *Studies* (L2) 161–70.
H. Jonas, *Gnosis* I (L150).
K. Rudolph, *Gnosis* (L141) 247–63.

This introduces us directly to the discussion about gnostic ethics and about the contradictory information that we possess on this subject. None of the questions from the *Excerpta ex Theodoto* is even remotely concerned with practical conduct. We do not find the question: 'What ought I to do?', which Immanuel Kant reckoned one of the fundamental questions to which even an idealistic philosophy had to find an answer. Gnosis is not able to see any obligation to make a positive contribution to the construction of the world or society, and is consequently unable to formulate such a requirement. All that remains on the horizontal level is a definition of the gnostic's relationship to his fellow gnostics within the same group. This is why Hans Jonas has coined the expression 'fraternal ethics', which he defines thus: 'common solitude in the world which has become an alien place' (171).

The directives for practical conduct which can be discovered in the texts are contradictory, since we find both a libertine and an ascetic line. The libertinism can be summarised by means of the slogan of the Corinthian enthusiasts: 'Everything is allowed to me' (1 Cor 6:12). Moral prescriptions and standards are merely arbitrary postulates which do not affect the true gnostic, who lives on the basis of his inner freedom, without paying heed to any external ties. Whatever he wants to do is right, as long as it serves the project he makes of his own life. Irenaeus accuses some gnostic groups of having this attitude. The first of the two relevant texts concerns more the theoretical programme – the one who does not consistently practise his freedom will lose it; hence, one must demonstrate this freedom – the other concerns rather the practical aspect (*Adv. Haer.* 1.25.4; 6.3f.):

> In their madness they have abandoned all restraints to such an extent that they assert that they are free to commit any godlessness and any crime, because they say that what one does is evil or good only in the opinion of human beings. In the course of their wanderings in bodies, souls must experience every life and every action ... If, for example, their freedom had not encompassed some particular experience, they would risk being compelled to return into a body once again, and the goal towards which one must work is to avoid this.

> This is why those among them who are 'perfect' do all manner of shameless deeds ... For example, they do not hesitate to eat meat offered in sacrifice to idols, and they believe that they do not contaminate themselves thereby. They are the first to take their places at all the joyous festivals that the pagans celebrate in honour of their idols. Some of them do not even shrink from looking at fights between men and beasts, something that God and human beings detest, and at gladiatorial contests in which men are murdered. Many are enslaved beyond all measure to the lusts of the flesh and say that one must pay one's dues to the flesh with that which is of the flesh, and to the spirit with that which is of the spirit. And some abuse women in secret, after they have given them instruction in their doctrine ... Nor does this exhaust the total sum of disgusting and godless things they do. But they pour abuse on us, who have fear of God and therefore take care to avoid sinning even in thoughts and words, as simpletons and idiots.

Irenaeus and the other fathers – especially Epiphanius, the 'hammer of the heretics', deserves a mention here – give us external testimony; we have very little evidence of the libertine tendency in texts written by the gnostics themselves, though we do find polemic in the *Pistis Sophia* (§147) and the *Second Book of Jeû* (§43) against various similar aberrations in gnostic circles. In the main (apart from the extreme example of the Manichaeans), the original gnostic writings breathe the atmosphere of a more or less strict asceticism. The gnostic ideal of a life separated from the world could also lead to a retired style of life, in which the gnostic kept himself far from worldly matters and renounced sensual delights and the enjoyment of life;

and it seems in most cases that these were in fact the consequences drawn from the ideal. Apart from this, the gnostic library of Nag Hammadi contains also non-gnostic exhortatory writings of a sapiential and popular philosophical character, viz. the *Sentences of Sextus* (NHC XII/1) and the *Teachings of Silvanus* (NHC VII/4).

The contradiction here can also be seen in the various interpretations. Hans Jonas insists that libertinism is typically gnostic, and almost necessarily the result of the gnostic starting point. Asceticism came only at a later stage, *inter alia* through assimilation to, or competition with, the worldwide Church. Thus the pneumatic morality bears 'in itself the revolutionary character in the most obvious manner, because this was a question of practical living. In the form of libertinism, we see the most complete dissolution of the traditional obligations which bound human conduct, and the excessive nature of a sentiment of freedom which considered the total lack of self-discipline to be evidence of one's own self, indeed to be a meritorious deed ... Thus libertinism is a central element of the gnostic re-evaluation of all things' (234). One almost has the impression that Kurt Rudolph wants to reverse the chronological order, so that the asceticism is considered original and the libertinism merely a later sign of decadence that appears in isolated cases here and there; but then Rudolph takes an intermediate position which is probably the only sustainable view. Both attitudes can be derived from the pneumatic self-understanding of the gnostics, and it is difficult to discern any chronological sequence in the sources. We must be cautious with the accusation of libertinism, and here again a further distinction is necessary between Epiphanius, who lacks subtlety and is overenthusiastic, and Irenaeus, who is much more prudent and who may have judged correctly in much of this area. In numerical terms, it was not the extreme positions that dominated. The majority of gnostics came to a moderate fundamental asceticism, linked to a defensive attitude vis-à-vis the world and society.

D. Conclusion: The 'Song of the Pearl'

List 159 (selected versions of the text and translation, mostly with commentary).
A. Adam, *Die Psalmen des Thomas und das Perlenlied als Zeugnisse vorchristlicher Gnosis* (BZNW 24), Berlin 1959, 49–54, 84–9.

O. Betz and T. Schramm, *Perlenlied und Thomas-Evangelium: Texte aus der Frühzeit des Christentums*, Zurich 1985, 19–33.

G. Bornkamm, in Hennecke and Schneemelcher, *New Testament Apocrypha* (L143), II.

H. J. W. Drijvers, ibid. German original II.344–8 [on the further 'genealogy' of this translation, ibid., 343 n. 155].

W. Foerster, *Gnosis* (L141) I.355–8 (quotations below are from this translation).

R. Haardt, *Gnosis* (L141) 159–67 (Eng. trans. based on K. Schubert's translation from the Syriac).

W. Hörmann, *Gnosis* (L141) 98–104.

H. Jonas, *Gnosis* (L150) I, 322–6.

——*Gnostic Religion* (L141) 112–29.

A. F. J. Klijn, *Acts of Thomas* (L143) 120–5.

K. Latte, *Religion* (L4) 68–71 (following Reitzenstein).

B. Layton, *Scriptures* (L141) 366–75.

H. Leisegang, *Gnosis* (L141) 365–70 (following Lipsius).

R. A. Lipsius, *Apostelgeschichten* (L143) I, 292–6.

P. H. Poirier, *L'Hymne de la perle des Actes de Thomas* (HoRe 8), Louvain 1981, 321–75 (detailed reconstruction of the text).

R. Reitzenstein, *Hellenistische Wundererzählungen*, Leipzig 1906, Darmstadt 3rd edn. 1974, 107–10.

W. Schultz, *Dokumente* (L141) 13–23 (in rhymed verse); 234–6 (in prose, following Lipsius).

List 160 (secondary literature, additional to L159).

G. Bornkamm, *Mythos* (L143) 111–21.

H. Jonas, 'The "Hymn of the Pearl": Case Study of a Symbol, and the Claims for a Jewish Origin of Gnosticism', in Idem, *Gnosis* (L150) II.346–59.

P. H. Poirier, *L'Hymne* (L159; important).

G. Quispel, *Makarius, das Thomasevangelium und das Lied von der Perle* (NT.S 15), Leiden 1967.

Despite the Nag Hammadi discoveries, the so-called 'Song of the Pearl' remains one of the most beautiful of gnostic texts, indeed perhaps the most beautiful of all; correspondingly, it has very often been translated and studied. It is found in Chapters 107–13 of the Acts of Thomas, on the lips of the apostle as he sits in prison, but it certainly has a prehistory independent of the Acts. It was originally composed in Syriac, and only subsequently translated into Greek (unlike the Acts of Thomas, which were composed in Greek and then translated into Syriac).

1. The contents

The clear narrative structure means that it is not difficult to summmarise the contents of the Song. A first-person narrator relates that he grew up as a little child in the royal court of his father (lines 1f.). His parents equipped him admirably for his journey, with gold, silver and precious stones (lines 4–8). All that he must leave behind him is the glorious garment 'which they had made in their love for me' (line 9) and the purple toga 'to match my height' (line 10). His parents send him from the homeland in the East with a charge that is written on his heart (line 11) and that runs as follows (lines 12–15):

> If you go down to Egypt and fetch from there the single pearl which is there beside the devouring dragon, you shall [again] put on the suit encrusted with stones and the robe which goes over it; and with your brother, our second, become an heir in our kingdom.

In keeping with this charge the king's son sets out on the perilous journey with two companions, and settles in Egypt near the dragon (lines 16–22).[19] Although he swathes himself in garments typical of the country, the local inhabitants see through this disguise and give him some of their food (lines 29–32), with the effect that the royal messenger forgets the charge he has received, and falls into a deep sleep (lines 33–5). When his parents in the distant country realise this, they summon an assembly of the council and compose a letter to him (lines 36–40), including this demand (lines 43–8):

> Get up and sober up out of your sleep, and listen to the words of this letter. Remember that you are a king's son. You have come under a servile yoke. Think of your suit shot with gold; think of the pearl on account of which you were sent to Egypt ...

The letter first takes the form of an eagle and flies in the form of the king of the air to the royal son. When it alights close to him, it becomes wholly

---

[19] It is somewhat difficult to discern the function of the episode in lines 23–8: the narrator, a lonely foreigner, finds a fellow countryman whom he informs about the charge that he has received, and whom he warns against the Egyptians.

word and voice (lines 49–52). The king's son awakens from his deep sleep, recalls whence he comes and the charge that he has received, casts a spell on the dragon so that it sleeps, and takes the pearl away (lines 53–61). Leaving behind the dirty, impure garment of the Egyptians (line 62), he sets out on his path home, with the letter as his travelling companion (lines 63–8). His parents send him the suit and the toga (lines 72–4); when the two envoys give him the suit, it changes into his image and double (lines 76–8; from this point on the directly mythological elements gain the upper hand). The motions of knowledge (gnosis) come alive everywhere on the garment, which gets ready to speak and whispers melodious words in his ear (lines 88–92).

When the royal son clothes himself in the suit and the toga, this means that he is reinstated in his earlier position. He is readmitted to the kingdom of his father, and the final lines say that he is now to appear with him and with the pearl before the King of Kings (lines 97–105).

2. On the interpretation

There is a widespread tendency to assume a priori that this narrative is gnostic, or to see the king's son, on the basis of the structure of the narrative, as Mani, the founder of Manichaeism; but the first observation we must make is that the text can also be understood in non-gnostic terms. It employs simple narrative structures that are very familiar to us from popular fairy tales: the royal son's search for the hidden treasure, which he must wrest from the dragon in a struggle, is one of the most widely attested topoi in such tales. Nor is it difficult to identify biblical motifs: viz. the lost son who is reintegrated into his rightful place when he receives the festal garment (from Lk 15:11–32); pearl of great price (from Mt 13:45); last but not least, Israel's liberation from Egypt and its entry into the promised land (in the Book of Exodus; in Philo of Alexandria Egypt is a cipher for bodiliness and addiction to the world). From Gen 3:1–16 to Rev 12:1–18, the dragon and the serpent provide the natural image for the rebellious opponent; the splendid garment may recall the robe of the high priest (cf. especially Wis 18:24). This presents a possible link to a theology that is found elsewhere in non-gnostic Syriac Christianity. In this perspective, the 'Song of the Pearl' would apply already existing metaphors to describe 'the human person's return from the demonic world into the state in which God created him, and the reuniting to his brother Christ, with whom he becomes an heir in the kingdom' (Drijvers 298).

It must, however, be affirmed with equal clarity that this text lends itself with great facility to a gnostic reading, and that it undoubtedly was in fact read and used by the gnostics (and applied to Mani). We recognise here most of the important components of the gnostic mythology that we have already observed: the *doppelgänger* motif ('syzyzgy'), the motif of the cloak of invisibility, the loss of the original heavenly homeland, the negative evaluation of the world and the body, the gnostic's temporary forgetfulness of self, his enslavement (mirrored also in what happens to the pearl), the summons that reaches him in various forms and awakens him, the overcoming of obstacles, the reuniting of what had been separated, the return into the *plērōma,* and not least, in line 88, knowledge (gnosis) itself. Thus, this narrative appears to the gnostic reader to be both unadorned and a work of high art; or more precisely, as something composed with such art that the artistic skill is no longer noticed, and all that is perceived is the simple narration. It is well known that this is an especially high achievement on an artist's part.

To look at the 'Song of the Pearl' in this way helps us to understand better the success that gnosis frequently had, irrespective of the fact that its mythology was often tangled and inaccessible. Despite the complex superstructure with its many levels, gnosis works with a simple and straightforward basic constellation which makes an immediate emotional appeal. It utilises archetypical patterns: the human being's wish to have a home, his unceasing striving towards an ideal homeland that he believes he has lost. Gnosis promised its initiates that all the contradictions and mysteries of existence would be clarified. It gave them a new identity, assigning each individual a place in the cosmos from which he could look with a feeling of superiority at all the business of the world around him, confident that this no longer touched him as it once had done, since he knew that he possessed an indestructible homeland in heaven, and that the best part of him would return thither.

We began with the first sentences of Ernst Bloch's *The Principle of Hope.* We can conclude with the final sentence on the last page of the last volume of that work, which puts precisely this idea into words: when the ideal condition is attained, without renunciation or alienation, then 'there arises in the world something which shines into the childhood of all and in which no one has yet been: a homeland'.[20]

---

[20] Op. cit. (above, p. 431, n. 1), III.1376.

Index of selected biblical texts

Index of secondary literature